DARTNELL is a publisher serving the world of business with business books, business manuals, business newsletters and bulletins, training materials for business executives, managers, supervisors, salesmen, financial officials, personnel executives and office employees. In addition, Dartnell produces management and sales training films and cassettes, publishes many useful business forms, conducts scores of management seminars for business men and women and has many of its materials and films available in languages other than English. Dartnell, established in 1917, serves the world's whole business community. For details, catalogs, and product information, address: DARTNELL, 4660 Ravenswood Avenue, Chicago, Illinois 60640, USA—or phone (312) 561-4000.

OTHER DARTNELL HANDBOOKS

Advertising Manager's Handbook
Direct Mail and Mail Order Handbook
Marketing Manager's Handbook
Personnel Administration Handbook
Public Relations Handbook
Sales Manager's Handbook
Sales Promotion Handbook

The Dartnell Office Administration Handbook

Sixth Edition
Revised and Enlarged

Edited by
Robert S. Minor
Clark W. Fetridge

DARTNELL

CHICAGO / BOSTON / LONDON

First Edition (Office Manager's Handbook) 1958
Second Edition (Office Manager's Handbook) 1961
Third Edition (Office Administration Handbook) 1964
Fourth Edition (Office Administration Handbook) 1967
Fifth Edition (Office Administration Handbook) 1975
Sixth Edition, 1984—Second Printing, June 1987

Library of Congress Catalog Number 67-16551

Standard Book Number 0-85013-142-1

Printed in the United States of America by
DARTNELL PRESS, CHICAGO, ILLINOIS 60640-4595

FOREWORD

By Clark W. Fetridge,
President, The Dartnell Corporation

THIS SIXTH EDITION of the *Dartnell Office Administration Handbook* reflects the changing physical structure of the modern business office. Office equipment, the tools used by those who work in the office, is undergoing radical change. Sometimes this change seems almost too rapid, but in truth it is a tribute to the thousands of administrators and office staff members who are adapting to new and sometimes exotic ideas at high speed.

In the previous edition, minicomputers were discussed in detail, especially in terms of applications. These new, smaller computing units brought keyboards into the general office, and operators were not always data processing systems specialists. "Package systems" were discussed, and it was pointed out that the very minimum for a system would cost well over $10,000.

In the previous edition, "package systems" and minicomputers were heralded as a new potential for bringing computer power into more offices with available keyboards and software applications that didn't always call for the data processing systems specialist. The word "microprocessing" was already being used as miniaturization was in full swing.

Today, people discuss 16K bytes vs. 8K, dot-matrix as compared to Daisywheel printing, modems, memories and ergonomics. Buzz words become standard talk in the office. Secretaries and clerical help use computers as easily as they used typewriters and adding machines.

In line with the constant change, the *Word Processing Society* changed its name in 1983 to the *Association of Information Systems Professionals*. The *Administrative Management Society* is exploring a possible/group name change, hopefully to better describe the activities of the membership. Managers in offices have new names— computer operations manager, data entry supervisor, applications programming manager, software systems programming manager, database administrator and information systems manager.

However, talk in many circles centers on the lack of productivity in offices, a loss despite the addition of new equipment. Since office productivity was never really easy to measure, it would be hard to determine if this is a fact or another misleading concept. Any office that is functioning well enough to meet the needs of a company is a productive office, and the productive office is usually the result of having a knowledgeable office administrator.

This *Office Administration Handbook,* therefore, concentrates on the basics of administration. It covers work simplification, long- and short-term planning, management by objectives, motivational theories and practice and day-to-day administrative problems and their solutions. Administration infers the direction of people as well as the care of people. People must be hired, trained, motivated, and, if necessary, terminated. None of these jobs can be carried out by a computer or some other office machine.

This gives rise to a pertinent question: "Where is the line between office administration and personnel administration to be drawn?"

Developments in both these areas have proliferated to the point where a handbook covering both subjects totally would become an unwieldly tome of several thousand pages. Yet "office management" means "people management," whatever else it may involve. That's why much of the personnel administration material in this book can be supplemented by the *Dartnell Personnel Administration Handbook.* However, personnel management cannot be ignored in a handbook on administration, neither can salary and wage administration or paperwork simplification. Dartnell does publish Management Guides specifically covering these areas for those who want specific, in-depth information.

Dartnell wishes to acknowledge the contributions to this Sixth Edition by Wilbert E. Scheer, author of the *Dartnell Personnel Administration Handbook;* William L. Davidson, author of *Wage and Salary Administration in a Changing Economy;* Dennis J. Zaiden, author of *Dartnell's Paperwork Simplification Manual;* Nicholas Rosa and Merl Miller, authors of "*Management's Guide to Desktop Computers;* Robert N. McMurry, author of many Dartnell publications on recruitment; and literally hundreds of other contributors, both individual and companies.

Since the First Edition of this book appeared in 1958 as the *Dartnell Office Manager's Handbook,* it has undergone total change. Even the name was changed in 1964 to the *Office Administration Handbook,* although the subject matter has remained substantially the same. It has dealt with the problems of the office administrator/ manager, and it has offered solutions.

Since Dartnell's founding in 1917, its editorial policy has been based on a major principle:

The most successful executive is not necessarily the individual who is most original but the person who can add to original knowledge by using the successful ideas of others.

A Handbook such as this, with its 1,000 pages, is not something most people read cover-to-cover beginning on Page 1. It is a single-volume reference source for problem solving, not a text book for teaching. The Contents Page, coupled with the complete Index, offers easy access to an administrator's immediate need. It is hoped that this volume will be of use to the reader for many years to come.

CONTENTS

Acting on the Results
The Carnation Poll
A Suggestion System
What Is a Good Suggestion?
Elements of a System
Training the Supervisors
Investigating Suggestions

A Working Agreement
Recognition and Purpose
Payroll Deductions
Grievance Procedures
Arbitration
Bargaining Meetings
Wages
Hours of Work
Overtime
Shift Differential
Holidays
Seniority
Job Postings
Benefit Plans

Forecasting
Inventory
Assessing Labor Market
Staffing
Employee Information System
Control
Temporary Help Services
Advantages of Using Service
Disadvantages
What Will it Cost?
Planning Early
What to Do When the Time Comes
Judging Results

PART 4   GUIDES THROUGH THE PAPERWORK JUNGLE

What Is Paperwork?
Fundamentals of Paperwork Simplification
"Total Systems" Approach
Basic Considerations
Challenging Every Detail
Implementing a Program

Who Doesn't Need a Manual?
Types of Manuals
Does My Company Need a Manual?
Planning
Preparation
A Company Manual Outline
Scheduling

PART 7   HOW TO IMPROVE ADMINISTRATIVE SKILLS

APPENDIX

INTRODUCTION

THE OFFICE AS A CONTROL CENTER

By Robert S. Minor

ORGANIZATION is the key word used in describing the successful operation of the control center we refer to as the office. Rapid-fire changes in the methods of doing business, radical changes in physical appearance of the environmental area and a growing complexity of operations have not eliminated the need for such a control center. It must function as home base for every company involved in producing goods or services.

The word "*office*" pictures white-collar workers sitting at desks and performing a variety of paper-oriented tasks. Interestingly enough, the workers in this picture can range from the chief executive of a multinational conglomorate down through the treasurer, controller, sales manager, secretary, receptionist and mail clerk. Even the dictionary offers two choices in definition: (*a*) *The place where the affairs of a business are carried on*, or (*b*) *the people working there.*

Organization of the activities of the people working within the physical confines of the area is the *primary function* of the office administrator. The job has changed radically—and hasn't changed at all—during the past 20 years. The office has been introduced to electronic and electric equipment of varying degrees of sophistication. But, people are still involved. They make up the "office" whether they are executives or clerks. They have jobs to perform and they must have the tools to perform them. They need physical space and comfort, and they need equipment. They need pencils and paper, paper clips, typewriters, copying machines, telephones, and perhaps computer terminals, microfilm readers, and electronic calculators.

The New Technology

Physical changes in the business office, especially related to new equipment and new methods, are obvious signs of a technological transition that won't end for years to come. The equipment seen in

1

offices of all sizes—computer terminals with cathode ray tubes, microfilm readers, word processing machines, printers, data transceivers—are being used by people who work in the offices. The office administrator must be fully briefed on every unit or be willing to give up authority in the area.

During the past decade, the data processing manager was joined by the management information systems manager in the corporate structure. In the future the MIS manager will help to develop most of the office systems, and the office administrator will either join the club or lose an important segment of control. Most of the technology necessary for the "paperless office" is available, but the rush to convert is tempered by many people who can't or won't accept radical changes.

Modern electronic workstations in the office provide the tools needed by the staff as well as the comfort and quiet necessary to get the job done efficiently.
Courtesy All-Steel, Inc.

The actual number of offices which have become fully "integrated" is still small and mainly limited to the largest of corporations, but the growth will be steady. There are those authorities in the office administration field who state that automation will be the only salvation for the small business which wants to compete in the future.

Automation will provide a means for any business office to handle transactions at high speed, equalling the speed of the larger companies. Orders can be processed, bills produced, files searched at the same rate (or very close) achieved by any large firm. Small offices will be able to use microcomputers, micrographic files, electronic mail and most of the other automated equipment that once could only be afforded by larger companies.

In many cases the stumbling block for automation is the office administrator who fears change and automation represents change. Whether or not administrators adjust, however, the equipment march will continue. By the end of the 1980s, there will be millions of small (micro) computers, millions of CRT terminals, millions of electronic calculators and millions of teleprinters in use. Would you believe the prediction for 160.6 million calculators in use in business offices by 1990?

The Role of the Office Administrator

As long as there are people in the business office, there will be a need for someone to administer that office—to supervise the activities of the people involved—and to coordinate the functions of the equipment.

This administrator performs a number of jobs and holds a number of titles. In many cases, the title may not convey the fact that the person does, in fact, administer an office. In other words, the administrative function may be secondary to a major function—such as vice president, treasurer, controller, etc.

In a Dartnell Target Survey profiling the office administrator, it was noted that approximately 60% of the respondents said the executive in charge of office operations holds the title of office manager, administrative manager, office services manager, etc. The "etc." includes "Manager, General Services," "Director, Organization and Manpower Planning," "Manager, Management Division," "Personnel Manager," and "Administrative Assistant."

Some 22% said their titles included "Executive Vice President," "Administrative Vice President," "Vice President, Corporate Services," "Vice President, Personnel and Administration," "Vice President-Controller," "Vice President, Finance," and "Vice President, Treasurer."

Although 20% of the firms responding still use the "office manager" designation, this traditional title continues to slip in favor of the more descriptive Director of Administrative Services or Administrative Manager. In fact, more than 50 position titles were submitted to describe the individuals charged with administering the office function. Worth noting is that the word "office" only appeared in 28% of all titles; "administrative," "administration," or "administrator" in 31% and "manager" or "management" in 54%. Additionally, 16% emphasized the service aspect of office operations by mentioning "service."

Just over half, 55%, of the administrators report to a corporate officer, with 25% reporting directly to the president. Fifty percent of those surveyed have served in their present capacities for 1–5 years: 25% have been on the job 5–9 years and 20% have put in 10 or more years.

How Many Employees Supervised?

There was a sharp difference in size of employee groups supervised, so this was broken down into two separate categories. One was set for employee groups of *less than 100* and the other was set for groups between *100 and 500*. (Actually, 450 was the top number of employees supervised by one executive.)

For firms with less than 100 employees at one location, the average number of employees supervised was 31. For firms with 100 to 500 employees supervised, the average number hit 232½ for the chief executive. Broken down into the three groups established by title (less than 100 employees), the data showed:

Vice President *37 employees (average)*
Treasurer-Controller *15½ employees (average)*
Office Manager *42 employees (average)*

How Many Supervisory Assistants?

The average number of assistants for these hard-working executives would come out at *3.3 per company*. This figure, by the way, includes the larger office groups as well as the smaller groups. It should also be noted that 24% of the office manager group had *no assistants*. Another 30% of the treasurer and controller group had no assistants, and all of the vice presidents rated at least *one* assistant. In the breakdown by title:

Vice President *4 assistants*
Treasurer-Controller *1.2 assistants*
Office Manager *2 assistants*

Administrative Responsibilities

The office administrator—be he or she the Office Services Manager, the Director of Office Services or the Director of Business Affairs—has the total responsibility for at least 14 major office functions. While not all administrators are totally responsible for all the functions, a majority reported they answer for 11 areas. The total breakdown follows

OVERALL DEGREE OF RESPONSIBILITY FOR 14 KEY AREAS

FUNCTION	Total Responsibility	Partial Responsibility	None
Salary administration (office)	43%	47%	10%
Purchasing office supplies	75%	18%	9%
Purchasing office equipment	58%	38%	4%
Purchasing office furniture	53%	40%	7%
Job performance evaluation	56%	38%	6%
Office planning (layout, facilities)	43%	53%	4%
Office security	50%	37%	13%
Inventory control	47%	38%	15%
Forms control	53%	37%	10%
Communications services	58%	36%	5%
Mailing services	65%	28%	7%
Filing services	62%	28%	10%
Records management	66%	29%	5%
Maintaining office discipline	62%	35%	3%

As the table indicates, administrative managers in 43% of the offices have full responsibility for salary administration in that particular area. This can be considered a high percentage when one looks at the majority of corporate structures today. Not as surprising in the survey was the 73% who reported full responsibility for purchasing office supplies. It was also to be expected that the majority would have total responsibility for filing, mailing and record-keeping areas.

The administrator is also responsible for the communications function, for purchasing office equipment and for purchasing furniture. While the majority shared responsibility for office layout and design, they were mostly expected to run the forms control program.

The table also shows that nearly two-thirds of the office administrators are responsible for maintaining office discipline, half are responsible for security within the office areas and slightly more than half have the forms control responsibility. Although only 43% reported total responsibility for salary administration, 56% indicated that performance and evaluation was a major duty.

In a related question, the administrators said that records management was the most time-consuming function, closely followed by job evaluation and communications services.

EDP and MIS Systems

According to the survey results, nearly one of every four offices (74%) now have some degree of electronic data processing (EDP) and a lesser 41% utilize management information systems (MIS). However, these are high technology areas and not all administrators possess the ability or authority to oversee these functions. The manager assumes some or all administrative authority over the EDP operation in 59% of the companies, while 57% exert *some* degree of control over the MIS function.

What Other Duties?

Office operations handled by the administrative executive go beyond the above listed number. As a matter of fact, more than 55% of the office services administrators have additional duties and some 65% of the vice presidents have other duties. Within the group reporting in this survey, *none* of the treasurers or controllers hold responsibilities in areas other than those listed in the questionnaire.

Some of the miscellaneous responsibilities of office administrators are security, technical assistance to customers, management systems, engineering services, reproduction department, and employee benefits. Other duties listed for vice presidents include finance, sales, home office properties, employee benefits, reproduction, systems and procedures, and security.

Vice Presidents—Office Managers

Office administrators who also ranked as vice presidents were asked to comment further on the scope of their duties, including any job descriptions they might wish to send along. The following are some of the direct quotes pertaining to the vice president's total job:

> "Complete responsibility for auditing, general ledger and payables section and section giving full clerical support to other departments." (Vice President-Controller)

> "Division head supervising six department managers in the fulfillment of their respective functions. Protection and preservation of the corporate powers and assets. Also functions as comptroller, assistant secretary and assistant treasurer."

> "Have total financial and work-load responsibility once budgets are established." (Title of this executive is vice president of finance.)

> "Responsible for all phases of operations." (Executive Vice President)

> "Responsible for all home office administration." (Administrative Vice President)

Following is a "position description" from a policy manual—indicating the scope of a vice president in charge of personnel and office administration.

```
POSITION DESCRIPTION

VICE PRESIDENT, PERSONNEL AND ADMINISTRATION

Reports to:  Executive Vice President, Administrative Services

Supervises: Five Section Heads

Basic Functions:
    Directs the development and application of personnel policies
    and procedures. Directs purchasing, mail, records, and main-
    tenance departments.

Major Duties and Responsibilities:
    1. Directs the development and administration of personnel poli-
       cies and procedures.
    2. Supervises the clerical and managerial employment function.
    3. Administers applicable salary administration programs.
    4. Directs the activities of the purchasing department.
    5. Directs the supply, mail, and copying department.
    6. Directs the central record and microfilm departments.
    7. Directs the activities of home office building and grounds
       maintenance.
    8. Conducts special projects as assigned.
```

Treasurer/Controller Office Managers

Treasurers and controllers, like vice presidents, have other specific duties besides the administration of the office operations (when they wear both hats). Here, then, are some specific quotes from this group:

"Handle all financial management and all personnel functions. Advise other administrative supervisors on systems and procedures. Schedule temporary help. Manage all company records." (Controller)

"Supervisor of all accounting functions. Supervise changeover to data processing. Responsible for systems and procedures in all departments. Responsible for office equipment and supplies." (Controller)

"Responsible for the preparation and maintenance of all financial records and activities, including deposits, revenues, collections, disbursement of funds, materials and supplies received and disbursed, and capital value of plant in service. Responsible for employing and supervising the activity of employees who may assist in carrying out these assigned duties. He is responsible to the board of commissioners and will report directly to them. In the absence of the general manager, he is in complete charge of all activities." (Treasurer-Assistant Manager)

Following is a specific description of the duties of a controller who functions as the chief office administrator:

DUTIES OF THE CONTROLLER

The duties of the Controller shall be to maintain adequate records of all assets, liabilities, and transactions of this corporation; to see that adequate audits thereof are currently and regularly made; and, in conjunction with other officers and department heads, to initiate and enforce measures and procedures whereby the business of this corporation shall be conducted with the maximum safety, efficiency, and economy. He shall report to the Treasurer and/or the Board of Directors as said Board of Directors may prescribe.

Other duties are as follows:

1. Principal accounting officer in charge of general accounting books, accounting records, and accounting forms.
2. Audit all payrolls and vouchers and cause them to be properly certified.
3. Obtain from departments of the corporation all reports needed for recording the general operations of the corporation, or for supervising or directing its accounts.
4. Cause to be enforced and maintained the classification and other accounting rules and regulations prescribed by any regulating body.
5. Cause to be prepared, compiled and filed, such reports, statements, statistics and other data as may be required.
6. Chairman of the Electronic Data Processing Committee; responsible to Management for the implementation, control and operation of the EDP department.
7. Prescribe (or act in an advisory capacity), implement, coordinate and maintain methods and systems related to office, administrative and accounting procedures.

Office Services Managers

As initially stated, this group has many titles and a variety of duties. *All* have greater responsibility than the job of merely supervising the office force. More than half of this group has the responsibility for the building, for employment and for purchasing of supplies. In most cases this would be supplies directly connected with the office operation. Here are some quotes from the office manager group, with titles in parentheses:

> "Head the management division (one of six managers reporting to president). Run all aspects of administration and control management systems." (Manager-Management Division)

"Responsible for the coordination of all personnel activities of non-exempt office personnel, screening and interviewing applicants. Direct activity of reproduction department, stenographic, telephone and mail departments. Has personal responsibility for the direction of the credit function and makes recommendations on policy changes within this function." (Office and Credit Manager)

"Supervises all office services including office space, mail, duplicating, telephone, and purchasing of office equipment and supplies. Also operate catered cafeteria, executive dining room and company store." (Manager-Office Services)

"Supervises stenographic pool, graphic arts, mail deliveries, reservation bureau, reproduction department, and audio-visual aids pool." (Service Bureau Manager)

"Formulate, plan, organize, direct, implement, coordinate and control all administrative policies, methods, and procedures in area of fiscal, accounting, data processing, engineering, service, office administration, personnel, wage and salary administration, legal, and public relations." (Administrative Assistant)

"In charge of all company property and facilities not directly used by production. This includes buildings, fleet, office furniture and equipment, and *installation* of new production equipment." (Properties Manager)

"Responsible for personnel function, general office function, reproduction function, communication function, security function, safety function, and the technical application (not EDP) of the computer function." (Director-Administrative Services)

"In addition to standard duties, is responsible for advertising, direct mail program, customer and stockholder public relations, and communications equipment." (Office Manager)

Following are examples of policy manual statements which define and outline the function of the office services manager. The scope of the duties outlined is sufficient to indicate the current work load enjoyed by administrative executives:

JOB DESCRIPTION

Title: Manager, Office

Department: Office Management and Services

Responsible to: Controller

JOB SUMMARY:

Responsible for operation of Office Management and Services Department. Print Shop, and for most personnel functions relating to salaried personnel, other than Sales Division.

Directly supervises three persons and indirectly supervises 34 other persons.

Interprets company policy for Department Managers and employees.

Administers salary program for all plant locations. Includes processing of Salary Change Requests, advising Managers on questionable changes, maintenance of Salary Classification Ranges, member of Salary Evaluation Committee, checks Time Reports, participates in salary surveys, reviews and signs salary pay checks.

Recruits new and replacement personnel. Interviews applicants and arranges for interviews with Department Managers. Recommends hiring or hires new personnel. Orients new personnel.

Counsels Department Managers and employees in personnel problems, and personal problems and complaints. Conducts exit interviews. Counsels retiring personnel.

Determines compliance with Federal and State laws governing hiring practices, work hours, minimum and overtime pay and separation of personnel. Recommends changes in company policies. Prepares reports indicating company practices and compliance.

Responsible for security of personnel files, salary information, contemplated personnel changes and corporate planning information. Determines personnel authorized access to confidential information.

Determines office space and equipment requirements. Authorizes purchases, assignment and reassignment of office furniture and equipment. Provides space as required.

Determines, with Corporate Secretary and Attorney, Records Retention requirements.

Responsible for preparation of Man Power Graphs, Salary Budgets, Capital Expenditure Budgets.

Represents company as member of American Management Society, and at various meetings relating to company participation in local civic projects.

May, on occasion, be required to perform duties other than those specified in this description. Performs various other related functions.

This job is exempt as to overtime pay requirements.

OFFICE SERVICES DIVISION

FUNCTION OF ADMINISTRATOR

As a division within the General Services organization, has the responsibility for coordinating the office services function throughout the company for the purpose of assuring efficient office services including adequate food service and office facilities; for coordinating office-wide activities for the general office; and for providing office facilities, building operation and maintenance, food service, and other office services for the general office.

RESPONSIBILITIES

1. Develops policies and plans relating to office design, construction, layout, and furnishings; food service; and other aspects of office services.

2. Devises methods and procedures to provide consistent administration of such policies and plans.

3. Serves as a staff advisory facility to members of management on matters of an office services nature.

4. Acquires and disposes of property for company offices; arranges for the construction or remodeling of office buildings; plans office layouts; and furnishes and decorates office space throughout the company to meet the requirements of organizational components.

5. Operates and maintains general office buildings and other related facilities.

6. Provides services that are needed for efficient operations within the general office, including food service, storage of inactive records, stenography, typing, calculating, reproduction, telephone, mail distribution, library, and various other types of office services.

7. Orders, stores, and issues office furniture, machines, equipment, and supplies for the general office and for other components of the company.

8. Carries on safety activities for the general office and promotes safety consciousness and practices in an effort to prevent accidents or keep them at a minimum.

9. Coordinates office-wide activities for the general office, such as supervisor and employee meetings; office hours, tours, and announcements; employee recreation programs; and time off work.

10. Provides information, advice, and staff assistance on office services including food service, and office facilities to the various components throughout the company.

11. Keeps informed on new developments in the office facilities, food, and other office services fields; and conducts studies needed to determine the knowledge, principles, techniques, and equipment that would have a practical application within the company.

RELATIONSHIPS

1. Is directly responsible to Vice President, General Services.

2. Operating and Auxiliary organizations, and Subsidiary Companies. Has a functional relationship with them; insures compliance with Office Services policies, plans, methods, and procedures; provides information, advice, and staff assistance to them; and provides services for their use.

3. Other Individuals and Components within the Company and its Subsidiaries. Provides or receives and utilizes available services, advice and assistance; cooperates in working relationships to effect desired coordination and avoid duplication.

4. Individuals and Organizations outside the Company. Establishes and maintains relationships that are in the best interests of the Company.

5. Discharges responsibilities in compliance with company policies and procedures, legal requirements, and in full cooperation with and respect for all other organizational lines of responsibility and authority.

Supervisor, Manager, Administrator?

Wilbert E. Scheer, author of the *Dartnell Personnel Administration Handbook* as well as hundreds of articles and reports in the field of management, personnel and human relations, also taught in the management field. He offered us this brief review of "Terminology" which sums up, to a fine point, the difference between the supervisor, manager and administrator—with a baseball point of view:

Many of the problems in dealing with human relations lie in the confusion caused by conflicts in responsibility and authority. Some members of management formalize policy; others execute policy. To minimize these conflicts let's arrive at an understanding. Let's get the terms and definitions straight.

The *supervisor* is the person who oversees a section of the whole; he is the one who gets things done.

The *manager* is the person who determines what should be done but not always specifically the methods to be used. He translates the several functions of subordinates to objectives and directs and reviews progress.

The *administrator* is the one who formulates the long-range objectives and the guidelines for their accomplishment. Administrative management is relatively removed in time and space from the "firing line" of business. Let's illustrate these distinctions by switching to baseball, which is appropriate and timely. The typical professional baseball club is an uncomplicated kind of organization which provides pretty clear examples of what we are talking about here.

In baseball there are usually several coaches on each team, each concerned with a single function, such as pitching, batting, etc. Each one is charged with his particular duty and held responsible for it. These are the *supervisors*.

The *manager* is the one who directs the total activity on the playing field. He determines tactics and integrates the various functions of pitching, batting, fielding, substitution, to produce the winningest combination. Winning each game is his immediate objective which must be harmonized with the longer-range goals of developing and improving the team. He is continually concerned with analyzing and appraising results, finding out what's wrong, and making sure it is corrected.

Above the field manager is the general manager, comparable to the *administrator* in business. While he is concerned about how the team plays he doesn't, or shouldn't, try to mastermind the tactics and second-guess the manager. He is concerned with more than the day-to-day performance of the team, the manager, and the personnnel. His concern involves attendance. finances, physical facilities, and long-range planning. The administrator is the mastermind behind the trades, the promotional activities, to stimulate attendance to pay for it all.

Whether in baseball or in business, too many of us in management are trying to play all the positions. In the area of human relations this confuses and confounds the individual player or worker who doesn't know who his boss is and to whom he is accountable. It even violates the Scriptures which tell us, in Matthew 6:24, "No man can serve two masters." For best results we'd better establish at the outset which job is ours, stick to it, and leave the other job to the other fellow.

What Qualifies an OA?

With a detailed report on the host of responsibilities that may fall on the office administrator's shoulders, it is fitting to run through the basic qualifications. He or she certainly should have a thorough knowledge of accounting if he or she is to participate in that department's function, or if he or she will be in charge of data processing. Each must have the ability to select the people who will be working in the various areas of responsibility.

He must be a manager because he will be managing the activities of these people even though he is not on the first line. He will make decisions that affect employees. He must also be fair and sympathetic in his dealings with people, since they are, in effect, his responsibility.

OFFICE ADMINISTRATION HANDBOOK

The office administrator must understand the forward rush of technology and its implications. She knows that new methods are being introduced all the time. Her job is to find those which will apply to the company and the department to improve its service. Part of his function, then, is to keep abreast of new developments at business shows, at business and administration conferences, and by reading business magazines and books. He should be the first to acknowledge the position of data processing people and of systems people. He may work as both or he may work with them. His education must be a continuing process, not unlike that of a physician or engineer.

Organizing the Office

It was stated at the beginning of this section that *"Organization is the key word used in describing the successful operation of the control center we refer to as the office."* Over the years, the commonest fault revealed in administration has been lack of overall supervision. In organizations where department managers run departments according to their own concepts, the lack of central authority shows itself in such ways as inefficiency, lack of morale and higher-than-needed costs.

There are 29 broad check points that the administrator can cover in a brief time and know that his areas of basic responsibility are intact:

ORGANIZATION CHECKING POINTS

1. Does each individual—worker, supervisor, or executive—know to whom he reports?

2. Does each supervisor, department head and executive know what individuals report to him?

3. Is there an organization chart?

4. Can a copy of the organization chart be found quickly?

5. Is the organization chart kept up to date?

6. Are individuals in the organization specifically acquainted with their respective sections of the organization chart and generally acquainted with the rest of it or appropriate divisions of it?

7. Is there an organization write-up describing each position on the organization chart?

INTRODUCTION

8. Are there standard practice instructions covering each operation standardized?

9. Is there a pamphlet for distribution to employees that tells of all office rules?

10. Is there an office manual describing the various routines and procedures and their relation to each other?

11. Is the work functionalized—that is, so far as possible is work of a similar kind assigned to specified workers (as in centralized departments like transcribing, calculating, statistical, and so on); and similarly with individuals where appropriate?

12. Is each individual responsible solely to one person for each function performed?

13. In sections, does one person at a time go to the supervisor?

14. Are technical and functional contacts and sources of information differentiated from lines of operating responsibility?

15. Does each executive have four or fewer subexecutives, department heads or supervisors reporting directly to him?

16. Is there a periodic inspection and checkup of department heads and supervisors?

17. Do executives and department heads know of the work, ability, special achievement and special shortcomings of their immediate subordinates' assistants, the men in the second rank below them?

18. Are expense accounts and budget items arranged according to the organization chart and, thus, according to regular operating responsibilities?

19. Are only those costs charged to divisions, departments and sections for which the division, department or section head is responsible and which he can regulate?

20. Are all costs allocated to divisions, departments and sections that can be allocated to them?

21. Are detailed analyses of their financial results available to division, department and section heads?

22. Is there a program for training men for supervisory and executive positions?

23. Is it recognized that anyone may appeal to the president or some other top executive?

24. Is decision-making decentralized as far as possible?

25. Are decisions made at the lowest point in the organization at which the decider possesses all the facts necessary for a sound decision?

26. Do men who possess the facts do the deciding?

27. Have nominal approvals that destroy subordinates' confidence in their ability and that encourage "buck passing" been eliminated?

28. In making executive changes is there too strict an adherence to a fixed organization plan regardless of the qualification of the executive personnel?

29. Are executives, department heads and supervisors in the same general level of similar intelligence and ability?

It was said that these check points can be "covered" in a brief time. That means it didn't take long to read them, but it may take a while to be assured that all are being observed. This is why the administrator plays such a key role, and this is why organization is the most important factor.

Effective Administration

The administrator's job is to get things done *through people*. Here are two dozen practical ideas on successful administration gathered from the experience of many successful office administrators. These have been a part of the Dartnell *Office Administration Handbook* for many years because they are "classic" reminders that will never become obsolete.

1. *Emphasize skill, not rules, in your organization.* Judge your own actions and those of your subordinates by their effects— effects in terms of increasing both the competitive strength of your business and the satisfaction of the human needs of the people who work in it. Go easy on pat rules for running a business. Doing it "by the book" isn't always the most satisfactory way. If an unorthodox solution works effectively and pleases the people who use it, don't discount it just because it doesn't seem exactly "according to Hoyle."

2. *Set a high standard for your organization.* If you are irregular in your work habits, late for appointments, fuzzy in expressing yourself, careless about facts, bored in attitude, your supervisors probably will be, too. If, on the other hand, you set a high standard for the organization, in all probability your supervisors will be eager to follow your good example.

3. *Know your subordinates and try to determine what is important to each.* Continuous study of individuals is a "must" for

getting things done through people. Motives and attitudes are important tools for the executive, and they can be determined only by study. Since security is the main drive in many people, giving recognition to the contribution of others and to their roles is a useful starting point in getting the best from people of future executive caliber.

Individuals vary widely in their other characteristics. Well-timed praise may spur one person to new heights of achievement, but it may only inflate another. A better key to the latter's effort might be constructive criticism. A third individual may wilt under any kind of criticism and some other approach is needed. The skillful executive constantly hunts for the appropriate procedure. He also searches beyond the office for background. People's motives and attitudes are heavily conditioned by their personal situations. For this reason, tactful drawing-out of subordinates can often supply invaluable information for understanding them. Remember that people often act on the basis of emotional, nonlogical reasons, even though they try to appear completely logical.

4. *Try to listen thoughtfully and objectively.* The executive who knows people—their habits, worries, ambitions, touchy points, and pet prides—comes to appreciate why they behave as they do and what motives stir them. The best and fastest way to know them is to encourage them to talk freely, without fear of ridicule or disapproval. Try to understand how others actually feel on a subject, whether or not you feel the same way. Never dominate a conversation or meeting by doing all the talking yourself, if you want to find out where your people stand. If both you and one of your people start to say something at the same time, give him the right of way.

One objection to the idea of being a good listener is that it takes time to draw people out. The answer is that it takes time to plan, too. Both are essential in the executive's job. The time invested will pay big dividends.

5. *Be considerate.* Few things contribute more to building a hardworking supervisory team than a considerate chief. Try to be calm and courteous toward your assistants. Consider the effects on them of any decisions you make. Take into account the problems they have of their own, both business and personal. Try to build up their pride in their work, and their self-respect. Start by treating personal characteristics as assets and being careful not to trample on them.

6. *Be consistent.* If you tend to "fly off the handle" and "set off fireworks" you are likely to frighten subordinates into their shells; if you vacillate wildly in reaction, mood, and manner you will probably bewilder them. Neither sort of behavior can win you the confidence and cooperation of your assistants, which you must have to get things done.

   You and your supervisors are in the position of a leader and followers. One wants to follow only the leader whose course is steady and whose actions are predictable.

7. *Give your subordinates objectives and a sense of direction.* Subordinates should know where they're going, what they're doing, and why they're doing it, in order to plan their time intelligently and to work effectively. Good supervisors seldom enjoy working just day to day. Therefore, make clear the relation between their day-to-day work and the larger company objectives.

8. *Give your directions in terms of suggestions or requests.* If your people have initiative and ability, you will get vastly better results in this way than you will by giving orders or commands. Issue the latter only as a last resort. If you find that you *have* to give orders all the time, maybe you'd better look for some new assistants—or reexamine the way you have been handling your own job. Be sure, also, to tell why you want certain things done. Informal, oral explanations are often as good as or better than written ones; let the individual circumstances be your guide here.

9. *Delegate responsibility for details to subordinates.* This is another "obvious" point that is frequently overlooked. Delegating responsibility is basic to competent administration. You are not doing your real job as an executive if you do not delegate, because, as office manager, if you insist on keeping your hand in details, you discourage your subordinates by competing with them. Moreover, by doing everything yourself, you prevent subordinates from learning to make their own decisions.

   Sooner or later the capable ones will quit and the others will sit back and let you do all the work. Ultimately, you will have no time for the thinking and the planning that are so important in your job. Think of your supervisors as working *with* you, not *for* you.

10. *Show your staff that you have faith in them and that you expect them to do their best.* Supervisors—and everyone else, for that matter—tend to perform according to what is ex-

pected of them. If they know you have the confidence in them to expect a first-rate job, that's what they will usually try to give you.

11. *Keep your subordinates informed.* Bring them up to date constantly on new developments and let them know well in advance whenever changes are in the offing. As members of a team, they are entitled to know what's going on. If they do, their thinking will be geared more closely to reality and their attitudes will be more flexible. Give them enough information about conditions and events in your company and industry to let them see themselves and their work in perspective.

12. *Let your assistants in on your plans at an early stage.* It's true that many plans can't be discussed very far in advance. They should, however, be discussed with subordinates before they are in final form. It will give your assistants that all-important chance to participate. Furthermore, because they will have taken part in shaping the plan, it will be as much theirs as yours, and they will feel a personal responsibility for its success. Hence, they will usually carry out the program with vigor and precision.

13. *Ask subordinates for their counsel and help.* Bring them actively into the picture. It will help to give them a feeling of "belonging" and to build their self-confidence. It will often make them anxious to work harder than ever. What is just as important, they may well have good ideas which may never be expressed unless you ask for them.

14. *Give a courteous hearing to ideas from subordinates.* Many ideas may sound fantastic to you, but it's important not to act scornful or impatient. There's no surer way to discourage original thinking by a subordinate than to disparge or ridicule a suggestion. That person's next idea might well be the very one you want—make it easy for that next idea to come to you.

15. *Give your subordinates a chance to take part in decisions.* When your people feel they have had a say in a decision, they are much more likely to go along with it cooperatively. If they agree with the decision, they will look at it as their own and back it to the hilt. If they don't agree, they may still back it more strongly than otherwise because of the fact that their point of view was given full and fair consideration.

16. *Tell the originator of an idea what action was taken and why.* If you do so, he or she will study other problems and make

suggestions on ways to solve them. If one idea is accepted, he or she will be encouraged by seeing the results put into effect. If the idea is not adopted, the person will accept that fact more readily and with fuller understanding if you indicate that the reasons for rejection are clear and sound. In addition, knowing exactly why the idea was impractical will help the suggester analyze the next problem more clearly.

17. *Try to let people carry out their own ideas.* Occasionally it happens that equally good suggestions on a particular problem come from two individuals at the same time; one person directly responsible in the situation, the other person essentially detached from it. In such cases, it's usually desirable to choose the recommendation developed by the person who will ultimately carry it out. He or she will then have a personal stake in proving that the idea is, in fact, workable. It's good administrative practice, therefore, to keep subordinates constantly aware of your willingness to have them work out their own solutions to problems in their particular operating areas.

18. *Build up subordinates' sense of the values of their work.* Most people need to think their jobs are important. Many even have to feel that they not only have an important job, but are essential in it, before they start clicking.

19. *Let your people know where they stand.* The day of "treat 'em rough and tell 'em nothing" has passed. A system providing periodic ratings for employees is the first step. However, the full value of such a system is realized only if ratings are discussed with each person individually so that each can bolster weak points, clear up misunderstandings, and recognize his particular talents.

A formal rating system may be worthwhile, but is not necessarily essential if the office manager talks at least once a year with each supervisor about his performance during the past period.

20. *Criticize or reprove in private.* This may, perhaps, seem obvious, but administrators forget to do it every day in hundreds of organizations. Reprimands in the presence of others cause humiliation and resentment instead of a desire to do better next time. Criticizing a subordinate when people from his department are present undermines his authority, his morale, and his enthusiasm to do his best for your company.

21. *Criticize or reprove constructively.* First, get all the facts; review them with those concerned, and reach an agreement on

them. Then be ready to suggest a constructive course of action for the future. When you criticize, concentrate on the method or the results, not on personalities. If you can precede the criticism by a bit of honest praise, so much the better. Note, however, *that some executives do this so regularly and unimaginatively that the compliments lose their value.*

22. *Praise in public.* Most people thrive on appreciation. Praise before others often has a multiple impact. It tends to raise morale, increase prestige, and strengthen self-confidence— important factors in the development of capable supervisors. But be sure that those you praise are really the ones who deserve it, and that you don't encourage "credit grabbing."

23. *Pass the credit on down to the operating people.* Taking for yourself credit that really belongs to one of your operating people tends to destroy his initiative and willingness to take responsibility. Giving him fair recognition for what he does has a double benefit; he gets appreciation for doing a good job, and you get the help and support of a loyal staff. If you take all the bows when somebody else played the leading role, you can rapidly lose the respect of your supervisors and other employees.

24. *Accept moderate "griping" as healthy.* In small doses, griping can serve as a safety valve for your people. If they worked under a perfect administrator they would probably still complain, just because he *was* perfect. Vicious, personal sniping is, of course, another matter; here, you should make every effort to have the cause discovered and rooted out. Remember, too, that without some dissatisfaction there would be little incentive to do or get something better.

"Anything and Everything"?

In replying to the Dartnell questionnaire, the Vice President-Office Manager of a relatively small (80 employees) sports-goods manufacturing company wrote, under the heading of Job Description: *"Anything and everything relating to the office that needs to be done."*

With or without new advances in technology, the apt job description covers the duties of the office administrator—today and tomorrow.

Part 1

Administrative Management— The Basics

CHAPTER 1

AN INTRODUCTION
TO ADMINISTRATIVE MANAGEMENT

By George F. Truell

ADMINISTRATIVE management can be one of the most satisfying professions on earth, and it can also be one of the most frustrating. Managing others is different from doing the actual work yourself. It involves a set of basic duties and responsibilities, an understanding of human behavior and an awareness of the changing scene. A person who moves into the job of managing must change *what* is done and *how* it is done. The changes a person experiences, the functions of management, the human element, and the impact of emerging trends are the subjects to be covered in this first section.

Changes That Occur

Let's take a look at what happens when a person becomes a manager. Most of us, when we finish our formal schooling, step out into the business world in search of a job. We've acquired certain knowledge and skills, which we might call "technical" or "professional," and we are anxious to apply them in an organization. After searching, we find a job where we are expected to apply our knowledge and skills in order to accomplish certain tasks.

Because we do our job well, our boss rewards us by increasing our duties and responsibilities, perhaps by giving us some status and some more money, and in time, a promotion to "MANAGER." As a manager, we are now required to apply certain knowledge and skills to other individuals who in turn are expected to apply their knowledge and skills to job tasks.

It soon becomes obvious that the knowledge and skills we applied as an individual, called "technical" or "professional," are different from the knowledge and skills we apply as a manager, which we might call "managerial."

An entirely different body of knowledge and skills is required when one becomes a manager. This information can be identified and studied, in the same way we learned the technical and professional capabilities we acquired before seeking our first job in business. In essence doing it yourself is different from trying to get others to do it for you. Unfortunately, many newly-appointed managers do not recognize this basic fact. They continue to function in the same way they did as an individual, and they fail as a manager. The organization loses a good individual performer and acquires a poor manager.

This does not mean that all of our capabilities as an individual performer are no longer needed. Actually a good portion of the day requires the application of these technical and professional skills, particularly at the lower levels of management. However, the percentage of time spent doing things ourselves and having others do things seems to change as we climb the organizational ladder.

At the first level of management, a small percentage of the day is spent in directing the work of others (applying managerial knowledge and skills). The major portion of the day is spent doing the same, or similar, type of work as those being supervised. Consequently, the manager should possess those technical and professional skills and know-how which relate directly to the work being performed. As a person moves into higher levels of management, more and more of the day is spent managing others, and less of the time is spent doing things. A manager relies less on his technical and professional skills and more on his managerial skills and competence.

Even at the very top levels of management, however, we often find some time still being spent in applying specific technical and professional knowledge and skill to certain tasks. Often this is jokingly referred to as the manager's "retained hobby." Perhaps it is calling on an old customer, tinkering with a certain piece of equipment, analyzing certain reports or designing a specific layout. When a manager has a choice of operating or managing, there's a tendency to choose the operating work. This is due to many different reasons. It requires less thinking, it's familiar, the results can be seen more quickly, one feels more secure doing it, one wants to set an example for others or just plain enjoy doing it. Yet the effective manager knows that he or she can make best use of time by concentrating on *management* responsibilities.

The Nature of Management Work

If the job of managing is different from doing it ourselves, then what capabilities are required? What knowledge and skills should a person acquire?

One way to start is to look at what managers do in terms of functions or the process of managing. There are as many different lists of functions as there are writers on management. However, in most cases, they can all be boiled down to four key groupings of duties and responsibilities:

1. **Plan**
2. **Organize**
3. **Direct**
4. **Control**

Let's take a brief look at each basic function.

1. Plan

The first task of a manager is to decide *where* he is going and *when* she wants to get there. What is the goal, the target, the objective, the end point of the activity? What does he want to accomplish with the group? When do they want to complete each part of their plan? What resources will be needed? When do they want to arrive at the end point?

2. Organize

Having decided where they are going, the manager must then divide up the tasks among the work group. He must decide *who* will do what, when and where. Questions of duties, responsibilities, levels of authority and relationships must be decided upon at this stage.

3. Direct

She then must implement the plan; i.e., put it into action. This requires they direct the work of others, and direct their own efforts in an attempt to attain the objectives.

4. Control

This function represents the closing of the system—the closing of the continuous loop. It is the activity that keeps all of the efforts "on target." It provides the manager with information as to how closely events are conforming to plans and where deviations or problems may be arising. The control function, by providing continuing feedback, enables the manager to modify actions in an effort to increase the chances of success in attaining the overall goals and objectives.

These four basic functions are the same, regardless of the technical activities in which managers are engaged, the level of any specific manager in the organization's hierarchy, or the nature of the organization itself. Planning, organizing, directing and controlling are being done by managers in production, sales and administrative positions, by managers "on the firing line," by managers in middle management and in the executive suite, and by managers in industrial, commercial, nonprofit, fraternal, educational, service and government organizations. *How* the functions are performed may vary from manager to manager, but the nature of management work remains the same.

The Human Element

The most complex, confusing, and at times the most rewarding aspect of the manager's job is the human element. In most organizations one person can accomplish very little alone. It takes the combined efforts of many people. It's the manager's job to coordinate those efforts. Yet trying to get others to do what you *want* them to do, *when* you want them to do it, and in the *way* you want it done is the ever-changing challenge of a manager. It requires great insight and understanding as to why people behave the way they do. Although all managers have some basic ideas about human behavior as a result of their lifetime of experiences living with and among other human beings, that storehouse of information is not usually sufficient to enable the manager to effectively direct others to work. Additional concentration and formal study are needed to prepare the manager for "people responsibilities"—to cope with the human element in the job.

Some Emerging Trends

The way managers carry out their four basic functions is greatly affected by a number of factors in our society. In essence, the ideas and strategies of managing must take into consideration and be compatible with a wide variety of forces and elements at work in our society at any given time. Today there are some emerging trends which are already shaping our ideas and strategies of managing for the years ahead. Let's look at a brief summary of some of these factors:

Environment

There are some changes occurring in our business and social environment—both on a national and international basis—which will have an impact on managers.

1. Rapid technologic change.

All around us we hear about the rapidly accelerating rate, complexity and intensity of change. The time lag between technical discovery and application for commercial use has reduced sharply in recent years.

2. **Knowledge explosion.**

   This continues to accelerate in all fields. It has been said that more new knowledge in technology has been developed in the last ten years than in the entire history of mankind.

3. **Greater interdependence of institutions.**

   There is an increasing interdependence of government, business, and education. Each is becoming more closely intertwined with the other. And on the international scene events in one part of the globe now have increasing impact on peoples in other parts of the world.

4. **Turbulence and uncertainty.**

   Rapid, unexpected events are occurring in all phases of our society. We see this in our companies, our schools, our churches, our governments and our labor unions. We also hear frequent reference to "revolutions"—technological, civil rights, students, moral, anti-establishment, women's rights, middle managers, etc.

5. **Large-scale, complex, multinational companies.**

   Bigness, on a world-wide basis, seems to be part of the future. Many large U.S. companies presently derive more than half of their income or earnings from foreign sales.

6. **Emergence of service-oriented companies.**

   There has been a definite shift from goods-producing companies to more and more service-oriented companies. Some calculations indicate that today more people are involved in services than in the production of goods. Increasing consumer pressure is causing an acceleration of this trend.

7. **Increasing importance of people problems.**

   More and more time, money and energy are being directed towards people problems—unemployment, discrimination, welfare, crime, housing, old age, schooling, etc.

8. **Increasing importance of environmental problems.**

   Greater attention is being paid to the planet Earth and the problems of pollution, conservation of resources, new sources of energy, etc.

9. **Reversal of roles for management and labor.**

   In many parts of the business scene, management is now viewed as the proponent of change and labor is seen as the champion of *status quo*.

Population and Our Work Force

Changes are occurring in our overall population and in the composition of our work force.

1. **More highly educated.**
   There is a steadily rising level of education in our population and in the work force.

2. **Trend toward continuing education.**
   Because of rapid technological change, there is an increasing problem of knowledge obsolescence in the work force. This requires people to view education as a continuing process all through their lifetimes.

3. **Increasing job mobility.**
   People are not only changing their home addresses more frequently, but there is greater mobility within and between companies as people seek new opportunities for growth and advancement.

4. **Population explosion.**
   Despite the increasing awareness of this problem and efforts to slow the rate of growth on a worldwide basis, total population continues to expand.

5. **New avocations and vocations.**
   Technology brings with it diverse new fields of endeavor, new vocations and avocations. A glance at the new job titles in the help-wanted columns of local newspapers provides ample evidence of the need for specialists in new fields.

6. **Increasing affluence.**
   With increasing material abundance has come a rising level of expectations. Whereas in years past, many people were taught to aspire, then to expect, today we hear the cry "What have you done for me lately?" People are seeking *more* and they want it *now*.

7. **Younger work force.**
   There is an increasing number of young people in the work force. Today many organizations find that more than 50% of their work force is under 30 years of age. The number is increasing.

8. **Increasing use of minorities.**
   As a result of social consciousness and awareness, group pressures, and many other complex factors at work, there

is an increasing number of women, blacks and other minority group members in the work forces of more and more organizations.

Work Attitudes and Values

Changes in the environment, in our population and in the work force are also reflected in changes in people's attitudes and values.

1. **Commitment to themselves.**

   More and more people in the work force have greater commitment to themselves, their field of work or their profession, rather than to the organization. They merely view the organization as a place to utilize their knowledge and skills and very quickly move on to another place if it provides a better opportunity. Loyalty to company is being replaced by loyalty to profession.

2. **Desire for more involvement.**

   There's a growing desire for more involvement, participation and autonomy—more say—much earlier in a person's work career.

3. **Changing attitude regarding work and leisure.**

   Years ago work was viewed as a duty; leisure as a reward. Today more and more people believe that work itself should be enjoyable and satisfying—it should be fun, not a chore.

4. **Higher level of wants and needs.**

   As more and more people obtain basic needs for food, shelter, and a sense of security, there is a growing attention to the higher-level needs in life—an opportunity to attain self-respect, respect of others, success, self-fulfillment, and a sense of accomplishing something worthwhile.

5. **Respect for knowledge, rather than rank.**

   Having a higher position or ranking in an organization is commanding less and less respect. Instead, people are turning towards those who possess the greater knowledge and expertise in any given field of work.

6. **Greater awareness of social responsibilities.**

   More and more people, particularly among the young, are seeking out those organizations which are fulfilling their responsibilities to the communities and areas in which they operate.

7. Revolt against conformity.

As more and more people search for individuality, there is a revolt against being pressed into the same mold as others. People want to operate in their own way.

These changes in the environment, the population and work force, and in peoples' work attitudes and values are having a significant impact on the nature of tasks, goals and organization structure. They're reflected in these emerging trends:

Tasks and Goals

1. More technical, complicated, and unprogrammed.

Rapid, unexpected changes create major shifts in the composition, sequencing and importance of tasks and goals.

2. Greater need for intellect.

The nature of tasks requires more and more intellect and less and less muscle. Technological changes are creating the necessity for workers with more knowledge as machines replace man's use of muscle.

3. Too complex for one person.

As tasks grow in complexity and technology, it is becoming more and more difficult for one person to comprehend and control all aspects of the task. Instead, a variety of skills and knowledge must be brought to bear on the tasks.

4. Require collaboration of specialists.

Because of the trend seen in 3, above, tasks and goals are being organized on a team or project basis to enable specialists from diverse fields to combine their efforts.

5. More complex, multiple goals.

As greater awareness of social needs develops and greater interdependence of organizations occurs, more complex, multiple goals arise. These require balancing the different needs and interests of various groups—employees, customers, stockholders, suppliers, the government, and the community.

Organization Structure

1. Temporary, adaptive systems.

Rapid change is necessitating the design of organizations which are temporary, adaptive and able to shift to meet new needs and objectives. People will move in and out of their work groups quickly and easily. The flexible nature of the organization helps to stimulate creativity, innovation and risk-taking.

2. Organized on basis of objectives.

Organizations will be pieced together based on the task at hand—the objectives or purpose—then will disband when that job is done. Different problems, objectives or tasks will necessitate different combinations of people at different times.

3. Executives will function as coordinators.

In rapidly-changing, task-oriented organizations executives will function as coordinators of various task forces and serve as a link between them.

The Challenge of Management

The transition from an operator (a person who accomplishes tasks alone), to a manager (a person who accomplishes tasks through others), is a difficult one. New knowledge, skills and attitudes are required for the functions of managing and how those functions can best be performed. To make this transition in an era of *rapid* change is an even more difficult task. If managers are going to avoid eventual obsolescence, they must not only acquire an understanding of basic management concepts and strategies, but must keep abreast of the findings of behavioral research. The manager must be alert to the emerging trends of tomorrow and what their impact will be on the management profession. It requires a person who can adapt and modify the knowledge and experiences of the past to fit the needs and demands of the future. It takes time, effort and determination to become a professional manager. The challenges are great, the opportunities are exciting and the personal satisfactions and rewards are unlimited.

The first step in the management process is planning. It is the function upon which all other management functions are based.

Unfortunately, many managers begin work each day without a clear idea of *where* they are heading and *why*. In essence they merely start where they left off from the day before and continue on—fighting fires and coping with the unexpected. It's little wonder that they soon become slaves to their jobs and victims of fate. Their jobs control them!

The Planning Responsibility

Planning is difficult mental work. It requires thinking out beforehand what is to be accomplished and how it can best be done. It's an integral part of the manager's job, not something that is done at occasional intervals only when time permits. It must be done by every manager *every day*. By careful planning a manager can exercise much greater control over the job and enhance chances for success. By knowing where she is going, she is much more likely to get there. Planning also enables the manager to effectively utilize all of the resources she is accountable for in the attainment of her objectives.

Planning is the responsibility of every manager at every level in an organization. It may be formal or very informal, in writing or merely in a manager's mind, very broad and general or quite limited and detailed, long range or short range. In general, planning done by managers at upper levels of an organization tends to be more formal, written, broad and long range. It may reflect top management's thinking concerning the overall organization's future goals and objectives such as: new markets, new services, new facilities, new products, major investments, acquisitions and shifts in the very nature of the business.

On the other hand, planning done by managers at lower levels of the organization normally covers much shorter periods of time (a shift, a week, a month, a year) and may be much more informal. It tends to be more detailed as to specific steps to be taken and deadlines to be met within the manager's own area of responsibility. Obviously these short-range plans must coincide with and support the long-range plans of the organization. In effect, short-range plans serve as stepping stones to the attainment of long-range plans.

In every case planning enables managers to anticipate future opportunities and problems, evaluate the probable effects of various forces and alternative courses of action, mobilize and allocate resources, and program a sequence of action steps which will maximize their chances for successful attainment of goals and objectives. Duplication of effort, waste of resources, employee confusion, unexpected events, and general chaos and operating ineffectiveness can be greatly reduced by sound, on-going planning by managers at every level of an organization.

Planning Is Future-Oriented

In order to plan, managers must look into the future. In view of the complexity, intensity and accelerating rate of change, many managers feel that such "crystal-ball gazing" is pointless. The future never seems to turn out as forecast. However, without a basic compass reading and road map for the future, a manager will never know whether he is on course towards his objectives or is merely drifting along aimlessly. It has been said that planning is akin to shooting a duck. If you aim where the duck is now, you will never hit it. You have to take into consideration the changes which are occurring in order to hit your target.

Even though the future will not be a mere extension of the past, it is helpful for managers to review their previous plans to see how closely the results actually matched the projected objectives. By evaluating those aspects of previous plans that seemed to help and those that seemed to hinder, a manager can improve his skill in the planning process. In addition, resource and staff people within and outside of an organization can provide useful special knowledge and technical know-how to a manager as he formulates his plans. Often one of the best sources of information is the employee group in the manager's own department. Employees like to be asked to express their opinions. Their suggestions about matters which directly affect them, and in which they're personally involved, are frequently extremely helpful to a manager who is developing objectives. and the specific steps to attain those objectives. Although the responsibility for planning is the manager's, the suggestions, advice and involvement of others can greatly improve personal effectiveness in carrying out this important function.

Types of Plans

A manager's individual planning, involving daily, personal actions, may be simply ideas which are mentally recorded. However, plans which involve others are usually written down in some format. These written plans may range from a simple daily desk calendar listing times, activities and appointments to a weekly schedule of events and projects. Or it may be a much lengthier and more detailed plan which summarizes objectives for an extended period of time, controlling policies and procedures, rules and specifications, a sequence of measurable action steps, allocated resources, target dates and criteria for measurement. Putting something in writing seems to increase clarity of thinking and makes it easier to communicate the plan to others. In most cases these plans will contain:

Units of time (man hours, days, month, years, etc.)

Units of resources (dollars, pounds, cases, truckloads, numbers, etc.)

Units of achievement (numbers, tons, barrels, etc.—expressed in both qualitative and quantitative terms)

Periods of time (within a month, by a certain date, etc.)

The nature of the manager's responsibilities and the situation determine the scope, detail and formality of the planning method. In all cases, it should be kept simple enough so that it can be changed quickly and easily when events are not conforming to plan. The actual plan itself is not the important thing; it is the *process* that counts.

A Dynamic Planning Approach

Effective planning requires a dynamic, systematic approach which enables a manager to collect relevant information, make and clarify existing estimates and assumptions about the present and the future, evaluate alternative courses of action, program a sequence of action steps, and build in a sufficient number of indicators to highlight progress. There are many different approaches to doing this; however, most planning systems attempt to answer the following questions:

1. **What must be done?**
2. **When must it be completed?**
3. **Under what conditions should it be done?**
4. **What steps shall we take to do it?**
5. **Where will these steps be taken?**
6. **What resources will be needed to get the results we want?**
7. **How will we measure our progress?**

The Answers

1. **What must be done?**

   The first step is to determine what end results are desired—what are the objectives we wish to attain. Perhaps there are several which exist at the same time. When this occurs, there is an additional question to be answered, "Which objectives are the most important at this time?"

2. **When must it be completed?**

   Once the objective is established, it should be stated in terms of a completion date. At what point in time do we want to attain our objective?

3. **Under what conditions should it be done?**

   Every manager works within a "ballpark." Policies, procedures, standards, rules and similar factors establish the parameters within which a manager must attain the objectives. Defining these helps the manager clarify beforehand those conditions which will control or limit a choice of action or implementation steps.

4. What steps shall we take to do it?

Here the manager considers various alternative steps which might be taken to attain the objectives. Based on time factors, resources, existing conditions and personal preference, the individual must select those which should best accomplish the job. These are then arranged in a sequence to form a program of action.

5. Where will these steps be performed?

It may be possible to have all of the action take place within the manager's own area of responsibility. However, in many cases, implementation may require the assistance and integration of efforts by others in the organization. Here the manager must coordinate and consolidate personal planning with that of others who are affected.

6. What resources will be needed to get the results we want?

Materials, machinery and equipment, money, manpower and time are required to attain objectives. The manager must determine how much of each will be needed and compare it with what is presently on hand. At this point a manager may find the necessary resources to do the job as planned are lacking. One then must rethink all action steps in order to attain the objectives with what is available, or one may seek additional resources to do the job.

7. How will we measure our progress?

If the manager is going to stay on course, he or she needs to have periodic readings which will indicate whether or not events are conforming to plan. How progress will be measured, at what frequency and by whom, must be determined at this stage.

Summary

Planning will not guarantee the desired results; however, effective on-going planning does enable the manager to have greater control over the job and make better use of all resources. It should optimize the likelihood of attaining objectives and minimize the impact of the unexpected.

THE MANAGERIAL MIND

By David W. Ewing

IN law, medicine, teaching, and other major professions, practitioners develop a distinctive point of view toward problems in their areas. They acquire not only a unique body of knowledge but also certain values, standards, and ways of thinking about the application of that knowledge. People often refer to this viewpoint or approach as a "mind." Thus, we say that a lawyer has a "legal mind," a doctor has a "medical mind," and a professor has an "academic mind."

Similarly, in management there is a "managerial mind." The managerial mind is not as easy to define as the other minds because it is newer, subtler, and more complex. Also, since management is not yet a profession in the usual sense, we do not have the benefit of written codes, annual debates over qualifications, specified curricula for training, and so forth. Indeed, we may never have the benefit of such criteria.

But this does not make the managerial mind any less real or important. In fact, the mangerial mind has an enormous impact on our daily lives and fortunes. To understand it is to understand a significant reason that organizations survive and grow in business, government, education, and the arts.

We tend to take organizational life for granted, but consider the odds against it, particularly in business. The most ordinary corporation operates in the face of endless strains, disruptions, and harassments. Inside it is torn by personal conflicts, group rivalries, apathy, stupidity, turnover, sickness, and other ills. Outside it fights competitors and predators not only in its same industry but in other industries competing for the same dollars in the consumer pocketbook. As if this were not enough, there is also the ever-present threat of attack from the antitrust department, pricing agencies, employment practices commissions, labor unions, dissident stockholders, and hosts of other critics. And if all these dangers cannot paralyze the corporation, there remains the ever-present threat of flood, earthquake, fire, freight strikes, civil disorders, war, and other such calamities. In a sense, therefore, it is a wonder that any corporation survives for long, let alone the thousands of them that actually do. This is one of those everyday miracles that we pay little attention to.

AN INTRODUCTION TO ADMINISTRATIVE MANAGEMENT

What accounts for the robust survival and growth rates of small, voluntary, vulnerable companies of men and women in such a hostile environment? Part of the explanation lies in human nature—our God-given capacities to cooperate, band together, and persevere. Part of it lies in our know-how and technology—our abilities to communicate, manufacture, distribute, and finance trade. But such explanations do not account sufficiently for the success of organizations. We must consider the managerial mind if we want a complete answer. For it is the managerial mind that makes a living corporation, like a living person, animal, or plant, more than the sum of its parts. It energizes the invisible but profoundly significant process that provides cohesion and fruitful cooperation among the functions. It does this by virtue of its will, its understanding, its power to make decisions.

Distinguishing Qualities

What is the nature of the managerial mind? How is it like other "minds"—and how is it different?

First, it consists in part, as other "minds" do, of a body of knowledge. In this case, the knowledge has to do with planning, control, and administration. As with law, medicine, teaching, and other professions, this knowledge is always changing.

Second, it incorporates certain values. The most important of these is the value placed on organization. For the man or woman with a managerial mind, the life of an organization has much the same vital, central, timeless importance that a client's rights have for the lawyer, that justice has for the judge, or that human life has for the doctor.

The preciousness of organizational life shows up in countless ways. People with managerial minds hate to see organizations die. They don't mind seeing them change but they will practically mortgage their own lives to keep an organization going. Viewing the desperate struggles some men and women wage to keep a company from going under, despite easier and pleasanter alternatives for a livelihood, psychologists sometimes say that managers "identify" with their companies, even to the extent of regarding death for the company as a kind of death for themselves. The manager, it is explained, seeks a kind of immortality by leaving a viable organization behind.

Whatever the explanation, the deep sense of commitment is real and tangible. Even the "job-hopping" executive, if he or she has a managerial mind, holds organizational life sacred. While serving with a company or division, he dedicates himself to its efficiency and growth as an organism, worries about its well-being, gives part of himself to it. A similar attitude is likely to hold for extra-curricular duties. I have seen executives come home exhausted at night only to rush out after supper to chair a meeting of a church or community organization. No matter how tired, they light up the moment they begin to feel involvement. "Organizations are sort of fascinating, sort of like children," one such man told me once. "They can have the same parents and many of the same committee members, but you know, each one is different!"

Such comparisons with people are common in managerial parlance. It is common to hear managers refer to companies as "healthy" or "unhealthy," "fat" or "lean," "aggressive" or "listless"; they may refer to the disbanding or selling off of a department or division as "corporate surgery"; they use such metaphors as "financial bloodstream" and "heart of the organization."

Investors and financial analysts are among those who can attest to the high value placed on organizational life by the managerial mind. From an investor's point of view, many companies would do well to concentrate on one or just a few endeavors. They would exploit the market while it is young and full, pile up all the profit they could, and liquidate when the market began to fall or be divided up among too many competitors. This would be to the investor's advantage, financial experts point out, because he would have many investments in his portfolio, and it is of no consequence to him which companies his money is in so long as each is maximizing its short-run profits.

But management usually takes a different view. It wants its organization to survive and prosper into the indefinite future, not burn itself out in a burst of glory like a Fourth of July fireworks display. So it may spend much time and money diversifying the products and services offered, taking on some lines that are not profitable today but should be good "insurance" for tomorrow. It may invest in research and personnel policies that can pay off only in the very long term. It may favor retained earnings over long-term debt as a source of funds because, while debt is cheaper for the professional investor, as a rule, retained earnings involve less risk.

At a well-known university program, executives from a variety of industries and localities were asked to consider the case of a venerable company which was in financial trouble. In the description of the case, a stockholder argued forcefully for selling out instead of trying to keep the organization intact. Most executives in the discussion objected to this view; their consensus was that everything possible should be done to save the organization. As one of them commented, it seemed almost "disloyal" to give up and liquidate, even though that was the economic thing to do for the owners.

It is not greed for money or power that explains the lengthening work weeks for many executives in business today, while other employees enjoy ever-shorter hours of work; it is the commitment of the managerial mind. The person who values organizational life in and of itself is incapable of saying, "The paperwork load is increasing, the demands of government regulations on my department are longer, and competition is more time-consuming, but I'll just have to do the best I can in a 40-hour week. If the company dies, it's not my fault." The managerial mind is like the doctor who goes without sleep to keep a sick patient alive, like the judge who keeps agonizing over a court case while vacationing in beautiful weather on Lake Michigan. She cannot let go. She cannot trick herself into thinking that the only thing that matters is her own welfare.

Third, the managerial mind emphasizes the understanding of relationships. Its unique approach to organizational problems is to look for the creative balance, the productive "fitting together" of people, money, plant and equipment, patents, markets, supplies, and the rest. No one of these elements by itself matters so much; what counts is its relationship with the other parts of the picture.

Not to grasp this way of thinking is to fail to understand the managerial mind. It is the mind of a "generalist" more than the mind of a specialist. This is one reason that staff people, academics, and other experts often fail to appreciate managerial decisions and to succeed in line management positions. What interests them is excellence in accounting, marketing, employee relations, or some other area by itself, not how such specialities can best blend together. Blending, balance, and "the big picture" tend to horrify the specialist because they mean compromising individual excellence. The managerial mind may value excellence, too, but what it reaches for most of all is the sense of wholeness, of productive interrelationship.

One time a task force of planning experts spent months studying a company's markets, building mathematical models showing the effects of different investment decisions, and formulating new decision rules for top management. The president studied the plan for a while and asked, "How does the purchasing department fit into all this?" The planners said they didn't consider that group because it was not important. "They have a job to do, too," the president answered. "You better work on this plan some more, because I don't think they could live with it."

Fourth, and in no manner least important, the managerial mind possesses the will to convert its knowledge, values, and understanding into acts of management. The man or woman with a managerial mind has no complexes or hang-ups about directing and controlling people. The dedication to organizational life is not contemplative or passive but energetically active. It becomes translated into such actions as giving instructions, calling meetings, setting deadlines, hiring people, checking on performance. It also becomes translated into such unpleasant but necessary tasks as firing employees who do not perform, making decisions that disappoint people, deciding to take big risks, and saying "no" when it would be nice to say "yes."

As veteran consultant Marvin Bower points out, what separates the men from the boys in management is often simply the will to manage. Nothing complex, subtle, or illusive about it—just the sheer, tough-minded determination to make up one's mind what actions are most likely to succeed *and then take them.* An executive once told me, "The main fault I find with the reports my subordinates give me is not that they are poorly written or unintelligent. They usually give the pros and cons and supporting facts fairly well. The trouble is they don't make up their minds which way to go." In other words, his subordinates may have had managerial knowledge and understanding but not the determination to decide. And if they didn't have that, what chance was there of having the will also to get involved, knock heads together if necessary, and see that decisions became implemented?

The will of the managerial mind shows up in many ways, but nowhere so conspicuously as in modern practices of control. In their philosophical moments managers may protest their emphasis on control—they may even give the impression that they interfere, intercede, and check up on their assistants relatively little. But watch one of these people in action and you will most likely get a very different impression. They are watching, investigating, checking, questioning, listening, evaluating, intervening all of the time. He or she *practically never* makes an important decision or gives an important instruction without following up on it. It is no accident that reams of the management literature focus on such qualitative control procedures as management by exception, management by objectives, span of authority, progress reporting, and program management; and on a nearly endless array of quantitative techniques, from cost analysis, profitability analysis, and cost-benefit analysis to various concepts of return on investment.

But mostly control is simple, direct, personal, and visceral. "Mr. Harrison, may I give you a little advice?" Billy Graham's business manager once told a young executive of a Georgia company who was upset because some work he had delegated had not been done right. "A good executive has to delegate, just as you have done in this case. And the power to delegate enables a man to multiply his abilities many times. But, in order to do this, he must learn one basic rule; *to keep his hand in* whatever he delegates."

A more extreme case is reported by Professor Chris Argyris. While studying the performance of a plant, he got to talking with supervisors about the plant manager. One supervisor said about the man: "I told him once that I didn't know how the hell to please him and he told me, 'Look here, I'm not going to let you alone. I'm not ever going to let you alone. If you ever get to a point where you think you know your job too well, then you become like a stagnant pool. I'm going to keep after you all the time.' " While this attitude may seem excessive to most executives, it dramatizes a willingness to intercede and become involved which is characteristic of the managerial mind. According to Dr. H. Edward Wrapp, a fine observer of top executive behavior, managers at this level do not withdraw to concentrate on the "big picture," as so many textbook writers and consultants think they should do. Instead, these executives habitually enmesh themselves in operating problems so they can keep their "feel" for what is going on.

Some Contrasts

Before turning to several important implications of the managerial mind for companies and other organizations, let us note what it is *not*. By contrasting it with other ideas and standards, we may be able to develop a clearer, sharper picture of it.

The managerial mind is *not* a certain philosophy or set of techniques. People with managerial minds employ many different kinds of approaches to their work, from seat-of-the-pants management to scientific management.

It is *not* a kind of personality or motivation. Some people with managerial minds are acquisitive and materialistic; some are idealistic and unmaterialistic; some love power and some don't. There is practically no end of variation in this respect.

It is *not* a certain kind or level of intelligence or education. A person may know everything there is to know about management, but if he cannot bring himself to decide, direct, and use muscle to get the task done, he lacks a managerial mind. As for I.Q., no doubt some people of this sort would score as high as any scientist or teacher; but others, I suspect, could just be called "shrewd."

It is *not* a title or position in an organization. Some people with "vice president" in their titles are not managers at all; they are analysts, staff specialists, experts of one type or another. Some people with "director" in their titles are power-hungry neurotics who have gotten near the top by political maneuvering or phenomenal capacities for work, not because they have an interest in directing people productively.

It is *not* some measure of financial success or authority. A person who manages a small firm or work project may have a managerial mind no less than one who directs a large corporation; in fact, many housewives apply managerial minds in running their households (a fact not well enough appreciated in the women-in-management controversy). A manager earning a small salary may have just as much of a managerial mind as a multimillionaire executive has. A person who, through misfortune or bad luck has never made it to the big time, may have as fine a managerial mind as one who has succeeded in that way.

In short, the measure of the man or woman with a managerial mind is tangible, physical contibution to organizational life made by directing the efforts of people in that organization.

Loyalty and Discipline

Life would be much simpler without the managerial mind. For one thing, there would not be some of the ethical dilemmas to ponder that regularly consume time and energy in countless companies, civic organizations, government agencies, and other groups. (But then there would not be so many vital organizations, either.)

Because of the value placed on organizational life, the person with a managerial mind demands a high degree of loyalty to the company, division, or other organization for which people work. To paraphrase Stephen Decatur's legendary slogan, "My country right or wrong, but my country," the managerial mind says, "My organization right or wrong, but my organization." Many companies used to post slogans mirroring that attitude—for instance, "The Corporation above Self," posted years ago at Dan River Mills.

Although that is not done very often now, loyalty to the organization is still very important in management thinking. Indeed, it has to be, for the alternative is anarchy. An organization of people with different tasks and specialties is organic in much the same way that a tree or animal is organic. The organism simply cannot live without a high degree of cooperation and discipline among the parts.

But this fact of life does not solve many ethical problems that arise. What does the assistant manager of a corporate division do when she sees her boss falsifying the reports sent to headquarters—distorting the figures not to feather her own nest but out of a desire (however mistaken) to protect the welfare of her employees? Does the assistant manager keep her silence out of loyalty to the boss and her associates, or does she send the word up to headquarters because of a sense of obligation to the larger organization? What does a supervisor do when she sees her company polluting a river with acids from a plant, urges management to correct the problem, and gets turned down? Does she shut up out of faith in the wisdom of the bosses and dedication to the life of the enterprise, or does she begin a protest movement that may attract community attention and hasten a political clampdown?

Pose questions like these to any group of managers and you will stir up a good argument in no time. Yet all is not confusion. In many companies thoughtful managers have worked on guidelines for use in such situations. And while the reality has been distorted again and again in popular novels and movies, these guidelines allow and encourage a high degree of individualism.

One important criterion is that nothing in the requirement of loyalty to the organization shall force an employee to alter his personal views so they conform with the view officially decided on. Recently an experience of AT&T's famous executive, Chester Barnard, was brought to light.* Early in his career Barnard found himself reporting to H. B. Thayer, at the time president of Western Electric Company. Barnard had been asked to study and report on a new rate system for the city of Detroit. Unfortunately, his conclusions were the opposite of those recommended by a man named B. E. Sunny, who was head of the company which gave service in Michigan.

When Barnard discussed his report with his boss, Thayer said to him, "Can't you modify your report in certain directions so as to harmonize with Mr. Sunny's view?" Barnard replied: "Look, Mr. Thayer, you people at the top managing this thing can and must take into account many considerations that a staff man working on one sector of a problem can't deal with. They are beyond my ken. Of course you can do what you want to, but what you are asking me to do is alter my statement of what my beliefs are. The minute you do that, if I accede, you destroy my usefulness. You just make me a yes man. I think you ought to go ahead and agree with Mr. Sunny if that's what you think is the wise thing, but I don't think you ought to involve me in doing that. I've made my report and I stand by it."

Thayer could have retorted, "You're an SOB and the hell with you," Barnard reflected when telling of the experience. But Thayer did not do that. What he said was, "My boy, you're right!"

Here is a good example of the managerial mind at work. The boss expected loyalty to the extent that it meant working hard and intelligently as directed. But loyalty did not mean to her that managers had to agree with one another or with her. Rather, differences of views were to be expected, in the very nature of things, and it was the boss's job to study those differences and make a decision as to

---

*See William B. Wolf, *Conversations With Chester Barnard* (Ithaca, N.Y., New York State School of Industrial and Labor Relations, 1973), pp. 42–43.

what action to take. Once the boss made that decision, she expected those who had dissented to do their best to help her, not because they agreed she was right but because only in that way could the organization stay productive.

When, as sometimes happens, a subordinate's feelings of disagreement become too strong to allow such cooperation, he or she is expected to resign. He or she is under no obligation to serve with any one organization, but so long as they do elect to serve it, they must do their best.

Some 3,500 U.S. executives gave their views on a series of questions I sent them on various ethical conflicts. A strong majority of these men and women did not expect an accountant, let us say, to falsify a profit statement because the boss said that was necessary in order to get an important loan; and if the boss fired him as a result, they would have countermanded the order. On the other hand, they would not have felt kindly toward the accountant if, while staying with the company, he had gone out of his way to tell an outsider about the distortions and thereby caused the company to lose an important piece of business.

Emphasis on Creativity

For many years professional managers have been under indictment as noncreative people. The "organization man" stereotype that William H. Whyte popularized in the 1950's still persists in the thinking of many critics. Among scientists and engineers, the person who breaks ranks to go into administration is often looked down on as a second-rate technical person who felt he could not make the grade with his peers. On the campus there is widespread suspicion of management in any field, business, government, the arts, or others. The very idea of controlling people somehow runs against the image of the creative life as students think of it. There is probably no business executive in the whole country who would get the high marks for creativity that, say, Ralph Nader would receive in a campus-wide poll.

The underlying assumption is that the manager is little more than a manipulator of ideas originated by others. He or she does not add anything new and vital to the organization, getting ahead not because of what he can do but because of whom he knows. Fresh thinking and originality, the critics say, must come from scientists, artists, youthful types not yet brainwashed by the establishment, or outsiders. Above all, creativity must come from individualists, not committee members.

It is understandable that management gets stuck with this drab and uninspiring image. For one thing, there are many companies that gain far more publicity for their resistance to change—to new air-pollution standards, for instance, or to new standards for truth in advertising—than for anything else they do. For another, the simple arithmetic of innovation produces a misleading image. A given company—even the largest and most profitable one—has limited resources. It has the time, manpower, funds, and facilities to concentrate on a certain number of new projects, but if it spreads itself too thin it will not be able to succeed in any of its new ventures. Employees and advisers whose ideas are shelved or rejected cannot always be blamed if they deduce erroneously from their experience that the company is "against change" or "doesn't like to do things differently." And since such people are numerous, their impressions may gain considerable circulation.

Yet another cause for misunderstanding can be traced to the fact that companies often seek uniformity in appearance for sales purposes. When Jersey Standard changes its name, each of its gas stations (Esso, Enco, and Humble) puts up an Exxon sign, every Jersey Standard office changes to Exxon letterheads. Every Howard Johnson's has the same cheerful, orange, family look. Every John Deere tractor has the same shade of green. Every McDonald's hamburger and cup of french fries are the same size. To the outsider, these appearances may seem like telltale symptoms of conformity. However, behind the customer displays, in the offices of the men and women who produce the products and services, innumerable contrasts and diversities exist. The "corporate identity" is simply a recognizable face for the outside world.

Appearances to the contrary, American business as a whole seems clearly to be under the control of innovators and individualists. Our cultural heritage, the competitive system, and private property get much of the credit for this—but not all of it. Something about the nature of the managerial mind, too, seems to keep conformity localized, like patches of blight on an otherwise healthy tree. The closer you get to the vital growth centers, the more you see individualism flourishing.

One convincing evidence of individualism is the diversity of personality one finds among people with managerial minds. A gregarious, easygoing department head will have an assistant who is introspective and hard-driving. A division president who commonly makes decisions on the basis of hunch and intuition will work closely with a vice president who thinks in terms of systems and statistics. In a large New York corporation with a predominantly conservative, "old guard" management, one influential top executive is as heretical, provocative, and liberal a thinker as can be found in any university "think tank." He has been with that company many years and no doubt will retire from it someday—for all of his odd-man qualities he is probably more secure than most of his more conventional peers. It is no accident that the managerial mind works in this way. As any botanist, zoologist, or anthropologist can confirm, organic life is a process based on relationships. The more contrast in these relationships, the more creative they can be. The highly creative act of reproduction, for example, requires opposite sexes, and the process of physical adaptation to the environment depends on responding to stimuli from hostile outside sources. The corporation is no exception to any of these rules. Intuitively if not consciously, the person with a managerial mind senses that an organization without internal contrasts and differences is an organization without much life expectancy.

Besides, any person with a managerial makeup is bound to thrive personally on diversity and challenge. For such a man or woman, a day spent with contrasting, divergent, colorful personalities is far preferable to a day of no surprises with yes men. Individualists like the late David Sarnoff of RCA would go further. Sarnoff once said that he was grateful even to his enemies around him because "in the long-range movement toward progress, a kick in the pants sends you farther along than a friendly hand does."

Innovation in business, even in the most common business activities, is not one whit different in principle from scientific innovation. It was inventor-businessman Edwin Land of Polaroid Corporation who once pointed out that the process of invention in merchandising is exactly the same as in a sophisticated science like rheology.

I recall a meeting at the Harvard Business School where a large group of executives from different industries got to reminiscing about the experiences which had helped them most to succeed. Man after man singled out some such factor as "I had a boss who let me throw out crazy suggestions" or "I worked for a man who would let me experiment and learn from my own mistakes—even though it made him grit his teeth to do it."

Critics of the corporation often ask: How can there be much creativity with so much control? Actually, the question would be a harder one if turned around: How can there be much control without continuous innovation and creativity? For the real threat to executive influence is not change but lack of change, not the fluid organization but the static organization. Innovation and revision are what give the manager his opportunities to govern effectively. It is when procedures get frozen and employees fall into ruts and rotes that he loses control, for then the "system" begins to control instead of managerial initiative and direction.

AN INTRODUCTION TO ADMINISTRATIVE MANAGEMENT

Executives have told me they would shake things up every so often even if they did not need to, because that is the best way they have of learning who can do what and how well and, most important, of challenging people to outdo themselves. The head of a prosperous large bank was asked by a friend why he was making a series of organization changes when everything was going so smoothly. "Look," he answered, "nobody likes to see earnings up more than I do, because it keeps the directors off my back. But what you don't realize is that every bank president is at war with the bureaucracy. If he leaves things alone when 'things are going smoothly,' he'll be just a figurehead. It'll be the bureaucracy that makes decisions, not him. You know how the President couldn't change the State Department when he wanted to. Well, every company has a potential state department on its hands."

Surely revolutionaries cannot be accused of conformity, and just as surely business executives with managerial minds must be ranked among the revolutionary forces in society. The late Benjamin M. Selekman, a great philosopher of the labor movement, used to point out that while business executives have been branded conservative in a political sense, their record has been anything but conservative in other respects. Radical changes in the quality and character of American life in this century have been brought on by management. Mass production, mass distribution, automation, modern food processing, electronic data processing, television, rapid transportation, teaching machines, pharmaceutical breakthroughs—these and other business-led revolutions have altered our daily lives more broadly, more profoundly, more irreversibly than any series of innovations in law, medicine, or the arts. These transformations, many of them carried out in the face of fierce opposition from labor and other groups, were not executed by conformists!

No letup of this revolutionary zeal is in sight. Every day the business press reports examples of work on new ideas, from novel methods of transportation and producing food to new concepts of providing community health care. In most of these cases, the idea itself is but a small part of the story, for behind the scenes enormous efforts must be made to muster support and solve developmental problems.

The Managerial Way

Persuading, inspiring, spending, innovating, investing, planning, revising, detailing, organizing, arranging, and engaging in all the many other activities that turn dreams into realities—this is the way of the managerial mind. It does not work in the solitude of a laboratory but in the hurly burly of deadlines, conflict, and tension, with telephones ringing and visitors interrupting and assistants coming and going.

To many people this may seem like an impossible world in which to innovate, and for certain types of creativity it is indeed. But this is the process through which creative relationships grow and make organizations come alive. True managers do not consider their creativity handicapped by "people problems." They know they could not be productive without them.

CHAPTER 2

ADMINISTRATION
IS COMMUNICATING

By Robert N. McMurry, Ph.D.

JUST about every company in the nation has a set of boxes (draw-ings, of course) pinned on the wall, with a big box (PRESIDENT) at the top, then a few smaller boxes below that (VICE PRESI-DENTS), and then rows of still smaller boxes, ad infinitum, all of which is called

"OUR ORGANIZATION CHART."

However, if my many years of experience has given me any in-sight, I call this "The Organization Chart Chimera." The conven-tional big-box-little-box charts show how the top executives *wish* the organization were functioning. But a much more realistic pattern is shown in the "Beehive Charts," on the next page.

The Beehive Chart

The conventional organization chart rarely reflects the existing *informal* relationships; it is therefore misleading because it assumes that everyone on a given level is psychologically equidistant from an immediate supervisor. In actual fact, this is practically never the case. Some supervisors are inevitably "closer" to their bosses than others.

Furthermore, these relationships are often quite unstable; certain individuals are constantly falling in and out of favor with their bosses. Because of the manifest inadequacies of the formal chart as a measure of relationships within the management hierarchy, it is useful to supplement it by the preparation of a circular or, even better, a three-dimensional beehive organization chart.

A beehive chart consists of a series of concentric circles, of which the innermost circle represents the apex of the management hierar-chy. (If it is not practical to construct a three-dimensional chart, perhaps one laid over a small globe of the world, then a flat chart

THE BEEHIVE TYPE OF ORGANIZATION

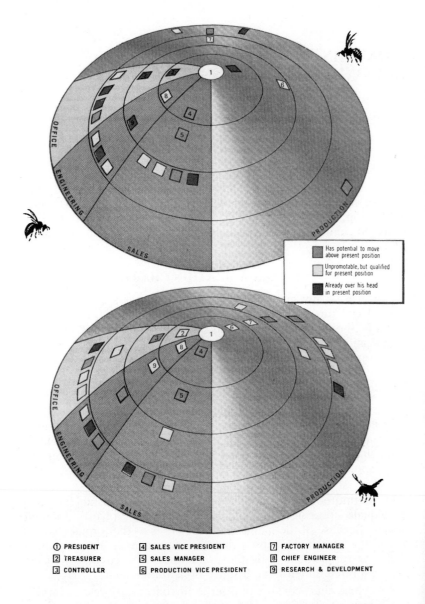

Has potential to move above present position

Unpromotable, but qualified for present position

Already over his head in present position

① PRESIDENT	④ SALES VICE PRESIDENT	⑦ FACTORY MANAGER
② TREASURER	⑤ SALES MANAGER	⑧ CHIEF ENGINEER
③ CONTROLLER	⑥ PRODUCTION VICE PRESIDENT	⑨ RESEARCH & DEVELOPMENT

The graphic illustration of the beehive type of organization chart clearly indicates at a glance where the various executives are ranked and how they are viewed in terms of potential.

should be thought of as in three dimensions—i.e., as a true half-dome, or beehive.)

The bands surrounding the apex constitute the supervisory echelons from top to bottom. The number of bands corresponds to the number of levels of management. The pie-shaped segments of varying widths represent the company's principal operating divisions or functions, such as sales, production, engineering, finance.

The symbol representing the chief executive (or administrator, in a departmental chart) is placed in the central circle, but not necessarily in the exact center. If he or she tends, for example, to favor one of the divisions over the others—perhaps because of being promoted out of it—his or her symbol is placed closer to it. If one has an associate, perhaps an executive assistant, who is very close, this person's symbol is also placed in the central circle. When the chief executive is also more closely identified with one of the organizational functions, his or her symbol is placed adjacent to it.

In the bands which surround the central circle, closeness to the chief executive—and to other supervisors in the lower echelons—is indicated by the location of the symbol for the individual within the circumferential band itself. If the supervisor is very close to the boss, this symbol is placed near the center of the circle; where the reverse is true, it is placed at the outer rim of the band.

If two supervisors within a department or segment are congenial, their symbols are placed side by side. In the event that they are not congenial, a space is left between them proportionate to the degree of their mutual hostility. Where a supervisor is indicated as the principal source of information for an executive, the supervisor's symbol is placed directly on the president-executive axis. A color code—green for those individuals who have the potential to move above their current level, yellow for those who are suitable for their current position but are not promotable, and red for those who are unsatisfactory—can also be employed to indicate the promotional status of each individual in the management hierarchy.

Diagnosis and Action

By studying a three-dimensional beehive organization chart such as this, the chief executive can readily see, in total perspective, the status of the supervisory staff. The executive can note at a glance who is promotable, who should remain where he or she is, and who should be replaced. By referring to the individual appraisal report, the chief executive can become familiar with the precise qualifications of each man. Furthermore, because these findings also picture the *informal* organization clearly, the executive can note realistically the groupings, alliances, cliques, and communication channels that characterize the organization. This is often invaluable in assessing the worth and significance of the information from those who report.

The greatest contribution of the beehive chart is its value in denoting those supervisors who are misplaced, overmatched, or whose performance is clearly unsatisfactory. But what about corrective action?

Occasionally, in situations where the individual has been obviously misplaced, corrective action is not difficult; the individual can be reassigned. However, in the majority of instances, the supervisor who is "over his head" is unwilling or unable to face his or her inadequacies. Hence, notwithstanding many experts to the contrary, "counseling" as conventionally employed is of little value in these cases. It may have a temporary palliative effect, but rarely yields a lasting cure *because the treatment fails to get at the cause of the trouble*.

Fortunately, these beehive appraisals not only distinguish those individuals in management who need help but also define in detail the nature of their strengths and weaknesses. With this diagnostic information, it is possible to pinpoint the sources of the trouble. On occasion, steps can also be taken to reconstitute the supervisor's job assignments in such a manner as to utilize his strengths to the maximum and minimize the demands placed on his areas of weakness.

In the final analysis, however, the major contribution of the appraisal program is that it takes a substantial portion of the guesswork out of management. The administrator at least knows much more about the supervisory people to whom major responsibilities in operating the business must be delegated. There is no need to "fly blind" with reference to their qualifications.

Constructive Steps

There are a number of constructive steps which the administrator can now take to better the functioning of the department.

First, one can strengthen the management team by realistically observing it and taking the necessary steps to identify, rehabilitate (when possible), and replace (where necessary) those members of the executive and supervisory staff who are imcompetent, misplaced, or maladjusted. This action *must* be taken when the supervisor is clearly incompetent and is, in consequence, undermining morale.

Second, one can build for the future by recognizing competent people with potential for advancement so that they are not frustrated and forced to leave, or permitted to wither on the vine in blind-alley staff positions.

Third, one can improve organizational efficiency by staffing the supervisory hierarchy in such a manner that the highest possible consonance is achieved between the formal (chart) organization and the informal ("natural") organization, as revealed on the beehive chart. This will ensure a more proper executive placement and minimize internecine (intra- and interdepartmental) conflict.

Fourth, an initial step can be made toward the betterment of employee morale by reviewing existing departmental conditions, policies, and practices in the light of employee attitudes toward them as revealed by the survey. In spite of the fact that some of these are hallowed by age and usage, it is usually better for the administrator to take prompt and drastic action to remedy what many people regard as legitimate grounds for dissatisfaction.

Fifth, the administrator can engage in a realistic morale-building program. Such a program will include the elimination of legitimate grounds for employee grievances—or if this is impossible, the exploration of why it cannot be done. Most difficult, but also most urgent, in this area is the prompt removal of incompetent, weak, or authoritarian first- and second-line supervisors. They may be technically proficient, of long service, and loyal, but if they can neither guide nor support their subordinates, they must go. It may not be necessary to discourage such employees, but they should be removed from a supervisory capacity.

Sixth, one can facilitate *upward* communication by supplementing conventional media (reports, the hierarchy of supervision, the union, the grapevine, and others) through the use of additional channels, particularly those which facilitate the cross-checking and verification of the information produced. The best of these are periodic (perhaps annual) employee survey polls, supplemented by regularly scheduled informal talks between top-management representatives and natural leaders, who will have been identified previously during the latest poll. (Just as a company's finances are audited annually, a department's personnel policies and practices, and the qualifications of its executives and supervisors, should be audited at least biennially.)

Seventh, it's possible to expedite *downward* communication by depending less on conventional, one-way-from-management media (i.e., house organs, bulletin boards, letters to the employees' homes, and talks by management and members of the supervisory hierarchy).

Communication Through Leaders

One of the best channels is through natural leaders. Ideally those who are judged most cooperative are assembled in groups varying in size from three to five or six, all from the same unit or department. After explaining to them that they have been very helpful in providing information, as a part of the poll, they are told that the company has a very important message which it wants communicated to all employees with as little modification as possible. Their help is desired in its dissemination.

The material is then presented to them, and they are encouraged to comment on it. (By meeting with several leaders in a group, discussion among the members can be stimulated, and this is usually revealing.) Normally, it does not require more than a few minutes to ascertain the extent to which the message is understood, believed, and accepted. If the message is not understood, believed, and accepted, it is expedient to discover immediately what is causing the difficulty and, if possible, to correct it. In most instances this is not too troublesome. Usually the problem is one of semantics.

The important point to keep in mind is that *if the members of the group, as natural leaders, understand, believe, and accept the message, then its dissemination, comprehension, belief, and acceptance by the employees as a whole will be successful.*

Good communications start at the top. If the administrator cannot face reality, he or she cannot expect that subordinates will open the door to it voluntarily. It takes an administrator with courage and resolution to face the facts of human relationships in business as they really are and not as they appear on a formalized chart.

CHAPTER 3

THE FOUR M's OF MANAGEMENT

IN order to fully understand the complexity of the directing function, it is helpful to look at the job of managing from a different perspective. Instead of talking about managing in terms of the four *basic functions* a manager must perform, it is helpful to look at managing in terms of the assets or resources which managers are given to use. All managers, regardless of the nature of their organization, have four basic assets:

Money

Material

Machinery and equipment

Manpower

The mark of a good manager is one who effectively utilizes those four assets to attain the goals and objectives of the organization. Most managers are periodically asked to account for their use or their stewardship of those assets. There are various ways this is done. We talk about money in terms of such factors as expenditures of funds versus budgeted amounts; about materials in terms of inventory levels, waste and new characteristics; and about machinery and equipment in terms of such things as downtime, preventive maintenance, and modification of machinery and equipment to get greater output. But, somehow, when we get to the fourth asset—manpower—it becomes more difficult to measure. Managers often shrug their shoulders and say, "What can you do—you're dealing with people!" Yet without that asset nothing happens. It's the most important asset a manager has.

It used to be the "in thing" to say that an organization's employees are its most important resources. Many companies, after they have devoted several pages of their annual reports to their use of physical assets (money, materials, machinery and equipment), include a line or two to say that their human resources are really their greatest asset. It's the "nice thing to say" and is certainly worth brief mention. However, other companies are beginning to view human resources from a very practical, pragmatic, dollars-and-cents standpoint. They are beginning to see that the only competitive difference that is left is the productivity of their people.

Years ago companies were able to establish and maintain an advantage over their competitors by developing and implementing improvements in the use of their physical assets—money, materials, machinery and equipment. Today with our rapid means of communication—with the fact that we can see a splashdown in the Pacific just about the moment it happens, the fact that communications media speedily carry word of developments throughout the world no matter where it happens—it is no longer possible to get the edge on a competitor through technological innovations. As a result, the only remaining difference lies in the fourth asset—people. If one company can get the same amount of money, the same materials, and the same types of machinery and equipment as another company, then the only thing that makes one company more competitive and more successful than another is the *productivity of its employees.* In fact, throughout the world, there is an increasing awareness of the need to find better ways to utilize this asset.

There's another important aspect about this asset that should be noted: it is the only asset that has the unique capability of *appreciating* in value. The other three assets—money, materials, machinery and equipment—basically *depreciate* over time. Human beings, however, based on the way they are utilized each day on the job, can actually increase in value through the acquisition of additional knowledge, skills, insight, understanding and the resulting overall contributions they can make to an organization. If managers are going to effectively utilize human resources, they not only must maintain them, they must find ways to increase the staff's value to the organization.

A person who becomes a manager takes on a tremendous responsibility. He must accomplish specific goals and objectives through other people. He must direct others in such a fashion that they will work willingly, enthusiastically, and as a unified whole in the attainment of the organization's goals and objectives. It requires a great amount of knowledge and a wide variety of skills to do the job. It is no wonder that directing is the aspect of managing that is the most complex and causes the greatest grief. It is no wonder we hear managers say: "I can do it myself, but how do I get them to do it?" Let's look at some of the approaches that managers have historically used in trying to direct the work of others.

Old Approaches to Directing Others

Whenever a group of managers is asked to list the various ways they attempt to direct others—to manage or motivate other people—they tend to give answers which can be placed under one or two categories. They are either examples of *Coercion* and *Threat* or some type of *Reward*. Sometimes these approaches are labeled the *Club* (or the stick) and the *Carrot*. In fact, many managers are familiar with the "Carrot and Stick" concept of motivation.

These approaches to directing—to managing or motivating people—do seem to work at times. However, many managers are beginning to find that their "tried-and-true" methods work less and less often with fewer people. Some managers refer to it as the "silent strike"—the difference between what people actually do and what they *could do* if they were motivated. Managers are spending more and more time trying to find new variations of these approaches to get people to do what they want them to do. New answers seem to be needed for the old question, "What is the best way to motivate people?"

The Impact of Behavioral Science

For years managers have been told that people will be motivated if they are treated better. Many books and courses have taught managers specific techniques, rituals, and simple "how-to-do-it" steps or formulas for handling people. Studies have been made of how people act on the job in an attempt to find new ways to motivate them. This activity has frequently been labeled the "human relations movement." Unfortunately it has not given managers the answers they were seeking.

Over the past 40 to 50 years there has been a growing body of research on motivation which *is* beginning to give managers some clues as to why some of the old approaches to managing and motivation don't seem to be working as well today as they did in the past. This research, which falls under the general heading of behavioral science, is a systematic study of people and their relationships to each other.

It embraces many different schools of thought regarding human behavior and many different academic disciplines including psychology, sociology, anthropology, economics, linguistics and education. It is based on the fundamental premise that there is a reason why people do what they do; i.e., all behavior is caused. Consequently, not only have behavioral scientists studied *how* we behave (which is fairly easy to do), but also *why* we act the way we do (which is the much more complex question to answer).

The overall objective has been to find out how to increase the productivity of organizations through optimal use of their human resources. The findings from these studies over the years have not given managers a new set of strategies or techniques for handling or manipulating people—in fact behavioral science rarely provides any specific, concrete answers. Instead, it has given managers a useful, analytical approach for gaining some *insight and understanding* of people, both as individuals and as members of organizational groups.

It has shown why certain managerial techniques work sometimes and don't work at other times, when to use one approach and when to try another. It points out how some "old rules of managing" have evolved and why they still make sense, and what has caused the development of newer concepts and strategies of managing which are frequently referred to today as the principles and practices of professional management. In order to develop more effective ways to perform the directing function, it is helpful for a manager to have a basic understanding of these findings from behavioral science.

The Fundamental Finding

Behavioral research has challenged the underlying "Push-Pull" assumption managers have held for years. The key message coming from all of these studies is that the answer to the question, "What Makes Sammy Run?"—as the old Broadway play used to ask—is not what managers *do to Sammy* in terms of pushing or pulling him, but *it's Sammy himself.* Sammy has his own built-in motor which is always running, i.e., he is *always* motivated. In fact, a person who is not motivated is dead—physically dead! The problem managers find is that often Sammy is motivated along lines that run just counter to what they want him to do. In fact, he is often most highly motivated when he is trying to "beat the system."

The reason that a person is always motivated is that he has needs. These serve as the fuel or nutrients for his motor. He acts, or he behaves, in an effort to satisfy those needs. If he is hungry, he looks for something to eat. If he is thirsty, he looks for something to drink. If he is tired, he lies down to get some sleep. What a person does—how he acts—how he behaves—*is perfectly sensible and justifiable to him.*

Managers, viewing his actions, may feel that what he did just doesn't make sense. A manager may not be able to see the logic of it. It appears ridiculous. However, what the individual does makes sense to him at that moment. This is because his actions are based on how he sees himself (his "self-perception") and how he sees the situation (his "perception of the environment") in which he finds himself at any given time. These perceptions are through *his* eyes—no one else's.

In order to more fully understand this, it helps to look at each of the two perceptions:

Self-Perception

Each person accumulates a storehouse of ideas in her mind concerning what sort of person she is. This storehouse consists of experiences she has had as she has grown up—things she has done, places she has been, things she has seen and emotions she has felt. This storehouse of an accumulated lifetime of experiences serves as a personal road map. It tells her just what she is like; and, it is different from anyone else's personal road map. Even though two people may have shared some similar experiences, or may have been at the same places together, or may have read some of the same books, the *total* accumulated data one person has will, in fact, be different from the *total* accumulated data of any other person.

Because each person's road map is different, it is difficult for a manager to try to change another person's road map. This is a task for men and women who are trained psychologists and psychiatrists. Most managers are not trained to do this kind of work. That would seem to indicate that a manager must take a person as she is and that she can do very little to bring about a change in that person's behavior. This is not entirely true, because there are some elements in the environment over which a manager may have some control.

Perception of the Environment

The environment in which each individual finds oneself, when at work, consists of several key elements:

1. **Job Content**
   What it is one is given to do.

2. **Managerial Style**
   The way in which one is managed.

3. **Organizational Climate**
   The overall organizational atmosphere in which the individual works.

All three of these elements can be changed by a manager. A manager can change what she gives a person to do; she can change the way in which she herself manages; and she can change to some degree the overall work atmosphere or climate. This then begins to indicate to a manager where she might turn her attention if she is going to try to bring about a change in another individual's behavior. Since the manager can't directly change the individual, she may be able to change the environment in which that individual works. By doing so she may gradually bring about a change in the individual. Let's look at how differences in perception may cause differences in actions.

How They See Themselves

Two people could be standing side by side and have identical needs at any given moment. One person sees herself as a winner—a capable individual, able to succeed in whatever she undertakes. Her experiences throughout her lifetime have shown her that she is the kind of person who can do things well. She's had a whole string of successes to reinforce this notion of hers as to what sort of person she is.

The second individual sees himself as a loser—a person who has been scarred for life by the fates. He is able to recount numerous examples of situations throughout his lifetime where he has attempted to do something and has failed. These failures are "evidence" to him of his own inadequacies and his lack of ability.

In this situation these two individuals could have identical needs at the same moment, but because they see themselves differently, they may act differently.

How They See the Environment

Take another example where two people see the environment differently. One person may see it as a world in which people are for him—it's a friendly place, it's a supportive atmosphere, the manager is a person who will help him. The second individual sees the environment as hostile. It's a world which she can't change. It has numerous barriers which prevent her from doing what she wants to do. The manager is against her, he will not provide help to her, she doesn't like him. These two people could have identical needs at the same moment, but because they see the environment differently, they may act differently.

Motivation Is Internal

In summary, we begin to see that motivation is not something we do to a person; motivation is something that comes from *within* each individual. What a person does makes sense to him because he chooses his actions based on how he sees himself (what sort of person he believes himself to be) and how he sees the environment (what kind of world he finds himself in). Therefore, a manager who is responsible for directing others, cannot do anything directly to them—in terms of pushing or pulling—that will have very effective results over any significant period of time. Instead, a manager must concentrate his attentions on trying to find out what a person's needs are at any given time and how that individual sees things. In essence, she has to try to get into the other person's shoes and see things the way that individual sees them, i.e., through the eyes of the other person.

There are elements in the environment over which managers *do* have some control. They can change the content of jobs, the way they manage and the overall atmosphere in their work areas. If a manager changes any of these so that people begin to see the environment differently, they may begin to act differently. Consequently, the area of maneuverability for a manager lies in understanding the impact that these various elements have on a person's behavior and how changes in these elements may bring about a change in that person's behavior. This requires a manager to spend less time criticizing someone's actions and more time in attempting to find out *why* the individual acted that way. Only by finding out *why* can a manager hope to have a chance to bring about a different type of behavior.

YOUR SUPERVISOR IS READY TO HELP YOU

Right now, when starting a new job, you're undoubtedly full of questions. There are a hundred and one things you'd like to know . . . and dozens of new situations to meet.

Your supervisor is always ready to help you. As leader of the group in which you work, he or she has a real interest in your welfare and progress and wants you, as a member of the team, to contribute to the overall accomplishments of the group.

So, when you have a question or problem, talk things over with your supervisor. With such friendly guidance, you'll soon feel right at home on your new job.

You will be given all the instruction and help you need. Your supervisor and your fellow workers want you to succeed.

The important thing to remember is to keep an open mind toward your job. Learn all you can about your work and the telephone industry by observation and by asking questions. Knowledge and sureness in your work will come gradually with experience.

Excerpt from employee-induction booklet

CHAPTER 4

MANAGEMENT BY OBJECTIVES

By James L. Dougherty

AT a time when management by objectives is becoming recognized as basic in the profitable operation of an enterprise, objectives are seldom mentioned in the same breath with personnel management. Yet this style of managing is so closely interwoven with action in the personnel area as to make them inseparable. Even where objectives are used in personnel management, they are all too often badly handled.

Most administrators embrace the concept of management by objectives. A few are quite expert in its use. Many others also manage by objectives, in the sense that they take the objectives handed them (or perhaps originated by themselves), break each objective into workaday pieces, operational goals, then set out to get them done. Perhaps more typically, many continue to do the things they have been doing, although perhaps more purposefully for having now better defined their goals.

Even skillful, objective-oriented managers will often fail to follow through, for any of several possible reasons:

1. They may fail to parcel out his goals, or subgoals, among the people reporting to him. Put another way, they fail to staff the program with the full potential of the personnel available.

2. They may fail to build in effective feedback on progress toward accomplishment of the goals, or to set time limits on the key mileposts (perhaps the completion of preliminary studies, a pilot run, or any well-defined intermediate point).

3. They may tend to be too rigid in setting goals. The feedback should do much more than mark off the weeks when actions are due. It should send up signals when the objectives are unreal—set too high or too low—and the goals should then be changed, or the whole idea dropped. The decision to stay on course should be a deliberate one.

More Than Division of Tasks

For an office administrator to parcel out objectives among the group of people who report to him or her involves much more than simply dividing the task as equally as possible among them, more than identifying, securing, or developing the people resources that will assume the responsibility for the future objectives of the enterprise.

Peter Drucker says, "The crux of a program of action is the allocation of resources, and especially the staffing decisions . . . In developing that scarce and most productive resource—high caliber people—the first-class people must always be allocated to *major* opportunities, to the areas of greatest possible return per unit of effort . . ." (italics mine).

Although obviously, it is unwise to permit *minor* opportunities to fend for themselves, neither would it be wise to demand or develop first-rate human resources for the lesser opportunities. Translating this concept to the real world, these not-so-attractive opportunities are the spot for the growing talent, or the sound, but perhaps not creative, worker—the "wheel-horse" type who, given a task, can be expected to follow through dependably but with minimum original creativity.

Drucker points out that it is a massive temptation to diffuse first-rate resources, rather than concentrate them; to avoid the irritating priority decisions that ought to be made by having the strong performer make himself available to assist weaker ones (not to be confused with on-the-job training which, at least on the professional level, is more like an apprenticeship of the learner than a dilution of the efforts of the first-rate performer).

Crucial Decisions

Staffing decisions are the crucial decisions. You may say, "Not at all—new product decisions are the crucial ones!" Or, "Decisions to change the process are the vital ones!" But consider: All the advice and technical and marketing know-how assistance you now have that will enable you to make a sound decision on new products or a changed process are the result of staffing decisions that may have been made—or put off—long ago.

So how to go about making staffing decisions, assigning the best-qualified people? Many administrators may reply, "Through our appraisal program." But often they will then behave as if that appraisal program were an objective itself, though one of no great priority, and make their staffing decisions on whatever facts, feelings, and people as are casually available at the time the decision must finally be met.

Nowhere are *clear objectives* more sorely needed than in personnel appraising and appraisal-sharing. Appraisal programs are the vehicle by which we arrive at accurate *decisions about people.* These decisions are increasingly successful as objectives are identified and formalized in all stages of the process.

What are these "People Decisions," besides optimum staffing of opportunities and goals?

Promotion

Further development or training

New assignment (for rounding)

Reward, and how much?

Delegation of additonal authority

Granting access to confidential information

Freeing from close control

Permission to set goals

Assignment to direct others

Expansion of job

Assignment to train others

Giving special attention

Retention on the payroll

It becomes ever more apparent that an effective, goal-centered, describable method must be achieved for making the sound appraisals upon which these decisions about people are based.

The Collapse of Appraisal Systems

Not infrequently, second-line supervisors don't fill forms out fully and promptly; when questioned, they may offer the defense that there is just no point in appraising some people, or that the form is inadequate, or that the process takes too much time. These are all unquestionably symptoms of a failing appraisal system, rather than merely of the supervisors. Yet these same supervisors, at the same time, continued to make salary recommendations, selecting people for development programs, awarding promotions, and making all the other "people decisions" spelled out above. It can be concluded that many managers believe themselves able to make these decisions without reference to or reliance upon the company's "official" record of an employee's performance, though these decisions are presumably based on the person's performance and potential, which the record presumably supplies.

Dangers of Dual Systems

A sick formal appraisal program can lead to a strange dual system. One goes on day-to-day: the actual evaluation of people that is used for determining reward, assignment, and movement. The other is a paper system carried out because it is part of an administrative procedure to which managers must adhere, "for the record." There is perhaps a little of this in even the most successful systems.

This failing in the more formal, deliberate, recorded appraisal process brings another less apparent danger: It casts a shadow over the integrity of every supervisor who must discuss an appraisal with an employee. If what is described to an employee is not the same description of that person as the description that is sent up the line; and if later personnel actions do not reflect the description of the performance that has been shared—then confidence in the appraisal system (and in the management) is weakened dangerously.

Profitability Is Key

There will be no failure of an appraisal system that recognizes that the general objective of any personnel program is primarily to contribute to the profitability of the enterprise by protecting and nurturing its human assets, its people investment, in such a manner as to achieve maximum productivity through employee efforts. The appraisal seeks to further this objective by providing early warning of recruiting and development needs in the employee group as a whole, and pointing the way to full employment of the potential of each individual. The message, then, to managers should be loud and clear: *Appraising is for profits.*

The process of appraisal-sharing with the appraised, whether called coaching, counseling, performance reviewing, or any other of a score of names and titles, serves important motivational purposes when properly used. Appraisal-sharing, too, is for profit, though its complications and difficulties have led to the collapse of so many appraisal systems that its value, on balance, has been questioned. But consider: College recruiters today are often dismayed to discover that interviewees will frankly state their concern about the avenues open to them in the company over the long haul, and they do not hesitate to express curiosity about the ways and means of getting access to these avenues. About appraising, they want to know who does what and to whom. Is there any evidence that these wishes change when a person takes regular employment?

The flip side of the employee's need for information is the appraisal-sharer's obligation to make judgments, and the accountability for these judgments.

Who Does What?

An accounting department of a company might have a line of progression that proceeds something like this: Junior Accountant, Accountant, Senior Accountant, Accounting Supervisor, Department Head. The new accountant is apt to enter at the level for which he or she is qualified, usually at the lower end of the scale. Besides the simple promotion progression, a progression of interest here is the deepening involvement with appraisal, appraisal-sharing, and people-decisions that come with supervisory authority. The levels may be described as:

1. little or no involvement;
2. directs others' work; personnel action recommendations usually honored;
3. recommendations almost fully effective;
4. final and personal decision-making authority.

The two progressions do not make a neat fit or correlation. Supervisors, as they progress, tend to retain people-decision authority at the expense of their successors; an administrator's style of managing may call for centralization of personnel decisions at a higher level; a new supervisor may simply lack qualifications for making these decisions, and so the authority shifts upward by default. While the advancement from level to level of the promotional sequence is clearly a step upward, the change from one degree of people-decision involvement to another is much more subtle and uncertain.

Levels of Decision

Another complication appears: Not all of the people-decisions about a given individual are made at a given level. Obviously, a decision to promote is of a different character than a decision to grant slightly increased responsibility. One constant, though, is the responsibility of the immediate supervisor to collect and supply the great majority of the facts upon which an appraisal is based. The supervisor must be on record with this information and is accountable for its accuracy and currency.

Another constant: Regardless of the shape an appraisal program takes, each supervisor must know the program thoroughly and must know his own accountability and authority in it. Without this knowledge on the part of each supervisor, communication about the system breaks down. He may be communicating doubt about, and contempt for, it even though he has no such intention.

Appraising: Formal vs. Informal

Let us repeat: The appraisal portion of the people-decision making has as its immediate goals identifying first-class people for assignment to first-class opportunities; identifying individual and group development and motivational needs, for a variety of appropriate personnel actions. With these goals before us, a number of questions about appraisals answer themselves.

In a profit-making enterprise, each person who is responsible for the output of others continually observes, evaluates, and coaches, seeking both to maximize their output and her own self-interest. It is a never-ending appraisal, and she constantly transmits the results downward through acceptance or rejection of work, assignment to major or minor opportunities, perhaps through nothing more than inflections of her voice. We must not underestimate the value of day-to-day appraisal and coaching. Properly done, these techniques contribute to improved performance on the job and heightened motivation. But they are not an adequate substitute for formal appraisals.

From the employee's point of view, day-to-day appraising is helpful in performing the job, and these appraisals, which often are merely sensed, give him a feel for his standing in the company. But this information is impalpable, and to a person concerned with new job opportunities, promotion, training, and pay raises, is frustrating. From the standpoint of the company, first-class people are not best identified by a backward look at hundreds of casual contacts—this should be done on no less a basis than a deliberate, authoritative, written appraisal of performance that represents an agreement between the person's supervisor and her supervisor's supervisor.

Appraisal-Sharing Is Not Easy

Questions about sharing official appraisals with employees will answer themselves, too, when we remember that the only defensible goal of divulging these appraisals is to keep the people you want to keep, at the same time upgrading the quality of their performance, expanding their contribution. Emphasis must center on demonstrated performance or, better yet, on success in reaching personal work goals. Remedial or productivity-increasing procedures for the individual must be enunciated. Performance goals and self-development goals should be set here.

Personal goals must be handled exactly like operational goals: A certain time must be set for reaching the milestones in completing the goals, checkpoints must be established, and when the feedback establishes that the individual performance or development goal was unrealistic, the goal must be realistically reconsidered. One dares not wait for the full-scale appraisal or performance review!

The employee has important questions to answer for himself; and if denied the information he needs—the representation of himself that is being passed up to higher management, his chances of promotion, higher pay, training opportunities, new job assignment—he may become disenchanted and seek a position elsewhere, even though the information might have been favorable had it been available.

Appraisal-sharing is not easy. We instinctively feel the sensitivity of the situation. It is a relationship of almost desperate interdependence: The supervisor depending on the performance of her work group (which ultimately determines how her own performance will stack up as compared to her peers), the subordinate depending on a good report of herself going up the line.

The supervisor asks herself many questions, prominent among which are:

Whom should I keep?

Whom should I dismiss?

Whom should I transfer?

Whom should I reward?

Whom should I upgrade?

Whom should I work with more closely?

Whom should I assign to the key project?

The subordinate, at the same time, is asking herself:

Should I stay?

Should I ask for a transfer?

Should I look around for other work?

Should I resign and then look around?

Should I try to improve my abilities?

The foregoing examples reveal how appraisal sharing is actually a process of matching supervisors' questions to workers' questions!

Making the appraisal itself has been a relatively simply process of gathering information, then unilateral decision-making, then agreement-seeking between the supervisor and higher management. But sharing the appraisal is anything *but* simple. It is a supremely social process under conditions of pressure, too often complicated by the absence of agreement on what constitutes a good or bad performance.

It is in appraisal-sharing that the need for performance standards becomes glaring. The subordinate necessarily must believe that his rewards are in some proportion to his ability to achieve the criteria set for the job in the organization. The supervisor will find that things go better when these standards are communicated to the subordinate. The counseling goes better as these standards are clearly defined and easily measured. If there is a single key to successful appraisal-sharing—and appraisal itself—it is in agreement on clear, easily measured standards.

A Balanced Program

To achieve the objective of keeping the people who are wanted, a balanced appraisal program should also provide the employee access to the official who is the effective people-decision maker. This is rarely an immediate supervisor who, however, has given the employee an outline of the company's official appraisal. The higher official will be able to provide authoritative information and advice concerning promotion and reward in the line of progression and the chances of moving to other departments and divisions of the company. Allowing the employee to get this information direct from authority works not only to the advantage of the employee but also helps the supervisor, who is too often called upon to discuss matters of which he or she is largely ignorant—information concerning other units of the company or, perhaps, the employee's standing relative to others of the same rank in other lines of progression.

Appraising Needs Objectives

A final remark about appraisal-sharing: Pursuing its proper objective, the supervisor should feel no compulsion to relate chapter and verse of each critical detail of an unsavory appraisal to the subordinate. Instead, he should set attainable goals for himself in the conduct of the interview, balancing the company's obligation to deal forthrightly with employees about their standing with the possible ill effects of a too-frank discussion of failings. The objective of keeping the people we want to keep, at the same time effecting performance improvement, dictates cautious handling of these cases of less-than-desirable performance.

It is thus clear that the execution of an appraisal and coaching program is not a single goal or a unified objective; rather, it is a vehicle—perhaps the single most important vehicle—for achieving both group and individual personnel objectives. An appraisal program that does not operate as a continuing function carries a high potential for failure, through lack of support from appraised and appraiser alike.

CHAPTER 5

THE LONG-TERM
PLANNING APPROACH

MANY managers have found that long-range planning involves asking some additional questions which may not be needed in planning for a more limited period of time. An analysis of various successful long-range planning approaches being used in business and industry today has resulted in the identification of the following six basic steps:

1. *Define our present status.*

In order to start the planning process, we first have to answer the question, "Where are we today?" (or "where are we starting from?") There are several different aspects to this question.

   a. What is the nature of our activity?
   What is its purpose?
   Why do we exist as a group—unit—department—company?

   b. What is the environment in which we operate?
   What's the nature of the economy at the present time?
   What's the financial status of our own business?

   c. Where are we going as we are? (What are our key strengths and weaknesses?)
   What do we do particularly well?
   What areas are there for improvement?

2. *Establish our targets*

The second step is to decide where we want to go—what are the goals or objectives for our activity? Goals are frequently thought of as broad statements of intent or direction. Objectives are frequently thought of as more immediate, measurable steps along the way toward the attainment of a goal. Probably one of the most helpful exercises in establishing targets is to identify and clarify the underlying assumptions that various managers in a group have at any given time. For example, what do we think will or will not happen during the months ahead regarding:

a. The overall world situation—the economy—our technology—our field of work—politics.

b. Our own organization—its stability—degree of success—direction of effort—top management.

We also have to decide the time periods within which the events will occur and by which our goals and objectives will have been attained.

3. *Summarize Ground Rules*

Having decided where we are now and where we want to go, we then have to decide the conditions under which we will attain those goals and objectives. This requires defining the policies under which we will operate and the procedures we will follow in implementing those policies. This step delimits permissible types of action and provides a ballpark within which we can all operate.

4. *Specify the Action Steps*

The fourth step is to detail *how* we plan to accomplish our goals and objectives. This requires a detailed summary of the specific strategies, programs, projects and courses of action we will take. These are then set in an order of priority and time sequence; i.e., an order of accomplishment so that one action properly follows and supports another.

5. *Allocate Resources*

Having decided where we are now, where we are going, the conditions under which we plan to operate, and how we plan to accomplish our goals and objectives, the next task is to determine *what* resources we will need, *when* we will need them and *where* they will be required. Lists must be prepared showing how much money, materials, machinery and equipment, manpower and time will be required. This step frequently indicates how feasible our plan may be.

6. *Establish Performance Measurements*

The final step is to decide how we plan to keep score and how often we plan to take a reading of our activities. In essence, we must determine what sort of criteria or yardsticks will be used to measure our performance, how frequently we plan to measure our activities, and how this information will be fed back to our group to help us keep on course.

THE LONG-TERM PLANNING APPROACH

This final step enables us to "close the loop" on our plan so that we can make adjustments as we go along. It is the built-in control or feedback mechanism for our activities.

Once a manager has clearly determined what the goals and objectives are and has developed a plan of action, the tasks must be divided up among the work group. It has to be decided who will do what, when and where. The group must be assigned individual activities so that their combined efforts will result in a successful attainment of the goals and objectives. This is organizing—the second basic function of management.

Most managers inherit their groups of subordinates when they are first placed in their managerial positions. It is unusual for a manager to have an opportunity to build an organization from scratch. However, just because a manager has a readymade department does not relieve her of the responsibility for organizing. Every time she sets out to accomplish some tasks with her employees, she faces some problems of organization. Consequently, as was true with the planning function, organizing is a responsibility of managers at every level in an organization. Whereas managers at the top levels of an enterprise may divide up major activities for large segments of the organization, managers at lower levels face the job of assigning tasks to specific individuals within their own areas of responsibility. It is, therefore, helpful for all managers to understand some of the principles and techniques of organizing.

Organizing—A Historical Perspective

The idea of dividing up work among a group of people seems to be as old as history itself. Anthropologists tell us that it is a common phenomenon found in most studies of human groups. In studies of primitive man, examples have been found of basic work assignments—some did the hunting, others were involved in fire building and food preparation, and still others in protection of the group, etc. The early records which described the building of the great pyramids made reference to quite detailed divisions of labor among the work groups. Some of our organization structures of today seem to closely parallel the works recorded in the Bible where Moses organized the Israelites into groups of tens, hundreds and thousands with rulers for each group. All of us carry around with us each day one of the finest examples of organizational structure and division of work—the human body. Various organs of the body, each having different responsibilities, work together as an integrated system to enable the body to function. Likewise, each day on the job the manager must decide what combinations of work must be performed and how to divide it up among people who will possess different knowledge, skills and capabilities. Organizing might be defined, therefore, as the process of logically grouping together *activities*, delineating *responsibility*, defining levels of *authority*, and establishing working *relationships* to enable a group to attain common goals and objectives.

In situations where there is lost time and motion, duplication of effort, reluctance to take action, friction among groups, politics and jealousies—in essence, basic inefficiency—the cause is frequently faulty organization. People can't operate effectively together if they don't have a clear understanding of what the objectives are, who has which responsibilities, how much authority they have, and to whom they relate.

Organizational Forms

It has often been said that any specific organization is an extension of its chief executive. He or she delegates to others what he or she wants them to do and how it should be done. While he or she may have an ideal organizational structure in mind toward which he or she is moving, he or she has to take into consideration and adapt the structure to match the interests, motivations and overall capabilities of the people working at any given time. An organizational structure is able to accomplish nothing by itself. It is the human element that makes it work. Consequently, both factors—organizational design and the organization's people—must be considered whenever the organizing process takes place.

The actual form an organization should take at any given time should be one which best supports its objectives. As new situations arise and different objectives are set, the organizational structure may require revision. Consequently, the structure should be under constant study and evaluation to make certain it is the best arrangement of people and activities to meet its current objectives. There are some basic organizational forms which managers use in designing an appropriate structure for their area of responsibility.

Functional

This is the form most frequently found in very small or young organizations. Activities which are the same, or very similar, are grouped together. These groupings, based on the nature of the work done, are then assigned to different individuals or groups of individuals. Each becomes a specialized function. For example, personnel in a manufacturing plant might be grouped together based on their involvement in sales, production, maintenance or accounting tasks. In effect, each person specializes in a specific phase of the business.

As organizations grow larger, other forms of organization begin to appear. The following are some of the most common found today:

1. **Geographical.** People or activities in different territories are linked together. These might be countries, cities, regions, different plants, buildings or even separate floors or areas on a floor.

2. **Product or Service.** People or activities who work on the same or similar products, or who provide the same or similar services, may be linked together as an organizational unit.

3. **Equipment or Process.** Activities involving the same or similar equipment or processes, or people who work with or have expertise in running certain equipment or in using specific processes, may be grouped together as a logical organization structure.

4. **Customer or Clientele.** Activities relating to or people serving the same or similar customers are placed in the same organizational group. Groupings often seen are those based on such breakdowns as wholesale versus retail, government versus private sector, and day customers versus night.

5. **Time.** Placing activities and people who work at different periods of the day under different organizational structures is a very common approach—particularly where you have round-the-clock operations. (Day shift, night shift, third shift, etc.)

6. **Task or Project.** Personnel and activities which have a direct bearing on the accomplishment of a specific task or project are brought together as an organizational unit for the duration of the project. This is frequently found in construction activities, installations of equipment or systems, research and related project-oriented activities.

It's rare to find any pure form of any of the above organizational structures. In most cases, managers use a combination of approaches according to the nature of the activities, the size of the organization, the capabilities of the people involved, and related factors. Consequently, it's not unusual to find a maintenance manager (functional approach) of warehouse B (geographical approach) on the second shift (time approach). In keeping his organization dynamic and efficient a manager may utilize any or all of these various approaches.

OFFICE ADMINISTRATION HANDBOOK

Span of Control

A manager has a direct working relationship with each of his or her immediate subordinates. The number supervised is called the "span of control" or "span of management." As the number of individuals increases, it becomes more difficult to keep track of what is happening, maintain effective communications, and to be responsive to the requests and needs of his subordinates. There is a limit to the number of people any one manager can effectively supervise and direct. It is not possible to state a definite figure as to how many. Actually the number may vary for any given manager over a period of time based on a number of factors:

1. **Manager's capabilities.** The amount of training, experience and skill the manager possesses in handling subordinates.
2. **Subordinates' capabilities.** The competence of subordinates to exercise self-direction, handle their jobs without frequent assistance, etc.
3. **Nature of the manager's work.** The amount and nature of the work the manager must do and the demands on time from others outside of the department.
4. **Nature of the subordinates' work.** The degree of difficulty, predictability and complexity of activities being performed by subordinates. The degree of similarity or diversity of the tasks performed. (Normally a manager can supervise more people performing similar, fairly simple and uniform activities than those who are performing diverse, highly complex activities with unpredictable problems.)
5. **Extent of standardized procedures.** The degree to which policies, procedures, performance standards, and similar yardsticks exist to enable subordinates to measure and control their own activities without advice and feedback from the manager. This makes it possible for only the "exceptions" to be discussed with the manager.
6. **Distance.** The physical distance or degree of separation and the frequency of contacts between the manager and his or her subordinates.
7. **Time.** The actual number of hours available in a day or a week for interaction with subordinates.

Chain of Command

A manager is only one link in a chain of responsibility and authority that goes all the way from the group of employees at the bottom of the organization to the managers at the top. This set of relation-ships, of a manager to her boss and a manager to her subordinates, is called the "chain of command." It basically answers the question, "Who's in charge here?" It helps to clarify responsibilities, authority and the ultimate accountability for actions of individuals up and down the line. While most individuals can work well with and serve many different managers, it is not fair to ask them to be responsible to more than one person for the same activities or tasks at the same time.

One of the problems frequently encountered in larger organiza-tions is that the chain of command becomes long and rigid. This makes it more difficult to exchange information and obtain deci-sions. Additional levels in an organization's hierarchy create delays, misunderstanding, misinterpretations, and a general breakdown in the overall communication process. Consequently, it is helpful to keep the number of levels in an organization to a minimum.

Delegation

In an attempt to overcome some of the problems that levels of organization create or to widen a span of control, many managers entrust some of their responsibilities and authority to their subordi-nates so that decisions can be made more promptly and closer to the scene of the action. This is referred to as delegation. While the manager may delegate responsibilities and authority down the line, he can never give up his ultimate accountability for the actions of his subordinates.

Delegation raises the question of "How far down the line do I delegate?" There are three criteria that are helpful to the manager who faces this question:

1. **Subordinate's competence.** The overall knowledge, skills and proven capabilities of the subordinate to make the type of decisions required. In addition, the degree to which the man-ager *feels* that the subordinate has the necessary competence. If the manager doesn't feel that way, he will continually dip down into the subordinate's area and eventually reduce the delegated authority to shambles.

2. **Availability of relevant information.** The degree to which the person who must make the decision will have the right infor-mation, in the right form, at the right place and at the right time. Decision making can't be pushed down below the point at which all of the information needed for the decision is available.

3. Scope of the decision impact. The ultimate impact of the decision. If a decision affects personnel and activities over which the person has no responsibility and accountability, he or she is being placed in a bad situation. Therefore, the decision should be made at that level where responsibility and accountability rest for all of the areas affected.

As will be seen in later sections, the art of delegating down the line not only helps in an organizational sense, but it has strong motivational implications for the people directly involved.

Steps in Organizing

With organizational forms and principles in mind, a manager then faces the task of deciding what should be done, who will do it, and how it will be done so that all of the activities will mesh together in order to accomplish the organization's goals and objectives. Five steps are helpful in this process:

1. **Define the objectives.**
2. **Determine what is to be done to achieve those objectives.**
3. **Divide, group and relate work in a logical, understandable combination.**
4. **Assign essential work.**
5. **Designate support groups.**

Looking at these steps in some detail, an organizational pattern emerges.

1. Define the objectives.

The planning process provides the goals and objectives for the manager. If she has been involved in the planning, she should have a clear idea of what end result is desired. However, before starting to organize, it is helpful to clarify precisely just what it is she wants to accomplish.

2. Determine what is to be done to achieve those objectives.

Here she asks, "What are the important tasks to be performed?" A helpful starting point is to construct a "Make—Sell" line. This is a straight line from the point of initial *input* (effort and resources) to the point of the final *output* (satisfaction of a "customer" through provision of goods or services). On this line are listed all of the activities that are needed to move the process from one stage to the next. This is often referred to as the "Line" organization.

In developing this sequence of events, the manager is also looking for obstacles that may be encountered at any point and is seeking possible ways to overcome those obstacles within existing policies and practices.

3. Divide, group and relate work in a logical, understandable combination.

Having decided what tasks must be performed, the manager is now able to examine the sequences and relationships which may have evolved. She seeks answers to the following:

- What are the logical sequences or relationships?
- What activity supports and reinforces prior steps?
- What combination makes best use of available resources?
- What other alternatives or combinations are possible?
- How will each combination overcome the possible obstacles we will face?
- Which is the best combination? Which will be easiest for others to understand?

4. Assign essential work.

Up to this point the manager has designed what might be called her "ideal organization." However, she now must take into consideration the people he has and their capabilities. She must then ask:

- How can the abilities of my present employees be best utilized?
- What additional knowledge and skills might they gain through specific assignments?
- What additional people might be needed?

Having evaluated her "people resources," she is now ready to designate *who* is to do what. Here she defines responsibilities, authority and relationships (both those within the organization as well as those outside of the organization). As the capabilities of people change, the manager may find that different assignments can be made. In essence, she may move towards the "ideal organization" through a series of stages which reflect the level of competence of her people at any given time.

5. Designate support groups.

In most organizations, additional specialized help is needed by the Line group in order to effectively carry out its activities. These groups are frequently referred to as "Staff." They provide three basic types of assistance to the Line:

- *Advice and Counsel*

  Some people serve as in-house specialists or consultants who have acquired and maintain in-depth knowledge about a certain aspect of the business. They may be specialists in such activities as finance, law, personnel, taxes, research, etc. In each case, they stay abreast of developments in their field and provide this special know-how or information to the line group.

- *Service*

  Frequently it is helpful to consolidate a group of activities under one or several people, rather than have each individual manager do it. An example might be purchasing, employment, accounting, etc. It is often cheaper and more efficient if someone performs an activity on a full-time basis for the various line managers, rather than have them dabble in it infrequently. As a result, the staff group frequently develops a degree of expertise or proficiency in the activity which aids the whole operation.

- *Control*

  This is a monitoring activity. In this case the line group decide how they want to operate, what sort of measurements they want to use in evaluating their performance, and what sort of data they want to accumulate to help keep them on course. They then can ask staff people to monitor their activities along these guidelines and to feed back information to them as they go along. This role frequently causes difficulty when line managers believe that the staff groups have usurped their responsibilities and authority. Clarifying the purpose of the staff group's function and the ground rules that are being monitored often helps to resolve these areas of conflict.

Whether staff groups provide personal assistance to one manager or to many, their role is primarily assistance and support to the line organization.

Need for Updating

Organizational structures seem to solidify and grow old quickly. They often take on a rigidity which is difficult to overcome. That's why every manager must view organizing as an on-going, never-ending process. Large, major, formal overhauls of entire departments may not be required often, but daily analysis of individual capabilities and organizational objectives should never cease. The way a manager organizes—the work to be done and who will do it—is a major factor in the successful execution of the manager's plans.

The following set of 10 questions is designed to enable you to check how well you have organized your area of activity. As you should be able to answer each question for your job, each of your subordinates should be able to answer the same 10 questions for his job. If all 10 can't be answered, you will have uncovered an area for improving the overall effectiveness of your work group.

1. What are the goals and objectives of the organization?
2. What is my role in attaining those goals and objectives?
3. What will I have to work with, in terms of resources, in carrying out my role?
4. What ground rules will exist while I'm doing it?
5. How much authority will I have to do it?
6. To whom will I relate, inside and outside of the organization?
7. What criteria will be used to measure my performance?
8. Where, when and how will I receive feedback on how I'm doing?
9. Where and from whom can I receive help and support when I want it?
10. What rewards and recognition will I receive for doing it?

GUIDELINES FOR IMPROVEMENT

1. What Are the Goals and Objectives of the Organization?

In many organizations, employees do not have a clear understanding of the overall purpose, function or target of the company, department, or unit to which they belong. Unless a person understands where he is heading, agrees with those goals and objectives, and believes that they are attainable and are worth doing, he cannot become very committed to them. Consequently, sharing information on organizational goals and objectives, and enabling people to have some say in setting them, provides some "ownership" and helps to develop their interest and commitment. Mutual goal setting appears to be the answer to the first question.

2. What Is My Role in Attaining Those Goals and Objectives?

Once a person understands what the goals and objectives are, he wants to know what *he* is to do—what his duties and responsibilities will be. A common practice in many organizations is to define duties and responsibilities in job descriptions. Unfortunately, most job descriptions are too long and are filled with "*how* to do it" phrases (methods), instead of "*why* to do it" phrases (end objectives). The descriptions are usually badly out-of-date. In addition, most descriptions do not give any indication of the relative importance or priority of the duties and responsibilities.

If you are wondering how useful your own job descriptions are, you might try the following test. Ask your subordinate to write down the three or four most important duties and responsibilities and rank them in the order of importance. You do the same thing for the job. Then compare your lists. If the two lists are not identical, you've uncovered an area for improving coordination and operating effectiveness. For unless a worker and the supervisor see the job in the same way, a great amount of slippage is occurring in that organization.

Streamlining job descriptions can be accomplished by arbitrarily limiting the duties and responsibilities to three or four in number. This flushes out the "how to's" and concentrates on the "why's," or the reasons for the action. In most jobs duties and responsibilities can be clustered under several major headings. Once these are identified it is easy to establish a ranking of importance for them and to relate them directly to the goals and objectives of the organization. The person is then free to exercise individual initiative and creativity in carrying out those duties and responsibilities.

A simple technique used by some managers to reduce the length of their job descriptions is to draw a circle and divide it into four parts. They then attempt to group all of their present duties and responsibilities under four different categories, i.e., in the four parts of the circle. At first this seems like an impossible task, particularly if the present description is several pages long. However, if the manager keeps asking "What is the reason, or end point, for this activity?", she will find that most of her duties and responsibilities easily fit under one of several broad terms or phrases, such as quality, quantity, cost, manpower, etc. These are the major tasks which differentiate her job from all of the other jobs in the organization. Once she has done this, it becomes quite easy to rank the tasks in their order of importance.

3. What Will I Have To Work with, in Terms of Resources, in Carrying Out My Role?

The resources allocated to a person are often reflected in budgets, schedules and timetables. These are essential tools in the overall planning process. Unless a person knows the amount of money, materials, machinery and equipment, manpower, space and time he will have to work with, he cannot put them to use effectively.

Participation in the initial process of allocating resources, establishing budgets, timetables and schedules helps to answer this question for the individual manager. This is why more and more organizations are now involving managers, at all levels of the organization, in the overall planning process. If a manager is to be held accountable for the stewardship of assets or resources and is evaluated on his utilization of those assets or resources, he should have a clear idea of the dimensions of that responsibility.

4. What Ground Rules Will Exist While I'm Doing It?

Once the target has been set, the individual's part has been defined, and she knows what resources she will have to work with, she wants to know how to play the game, i.e., what the "rules of the game" will be. Policies (ground rules), and procedures (the application and implementation of those ground rules), define the parameters within which a person can operate. They act as controls on the individual's current and future activities. Knowing in advance what the ground rules are enables the individual to control her own actions and reduces the need for continuous surveillance by the boss. As organizations become larger, it becomes more and more necessary to replace "imposed control" by a superior with "self-imposed control" by the subordinate.

An effective way for an individual to learn the policies and procedures is to participate in establishing them, reviewing them, and modifying them in response to the changing goals and objectives of the organization and taking a personal role in helping to attain those goals and objectives. As is true in so many other aspects of the managerial job, involvement helps to increase a subordinate's understanding and commitment.

5. How Much Authority Will I Have To Do It?

One of the problems frequently encountered in organizations is a difference in opinion concerning how much authority a subordinate has to carry out duties and responsibilities. Subordinates often complain that their bosses keep them under tight control, don't let them make decisions and don't let them act on their own. They have responsibilities, but no authority. At the same time their bosses complain that the subordinates don't stand on their own two feet, don't make decisions and don't act on their own like a capable manager should. Instead, bosses say, their subordinates keep running to them for answers. Think how much effort and talent are being wasted in those situations where the boss and the subordinate don't have a clear understanding and agreement on the scope of authority.

One helpful way to remedy this dilemma is to have subordinate and boss define ahead of time how much authority the subordinate will have to carry out each of three or four major duties and responsibilities. Often a simple code is placed alongside of each duty and responsibility to indicate the level of authority that applies, such as: A = may *act* on his own; AA = may *act* on his own, but is expected to *advise* the boss of actions after the fact; and SR = is expected to check with the boss first with *suggestions* and *recommendations* before acting.

An interesting by-product of this activity is that periodic discussions of this sort often indicate how well the subordinate is developing on the job. Even though duties and responsibilities may stay the same, changes in levels of authority for a given duty or responsibility indicate growth in knowledge, skills and competence in performing the task.

6. To Whom Will I Relate, Inside and Outside of the Organization?

Formal organization charts and diagrams give some clues as to the relationships that will exist; however, they only provide one dimension. In most situations individuals must not only observe the reporting relationships up and down the line, but they must also coordinate their activities and maintain liaison with persons in other departments as well as with persons outside of the organization. These people compose the informal organization and the various "publics" with whom managers must deal in their attempts to perform their jobs. Clarifying these organizational relationships in advance—who they are or the functions involved, and the nature of the relationship—is a valuable step in developing improved teamwork and effectiveness.

7. What Criteria Will Be Used To Measure My Performance?

One of the saddest events in an organization is when an individual learns how she is being measured on the job *after* she has acted. Sometimes she learns this for the first time when she is being terminated. It is then she learns that the yardsticks she was using to measure performance were different from those being used by the boss.

Many organizations are now attempting to establish standards of performance for each person's job in an attempt to clarify performance measurements beforehand. In those situations where this process seems to be working well, the individual herself has had an opportunity to participate in setting the performance standards and is, therefore, willing to have her actions measured using those criteria. She considers them fair and sees them as factors over which she has some control. Because she understands the measurement criteria and system, she is often able to keep her own score as she goes along, rather than having to wait for her boss to give her clues.

Performance standards are statements of conditions which will exist when the job is performed satisfactorily. These statements consist of specific results, symptoms, or efforts which can be measured in terms of factors such as: quality, quantity, cost and timeliness. Since they serve as a floor, it is easy to measure any activity falling below them as failure and any activity which exceeds them as excellence. As new goals and objectives are established, responsibilities change, and an individual's competence increases, new standards of performance may be needed to fit the changing conditions. The key is that "there are no surprises!" The manager knows *before* the game starts how his performance will be measured and while he is playing the game, he can keep his own score.

8. Where, When, and How Will I Receive Feedback on How I'm Doing?

Many organizations have formal performance appraisal systems in an attempt to provide periodic feedback to an individual on how he is doing. Unfortunately, these often represent nothing more than involved form-completion and paper-processing activities at a specific time of year, such as the beginning of a new calendar year, a person's anniversary date with the organization, or some other irrelevant point in time.

People involved in any sport want to know how they're doing while they are playing the game. They aren't content to wait until the game is all over before getting any feedback on their performance. The same thing is true in any organization; people want feedback as they're doing the job. In those cases where appraisals of performance seem to be helpful, we find that they are being done frequently. This doesn't require formal, involved forms and procedures. If a person can answer the preceding seven questions for her job, at any time she can stop to take a reading on where she is versus where she had hoped to be, in what areas she is performing well, and where she is running into difficulty. The *process* of receiving feedback is the important thing, not the formal *procedures* and *paperwork* that often surround it. Therefore, knowing where to get information on one's progress, in what form it will be and how frequently it can be obtained is an important step in self-control and self-improvement.

9. Where and From Whom Can I Receive Help and Support When I Want It?

One of the valuable resources available to any individual manager is advice, counsel, assistance and support from the boss and from other individuals and functions inside and outside of the organization. Unfortunately, in many organizations this resource is not being tapped. The boss is not viewed as a coach and counselor and staff groups are seen as threats, hindrances, and obstacles which get in the way of the individual trying to do a job. Frequently this image can be traced directly to the actions of the boss and the behavior of personnel from the various staff departments who see their role as making themselves look good by making others look bad. Bosses often criticize subordinates for not utilizing resource departments within the organization. On the other hand, subordinates often view the use of resource departments as a sign of weakness. As a result, they try to "go it alone."

A solution to this problem rests with the boss. He must clarify with his subordinate what role he, the boss, wishes to play in helping the subordinate carry out his duties and responsibilities. One way he can reinforce this is to periodically ask his subordinate what he could do more of, less of, or do differently to help the subordinate. In addition, the definition and delineation of the role and availability of various other groups which the individual might turn to for assistance is valuable preparation for a person who is trying to improve his effectiveness.

10. What Rewards and Recognition Will I Receive for Doing It?

From each individual manager's standpoint, this is probably the most important question of them all—"Is it worth it?" "Having performed effectively, what can I expect to receive?" Continuity of employment and a possibility of a wage adjustment are only two of the "rewards and recognition" that many employees are seeking today. Opportunities to see the results of their contributions, to have some responsibility on their shoulders, to have a sense of achievement from something they did, to see what they might learn next, and where they might advance to in the future, are all additional reasons for putting forth the effort. Consequently, time spent in this area pays off in greater motivation, interest and commitment among managers.

With this in mind, many organizations are reexamining their wage and salary plans to make certain that they relate to accomplishments and contributions (performance) rather than to activities, energy expended, or personality characteristics. They're making these programs known so that individual managers can see what's ahead, rather than keeping the salary systems top secret. Opportunities for transfer and promotion are being widely communicated and special recognition systems are being geared directly to behavior that *supports* the attainment of goals and objectives, rather than to other irrelevant factors or activities. In effect, individuals are able to examine and determine beforehand whether or not the game is worth playing.

No coach would think of fielding a team unless each player could answer fully each of the 10 questions listed above. Yet, in many organizations, managers are attempting to field teams where great gaps in understanding exist. Improving performance doesn't have to wait for a grand overhaul of the entire organization. It can get underway immediately with each manager in his own area of operation. Developing answers to each of the 10 questions above is a key step in getting that improvement process underway.

The fourth basic function of management is controlling. It is an on-going process that involves the measurement and evaluation of what's happening versus what should be happening, and the adjustment of actions, when necessary, to assure the attainment of objectives. Controlling is essentially a forward-looking activity. By looking at what has happened and what is presently taking place, a manager can decide what should happen in the future to keep all of the group's efforts on target. Based on this feedback of information, a manager may decide to change plans, the organization of the area, or the way the operation is directed. This opportunity to modify behavior, based upon a continuing monitoring of events, is the reason the control function represents the final link in the management closed-loop system.

A Negative Image

Unfortunately, the controlling process is frequently viewed in a negative light. Many managers feel that controls represent restraints or criticisms of their actions. This perhaps stems from the fact that an aspect of control involves changing a person's behavior or activities. This occurs whenever actions or results are not conforming to plans and policies. When these deviations or problems are discovered, an effort is made to have the manager and his group get back on course. This corrective action is often viewed as a restriction on a person's activities or a criticism of his actions.

In addition, staff groups (such as accounting, engineering, personnel, etc.) often provide information to a manager on his group's performance. When this information is not complimentary, the manager frequently sees it as a nuisance and as an example of how others are always trying to make themselves look good by making him look bad. It is no wonder then that many managers have a negative view about the controlling process.

Despite the role often played by others in providing feedback, and despite the fact that the word "control" conjures up negative feelings, managers at every level of an organization must become proficient in controlling operations if they are going to be successful in achieving or exceeding their goals and objectives. As is true with each of the other management functions, controlling is a vital, ongoing responsibility of every manager—regardless of her level in the organizational hierarchy, the size of his group, or the nature of her assignment.

Imposed vs. Self-Imposed Control

In attempting to control his operations, a manager may decide to do it all himself. He may personally watch his subordinates as they perform their activities, check their work and ask them for frequent status or progress reports. This personal presence, visual scrutiny and assemblage of data may enable the manager to keep a close check on operations, spot deviations as they occur and take prompt corrective action. This approach, frequently called "imposed control," can be effective in small groups where the operations are fairly simple, quite repetitive and in a compact area. However, as a manager's responsibilities increase and his operations become larger, more spread out, more varied and complex, another approach to control is required—*self-imposed control.*

Self-imposed control enables the manager to multiply her own efforts by placing some responsibility for control in the hands of subordinates. When subordinates are given an opportunity to participate with the manager in planning and organizing the work, establishing standards and yardsticks for measuring performance, and receive direct feedback on their progress, they can spot deviations themselves and can take the required corrective action to keep themselves on target. In essence, the manager is able to maintain control over her operations, not by her own efforts alone, but by the capabilities of subordinates to exercise self-direction and self-control over their own activities. Not only can a manager multiply her effectiveness in performing her control functions through this approach, but there is a motivational impact on subordinates (as will be seen in later sections) when an opportunity exists for self-control.

Having developed a basic self-imposed approach, many managers then build in a reporting system which highlights "exceptions" or major deviations from what is planned. These alerts help to focus the manager's time and attention on those areas where he is really needed and where he can make the greatest contribution.

The Focus of Control

The control process has its roots in the planning process. As has been often stated, if a manager doesn't know where she's going, she can't tell when she's lost. A manager must have a plan against which to measure performance. The results she obtains and the actions she observes tie in directly to the first six planning steps as follows:

THE LONG-TERM PLANNING APPROACH

Planning Steps	Focus of Control
1. What must be done?	
2. When must it be completed?	Results
3. Under what conditions should it be done?	
4. What steps shall we take to do it?	
5. Where will these steps be performed?	Actions
6. What resources will be needed to get the results we want?	

Having developed her plans, a manager can then measure and evaluate the *results* (output in terms of goods and services) she obtains in terms of:

Quality (Match quality specified?)

Quantity (Right amount?)

Cost (At the right cost?)

Timeliness (On time?)

In addition, on an ongoing basis she can measure and evaluate the degree to which actions are in conformance with the methods, approaches, or ground rules which were established, such as:

Policies (within the conditions specified?)

Procedures (at the proper place, by the right people, and using the standards or practices specified?)

Budgets (using the proper amount of resources allocated in advance?)

The seventh step in the planning process, "How will we measure progress?", provides the manager with a basic framework for the control function. Having some idea as to how she wants to measure her progress, at what frequency, and by whom, the manager can then set to work designing her on-going control activities.

Types of Controls

There are two basic types of controls:

1. Preoperational.

2. Postoperational.

Preoperational controls are those that are established before the activity begins. One of the most familiar preoperational controls is budgets. Budgets represent plans with price tags. They indicate what resources (money, materials, machinery and equipment, and manpower) will be needed and how they will be used over a period of time. By comparing actual usage of resources against budgeted allocations a manager can easily determine whether his operations are under control or beginning to get out of control.

Schedules are another common form of preoperational controls. By indicating in advance what results are expected by what dates, a manager can evaluate actual progress and determine whether or not his output or progress is on schedule. Specifications, standards, quality requirements, etc. are also established in advance of events. Measurements of results against these predetermined criteria serve as useful guides to the manager in evaluating his performance.

Postoperational controls include all of the various types of records and reports that reflect what has happened. Daily or weekly reports on production, downtime, quality, absenteeism, shipments, orders received, requests for service, product complaints, man hours used, etc. are all examples of common progress or status reports. All provide data to the manager, just like a speedometer needle provides data to an automobile driver, as to how he is progressing. By comparing what is happening with what he wants to happen and where he expects to be, a manager can determine whether or not corrective action is required to put himself back on course. The closer in time the feedback is to the action itself, the quicker the manager is able to make any necessary adjustments.

Basic Steps in Control

Setting up a control process involves four basic steps:
1. **Establish standards.**
2. **Report what's happening.**
3. **Evaluate actions and results.**
4. **Adjust as needed.**

1. *Establishing standards.*

In establishing a control system, there are three questions a manager should ask first:
1. What do I need to know to tell me whether or not events are conforming to plan?
2. When do I need to know it?
3. In what form will it be most helpful?

Unfortunately, it is not possible for a manager to keep track of everything that is going on in his or her area of responsibility. Therefore, one must select those *critical* factors in the operation which will have the greatest impact on the attainment of objectives. In most situations there is a relatively small number of items, often 10 to 15%, that have the most significant impact on final results.

Finding these "make-or-break" factors is a key step in developing meaningful control systems. To do so a manager asks questions such as the following:

- What is likely to go wrong?
- How, when and where might it occur?
- How soon would we know?
- What impact would it have?
- What corrective action could we take?
- Who could take the action?
- How soon could we act?

Once these factors are identified, the manager must then choose which ones to measure. This is done by evaluating the cost of measurement versus the benefit received. Any control activity requires an expenditure of time and effort. This amount of time and effort is, therefore, not usable for productive purposes—the production of goods or services. The manager must ask whether or not the control system is worth the time and effort spent in implementing it. If it is undercontrolled there is a risk of failure in attaining all objectives; if overcontrolled, needless time and effort is wasted. Each of the critical factors should be evaluated along the following lines:

- How available is data on this factor?
- How sound is the data?
- What is the cost—in time and effort—of obtaining these data?
- What is the potential value in controlling variations in this factor?
- Is there any other way to measure this?

Having decided what factors to monitor, a manager can then select from his planning and organizing functions those items that will serve as preoperational controls (budgets, schedules, specifications, job definitions, performance standards, etc.) and can design those reporting methods and procedures that will serve as postoperational controls (a variety of status and progress reports).

2. *Reporting what's happening.*

The manager's postoperational control systems will tell her *what* is happening, *where, when, how* (all relate to her planning activities) and by *whom* (relate to her organizing activities).

3. *Evaluating actions and results.*

The information received in step 2 is then compared against the desired actions and results. In doing so, the manager asks such questions as:

- What deviations or problems are there?
- What may be causing these?
- What adjustments should we make in our planning, organizing, or directing activities to correct the situation?
- What are the likely consequences of those adjustments?
- What would happen if we did nothing?

4. *Adjusting as needed.*

Having decided when adjustment is needed, the manager acts promptly to put the situation under control. In some cases, as a result of a heavy emphasis on self-imposed controls, the manager may merely have to provide feedback to subordinates on the status of operations and assist them in bringing the situation back on course. In other cases, where major adjustments are required, the manager may have to take a much more active personal role in correcting the situation. How a manager works with his subordinates in adjusting a group's actions or individual behavior will determine how the control process is seen—as a negative, hindering and critical activity, or as a positive, helpful and supportive activity. Control systems, by themselves, are neutral. How managers apply those controls—particularly in this fourth step—determines how they are seen by their subordinates.

Summary

Effective managers maintain control systems which enable them to keep on top of their operations with a minimum amount of data about the actions and results which count the most, in the briefest period between action and feedback, and with the least expenditure of time and effort. To do this requires an approach to controlling that is planned, systematic and dynamic to meet the ever-changing objectives and needs of the organization.

Of the four management functions directing is perhaps the most difficult to perform. After the manager has planned and organized his work, he then must put it into effect. He must implement those plans and make his organization work effectively. This he does through directing—directing his own efforts and the efforts of other people.

Most managers are able to direct their own efforts quite successfully. However, when they attempt to direct the efforts of other people, many managers run into difficulty. In fact, frequently managers are heard to say, "It's easier to do it myself than to get my employees to do it." People are complex; one person is different from another, and they seem to be constantly changing from one day to the next. And because people are both rational *and* emotional, directing tends to have the greatest emotional content of all of the management functions. As a result it becomes a major problem to get other people to do what you want them to do, when you want them to do it and in the way you want it done. Yet, a manager can only accomplish set objectives with the help of other people. He or she cannot do it alone!

Part 2

OFFICE PERSONNEL—RECRUITING AND SELECTION

CHAPTER 6

THE GAMUT OF PERSONNEL ADMINISTRATION

By Clark W. Fetridge

COMPANY SIZE, of course, has much to do with the amount of direct responsibility the office administrator has in terms of recruiting and selecting personnel. On the other hand, it is necessary in this age of automation to make sure that office personnel can function efficiently and profitably.

While a company may not have a word processing department, per se, chances are it still has electronic equipment designed for that function. It is vital that people who will handle the equipment will be able to do so with a minimum of effort. Many companies retain micrographic records, many companies use computer technology in one form or another. Automated offices and even partially automated offices can receive and store data and transmit information at high speeds. Video display terminals are appearing in more and more office operations. While it doesn't take a college education to work with this equipment, it does take the ability to cope with the machines on a daily basis.

Job Descriptions

The office administrator—as an executive, a manager or a supervisor—is responsible for clear-cut job descriptions. These will either be used by the personnel department in recruiting or by the office administrator who must perform the selection. If it is known that a department will be automated or partially automated in the near future, it is the responsibility of the administrator to build this into the job description.

Each individual job applicant offers a unique combination of education, experience, aptitudes, skills, interests, needs, values, goals and qualities. Working within all the guidelines—E.E.O., Affirmative Action, etc.—the administrator is still responsible for recruiting or at least selecting the right person for each job. The job description is the first step in the process. It provides the applicant with a picture of the now and future job, and it tells the personnel or human resources department what they must find.

Bringing Personnel Administration into Focus

Once a person is brought into the office, the personnel administration job begins. Probably the most important single characteristic of personnel-administration development in recent years has been the recognition of behavioral-science techniques and discoveries. Guessing and crystal-gazing have been replaced by legitimatized aptitude testing, recognition of sociotechnical-interface applications, and the development of personnel administration along systematized, rather than purely opportunistic, lines. This trend has been coded in the term Organizational Development (OD), for which a leading exponent has been Harold M. F. Rush, of The Conference Board, Inc. To quote:

> "*Organization development:* a planned, managed systematic process to change the culture, systems and behavior of an organization, in order to improve the organization's effectiveness in solving its problems and achieving its objectives. In practice, organization development is a group of activities with the common aim of improving the organization's effectiveness. It is a problem-centered process that addresses itself to real organizational problems—existing and anticipated—and seeks to solve them through a variety of appropriate methods. Solving these problems usually involves identifying and removing impediments to the effective mobilization of the organization's resources, both material and human, for the achievement of the objectives."*

Certain activities and practices are considered by experts to be characteristic of the OD process. They are: attitude and opinion measurement, interviewing for diagnostic purposes, problem identification and problem solving, goal setting and methods of achievement, communication improvement, conflict identification and resolution, task forces and temporary systems, job design for motivation and productivity, and measurement and evaluation. Responses from 147 "Blue Ribbon" companies participating in a Conference Board survey showed that the companies were practicing major areas of organization development in the following proportions:

1. *Goal-setting methods* appeared in 98 percent of the OD companies and 81 percent of the others. One notable difference was that in the OD companies, a much larger group of firms allow work groups to set their own short-term goals.

2. *Participative and group problem-solving methods* showed up in 98 percent of the OD companies and 47 percent of the others. Behind this is the idea that people are more commit-

---

*"Organization Development: A Reconnaissance," by Harold M. F. Rush. The Conference Board, 845 Third Ave., New York, N.Y. 10022. (By permission.)

ted to achieving goals if they have had a hand in setting them.

3. *Special activities to improve communication* appear in 87 percent of the OD companies and 60 percent of the non-OD group. The OD group were also more likely to emphasize such activities as team-building and laboratory training as opposed to constant tinkering with conventional communications channels.

4. *Attitude surveys* used by 82 percent of the OD companies and 38 percent of the others. The OD companies were also more likely not only to report results to everyone in the organization, but also to actually intervene to bring about changes needed.

5. *Job design activities* also turned up in more of the OD firms—73 percent as compared to 59 percent among the non-OD companies.

6. *Diagnostic interviewing* to get additional information about trends showing up in attitude surveys was used in 71 percent of the OD companies and 38 percent of the others. OD companies were more likely to use internal OD specialists for this, while the non-OD companies were more likely to use personnel managers.

While not all functions, obviously, are applicable in all types and sizes of companies, personnel can be oriented and—what is most vital—integrated by such OD applications as *are* practicable. The worker then becomes "in" rather than "at" his/her job, and the discoveries of the behavioral and motivational sciences become more realistic and productive.

"PERT"

Later in this Handbook you will be reading more about PERT. The use of this administration tool is constantly increasing as office management becomes more complex and ramified.

PERT (Program Evaluation and Review Technique) is a method for planning, controlling, and monitoring the progress of complex projects. Originated to coordinate the work of a large number of subcontractors engaged in the development of the Navy's Polaris missile, PERT is credited with having cut two years off the time span of that project.

The emphasis on PERT is on time scheduling. A project is broken down into its component steps. These steps are represented graphically in a network to show their interdependence. The time required to complete each step is estimated and potential bottlenecks are identified. A determination is made of the critical path (i.e., the sequence of events that can be expected to take the most time to complete). Having this information, management is able to reassign manpower and resources to speed up the steps that might cause the project to fall behind schedule.

To provide an additional dimension to PERT/time, the PERT/cost system has been developed for the specific purpose of integrating financial data with the associated time data of project accomplishment. In terms of control, the integration of PERT/time and PERT/cost provides substantial assistance in determining whether various levels of management are meeting schedule commitments, cost estimates, and technical performance standards.

Because PERT incorporates a method for estimating the time it will take to do something that has never been done before—and for which, therefore, no time or cost standards exist—it is particularly useful with research and development projects in the office area.

PERT does have some limitations in its application. To some, it seems too scientific to be practical. A second limitation is that estimates tend to be established as firm time and cost commitments, despite the fact that numerous revisions are generally anticipated. At the same time, cost estimates are not often easily identifiable in the normal activities of a department. As a result, the data are sometimes manipulated to make a specific aspect of the project look good at the expense of accuracy and reliability.

These limitations, however, are common to many control tools because of human behavioral considerations, and office administrators who have used PERT conscientiously have found it to be worth the time it takes.

The "New Look" in Personnel Administration

PERT is mentioned only as a foretaste of the many borrowings from heterogeneous disciplines that have found their way into the gamut of today's personnel administration. The "office manager" is now—if he is willing to be—a major administrator, with an impressive armamentarium of scientific tools. As Wilbert Scheer has written:

> "As long as you're content to be just a department manager, then concentrate on your personnel procedures, all the while administering in your central office other people's ideas and policies, many of them perhaps unsound. However, if you aspire to become a company executive, then rise above these necessary techniques and concentrate on their meaning, all the while training and developing your line managers to perform the personnel functions. Don't think of yourself as dealing only with people but rather as dealing also with the factors that affect people. There is quite a distinction here. The landscape is the same; the difference is in the beholder."

CHAPTER 7

THE FUNDAMENTALS OF EQUAL EMPLOYMENT REGULATIONS

By Raleigh F. Seay, Jr.,
Vice President, Sesco Management Consultants, Bristol, Tennessee.

THE FIELD of fair employment practices is one which has mushroomed quite rapidly in the last several years, ever since the passage of Title VII of the Civil Rights Act of 1964. Prior to this Act's being passed, there were no definitive regulations indicating what an employer could and could not do regarding this aspect of employee relations. Now, the entire spectrum has changed. Regulations have become extremely stringent and in many cases difficult to understand.

Employers are swamped with conflicting and hard to understand requirements. It has been our experience that most employers become involved with alleged charges of discrimination *not* because of any intent or desire on their part to discriminate, but because of a lack of complete understanding concerning the manner in which the regulations are being enforced—a situation which is entirely understandable because of the sometimes capricious and arbitrary nature which characterizes many bureaucratic decisions. Most EEOC charges we know of arose out of situations where the employer did not intend to discriminate and in fact did not even know that discrimination had existed.

The purpose of this publication is to offer a very general guideline concerning the basic fundamentals of Equal Employment regulations, in the hope that this knowledge, when put into effect by the employer, will preclude inadvertently committing a violation which would involve one of the Civil Rights enforcement agencies.

Bear in mind, however, that the field of equal employment is one which changes rapidly—therefore, the items which we discuss in this report may be subject to change on a very short notice. Nevertheless, we feel a tremendous need to communicate these basic fundamentals to interested, concerned managers in order to help comply with the letter and spirit of these regulations in a manner which is both practical and economically feasible.

Summary of the Most Important Laws and Executive Orders

Title VII of the Civil Rights Act of 1964—Covers every employer who is involved in interstate commerce (virtually everyone) and who has at least fifteen (15) people employed. It specifies that an employer may not make any employment decision based on race, creed, color, religion, sex, or national origin. Additionally, an employer may not limit, segregate, or classify employees or applicants in such a way as to discriminate against them, which means that you may not have jobs listed as male jobs and female jobs, black jobs and white jobs, etc. These regulations are enforced by the Equal Employment Opportunity Commission.

Age Discrimination in Employment—Covers all employers of twenty (20) or more persons and states that an employer may not make any employment decision based on age, for those persons between forty and seventy. It is enforced by the Equal Employment Opportunity Commission.

Equal Pay for Equal Work—Passed as an amendment to the Fair Labor Standards Act, and enforced by the Equal Employment Opportunity Commission, it states that men and women performing the same or similar work in the same establishment and under similar working conditions, must receive the same pay if their jobs require equal skill, effort and responsibility. However, a differential may exist if it is based on a factor other than sex, such as merit, performance or seniority.

Executive Order 11246—A Presidential Decree having the force and effect of law, which requires employers doing business with the federal government to develop and implement a written affirmative action plan. Essentially, it covers employers who have federal government contracts exceeding $50,000 and who also have 50 or more employees. Financial institutions are covered if they handle federal funds and have 50 or more employees. Executive Order 11246 is enforced by the Office of Federal Contract Compliance Programs.

Vocational Rehabilitation Act—Covers employers having government contracts exceeding $2500 and prohibits employment discrimination based on mental or physical handicap. It requires a written affirmative action plan for handicapped persons, if the government contract exceeds $50,000 and if the establishment employs 50 or more persons. It is enforced by the Office of Federal Contract Compliance Programs and the Department of Labor.

THE FUNDAMENTALS OF EQUAL EMPLOYMENT REGULATIONS

Viet Nam Era Veterans Readjustment Act of 1974—Prohibits discrimination against qualified disabled veterans and veterans of the Viet Nam Era. It requires a written affirmative action plan for veterans if the government contract exceeds $50,000 and if the establishment employs 50 or more persons. It includes a requirement to list available job openings with the local state employment office and is enforced by the Office of Federal Contract Compliance Programs and the Department of Labor.

Statistical Inference

One of the most controversial areas of equal employment enforcement today deals with an "inference" of a violation based on the statistical population of a work force. Recently, enforcement agencies such as the EEOC have found establishments in violation of EEOC regulations where the percentage of minorities in an establishment's work force did not reasonably approximate the percentage of minorities in the work force of the surrounding community.

This area is a very sensitive one in that Title VII includes a very specific ban on "quota hiring", and this particular type of charge is usually initiated only after an investigation of another charge. However, it is our opinion at this time that any establishment whose minority population does not reasonably approximate the minority population of the surrounding work force has a liability of being found in violation and may be required to establish numerical goals and timetables by which to move women and minorities into and upward through the work force.

As an example, a small company in the southeast was undergoing severe economic problems and was forced to lay off some of its employees. Following good personnel procedure, it chose the *least senior* employee in the entire company, a black mechanic, who immediately filed a charge of racial discrimination with the EEOC. After conducting an investigation, the EEOC said that it found *no reasonable cause* to believe that racial discrimination occurred regarding the charging party.

However, blacks represented only 12 percent of the company's work force but 25 percent of the city/county work force—therefore, this company was required to set hiring goals and timetables until its work force attained a minority representation of approximately 25 percent.

Many employers believe that they are meeting the requirements of EEOC regulations by simply not engaging in any overtly discriminatory acts. However, we know of many situations where an employer has been charged with a violation, investigated and found innocent of the alleged charge, yet determined to be in violation of the additional charge of having too few women or minorities. If you as an employer will take positive action to seek out and train qualified minority employees, then you will alleviate the possibility of being found in violation, based on statistical inference.

Recruiting, Screening and Hiring

Recruiting—One of the most frequently violated areas of the fair employment regulations deals with advertising for employment, whether by radio or by newspaper. The enforcement agencies have developed guidelines which outline the types of advertisements which may be considered discriminatory.

First, no advertisement should contain any indication of preference for one sex over another. Examples of this type of situation include "seamstress wanted" or "tailor wanted". Even the word "salesman" would probably be better described as "salesperson".

Secondly, no advertisement should express any preference for age which would tend to discriminate against those persons between the ages of forty and seventy. As an example, the statements "Young person wanted" or "Must be between twenty-five and thirty" or "Recent high school graduate" would all be viewed as discriminatory by the enforcement agencies. No maximum age may be set—however, you may set a minimum age below forty.

Automation in the office has contributed to equal opportunities for women, minorities and the handicapped who are trained to operate the new machines and devices. Training, however, is a very important factor in job placement.

Courtesy Microdata Corporation

THE FUNDAMENTALS OF EQUAL EMPLOYMENT REGULATIONS

Additionally, newspaper advertisements should not be listed under a "male" or "female" heading. Many newspapers have abolished such headings, but if yours has not, we suggest that you place your advertisements under one which says "Male or Female".

Of course, neither should an employer express any preference for a certain race or religion (although such violations are relatively rare), except in those rare circumstances where the "bona fide occupational qualification" applies. As an example, it is all right to advertise along denominational lines when searching for a professor in a Baptist seminary. The "bona fide occupational qualification" also has a very narrow application to sex discrimination.

At the conclusion of each newspaper or radio advertisement, always include the words, "We are an equal opportunity employer—M/F."

Other forms of recruiting are acceptable so long as they do not serve to screen out more minorities than non-minorities or have the effect of referring only to non-minorities. As an example, if you rely strictly on walk-in applicants, and if you receive only white and male applicants, then you should consider seeking some other form of recruitment.

Application Forms and Pre-employment Inquiries—We recommend that you obtain a completed application form for each employee you hire. The name of today's personnel management game is documentation.

We do not, however, recommend that you receive applications unles you currently have or anticipate a bona fide job opening. Of course, if you are in a situation where job openings always exist, you may wish to receive applications on a regular basis.

On those days during which you receive applications, you should offer one to every person who applies. Additionally, your application form should have a statement to the effect that—"We are an equal opportunity employer—M/F."

During any pre-employment inquiry (which includes an application form or an interview), there are certain questions which you should not ask. These questions are ones which are not discriminatory in themselves, but which have the *potential* for discrimination under the right set of circumstances. Furthermore, the EEOC will consider these questions as evidence of discrimination, should you be investigated.

As an example, suppose you received an application from a divorced woman, but decided not to hire her for some good reason. If this woman filed a charge of sex discrimination, then the fact that "marital status" appears on your application form will be evidence that you did in fact engage in sex discrimination.

One of the most important aspects of equal employment which you should understand if you wish to deal effectively with your employment practices is this one—Any device which you use or any question which you ask, which has the effect of screening out more minorities than non-minorities, even though applied equally to everyone, will be looked upon as discriminatory by the EEOC, unless it is job related and you can prove it.

As an example, if you ask a question such as "Have you ever been convicted of a crime?"; and if you use this question to screen out applicants and this action results in a disproportionate screening out of more minorities than non-minorities, the question is discriminatory.

Accordingly, the two questions which you must ask yourself concerning any pre-employment inquiry are these—(1) is it job related? and (2) does it screen out a disproportionate number of minorities? If the answer to either of these questions is unfavorable, then you should give serious consideration to eliminating the question or device.

As you can see, there are a series of questions which fall into this category—that is, the category of potential discrimination. Some questions are blatantly discriminatory and we recommend that you do not ask them at all, such as race or sex. Other questions which have the potential for discrimination are:

1. **Do you have any friends or relatives working here?**
2. **Color of hair or eyes.**
3. **Arrest/conviction record.**
4. **Height/Weight.**
5. **Marital status.**
6. **Dependents.**
7. **Do you have any babysitters for your children?**
8. **Questions concerning credit and/or credit rating.**
9. **Questions concerning debts and to whom debts are owed.**
10. **Home ownership.**
11. **Family background.**
12. **Clubs and societies.**
13. **Questions concerning garnishment.**

Dealing with the question of convictions for a moment, we do not mean to say that you must hire a minority or anyone else who has committed a serious crime; however, you should not use the simple *fact* of a conviction of a minor crime which is non-job related as a reason for failure to hire a minority applicant.

Obviously, you would not want to hire a minority teller who had been convicted of stealing money. The fact that he had one conviction would lend credibility to the belief that there might be another, thus constituting a good non-discriminatory reason for not hiring the individual in this case.

But, if the minority teller had been convicted of evading the draft, you would not be able to use that conviction as a reason for not hiring the person. You see, the simple fact of conviction itself may not be used as reason for failure to hire, but a *job-related* conviction may be used in most circumstances.

Employers covered by the Vocational Rehabilitation Act have restrictions on the questions which may be asked regarding an applicant's health.

Pre-Employment Tests—Many employers administer pre-employment tests, and many of these tests have proven to be very effective in screening potential employees. Although the Equal Employment Opportunity Commission has stated that it is perfectly all right to give and act upon the results of employment tests, certain conditions must be met first. These conditions make it difficult for most employers to utilize pre-employment tests, not because of their discriminatory intent, but because of the difficult administrative procedures and guidelines which must be met prior to their use.

For many years, the federal agencies concerned with civil rights enforcement have been attempting to agree on a uniform set of employee selection procedures. Until very recently, one or two of the agencies would agree while the others would not, thus leaving the employer with, as an example, one set of selection procedures for affirmative action purposes and another set for EEOC purposes.

Now these agencies have agreed upon a uniform set of employee selection procedures. They have published these procedures and they are the ones by which we must abide and to which we must look for guidance in making selection decisions.

An employee selection procedure is any device, any test, any form, or any policy which an employer uses to make an employment decision. This definition includes pre-employment tests, applicant screening profiles, the application form itself, informal interviews, unscored interviews, and other vehicles.

You are free to utilize any type of pre-employment test or any type of employee selection procedure desired, so long as the test or procedure does not have a disproportionate impact upon minorities or women as compared to non-minorities. Further, the employer must maintain records to document, prove and defend this position. Tests may not be utilized to make an employment decision during the time that "adverse impact" information is being gathered. (The technical term for the fact that a test has a disproportionate effect on minorities or women is called "adverse impact".)

Where an employee selection procedure or test does not have an adverse impact on applicants, then the employer is free to continue to utilize the test or selection procedure. However, records must be maintained continuously and the selection procedure or test must be reviewed with regard to adverse impact at least once a year.

Now, what happens when statistical data show that a test or selection procedure does have an adverse impact on women and minorities? In that case, the test or selection procedure must be professionally validated by a person who has been trained in this field. Each test or selection procedure must be validated for the particular use to which it is being put. "National" validation studies or validation studies conducted by the test maker normally will not be acceptable to the EEOC. Each test must be individually validated for each individual position.

In order to help determine whether a test or selection procedure has "adverse impact", the EEOC has established a "rule of thumb" which is not law but which will be used by the EEOC in making these types of decisions. This rule of thumb is called the "four-fifths rule". By means of this rule, a selection rate for any minority group which is less than four-fifths of the selection rate for non-minority groups will be regarded as discriminatory.

As an example, if a test or employment procedure results in selecting 80 out of 100 white applicants, then the selection rate is 80 percent for that group. By means of the "four-fifths rule", the minority selection rate can be no less than four-fifths of 80 percent, or 64 percent. If the minority selection rate is less than 64 percent in this instance, then EEOC will say that discrimination exists with regard to the test or selection procedure in question. Similarly, if the white selection rate is 50 percent, then the minority selection rate can be no less than four-fifths of 50 percent, or 40 percent.

Now, along this same line of thinking, the burden of proof is always on the employer. Additionally, these rules and regulations state that the employer must keep records to justify the use of any test or selection procedure.

Where an employer has no records indicating that selection procedures are justifiable and proper, and where also the organization has fewer minorities than are represented in the work force, then the EEOC will infer or assume that discrimination exists.

Now—remember this point—there is no law or regulation anywhere which says that you must hire an unqualified person. On the contrary, hiring an unqualified person will nearly always result in unnecessary problems, expense and trouble.

But—and remember this point, too—you must be able to document in detail the reasons for not hiring someone. "Intuition" won't work any more—you must be able to offer sound and detailed reasoning for all your employment decisions, and it must be reduced to writing.

Employment Conditions

Many of the early, overtly discriminatory acts (such as segregated restrooms, cafeterias, social activities) have been eliminated, but strangely enough, some still exist. All facilities should be open to all people.

You may not classify jobs as black/white or male/female, or have departments which are all one way or the other, without a good reason and upward mobility for those minorities and women within the department. In other words, if you have any job category which is totally minority or totally non-minority, then you have a potential problem area. Even though your policies are not intended to keep minorities from entering these other positions, the enforcement agencies will probably assume that your policy has the effect of keeping minorities down.

All jobs must be open to all people. Women should be allowed to fill jobs which have traditionally been handled by males, and vice versa. Examples are switchboard operator, lineman, loom fixer, construction worker, miner, supervisor or manager. You may not refuse to give a job like that to a woman simply because she is a woman. If you use reasons such as (1) she has to be home with her children, (2) her husband may move and take her with him, (3) women have more turnover than males, then you may still be in violation, since these are looked upon as sexist-linked reasons for failure to hire or promote.

There is, however, such a thing as a "bona fide occupational qualification". A bona fide occupational qualification, BFOQ, is a job qualification for which only one sex or one religion would be appropriate. However, this exception is being construed very narrowly and, as a result, is almost unavailable to most employers.

An example of a job for which a BFOQ would exist would be something like a chorus dancer, actor for a shaving commercial, model for maternity clothes, or professor of religion in a Baptist seminary. Prior to applying this special situation in your work establishment, you should contact a knowledgeable person in order to ensure that it is permissible.

State Protective Laws—Many states have laws on their books which indicate that a female can work only a certain number of hours or lift a certain amount of weight. As an example, one southern state has a law which says that women cannot work past 12:00 at night. But—you may not rely on any of these laws since they have been superseded by federal regulations. Males and females must be treated equally in every respect.

Benefits—Of course, all benefits must be open to all employees on an equal basis and until recently the great area of unresolved questions centered around the issue of maternity.

On October 15, 1978, Congress finally passed an amendment to Title VII of the Civil Rights Act of 1964 which prohibits discrimination based on pregnancy. Generally, this new amendment says that employers must offer the same benefits to pregnant employees which it offers to other employees who experience a sickness or disability. There is no requirement for employers to grant special privileges to pregnant employees simply because of the fact that they are pregnant, but it does require pregnant employees to be treated in the same manner as other employees who are sick or disabled.

When the Civil Rights Act was passed in 1964, the prohibition of discrimination based upon sex was added at the last moment in an apparent attempt to block passage of the bill. Obviously, the addition of sex discrimination did not block the bill's passage, but it *did* have the result of providing employers with very little background regarding the exact intent of Congress in this respect.

Shortly, the Equal Employment Opportunity Commission developed "Guidelines on Sex Discrimination" which stated that pregnant employees must receive the same benefits as other employees who are sick or disabled. These guidelines also state that pregnancy must be included in an employer's disability insurance program.

A number of employers disagreed with EEOC's guidelines and took the issue to court. In 1976, the United States Supreme Court decided in *Gilbert vs. General Electric** that pregnancy need not be included in an employer's disability program. As a result of this decision, Congress immediately began work on a bill designed to overturn *Gilbert* and provide pregnancy benefits for female employees.

That movement reached fruition and the bill was finally passed during the final, hectic days of the Ninety-Fifth Congress. The bill has an effect on your policies from the following five (5) standpoints:

---

*Gilbert vs. G.E., US SCT (1976).

THE FUNDAMENTALS OF EQUAL EMPLOYMENT REGULATIONS

1. **LEAVES OF ABSENCE**—You must grant leaves of absence to employees who become pregnant in the same way that you grant leaves of absence to employees who are sick or disabled. Generally, the duration of this type of leave should be based on a medical determination by the pregnant employee's physician. Employers may not set arbitrary limits.

2. **SICK PAY**—If you have a sick pay plan which provides "sick days" to employees who are absent due to illness or disability, then this sick plan must be available to employees who are pregnant.

3. **DISABILITY**—A long-term or short-term disability insurance program may not exclude pregnancy from its coverage.

4. **MEDICAL INSURANCE**—A medical insurance plan may not exclude pregnancy from its coverage. Similarly, a medical insurance plan which provides for complete payment of the other disabilities must also provide for complete payment of pregnancy. It would be improper to have a medical plan which paid 100 percent of other disabilities, but less than 100 percent for pregnancy.

   Also, it would be improper to have an insurance program in which pregnancy coverage only extends to those employees who have "dependent" coverage.

5. **ABORTIONS**—You are not required to include medical benefits for abortions (unless they are therapeutic) in your insurance program, but you are required to pay the employee for being absent during that time, if you also pay other employees who are absent for illness or disability.

The bill was signed by President Carter on Halloween, October 31, 1978. Since October 31, 1978, employers may not make any employment decision based on an employee's pregnancy.

Equal Pay for Equal Work—Briefly, employees who perform the same or similar jobs must receive equal pay, without regard to sex, except that any differential may be based on something other than sex, such as merit, seniority or performance.

If you employ both males and females, the chances are very good that you have an equal pay violation and don't even know it. These types of violations creep into the payroll very subtly over a number of years. Many times, we find males and females working alongside each other, the female receiving less pay than the male for no apparent reason. In the past this discrepancy has been based on the fact that the man must support the family, the man can work harder and do more, etc. None of these reasons are sufficient any longer. You must compensate people equally, unless the differentiation is based on something other than sex, and you must be able to document your position.

Terminations

In dealing with terminations, you can apply most of what we've already discussed. An employer may not terminate an individual for most of the reasons that he may not refuse to hire an individual. There is no law or regulation which says that you can't terminate an employee who is performing poorly or who commits some serious indiscretion. However, your reason for termination may not be based on race, creed, color, religion, sex, age, national origin or a handicap which doesn't affect job performance.

We would offer three (3) recommendations for your consideration when you wish to terminate an employee:

1. Have a good reason for the termination and be able to prove it.
2. Thoroughly document the termination to the last detail.
3. Should it be necessary to lay off, do so by seniority if at all possible.

With respect to documentation, if you wish to discharge an employee for absenteeism, do not simply list "excessive absenteeism" on the termination form, but list "Excessive absenteeism—missed five (5) days in a row without calling in", or something of that nature. The point is to document the termination completely and thoroughly.

Additionally, you should ensure that your disciplinary actions are applied equally. You may not discharge a minority for fighting on the job without discharging the non-minority who provoked the fight. Likewise, you should not discharge a minority employee who has a bad absentee record without taking similar action against a non-minority employee who has an equally bad absentee record.

Charges of Discrimination

Any applicant for employment, any employee or anyone on behalf of an applicant or employee may file a charge of alleged discrimination against your establishment. If you live in a state or political division which has a local enforcement agency, then the charge must be filed with it first. If there is no state or local agency, the charge is filed directly with the Equal Employment Opportunity Commission or one of its district or regional offices. The charge must be filed within 180 days after the occurrence of an alleged unlawful employment practice, unless the charge is "continuing" in nature. As an example, if you refuse to hire an applicant for employment on Monday, then the EEOC says that you "continue" to refuse to hire that person every day, so that the 180-day period never runs out.

But, if you discharge an employee, then that action occurs on a one-time basis and is not of a continuing nature. Most charges are the continuing type.

After filing, the Commission must serve a notice of the charge on the respondent (in other words, the employer) within ten (10) days. The Commission must then investigate the charge, after which it must make a determination concerning whether or not there is "reasonable cause" to believe that the charge is true. A reasonable cause determination should be made as promptly as possible, but we have found that this determination is taking from one to four years due to the tremendous backlog of cases which the Commission has on hand.

If the Commission finds no reasonable cause and no other charges, it dismisses the charge. If, however, reasonable cause is found or other alleged violations are uncovered (such as statistical inference), it will attempt to conciliate the case (see below). If the Commission is unable to secure a conciliation agreement that is acceptable, it or the charging party, may bring a civil action in an appropriate U.S. District Court.

Conciliation—Conciliation comes into play when an investigation by the Commission results in a determination that there is probable cause to believe that the charge is true or when additional violations are uncovered. This finding is not one of guilt, simply a determination that the charge is *probably* true. The Commission then negotiates with the employer and the charging party, attempting to reach a satisfactory agreement. This agreement is called a conciliation agreement. The advantage of a conciliation agreement to both the employer and the Commission is the avoidance of the time and expense of litigation.

The Commission will try to resolve the case at the conciliation level if at all possible but will not hesitate to sue. You should have an experienced negotiator by your side, should you find yourself in this situation.

Negotiated Settlements—In order to eliminate some of the backlogged cases, the EEOC is trying several different techniques, one of which is called negotiated settlement.

By means of a negotiated settlement, the employer, EEOC and charging party attempt to reach some sort of settlement agreement prior to an on-site investigation by the Commission.

Most of the time, engaging in these discussions will result in an advantage to the employer in that an on-site investigation can usually be avoided. A negotiated settlement should almost always be discussed, since nothing in the discussions can be used in a subsequent investigation should negotiations break down. Other types of settlement proceedings are being introduced by the Commission including fact-finding conferences and others.

Recordkeeping

There are only three (3) basic recordkeeping requirements but there are several situations which may require keeping other records. The three (3) main requirements are as follow:

1. All personnel records should be kept one year from the date of the action.
2. All discharged employees' records should be maintained for six (6) months.
3. The latest EEO-1 Report must be on file. (Employers of 100 or more people must file an EEO-1 Report each year. Employers of 50 or more must file if subject to Executive Order 11246.)

We recommend, however, that all personnel records be maintained for a period of 24 to 36 months. This recommendation coincides with the Wage and Hour regulations, but also may be necessary due to the fact that most charges take from 18 months to four years to resolve. In addition, when a charge has been filed, all personnel records must be maintained until the charge is concluded, including records of other employees who may be affected by the outcome of the charge.

A Word About Affirmative Action

If your company, hospital, financial institution or establishment has at least one contract with the federal government of $50,000 or more and if you have 50 employees on your payroll, you are subject to Executive Order 11246 which, among other things, requires that the establishment have a written affirmative action program. A bank, savings and loan association or other financial institution falls under this Executive Order if it has 50 employees and handles government money (U.S. Savings Bonds, VA and FHA loans).

This program is extensive, technical, complex and cumbersome to develop. Basically, it includes a discussion of your employment practices along with numerical goals and timetables for moving mi-

SEXUAL HARASSMENT

As you know, the Equal Employment Opportunity Commission is an agency which is charged with investigating alleged charges of discrimination and resolving them. To do so, they have issued various sets of guidelines concerning subjects such as pregnancy, testing, pre-employment inquiries, and others.

The latest set of guidelines which the EEOC has issued and which is receiving a lot of press right now deals with "sexual harassment." Sexual harassment is defined as the conditioning of an employment benefit on a sexual favor. It exists when a supervisor, member of management, or other employee indicates that a person will not receive a promotion, as an example, unless (s)he submits to a sexual favor.

However, that's the obvious example—sexual harassment can also exist where other employees flirt or make statements which are construed as harassment.

As an example, if you have an employee who is constantly teased in a sexual way, and if that employee objects to the teasing, then that type of situation would also constitute sexual harassment.

In my judgment, there is a real danger here in that we could claim that some particular supervisor was guilty of sexual harassment, simply because the employee misinterpreted a statement or remark that the supervisor may have made.

Now, I'm discussing this information with you just to let you know that it exists, and it seems to be something of a hot item right now. We would offer three recommendations in this regard:

(1) Simply be aware of the fact that sexual harassment is a prohibited activity from the standpoint of the Equal Employment Opportunity Commission. It is prohibited no matter whether the harasser is male or female.

(2) A statement regarding sexual harassment should be included in the next revision of your affirmative action plan. It should state that sexual harassment is not permitted at your company, and you should go on to include the company's position in that regard.

(3) We think it would be a good idea for you to have a meeting of your management staff in which you discuss this particular subject. I believe that it is important enough for your managers to know about it to the extent that they should be careful of their remarks and actions, and they should be charged with the responsibility of ensuring that the employees who work for them do not engage in sexual harassment.

I believe—given the current enforcement posture—that these three actions should be sufficient.

Of course, should you detect a case of sexual harassment, then the company should take steps to eliminate it right away.

norities into and upward through the work force, based on formulas and formats outlined by government agencies.

These plans cover the areas of race, creed, color, sex, religion, age, national origin, physical or mental handicap and veterans.

The penalty for not having developed an acceptable affirmative action plan could be the loss of your government contracts. In the case of federal depositories, it could mean the removal of federal money.

Summary

In this rapidly developing field of personnel management, changes occur on a very frequent basis. The purpose of this discussion has been to provide you with information concerning the overall general guidelines which have developed during the implementing years of the Civil Rights regulations. You should remember, however, that each case is an entity in itself and all appropriate facts must be considered and analyzed prior to reaching a final decision.

HOW TO IMPLEMENT EQUAL EMPLOYMENT OPPORTUNITY POLICIES

RECOMMENDATION NO. 1—Put Your Equal Employment Opportunity Policies in Writing

1. Draw up a written corporate policy on nondiscrimination setting forth your objectives to comply with applicable federal and state nondiscrimination laws.

2. Reproduce your nondiscrimination policies in all company policy manuals.

3. Print your nondiscrimination policy in all employee handbooks.

4. To protect your company's interest—and intent to comply with current laws—include the nondiscrimination policy in your union contract. Unions *and* employers are equally responsible for complying with current E.E.O. laws.

RECOMMENDATION NO. 2—Establish Internal Procedures for Hiring, Selecting and Placement

1. Make sure that staff recruiters cover minority group schools, and colleges in your area. Explain *your* policy to school officials.

2. If there are minority group employees within your organization, let them know they can recommend others of the same group for employment consideration.

3. Make very sure that interviewers carefully document reasons for turning down any minority group job application. The interviewer should also try to verbally communicate to a minority group applicant why he could not be hired because of objective or personal reasons—rather than race, color, sex, religion or national origin.

4. Check out types of psychological tests presently being used in your organization. Make sure that your tests are professionally developed and scored.

5. Draft a written guide for interviewers outlining areas of questioning that may be asked all job applicants and those types of questions which must be avoided to prevent charges of discrimination.

6. Display Federal Equal Employment Posters in job applicant waiting rooms or areas where applicants await employment interview.

7. Print on all employment applications and other personnel forms required to be filled out by applicants a statement such as the following:

All qualified applicants will receive consideration for employment without regard to race, color, creed, sex or national origin. This company offers equal opportunity and treatment to all employees and qualified applicants.

RECOMMENDATION NO. 3—Communicating with Supervision

1. Be sure supervisors have copies of *all* company policy statements and procedures on E.E.O. in your organization.

2. Tell all levels of supervision that employees, regardless of race, color, religion, sex or national origin, will not be discriminated against in hiring, induction or training, layoffs, promotions, transfers, discipline, the filing of grievances or in any other phases of the employer-employee relationship.

3. Provide supervisors, who have hiring responsibility, with written instructions on prohibited pre-employment inquiries under state and federal laws or regulations.

4. Most important, set up formal training programs for present and new supervisors that will emphasize their role in practicing your equal employment opportunity policies.

RECOMMENDATION NO. 4—Communicating with Employees

1. Your equal employment opportunity policy should be recorded in your current employee handbook, and it should be repeated from time to time in company publications.

2. Make sure that company publication editors are aware that *all* employees receive equal treatment in the reporting of promotions, transfers, retirements or similar company news. At the same time, emphasis on the fact that the employee is a member of a minority group must be eliminated completely.

3. If necessary, hold group meetings with employees to explain your current policies on nondiscrimination. During these sessions you should:

   (a) Detail your company's hiring policy with emphasis on the employment of minority groups.

   (b) Explain that all job candidates must be considered for employment on the basis of their qualifications, skills, aptitude, previous experience and education.

   (c) Ask employees for their help and cooperation in making new minority group employees feel at home.

   (d) Explain that the progress of the company and the employees' job security requires that you utilize all available manpower to the fullest, regardless of race, color, religion, sex or national origin. Remind employees that the company must always comply to the best of its ability with all aspects of the federal equal opportunity laws as well as state laws if there are such.

   (e) Ensure employees that no reverse discrimination will be practiced in hiring, promoting or firing procedures.

RECOMMENDATION NO. 5—Communicating With Your Community

1. Visit or phone local schools and colleges (if you currently recruit from these schools) and inform them of your equal employment program. They should be interested.

2. If you conduct open house tours, be sure to invite minority group teachers, school officials or community leaders.

3. If you are contacted by minority group community leaders, be sure to invite them to visit your company or offer to send them copies of your printed equal employment opportunity policies.

4. Make an effort to advertise job openings in *all* community news media, and use all reliable employment agencies including your state agency if there is one.

5. When you do advertise for help, make sure your ad carries the tag line "An Equal Opportunity Employer" with an M/F when possible. This helps in conforming with most regulations.

CHAPTER 8

PERSONNEL SELECTION—
RECRUITING

UNLESS a company's selection process has been carefully conceived and is properly administered, there is little hope that any office is going to run efficiently and economically. The emphasis on the proper selection and placement of office personnel has long been understood by those who are charged with this responsibility.

Certainly, when business is in a downturn or the job market is loaded with excellent talent it is a simple matter to hire people with appropriate skills—even people who have extra skills. This can be as wrong a move as hiring someone with no aptitude at all. One of the most important factors in labor turnover has been, experience shows, the proper screening and placement of workers.

The key is to find an employee who can (1) handle the job if it calls for a particular learned skill, or (2) be trained in a brief period of time. Many office jobs call for special skills as a basis for employment. If this is the need, it is wise to match the abilities of the candidate with *all of the factors* affecting the position. The salary offered must be equal to the person's basic skill. There must be some opportunity for growth. There must be some challenge.

Skilled people normally will demand an equitable salary (except in times of downturn), but they might not be as demanding in some of the other basic areas when they are interviewing for the position. It is up to the interviewer to find out *why* they have less interest in growth and achievement.

The administrator who will direct the activities of office personnel may not be directly responsible for the hiring of individuals, but he or she must at least understand selection techniques, the following of company policy on selection, and the availability of people in the local job market.

The administrator must, within his realm of authority, make his own decisions when he meets a potential employee for the first time. He can set his own standards, and he can stick to them, but he must function with an open mind when a candidate gets to his desk.

Assessing the Labor Market

Not every job opening can be filled from within the company although this is a desirable practice whenever it is feasible. Employees like to advance and "upward mobility" has many advantages for the company as well as the employees.

But there are occasions, many times, when a job vacancy must be filled from the outside. The opening is a critical one and the necessary talent is not "in the house." In most cases, however, the jobs to be filled are at or near the bottom, or entry level, as previously-hired beginners gain experience and are promoted.

Because of the need to hire from the open market, interviewers should be surveying the situation constantly. Companies should know the availability and cost of acquiring the number and types of people necessary to fill jobs. It should have ready information about:

1. The best sources of applicants.
2. The going rates of pay for starting jobs.
3. The availability of qualified candidates.
4. The waiting or "lead time" for newly-hired workers.
5. The cost of acquisition.

While it is axiomatic that for best results every position should be filled by the best qualified candidate who is available—from the inside or the outside—the truth is that the jobs are often filled by the handiest persons. Oftentimes it is easier to obtain an already-trained employee from the outside than to take the time to prepare someone presently on the payroll. Taking the easy way out and hiring a stranger often overlooks talent the company is unaware it already possesses.

The best way to fill job vacancies by a given time, by either internal transfer or external recruitment, calls for a company to assess both the workforce and the labor market. Over the long pull, a company's investment in its employees is greater than any of its other capital investments. Hiring employees deserves careful attention, and this means a company should know how to assess the market.

Acquisition Cost

The employment function is a continuing one in every company, regardless of whether or not the procedure is formalized. The selection and retention of efficient workers is one of the most important operations of any company. In a tightening labor market this is also one of the greatest problems.

The reason this becomes a problem of dimensions is not simply to keep jobs in the company filled. The problem is concerned with cost. The cost of hiring applicants has been variously estimated in different companies and in different regions of the country. For female clerical workers, for instance, the employment agency fee itself, often paid by the employer, is sizable. For this fee the agency does little more than refer applicants; there is no testing and very little screening.

For certain types of jobs newspaper advertising is effective; for other jobs it is of little value today. For instance, an advertisement in a local newspaper for housewives to do typing for a few hours each day will bring in an avalanche of inquiries. On the other hand, an advertisement in a big city daily for a secretary will bring in little response, especially when such notice is included among hundreds of other similar ads for stenos and secretaries. In such case the few referrals and the limited selection resulting from the advertisement make newspaper classified or display ads quite expensive. It is not sufficient to think of the cost of the ad itself; the number of ads and the amount of work in connection with replies must be considered in relation to results obtained.

Many companies have found it profitable to reward employees who refer their friends or relatives for employment. This payment may take any of many forms, such as cash, government bonds, time off, and the like. This practice has two distinct advantages. First, it is the cheapest form in use, for surely a government bond or two is less in cost than an advertisement and all the screening work this entails, or an agency fee. Second, it tends to bring in the same type of person who has already been found acceptable to the company, and with affirmative action programs now firmly established, this practice of having employees refer friends and relatives is no longer considered discriminatory.

There is another intangible benefit that many companies recognize as valuable: The employees who recommend their company to other persons not only sell the company and its favorable working conditions to their friends but in so doing also resell this to themselves.

Whatever method is used, we can be almost certain that the cost of each new worker is high, much higher than we realize. Add to this the expense of interviewing, low production during the beginning or training period, the time of the person who does the training, and all the many other obvious as well as hidden costs, and we get some idea of the cost of employment.

It is, therefore, advisable to analyze the cost against results. The following acquisition cost analysis chart should be helpful.

OFFICE ADMINISTRATION HANDBOOK

ACQUISITION COST ANALYSIS

Newspaper	Telephone Responses					Total	Mail Responses					Total	Personal Interviews					Total	Acceptances					Total
	M	T	W	Th	F		M	T	W	Th	F		M	T	W	Th	F		M	T	W	Th	F	
1.																								
2.																								
3.																								
4.																								
5.																								

Newspaper	Cost of Ad	Total Leads	Cost per Lead	Total Acceptances	Cost per Acceptance
1.					
2.					
3.					
4.					
5.					

Employment Costs Outline

1. Acquisition
- 1.1 Advertisements
    - 1.11 Preparation of advertisement (writing it)
    - 1.12 Blind advertisement
        - 1.121 Writing the advertisement
        - 1.122 Screening replies
        - 1.123 Contact applicant by telephone or letter
- 1.2 Agency (free or fee)
    - 1.21 Preparation of job orders
    - 1.22 Time and cost of phone orders
    - 1.23 Those interviewed who are rejected at once
- 1.3 Bonus payment for employee referral
- 1.4 Recruitment
    - 1.41 Membership in organizations for applicant contact
    - 1.42 Visiting high schools and colleges
    - 1.43 Participation in career days
    - 1.44 Expenses of entertaining
    - 1.45 Work study or work experience program costs

2. Employee Processing
- 2.1 Receptionist
    - 2.11 Supplies
        - 2.111 Application blanks
        - 2.112 Other forms
    - 2.12 Interviewer
        - 2.121 Time of interviewing
        - 2.122 Education to improve oneself
        - 2.123 Cost of tests
            - 2.1231 Supplies themselves
            - 2.1232 Administration and interpretation
            - 2.1233 Training on improved methods
            - 2.1234 Reports kept to establish company norms
        - 2.124 Reference checks
            - 2.1241 Time and cost of phone inquiries
            - 2.1242 Letters

       2.125 Investigations

             2.1251 Personal followups (especially in negative cases)

             2.1252 Professional inquiry services

3. Break-in Costs

   3.1 Indoctrination

   3.2 Orientation program

       3.21 Planning the program

       3.22 Executing the program

       3.23 Material used for program

           3.231 Pamphlets

           3.232 Films

           3.233 Equipment

   3.3 On-the-job training

       3.31   Training supervisor

       3.32   Lower production during learning period

   3.4 Tying up other workers

   3.5 Double worker costs

4. Separation Costs

   4.1 Processing procedures

       4.11   Discussion with supervisor

       4.12   Counselor's exit interview

   4.2 Slowing down of production rate

   4.3 No new work assignments

   4.4 Separation pay

       4.41   Terminal pay

       4.42   Unpaid vacation time

       4.43   Cost of payroll in special handling

Help Wanted Requisitions

A help wanted requisition is used to control the size of the employee group. Without such a simple device an organization could grow without restriction.

Such a requisition is completed by the department manager when a job vacancy occurs or a new job is authorized. On it the manager lists the job title, location, work hours, classification, starting salary, qualifications, description of duties, date to be filled, and other information needed to fill the job. After it is signed and authenticated, it is forwarded to the personnel or employment office.

Upon receipt of such requisition, the employment interviewer will take whatever action is deemed appropriate to recruit and process candidates. Ideally, the interviewer will find more than one applicant who measures up to the requirements of the job, in order to give the line manager a choice.

It is advisable to have a different requisition, or the regular one in a different color, for jobs that are temporary, emergency, summer vacation, or otherwise short-term. Filling one of these short-term jobs does not necessarily cancel out a regular requisition.

In a stable organization the manager is ordinarily permitted to hire replacements for regular established jobs. Even then, jobs that remain open for a while should be investigated for possibly they are not needed. Additional jobs should carry the approval of a top officer, preferably the president or comptroller. This precaution requires divisions or departments to justify creating jobs and assuring that necessary budgetary support has been provided.

The Art of Recruiting

The employment of workers begins with the act of recruiting. Recruitment, as this is called, is like the outstretched arms in the employment picture. Ideally it should gather in enough applicants from whom the final selection can then be made.

The problem of recruiting varies by type of job, industry, location, and current labor market. The company must: (1) establish and maintain the most productive sources of supply, and (2) devise the most effective and efficient means of reaching applicants. Then it must succeed in encouraging them to inquire about the job opportunities offered.

There are two sources of applicants to fill vacant positions: internal and external. The internal source is inside the company for lateral transfer and promotion. This rewards faithful and loyal workers with more remunerative positions or with work that is more to their liking. But it could have the disadvantage of inbreeding.

For some jobs it might be better to go outside. Most job vacancies, especially beginner positions, are filled from the external source. This consists of many aspects. Wilbert E. Scheer, author of the Dartnell Personnel Administration Handbook, has developed this listing of sources of external applicants:

1. Employment agencies
   a. Private—or fee
   b. Government—or free

PERMANENT HELP REQUISITION

To: Personnel

DATE _____

JOB CLASSIFICATION _____ DEPARTMENT _____

Recommended Salary to Start—from $ _____ to $ _____

Duties (including machines to be operated) _____

_____

Replacement for _____

If additional job, explain fully _____

Education _____ Experience _____

Requested by _____ Approved _____ Approved _____
         Manager   Vice President   President

TO BE COMPLETED BY PERSONNEL

Job filled by _____ From _____

2. Advertisements
    a.   Metropolitan newspapers
    b.   Neighborhood weeklies
    c.   Trade publications
3. Schools
    a.   High schools
        (1) City public
        (2) Suburban
        (3) Parochial
    b.   Junior colleges
    c.   Universities
    d.   Business colleges
    e.   Trade schools
4. Employee referrals
5. Miscellaneous sources
    a.   Churches
    b.   Clubs
    c.   Fraternal organizations
    d.   Minority group headquarters
    e.   Handicapped
    f.   Business associations
6. Unsolicited applications
    a.   Walk-ins
    b.   Write-ins
    c.   Job-shoppers

You can add radio and even TV to this list under advertisements today, for this form of recruiting has been popular in smaller city areas where spot announcements are not too expensive. It is also working in metropolitan areas for high technology companies. Those who have used these media find them very successful. Where there is cable TV, it is even easier for a company to use TV for recruiting. The smaller stations have low rates, and it has been possible for companies to use their own closed-circuit TV equipment to produce their own recruiting messages. These have proved to be very effective.

ADVERTISING FOR HELP

Classified ads pull well for many companies, especially in the large metropolitan areas. Since classified sections have been de-sexed—meaning all positions are offered to Men/Women, this calls for care in describing the position in the first sentence (first word if possible), because of the alphabetical listing. An ad starting with the phrase: "Wanted, Secretary" could be printed down the list with Waffle Cooks, Watchmen, Welders, and Woodworkers.

Studies have been made to see if tricky ads or clever ads draw better response. In general, they do not. A Chicago oil company once ran a misspelled message to dramatize the need for stenographers. The ad pulled five replies—and only one was from a likely candidate.

On the other hand, a classified ad does not have to be deadly dull. A simple "Secretary Wanted, Five Days. Phone 000-0000" isn't going to set any young lady's imagination on fire. Which brings up the use of the word *young*. This is still used by some companies, but it is in danger of attracting the Equal Opportunity people since age requirement is considered a discrimination under law; likewise, "lady."

A classified ad should stress some advantage offered by the company. The new four-day week might be one such advantage. The term "Excellent Salary" or better still a figure can attract immediate attention. The location of the company can attract or turn away people. Size of the office has the same effect.

Following is a checklist and outline which should stimulate some thinking about the development of a classified ad.

CHECKLIST

A well-written help-wanted advertisement contains the following information:

1. *Hours*
2. *Remuneration*
3. *Distinguishing features of work or product*
4. *Benefits*
5. *Transportation and location*
6. *Requirements and references*
7. *How to apply*

TO WRITE AN AD THAT WILL BE READ

I. Attract reader attention.
   A good opening line or phrase—a catchy head in big type helps to get an audience.

II. Hold their interest.
   A. *Be natural.* A few lines in informal, friendly style will attract more readers than a hundred lines of dull print.
   B. *Be specific.* Tell exactly what type of person you want to hire, to avoid excessive screening of misfit applicants.
   C. *Be different.* To attract high-quality applicants, appeal to the imagination with attention-getting phrases.
   D. *Be explanatory.* Don't leave out important facts that will cause the person you want to hire to pass over the ad. The sin of omission is a costly one.
   E. *Tell them what they want to know.* What business are you in? What conveniences do you have? What hours do you require? What experience is necessary? Where are you located? What salary range are you planning? What will your job *do* for the applicant? What are the opportunities for advancement? What are the qualities you are seeking?

III. Invite action.
   A. Tell them how to apply or whom to call.
   B. Tell them to *do it now.*
   C. Give them a specific person to contact (they'll feel more confident, more inclined to apply for the job).
   D. Make them feel welcome.

"The NATURAL way makes want ads pay"

To Sign or Not to Sign

Should you sign your ad with company name, address and telephone number? If you look at the classified pages, you will find that there are a larger number of unsigned ads. Do they draw as well? In many cases, they do draw a large number of responses, especially if they make an attractive offer of employment or indicate a salary level.

But, the experts agree, you will get a better quality of respondent with a signed ad. The manager of the classified advertising department of the Detroit News once explained: "Advertisers are using them (blind ads) more and benefiting less than they were a few years ago." He offered three reasons:

1. Unless employment is very hard to get, people don't respond to an ad that offers little more than they now have.
2. There is a growing reservation about blind box numbers. Some people resent (or are suspicious of) the secrecy and do not apply.
3. Employees may fear that they might be answering an ad placed by their own company.

Many, if not most, firms do not bother to answer all applicants, especially those who do not meet qualifications. This irritates people who respond in good faith. They have spent energy, and postage money and are not pleased when they receive no answer—not even a "Thank you for responding but . . ." Common courtesy—and good public relations—suggest a reply, if only a form letter.

Dartnell conducted a short survey by answering ads for executive and semi-executive level positions open . . . with blind ads and box numbers. Only 20% of the companies responded in any way, despite the fact that the qualifications required were carefully listed in the response and resume offered.

The type of form letter used by many companies is very simple and direct in its approach:

Dear Ms. Jones:

Your application for the position of secretary with our sales department has been received and studied by our personnel department.

While your experience is most impressive, we have received applications from several candidates who appear to have more exactly the qualifications we are looking for.

Thank you for responding to our advertisement. We hope that you will find a satisfactory position in the near future.

While this response is obviously a brush-off, it at least gives the satisfaction of knowing that the company is courteous and has looked at their application.

Some time back, Ted MacDonald, *Harrison C. MacDonald & Sons, Inc.,* an Indiana firm which has served classified advertising departments for nearly 50 years said:

> "For as long as I can remember, it has been the opinion of experienced classified professionals that a box number is less effective than an identifiable ad. There is a natural inclination on the part of the applicant to feel that the advertiser has something to hide if he is not willing to identify himself."

RECRUITING AT SCHOOLS

Local high schools as well as colleges and universities provide the biggest potential for new employees in white-collar positions. If your company is large enough to recruit beyond its community in universities, then you have a professional recruiter who is doing the job. If you have need of bright young people from local high schools and junior colleges, then you may be doing the recruiting yourself.

No matter what the economic situation, there is usually a demand for young people trained in office skills in any community. There is also a growing demand for those trained in advanced skills, such as computer programming and in bookkeeping or accounting. This means an extra effort must be put forth if you want the best available.

Junior Colleges

Many junior colleges turn out graduates, after two years of study, who have very definite business and technical skills. It is very easy to talk to the dean or placement officer at these institutions. They will make your needs known to upper-grade students and send you any number of possible candidates.

The advantage of recruiting at a junior college level is that it is local and the students have less of an immediate desire to leave for another city to obtain work. A straightforward presentation to these young people—especially outlining their opportunity to advance with the company—will provide a constant source of new talent if you need it.

It is also well to set up a policy whereby they can continue their education while they are working. This may be through night-school or university extension courses. If you can help them obtain a degree, they will be loyal employees in most cases.

Colleges and Universities

Small companies, as well as large corporations, want the best qualified men and women available when they seek new personnel. Often, the best qualified applicants are to be found among college and university graduates. Dr. Frank S. Endicott, former Director of Placement, Northwestern University, reported this especially true in specialized fields such as science, engineering, and accounting.

Large corporations, with well organized recruiting teams, regularly canvass the crop of college seniors in search of outstanding graduates. These companies compete with each other for what they consider to be the top group. It is this competition which the small company must try to meet successfully.

True or False?

Before outlining some of the procedures which the small company can utilize in employing college graduates, let us consider briefly a few of the comments frequently made by executives of small companies.

"College graduates are only interested in large companies." This is not necessarily true. Some graduates prefer a smaller company. Others will consider favorably a job with a smaller company when they have an opportunity to investigate and learn about the position.

"The college graduate is likely to get lost in a big corporation." Definitely not true. Large companies are often divided into small

sections, divisions, or district and local offices. The young graduate has fairly close personal relationships with a few men with whom he works, much like the experience he would have in a small company. Furthermore, large companies, through carefully developed personnel procedures, keep track of the new graduate and try to see that he does not get lost.

"Placement agencies are only interested in serving large companies." Not true. Most personnel agents welcome an opportunity to refer graduates to small companies. Requests for applicants and for interviews on the campus are handled in exactly the same way for all types and sizes of companies.

"Small companies can't compete with large corporations in salaries." In many cases, this is not true. Studies have shown that the small company often has a general salary schedule which is as good as that of the large corporation. Large corporations continually lose good men to smaller companies because of greater opportunity and salary.

"Advancement in small companies is more rapid than in large corporations." Often this is true, but there may be fewer higher-level jobs in the small company. If the sales manager of a small company has only 10 salesmen, opportunity for advancement into sales management is limited. If a large company has 200 salesmen in 20 different local or regional offices, there is usually considerable opportunity for outstanding men to move into sales management.

"Small companies are handicapped because they can't have full-time recruiters and fancy brochures." This may be true. Nevertheless, since the small company needs fewer graduates, operating personnel can keep in close contact with a small number of schools. Mimeographed or typewritten information about the company and about the job is often as effective as a four-color booklet.

CHECKLIST FOR COLLEGE RECRUITING

Effective procedures for contacting colleges and universities and for hiring college graduates have been fairly well determined by those companies which have been successful. These procedures are outlined briefly below:

1. Be sure to get the approval and unqualified support of top management. Executives must be throroughly sold on the need for college graduates. They must be willing to make the employment of college graduates an important part of company policy.

2. Make certain that the job is one which requires college training. It is a great mistake to give college graduates a job which

a high-school graduate can handle reasonably well. College graduates need to be challenged. They want to use their knowledge and skill. If they are kept too long on a routine assignment, they lose interest, and will seek another position.

3. Establish a competitive starting salary. Starting rates for college graduates in various fields are fairly well known among personnel executives. A telephone call to a few placement directors in representative colleges or universities will bring helpful information on starting salaries and college graduates.

4. Make a personal visit to selected schools in order to meet the placement officer and to acquaint him with your company and its needs. This should be done at least six months in advance of the hiring date. On this visit the company representative can find out how the office operates, how interviews are scheduled, what type of information is needed about the job and the company, and how a continuing relationship can be maintained.

5. Develop appropriate descriptive information about your company and the positions. Such information can be presented in a helpful way without printing an expensive booklet. The placement officer will have suggestions concerning what type of information interests the graduates. Of special importance is information about the nature of the work assignments and opportunity for advancement.

6. Make arrangements with the placement officers on selected campuses to interview or contact graduates. Most placement officers have limited space. Many companies schedule interviews on very short notice.

7. Send to the campus the best qualified interviewers. Many operating managers need training or experience in order to do a really good job as a recruiter of college graduates. There are special skills involved which some executives may not have.

8. Arrange for selected applicants to come to the office or plant for further interviews. It is especially important to see that the graduate is well received and that the necessary executives are prepared to talk to the candidate.

9. Following plant or office interviews, offers should be made promptly. It is likely that other companies have interviewed the applicant and that other offers are being considered.

10. There should be a carefully planned program of induction and training for each graduate employed. In smaller companies, on-the-job training is often most practical and success-

ful. Even so, there should be a plan and a purpose for the program.

11. Be sure that those who supervise the newly hired graduate are aware of their responsibilities and that they are sympathetic and helpful.

12. Close personal contact regarding progress is important. Good personnel procedure includes regular appraisal and advancement on merit.

Companies, both large and small, may find it helpful to use these twelve steps as a checklist in evaluating and improving current recruiting procedures or in initiating a program for the selection and employment of college graduates.

Spectacular results should not be expected at once. Most companies which are successful in hiring college graduates have been recruiting for many years. It may take several years for a company to become well known on a particular campus.

Can a small company successfully recruit college graduates? *The answer is Yes!*

EMPLOYEE REFERRALS

Your firm may or may not have a written or stated policy on employee referrals. It is usually the company that has excellent employee relations that does the best business in gaining new recruits through its own employees' efforts.

Some firms have paid bonuses in the past and probably will do it again in the future when they find that current employees can bring in skilled personnel. Of course, no employee is going to lure a friend to work for a company that he or she is considering leaving, so any effort on the part of the employee is based on honest belief that his company is a good place to work.

If a company is going to actively seek the aid of employees in searching for job candidates, several points should be cleared:

1. The company must announce jobs available to the employees, and in most cases this means that the employees have first opportunity to try for the jobs themselves. Once the opening is definitely established, then the request should be made to the employees.

2. The company should establish a policy on hiring or not hiring relatives of employees.

3. If a bonus is to be paid, the amount and method should be explained in the company manual, house organ, or at a meeting.

4. E.E.O. guidelines must be followed.

Administrators must recognize the possible disadvantages as well as the advantages of hiring people on referral. One advantage is the saving incurred by not having to advertise for the position or use the services of an employment agency. One disadvantage is the possibility of hiring a new employee referred by someone who may not be performing adequately. It would be difficult to say: "Sorry, Mabel, we can't hire your friend because we are considering your dismissal." This would be a rare but uncomfortable experience.

Also to be considered is the possible unpleasantness that might result from the dismissal of an employee who was brought in by referral. If a referral policy should be adopted, more than casual care in selection is needed to be sure the referred applicant offers reasonable hope of permanence.

USING EMPLOYMENT AGENCIES

The use of employment agencies, especially in the larger cities, is wide-spread for many reasons. The major reason is *convenience.*

Smaller firms, especially, which do not have personnel departments to back up administrators in the selecting and recruiting processes, must often turn to an agency to save time and money—despite the fact that a fee payment is involved. The modern agency acts as a personnel department in the areas of initial screening for skills, in testing, and in handling the advertising for employees. The agency personnel in a first-class operation are trained recruiters who are sincerely interested in obtaining good employees for a company client.

An agency that doesn't satisfy its customers isn't likely to stay in business very long, so the fact that many agencies are well-established testifies to their ability to satisfy. The administrator who is going to work with an agency should quickly learn how interested the agency is in securing future employees. Initial contact should require some lengthy discussions on the types of jobs that will be available, the company's employment policies and practices, and the role the agency will play.

Finding an Agency

State regulations govern the business conduct of employment agencies in most instances, but the regulations vary, and as it is in every type of business, there can be bad agencies in the bunch. The administrator who is turning to an agency for the first time can ask his associates about their experiences. Many agencies are members of local Administration Management Society chapters, and here the administrator can make personal contact with the agency people as well as business friends who use them.

Experience is the best teacher in dealing with an agency. If you like the type of people the agency chooses for you, you will like the agency. You can also question the candidates about their experience with the agency. This, often, can be an excellent clue. You should be sure that you are making your needs clear so that the agency is not sending you the wrong candidates. Often the fault lies more with the person hiring than with the agency, although a good agency will clear up this situation quickly once the problem is spotted.

The Public Employment Service

The public employment service was established in 1933 under the authority of the Wagner-Peyser Act. It was created as a nationwide Federal-State system of no fee local employment offices to assist workers to obtain employment. It is administered by the U.S. Employment Service (USES) of the Employment and Training Administration (ETA), Department of Labor, which formulates programs and policies, issues regulations, apportions funds to State employment security agencies for employment service operations, provides technical assistance, and monitors program progress.

Nearly all State employment security agencies are now using "Job Service" to more accurately reflect their primary role as a labor exchange agency. The Job Service consists of nearly 2,500 local offices and about 30,000 staff members who serve people seeking employment and employers needing qualified workers. General services include applicant registration, interviewing, testing, counseling, job development, recruitment, and other services for employers, referrals to jobs and referrals to training or other services concerned with preparing people for employment.

For Applicants

Local Job Service offices provide job placement services to all jobseekers. Job Service staff solicit information on job openings from employers. Applications from job seekers are screened regularly against available job openings. Applicants are referred to job opportunities for which they are qualified. Computers are now being used in many offices to speed up selection and referral and to give jobseekers a wider exposure to job opportunities available.

For Employers

Job Service staff maintain contact with employers to assist them in recruiting new workers and in achieving or improving stability of current workforces. Employers with Federal contracts who are required to list job openings with Job Service local offices are assisted in meeting their veterans affirmative action obligations and in obtaining qualified workers.

The Job Service is moving to strengthen its services to help reduce unemployment; a productivity increase of 10% for individuals placed has been set as one of its goals. Emphasis is being given to increasing placement services for migrant and seasonal farm-workers. Special efforts are being made to help more veterans find jobs or training leading to jobs. As youth unemployment is still far too high, the Job Service is also focusing on helping young people make the transition from school to work and on improving the summer jobs program.

Hiring Older Workers

Although there is an Equal Opportunities Employment law that protects the older worker from discrimination in employment, there is a tendency on the part of the administrator to choose a younger person for many of the available office jobs. The selection process, if well-based, should seek out people with qualities or abilities to perform the work. If the administrator can realize that older people can do the job, he both avoids breaking the law and serves himself to an employee who will probably have less absenteeism, less tardiness and less desire to move on.

The biggest advantage in an office situation is that the department gains a stability of performance from someone who knows the value of work. A woman whose family is raised, or old enough to take care of their basic needs, enjoys the opportunity to work in an office. In most cases, she will adjust rapidly and will be cooperative, quickly learning office routine. Thousands of companies have learned to rely on this work force, and there will probably be a continuing market for the older worker.

MISCELLANEOUS SOURCES

There remain several other sources for recruiting of employees—neighborhood clubs, the YMCA, church groups, business associations and temporary help organizations.

When the word is passed to most of the above groups, someone may be available to refer your company to a prospect. You normally will find that the person nominated is local, willing, and may be fully qualified. Although the selection process must be carried through under any circumstances, the saving involved in not having to advertise or not having to go through an agency makes the effort worthwhile.

Temporary Help

The temporary-help industry, which started in Chicago in 1935, has mushroomed into a quarter of a billion dollars per year business. It currently employs a million wage earners. Under its arrangements workers are hired by the temporary help agency (which does not charge them any fee), then leased to industrial and professional firms on a short-term basis.

The company pays a flat hourly rate, based on the skill. The employee is on the payroll of the agency, not the company where the work is performed. The agency assumes the obligations for Social Security taxes and records, insurance, vacation, and other benefits. The big item, of course, is that the agency recruits, interviews, tests, selects, and hires the employees and either finds them qualified in a specialty skill or trains them. The employing company gets a fully trained worker. Temporary workers are mostly women, especially married women. These are often well-trained and skilled workers who for reasons of their own are unable or unwilling to accept full-time employment.

The temporary-help industry is a blessing for wives who want extra money. But it may also be the answer for career women who like to travel, students working their way through college, actresses between engagements, athletes during the off season, and older people who need new jobs.

Job arrangements can be tailored to the worker, who can work those weeks when he or she is available, certain days of the week, and occasionally even limited hours of the day. Mothers can take the summer months off to be home with school-age children simply by making themselves unavailable during that period.

Travel for single women is more than saving money while working for a vacation trip. Companies which have offices in different cities have been known to certify employees in their home city and then assign them out of offices in other cities. An example is the British secretaries recruited and hired in London for six or 12 months' work, then assigned to companies in various cities in the United States.

Many workers like the variety which this kind of service offers. Creative types may find working for the same company somewhat stifling. As temporary workers they can move about, actually pick and choose the kind of work they prefer.

Temporary workers are mostly typists and secretaries. But there are also many other types of office skills—calculating machine operators, clerks, bookkeepers, file clerks, key punch operators. Some are trained as computer progammers, receptionists, demonstrators, convention registrars, ushers, pollsters, survey interviewers, etc.

A few agencies are now specializing in men for temporary jobs. Some of these supply laborers, freight handlers, watchmen—hired and paid by the day. Others are office and factory workers, product demonstrators, booth attendants, sample distributors, and so on.

Temporary personnel is a new industrial cost-saving tool. Apart from the savings in recordkeeping, payroll taxes, workers' compensation, and fringe benefits, the big item is direct labor cost savings. Temporary workers are used only when there is work for them. Whereas regular employees remain on the payroll even when the volume of work decreases, the temporary workers are released. No work, no direct labor cost.

APPLICATION BLANK

In applying for a job in the office, the applicant is asked to fill out an "Application for Employment" form. This is usually done in the office of the employing company but it is occasionally completed away from the premises and then mailed in or carried in.

The application blank is used to obtain information. By the use of a standard form the information is always in the same place and the interviewer is spared the time and annoyance of having to hunt for specifics. The form may be professionally prepared and purchased from an office supply store, or individually developed by any one company to suit its own circumstances.

The information asked for depends upon company requirements and job demands. In all cases certain basic data, such as name and address, are essential. But questions to a sales applicant will vary from those to a shop worker.

Different application blanks may be used for:
  1. **Office personnel.**
  2. **Factory workers.**
  3. **Salesmen.**
  4. **Technicians.**
  5. **Supervisors and managers.**
  6. **Executives.**

Since different information is often needed for higher positions, the appropriate application blanks are more detailed. They provide for information about the applicant's background and stability, extracurricular activities, scholastic honors, leadership positions, military accomplishments, civic responsibilities, interests, and the like.

In general, the sections of an application blank are usually these:
  1. Personal data: name, home address, telephone number, social security number.

2. Helpful information: type of work sought, salary desired, when available to begin work, reason for wanting to change jobs, and from what source the applicant was referred.

3. Education: chronological education history, highest level attained with everything leading to it detailed out by names and locations of grammar school, high school, trade or business college, correspondence school, college or university, night school: years attended, whether graduated, courses of specialization.

4. Work experience: work history in inverse order, names and addresses of companies worked for (listing most recent one first and working back), dates of employment, earnings, types of work done, progress made, reason for leaving, and name of supervisor who may be contacted for reference.

Other information requested may pertain to machine skills learned in schools or on previous jobs, military experience, if any, and specialized training received, and talents or hobbies that could be useful in employment. Job reference may be asked for but references from personal acquaintances are not used much anymore because they have little value.

Provision should be made for the applicant to supply additional data that could enhance personal qualifications. Usually, the bigger the job, the more information is asked for.

It is advisable to have the applicant sign the form. Above the space for the signature enter a "clearance" statement that guarantees all information to be accurate and gives the prospective employer the right to investigate any of it. Quite often, however, the interviewer will be asked not to check with the present employer, and this request, of course, should be respected.

Questions Cannot Conflict with Legislation

Because of the usually tight labor market, as well as the pressure to hire marginal applicants, some companies are purposely expanding their application blanks to ask for more personal data. As protection for the company that wants to cooperate but does not want to hire bad risks, and also to protect the applicants from being hired for work for which they are unsuited, these firms now ask more in-depth questions about an applicant's preparation and readiness to become a trouble-free employee. This is a delicate matter and care must be exercised in not asking for data which conflicts with legislation.

It is unlawful to ask questions about:

1. **Name:** original name if name has been changed.
   if the applicant ever worked under another name.

however, a married woman may be asked to tell her maiden name.

2. **Birth:** birth place of applicant.
   birth place of applicant's parents, spouse, or other relatives.
   birth certificate, baptismal record, or naturalization or first papers.

3. **Citizenship:** citizen of what country.
   where applicant was naturalized.
   whether parents or spouse were naturalized.

4. **National origin:** lineage, ancestry, descent, parentage, nationality.
   what is the mother tongue.
   language commonly used at home or with parents.
   how applicant learned to read, write, or speak foreign language.

5. **Race:** complexion or color of skin.
   require applicant to affix photograph.

6. **Religion:** religious affiliation.
   religious holidays observed.

7. **Age:** unless to satisfy minimum age statutes (Ex: under 18?) or to determine if applicant is over 70.

8. **Sex and marital status:** sex of applicant.
   marital situation past and present.
   dependents.

9. **Physical characteristics:** height.
   weight.
   hair length and style.
   handicap, unless this is a bona fide occupational limitation.

10. **Organizations:** membership in what clubs, societies, or lodges to which applicant belongs.

The "Application for Employment" blank is one of the chief tools in the selection procedure. It is important that it be properly designed and correctly interpreted.

JOB POSTING

Job posting, or open posting, is a method of publicizing to employees, possibly on bulletin boards, the jobs that are open in the company. The purpose is to fill as many jobs as possible from within the company and also to aid in the promotion of employees who are ready to be rewarded.

This can be a time-consuming procedure since many workers could apply for the same job and all have to be dealt with. Everyone who responds must be interviewed. During the interview the duties are explained and the requirements outlined. The applicant's training and experience are reviewed. Every qualified employee who expresses interest must then be considered to be "in the running" for the job. When the final selection is made the decision must be reported individually to all remaining candidates in such a way as to get their understanding and also to maintain their willingness to apply again when other jobs appeal to them.

When job vacancies are made known to the workforce, good and bad results may follow.

Good:
1. Keeps employees informed.
2. Present employees bring in applicants.
3. They apply themselves, thereby making their interests known.
4. They reveal feelings in present placement.
5. Lets jobs and salary grades for jobs be known.

Bad:
1. May encourage job hoppers.
2. May let disgruntled employee "run away" instead of meeting problem in present job.
3. May attract applicants who are more interested in money than in using their skills.
4. Results in a long chain reaction at times, with bumping involved.
5. Sometimes hard to select if ability is the criterion; usually it becomes seniority, especially where a union contract is involved.

Rules:
1. Use a definite posting period and close it, after which accept no more bids.
2. Announce in a definite place, openly, to avoid suspicion.
3. Must be controlled by some neutral agency, like Personnel, not by a line department.

TRANSFERS

Transfers and promotions should not be confused. They are not the same and the two terms are not interchangeable.

A transfer is a lateral move, within the same labor grade, or from one job to another job of like value and importance. A transfer is a movement from one job to another, with changes in duties, supervision, work conditions, but not necessarily salary. A promotion, on the other hand, is an upgrading from one level to a higher one, and should carry with it a corresponding increase in salary.

Transfers are made for the convenience of the company, the convenience of the worker, or to increase the flexibility of the workforce.

From a company standpoint, transfers are made for negative or positive reasons:

Negative

1. A worker is not suited for the present job.
2. The present job is eliminated.
3. Friction exists.
4. There is a physical handicap.

Positive

1. The environment needs improving.
2. Morale can be raised.
3. Worker acquires more prestige duties.
4. Worker adds experience.

A transfer, while it does not carry with it any automatic consideration for more money, has other advantages. It could offer the employee any of the following:

1. A chance for broader experience.
2. More suitable work.
3. More interesting duties.
4. More congenial work group.
5. Better supervisor.
6. Better hours.
7. Location closer to home.

Quite often a manager or foreman is reluctant to suggest a transfer because a wage increase is not included in the deal. This would be unfair to the employee who might eagerly accept the move for any of the above reasons, or others which are understandable to the employee.

Correcting Misplacements

A company may wish to transfer an employee who is worth keeping but who is obviously mis-assigned. A misfit in one type of work, provided work habits and attitude are good, might find a niche in another line of work. For example: a clerk who goes home tired every night might be better off on the next desk where less math is required.

Beware, however, of the person who seeks transfer as a means of running away from a situation he or she refuses to correct. Instead of admitting to shortcomings and agreeing with the supervisor to change a bad habit, such as excessive tardiness, the employee moves out, taking the unsolved problem along. Before anyone is transferred, performance and conduct should be carefully checked. Is the record clear?

Temporary transfers are a stop-gap measure for an emergency situation. One or more employees may be transferred temporarily because another part of the company is shorthanded or overloaded and extra people are needed until the problem can be solved. In such cases, the employees may be moved bodily but not on paper; that is, no actual re-assignment is effected. If their wages for this interim period are to be charged to the new department, this becomes an accounting transaction. Should the duration of the temporary transfer be more than just a short time, it might be advisable to keep the records straight by issuing the necessary transfer papers when the first move is made and reversing them when the people return to their regular jobs. In all these cases, employees transferred for company convenience to a lower rated job should not be penalized in the paycheck. Should they be working in their temporary duty in jobs which rate higher, some consideration might be given to paying them accordingly.

Transfers are part of the "bumping" process that goes on during a cut-back in the workforce. Rather than lay off a worker whose job has been eliminated, a company may permit an employee to bump another worker with less seniority or tenure.

Seniority generally accompanies a worker who moves. This could be a deterrent since the new department, in addition to getting a loyal and experienced worker, also inherits all that goes with seniority— longer vacation with possibly an early choice, rate of pay possibly higher than others in the same job, etc. Seniority is company-wide and refers to length of service in the total organization. In those few cases where seniority is not plant-wide but departmental, or worse yet, job-line, the terms better be clearly spelled out and understood by all concerned.

PROMOTIONS

The best practice of filling any job vacancy is to select the best qualified candidate who is available, whether from the outside or inside the company. When the selection comes from within, the employee is moved into the new job by either transfer or promotion. There is a difference.

A horizontal promotion is really not a promotion but a lateral transfer. This results in a change of duties and opportunities but not in degree of responsibility, or job value, and therefore at no change in salary.

A true promotion is an upgrading of a worker's job from one level to a higher one with a correspondingly higher rate of pay.

A vertical promotion is an upgrading in the same area or type of work. **Example:** a stenographer to secretary.

A prestige promotion or transfer takes a worker to a less strenuous but more attractive job, sometimes at the same pay, but with certain more desirable features. **Example:** a typist clerk to receptionist.

A systematic promotion is one step in a sequence of jobs planned for workers to enlarge or broaden their understanding of overall operations. In management jobs this could be called job rotation, when the movement is made more in the employee's interest and not only for company convenience. Systematic promotion is a device for getting workers out of blind alley jobs.

Practically every employer boasts of having a promotion-from-within policy. But if a check were made, it could well be that the employees think otherwise.

Avoid Blanket Policy

A blanket statement of promotion-from-within in an employee handbook is not only erroneous but also foolish. No company today fills all its higher job openings from within. Some jobs require background and experience which cannot be found in the present workforce. As soon as the first outsider is hired for one of these jobs, the employees know the promotion policy mentioned in the handbook is untrue, and they could be expected to distrust similar statements about other aspects of the employee program.

When an employee is ready for a bigger challenge, and an opportunity for promotion presents itself, it is well to consider the employee. This not only makes it easy for the company to fill the job, but it also offers more responsibility and a better earnings opportunity to a deserving worker. When employees are by-passed, there is the likelihood of losing them as they acquire a "what's the use" attitude.

This does not mean that all or most jobs should be filled from within the organization. Promote from within is good policy but should not be a rigid rule to close the door to qualified outsiders. Nor should better jobs be offered to outsiders and denied to present employees. Too much promotion from within results in in-breeding of ideas and experience, and does not take advantage of ideas from outside. An outsider's different viewpoint may be invaluable in some situation.

On the other hand, filling all or most of the job vacancies from the outside does not take advantage of valuable experience gained by employees. In many cases there is no substitute for on-the-job training and know-how. It should also be realized that too little promotion from within results in low morale and high turnover because of lack of opportunity.

Jobs should nòt be filled by a company policy that says blindly that one course or the other must be followed. The most practical company policy is the one which says simply that jobs should be given to the best qualified, and best suited applicant, whether from within the company or outside of it. Anything less, no matter how altruistic it may sound, shortchanges both the company and the workers.

Make Employees Promotable

What usually happens is that two types of jobs are filled from within: (1) those which are in the same field but are heavier or carry more responsibility, and (2) those which call for general training and not for a peculiar skill or special talent.

The better secretarial jobs can often be filled by up-and-coming stenographers who have improved their skill through practice and increased their knowledge of company operations through experience to the point where they are ready for something bigger. A company is fortunate when it has enough movement in its workforce to be able to offer bigger job opportunities to employees who have outgrown their present assignments.

Similarly, a job as order-checker in a jobbing warehouse can usually be filled by an experienced order-filler. Here knowledge of the company and its products is more important than the unique skill of checking. It is easier to teach a loyal company employee the new checking procedure than to acquaint a stranger with the thousands of products in the line.

There are two avenues which lead to a successful promotion-from-within program:

1. Training programs, to help employees develop beyond present duties. Without this the better jobs will, of necessity, be filled from the outside.
2. A system for recognizing and rewarding growth in individuals. Without this, promotable employees will leave to take their chances elsewhere.

One value of promotion from within lies in its chain reaction. To fill one higher job, which in turn creates a vacancy lower down, at least two persons, and oftentimes more, are involved. Movement in jobs is generally desirable, especially when boredom may be a factor. It is not desirable in all cases as, for instance, a worker who is peculiarly adapted for a certain type of work, or a skilled worker who would have to abandon the one talent that sets him or her apart from co-workers.

Some jobs never change; some people do not change. But in those cases where jobs grow bigger, we can be grateful that some people grow bigger too, so that these jobs can be filled. One of the basic job satisfactions workers require is to enjoy their work and be interested in what they are doing. Work that challenges a worker at first becomes boring once it is mastered; it no longer provides the same degree of satisfaction. Ideally, employees ought to have jobs that are just a bit "over their heads." This would keep them "on their toes." Promotion is the answer.

CHAPTER 9

PERSONNEL SELECTION—
TESTED SELECTION PROCEDURES

AS THE office administrator you may not do the interviewing or participate in the techniques of personnel selection. However, you are responsible for setting the *exact role* (job description) that the candidate will fill. It is your job description that will guide the personnel department in making a selection. It is still the job description that will set the standard for the employee even if the administrator does the selecting.

So the first phase of the process could be viewed as the "philosophy" of the company's selection policy. For example, the company (or administrator) can have a policy of picking people with high potential who can be trained and developed for higher-level positions. This type of policy requires that such positions will become available at regular intervals. Hiring high-potential individuals and having no place for them to go is going to lead to high turnover.

A good question to ask yourself is: "Will the company (my department) be expanding or contracting in the future?" An expanding business requires different personnel in low-level jobs than if the *status quo* is to be maintained. The expanding business or department requires people who can move up rapidly.

In addition to a complete job description, the administrator should be able to specify and describe successive jobs for the person filling the original position. Can a pool typist move up to a secretary? Can a file clerk move along a choice of several paths to better and more demanding positions? Are the paths to better positions open to all people hired? Is there a set time limit for their advancement? Are the interviewees told of the advancement policies? Does the policy give the administrator, the supervisor or the the personnel department the authority to move people into better positions?

Looking at the Job Market

Today's administrator, by what could be called yesterday's standards, is a younger person than he or she was a generation or so ago. But the job of managing people doesn't really change. True, today's managers are certainly more informed in the area of human relations. The company spends money sending them to seminars and management training courses, but their problems are only too similar.

The change is in the employees. The young people coming into the business world are generally better educated, more sophisticated, and *hopefully* more concerned about their role and their company's role in the overall social structure. They are said to have less *loyalty* to a company and they say they have more loyalty to *themselves*. There is truth in both of these facets, and it is up to the administrator to recognize this as fact.

There is no evidence to prove that today's young people will not make good employees (and loyal employees) because they express concern about ecology, environment, and the social responsibilities of corporations or businesses. Faddish hair styles and clothing do not indicate social awareness, so the administrator must look beyond current style to probe for personality and ability.

SELECTION

The employment function is a continuing one in every company, regardless of whether or not the procedure is formalized or the job is centralized. The selection and retention of efficient workers is one of the most important operations of any company. In any kind of labor market the proper selection of applicants for jobs poses one of industry's greatest problems.

A big concern is that of cost. There are statistics available to tell us how many dollars were lost last year because of fires, termites, floods, and hurricanes. Unfortunately, not even an estimate exists for the loss that is due to incompetent employees, the result of poor hiring practices and improper placement. But if such a survey could be made, the total would undoubtedly be in the billions of dollars. Add to this staggering cost the waste of human capacities and the countless cases of tragic frustration, and the signficance of proper selection and placement becomes apparent.

This cost item is many things. Acquisition costs are more than agency fees, newspaper ads, or employee referral bonds. The cost of interviewing and screening applicants, including the many who are rejected, must be taken into account. Medical examinations, if given for new employees, will add substantially to the cost. Whatever method is used, and whatever steps are taken, we can be certain that the cost of each new worker is higher, much higher, than we realize.

Add to this the expense of low production during the beginning or training period, the time of the other person during the training, and all the many other obvious as well as hidden costs, and we get some idea of the cost of employment, and the importance of good selection.

Poor selection, hurried placement, and such considerations add even more to the hidden cost of employment. The employment of incompetent, unstable, and non-productive workers can be a very costly item in terms of direct expense.

Costly Investment

Then think of the less desirable employees who get into the work-force who are not released for any of many reasons. Sometimes a contract complicates the firing of such employees. In other instances seniority or company policy keeps these people on the payroll. And don't think for a minute that there is no sentiment in business. Otherwise, how can we justify the retention of workers who obviously have lost their usefulness.

Add all these factors together and we begin to understand the investment companies have in their people. An investment decision of this magnitude in other departments would be given very close scrutiny and consideration. Yet, investments of this amount are made in newly-hired employees every day with very little caution. Employment is the one item that is governed by little objective decision. Everybody who hires new workers seems to be somewhat of an amateur psychologist and a certain measure of subjective opinion influences the decision to hire or not to hire an applicant.

This kind of approach has some consequences. One of the consequences of ineffective selection of employees is a drag on efficiency, low production, and poor morale. The notion that these people will somehow fit into the scheme of things is wishful thinking. Unsatisfactory work habits in people are usually the result of long-established habits and character traits that are very difficult, if not impossible, to change in the average work situation.

A Series of Rejections

The selection procedure covers the entire period from the initial contact with the applicant to final acceptance or rejection. The screening out of unqualified applicants should be accomplished in the quickest time consistent with good community relations since this is costly and, of course, non-productive.

Selection begins as soon as an applicant becomes available for employment, either in person or by mail. Sight screening eliminates the obviously unqualified. Knock-out questions eliminate those who cannot meet specific job requirements. Interviewing is done to reduce the number of candidates. Defensible testing programs eliminate some applicants and serve as aids in interviewing the others. Reference inquiries, physical examinations, and multiple interviews are additional devices used in the selection procedure.

Selection actually is a normal process of a series of rejections:

1. **Preliminary interview**	**if not rejected, then . . .**
2. **Application blank**	**if not rejected, then . . .**
3. **Interview**	**if not rejected, then . . .**
4. **Check on references**	**if not rejected, then . . .**
5. **Physical examinations**	**if not rejected, then . . .**
6. **Mental tests**	**if not rejected, then . . .**
7. **Multiple interviews**	**if not rejected, then . . .**
8. **What is left**	**make final selection.**

The sequence might be slightly rearranged in some companies or under some circumstances, but the idea of a series of rejection steps remains unchanged.

Six Appraisal Factors

For better selection, and a corresponding reduction in the size and cost of the problem of selection, it is well to know just what we are looking for. There are six appraisal factors involved in the selection and employment of applicants:

1. **Informational:**	**abilities and personal data.**
2. **Motivational:**	**drives and personal goals.**
3. **Emotional:**	**maturity and business outlook.**
4. **Attitudinal:**	**sense of values.**
5. **Behavioral:**	**habit patterns and conduct.**
6. **Physical:**	**health and peace of mind.**

In selecting employees to work with us, these are the qualities we try to identify and evaluate. It is necessary, therefore, that the interviewer understand what is involved.

THE INTERVIEW

"Interviewing is a big part of every manager's or supervisor's job." These words are from the *Dartnell Personnel Administration Handbook,* and they express a basic fact of business life. Author Wilbert Scheer looks at this function as belonging to the personnel department, but in the truth the administrator is going to do his share of interviewing because he is interested in the people who are coming into this area of responsibility.

Even though you are armed with a detailed job description and you know your company philosophy, you are usually a little unsteady in an interviewing situation—perhaps almost as much as the

SELECTION PROCESS

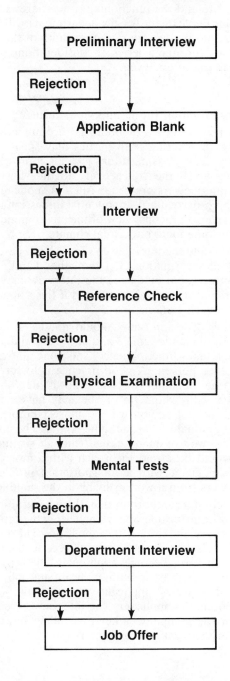

interviewee. This is a human relations function which literally involves a person's life and the functioning of your area of authority. The people in your department (or his department) will be affected by the newcomer—no matter the size or breadth of the work area. By the time you get through a series of considerations, you may be more nervous than the interviewee.

Interview Essentials

Some necessary essentials for all interviews include:

1. Privacy. A private office or booth is recommended in many situations, on the theory that both parties may speak without restraint. Sometimes clear-glass partitions give an impression that the candidate is being given the "once over" to the viewers outside. Many successful interviewers prefer to visit with applicants out in an open office, since no particularly confidential discussion takes place. The applicant is given a practical view of the environment instead of being sheltered in some ideal but unreal climate.

2. Comfort. Certainly the interviewee should be at ease, to permit a free exchange of information. On the other hand, letting him smoke in the waiting room or during the interview may lead to an erroneous impression of working conditions if this same privilege is not granted at the work station.

3. Understanding. The interview should not be attempted, nor should any decision be made, unless and until mutual understanding is reached. It often takes time, patience, and some innovation to get through to the other person. A good practice is to turn the applicant—especially the beginner or one who is nervous—over to another employee with whom he or she may have something in common. A high school senior will be more comfortable in the hands of a recent graduate from the same school. The applicant will ask such a clerical worker many casual (though significant) questions which he would be afraid to broach with a more formidable interviewer. An applicant with a transportation problem will get more helpful answers from a worker living in the same locality.

4. Attitude. Much more important than the fine furniture, modern environment, and other visible appurtenances is the attitude of the interviewer and company toward the applicant. The best physical facilities will not offset insincerity, annoyance, or "going through the motions" which soon become apparent to the applicant. The interviewer's interest must be in both applicant and job, and it must be equally divided. The best applicant will not fit the job unless at some time the job fits the applicant. The interviewer's concern over filling the job for the company rather than filling the need of the applicant is one of the weaknesses of interviews.

Making the Interview More Effective

1. Decide carefully in advance just what you wish to and can determine by the interview. Review the appliction blank in advance as a guide.
2. Examine and discount your own prejudices.
3. Give personal appearance its proper weight, but no more.
4. Endeavor to talk to the applicant alone, preferably in a closed office or a desk away from ordinary distractions.
5. Open the interview by conversing briefly and informally about some subject of mutual interest. Be sure to introduce yourself and lead into the interview itself as soon as you feel the applicant is at ease.
6. Ask questions which call for narrative statements, things done that have demonstrated the possession of certain qualities, rather than questions that call for an expression of opinions or a mere chronological statement of experience.
7. Avoid leading or suggestive questions.
8. Listen attentively and show evidence of being interested.
9. Talk only enough to keep the conversation informal and friendly; avoid expressing opinions.
10. Encourage the applicant to ask questions about the work and working conditions.
11. Do not let the interview become mechanical; keep on the alert for unexpected evidence.
12. Guard against the "halo effect." Don't let a single favorable or unfavorable trait warp your judgment.
13. After the close of the formal interview, watch for additional evidence.
14. Be careful not to make too many notes during the interview.
15. Record impressions and reasons for them *immediately* after the applicant leaves, before starting the next interview.
16. Provide for a second interview whenever practicable.
17. Be especially careful as to what is said and how it is said when explaining an applicant's unsuitability for a position.

Remember:

1. The chief problem is not getting the facts but interpreting them.
2. Pause occasionally, pretending to look the applicant over, giving the applicant the opportunity to talk.

3. Be objective.

4. The correct methods of interviewing can go a long way to reduce turnover.

5. The personal interview is the supervisor and the applicant sizing each other up well enough to judge whether they'll work together satisfactorily.

6. A competent interview takes the form of a conversation rather than a question and answer period.

7. An interviewer should be a good listener, impartial, a good judge, well acquainted with the requirements of the job being discussed.

8. What the applicant has done in the past in school and on the job is a good indication of what can be expected in the future.

9. The following factors should be considered before a final decision:
   a. appearance
   b. education
   c. work background
   d. test scores
   e. references

10. Verify dates to make sure no period of time is overlooked which might be covering up a bad employment record.

These are general suggestions, of course, and must be individualized to fit each particular situation.

The applicant must understand such things as:

- The job for which he or she is being considered.
- The reason the position is open.
- Why she or he would want to work in the company.
- Wages, hours, conditions of employment.
- Promotions and opportunity for growth.
- Benefits.
- Stability of employment in the company.
- The philosophy of the company toward its workers.

Finding the right person for any job is, however, only half the task. The applicant must feel that he or she too has found a job opportunity which meets or exceeds expectations. Only when there is a happy job marriage, in which both sides are satisfied, does the placement stand a chance of being successful. In that case the company will provide the worker with the job satisfaction needed in order to be happy; and in turn, the new employee will have that built-in motivation a company looks for in order to make the employment pay off.

The Patterned Interview

Many companies have established some sort of standards for the interview in selecting and placing personnel. But the interviewing technique has three weaknesses:

1. Many interviews do not get complete or relevant information necessary to make a decision. Many interviewers do not know what information they are actually looking for.
2. Experienced interviewers may be able to determine from the information obtained what an applicant *can* do, but they lack a means of judging what he *will* do on the job.
3. Personal feelings enter into the interview; the interviewer is influenced by promises and general rationalizations of the applicant rather than unbiased, objective, factual information.

Some years back, *Dr. Robert N. McMurry* developed a patterned interview form for *The Dartnell Corporation.* It has been used by hundreds of companies for many years because it helps to overcome some of the faults and limitations mentioned above. Here are the major advantages of this form or of any good form:

1. It guides the interviewer in getting the facts and discovering valuable information about the applicant.
2. It makes possible a systematic coverage of necessary information upon which to predict the applicant's probable chances for success.
3. It provides a set of principles for use in interpreting the facts obtained for the purpose of judging what the applicant will do besides what he obviously can do.
4. It provides a means of minimizing the interviewer's personal biases and prejudices.

Applicant Screening Form

Along with the interview form, it is suggested that the interviewer have an applicant screening form (profile) as well. This form is to be used by the interviewer immediately after completing the interview. It gives one an opportunity to record findings and to establish reasons for hiring or rejecting an applicant. This written data also provides protection against possible discrimination charges in that it gives an on-the-spot record to support the minimum standards previously established for the job.

APPLICANT
SCREENING PROFILE

Name _____ Date _____

Address _____ Telephone _____

Applying For Job As _____ Date Available _____

Present Job _____ Education _____

PERSONAL GROOMING	Unkempt; noticeable lack of neatness	No special care in dress or appearance	Neat and clean	Pays special attention to personal details	Immaculately dressed and groomed
	1	2	3	4	5
VOICE QUALITY	Harsh, irritating	Indistinct, difficult to understand	Pleasant tone and voice	Clear, understandable; good tone quality	Unusually expressive; excellent voice
	1	2	3	4	5
PHYSICAL APPEARANCE	Unpleasant, unhealthy appearance	Appears to lack energy, listless	Good physical condition; pleasant appearance	Appears fit, alert, energetic	Especially energetic, good carriage; appears in excellent condition
	1	2	3	4	5
PERSONAL MANNER	Nervous, embarrassed; compulsive mannerisms	Stiff, uncomfortable; ill at ease	No unusual tension, comfortable, at ease	Appears alert, free of tension	Unusually self-possessed and composed
	1	2	3	4	5
CONFIDENCE	Shy, retiring; arrogant, "cocky"	Submissive; argumentative	Reasonably self-assured; forthright	Shows self-confidence	Unusually self-assured; inspires confidence
	1	2	3	4	5
EXPRESSION OF IDEAS	Unclear, illogical; speaks without thinking	Dwells on non-essentials; thoughts not well defined or expressed	Thoughts clearly expressed; words convey meaning	Convincing; thoughts developed logically	Unusual ability to express ideas logically
	1	2	3	4	5
MENTAL ALERTNESS	Dull, slow to grasp ideas	Comprehends ideas but contributes little to discussion	Fairly attentive; expresses own thoughts	Quick-witted, alert; asks intelligent questions	Unusually quick thinker, keen mind; grasps complex ideas
	1	2	3	4	5
MOTIVATION AND AMBITION	No drive, ambition limited	Little interest in development; seems satisfied	Interest and ambition fair; reasonable desire to work and develop	Definite future goals; wants to succeed and grow	Ambitions high, future well planned; evidence of personal development
	1	2	3	4	5
EXPERIENCE AND EDUCATION	Education and experience unsuitable for the job	Education and experience not directly applicable, but helpful	Good educational and work background; experience fair	Education and experience fit job; above average qualifications	Background especially well suited; continues to study
	1	2	3	4	5
PERSONALITY	Immature, impulsive; indecisive, unstable	Opinionated; difficulty in accepting others' ideas	Reasonable stability and maturity.	Stable, cooperative; accepts responsibilities	Very mature, a "self-starter"; outstanding personality
	1	2	3	4	5

TOTAL [   ]

Remarks: _____

_____

Recommended For Further Consideration: _____ Not Recommended: _____

FORM NO. 7
EMPLOYER'S SERVICES CORP.
BOX 314 — BRISTOL, TENN. 37621

Signature of Interviewer

Screening profile developed for job applicants by the Employer's Service Corp. of Bristol, Tennessee, makes it easier for interviewers to judge personal qualities of applicants.

REFERENCE INQUIRIES

Reference inquiries, or checking references, is a very important part of the employment procedure. Inquiries are made about prior work experience, character, education, and whatever else may be considered necessary to help arrive at a decision to hire or not to hire an applicant. Inquiries are chiefly addressed to former employers, schools, and personal acquaintances of the applicant.

The names and addresses of the individuals, schools, or firms are taken from the information supplied by the applicant on the application blank.

Former employers are queried about the applicant's dates of employment, the nature of the job, quality of performance, any strong or weak points that stand out and can be remembered, the reason for leaving, and so on. These are mechanical questions seeking factual answers. Whatever else is asked, the *key* question is "Would you rehire?"

Schools are asked about levels of academic achievement, such as completion of courses, graduation, degrees, and majors or concentration of study. They can also report on the former student's attendance record. One of the useful services schools can furnish is that of checking ages of people. School records are kept indefinitely and reveal the age of an individual accurately as a student, before the person might have been tempted to lie about the age and try to alter the year of birth.

As a suggestion, do not send schools a form letter listing a string of questions. Some details of a former student's record may no longer be accessible in the front office, and a conscientious and cooperative clerk might have to spend hours in the archives hunting for an answer to a question that really does not deserve this much time and trouble. Usually the information that is readily available in the school office is more than sufficient.

Personal references are not used much anymore since their usefulness is questionable. Friends, relatives, acquaintances, and clergymen are likely to give favorable reports. The only value might be to specific questions such as, "How long did the applicant work for his last company?" or "Where did the applicant reside before moving to the city?"

Police records are worth checking for certain jobs. Local and national bureaus of information could come up with information not obtained in routine inquiries.

Military service records provide data that is useful, particularly as it relates to skills and training acquired. Discharge papers tell about the length of service, duty performed, advancement, and type of release from service. It might be well to ask to see such papers, especially for a veteran whose military service is not too far in the past.

Types of Inquiries

Most references are checked by mail because this can be done in an easy routine manner. The signed replies form a permanent record, easily filed for possible future use. But written references also have disadvantages. Most people are reluctant to tell the truth if they think it will hurt someone. They tend to minimize adverse comments. Besides, once the former employee is gone and forgotten, and the sting of the termination no longer felt, a manager is inclined to brush off a written request with a response that has little substance. The tip-off comes when the answer is "No" to your question, "Would you rehire?" The former manager is trying to tell something without running the risk of putting damaging remarks on paper. In effect there is the hint, "Why don't you phone us and we'll talk about it."

The telephone is used because it is faster and more intimate. A direct two-way conversation can clear up questions. The telephone brings two people close together immediately, whereas it is usually total strangers who exchange letters in a routine mail inquiry. For the more important jobs telephone reference checking may be better. In these cases it is advisable to make a written report of the call, documenting the answers received.

The personal visit to a former employer or school is used infrequently since it is time consuming. It is done when the job is unusual or highly important, or when some questionable record needs to be looked into.

There are credit agencies that will check out an individual and report in writing their findings. Their detailed reports tell about the person's family, neighborhood, education, age, employment history, character, reputation, financial stability, and anything else that may be requested. In the process of checking the individual they will uncover any lawsuits, bankruptcies, or criminal background.

It takes time and talent to get useful answers to reference inquiries. It is safe to say that the value of any reference reply is worth very little unless the answer is negative. If it tells nothing new then it merely confirms what is already known. It verifies the information supplied by the applicant. This makes it safer to assume that other information may likewise be taken at face value.

A negative reply, on the other hand, alerts the employer to be on guard and suspect all the information given. If prior dates of em-

TELEPHONE REFERENCE CHECK

Date: _____

Name of Applicant _____

Organization Name _____

Organization Address _____ Telephone _____

Person Contacted _____ Position _____

Verify:

Dates of Employment _____ Last Salary _____

Nature of his/her work assignment _____

_____

_____

Reason for leaving _____

Explore:

Skill level at which applicant is operating. Capacity to handle the position for which he/she is applying: _____

_____

Relationships with associates, clients, supervisors? Can he/she follow instructions, ask for and take help? _____

_____

What is applicant's record of illness? Is he/she punctual? _____

_____

How about dependability, cooperation, initiative, ambition? _____

_____

Are there areas where applicant could use additional training or supervision? _____

_____

Would they rehire? _____ If not, why _____

Comments _____

_____

(Use other side if necessary)

A telephone reference check form for recording the information obtained in a reference inquiry.

REFERENCE INQUIRY FORM

Date: _____

May we verify the following information given to us by one of your former employees who has applied to us for a position?

_____
Name

_____
Position Held

_____
Employment Dates

_____
Earnings

_____
Reason given for leaving your firm

Is the above information correct?_____

Would you care to give us additional information on the following questions:

Were services satisfactory? _____

Would you rehire if you had an opening? _____

Do you know of any reason why we should not employ? _____

Is there anything outstanding about this employee that you would like to tell us? _____

Do you suggest we contact you by telephone? _____

Thank you for your cooperation.

_____   _____
Signature   Employment Manager

_____
Title

ployment, for example, are not correct as shown, perhaps the applicant is deliberately trying to gloss over an employment gap. A negative reply should be followed up immediately by a telephone call, possibly a personal visit, or a report from an outside agency.

Letter inquiries are usually done by form letter. The one standard letter for all applicants contains vacant spaces that are filled in from data taken off the application blank. The former employer is asked to verify this information. Usually this is followed by a few questions the new employer would like to have answered.

Some forms are elaborate, designed to be "cute," and to impress the recipient. But the purpose of the form inquiry, it should be reminded, is to inform. Much to be preferred is a simple and direct request along the lines illustrated in the request form on the next page.

TESTING AND THE EEOC

Tests for employment and promotion are declining in use for reasons other than their accuracy. The biggest stumbling block is the Equal Employment Opportunities Commission (EEOC) and its inflexible rules. To many employers testing under their rigorous guidelines is impossible. It is simpler to chuck the testing program altogether.

In a spasm of anxiety about compliance requirements, employers are afraid they cannot support decisions based on test results. This may be a case of over-reacting but it is the easier way out.

Hiring and promoting cannot be justified solely on qualifications but must take into account local minority group percentages as determined by the EEOC. Companies cannot afford to become involved in statistical discrimination.

To continue to be influenced by test scores, a company must be able to show that the tests it gives for a specific job are necessary because they are related to what an employee actually has to do on the job. Most tests are developed outside the company and are too general in their application to serve the unique requirements of different jobs. The validations are, in most cases, impossible to prove; they just do not hold up in court.

Further, the validations of tests, which are customarily developed in the university laboratories, are not related to sex and race. As such, they are indefensible when challenged.

Established tests keyed to the qualifications of a given job are an efficient tool for a proper hiring decision. Once companies are scared off of testing they resort to less objective means and are influenced by pleasing or unpleasing appearance, references that are usually lackluster, performance in previous jobs that is difficult to assess, interviews that rub the interviewer the wrong way, and the untouched, built-in biases of managers.

Why such subjective involvement is supposed to be better than objective testing is not easily understood.

WHAT PSYCHOLOGICAL TESTS CONTRIBUTE

All too often psychological testing has been enshrouded in mystery. Sometimes it has even been regarded as a magical device which provides a sovereign remedy for all of the problems which beset employment departments. Some executives favor testing because it takes such vague and intangible qualities as intelligence, aptitudes, and personality and reduces each to neat, numerical indexes. A great many companies have found, however, that a more realistic approach is to recognize that, while tests have a distinct contribution to make to employee selection, they definitely are not cure-alls. Tests are but "tools." There are distinct limitations to their functions and dangers in their use if improperly handled.

Experience has conclusively shown that the best use of tests lies in measuring what an applicant can do. Tests have proved to be admirably suited to measuring such elusive qualities as mental ability, aptitudes, proficiencies, and skills. In many instances they provide the only reliable means for quickly evaluating these characteristics.

Since tests provide a useful (although not all-inclusive) measure of what an applicant can do, they logically constitute a next step in the processing of applicants who meet the screening standards. If the candidate obviously does not possess the requisite mental ability, proficiencies, skills, and other can-do qualifications for the job, it is futile to consider him any further. By eliminating such applicants as quickly as possible, the selection procedure can be streamlined still more, thereby saving the time of applicants, executives, or the employment department staff.

Five Kinds of Tests and Their Uses

Although most psychological tests are commonly referred to as measures of "aptitudes," there are actually five distinct types of tests:

1. *Measures of mental ability, alertness, or intelligence.* Intelligence, as measured by tests, is essentially the capacity to learn, to solve problems, and to comprehend and work with intangibles. A measure of an individual's level of mental ability is particularly useful in emloyee placement. Each job has an optimum range of intelligence required for success in it. Mental ability tests provide a quick, efficient measure of whether an individual is bright enough, or too bright, to perform the job well.

Executives, supervisors, research workers, creative thinkers—advertising copywriters, accountants, and persons dealing with intangibles—need a higher level of mental ability than do persons performing routine jobs. Their jobs require the ability to see abstract relationships at their intangible level. They must plan, organize, anticipate possibilities, think creatively, solve unusual problems, and handle human relations. People with limited mental ability find it difficult, if not impossible, to cope with such problems.

On the other hand, people with a high level of mental ability usually do not do well on routine, repetitive jobs which provide little or no challenge or opportunity for advancement. They find them boring and monotonous. Mental tests can, therefore, be an invaluable aid in matching the candidate against the intellectual demands of a position in order to insure that he is not too dull nor too bright for the job in question.

2. *Measures of proficiencies, skills, and job information.* Such tests measure the level of skills which a person has already acquired in such techniques as stenography, typing, calculating; as well as his knowledge of such trades as carpentry and bricklaying.

Measures of proficiency, such as tests of typing and stenography, are performance tests. They require the applicant to demonstrate his competence on an actual work sample. Trade tests, on the other hand, measure proficiency indirectly by asking for information which is supposedly only known to persons who are skilled in the occupation.

It is assumed, for example, that a machinist will know the name of the instrument used to check the inside dimension of a cylinder, while one not so skilled in the craft or trade will not. Published proficiency and trade tests are available for a number of the more common occupations. A good many companies, however, prefer to design their own performance and trade tests tailored to fit their exact needs.

3. *Measures of aptitude.* Such tests measure inherent or unlearned knacks or predispositions toward various types of activities as, for example, mechanical or clerical aptitudes. Some measure single qualities—such as finger dexterity—which can be useful on many different jobs. Other tests incorporate a "yardstick" for a number of different traits and are designed to measure trainability for certain definite types of work.

Aptitude tests do not indicate the degree to which a subject is presently skilled in a specific type of work. They are often helpful, however, in determining how skillful he can become with training. As an example, a test of tonal discrimination will help in determining the extent to which a subject has latent talent as a violinist. If he is tone deaf he has no potential whatever. On the other hand, the fact that a person has excellent tonal discrimination does not automatically ensure that he will ever be an accomplished violinist—he still must have digital dexterity and be willing and able to study the violin.

A major problem exists with regard to the choice of aptitude tests for use in selecting personnel for specific jobs. Unfortunately, a number of companies have found that the name of a test is not always a good indicator of its value in determining trainability and potential suitability for a specific type of work. There are, for example, many "mechanical aptitude" tests on the market, and not all of them measure the identical qualities. There are, furthermore, all kinds of "mechanical" jobs. For these reasons it is advisable to first read the test manual for evidence that the test has been standardized on activities at least similar to those for which the test is to be used.

Even then it is not always certain that the test will serve as a reliable and valid instrument in selecting people for particular occupations. A large electronics firm reports this experience:

> We found a hand-eye coordination test which seemed ideally suited for use in selecting assemblers on tape recorders. The motion involved in the test was almost identical with one used on the job.
>
> However, a comparison of test results obtained at the time of hiring, with subsequent job success, showed the test was worthless in predicting competence as an assembler. It's a good thing we didn't actually use the test in making our hiring decisions, because we would have turned down some of our very best assemblers!

As this comment indicates, the choice of proper aptitude tests is very tricky. Care must also be used in setting critical (passing) scores where aptitude tests are used. Validation studies, which will be discussed later, are usually necessary.

4. *Measures of vocational interest.* Such tests are designed to ascertain the areas of the subject's principal occupational interests. Tests of this character are chiefly useful in vocational guidance work. They are designed to aid the subject in finding a vocation in which he will be interested and which hopefully he will find to be temperamentally congenial. For employment purposes, these tests have been found to have less value. This is because interest in a field of activity does not necessarily guarantee competence in it.

Studies also indicate that less sophisticated interest tests are easily faked. If an applicant has a keen desire to obtain a particular position, he may try to slant responses and give the answers which he thinks are the "right" ones for that opening. He may, for example, actually be quite timid and dislike meeing people. In applying for a sales position, however, he may state that he always prefers contacts with other people to solitary activities, and that he is a joiner and leader, which he is not. He "knows" that salesmen are supposed to answer that way. Since the person scoring the test has no control over the truthfulness with which it was answered, the results may be seriously misleading.

Because of these limitations, this type of test is not thought to have particular value in selection work.

5. *Measures of personality or temperament.* Tests in this classification are designed either to measure specific personality qualities such as introversion-extraversion or dominance-submission, to serve as aids in the evaluation of the subject's total personality structure, or to help in the diagnosis of existing emotional maladjustment and mental illness.

Measures of personality are of two basic types: Paper and pencil tests and projective tests. In paper and pencil tests, the subject answers a series of specific questions relative to his likes, his dislikes, or his fears. In addition, it probes for symptoms of other personality problems such as the extent to which he worries excessively, believes that people are watching him, or smokes excessively.

Paper and pencil tests are well suited to clinical or vocational counseling work, since the subject *is motivated* to answer the test questions frankly, fully, and honestly. In personnel selection, however, this is seldom the case—the applicant's motive is a desire to get the job. As with interest tests, the applicant may deliberately slant answers to create what is regarded as a favorable impression.

Many companies have found projective measures of personality— such as sentence completion, the Thematic Apperception and Rorschach Tests—to be useful in employment work, particularly for higher level jobs. In such tests, the subject responds to a partially or wholly unstructured stimulus—stubs of sentences to be completed, a series of pictures or simply a number of ink blots on a card. In the Thematic Apperception Test, for example, one is required to make up stories about pictures which are shown. Since, generally speaking, such stories are largely autobiographical, without the subject being aware of it, they reveal to the skilled clinician a great deal about the applicant, particularly underlying personality makeup.

Experience has shown that these projective measures can be helpful in determining the individual's basic personality structure and motivations, as well as in predicting how he or she will react to the stresses and pressures encountered if employed. Tests are truly professional tools, however, and must be used only by experts. For that reason, most companies have employed outside assistance in using them. The American Psychological Association can supply the names of clinical psychologists who are qualified to employ these techniques.*

Advantages of Psychological Tests

In summarizing their experiences with psychological tests as selection instruments, experienced executives point to two major advantages: First, tests are quite objective. Every applicant is given identical tasks. Where the tests are timed, everyone has precisely the same period in which to complete them. In every possible way, the conditions of administration are kept uniform. The possibility of bias or prejudice in their interpretation, while always present, is minimized. In the areas where they are applicable, therefore, tests have the advantages of objectivity over most of the other selection devices.

The second advantage reported by users of psychological tests is that their use provides a relatively quick and precise measurement of such qualifications as intelligence, proficiencies, and certain aptitudes, which cannot be as reliably measured by other means. Illustrative of this fact is the comment of one personnel executive regarding the use of tests as a measurement of intelligence:

> Nothing is more difficult nor potentially more misleading than an attempt to judge an individual's intelligence from appearance, manner, or responses in an interview. Even a school record does not always provide a precise measure of intellectual equipment. On the one hand, a person may have been brilliant but lazy or preoccupied with other activities, or, on the other hand, dull but exceptionally industrious. An intelligence test, in a space of from 10 minutes to an hour, provides a fairly precise measure of the person's intelligence. In addition, it is possible to compare the scores with the performance of many others who have taken the same test so that a relative standing—the extent to which the subject is a genius, above average, average, below average, or subnormal—can be easily ascertained by reference to a table of norms.

Similar benefits are also noted in measuring specific skills and proficiencies. When asked directly about their proficiencies and skills, some applicants tend to be overly optimistic about what they can do. Others take the opposite position. Tests provide a control on such self-evaluations by providing an objective measure of what each applicant can actually do. An illustration showing the value of

---

*1515 Massachusetts Avenue, N.W., Washington, D.C. 20005.

this method of testing is found in the following report by an official of a nationally known insurance company:

> A candidate for a position as secretary modestly stated that she could take shorthand at 120 words per minute, type 80 words per minute, and that she had exceptional abilities in spelling, punctuation, the use of grammar, and in turning out neat work. However, when she was told she was to take a few simple tests to determine the extent of her skills and proficiencies, she began to hedge. She shyly confessed that it had been some time since she had used her shorthand and that she might be a little rusty on her typing. All this was subsequently confirmed by the tests. In reality, she could take shorthand rather inaccurately at 50 words per minute, type with numerous strike-overs at 35 words per minute, and was quite innocent of any real knowledge of spelling, grammar, and the rules of punctuation.
>
> If her prospective boss' work had been of such a nature that a relatively unskilled person was adequate for her needs she would have been content to hire her. At any rate, by determining these qualities in advance, she could have experienced no unpleasant surprises. She would know what she was getting before she put the girl on the payroll. But, since her work really required topnotch stenographic proficiency, the applicant was not hired. Thus, in a relatively short time, tests gave a specific measure of competence which it would have been difficult if not impossible to get in any other manner than by trial and error after she was employed—which would have been too late.

Limitations of Psychological Tests

In addition to the hazards of the uncritical use of tests which have already been mentioned, several others must also be taken into account. Chief of these is the fact that to the uninitiated tests appear to be instruments of a high degree of precision. There is, therefore, a temptation to assume, for example, that A is better qualified for a particular position than B because he or she scored five points higher on a test. In some instances this may be true, but only rarely. A five-point difference on most tests is not significant.

There are conditions, furthermore, under which a lower level of competence is actually preferable: It is possible for an applicant to be overqualified. Psychological tests, for all their apparent precision, are actually very rough and only partial indexes even of the qualities they presume to measure. A test of intelligence, for example, measures only certain aspects of the subject's mental ability. In addition, not more than from 10 to 30 percent of all of the traits, aptitudes, motivations, and attitudes which affect job performance are susceptible to measurement by tests of any kind. It is easy to assume that a test actually measures the qualities its name indicates, i.e., that it is valid, because it was developed by a recognized authority, is published by a reputable house, is reliable, e.g., has norms for various groups, and is widely used. Unfortunately, this is not always true. It is quite possible that while it is technically a well designed instrument it is not suited to the selection of persons for particular jobs (jobs vary widely in their content and demands so that the name of the position is not always a sound basis for deciding what tests to employ). For example, a test of clerical aptitude may be well suited to work as a file clerk and have little value in accounting work, even though both are essentially clerical activities. Therefore it is extremely dangerous to make use of any test without the conduct of a properly controlled validation study.

Validating All Tests

The danger of the misuse of mechanical aptitude tests has already been pointed out. There are, for example, more than 1,000 tests which purport to measure clerical or related aptitudes. At the same time, there are an infinite number of variations in the job activities which are termed "clerical." It is, therefore, possible for a given clerical test to be well suited to the selection of personnel for one type of work and to give dangerously misleading findings when used to select personnel for a superficially similar although basically different position. For this reason a test should never be chosen and used simply because its name implies that it will measure some quality which the employer, solely on an *a priori* basis, assumes is related to job success.

Tests of intelligence, aptitudes, temperament, and similar characteristics, must be *validated* before being used as actual selection instruments. For this reason, standard or universal batteries of tests—where identical tests are used to select for a wide variety of positions—are particularly dangerous. They may yield impressive looking profiles, but unless each measure in the battery has been individually validated for each specific position for which it is to be employed, its findings may be seriously inaccurate.

Illustrative of this point is the unfortunate experience with a battery of tests reported by a leading airplane parts manufacturer:

> "We had, at one time, a personnel manager who might be described as 'test happy.' He installed a battery of 10 tests which were to be given to all applicants for plant jobs—regardless of the type of job involved. For each different job he established what he termed an 'ideal profile' by averaging the scores on the various tests made by our 10 best workers in each particular job category. All told, he worked out 87 different 'ideal profiles.' When each applicant was considered, his test scores were compared with the 87 different 'ideal profiles,' and he was then recommended for the job in which his scores best matched the 'ideal profile.' If his scores didn't match up too well with any 'ideal profile,' he wasn't hired.
>
> "It all seemed very impressive and very scientific. In fact, there was only one problem—the procedure didn't seem to be helping us select

better employees. Merit ratings were as poor as ever, and there were many supervisory complaints about the quality of new employees. Fortunately for us, however, the personnel manager resigned to take another job, and his replacement really understood the ins and outs of psychological testing. She examined the program and then began to ask some very embarrassing, yet stimulating, questions about how it had been set up. Among these were:

"1. Didn't we think that 10 people might be a rather small group to use for establishing a screening 'profile,' since, statistically, a group of 50 or more would be necessary to rule out random variations?

"2. What about the poorest employees on the 87 jobs? What kind of scores did they make on the same tests? How did we know that they didn't show the same 'profile' as the best employees—and, if they did, then how were the tests helping us to discriminate between potentially good and potentially poor employees?

"3. How did we know that each of the tests was equally valuable in selecting employees for any particular job? Our profiles assumed this, but was it true? Wouldn't we be better off to study each test separately and also in relation to the others?

"As a result of the admitted doubts raised both by her questions and the unsatisfactory results we had obtained, we authorized our new personnel director to make careful validation studies that would definitely check the effectiveness of the testing program. These studies revealed the following information:

"1. Seven of the 10 tests were completely worthless in helping us select employees for any of our 87 jobs!

"2. One test was useful on only 13 jobs.

"3. The other two tests were mental ability tests which overlapped so much that only one of them was really useful, and it was helpful on 47 jobs.

"4. All told, there were 34 jobs for which the tests could not be used and 53 jobs where one or both of the tests were helpful.

"While we were naturally disappointed that the tests were not of broader usefulness, we were also highly pleased with this study. It gave us a firm foundation for the proper and effective use of tests in our selection of factory employees. Subsequent studies show that our present limited testing program is of real value to us."

The use of tests which will not discriminate satisfactorily between potentially employable and unemployable applicants is undesirable on two counts: (1) They will not reduce the error of prediction significantly, that is, they will not improve the quality of the personnel hired; and (2) they will reduce the number of persons available for subsequent processing and employment. If 25% are erronously rejected by the tests, the available supply of applicants is reduced by this number. In a tight labor market, this may create a costly shortage of qualified applicants. Consequently, if tests are to be employed at all, their choice and standardization must always be under the supervision of someone trained in their use.

OFFICE ADMINISTRATION HANDBOOK

How Tests Should Be Administered

Experienced users of tests emphatically and continuously stress the fact that to obtain full benefit from their use, tests must be properly administered. Otherwise, the scores obtained may be meaningless or even misleading.

Not all tests are administered in precisely the same manner. It is essential, therefore, to follow explicitly the detailed instructions set forth in each test manual. General rules applicable to most tests are:

1. *The testing room should be quiet and private.* It should have good lighting and good ventilation. Comfortable and sturdy seating facilities and work space should also be provided. All necessary equipment such as typewriters, stenographers' notebooks, pencils, paper, and answer sheets should be available and in good, usable condition.

2. *Test must be administered only by persons who are thoroughly familiar with the procedure to be followed and the importance of giving tests under uniform conditions.* The test administrator need not be a psychologist as long as the program used has been developed by a professionally competent technician.

3. *The instructions to be given each applicant must be precise, complete, and uniform.* This is necessary to make sure that each person taking the test has a complete understanding of the instructions, and knows exactly what he is expected to do. Most test manuals contain a detailed information guide to the manner in which the test is to be administered. This includes the instructions which are to be given the subject and the manner in which they are to be presented. Many test instruction sheets also include practice problems. To be sure that he completely understands the instructions, these must be checked after the subject has completed them and before he starts the test.

4. *During the test no interruptions must be permitted.*

5. *If several applicants for the same position are being tested simultaneously, it is advisable to use what are known as equivalent, or parallel, test forms, if available, to eliminate the possibility of copying.* The test manual will indicate whether such forms are readily available.

6. *If the test has a time limit it must be accurately timed.* Variations of even a few seconds can make significant differences in scores on many tests. A stopwatch is recommended, but a

watch with a second hand may be used. If a mistake is made in timing, the subject must be retested, using a parallel form of the test initially administered. Attempts to "adjust" scores for errors in timing must never be made.

7. *Scoring instructions must be followed exactly.* Many tests have special scoring methods such as, "the score is the sum of those right minus one-half of those wrong," or, for certain items, special weights are provided. If these instructions are not followed exactly, the results will be misleading.

Companies which have used tests effectively are well aware that they are not gadgets or playthings and must not be regarded as such. They are delicate tools to be used only with care and understanding.

How Test Results Can Best Be Used

Psychological test results may be used in either of two ways: They can be employed as clinical aids to the interviewer, where, for example, the applicant's performance is to be evaluated on a clinical-commonsense basis; or they may be used as a secondary set of "Go/No Go" screening standards.

Using tests clinically. In many situations, particularly where validation studies cannot be conducted, it is nevertheless possible to use tests as clinical aids to the interviewer. Companies which use tests in this manner stress that the user must be trained to an understanding of test interpretation. They are convinced that this is definitely not a field for well-meaning amateurs.

Test results are often influenced by environmental and personality factors which can be evaluated and compensated for only by persons who have a thorough understanding of the strengths and limitations of tests. A steel company, which uses tests to hire for semiskilled jobs, points out that a subject's performance on a typical intelligence test may be greatly influenced by the fact that he has come from a home where English is not spoken regularly. Performance on verbal intelligence tests is influenced to a large degree by the individual's knowledge of word meanings. The amount of a subject's schooling, therefore, together with the fact that he has a bilingual home background, may unfairly handicap him in his test performance. A non-verbal intelligence test, which is not influenced by these conditions, may reveal that he is actually very bright. Unless the person interpreting the tests is aware of this situation and its implications, as well as of the many other factors which can affect test performance, the scores obtained may be both definitely misleading to the employer and grossly unfair to the applicant.

Establishing the Critical Score

Many companies report that a secondary advantage gained from a validation study is that it permits the establishment of critical or cutting (passing) scores. On some tests only one critical score need be established—for example, all applicants who score under 50 on a particular test can safely be eliminated. On another test, 2 critical scores may be required to establish an acceptable "middle range," so that, for example, applicants who score less than 10 *or* more than 62 may be eliminated.

Critical scores are established by reviewing test validation data to determine the scores which, when used as a basis for rejecting applicants, will lead to the exclusion of the greatest number of unsatisfactory applicants without the simultaneous loss of potentially desirable personnel. Simply stated, the aim is to set a score by which the greatest number of poor job risks can be screened out without losing too many good prospects.

These critical or cutting scores then become the absolute, or "Go/ No Go," standards which are employed when the test is used as an arbitrary means of rejecting applicants. If the applicant attains the right score she "goes"; if she fails to, it is "no go" as far as the job in question is concerned. Once these scores have been established, companies report that an intelligent, conscientious personnel clerk can administer and score the tests, and handle this secondary screening of the applicants.

Small Company Experience in Validating Tests

While it is not easy to conduct validation studies in small companies, or where the number of persons engaged in a particular occupation is small—less than 50—many companies have found that this can be done over a period of time by administering tests to applicants as they are hired and permitting the material to accumulate. It usually requires a year or more to secure the minimum number of cases, but, in the long run, this process will yield the information that is necessary. If the circumstances are such that no validation studies are possible even on this basis, then the tests must be used strictly as clinical instruments.

What Tests Should Be Used

There are reported to more than 25,000 different psychological tests on the market. The decision as to which of these many tests should be used by a particular company for particular positions is a crucial one requiring expert advice. The effectiveness of a testing program depends almost entirely on the competence of the person who (1) chooses the tests, (2) conducts the validation studies, and (3) sets the standards. In no event should a company entrust this assignment to amateurs or halftrained technicians, no matter how well-intentioned they may be. This is a highly technical field, and if good results are to be obtained only skilled specialists should be employed.

Companies contemplating a testing program can assure themselves of skilled assistance and counsel by contacting the American Psychological Association for names of qualified consulting psychologists.

Contribution of Tests to the Selection Program

Since they provide excellent measures of what the applicant can do, tests, when properly used, can make a worthwhile contribution to the selection procedure. Experience has shown, however, that the principal danger in the use of tests is the assumption that, because a person can do a particular task, he necessarily will do it. It is for this reason that it is necessary to supplement tests with such other fact-finding techniques and interpretative material as obtained by the telephone checks and the interview.

These are needed to provide answers to such questions as: "What will the applicant do?" To what extent will he make good use of his intelligence, skills, proficiencies, and aptitudes by staying on the job; working hard; getting along with people; being loyal; showing sufficient leadership, self-reliance, and perseverance; and being free from too many tendencies toward poor judgment and lack of self-control?

Legal Status of Psychological Testing

The employer today has lost much autonomy in hiring. While free to take on or hire anyone desired, the right to reject candidates has been seriously restricted as a result of the Fair Employment Law of 1964, Title VII, and its numerous supplementary rulings.

Briefly summarized, it is no longer permissible for an employer to *reject* an applicant because he or she is a member of a minority group, i.e., on the grounds of race, religion, nationality, country of national origin, political affiliation, sex, or on the grounds of age if the candidate is between the ages of 40 and 65. Furthermore, the employer's standards must be relevant, valid, and nondiscriminatory against those who are educationally and culturally deprived. This precludes the use in many instances of arbitrary selection standards, e.g., the requirement that the candidate be a high-school graduate. It also precludes the use of any tests that discriminate against the educationally and culturally deprived, e.g., verbal tests of intelligence such as the SRA verbal test, the Otis, or the Wonderlic.

The enforcement arm of the Act is primarily the Equal Employment Opportunity Commission, although if the employer happens to have Government contracts, he can be subject to the jurisdiction of the Office of Federal Contract Compliance. The Equal Employment Opportunity Coordinating Council has established standards for use in evaluating candidates' qualifications for employment.

EEOC is empowered to investigate all charges of discrimination by employers of 25 or more persons, and has the power of subpoena to come into the employer's place of business and investigate not only the case from which the charges originated but also all of the company's hiring, promotion, and placement policies. The Agency can enforce its findings by giving the offending employer bad publicity, by canceling any Government contracts the employer may have and by filing a class-action suit in a Federal District Court.

The courts have supported the findings of the EEOC in many cases. Typical of this, a Federal District Court judge found the Detroit Edison Company guilty of discriminating against blacks in the hiring, testing, and promotion of workers and fined the utility $4 million. As a part of his ruling, Federal Judge Damen Keith ordered the Detroit Edison Company to: 1) hire blacks until they represent 30 percent of its work force; 2) hire blacks to fill technical and craftsman jobs until they represent 25 percent of this skilled work force; 3) promote one senior black employee to a foreman or supervisor post for every white so promoted; 4) stop giving intelligence and aptitude tests that weeded out a higher proportion of black applicants than white without evidence that the tests were inherently valid, i.e., that the qualities the tests measure are necessarily related to success on the job.

The EEOC is primarily concerned with the prevention of discrimination against minorities, women, and applicants between the ages of 40 and 65, hiring, upgrading, transfers, and rates of compensation. For practical purposes minorities include principally blacks, Puerto Ricans, Cubans, American Indians, and Chicanos. To prevent discrimination in the employment of minorities, the employer is forbidden to ask questions of applicants relative to their race, religion, nationality and country of national origin, or require photographs (which might reveal race). Other restrictions come and go, as state legislatures act and react.

More specifically, as already noted, employers' standards for selection must be "relevant." By this is meant the employer must be in a position to prove (in this context the employer is always considered to be guilty until he can prove himself innocent) that whatever standard he uses, e.g., high-school graduation, is not only prerequisite to success on the job but also that he does not have anyone already in the same job who does not meet this standard. In a case adjudicated by the Supreme Court, the Duke Power Company required high-school graduation for many of its operating and clerical positions, which excluded a disproportionate number of blacks. Simultaneous investigation, however, revealed that some whites who were not high-school graduates had been employed for these positions and were performing satisfactorily. It was on this basis that the Court held that high-school graduation is not a relevant employment standard for the positions in question.

The courts have also held that whatever selection instruments, e.g., psychological tests, are employed, they must be demonstrably "valid." The purpose of a validation study is to demonstrate statistically that there is a consistent and significant relationship between performance on the test and competence on the job. Validation studies are of two types: concurrent and predictive.

Concurrent Validation Studies

In the *concurrent* type of validation study, *present* employees are tested and their performance is rated or evaluated, following which a comparison is made between test scores and measures of job success to determine the degree of correlation between the two, using a sample of at least 50 cases. Concurrent validation studies of this sort often tend to be unfair to tests, since the sample of employees used is rarely representative; the less qualified employees will have left the company either voluntarily or by termination, so that the lower end of the sample will have been truncated. Hence, it will not include the less-qualified employees.

Predictive Validation Studies

The *predictive* type of validation study is much more reliable. Here everyone employed is given the tests at the time of hiring, but they are not used for selection purposes. The test findings are put away, so that they have no influence on initial selection or subsequent measures of job success. Only after six months or a year, during which time the employee's competence will have been established, is a study made of the relationship between test performnce and job success. This is called a "predictive" study because it is designed to indicate the extent to which the tests in question have *predicted* subsequent performance on the job. This type of validation is also much fairer to the test because the sample includes *everyone hired,* hence is truly representative. Everyone is included, even those who after being hired never appeared to go to work.

The resistance of the EEOC to *verbal* tests of intelligence lies in the fact that it holds that persons of limited education are discriminated against when asked questions necessitating a knowledge of arithmetic, grammar, etc., which can be obtained only in school. The EEOC also holds that applicants are discriminated against if they are asked to define word meanings or interpret proverbs, when they have been raised in a culture where most of the members are illiterate or speak a foreign language, e.g., Spanish.

This restriction is avoided in the case of the so-called "pictorial" or "culture fair" tests. Here the subject evaluates pictures and diagrams which have been carefully chosen and pretested on minority-group members to ensure that the objects or designs shown are comprehensible to those with little education or are foreign born.

Summary of Legal Status

Briefly stated, no psychological test of any type may be used as a basis for *employee selection* unless the test is demonstrably *valid*. By this is meant the employer has conducted studies which indicate that there is a statistically significant relationship between performance on the test and success on a particular job. This requires that a comparison be made between test performance and whatever measures of job competence and performance are available. This normally requires a minimum of 50 cases and ordinarily should be conducted by trained specialists in the field of test development and evaluation. Unless a statistically significant correlation (.30 between test scores and the criterion) is obtained, it is not recommended that the test be employed as a go/no go criterion of employability. The only possible exception to this is the case of proficiency tests, e.g., tests of typing skill, trade tests, etc., which are job samples, i.e., measures of acquired skills.

If questions should arise relative to the suitability of any particular test, it is recommended that counsel be obtained from recognized specialists in the testing field, the publishers of the test in question, or the Equal Employment Opportunity Commission.

There is no legal restriction on the use of tests for selection purposes. However, in the event that tests are employed and the applicant is not hired, he can always file charges with the EEOC alleging that he has been rejected because of his performance on the test. The burden of proof of the legitimacy of the rejection then falls on the shoulders of the employer to prove either that the tests employed have been validated and are demonstrably useful measures of job suitability or, if this is not the case, that the reason for rejection was something other than test performance.

Furthermore, the statute of limitations for a charge of discrimination must be filed with the EEOC within 180 days after the alleged unlawful employment practice occurred. However, when the person aggrieved has initially filed charges with a state or local agency, the statute of limitations for filing the charge with EEOC is 300 days.

If the EEOC, which has subpoena power to examine all records, finds for the plaintiff, the latter must be employed, paid back wages to the date of his initial application (which can be up to two years) and be given any promotions received by the employee hired in his place. For the the foregoing reasons, it is not recommended that tests be employed unless their validity has been established and that they meet the standard for validity set by the EEOC.

Part 3

Office Personnel—Administration

CHAPTER 10

WAGE AND SALARY PROGRAM ADMINISTRATION

IN establishing pay objectives, the administrator is concerned with the need to attract and retain qualified workers. This objective implies establishing incentives for self-advancement, consistency and confidentiality in pay matters, and a pay scale that is in line with industry and area trends as well as with public and government policy.

The role of the office administrator often includes that of pay administration. Any company program, especially one that touches the purse as well as the ego, is only as effective as its administrator. The person must be sensitive to the needs of both the company and the individual worker—a job that can sometimes be compared with walking a tightrope. In addition, he or she must keep one eye on the company's responsibility to comply with appropriate laws and statutes such as the Equal Employment Opportunity law, under which the federal government specifies that no discrimination shall be allowed on the basis of sex, race, creed, color, nationality, religion, or age in matters involving hiring, pay, transfers or promotions, or layoffs. Thus the office administrator must be not only a balancer but also a juggler.

Communicating Program Objectives

In matters of compensation, employees today expect to "hear it like it is" from company managemnent. A program keyed to pay objectives, formally committed to paper, understood by all, and followed by management can be a strong force for reducing employee turnover, facilitating the training process, and fostering that important personal identification with the company. Hence communications concerning pay programs should include the intent of the program, as well as its more mechanical or operational aspects.

Meetings between the office administrator and employees provide an excellent opportunity for discussing the pay program. First, they clearly identify the department head as having direct responsibility for pay recommendations involving the workers in a department. Further, they involve the employees in the program and tend to remove some of the mystery and possible resentment "edicts from above." Most important, the employees are the only ones who can definitively and realistically describe their duties, their responsibilities, and their position requirements.

Meeting Format and Questionnaires

The format of a department meeting might include opening statements by the company president or other top executive concerning overall compensation aims and goals. More specific details by the department administrator regarding department objectives and procedures, and instructions for the completion of a position-description questionnaire form handled by the pay administrator or executive charged with pay administration responsibility, might follow, when and if needed.

Employees will invariably ask where they should complete the questionnaire, and how long they should spend on it. Actually, the best place is at the employee's home, away from the demands and pressures of the work place. Following questionnaire completion, each employee is told to review the form with his or her immediate supervisor, after which the job will be analyzed, ranked, and graded.

Using Company Publications

Another communications tool is the employee house organ or newsletter. This medium can be used to introduce a new program before employee meetings begin, and to keep them advised of the program. The newsletter can serve especially well as a means for informing employees of changes in existing programs, new developments, and government pay regulations, as they change from time to time.

Some organizations publish supervisory newsletters to keep supervisors up-to-date on changes in pay policy *in advance* of that information being given to employees, thus preserving effective communications channels within the organization and helping the supervisor to know his business.

Other companies maintain a formal organization manual which is distributed to executives, managers, and supervisors. This manual includes an organization chart, position descriptions, and procedures which guide the company's policies and actions in pay matters. Such a manual keeps executives up to date on new or changed procedures, so they can assure employees of the uniformity and fairness in the company's compensation policies and practices.

PREPARING REALISTIC JOB DESCRIPTIONS

The job description, a detailed written statement of duties and responsibilities of any particular position or job as it is being *presently* performed, is the foundation stone of any wage and salary program. It also provides the documentation for later job evaluation.

In addition, the job description is an effective vehicle for comparing pay within a company with pay for similar jobs elsewhere. Jobs that adapt to intercompany comparisons are called "benchmark" jobs, since they "compare apples with apples" and thus assure the establishment of a realistic and competitive pay struture. A well-written and documented job description also highlights the specific duties and functions the employee should be performing. Unless the employee's superior has this information when rating performance, he cannot be as fair and objective.

The supervisor who orients and trains new employees will find the job description a real help in delineating the key points of and reasons for the job routines which must be emphasized in teaching correct procedures and quality standards. Properly prepared job descriptions are a means of achieving unanimity between superior and employee in regard to the specific duties of the employee's job, thereby reducing misunderstandings concerning performance expectations. Good descriptions also serve to clarify relationships between jobs, functions and departments, to establish harmony and balance, to clearly delineate responsibilities and authorities, and to establish lines of communication. Further, labor grievances can be worked out more easily when job descriptions outline clearly what job is responsible for what duty and carries what pay rate.

Finally, a department promotional sequence can be established through the use of job descriptions, which show the real differences between present and contemplated assignments. They highlight what the employee to be promoted needs to know to perform his new duties.

One of the best sources for establishing standard formats for job descriptions is the *Dictionary of Occupational Titles,* published by the U.S. Department of Labor. Over 30,000 jobs are described, which can then be adapted to specific company requirements by the job analyst.

ANALYZING AND CONSTRUCTION JOB EVALUATION PLANS

Once job descriptions are formalized, the next step in the pay program is to evaluate the jobs. This is defined as a systematic method of determining the *relative differentials* between jobs in an organization. Job evaluation is concerned with job requirements, not the qualifications of the employee in the job, or the wage paid him. The end result of job evaluation is job ranking in which the more complex, responsible, and skilled jobs are grouped at the higher end of the hierarchy, while the less complex and less skilled jobs fall at the lower end of the job hierarchy.

Objectives of job evaluation include:

1. **Elimination of wage or salary inequities resulting in a reduction of complaints concerning inequitable relations of wages paid different jobs.**
2. **Establishment of a framework for determining pay for new or changed jobs.**
3. **Determination of employee qualifications for jobs.**
4. **To aid in determining promotions and transfers.**
5. **Training of supervisors in wage determination.**
6. **Establishment of bases from which individual performance may be measured.**

Companies considering the installation of a job evaluation program should be aware of the strengths and weaknesses of such a program.

Advantages and Disadvantages

A proven, recognized tool used by both managements and unions for years, job evaluation emphasizes a common understanding of the complex problems involved in establishing fair and equitable pay. It takes the guesswork out of establishing pay rates through use of a planned method based on logic, and provides a basis for easy auditing and updating. It commits the program to writing, and thus removes it from the personalities of supervisors who are transferred or leave the company—and at the same time, communicates management's pay philosophy to each employee. Formalized job evaluations permit intercompany comparisons, particularly those in the same industry negotiating with the same international union; and finally, on the plus side, it is the basis upon which incentive programs and fringe benefits are built, for these are invariably keyed to the base wage or salary.

One of the weaknesses of job evaluation is that it assumes that organization and shop procedures are correct and effective. This may not necessarily be the case. Assume that the methods involved in operating a punch press are slow and cumbersome, requiring an inordinate amount of physical energy to operate the machine. This defect will show up in the job evaluation, since physical energy is typically one of the factors used in analyzing job worth. In addition, it emphasizes the down-play of worker qualifications, but because in most cases, the employee supplies the basic job description and requirements, it is impossible to obtain a completely objective result. Assume that one employee occupies a job classification, and his performance is below standard. This performance level invariably will make itself felt in the job evaluation for his classification.

While job evaluations presuppose that the supervisory and management staff initially evaluating jobs will be broad-minded, and that union representatives will be thinking only of the company's good, such is unfortunately not always the case. In some cases, job evaluation decisions are made on the basis of expediency or politics so as not to "rock the boat."

THREE EVALUATION TECHNIQUES

Overall, however, advantages outweigh the disadvantages, and a company would be well-advised to consider the installation of a job evaluation plan based on one of the three types which have evolved through usage.

1. Ranking

The ranking technique is the simplest. It utilizes the job description, the salary or wage survey, and supervisory knowledge to analyze and group jobs. No attempt is made to evaluate specific job requirements or to compare similar jobs in a company.

Using this technique, company management decides how many job levels or grades will be in a specific group of jobs or positions. In a shop hourly classification evaluation study, dependent upon the range of skills, typically 10 to 12 jobs levels or grades are determined. Those jobs which pay the same as or close to wages reported in industry or area surveys are grouped together at the same job level, up and down the hierarchy. This form of evaluation sets a company's wage structure in a competitive posture, and assumes that the company's jobs follow the area or industry in wage patterns. Such may not be the case; in fact, the matter of intra-company equity in job ranking has been overlooked completely. Research data indicate that 24% of manufacturing firms and 14% of service firms use this technique.

2. Factor Comparison

The factor comparison evaluation technique is more analytical and widely used than the ranking method. It compares jobs by assisting management to make judgments as to which jobs encompass more requirements, skills, and responsibilities than others. This technique emphasizes the consideration of "universal factors" such as mental requirements, physical requirements, skill requirements, responsibility, and working conditions. It requires a custom-built utilization of these factors by which the bench-mark or key jobs are firmly set; other jobs are then compared to the key jobs and appropriately slotted. No numerical values are attached to the factors.

While the advantage of custom-building an evaluation plan is highly desirable as in the factor comparison technique, one of the disadvantages is its complexity, as well as the fact that key jobs change over a period of time, rendering their use as "standards" meaningless.

3. Point Factor

The quantitative point factor plan technique is the most widely used of the formal job-ranking plans. Quoting from the Dartnell *Wage and Salary Administration Guide to Current Practices,* 53 percent of manufacturing companies and 66 percent of service organizations use this plan.

A point factor plan features clearly-defined, job-related factors, to which are assigned numerical values, or degrees. Each job is considered separately, and evaluated for the appropriate factor and points.

Let us assume that education is considered an important factor by a particular company seeking to develop a factor scale for a set of clerical jobs. The scale might be developed in the form illustrated on the next page.

JOB FACTOR: EDUCATION

The factor must be carefully defined. The following is suggested: *"Education consists of the basic knowledge acquired by formal education, outside study, or training on jobs of lesser degree, necessary to achieve normal job performance." The factor-point degree development might take this form:*

WAGE AND SALARY PROGRAM ADMINISTRATION

Degree	Point Value	Requirement	Equivalent
1.	40	Knowledge of simple clerical routines—checking, posting, typing. Blueprint reading.	High school.
2.	70	Knowledge of stenography, calculator operation, basic drafting, key punching.	High school, plus additional technical or specialized training up to ½ year college.
3.	100	Knowledge of secretarial procedures, basic accounting, personnel interviewing.	Equivalent to 1 year college.
4.	130	Knowledge of cost accounting, time study, computers, manufacturing methods.	2 years college.
5.	160	Knowledge of general or technical field—chemistry, engineering, accounting.	4 years college, Bachelor's degree.

It will be noted in the table that the point values increase algebraically, that the *requirements* are expressed in terms of educational levels, and that *the equivalent* is clearly expressed in years of education. This type of factor development is quite commonly used and easily understood.

Other factors and degrees are developed in the same manner. A company engaged in developing its own plan, should ensure that the factors used are tied squarely to job conditions and requirements (which can be ascertained from job descriptions), and that the terms used are understood by the employees charged with administering the plan.

There are both advantages and disadvantages to the point factor approach. It features development of a fixed point scale for each factor which results in greater consistency, and acceptance by the parties using it. Once the point scales are developed, they may be used for a long period of time (they do not change, as the key jobs under the factor comparison technique may). Further, the management decision-making process is quantified. On the other hand, the point factor plan is more complicated than the other types, and may be more easily understood. Also, to install a point factor plan takes more time.

Standard Plans

References have already been made to some of the steps necessary in constructing a tailor-made plan. There are a number of standard plans available which have been widely tested, and proven in a variety of installations. These include:

1. *National Metal Trades Association Job Rating Plan.* This plan has been broadly used in the metal-working industries. It is a point factor plan, based on 11 factors covering production job requirements in terms of skill, effort, responsibility, and job conditions.

2. *National Electrical Manufacturers Association Job Evaluation Plan.* Quite similar to the NMTA plan, this plan has been widely applied in the electrical industries. It, too, is based on 11 factors, and covers spectrum of production job requirements.

3. *The Cooperative Wage Survey (CWS) Plan* was developed jointly in 1944 by steel industry management and the United Steelworkers of America union to arrive at a common basis between management and union for settling wage disputes under wartime conditions. Since then, it has been extensively used in basic steel and heavy industry. Also a point-factor plan, it utilizes 12 factors in determining production job requirements in terms of skill, responsibility, effort, and working conditions.

4. *Combinations* of these plans, as developed by industrial job analysts and consultants. Each standard plan has its strengths and weaknesses, and should be evaluated by a company in the light of its unique requirements.

The decision whether to adopt a standard or custom-made plan should be based first on the availability of company staff to develop a custom-made plan. Such a plan requires a competent pay administrator or job analyst, in wage and salary administration, industrial statistics, and company organization, who has the ability both to "sell," install, and administer the program. This type of installation assumes that the company has the necessary time and resources to develop its own plan. Another factor is the availability of a standard plan which will answer the company's needs. These standard plans invariably are bound in manual form, backed up with tables of data and instructions for use, and therefore possess an aura of authority.

Job Evaluation Data

Detail your job in terms of the minimum requirements necessary to achieve normal performance.

1. Education

   The basic knowledge acquired by formal education, outside study, or training on jobs of lesser degree necessary to achieve normal job performance.

   Please check:

   A. High school.

      Knowledge of simple clerical routines, checking, posting, typing, blueprint reading.

   B. High school, plus additional technical or specialized training up to ½ year of college.

      Knowledge of stenography, calculator operation, basic drafting, key punching.

   C. One year college.

      Knowledge of secretarial procedures, basic accounting, personnel interviewing.

   D. Two years college.

      Knowledge of cost accounting, time study, computers, manufacturing methods.

   E. Four years college. Bachelor's degree.

      Knowledge of general or technical field —chemistry, engineering, accounting.

Once a job evaluation plan has been adopted, a form should be constructed to accompany the job description questionnaire upon which the employee indicates what he thinks the job requirements are in terms of each evaluation factor.

The employee is asked to check the appropriate education degree which he considers pertinent. Only *one* is checked. In like manner, detailing other factors can be accomplished in questionnaire form.

Unions are more apt to accept a standard plan when bargaining unit jobs are involved in an evaluation program. A third consideration determining which type of plan to use is the manner of conducting union wage negotiations. Some companies and unions bargain for wages on an industry-wide basis. The presence of a common job evaluation plan could easily facilitate resolvement of wage disputes.

There are undoubtedly other considerations. One fact favoring a custom-made plan is that such plans tend to be more valid because they are keyed to specific company conditions and jobs.

DETERMINING THE PAY STRUCTURE

There are two kinds of pay structures that are useful within their own specific situation: the single rate structure and the rate range by class or grade.

Types of Pay Structures

A single rate structure is composed of a single wage or salary for a given job classification or grade. A single rate structure is more typically found in hourly paid classifications, as the survey data above indicate. Survey data further indicates that it is not widely used either in manufacturing, service or distribution organizations. A single rate structure is often used in production occupations where incentive rates are applied. The measure of performance, then, is indicated not in the base rate, but in the degree to which the employee produces on the incentive scale. Examples of single rate structures are also found in the crafts; for example, the building trades.

A disadvantage to the single rate structure is that there is no opportunity for merit increases in the base rate. So, there is no opportunity for the company to exercise individual treatment of employees deserving merit increases. However, this is an advantage for the pay administrator who does not have to justify specific merit raises. Favoritism is taken out of the pay procedure, but it must be remembered that favoritism can be demonstrated in many other ways.

As the survey data indicate, the rate range by class/grade pay structure is more widely used by all three types of reporting organizations. Under this type of structure, a range of pay is indicated for each job classification or grade.

Under these pay ranges, the new employee starts in pay at the minimum rate of the classification or grade in which the job falls. Depending upon the type of plan used, he advances in pay within the range on *either a merit increase or an automatic increase* to the midpoint of the range. The *mid-point* is usually considered as the "going rate" for the job and is indicative of average or standard performance by the employee. Increases above the mid-point are awarded to those employees capable of doing above-average work.

Automatic increases are those which are given to employees who complete certain periods of service on the job, and are given more often in hourly paid structures. These periods of service range from one to three months.

Although the increases are automatic, it is assumed that the employee is learning the basic requirements of the job and is making satisfactory progress. Some union contracts specify that management has the right to withhold an automatic increase if the employee is not performing at the level required.

In some pay structures, the concept of average performance is not considered to be at the mid-point of the range, but rather at the maximum of the range. In this case, the approach depends upon whether superior performance can be realized on the job. In factory jobs involving conveyorized operations and a group effort on the part of employees, it is doubtful whether superior performance can be gauged on the individual performance basis. In that situation, the maximum of the range is considered to be average performance.

In the case of salaried positions, increases are often given not on an automatic basis, but on an individual performance basis unrelated to length of service. To assist in awarding merit increases, some companies use "step rates." Step rates are fixed equal increments within the range. An example would be if the range were from $800 to $1000 a month with a total range of $200, four equal step rates each $50 apart, would be used. Employees would be advanced in pay in line with these equal increments. The disadvantage of this plan is that it tends to standardize the amount of increase awarded and to underplay the individual performance of an employee. For example, an employee might be judged in performance to be worth a $70 increase, but the most he or she could receive would be $50. In this sense, it is rather inflexible.

Establishing a Pay Structure

Upon completion of the pay survey, the next phase in establishing a pay structure is to determine statistically the best relationship between the job's evaluation points and the survey rates of pay. Since the majority of organizations use some form of point factor plan, discussion of pay structure determination is done with this in mind.

First, a "*scattergram*" is made. A scattergram is a chart which plots the position of each job by evaluation points and survey rates of pay. See the illustration on the next page for an example. The horizontal (X) axis, or abscissa, represents the spread of evaluation points from the lowest grade through the highest grade. The vertical

(Y) axis, or ordinate, represents the range of the survey pay data and can be indicated by hourly, weekly, monthly, or annual rates. An examination of the scattergram indicates the trend of the data. The next step is to draw a line which best fits the distribution of points on the scattergram. There are two basic techniques in calculating a line of best fit: the inspection technique and least squares technique. No matter which technique is used, the theory is to determine a trend line that allows the least vertical deviation from the line to each plotted job position. The charts following graphically demonstrate this principle.

TWO EXAMPLES OF TREND LINES
DRAWN BY INSPECTION
STRAIGHT

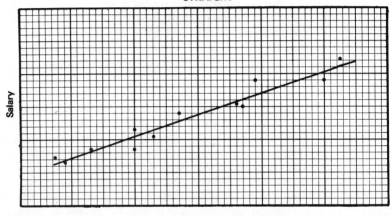

CURVILINEAR

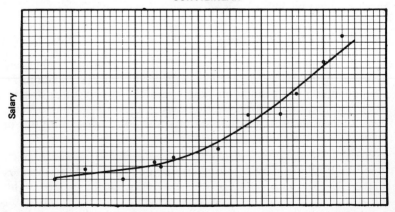

Using the *inspection* technique, the trend line is drawn free-hand. "Eye-balling" the line is done by sighting the concentration or clusters of jobs. See below. When drawn by experienced job analysts, the free-hand trend line can closely approximate the line of best fit. However, the technique is open to criticism because of the judgment factor involved.

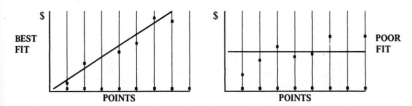

Statistical Correlation Techniques

A more reliable, statistical means of drawing pay structures is the "average plots" technique. It is often used along with the inspection technique. The technique calculates the means of the total points and survey pay rates for each cluster of jobs. When the trend appears to be linear, simply divide the data in half, calculate the two means, plot the two points, and draw the line. This technique is especially helpful when the trend is curvilinear. The means for the several job clusters are plotted, and connecting lines drawn. Then some adjustments by inspection may be needed to "smooth" the curve.

The method of least squares is the more accurate of the techniques described. It should be used when the pay administrator is less experienced in the inspection technique or when a skeptical management needs assurance that the approach is statistically valid.

Displaying Data

The limits can be in one of two forms; either as a series of boxes representing each job grade or as continuous lines corresponding to the survey trend line. Note the following graphic display of these two approaches. There are advantages and disadvantages in each approach that need to be evaluated.

The box approach sets the upper and lower limits by using the mid-points of the survey trend line for each job grade. The degree of overlap should be evaluated once the pay structure has been established. Overlap means that the highest pay rate in one grade is above the minimum of the range for at least one successive grade. Too many grades do not allow a distinction between levels of skills.

Good practice indicates there should be at most a two successive grade overlap. If there is excessive overlap, then the number of grades should be reduced.

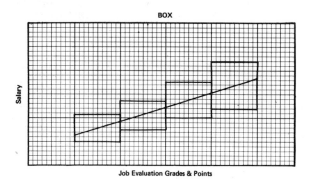

BOX

Salary

Job Evaluation Grades & Points

The box approach is the more commonly accepted. Employees can readily visualize the limits. This approach assures a more equitable treatment of employees. Some people dislike the boxes because they feel the boxes create a rigid, confining situation. Certainly, this is a perceptual bias and understandable. The fact is that it provides a good, easy-to-communicate and understandable method which employees readily grasp.

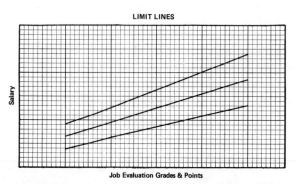

LIMIT LINES

Salary

Job Evaluation Grades & Points

The continuous line approach sets the upper and lower limits typically by drawing a continuous line using the mid-points of each job grade. Virtually all job evaluation plans have some form of grade scale to the total point values. When the emphasis is placed upon points and not grades, employees have a greater tendency to "nit-pick" the job point worth to get the few extra dollars. Also, the table which represents the pay structure is more complex because each successive point value has a different pay range.

The percent spread of the limits varies in proportion to which performance differences are possible. In the case of a file clerk, for example, where standard procedures are used, the opportunity to demonstrate performance is limited. On the other hand, in the case of a department manager, the opportunity for demonstrating performance is much broader. This individual has responsibility for delegating work to subordinates, training new employees, meeting department goals, and maintaining standards of quality and quantity. Also, lower-level jobs are not usually career-oriented and have more potential for advancement; whereas, high-level jobs are career-oriented and need a wider range to recognize longer time-in-position performance. Wage and salary administration practice suggests that the minimum to maximum range spreads for varying levels of jobs should be as follows:

Type of Job	Width of Range Percent Minimum to Maximum
Hourly	10 to 15
Office Non-Exempt & Exempt	25 to 30
Management & Professional	30 to 50

The varying pay range spreads are done on the basis of job grade. Each grade is broken down generally into an equal number of points on the total point scale. The pay ranges are computed from the mid-point of each grade using the survey trend line. Observe the table of the pay structure with the ranges included. The percentage spread distribution for this particular example is as follows:

Grade	Percent Minimum to Maximum
7–8	30
6	25
5	20
3–4	15
1–2	10

The Finished Product

Graphic presentation of the relationship between the incumbents' pay and the survey pay structure can be done in two ways, a line of best fit can be calculated by the plotting of the actual pay for the positions evaluated. This approach can readily point out group inequities by the slope of the line at the lower, middle, or upper end of the total points scale. The figure clearly demonstrates this situation: namely that those jobs at the lower end of the structure are paid lower than the survey trend line in comparison to the other jobs, and conversely, higher level jobs are paid higher than the survey trend line.

Some companies follow a policy of paying below the survey trend line, others meet the survey line and still others pay above the line, the latter being the most favorable competitive pay structure. This decision must be made by top management considering all factors involved.

ADMINISTERING THE PAY PROGRAM

The job evaluation plan is a flexible approach used to define and clarify the content and reporting relationships of jobs. Because the company experiences continual change due to growth, change of product mix, procedural changes, economic depression, etc., it is vital to establish a policy of continued maintenance of the pay system.

Responsibilities of Administrator

The system maintenance is usually delegated to the *Personnel Manager* or *Compensation Specialist,* or, in small companies, to the *Controller.* The *Pay Administrator* is responsible for the following activities:

1. Establish procedures to ensure that supervisors notify him of changes in job content. Notification of supervisors and a company-overall review are good practices to follow.
2. Review new jobs using prescribed evaluation procedures.
3. Resolve arguments among employees concerning specific job ratings. The pay administrator must be experienced in job evaluation and keep up-to-date on current developments in order to instill confidence in the employees using the system.
4. Conduct wage and salary surveys of industry-related companies and companies in the same geographical locale.
5. Summarize data and construct pay structures in the form of graphs and tables to reflect competitive pay rates.
6. Develop pay trends and projections for use by top management.
7. Recommend new or improved compensation policies and procedures.

8. Coordinate with *Data Processing* the preparation of summary reports for use by departmental personnel.
9. Keep current and accurate records of all pay matters.
10. Maintain file of individual employee performance review dates and notify supervisors to ensure prompt performance review and up-to-date pay rates.
11. Conduct job evaluation training programs for supervisors so they understand the basic principles of the system.

Responsibilities of Supervisor

The supervisor should have a working knowledge of the job evaluation plan and how it relates both to his or her job and to subordinates' jobs. He or she should have complete familiarity with the employees' descriptions and ratings. The description can be used to determine whether the employee is performing the duties of the job. The factor evaluation data provides information necessary for hiring replacements, for example: education, experience, and any special skills required.

The supervisor should be made aware of the fact that the description and rating forms can and should be used in indoctrination of new employees. This information helps the new employee gain a basic understanding of job responsibilities and the limits of his authority.

Additional specific responsibilities include:

1. Review new and revised job descriptions and ratings to assure that they accurately reflect the duties and demands of the job.
2. Report to the pay administrator changes in job content.
3. Recommend pay raises and promotions within prescribed policies and procedures.
4. Communicate to subordinates the purpose of the job evaluation and pay administration system.
5. Maintain accurate records of subordinates' pay rates, the pay ranges for subordinates' jobs and performance review date.
6. Conduct subordinates' performance reviews as close to prescribed review date as possible.
7. Control the amount of overtime work, distribute the overtime work assignments equitably, and evaluate gross pay relationships with other departments and jobs in the company to remain in line with overall pay standards.

Setting Pay Rates

Once the pay structure has been calculated, it is clearly evident where a specific employee's pay falls relative to the appropriate pay range. Some pay rates will fall above the maximum of the range, some will fall within the range, and others will fall below the minimum of the range. Initially, those pay rates above the maximum or below the minimum should receive the most attention. Each situation is inequitable both for the employee and the employer and should be resolved as quickly as possible.

When pay rates have been set by union negotiation, rate adjustments must not be made until the union has been contacted. Those rate adjustments must conform to the union contract.

"Red circle" rates fall above the maximum of the pay range. It must be remembered that every job has only so much worth to the company. It's a hard line for the employee to accept, but it is a reality. Obviously, the employee is not at fault for being overpaid. However, the company must consider the inequities created among all the other employees when overpayment occurs.

Various approaches have been taken to consider both the employee's and the company's situation. No approach will completely satisfy both parties. It is a tough problem for the pay administrator and requires considerable tact and persuasion to make the situation at least acceptable, if not agreeable, to the employee. Several approaches can be taken:

1. Freeze the rate until the structure shifts sufficiently due to the cost-of-living increases.

2. Promote the employee to a higher pay range.

3. Allow a 6-month period for the employee to train and develop into a more responsible position. If not successful, adjust the rate downward to the maximum.

4. Offer a job with higher responsibilities and, if refused, adjust the rate downward to the maximum.

5. "Personalize" the rate. This approach can be used for long-service employees, for example, who helped get the company started, but who can not now accept more responsibility. The value of job evaluation should be noted because it can determine the worth of the job for the next incumbent.

6. Sometimes "red circle" rates are created by tight market conditions for people with special talents. In this case, the range should be ignored and these employees should be paid what the market demands. It is not a good practice for

maintaining internal equity, but many times it is economically essential.

"Green circle" rates fall below the minimum of the pay range. In some respects, these rates are easier for the pay administrator to resolve. In general, appropriate action is to raise the pay to the minimum of the range as quickly as possible. Otherwise, the company must face the possibility of losing the employee to a higher-paying competitor. Raising the rate to the minimum can be done in steps if the pay increase is substantial.

Raising the rate to the minimum, of course, assumes that the employee is qualified for the job. Should the employee be considered a trainee, it is not unusual for the starting rate to be 10% below the minimum of the range. Generally, there is an agreement between the employee and the company that increases will be awarded on the basis of time on the job and performance. This probationary period should be for only a short time, or the employee may leave.

Distinguishing between employees can be done on the basis of length of service or performance, or a combination of the two. The concept of pay range allows different pay for employees on the same job.

Many companies divide the rate range into a series of equal steps. This is called the *"step-rate"* approach. At least three steps are provided, and sometimes more, depending upon the size of the range and the time it takes to learn and perform the job satisfactorily. Other companies consider the step-rate approach to be inflexible and the pay range to be less motivating by specifying the amount of increase per step.

Types of Increases

Step-rates are necessary when the *"automatic progression"* technique is used. This technique moves the pay rate from the minimum using equal interval steps based upon the length of service only. Performance is expected to be at least satisfactory after the designated period of time has passed. For example, the minimum of the range is $500, the maximum is $650 and there are four steps based upon a three month's rate, a six month's rate, and the final rate at the end of one year. Each step equals $50. This technique assumes proficiency by the end of the year.

"Merit progression" may or may not use step-rates. The merit progression technique operates on the principle that pay increases are earned by improved performance. The pay range is well suited

to this technique because it is really, in theory, a bell curve (normal distribution) up-ended. The less than satisfactory employee (or trainee) falls in the minimum to mid-point portion of the range, the average or acceptable employee falls close to the mid-point and the maximum of the range, depending upon the quality of that person's work.

While the merit progression approach has much to offer, failure to use performance appraisal techniques properly can create serious inequities. Careful use of this technique is a must.

The amount of merit increase varies with the job level. Nonexempt and lower-level exempt employees should receive no less than a 3 percent *merit increase.* No less than a 5 percent merit increase is appropriate for supervisory, professional and managerial personnel.

A popular combination of these two techniques is the *step-rate approach to the mid-point.* The merit approach works from the mid-point to the maximum of the range. This approach assumes that those employees still working for the company after their probationary period (for example, one year), are performing at least satisfactorily or they would have been fired.

Promotional increase is a third way to reward an employee's performance. Oftentimes, the company will place an employee in the more responsible job and hold back the promotional increase until the person proves himself. This treatment is not a justifiable approach because recruitment from the outside world would necessitate the higher pay rate. Good practice is to award the pay increase at the time of promotion. Generally, the size of the increase should not be less than 5 percent or more than 20 percent.

Pay Review

Pay review schedules are based upon the level of the job and the time on the job. A general rule is to review the employee six months after the date of hire and subsequently, on an annual basis.

Management salaries can be placed on an 18- or 24-month review schedule because performance takes longer to observe. For low-level jobs which take a relatively short time to learn, a three month, six month, and then an annual review schedule is recommended.

Secrecy

There are no final answers to the question of whether or not to keep pay matters secret. It is a fact that equitability of pay among employees *within* the company is more important than equitability among employees at other companies. Consequently, the manner in which pay matters are conducted has a real impact upon the needs of the employee.

Proponents of secrecy believe:

1. "My pay is no one else's business."
2. Excessive comparisons and demands that job ratings are incorrect are reduced by not publishing pay data.
3. Publicizing pay rates would tend to "homogenize" the pay rates as can be seen in the pay trends in union contracts.
4. Motivation to compete is reduced.

The critics of pay secrecy will certainly disagree with each of the points given above. *Edward Lawler,* a well-known behavioral scientist at Yale University, has conducted research studies in the area of pay secrecy. He believes that secrecy creates an unrealistic reaction, an illusion, by employees to other employees' pay levels. The employee tends to overestimate the pay of peers and subordinates, and underestimates the pay of superiors. So, the employee is dissatisfied with his own pay level because he perceives peers and subordinates to be making more than they actually may be and is not motivated to progress to a more responsible position because he believes the pay rewards are not sufficient for the extra effort. Also, some critics believe secrecy is a cover-up of poor administration of actual employee pay rates.

An alternative to complete pay secrecy is to publish only the pay structure which provides the employees with the minimum, midpoint, and maximum of the pay ranges. Individual pay rates would be considered privileged information. This approach affords the employee some means of comparison, and reduces the possibility of haggling over each and every pay raise.

Possibly the most important factor for the pay administrator to consider when establishing policies about pay secrecy is the employees' trust in the company. Employees who have a high degree of trust and faith in the company can more readily accept pay secrecy because they genuinely believe they are being treated equitably.

It has been said that the skill and knowledge of the pay administrator and supervisors are essential in implementing the pay program. Continued communication and cooperation among these persons must occur if the pay program is to be successful.

To help this relationship, certain pay guidelines in the form of specific policies and procedures, should be developed. Following is a checklist that covers most of the areas which need to be considered when developing a formal wage and salary administration program.

POLICY AND PROCEDURE CHECKLIST

Check those areas which are pertinent to your company.

_____ 1. Basic wage and salary policies.

2. How wages and salaries are determined:
_____   A. Job evaluation plan.
_____   B. Merit or performance rating plans.
_____   C. Rate range by classification.
_____   D. Length of service raises.
_____   E. Incentive wage policies.

3. Wage and salary differentials:
_____   A. Shift differentials.
_____   B. Working conditions differentials.
_____   C. Differentials for learners and apprentices.
_____   D. Handicapped employees.
_____   E. Group leaders.

4. Overtime pay policies:
_____   A. Employees subject to overtime pay.
_____   B. Employees exempt from overtime pay.

5. Method of payment:
_____   A. Check.
_____   B. Cash.

6. Time of payment:
_____   A. Pay period.
_____   B. Pay day.
_____   C. Pay advances.
_____   D. Employees absent on pay day.

7. Payroll deductions:
_____   A. Required by federal and state.
_____   B. Required by employer.
_____   C. Garnishments and wage attachments.
_____   D. Deductions authorized by employee.
_____   E. Employee authorization in writing for deductions.

_____ 8. Personnel forms used in administering pay policies.

WAGE AND SALARY PROGRAM ADMINISTRATION

ESTABLISHING GRADES AND RANGES

Pay Grades and Rate Ranges

1. Jobs are evaluated into a pay grade which is then related to the Company Rate Structure for the specified "dollar and cents" range.

2. An employee assigned to and proficiently performing the duties of a given job a majority of the time will normally be paid at least the minimum of the rate range, unless governed otherwise by probationary or beginner rates. Progression through the rate range is governed by the Performance Review Program. Normally, jobs classified as "Lead . . ." will be evaluated in pay grades higher than the jobs over which an individual is a Lead. Also, any individual so assigned and classified as a "Lead" should normally receive a certain minimum rate differential above those led. For specific instances, see the Wage Administrator.

3. The Wage & Salary Administrator will determine the rate of pay for "beginner" type or "trainee" type employees. The rate will then be coodinated with the Employment Manager and appropriate line supervisor.

4. Those employees with present rate of pay *above* the established Rate Range for the job to which they are classified are to be considered as having a "Red Line" rate of pay. Being at the top is not considered "Red Line." Such employees are not eligible for normal performance review increases until such time as their pay is within an established rate range and below the maximum of the range. The Wage & Salary Administrator will review any "Red Line" rates to determine appropriate action. The Supervisor should consider that employees with "Red Line" rates can be transferred to more complex and higher classified jobs.

5. If an employee requests to know his rate range, he may be told by his immediate supervisor what the rate range is for the job to which he is classified. The rate range for a classification other than that to which the employee is assigned will not be made known to the employee, except for instances in which an employee is being considered for transfer, promotion, demotion, etc.

WAGE INCREASES ABOVE ESTABLISHED
RATE RANGES

Occasionally, requests are made to establish a provision to permit the granting of wage increases above the top of established rate ranges for Hourly and Monthly jobs.

Such a provision is considered not a good practice. It would defeat the purpose of job evaluation and rate ranges. Rate ranges define the limits of worth for jobs and have been established following an evaluation to ensure equitable relationships between jobs within the company and to ensure proper rates when compared with other companies. Going a small amount above the established rate range would in effect be the same as broadening the range and after a period of time this too would be considered inadequate.

It should be re-emphasized that the minimum of the rate range is a competitive rate. To be paid more than that, an employee is expected to maintain above normal performance. Only those whose performance is exceptional should receive the top of the range. Movement through the rate range is to be based on the individual's performance and not automatic progression based on length of service.

Employees who have been at the top of their range for a considerable time should be considered for transfer or reclassification to jobs requiring greater responsibility and therefore higher pay grades. There are of course those who have reached the top and there are no other jobs to go to. However, they will normally continue to participate in general increases.

Recognition for long-term, loyal and proficient employees is most commonly accomplished by means of fringe benefits. These require long-range planning and are provided or improved at such times when it is economically feasible and when it is most beneficial to both company and employee.

PERFORMANCE EVALUATION

Supervisors and managers, as a practical matter, rate performance of their employees constantly, whether formally or informally. Decisions bearing on pay increases, promotions, layoffs, transfers, training which must be done periodically, all require the supervisor to draw on his observance of the performance of a given employee. Some decisions are routine; others must be made quickly. The supervisor must be prepared for either situation.

The formal rating implies that a written record is made by the supervisor of the subordinate's performance. This is the type most used because it is often more factual and carefully prepared. In that sense, performance evaluation is an established plan for appraising employee performance based on an objective rating of traits and goals directly tied to job responsibilities, duties, and requirements. The best method, therefore, of initiating an employee performance program involves a careful review of job descriptions for comparison of job expectations to actual performance.

Properly made, such evaluations can be of immeasurable assistance to the supervisor as he ponders such typical decisions as:

1. *How large a merit increase should be awarded to this employee?* First, a performance rating establishes whether, in fact, the employee is eligible for more pay. Secondly, while a pay increase should be awarded on the basis of such factors as increased output, improved attitude, and cost reduction, there are degrees of merit which bear on the amount of the award. The performance rating can specify this, based on actual job output.

2. *Is the employee in the right position?* Perhaps, the employee has been in a position for a number of years, but seems unable to adapt to changing job conditions—position requirements are out-pacing his or her qualifications. A carefully prepared performance review will indicate areas of performance weakness, and be instrumental in placement in a job suited to his abilities.

3. *Why is this employee becoming uneasy in her position?* She is performing well, let us assume, in most job funtions, but a performance review shows that she is experiencing difficulty in supervising those who report to her. She needs to develop her human relations skills. Through use of the job description, interviews with the employee and her subordinates, the manager can pinpoint specific performance weaknesses and note them on the performance rating form. Perhaps having her attend a class in supervisory human relations would be a partial answer.

4. *Which of these three employees should be promoted?* Again the performance review can be a useful tool. Performance rating forms of all three should be carefully scrutinized by the supervisor, and the qualifications of each compared with the job description and evaluation of the position to be filled.

5. *What can I, as his supervisor, do to increase the employee's effectiveness?* In rating his subordinate's performance, the supervisor is also testing personal ability to train, motivate, and direct the subordinate. Perhaps the reason the employee does not fully comprehend the requirement of his new position is

that the supervisor has been ineffective in training the employee during the probation period.

6. *How can the union be convinced that this shop employee should be promoted?* It is assumed, for the purposes of this discussion, that the union contract specifies that both seniority and ability are of equal value in determining which employee is promoted. Admittedly, ability is somewhat subjective and therefore open to emotional discussions between union and management. Performance ratings, carefully and objectively done, can provide factual evidence upon which the decision can be based, even under union pressures.

Review Techniques

Several techniques for the review of employee performance have evolved through research and application. One of these involves the ranking of each employee by the supervisor on the basis of the employee's overall worth to the company. The supervisor is supplied with a list of employees, by job classification. Each employee in any one classification is compared with each of the other employees in the same class and a check mark is placed opposite the name of the employee who is the better of the two. The number of check marks is then totalled for each employee in the classification: the employee getting the highest number is the highest-rated employee.

While this rating technique is undoubtedly the simplest to use and understand, it does have certain drawbacks: there is no attempt to differentiate the various elements in performance, as the rating is done on the basis of "Which is the better employee of two?"

Furthermore, ranking restricts the choice of degrees of performance. It emphasizes a "Yes" or "No" answer, whereas, comprehensive rating of employee performance requires a wider choice of degrees of achievement.

Under the forced distribution technique, the rater is asked to classify employees according to their performance so that a specified percentage of employees is assigned to a scale of distribution, i.e. lowest 10 percent, next 20 percent, middle 40 percent, next 20 percent, and highest 10 percent. This type of distribution follows the "normal curve of distribution" concept, or the so-called bell-shaped curve. In other words, the poorest performers would be placed in the lowest 10 percent, the less-than-average performers would be placed in the next 20 percent, the average employees would be classified in the middle 40 percent, and so on. When the distribution has been completed, all of the employees reporting to the supervisor would be classified. The employee distribution can be facilitated by the use of cards upon which each employee's name is written. The supervisor then places the cards in five piles, according to the employees' performance in the percentage distribution indicated.

A supervisor using the so-called *"critical incidents"* observes *the daily behavior* of employees, classifying some as *positive* and some *negative.* An example of positive behavior would be improvements in quality of work, while negative behavior might be characterized as a worker's inability to report to work on time. Such examples deemed significant by the supervisor are noted daily in a record book. At the end of the rating period, the supervisor summarizes the notes taken and rates the *overall performance* of each employee.

This type of rating technique has the advantage of keeping the supervisor alert to *significant behavior patterns* in employees. However, the data recorded by the supervisor does not yield comparisons with other department employees on standard performance bases. His rating technique is best used in combination with the *Graphic Rating Scale.*

The graphic rating scale, the technique actually the most widely used, involves the supervisor's judgment in comparing employee's performance to a standard. Various performance factors—similar to job evaluation factors—are used to aid the supervisor in rating employees. For example, in the case of an office typist, a review of the job description might indicate the use of the following performance factors: quality and quantity of work, job knowledge, cooperation, etc.

In the case of the first factor, *Quality of Work,* the supervisor is asked to rate the neatness and accuracy of the typist's work. Therefore, a series of description phrases—from *very poor* quality to *exceptional* quality—is developed as follow:

Quality of Work

Check the statement most characteristic of this employee's accuracy and neatness.

| Extremely careless.— | Not very accurate or neat.— | Work quality acceptable.— | Few errors. Usually neat.— | No errors. Neat work.— |

Similar phrases are then developed for other factors listed. It is fairly common practice to put a weighting on the rating phrases so that a total score can be summed up for an employee on all factors rated. In the above illustration, the weighting might be:

| 0. Extremely careless. | 5. Not very accurate or neat. | 10. Work quality acceptable. | 15. Few errors. Usually neat. | 20. No errors. Neat work. |

An employee doing "acceptable" quality work as rated by the supervisor would thus receive a score of 10.

The graphic rating scale has the advantage of wide usage and is easy to use. The parameters of each factor are well defined. However, it has the disadvantage of the "halo effect," i.e. some supervisors have the tendency to rate an employee's performance high on *all* factors because of excellence in one. For example, an employee's ability to do high-quality work may affect a supervisor's ability to properly rate the employee's quantity of work (which may be unacceptable). Also, many companies neglect to provide training necessary so that supervisors, in rating performance, use consistent evaluation standards. Improperly trained, one supervisor may rate an employee as acceptable; another might rate the same employee as "below average."

Frequency of Review

How often an employee's performance should be reviewed is a question that has no one or easy answer. Many organizations set the end of the job training period as the time for first review. If the training period is three months, performance of a new employee would be rated at this time to determine his mastery of the job fundamentals. Many union contracts specify a probationary period of 2–3 months for new employees before they are required to join the union. It is vital for management to correctly assess performance during an employee's probation to prevent a weak performer from winning union status.

After the probationary period, it is recommended that performances be reviewed at periodic intervals. A yearly check is typical so that management may keep a current assessment of the varying levels of their employees' output, and so that effective decisions on employee status may be made. Also periodic review assures the employee that is he is not being overlooked.

Motivation

One of the primary responsibilities of a supervisor is to motivate employees to high quality performance through counselling and coaching. This is done in several ways.

Informal daily chats with each employee—*"How is the work going?" "What do you think of the new incentive system?"* This provides the supervisor with information on employee attitudes, problem areas, etc. and enables him to relate to the employee on a more personal basis. By understanding the employee, the supervisor can help develop an effective plan to meet specific needs and motivate them toward further self-improvement.

Another motivational method is to communicate with the employee about suggestions for work improvements, grievances, or reactions to company procedures, thus involving her in procedural decisions.

It is important also that the supervisor be fair in rating the employee's performance and discussing strengths and weaknesses frankly. Equating performance with pay is one of the surest ways to motivate an employee. Denying a marginal employee a pay increase may improve his performance. The high performers, however, should receive pay increases commensurate with their worth.

Performance Interview

Most formal performance review plans in existence feature a supervisor-employee interview. This interview takes place after the rating form has been completed by the supervisor and provides the opportunity to discuss results and consequences on that all-important one-to-one basis. As a guide for the supervisor, the rating form should lead to questions pertinent to this interview:

1. What should the employee do to improve performance?
2. What can I, as a supervisor, do to help?
3. Is this employee promotable? To what job? When?
4. What are the employee's strong points? Weaknesses?

These kinds of questions raise points basic to the objectives of performance review—to improve job performance, and enable the supervisor to coach and motivate more effectively.

The attitude which the supervisor has toward the performance interview will determine its success. If the interview is used to criticize only, the end result will be a complete breakdown of communication between the two which can only lead to low morale and mutual dissatisfaction. If on the other hand, the supervisor assumes the role of interested counsellor, listening to the employee's conversation patiently and reacting constructively, the outcome will be positive and motivating.

The interview should be held in a private place away from the distractions. The supervisor opens the interview by indicating the employee's strengths, then proceeding into review of areas of weakness and determining a basis for improvement through discussion and mutual agreement.

"Case History" Approach

As pointed out previously, it is of the utmost importance that supervisors rate consistently. The best way to ensure this is through supervisory training sessions. One method that we recommend is the *"case history approach."* Each supervisor attending the session is given a blank performance review form, and a *"John Doe" sheet.* The John or Mary Doe sheet consists of a job description and characteristics of performance. The job description includes the following requirements:

1. Interpret customer order requirements from written or verbal inquiries.
2. Derive estimated costs from standard data, profits, commissions, etc.
3. Dictate quotations and proposals.
4. Communicate with customers by letter or telephone to obtain or clarify details as to specifications, materials, etc.
5. Check progress of orders to ensure delivery by the date specified.

After the supervisors have been familiarized with the review form, to be used to make the final evaluation, and the job description details, facts of the case history are explained to the group. The facts are:

1. John Doe has been a sales correspondent for the ABC Company for the past 2 years.
2. He is 32 years old, married, 6'2" tall, weighs 210 pounds, and has had some previous outside sales experience with a different company.
3. He holds a college degree in Marketing; however, the job evaluation factor on education for his position specifies 2 years of college.
4. He has a good technical mind, but needs coaching in engineering applications of his company's products.
5. He is inclined to be late for work about twice a week, though he has been warned about this by his supervisor.
6. He is hard-headed—doesn't change his mind easily.
7. He has to be goaded by his supervisor to get going, especially on detail work involved in his duties.
8. He works in spurts and has to work overtime occasionally, because his work piles up on his desk.
9. He gets along quite well with customers and company dealers; in fact, his supervisor has received good comments

from the field on John's handling of several "sticky" customer problems.

10. He makes mistakes occasionally in quotations and in correspondence with customers; therefore, his work must be more closely checked than that of other correspondents.

As each fact is given, the group is encouraged to make notes under the factor on the performance review form to which the specific fact applies. Then, using the above information, John Doe's performance is evaluated by each participant on the first five factors—*Job Knowledge, Application of Knowledge, Planning and Organization, Initiative, and Cooperation.*

The ratings made by five supervisors on John Doe might be as indicated on the following review form which shows a consistent and valid approach by all concerned in rating the performance of this individual. In the supervisor's training, the basis of each judgment should be discussed and evaluated to ensure consistent results. Study of this rating effect indicates that John Doe was misplaced as an inside sales correspondent leading to the decision to put Doe into the field as a salesman where he should perform well.

The types of performance-review procedures already discussed are generally applicable and valid for hourly-paid, clerical, and lower-level supervisory employees.

Because middle and upper management employees have broader responsibilities, and their decisions are more critical, different approaches in appraising their performance are required. One approach is *management by objectives.*

This method emphasizes indentification of *job-oriented goals* for a given budget period, the definition determined by the manager and his supervisor of *specific manager's performance goals* for the budget period. This method also provides for periodic feedback to the manager in the matter of meeting or not meeting goals.

The advantages of this review technique are the realistic bases upon which performance decisions can be made, and the subordinate's role in setting the initial goals. A disadvantage is the difficulty in evaluating causes not under the manager's control which prevent him from reaching his goal.

SETTING UP PAY CONTROLS AND RECORDS

One might well question the necessity for pay controls with the use of such tools as job descriptions, job evaluation, salary ranges, performance rating, and others described. Change, over which a company has no control, however, is the order of the day—improved technology, changes in management personnel, inflation, all have an influence on the company's pay system. Therefore, to stabilize the system, controls are required.

Pay controls should be the responsibility of one person, typically the wage and salary administrator. His or her authority would include auditing the existing pay program periodically—job descriptions, evaluation data—to ensure accuracy and pertinence. This should be done at least once a year. The administrator should also see that wage and salary surveys are used as a basis for recommending changes to management to maintain a competitive pay structure. This should also be done over a year. Ensuring that employee pay is being administered fairly across the company is the ultimate charge.

Types of Pay Controls

One method for analyzing the distribution of pay company-wide is the *"compa-ratio,"* the ratio of actual salaries in each department, or pay grade, to the grade's mid-point. An overall ratio for the company, or each department or division, or each pay grade may be computed. A ratio of 100.0 indicates that the average of actual pay ratio is identical with the midpoint. If the ratio is below 100.0, it indicates that the actual pay average is below the midpoint, while, if above 100.0, the actual pay average is above the midpoint value.

Here is an example that will serve to illustrate the compa-ratio. Let us assume the following pay rate averages and midpoints for the *XYZ Company:*

Department Name	Annual Pay Rate Average	Total of Range Midpoints	Compa-Ratio
Accounting	$ 9,625	$10,200	94.3%
Sales	11,860	10,950	108.3
Manufacturing	10,450	10.100	103.4
Personnel	8,780	8,650	101.5
Engineering	10,120	10,900	92.8
Average			100.1%

This illustration indicates that employee salaries are lower than the range midpoints in the Accounting and Engineering departments (thus a percentage of *less* than 100 is shown), but higher in the Sales, Manufacturing and Personnel departments (thus a percentage of *more* than 100). However, the all-department average is 100.1 percent, indicating a workable balance.

If the compa-ratio for one department is high, e.g., the Sales department's 108.3 percent, it may mean that some employees are receiving higher pay than is warranted, and that pay increases should be carefully checked. On the other hand, the Sales department may have some long-service employees who are top producers and therefore are earning top salaries.

In any event, the compa-ratio indicates company department pay relationships as a means of assessing internal pay equity.

Another technique organizations use is the *salary budget.* Using this technique, each department head and supervisor projects pay costs ahead for one year, usually to coincide with the company's budget year. Such factors as timing and amount of merit increases, hiring of new employees, changes in job skills, turnover due to retirements, etc. are considered in making up the budget on a monthly schedule.

This approach forces the supervisor to logically and critically plan pay decisions, and provides top management with meaningful data when preparing a profit or financial plan.

In the final analysis, employees respond positively to fair and consistent treatment in pay matters. Management has the responsibility for designing a pay program that will serve to inspire employee motivation and productivity. To accomplish this, a well-defined written pay program indicating the extent of the supervisor's authority and communicating details of the program to employees is essential. Typical statements of pay-control policies follow:

New or Transferred Employee Starting Salaries

Salary rates of newly-hired or transferred employees shall be at, or close to, the minimum of the salary range in which their position classification falls. In no case shall such salaries be set above the midpoint of the salary range.

If the employee's qualifications do not meet the minimum requirements of the position as evaluated, beginning salary may be set below the minimum of the salary range for the position, but in no case, less than 10 percent of the minimum of the range. Compensation shall be reviewed by the superior within three months, as performance warrants.

Frequency of Salary Review

Once each year, the performance of each employee will be reviewed by a superior. As a guide to this review, the Performance Review Form will be completed by the superior three (3) months prior to the salary review.

A salary increase form will be completed by the employee's superior and forwarded through channels for approval and action.

Amount of Merit Increases

The following table indicates a range of merit increases as a percent of base salary, for guidance to top management in determining the amount of an individual merit increase as related to *performance*.

Performance Evaluation	Merit Increase %
Unsatisfactory	0
Less than average, but	
could do better	3–4
Average	5–6
Above Average	7–8
Exceptional	9–10

In no case will a merit increase of *less* than 3 percent *more* than 10 percent be approved.

Cost-of-Living Adjustments

Because of continuing upward trends in the cost of living and the effect of those trends on executive pay, it is mandatory that the salary ranges be reviewed once a year and adjusted, as required.

Pay Records

One of the important responsibilities of the pay administrator is the maintenance of appropriate pay records. Such records substantiate an employee's seniority date, necessary to establish vacation, pension, and benefits eligibility. They provide scheduling for pay and performance reviews. By providing the pay administrator with data for personnel research, they are helpful to management in determining which employee to promote, transfer, or lay off. Without them, the personnel department would be unable to provide references on past employees regarding dates of employment, job title, and reason for leaving.

In establishing a pay record system, a company should study its personnel and pay record flow, simplifying it where possible, and routing it so that necessary forms reach the pay administrator's department. It is helpful to list on the forms the people or departments involved in processing the form, which should be made multi-purpose wherever possible.

A permanent pay record (*Personnel Record Card*) enables the pay administrator to keep all pertinent facts on each employee on a card on which data may be entered easily.

When, because of the size of a company, it becomes impractical to keep individual records manually, computerizing those records should be considered. The pay administrator considering computerization should determine in advance those personnel variables required. After the variables have been established, the mechanics of feeding the data to the computer, frequency of report preparation, etc., can be worked out easily.

GOVERNMENT PAY CONTROLS, REGULATIONS AND LAWS

Living with pay controls in some form is nothing new for the American people. Wage stabilization programs were instituted both in World War II and the Korean War. Limits on pay increases resulted in a slowing-up, but not stopping of the wage spiral.

Regardless of the form that wage and salary control procedures might take, a company should take steps to lessen the impact upon its compensation programs. A *formal* wage and salary program allows the most flexibility because stabilization regulations emphasize formalized pay procedures and company pay administration within broad control guidelines. A company which uses an *informal* pay program will undoubtedly have to secure, at some point in time, government approval on such routine matters as pay increases, increases in benefits, and necessary cost-of-living adjustments. Individual documentation of pay decisions can be much more costly than installation of a formal pay program.

Flexibility in Formality

A company should initiate, review and improve the following aspects of its pay program to ensure the greatest administrative flexibility, especially while controlled by pay stabilization regulations:

1. Formally organized wage and salary administration, including fringe benefits.

2. Job evaluation for *all* positions. Job descriptions which are part of the documentation should be reasonably detailed to ensure an accurate profile of the specific duties or responsibilities.

3. Formal written documentation of the wage and salary program. A Pay Administration manual should cover all con-

ceivable situations which relate to changes in pay and benefits.

4. Communication techniques that ensure employee understanding of the program.

5. Establishment and maintenance of sources of current information for wage, salary and fringe benefit changes and trends in industry, and for new and changed laws and regulations relating to these matters.

The presence of pay controls should not be the only reason for having a formalized pay program. Experience with many kinds of organizations has shown that formalized pay programs have always provided many advantages that have served their long-term goals. The important point is that a company should not allow its pay program to fall into disuse once the controls are lifted.

Government Laws and Regulations

The federal government has enacted specific laws throughout the years to protect the pay of the employee and to control the payment of wages and salaries by the employer.

The Wage-Hour Law, technically known as the *Fair Labor Standards Act,* was enacted in 1938 to cover minimum wages, hours of work, overtime, record-keeping, and specific employee groups including minors, handicapped workers, apprentices and full-time students. This law has had the greatest impact upon legislation governing wage and hour practices.

The law has undergone many revisions and the following text provides a brief outline of these changes and their impact upon employees' wages and hours of work:

1. The original Wage-Hour Law set a minimum wage of $.25 per hour. The current (1981) federal minimum wage rate is $3.35.

2. Overtime pay must be at the rate of one and one-half times that of regular pay for all hours worked after 40 hours per week and applies to every covered employee regardless of pay level. Originally, the intent of overtime pay was to reduce the overtime work at a time when spread of employment was desirable.

3. No oppressive labor may be employed in the commerce or in the production of goods for commerce or in any related enterprise. Generally, the minimum acceptable age is 16, and for hazardous work, 18 years old.

4. A good rule-of-thumb for retention of records is at least three years.

One of the most recent amendments made in 1966 has considerably reduced the number of business exemptions from this law. For example, coverage was extended to hospitals, schools and related institutions that are operated by state and local governments. In fact, Congress now has the power to extend coverage to all employees of any enterprise.

It should be noted that most state legislation on wages, hours, and child labor preceded the federal law and, in many cases, is more strict. In the case where both federal and state laws exist, good practice is to follow the stricter requirements.

CHAPTER 11

THE JOB EVALUATION PROCESS

AFTER the job evaluation plan has been thoroughly researched and approved by top management, the next step is to apply it to the group of jobs to be evaluated, represented by description and factor evaluation questionnaires as approved. See Chapter 10.

This phase can be consummated in one of three methods: the pay administrator does the job evaluation inasmuch as he or she has constructed the plan and understands the procedures involved; the pay administrator does the job evaluating with the immediate supervisor of the job being evaluated, inasmuch as the supervisor is responsible for wages and salaries of employees; or job evaluation can be done by a committee, composed of the pay administrator, the job's supervisor, and two or three members of management who know the company and its organization.

Of the three methods mentioned, the last is the preferred one because with the varying management disciplines represented, a higher degree of objectivity is secured. Moreover, the committee approach emphasizes insight into the solving of inter-departmental problems as the job study is in essence an organization analysis. Lastly, the committee members would be more apt to be "sold" on the equitable results since each would have a voice in the decisions arrived at.

EVALUATION METHODS

Job evaluation can be done in several manners. One means is for the committee to evaluate all positions in one department, usually from the top down. Another is to evaluate peer-level positions or jobs as they appear on the organization chart, e.g. foremen, engineers, skilled trades. Still another is to evaluate "bench-mark" jobs in all departments, those jobs which are common and more easily understood, such as clerk-typist, draftsman, punch-press operator, etc.

Each method has its advantages. Which one to pick will depend upon the variety and number of jobs to be evaluated, the sophistication of the evaluators and other factors. The preferred approach, in line with pay adminstration practice, is to use the "bench-mark" route. This has the advantage of training the evaluation personnel or committee in applying the evaluation plan to a variety of jobs which can be readily related to. Then attention can be given to the job hierarchy of a department with the supervisor present.

Final ratings of jobs are the result of the committee's pooled judgment. In effect, evaluation ratings are made after a thorough discussion among the committee members present. Occasionally averaging the members' ratings occurs. Generally, it is not a matter of majority rule, but of members being convinced to go along with the majority rule.

A union's participation in the job evaluation process requires different approaches, and is described in a following chapter covering union negotiations and policies.

The pay administrator keeps a record of the committee's evaluation decisions. A "score sheet" can be set up as shown:

JOB EVALUATION COMPARISON

Job Title	Dept.	Total Points	Job Grade	Evaluation Factors		
				Educ.	Exp.	Etc.

This record assists the administrator in making evaluation-factor comparisons, and keeping necessary point differentials between supervisor and subordinate positions, for example.

Validating Evaluation Results

After the committee or evaluation personnel have finished their job ratings, the pay administrator has the responsibility for comparing the job ranking and grading to insure that a high degree of validity exists. This can be done by making an interfactor comparison of all jobs in the study.

If education is an evaluation factor, list all jobs by title rated at the highest numerical degree, then list jobs falling at the next highest numerical degree, and so on. This procedure tends to highlight inconsistencies when the question is asked, "Does the maintenance machinist job require the same education as a tool and die maker?" (The answer is probably "Yes," since both typically require completed apprenticed training.)

Another procedure which the pay administrator can utilize to substantiate job ranking is the *Chart of Positions*. This chart indicates the relationships between jobs by job grade and function or department. It can be set up in this manner:

CHART OF POSITIONS
Departments

Job Grade	Accounting	Sales	Manufacturing
1	File-Clerk		
2		Clerk-Typist	Clerk-Typist
3	Steno, Jr.	Receptionist	
4	Keypunch Operator		Production Clerk
5		Sec'y-Steno	Shipping Clerk

The pay administrator, in reviewing the job ratings, should also review the job descriptions and titles to be sure that the particular job is a viable entity, capable of standing on its own legs. The tendency for some evaluation committees is not to combine similar jobs into one classification where the requirements are indeed identical. For example, if the position of junior stenographer occurs in several departments and is used as a training job for inexperienced employees, there is no reason why more than one job description is required, inasmuch as the duties and requirements are identical.

Job titles are important. They should realistically portray the extent of the major duties, and indicate the level of the position in the organization. Occasionally, organizations using informal pay systems assign honorific titles to employers, which are not in keeping with the actual duties. The pay administrator must use discretion in changing titles under these circumstances; one might identify the position by proper title on personnel and payroll records, but allow the employee to continue to use the honorific title.

Titles are very important among exempt salaried supervisors, managers, and executives. The following table is suggested for company use in establishing titles for this group:

Organizational Component	Position Title
Major functions or divisions of the company	Vice-President; General Manager; Director
Major divisions of functions; depts.	Manager; Chief Engineer
Sub-division of depts.; sections	Supervisor; Foreman

Once the pay administrator has completed the appraisal, he or she should review the job title, description, evaluation, and grading of all jobs reporting to each department head with that individual, and secure concurrence. Then the same data for all jobs studied should be reviewed with the top executive staff and president. It goes without saying that the program to be successful must have the president's blessing and endorsement.

Field-Testing Program

With the job evaluation program in actual use, the pay administrator must continually "field-test" it and apply the criterion of workability. Is the company, employee, and union satisfied with the plan? The degree of feeling can be determined through an attitude survey in which statements like the following concerning pay are found:

1. **The pay here is lower than in other companies.**
2. **I'm paid fairly compared with other employees.**
3. **My pay is enough to live on comfortably.**
4. **My boss does not talk to me about my pay or performance.**

Research studies have indicated that a high job-evaluation reliability can be secured through realistic job descriptions, improved job-rating factors, evaluator training, and reducing rating biases.

Like any management device, the evaluation program must be audited periodically by the pay administrator. This involves a review with each supervisor of the description and evaluation data, job titles, and employee assignments. Typically, this audit is performed yearly, or more frequently depending upon the tempo of organizational change.

A typical "tailor-made" job-evaluation plan, developed by a consultant for a company with manufacturing and research activities, to cover a wide range of clerical, technical, administrative, supervisory, and management positions, is described as follows:

JOB EVALUATION PLAN FOR PRODUCTION AND MAINTENANCE JOB CLASSIFICATIONS

1. KNOWLEDGE

This factor is a measure of the general level of knowledge that is required for the satisfactory performance of a particular job. Formal school attendance is not essential in acquiring this knowledge; it may be acquired through equivalent home study.

Level of Knowledge Required	Points Allotted
1st Degree— No formal education is needed beyond the ability to understand verbal instructions and to read signs.	10
2nd Degree— Requires ability to read and understand written instructions; to count; to add and subtract whole numbers; to understand simple processes and routine operation of machines. Equivalent to grammer school.	30
3rd Degree— Knowledge is necessary to understand basic manufacturing processes and their related equipment; to prepare production records; to comprehend temperature and pressure charts. Equivalent to two years of high school.	50
4th Degree— Requires knowledge necessary to perform work involving the application of chemical or physical principles to fairly complicated processes. Level of knowledge equivalent to four years of high school.	80
5th Degree— Jobs requiring knowledge to comprehend the operation of manufacturing processes involving advanced chemical or physical systems and equipment. Level of knowledge equivalent to four years of high school plus additional specialized or technical courses.	110

2. EXPERIENCE

This factor measures the amount of training and experience on the job an average employee must possess in order to perform the job duties satisfactorily.

Degree of Experience on Job Needed	Points Allotted
1st Degree— One week or less	10
2nd Degree— From one week to one month	15
3rd Degree— From one month to three months	25
4th Degree— From three months to six months	45
5th Degree— From six months to one year	75
6th Degree— Over one year, to two years	115

3. MENTAL EFFORT

This factor measures the degree of judgment and decision-making required because of the complexity of operations and the nature of problems related to the work.

Degree of Mental Effort	Points Allotted
1st Degree— Little mental effort required. Work is routine and simple in nature. Essentially a physical job.	10
2nd Degree— Repetitive work. May make minor decisions, usually of relatively little importance. Problems are few and easily solved.	25
3rd Degree— Semi-repetitive work. Decisions will have limited effect on results. Operate within clearly prescribed standard practice.	45
4th Degree— Work generally standardized involving choice of action within guidelines and procedures. Decisions will affect quality, quantity, or utility of results.	70

Degree of Mental Effort	Points Allotted
5th Degree—	105

Diversified work involving considerable concentration of thought. Requires judgment in the application of broader aspects of established practices and procedures to problems not falling clearly or concisely within accepted standards.

4. RESPONSIBILITY FOR WORK OF OTHERS

This factor is a measure of responsibility for the utilization of time, equipment, and materials by others doing similar or closely related work. It is not intended to appraise supervisory responsibility for results.

Degree of Responsibility for Work of Others	Points Allotted
1st Degree—	10

Has responsibility for instructing and maintaining flow of work of one or two helpers, or those involved in process control.

2nd Degree—	25

Regular duties involve instructing, maintaining flow of work, or setting up two to five workmen in the execution of prescribed work, or in process control.

3rd Degree—	40

Responsible for instructing, or maintaining the flow of work in a group of more than five employees, or those involved in process control.

5. RESPONSIBILITY FOR PRODUCT QUALITY

This factor is a measure of the responsibility for producing a quality product, or to prevent or minimize loss of or damage to a product in process. It evaluates the responsibility for preventing waste or loss of raw material, partially finished product, or finished product through error, carelessness, or negligence. The cost of losses may be either—

(1) Cost of damaged product less salvage value or

(2) Reduction in value of product by downgrading product.

See Table following

5. RESPONSIBILITY FOR PRODUCT QUALITY
Degree of Attention
Required

Extent of Probable Loss or Damage

	Small loss.	Fairly large loss.	Significant loss.	Sizeable loss.
	Seldom over $10	Over $10 but seldom over $100	Over $100 but seldom over $250	Over $250
1st Degree— Little attention required	5	15	25	35
2nd Degree— Part-time attention required.	15	25	35	45
3rd Degree— Ordinary attention required.	25	35	45	55
4th Degree— Special attention required.	35	45	55	65

6. RESPONSIBILITY FOR AVOIDING EQUIPMENT DAMAGE

This factor measures the responsibility for performing work without damaging machinery or other equipment used in the performance of the job. Consider the probability of loss, and the dollar value of recovering part of the loss or damage in determining the dollar value.

See Table Following Page

7. RESPONSIBILITY FOR SAFETY OF OTHERS

This factor measures the extent to which careful action by the employee is necessary to prevent injury to other persons. Carelessness in operation of machines or in handling tools, material, or other equipment often results in possible injury to other workers.

6. RESPONSIBILITY FOR AVOIDING EQUIPMENT DAMAGE

Degree of Attention
Required

Extent of Probably Loss or Damage

	Small loss.	Fairly large loss.	Significant loss.	Sizeable loss.
	Seldom over $10	Over $10 but seldom over $100	Over $100 but seldom over $250	Over $250
1st Degree— Little attention required	5	15	25	35
2nd Degree— Part-time attention required.	15	25	35	45
3rd Degree— Ordinary attention required.	25	35	45	55
4th Degree— Special attention required.	35	45	55	65

Responsibility for Safety of Others	Points Allotted
1st Degree— Little responsibility for safety of others. Job performed in isolated location.	10
2nd Degree— Reasonable care required. Accidents to others would be minor: cuts, abrasions, bruises, etc.	20
3rd Degree— Carelessness in job performance may cause lost-time injuries to others: crushed foot or hand, eye injuries, extensive burns, loss of fingers or toes.	35
4th Degree— Constant care required. Accidents to others might result in disability: loss of limbs, permanent impairment of eyesight, etc.	60

8. PHYSICAL EFFORT

This factor measures the expenditure of energy or the physical exertion required by the job and gives credit for the effort exerted in lifting, pushing, and pulling, and in work such as operating levers and valves or using hand tools. The measure of effort is reduced to terms of average weight and frequency.

Average Weight Lifted or
Equivalent Exertion   Frequency of Effort

	Low 10% or Less Time	Moderate 10%–25% of Time	High 25%–50% of Time	Sustained Over 50% of Time
1. Less than one pound	0	5	15	25
2. One to five pounds	5	15	25	35
3. Five to twenty-five pounds	15	25	35	45
4. Twenty-five to sixty pounds	25	35	45	55
5. Over sixty pounds	35	45	55	75

9. UNAVOIDABLE HAZARDS

This factor serves to recognize the hazards of each specific job and the probabilities of injury to which the worker is exposed *after* all practical safety devices are installed.

Degree of Unavoidable Hazards	Points Allotted

1st Degree—   10
Little exposure. Accident hazards almost negligible.

2nd Degree—   20
Injuries improbable, except minor cuts, abrasions, bruises, etc.

3rd Degree—   35
Job hazards could result in loss-time injuries to employee: crushed foot or hand, eye injuries, extensive burns, loss of fingers or toes.

4th Degree—   60
Constant exposure. Accident to employee might result in disability: loss of limbs, permanent impairment of eyesight, etc.

10. WORKING CONDITIONS

This factor measures the environment of physical conditions under which a job must be performed and over which the employee has no control. The intensity and severity of the elements and the continuity or frequency of exposure must be considered. Dust, dirt, heat, cold, fumes, dampness, grease, oil, noise and vibration are examples of elements which make a job less desirable.

	Elements to Which the Worker is Exposed			
	Not Disagreeable	*	**	***
1. Occasional	0	10	20	30
2. Frequent or seasonal	10	20	30	40
3. Continuous	30	40	50	70

DESCRIPTION OF FACTORS IN VARIOUS GRADES COMPLEXITY-JUDGMENT FACTOR

GRADE

1. Routine or highly repetitive work, simple in nature, in which the employee is allowed little or no choice of action.
2. Repetitive work, following clearly prescribed standard practice and involving straight forward application of readily understood rules and procedures. May make minor decisions, usually of relatively little importance and affecting efficiency of operation rather than accuracy or quality of work.
3. Work generally standardized but involving choice of action within limits defined by standard practice and instructions. Requires application of various established rules and procedures and decisions that may affect quality, accuracy or utility of results to some degree.
4. Work generally diversified. Requires judgment in the application of broader aspects of established practices and procedures to problems not falling clearly or concisely within accepted standards or precedents. Work toward assigned objectives, sometimes adapting or modifying methods and standards to meet variations in controlling conditions.
5. Work governed generally by broad instructions and objectives usually involving frequently changing conditions and problems. Requires considerable judgment to apply factual background and fundamental principles in developing approaches and techniques for the solution of problems.

*Exposed to any number of the above elements and with one present to the extent of being objectionable.
**Exposed to any number of above elements, with several present to the extent of being objectionable.
***Extremely disagreeable conditions due to intensive exposure to a number of particularly objectionable elements.

EDUCATION FACTOR

GRADE	Approx. Time Beyond Elementary School
1. Minimum requirements; read and understand simple instructions, use ordinary arithmetic, etc. Roughly equivalent to elementary school education.	None
2. Additional knowledge, on the order of understanding decimals and using arithmetic involving decimals; comprehension of simple drawings, charts or diagrams. Equivalent to partial (technical) high school education; or comparable brief shop training.	1 or 2 years
3. Training or education beyond that specified for 2nd degree, embracing such knowledge as: understanding of somewhat complicated drawings, diagrams, charts; shop arithmetic and ordinary shop mathematics, including use of handbook formulas, tables; basic principles and methods of setup and operation of several machine tools (or highly specialized knowledge of one or two types of machine tools); or broad knowledge of other types of shop operations, such as plating, heat treating, sheet metal work, foundry practice and comparable trade knowledge. Equivalent to partial high school education plus 2 or 3 years of apprenticeship or trades training; or equal to about 4 years of trades training, when high school equivalent is not required (as in some foundry jobs).	3 to 5 years
4. Training or education in a highly skilled trade, such as toolmaking, pattern making, or all around machinist, usually requiring 3 to 4 years apprenticeship or its equivalent in addition to two or more years of technical high school education (mathematics, mechanical drawing, etc.).	5 to 7 years

EXPERIENCE FACTOR

This is to be considered after the Education requirement has been determined. The Experience requirement should indicate the time required, on the average, for an individual having the specified educational background to acquire sufficient general knowledge of Company or Departmental activities and to learn the specific job.

GRADE	EXPERIENCE REQUIRED
1	Under 1 month
2	1 to 3 months
3	3 to 6 months
4	6 to 12 months
5	1 to 3 years
6	3 to 5 years
7	5 to 7 years
8	7 to 10 years
9	Over 10 years

INITIATIVE FACTOR

GRADE

1. Work under immediate supervision or completely detailed instructions. Employee is permitted little or no latitude in method of performing work and refers all questionable problems of whatever nature to supervisor.
2. Work under close supervision with frequent guidance and check, or follow standard practice in the performance of routine work, referring all questions to the supervisor that do not fall within standard practice and established procedure.
3. Work under direction and follow established practice in performing majority of duties. Make decisions when general instructions, established methods and clearly defined precedents indicate action to be taken but refer unusual problems to superiors.
4. Work under general direction and guidance, planning details of procedure and methods to attain definite objectives. Make decisions within broad limitations of standards widely accepted within the occupation or vocation.

ERRORS FACTORS*

GRADE

1. Errors would have only minor effects. Damage to equipment or spoilage of material possibly up to $5.00, never more than $10.00.

*Note: Apply 2.5 factor to above dollar values to allow for cost increases.

2. Nature of equipment used and work performed is such that normal errors may cause damage or loss of more than $10.00 but seldom if ever over $100.

3. Errors may cause losses over $100 due to use of expensive machinery, or other equipment such as special gages, testing apparatus; or because of operations of a difficult nature on unusually costly materials, or on parts of considerable value due to preceding operations. Or errors may cause appreciable delays in related or succeeding operations.

4. Errors may have serious results beyond immediate equipment damage or material waste, as when shortage of essential parts or equipment, or failure to provide correct tools when required, cause serious production delays.

CONTACTS FACTOR

1. Contacts of little importance and usually with immediate associates. Requires only ordinary courtesy to avoid friction in relationships incidental to working with others.

2. Contacts occasionally with others beyond immediate associates but generally of a routine nature. May obtain, present, or discuss data, but only as pertinent to an immediate and specific assignment. No responsibility for obtaining cooperation or approval of action or decision.

3. Contacts of some importance within the department, such as those required in coordination of effort or in supervising others on closely related work. Or frequent contacts with other departments, generally in normal course of performing duties; requires tact in discussing problems and presenting data and making recommendations but responsibility for action and decision reverts to others.

PHYSICAL DEMAND FACTOR

GRADE
1. Usual office jobs.
2. Light shop jobs, such as small bench assembly (not straight line or paced work), watchman; also some machine operations, usually on automatic or semi-automatic machines, when loading etc. is light and infrequent. Or "salary" type jobs involving considerable moving around (as foreman, dispatcher).
3. General run of machine shop operations, floor assembly, usual shop maintenance jobs.
4. Unusually heavy machine shop jobs, such as those requiring frequent loading and unloading of heavy work. Laborers, handling

material majority of time, but not excessively heavy and with intervals on work such as pushing empty hand trucks.

5. Heavy labor—almost continuous loading and unloading of freight cars; "bull gangs."

6. Exceptional.

WORKING CONDITIONS FACTOR

1. Office and comparable.

2. Best shop conditions—slightly dirty. Small, clean assembly and bench work. Or office and supervisory jobs, in shop or requiring considerable time in shop, but with little exposure to dirt, oil, heat, noise, etc. Or strain as in Draftsman-Detailer, continuous comptometer operation.

3. Average run of machine operations; assembly or bench work that is oily and greasy; otherwise clean and pleasant jobs in noisy, dusty location, or subject to fumes part of time.

4. Especially dirty, oily, noisy jobs—typical example—auto-screw machine operators in battery of machines (oil spray, noise). Platers (modern installation, with exhaust system). Polishers (properly exhausted). Usual welding jobs (arc or gas).

5. Continuous exposure to heat and fumes, or to a combination of other conditions, where continuous attention to job is possible.

6. Exceptional. Jobs of such nature that workers must be relieved frequently.

HAZARDS FACTOR

Supplement to Working Conditions Factor

This factor measures the hazards connected with the performance of the job. It is based on the probable occurrence of accident, considering that reasonable precautions have been taken and safety rules have been followed.

POINTS	GRADE	
5	a)	More than occasional exposure to injuries such as lacerations, eye injury from flying particles, serious bruise of hand or foot.
10	b)	More than occasional exposure to serious injuries such as severe burns, severe fractures causing partial disability, loss of arm or leg.

     15   c)   More than occasional exposure to accidents which may result in total disability to death.

The point value for the grade scored for existing hazards, as defined, will be added to the point scoring of working conditions factor as supplement a, b or c. If the conditions listed above do not exist in an occupation, no supplementary points will be allowed.

SUPERVISION FACTOR

GRADE

1. Direct one to five assistants or helpers, with responsibility for correct completion of assignments but generally working along with those supervised.
2. Leader of a group, usually more than five in number, seldom over 10 or 12. Assign and check work, assist and instruct as required, but perform same work as those supervised or closely related work, most of the time. Strictly supervisory and administrative duties generally occupy no more than 25% to 35% of time.
3. Supervisor or leader of a group, usually about 10 to 25 in number, but possibly smaller if on difficult technical work requiring considerable direction and assistance. Plan, direct and coordinate work, make decisions, and perform personally the more difficult aspects of the same broad assignment. Supervisory and administrative duties generally require more than 50% of time.

HOURLY JOB EVALUATION PLAN

If an employee or the Union finds a job scoring inaccurate, or there has been a change in a job's requirements totaling twenty or more points, then either the employee or the Union may, within six months of the establishment of such job or of such change, submit a grievance thereon. If the re-evaluation of the changed job does in fact result in a twenty or more point change in scoring, the job will be rescored and the employee's rate adjusted effective from the date of the grievance. If the re-evaluation of the changed job results in less than a twenty point change in scoring, then neither the job scoring nor the rate of the employee will be changed. No such grievances shall be considered timely if filed more than six months after the establishment of the job requirements or the change in the job requirements.

If the Company finds there has been a change in the job's requirements then it may rewrite and rescore such a job's requirements. The employee or the Union would have the right to submit a grievance thereon. If it is finally determined that the change in the job had in fact resulted in a change in scoring, the job scoring would be corrected, and the incumbent employee's or employees' rate would be red circled.

Wage Administration and Job Evaluation

A sound Wage Administration program has as its objective the payment of fair and equitable wages to all employees. The most effective procedure for attaining this objective is to install and maintain a job classification system based upon job evaluation.

The Job Evaluation plan that we have adopted is of the general category of factor analysis and comparison. It is based upon the premise that there are certain job elements or factors that exist in some measure as requirements of all jobs. Training, experience and physical effort required on a job are among the common job characteristics that have been considered by foremen and other supervisors for many years; for it will be noted that the majority of executive and supervisory personnel have always had to "evaluate" jobs in order to determine rates of pay. However, each has done this in his own way, with no formal method usually, and a resulting lack of consistency in the relative values of jobs of different types.

The method described uses eight factors for the evaluation of any job of whatsoever nature, with an additional factor of "Supervision" when the job requires supervision of others.

The prime necessity and very core of the Evaluation method is the careful analysis of the job and an adequate job description in substantially clear terms. This job description is used as the basis for determining the scoring.

Our first factor, which we call "Complexity—Judgment," is especially difficult to define in general terms, but we may say in part that the scoring is dependent upon the number and difficulty of the job elements that require original thought in deciding what to do, as well as skill in performance.

The factor "Education" refers to the preliminary training necessary to prepare an individual for learning the job and does not always need to be formal schooling, but the specific and general knowledge requisite to the learning of the job is more readily expressed in terms of formal education.

The "Experience" factor indicates the time that must be spent on the work under consideration, on similar work wherein the same principles come into play, or related work that tends to build up a body of knowledge essential to the proper performance of the job.

"Initiative" is the fourth of our factors, and is a measure of what the job demands in terms of ability to proceed alone and unguided and to make decisions in the course of performing an assignment. It takes into account the frequency and immediacy of the supervision normally received, as well as the impersonal guidance supplied by standard practice, precedent, or written instructions.

We use two factors that may be called "Responsibility" factors, namely, "Errors" and "Contacts." These factors take into consideration the probable results of normal errors in terms of losses to the Company; and the responsibility for effective handling of any personal contacts that are essential for adequate performance of the job.

The "Supervision" factor has only minor application in shop jobs, as we are not here discussing those jobs that are primarily supervisory in nature. However, a job that requires working at times with one or more helpers will be scored at the minimum value for this factor.

When a job has been described and scored, use of point scoring is warranted by the fact that the entire method is dependent to some extent on the judgment of the evaluator. In practical terms we are saying in effect that his judgment is not accurate enough to bring out differences in the relative values of jobs within a cent or two. Rather we prefer to attempt through careful analysis and review to place a job in a general grouping or in other words, in a job level.

Job Evaluation determines relative values only. The next step is to set up a wage scale using a minimum and maximum rate for a particular plant as determined by "going" rates in the community or industry insofar as such rates can be determined. The preferred wage scale will show a rate range for each job level rather than a single rate.

This method forms the basis for a sound administrative and control of wage rates and are, we believe, superior to the unsupported opinions of supervisors and executives in determining the worth of jobs to the company.

JOB EVALUATION PLAN

(Office Positions)

FACTORS

A. Training and Experience

(1) Practical Experience

(2) Formal Education or Equivalent

B. Application

(1) Special Knowledge

(2) Analytical and Other Special Skills

C. Responsibility	E. Working Conditions
(1) For Supervision	(1) Mental Demands
(2) For Dependability and Accuracy	(2) Physical Demands
(3) For Initiative and Achievement	(3) General Surroundings
D. Contacts	F. Physical Skills

Points by Factor Degree

Factors	Degree 1st	2nd	3rd	4th	5th	6th	7th	8th
Experience	5	10	15	30	45	60	75	90
Education	10	20	40	55	80			
Special Knowledge	10	20	30	40	50	60	70	80
Special Skills	10	20	30	40	50	60	70	
Supervision:								
Quantitative:	10	20	30	40				
Qualitative:	1	1.5	2	2.5				
Accuracy	10	20	30	40	50			
Initiative	15	30	45	60	75	90	105	
Contacts	10	20	30	40	60	80	100	
Mental Demands	3	6	9	12	15			
Physical Demands	3	6	9	12	15			
General Surroundings	3	6	9	12	15			
Physical Skills	10	20	30	40				

A. *Training and Experience*

This factor gives recognition to the total time normally required for an individual to acquire the necessary specialized knowledge needed for fully satisfactory performance of the job. Consideration is given to the time required for training, acquired through experience on other jobs, learning time on the job.

1. *Practical Experience*

Degree		Points
1	Less than 3 months practical experience	5
2	Three to 6 months practical experience	10
3	Six to 12 months practical experience	15
4	One to 3 years practical experience	30
5	Three to 5 years practical experience	45
6	Five to 7 years practical experience	60
7	Seven to 10 years practical experience	75
8	Over 10 years practical experience	90

OFFICE ADMINISTRATION HANDBOOK

2. *Formal Education or Equivalent*

Degree		Points
1	Formal educational equivalent to high school graduate.	10
2	Formal education equivalent to 2 years college or business school.	20
3	Formal education equivalent to BS degree.	40
4	Formal education equivalent to MS degree.	55
5	Formal education equivalent to Ph.D. degree.	80

B. *Application*

1. *Special Knowledge*

This factor measures the scope and requirements of a job as regards the application of knowledge needed for satisfactory performance. Consideration is given to the special problems, procedures, products, and operations of the company. Performance of the duties of the job requires ability to:

Degree		Points
1	Apply and understand written or oral instruction. Use simple arithmetic and post, check, or file accurately. Operate simple office machines, such as simple calculators or adding machines.	10
2	Operate more complicated office machines such as typewriters, calculating, bookkeeping, and tabulating machines. Perform simple manufacturing or laboratory operations or routine office functions. Some charting or computing.	20
3	Apply elementary principles of a science which can normally be gained through high school or 1 or 2 years of college. Understand basic office methods and/or ledger processes and develop simple procedures according to general instructions. Understand and apply principles of electronic word processing equipment. Use of shorthand in addition to Degree 2. Some use of chemical formulas. Translations.	30

Degree		Points
4	Apply a thorough working knowledge of plant operations, business procedures or laboratory processes. Understand basic formulas and engineering drawings, advanced shop mathematics, industrial laws and regulation; cost, distribution, and accounting practices. Use practical knowledge of a science, such as chemistry, or a technical subject. Idiomatic usage of two or more foreign languages.	40
5	Apply complex principles of a general technical subject, such as chemical engineering or chemistry, industrial engineering, or cost and general accounting.	50
6	Function as a specialist in a technical or professional field such as chemistry, industrial relations, sales, data processing, computer programming or general accounting.	60
7	Apply original and independent action in complex technical or professional fields. Assist in formulation of policies.	70
8	Formulate and be responsible for policies and administration in a complex technical or professional field.	80

2. Analytical and Other Special Skills

This factor measures the requirements of a job as regards the ability, ingenuity, and special mental skills needed to perform the job.

The factor gives consideration to requirements for skills, such as analytical ability, ability to recognize errors, creative ability as in writing or devising better ways of doing things, and the ability to evaluate trends and anticipate difficulties.

Degree		Points
1	Routine repetitive work offering little or no alternative method, such as filing, posting, and routine clerical work. Not much reasoning required but ability to solve simple problems or recognize and correct errors in routine work.	10

Degree		Points
2	Simple analysis of figures, copy typing test or data from which a logical answer can be readily ascertained. Methods and routine to be followed are largely predetermined. Copy typing or dictation typing with word processing equipment.	20
3	Ability to analyze figures or data often varied in nature in order to arrive at a logical solution to a problem such as material control or production scheduling. Ability to analyze new situations in a limited and familiar field, such as computer programming, direct selling, and direct supervision of simple or well-organized functions.	30
4	Ability to evaluate complex figures, results, trends, or data varied in nature, and to reach sound conclusions. Use of independent judgment is needed in gathering diversified data. Creative ability, imagination and originality in a field such as sales promotion, public relations, or advertising.	40
5	Frequent use of independent judgment in analyzing and appraising figures, results, trends, or data of a specialized and/or technical nature. Analysis and evaluation of considerable scope representing coordination of a major section, laboratory, or department. Outstanding creative ability, imagination, and originality.	50
6	Continual appraisal and analysis of figures, results, trends, and data of all types and wide scope pertaining to Company policy or a number of major departments. Ability to solve unusual or exceptionally complex manufacturing, technical, business problems of production, sales, or accounting.	60
7	Top management or administration.	70

C. *Responsibility for*

1. *Supervision*

This factor measures the requirements of a job as to acceptance of responsibility for the organization, selections, leadership, and the guidance or direction of others. Consideration is given to the accountability for results as measured in terms of costs, methods, and determination of policies. Supervision is to be evaluated in two parts; *quantitative* or number of people supervised and *qualitative* or amount of supervisory authority exercised. Point totals for supervisory responsibility are the product of the two factors. Supervision must include responsibility for selecting, training and disciplining.

Quantitative

Degree		Points
1	Direct supervision of a few, such as 2–6, or 1 in case of work or function responsibility of assistant.	10
2	Direct supervision of a number, such 7–25 or direct supervision of few plus indirect supervision of larger number.	20
3	General supervision of a production or staff department through a few subordinates.	30
4	General supervision of one or more production or staff departments through a number of subordinates.	40

Qualitative

Factor		Multiply by Factor of
1	Assignment of routine work and minor responsibilities for selecting, training, and disciplining subordinates. Work direction.	1
2	Assignment of work and responsibility for selecting, training, disciplining, and recommending rewards for subordinates in relatively routine work.	1.5
3	Assignment of work and full responsibility for selecting, training, disciplining, recommending rewards for subordinates in directing complex or highly technical activities, subject only to general policy or budget limits.	2
4	Full responsibility for policy and budget limits.	2.5

2. *Dependability and Accuracy*

This factor of responsibility measures the integrity and discretion, accuracy, and thoroughness required in performing the task or for safeguarding confidential data. Also, the opportunity the work offers for errors and the probable effort of errors. Consideration is given the degree to which the work is checked or verified and the probable frequency and the direct or indirect loss to the Company for unreliable performance.

Degree		Points
1	Little or no confidential data involved. Possibility of error is negligible and errors can easily and quickly be detected.	10
2	Occasionally works with confidential data but result of disclosure would be insignificant. Probable errors would be detected in succeeding operations involving some trouble in backchecking but only slight loss.	20
3	Regularly works with confidential data which, if disclosed, would have an adverse internal effect. Most of work not checked or verified and loss through errors may cause delay of productions, waste of materials or damage to equipment, or loss of prestige.	30
4	Regularly works with confidential data of major importance which, if disclosed, may be detrimental to Company's interest. Considerable accuracy and dependability required. Errors would be difficult to detect and may involve substantial loss.	40
5	Responsibility for Company assets.	50

3. *Initiative and Achievement*

This factor measures the amount of supervision received on the job and self-reliance, adaptability, independent action, and aggressiveness required to anticipate and provide for changing conditions, over-coming obstacles, and completing the job. It measures the extent to which responsibility is final for conceiving plans, initiating projects through to completion.

Degree		Points
1	Perform routine and simple tasks under direct supervision, which require few decisions and a minimum amount of independent action.	15
2	Perform repetitive operations covered by detailed instructions or standardized proce-	30

Degree		Points
	dures. Work is checked by others but some independent action is needed in making minor decisions within limits of established routine.	
3	Under changing conditions perform diversified but semi-repetitive operations covered by standardized procedures. Some independent action and more than average perseverance is required.	45
4	Under general supervision, perform a series of operations in a well-defined field where changing conditions require independent action. Sets precedent.	60
5	Solve complex problems in an established field under frequently changing conditions where supervision received consists of assignment of the problem and discussion of its nature.	75
6	Originate new ideas and act independently in an established field under continually changing conditions. Work is performed under general over-all administration.	90
7	Provide general over-all administration and formulate Company policies.	70

D. *Contacts*

This factor measures the tact, cooperation, persuasiveness, skill in presenting facts, and ability to inspire confidence required in dealing with or influencing other persons either within or outside the Company. In rating this factor, consideration is given the frequency and importance of associations with others and their possible effect on Company operations, employee, customer, and public relations.

Degree		Points
1	Routine contacts with co-workers and superiors for exchange of information and for instruction, not involving "sale" of ideas, but generation of mutual respect and general cooperation.	10
2	Adaptability to meet changing conditions including some contact within and outside of Company. Part-time telephone relief.	20

Degree		Points
3	Obtain specific cooperation or willing work from personnel directly supervised and those from whom work is received, or to whom it is delivered in normal operations. Adjust minor grievances. In case of telephone operators or receptionists, can include frequent contact with customers and public.	30
4	Maintain satisfactory relations with other departments or with customers in routine matters, which may include collaboration in executing established policies, discussion of ways to reach agreed-upon objectives, securing compliance with approved procedures, but not putting across new or highly controversial programs. Direct selling at junior level. Presentation of data, reports, and participation with other technologists in seminars and as members of technical committees and associations.	40
5	Administration at department or division levels which may involve frequent presentation of new methods or programs to improve traditional practices or to meet changing conditions or settle controversial issues. Direct selling at intermediate level. Selling of technical ideas through teaching or to technical societies. Direct representative of Company as a technical expert.	60
6	Administration of advertising, personnel relations or public relations at executive level. Top management. Development of effective teamwork and smooth operation. Direct selling of highest level.	80
7	Administration of sales programs at executive level.	100

E. *Working Conditions*

1. *Mental Demands*

This factor gives recognition to the mental alertness and nervous energy required as measured by the intensity and continuity of application rather than the complexity of the work.

Degree		Points
1	Minimum of mental concentration on largely repetitive operations where routine is closely defined and continuity frequently interrupted.	3
2	Light mental concentration on largely repetitive operations where continuity is only occasionally interrupted.	6
3	Normal mental concentration on largely variable operations for short periods, or moderate mental concentration on largely repetitive operations for long periods.	9
4	Considerable mental concentration on variable operations for long periods.	12
5	Close mental concentration on highly variable operations for long periods.	15

2. *Physical Demands*

This factor measures the physical effort required and the fatigue due to the intensity and continuity of the work. Consideration should be given also to manual dexterity, coordination, and working conditions.

Degree		Points
1	Light tasks requiring a minimum of tiring physical effort. Performance of work provides intermittent sitting, standing and walking.	3
2	Light physical effort required in working with lighweight materials and supplies. Occasional operation of office machines or equipment resulting in some fatigue.	6
3	Almost constant or repetitive work of a mechanical or machine nature. Almost continuous sitting or walking. Occasionally difficult working position. Small amount of lifting and carrying.	9
4	Sustained physical effort required in working with average or lightweight materials and supplies with continuity of effort. Continuous sitting or walking. Continuous operation of office machines or equipment resulting in considerable fatigue.	12

Degree		Points
5	Continuous standing or working in difficult positions. Working with average or heavy-weight materials and supplies.	15

3. *General Surroundings* (miscellaneous unfavorable job conditions)

General surroundings and prevailing circumstances, including consideration of relative noise, light, ventilation, health and accident hazards, inside and outside work, and requirements for travel.

Degree		Points
1	Good conditions and no disagreeable elements or factors.	3
2	Good conditions with minor features which disturb the physical or mental well-being of the employee, such as disagreeable appearance of work place, necessarily poor ventilation, uneven temperature, or slight possibility of damage to clothing. About one-quarter time spent in travel.	6
3	A periodical disagreeable element or combination of factors, such as heat, cold, dampness, fumes, noise, vibration, and intermittent schedule deadlines. Infrequent exposure to less serious lost-time accidents. About one-half of time spent in travel.	9
4	A disagreeable element or factor which is continuous, such as heat, cold, dampness, fumes, noise, or vibration. Occasional exposure to lost-time accidents.	12
5	More than one disagreeable element or factor which is continuous. Chance of bodily injury relatively great.	15

F. *Physical Skills*

This factor measures the degree of physical development or proficiency required in the position. Consideration is also given to the need for special skills of the senses, such as taste or smell.

Degree		Points
1	Ability to operate simple office machines or simple laboratory equipment. Demonstration of the use of products.	10

Degree		Points
2	Ability to operate with proficiency one or more office machines, such as electric typewriters, calculators, micrographic equipment or adding machines.	20
3	More highly developed skill of a specialized nature, such as expert stenography or expert operation of more complex machines.	30
4	Ability to render expert opinion on basis of highly developed skills.	40

POINT FACTOR SCHEDULE

Clerical Group

Factors	Skill	1st Degree	2nd Degree	3rd Degree	4th Degree	5th Degree
1.	Education	14	28	42	56	
2.	Experience	22	44	66	88	110
3.	Initiative & Ingenuity	14	28	42	56	
4.	Contacts with Others	14	28	42	56	
	RESPONSIBILITY					
5.	Supervision Received	10	20	35	50	
6.	Latitude & Depth	20	40	70	100	
7.	Work of Others	5	10	15	20	
8.	Trust Imposed	10	20	35	50	70
9.	Performance	7	14	21	28	35
	OTHER					
10.	Work Environment	10	25	45		
11.	Mental or Visual Demand	10	20	35		
12.	Physical Effort	28				

1. EDUCATION

Education is the basic *prerequisite* knowledge that is essential to satisfactorily perform the job. This knowledge may have been acquired through formal schooling such as grammer school, high school, college, night school, correspondence courses, company education programs, or through equivalent experience in allied fields. Analyze the minimum *requirements of the job and not the formal education of individuals performing it.*

1st Degree

> Requires knowledge usually equivalent to a two year high school education. Requires ability to read, write, and follow simple written or oral instructions, use simple arithmetic processes involving counting, adding, subtracting, dividing and multiplying whole numbers. May require basic typing ability.

2nd Degree

> Requires knowledge equivalent to a four year high school education in order to perform work requiring advanced arithmetic processes involving adding, subtracting, dividing, and multiplying of decimals and fractions; maintain or prepare routine correspondence, records, and reports. May require knowledge of advanced typing and/or basic knowledge of shorthand, bookkeeping, drafting, etc.

3rd Degree

> Requires knowledge equivalent to four year high school education plus some specialized knowledge in a particular field such as advanced stenographic, secretarial or business training, elementary accounting or a general knowledge of blueprint reading or enineering practices.

4th Degree

> Requires knowledge equivalent to two years of college education in order to understand and perform work requiring general engineering or accounting theory. Must be able to originate and compile statistics and interpretive reports, and prepare correspondence of a difficult or technical nature.

2. EXPERIENCE

Experience appraises the length of time usually or typically required by an individual, with the specified education or trade knowledge, to learn or perform the work effectively. Do not include apprenticeship or trades training, which have been rated under Education. Include under Experience only the *time required to attain production standards.*

1st Degree

Up to three months.

2nd Degree

Over three months and up to one year.

3rd Degree

Over one year and up to three years.

4th Degree

Over three years and up to five years.

5th Degree

Over five years.

3. INITIATIVE AND INGENUITY

Initiative and ingenuity appraise the independent action, exercise of judgment, the making of decisions or the amount of planning which the job requires. This factor also appraises the degree of *complexity* of work.

1st Degree

Requires the ability to understand and follow simple instructions and the use of simple equipment involving few decisions, since the work is outlined in detail for the employee.

2nd Degree

Requires the ability to work from detailed or semidetailed instructions and the making of minor decisions involving the use of some judgment.

3rd Degree

Requires the ability to plan and perform a sequence of operations where standard or recognized operation methods are available, and the making of general decisions as to quality, operation and set-ups sequence.

4th Degree

Requires the ability to plan and perform unusual and difficult work where only general operation methods are available and the making of decisions involving the use of considerable ingenuity, initiative and judgment.

4. CONTACTS WITH OTHERS

Contacts with others is the extent to which the job requires cooperation and tact in meeting, dealing with or influencing people, whether by telephone, correspondence or personal contact. Consider the *frequency and importance of* contacts, the fact required to maintain harmony and efficiency within the Company and goodwill of the general public.

1st Degree

> Contacts usually limited to persons in the same section or department.

2nd Degree

> Contacts with persons outside the department or outside the Company, *furnishing or obtaining routine information only*.

3rd Degree

> Contacts with other departments or other companies, furnishing or obtaining information or reports, *under conditions requiring the use of tact to obtain cooperation and maintain goodwill.*

4th Degree

> Contacts with other departments or other companies involving carrying out company policy and programs and the influencing of others, where improper handling will affect operating results; or contacts involving dealing with persons of substantially higher rank on matters requiring explanation, discussion and obtaining approvals.

5. SUPERVISION RECEIVED

This factor appraises the degree to which the immediate superior or prescribed procedures outline the methods to be followed or the results to be attained, and the degree to which the immediate superior checks the progress of the work or handles exceptional cases. Consider the *proximity, extent and closeness* of both kinds of supervision in rating this factor.

1st Degree

> Under immediate supervision with short assignments of work at frequent intervals and a regular check of performance, or work usually repetitive and routine, well covered by instructions, requiring but minor initiative, within limits of routine.

2nd Degree

> Under general supervision, work may be variable but precedents usually have been established and standard practice enables the employee to proceed alone on routine work, referring questionable cases to the supervisor.

3rd Degree

> Under direction where a definite objective is set up, the employee plans and arranges his own work in the performance of a sequence of operations and in a specific field where precedents are accessible for application to changing conditions and only unusual cases are referred to the supervisor.

4th Degree

> Under general direction, working independently in an established field, setting up procedures when necessary, but working from policies and general objectives. Rarely refers specific cases to superiors unless interpretation of company policy is involved.

6. LATITUDE & DEPTH OF RESPONSIBILITY

This factor appraises the degree to which the job allows the incumbent to develop and *perform beyond the point of usual production standards*. Consider the extent to which creativity may be exercised, and additional responsibilities assumed as the incumbent progresses in skill and knowledge.

1st Degree

> Allows little or no development beyond the upper limits of production expected in this job except for further attainment of speed, precision, or skill in performing the duties of the job.

2nd Degree

> Allows *minor* latitude, depending upon the individual incumbent, to exercise creativity or assume additional responsibilities over and above the upper limits of production standards expected in the job.

3rd Degree

> Allows sufficient latitude in creativity or assuming additional responsibilities so that the performance of the incumbent can be evaluated in terms of possible future management candidacy.

4th Degree

> Allows considerable latitude in creativity, judgment, and assuming increasing responsibilities beyond the basic requirements of the job. The nature of the job is such that the performance of the incumbent can readily be appraised in terms of management candidacy as the next step in his progress.

7. RESPONSIBILITY FOR WORK OF OTHERS

This factor appraises the responsibility which goes with the job for assisting, instructing or directing the work of others. It is not intended to appraise supervisory responsibility for results.

1st Degree

> Responsible only for own work.

2nd Degree

> Responsible for instructing and directing one or two helpers 50% or more of the time.

3rd Degree

> Responsible for instructing, directing or setting up for a small group of employees, usually in the same occupation, up to 10 persons.

4th Degree

> Responsible for instructing, directing and maintaining the flow of work in a group of employees up to 25 persons.

8. RESPONSIBILITY FOR TRUST IMPOSED

This factor appraises the extent to which the job requires responsibility for safeguarding confidential information and the effect of such disclosure on the Company's relations with employees, customers or competitors.

1st Degree

> Negligible. Little or no confidential data involved.

2nd Degree

> Some access to confidential information but where responsibility is limited or where the full import is not apparent.

3rd Degree

> Occasional access to confidential information where the full import is apparent and where disclosure may have an adverse effect on the Company's external or internal affairs.

4th Degree

> Regularly works with and has access to confidential data which if disclosed could seriously affect the Company's internal or external affairs or undermine its competitive position.

5th Degree

> Full and complete access to reports, policies, records and plans of Company-wide programs, including financial cost and engineering data. Requires the utmost discretion and integrity to safeguard the Company's interests.

9. RESPONSIBILITY FOR PERFORMANCE

Responsibility for performance is the degree of accuracy, thoroughness and reliability required in the performance of the job. Consider the probability of errors and the degree of resulting damage which could normally be expected.

1st Degree

> Work is routine and errors can be quickly checked and would result only in minor confusion or clerical expense for correction.

2nd Degree

> Probable errors usually detected in succeeding operations and generally confined to a single department or phase of company activities. Correction involves some trouble in back checking by others.

3rd Degree

> Work requiring accuracy of performance and reliability. Errors may result in loss or hold up of production, waste of material, damage to equipment or monetary losses of a related nature. Effect is usually confined within the Company.

4th Degree

> Work requiring a high degree of accuracy and responsibility. Probable errors are difficult to detect and may seriously affect costs, planning or production.

5th Degree

> Work of major importance in which there is considerable opportunity for making errors of serious consequence, resulting in substantial losses to the Company, either in costs or damage to property or in public or customer relations.

10. WORK ENVIRONMENT

This factor appraises the physical surroundings and the degree to which noise is present at the work location. Consider the extent of distraction and commotion caused by the sounds.

1st Degree

> Normal office conditions. Noise limited to the usual sounds of typewriters and other equipment.

2nd Degree

> More than average noise due to the intermittent operation by several employees of adding machines, typewriters, printers, bursters or copiers.

3rd Degree

> Considerable noise generated by constant machine operation such as is present in the Data Processing section.

11. MENTAL OR VISUAL DEMAND

This factor appraises the degree of mental or visual concentration required. Consider the alertness and attention necessary, the length of the cycle, the *coordination of manual dexterity* with mental or visual attention. Consider, also, the *tediousness of the principal duties* on this job.

1st Degree

> Varied duties. Job not tedious. No special manual dexterity required.

2nd Degree

> Job partially repetitious and tedious. Frequent mental or visual attention or concentration. More than average dexterity required.

3rd Degree

> Constant mental or visual attention. Job very tedious or repetitious.

12. PHYSICAL EFFORT

Consider the requirement for physical work such as regularly lifting or moving materials and supplies, continual driving, and other similar activities not normally associated with general office work. Also consider the requirement for standing while working, such as is necessary in certain office machine operation. (One Degree Only)

CONDUCTING A WAGE AND SALARY SURVEY

After the evaluation of jobs has been completed, the company should apply dollar values to the worth of each job. The wage and salary survey is conducted in order to determine the cost of maintaining a work force that is competitive with companies in its industry and in the community.

The approach usually taken is to conduct a wage or salary survey of the company's industry and area of operation using "benchmark" jobs—those similar enough in content to allow intercompany comparisons. In making a survey of this type, it is very important that comparisons be made by careful consideration of job responsibilities, not on job title alone.

The job evaluation plan provides the data necessary to make bench-mark comparisons. The job descriptions define the specific responsibilities for each job and the job title of the superior. Supportive factor evaluation data provide other pertinent information such as education and experience required to do the job, the number and kind of individuals supervised, if any, reporting relationships, and internal and external contacts.

Many jobs share common responsibilities with jobs in other companies within the same industry and in the vicinity. However, not all jobs can be used in the survey data comparison. In every company, there are jobs which are unique. Such an example can be found in a small manufacturing company where one job has responsibility for general accounting, office services, personnel, data processing and systems, purchasing, customer service, and materials control.

Use only bench-mark jobs for the survey. Do not attempt to make comparisons using the unique jobs. The latter will easily slot into the salary structure because they are related numerically to the bench-mark jobs through the job evaluation plan.

The bench-mark jobs selected should cover the range of jobs to be evaluated. There is no magical formula in determining the number of jobs. A large sample does not mean excellent results if careful, accurate bench-mark comparisons are not made. It is best to rely on a smaller sample which uses an accurate, methodical approach. A carefully selected sample will yield data as reliable as that gathered from a large sample.

In determining which companies should be requested to participate in the survey, three factors should be considered. One is that they should be comparable in size. Two, they should have similar product lines or operations, if possible. Three, they should be in the same area, or at least, recruiting in the same area.

In surveying hourly rates of pay, it is best to analyze these rates on a localized or metropolitan basis because they tend to be determined in this manner. An exception to this approach is where a company is unionized and whose rates could be at variance with those of other companies. In the case of salaried and managerial pay surveys, however, care must be taken to determine the impact of industry and national trends. Management salaries above the level of $20,000 a year, for example, tend to follow national trends. However, there are wide variations in management salaries from one industry to another. The cosmetics industry may pay as much as 25–35% higher than the heavy equipment industry in comparable sales executive positions.

The Survey Format

Careful consideration of the survey questionnaire information to be collected is essential in securing workable results. The following list indicates those points generally considered as important general information:

Company Name (or code number)
Geographical Location
Size by Sales Volume
Corporate versus Division
Product Line(s)
Number of Employees

Supplemental information can be obtained at very little additional time and expense. These data could include distinction of pay and benefits between hourly and salaried employees, the type of position evaluation plan used, the type of wage incentives and bonus plans used, starting rates, and rate-increase policy.

The Questionnaire

The questionnaire should include an organization chart which shows the reporting relationships and responsibility levels of the jobs being surveyed. For each job, a description of its responsibilities and space for describing any variations should be included. Space should be provided for multiple entries of base pay, incentive earnings and other bonus payments if there is more than one employee in the job. Additional information may be requested to get better understanding of the breadth of the position. For example, the following data requested may be included on the form for *Personnel Supervisor:* the number of employees supervised, the position title of the superior, the number of labor unions (if any) and the number of bargaining units. Data for a *Purchasing Agent* may include the number of employees supervised and the value of the annual purchases made by the Agent.

The design of the survey form should stress a simple format, easy-to-understand instructions, easy-to-answer questions, and should have ample space to report information.

Collecting Data

The collection of the survey data can be done in one of two ways: by personal interview or by mail questionnaire. The personal interview gives a company more assurance that the survey data are completely comparable. Discussion of the bench-mark jobs in person can quickly resolve many questions the participant may have about the comparisons. However, this involves considerable time and expense. The mail questionnaire is a more economical approach, but can yield less accurate results because each respondent's interpretative ability must be relied upon. When this approach is used, clarity of format and instructions is essential.

Regardless of the approach used, an introductory letter should be sent to the participants indicating that their data will not be identified and that they will receive a copy of the survey results.

Available Surveys

It is not always possible to conduct a "do it yourself" survey. If that is the case, there are many reputable wage and salary surveys available. Employees' associations, chambers of commerce, trade associations, consulting organizations, and others make such surveys on a periodic basis. Interpreting these survey data should follow the same basic guidelines as set for conducting an independent survey. Descriptions of responsibilities, the industry, the size of the company, and other supplemental data should be carefully analyed.

As mentioned earlier, the geographical locale does affect pay level. Historically, the South has had a lower cost-of-living than elsewhere in the United States, and Boston is one of the highest cost-of-living areas. Experience indicates that pay differentials still exist, although not as much for the managerial positions as for lower-level positions.

The Consumer Price Index published by the Bureau of Labor Statistics (BLS) of the U.S. Department of Labor provides data showing intra-city cost fluctuations. It is a misconception that this Index can be used for inter-city comparisons. In short, it is strictly for cost fluctuations within a specific city only. A "market basket" of 400 items is priced in 56 cities in the United States. These data are used to calculate the individual city indexes which show how much prices have changed from time to time within each city.

One means of determining a city's level of cost-of-living in comparison to other cities is by the use of a study done by the U.S. Department of Labor's Bureau of Labor Statistics. Another approach that can be used to determine inter-city pay differentials is either BLS wage data or similar multi-city surveys. The important thing to remember is to assure accurate identification and use of the bench-mark jobs.

The primary use of the wage and salary survey is to determine what the market place is paying people with similar jobs, but the survey does not tell why those companies are paying that way. Pay administration policy decisions can only come from within. The survey does have other uses which include validation of the current pay structure, the relative importance of evaluation or incentive plans, and provides a basis for controlling pay. The time interval between surveys is based upon several factors. Annual surveys would be appropriate when a stable economy and working force exist. High labor turnover and unstable economic conditions call for more frequent surveys. Other factors affecting the survey frequency are the quality and time spent in data collection and analysis, the willingness of companies to participate, and management's belief in their usefulness.

Reporting Results

The final report should present the appropriate statistical data in a concise format. A glossary of terms should be included to define the statistical terms. For example, the list following presents those terms frequently used in pay survey reports.

Mean Average	the arithmetic mean—the total sum of the salaries or bonuses reported, divided by the total number of salaries or bonuses reported.
Median Average	value in salary or bonus scale for any one position below which one-half or 50% of the values fall. Thus, if individual salaries are $12,000, $13,000, *$16,000,* $19,000, $20,000 the median or middle figure is $16,000.
High	highest salary or bonus reported for any position.
Low	lowest salary or bonus reported for any position.
Bonus	the figure includes only additional compensation above base salary for the year reported. It does not include deferred compensation such as profit sharing, pension or stock option plans.
Total Average	the weighted average of total base and bonus payments for a position.
Total Median	the median of total base and bonus payments for a position.

The time period during which the data was accumulated and the method of accumulation whether by mail or personal interview should always be included in the report.

"SYNERGETIC JOB EVALUATION"

The Personnel Department of COPCO PAPERS, INC. employed what it called a Synergetic Job Evaluation, performed with each salaried employee, within a reasonable amount of time after his or her first year of employment. The interview is conducted whenever practical *by the employee's supervisor once removed.* Employees hired prior to the inception of this evaluation format are considered new hires for the purpose of applying this policy.

Repeat interviews ongoing are at the option of the Division Manager or by request of the employee. Repeat interviews should be considered a must if supervisors have changed within the past two years or no interview has been conducted within the past four years.

The response to each item on the form must be agreed upon by the interviewer and the employee. The collective response will require considerable discussion about many of the items before the parties are confident the question and response are understood and can agree. Should the parties not be able to agree, the immediate supervisor will be consulted to help determine the correct response.

Those items on the form that call for ratings on a satisfactory scale will be indicated as satisfactory unless specific instances can be recalled that would indicate otherwise.

Individual responsibilities are determined by the employee prior to the interview. The response should reflect the employee's understanding of the job, and not copied from meaningless job descriptions. The section for rating performance of general responsibilities of the employee, supervisor, and interviewer/administrative committee generally result in a "yes" or "no" response. This "yes" or "no" must be synergetically interpreted to the AA, S, or NI rating.

It is believed that the interview with a supervisor once removed, will polarize the confidence of the employee that management is interested in him, and should enhance communications. This approach also educates the interviewer by bringing him in direct contact with employees responsible for making the programs, that he implemented, work.

The responsibility for scheduling the interview rests with the Division Manager.

CHAPTER 12

MERIT RATING/INCENTIVES
AND PERFORMANCE REVIEW

OFFICE managers, perhaps more than most executives, are on their toes when it comes to saving time and money in their departments. They are constantly on the lookout for better ways of doing the work of the office. As a result, office management in America is far ahead of any other country in the world today. Perhaps the very fact that office management is so receptive to new systems and techniques is one reason for the amazing innovations which are constantly being made to simplify the paperwork of business.

Deadwood on the Payroll: In periods of good business, when overloads are heavy, employees are taken on to speed the work through the office. Then the load lightens, and, unless there is rigid control and alert supervision, these employees sometimes remain on the payroll. The excuse is that trained employees should be "stockpiled." Then again there is the very human desire of some supervisors to be "empire builders." Business executives are natural optimists, and the temptation to hang on to trained men after they are no longer needed is very great. At any rate, the net effect is that without some method of control, payrolls tend to become top-heavy and office organizations are cluttered with employees who have acquired a sort of vested interest in their jobs and have become fixtures in the department.

The installation of a merit-rating system, and the periodical audits of employee efficiency which it requires, is one way to guard against deadwood on the payroll. But something more may be needed. One way is to set up a methods-improvement committee. The assignment of this committee is to find better ways of doing things in the office. Nearly every company has a different name for these committees and the name is not important, but the job is extremely essential if a company is to grow.

One particular committee was composed of executives who had proper authority to reach decisions on the majority of all ideas submitted. The meetings were at the policy level and the participants worked sincerely and persistently. Vague and misty ideas were quickly dismissed, or the proponents told to present the ideas in logical, written form with cost estimates.

One of the by-products of the work of such a committee is to evaluate the worth of the employees of the business. It soon discovers which departments are overstaffed, which employees are "piling bricks," and which supervisors are dying on the vine. Its duties go beyond simple job analysis, important though that is, for by studying the responsibilities of each supervisor and the employees, the committee is in a position to make recommendations to top management.

Whether the responsibility for administrative efficiency rests with a committee, with a continuing department, or with the office manager, it is important to analyze periodically the work being done by each employee. Such analysis differs from the so-called "job" analysis which concerns itself with who does what, whereas work analysis is concerned with most efficient use of an employee's time. It affords a basis for establishing reasonable standards for clerical production, and locating inefficient operations as well as work overloads.

One manufacturing firm has a department known as the "Office Methods and Equipment Division," which makes continuous studies to determine ways of reducing administrative costs in the office. Employees are required to fill out a form daily for six days stating just what they do with their time during that period.

A company spokesman told a Dartnell editor:

"With this data available we determine the loading of each employee in the given department or unit. The mass of data from the analysis forms is broken down into appropriate and useful classifications. These various subdivisions are studied; tentative production norms are established and variations from these norms are investigated.

"Actually, when we begin these studies we don't know what we will find; it is important to begin with an open mind and no preconceived ideas of what methods a department should use.

"The 'work analysis sheet' plays an important role in our study of the data accumulated on the analysis form. It is on this that the variations I referred to earlier show up. By this time, the analysts of the methods department have become extremely familiar with the operations and procedures of the department being studied. They have a good idea of the time needed for many or all of the department's operations. They may suggest revisions based on their knowledge of motion-economy techniques.

"Studies of one department lead into other departments. Recently an analyst investigated a department and found that its employees did not know why they were receiving a copy of a certain operating form from the billing department; each day they had to file away a large pile which, once stored, was never referred to. The analyst went to the originating department, told its supervisor about the unwelcome and unnecessary copies, and the latter had the procedure immediately changed to eliminate this waste of time and paper.

"When the survey and the study and investigation of its findings have been completed—it can be easily seen that the time required will vary considerably from survey to survey—the analysts write a joint report with only the essential ideas in it. This report is given to the supervisor who originally requested the survey. It is divided into two general sections:

1. **Corrections which have been made.**

2. **Corrections which should be made.**

"This second section does not necessarily consist of recommendations of the analysts which have been turned down. In many cases, the time is not appropriate to make the corrections—a more appropriate time-frequently occurring when we make changes in models.

"The supervisor now has a fairly definite idea of departmental assignments and the standard time required to do each of these. In setting standard times, our only aim is to try to find out what constitutes a reasonable day's work by employees. We pay very well, require applicants for office positions to pass job-sample tests (55 words per minute for typists is a typical preemployment requirement), and expect our employees to do their share. A further example of this liberal policy is that if the hourly standard is 100, the daily standard is not 800, though we have an 8-hour day, but 700. We make allowances for rest periods, and personal time.

"Surveys reveal from time to time that changes should be made in the general administration of the department as well as individual job procedures. If, for example, a worker frequently lists 'waiting for work' on the analysis form, it is obvious that some correction should be made.

"Upgrading is based on job performance and employees are moved to a higher classification when they are able to do the work required. This is an important reason why our departmental and section supervisors keep records of individual production. We have encountered a little resistance on this score, but when we demonstrate that no sound and accurate estimate of manpower requirements—upon which are based requisitions for additional employees—are possible without such records, we never have had any further trouble."

This situation exists in many offices: Somebody gets an idea for a "system." At the time it seems like a good idea. But as time goes on, one of two things usually happens: The system is not kept up and soon becomes useless, or the need for the system diminishes as conditions change. In either case, whatever is being spent to maintain the system is largely wasted, and the flow of work through the office is slowed down. If the equipment used with the system requires floor space, a further loss is incurred. This cost may be considerable.

A periodical check of the use made of office records, systems, and procedures should be made by the controller. Such a check should determine the approximate time spent annually to maintain the system, the cost of materials used over a year's time, the rent of the office space, and a fair charge for supervision and other overhead expenses. Against that expense a computation should be made of the probable savings or other benefits resulting from the use of the system, as compared with doing the work in some other way or not doing it at all. Audits of this sort put the finger on systems which have not been properly maintained, and on which a considerable amount of work must be done to make them fully effective. Mailing lists are a good example of this. Purchasing agents seem to have a fondness for setting up systems and then failing to keep them up, due to clerical shortages in the department.

Top management sometimes takes a notion that it needs certain kinds of information upon which to make decisions. Then conditions change, and that sort of information is not as important as it was. But the system to furnish the information is still maintained. The controller, not having been informed that the information will no longer be required, continues to keep up the system just in case the front office should call for it.

The Average Letter Cost: In order to determine the cost of completing the average letter of a certain type during a certain month, the following unit costs are added: Payroll cost of operation performed (dictator's time), plus stenographic costs for the particular type of letter, plus variable costs per letter, (paper, postage, etc), plus percentage of fixed-time productive payroll cost.

In addition to these records, general ledger accounts are, of course, maintained. The accounting statements show the cost items arranged according to fixed and variables, similar to the generally used statement.

The first step in cost-control procedure must always be to predetermine or budget what is to be accomplished. Usually budgeting is based on the accounting statements for previous years, with possibly some additional information as to anticipated volume obtained from customer departments. It should be obvious that the more detailed the data gathered for budget purposes, the more accurate the resulting estimates. This means that budgeting necessarily is a synthetic process when a series of factual breakdowns are available. Estimates based on the available data should be made, and from them the desired final budgets computed.

Work Measurement Techniques

Research in the field of office work measurement indicates that the five most widely used work measurement techniques applied in establishing clerical work standards are historical data, work sampling, time study, motion pictures and predetermined times. *Robert E. Nolan,* an industrial engineering consultant, presents a very concise account of each of these five techniques in his article entitled *"Various Methods of Measuring Office Activities."*

"*Historical Data:* This is one of the easiest and most commonly used methods: The analyst simply takes what has been produced by a clerical group in the past and uses this as a means of gauging how the group performs in the future. For example, suppose the billing department consists of three people—each working eight hours a day. This means that the billing function apparently requires 24 hours per day. If this group turns out 100 invoices per day, we could state that each of the invoices apparently required .24 hours or 14.4 minutes to process. This is called measurement based on past history. Now to review what happens under varying degrees of work volume.

"If the billing department turns out 120 invoices per day with the same three employees, we could say that the department was 120 percent efficient. On the other hand, if they turned out only 80 invoices with the same three employees, we could say they were only 80 percent efficient. The supervisor could justify the need for a fourth employee if the volume were to stay at 120 invoices per day, since it is unreasonable to expect employees to perform better than 100 percent.

"What's wrong with the historical data method of work measurement? First, we do not know under what conditions the 100 invoices were originally prepared. We do not know if the method of invoicing is up-to-date and efficient. We do not know how well the three employees performed when they processed 100 invoices per day.

"Historical data, therefore, affords some degree of control but certainly is not precise. Its biggest flaw is that it shows you what you did rather than what you should have done. Historical data could be your first step to control clerical costs. It should not be your last.

"*Work Sampling:* This technique, also known as ratio delay, is merely a statistical method of determining what is occurring in a clerical area and what percent of the time it is occurring. It is accomplished by taking random samples or reading and recording what is going on at various times throughout the day. For example, if we make a thousand random observations in a clerical area and find that 700 instances showed people actually working, 100 showed the person observed idle, 100 showed the person to be observed was not present at the work place, and 100 showed the person observed talking to the supervisor we could say that 70 percent of the time this clerical group was working, 10 percent of the time they were idle, 10 percent of their time they were away from their work station (probably at the rest room or coffee machine), and 10 percent of the time they were discussing problems with the supervisor. From this information we could arrive at a time per unit of work processed.

"What's wrong with work sampling or ratio delay? Suppose a speaker wanted to take a ratio delay study of the people in an audience. He might say that part of them were working because they were taking notes and part were working because they appeared to be listening. But some of the audience might have been bored and not listening at all. By assuming what the individual is doing, you may assume wrong, and this is a serious fault of work sampling.

"Work sampling is no longer true work sampling when you define everything you are sampling, including how fast the work is being done. Applied this way, work sampling may be more expensive than other techniques. To be sure, work sampling has a place in office and clerical measurement. It is a helpful method of determining which areas of an office should be studied, what allowances are needed, and the frequencies of certain items such as telephone calls, trips to other departments.

"*Timestudy:* This method is probably the oldest approach to work measurement. It gives an accurate time for performing a job provided the study is rated correctly. The big objection to time study is that it involves rating the person performing the operation, and making a time study requires visible stopwatch observation of the person being timed. Office personnel look down on it since they connect it with factory work. Time study, however, can give just as good results as any other approach to office work measurement. The only thing it lacks is detailed description of what actually is done by the person being studied. This also can be included with good time study, but may cost more than when it is done by other techniques. Time study requires many observations to get accurate times for establishing clerical measurement.

"*Motion Pictures:* This technique makes use of a motion picture camera and micromotion analysis. Motion picture study is very costly and time consuming, but it does furnish a good description of the method being performed and a great deal of detail concerning the operation. Taking movies in the office may be very objectionable, and may cause morale problems. If you want to use this technique, be sure to prepare the employees at least a day or so ahead of time. It is not recommended to use this method of clerical work measurement. It's too costly unless you can apply the data to many offices throughout your company.

"*Predetermined Times:* The so-called 'canned' data, or predetermined times, are a catalog of clerical work elements that can be, depending on the technique, applied to approximately 95% of office work. In this approach you obtain all of your information for measuring clerical work through discussions with office supervisors and employees. During these discussions you learn what people do, how they do it, and what is done with the work once they have completed it. You have a detailed description of the methods and the work produced.

"From predetermined times you cannot only develop a time for the way it is presently being done, but you can analyze it and, many times, improve the methods used. This type of clerical measurement serves two purposes. It gives you a time for performing an operation and the basis for improving the method."

Following a thorough review of the various methods used in measuring clerical work the next step is to choose the method(s) which could be most readily applied to your own office operations. The table on the following page gives a capsule account of the positive and negative characteristics of the five clerical work measurement techniques discussed earlier as presented by Nolan.

HOW TO APPLY INCENTIVES

An initial step in investigating the application of incentives for office use would be to examine the job descriptions of clerical employees in the various departments of the company to determine if there exists a homogeneous group of four or more people. There should be a continuous supply of work and the duties should be of a repetitive and routine nature, with procedures in governing the employee's duties set by definite rules. The rate of production should be under the control of the person assigned to the specific job, and finally, the supervisor of the groups being considered for the incentive program should be receptive to the idea of incentives.

Subsequent to determining whether or not a company, department or given set of employees fit the five guidelines noted above, company executives must decide whether to follow the path of *individual* employee incentives or *group* incentives.

In focusing on a more scientific approach to office management, whether the direction be toward an individual or group incentive program, the first step is to clearly define the goals intended by conducting a clerical work measurement and incentive study. Once these targets have been established, a comprehensive study of existing clerical work measurement plans must be made.

If the company has no qualified employee with experience and skills in clerical incentives, consideration should be given to hiring a specialist with professional clerical measurement experience or contracting with a professional management consultant. The professional would assist in the fact gathering and analysis processes necessary for establishing the work measurement and clerical incentive program best suited for your own company.

Management Support

As in the plant, prior to initiating a search for a mutually acceptable clerical incentive program, it is necessary to engage the *full*

PROS AND CONS OF THE FIVE CLERICAL WORK-MEASUREMENT TECHNIQUES

TECHNIQUES	PRO	CON	COMMENT
Historical Data	Gives some degree of control.	Imprecise.	A good first step.
Work Sampling	Helpful in pinpointing best areas for detailed study.	Involves dangerous assumptions regarding "work."	Fine for determining allowances and frequencies.
Time Study	Actually measures work.	Requires subjective rating and use of hated stop watch. Factory overtones. Usually omits method description.	Useful in spot-checking standards developed by other methods. Essential for process or machine times.
Motion Pictures	Provides detailed, easily understood description and record of method.	Costly and time-consuming. "On camera" problems.	Valuable as a teaching aid for new employees.
Predetermined Times	Fast. Easy to apply. Eliminates feeling of being studied.	Danger of misapplication because of apparent simplicity.	Best applied in streamlined form rather than basic pre-determined time data.

support of the company's top management staff. Once this has been accomplished, the next step is to discuss with the clerical employees to be affected by the incentive program, as well as their supervisors, exactly what the company executives have planned. A guarantee must be made against a standards increase unless there is an equipment change or change in operations methods. It is also important to assure the employees considered for the incentive program that they will be paid a basic salary during nonincentive work hours.

Offering Incentives

Here is how a large mail order firm developed and implemented office incentives. The first area was "Control of Office Operations."

Control of office operations, just as for other types of operations, requires the manipulation of personnel, methods, and equipment so as to achieve the best results at the lowest, comparative cost. The purpose of management control, of course, is to produce the best profit at any level of operations. Most of us will agree that the objectives of any business are:

1. To produce a profit for the stockholders.
2. To give good service to our customers.
3. To maintain the best possible employee relations.

And you could put these in any order you desire. But isn't it true that when we achieve the optimum level for each of these objectives, that we also produce the best possible profit?

Controlling operations of any kind, and that includes office operations, requires the use of "tools" to provide the means for good control. The controls we use are:

1. An incentive plan for controlling wage payments based on productive output.
2. Time studies and the setting of time standards for each job.
3. The accurate reporting of production units (signout control).
4. Job descriptions, job evaluations, and the determination of proper wages or rate grades for each job.
5. Operating audits as a follow-up on the proper use of rate grades, standards, signouts, and the calculation of each worker's efficiency.
6. Man hour controls for establishing budgets.
7. Budgets for payroll and expense control at various levels of operations, and follow-up to see that these budgets are attained.
8. Quality control by inspection and the statistical sampling of work.

There is an interrelationship of these controls which produced that condition which we believe is a controlled operation. Profit performance, over a number of years, indicates that we have achieved that condition.

There are two other old-fashioned basics which are needed for the control of office operations: good supervision and constant follow-up. They are just as important today in the jet age, as they were years ago.

Wage Control

The mail order company has used an incentive plan for wage payment in office operations since 1926. This plan has undergone some changes since that time, but with variations has effectively lowered costs and improved control over our operations since then. Prior to 1926, the firm used a unit method of cost control. However, these unit costs were based on records of past performance—not established by work measurement methods. As a result there existed a great possibility for wide variations in costs between departments, and these could not be detected. The cost of similar jobs in different departments varied greatly, and the managers explained these as being due to differences in handling. To some extent this may have been true, but to what extent? The greatest danger in this type of control is that bad performance can be perpetuated.

Recognizing the fact that it did not have the means for effective control, management decided to do something about it. A firm of consulting engineers was called in to survey needs in 1926. This was necessary because the company had no qualified staff to undertake a task of that kind at that time. Not only was a control plan needed, but it was also very important that an effective selling job be made to managerial and supervisory staffs. It was felt that a management consulting firm was best qualified to do that job. The full backing of top management was behind the survey.

The consultants selected a plan and tailored it to fit the company's needs after a thorough investivation and a series of meetings with management. Along with it was a recommendation that each operation be studied, and that production standards be established.

The selling of the plan to the managerial staff was even more difficult than anticipated because the first studies indicated that most jobs were being performed *at 30 percent to 50 percent efficiency*. Many managers, who were convinced that their employees were producing at a high rate of efficiency, were skeptical of these results. They couldn't be convinced that their people could possibly produce more than twice their regular output. Some agreed to the plan in full belief that the engineers were wrong, and that the plan would eventually be thrown out. They also felt that the "Speed-Up" plan would cause an abnormally high error ratio.

It's not possible to cover all of the problems of installing a wage control plan. However, one experience in the Mail Opening Department should be interesting. This department handled all incoming mail and performed the following operations:

- Opening and sorting mail.
- Abstracting cash and jacketing orders.
- Listing cash on NCR machines and banking the cash.
- Reading and classifying the orders.

Four employees in this department were rated as top producers by their manager. Under the merit rating system then in effect they were the highest paid employees in the department, and were considered to be the backbone of the department by the supervisor and manager. The studies showed them to be producing at 31% efficiency.

This brought an immediate reaction from the department manager—the standards must be wrong—it was impossible to increase their production from this so-called 31% to the goal of 100%. ("What you're expecting is an increase from 100% to 300% in efficiency.")

In spite of these objections the plan was installed in the Mail Opening Department. Within two months some surprising results were evident. Production began to increase while costs were reduced. Further, the four operators who were rated so highly by the manager were proven to actually be the poorest producers in the department. (They just looked busier than others.) *Production doubled by the end of six months and no further selling of the plan was necessary.* The manager also found that, contrary to what he had feared before the plan was put in, errors were reduced. Everyone was convinced of the value of the plan and management accelerated the installation in all departments. Two years were required to complete the installation. Results were the same in each department—*substantial increases in production, with corresponding reduction in costs.* The plan was installed in all order clerical departments; in the order handling and merchandise handling departments; and in the Billing, Shipping, Adjustment, and Credit Departments.

It is easy to see why efficiencies of only *40% to 50%* are achieved on operations which are not placed on standard by work measurement. The methods review which takes place before the operation is timed produces work improvement and the standardization of similar jobs in different departments. Managers insist on setting standards on any job where work can be measured. It is also felt that work of higher quality is produced by people who operate at higher efficiencies. (*They develop good work habits which produces work of higher quality.*)

What Are the Benefits?

First, there is an accurate measure of production (and cost) instead of work units dependent on a manager's judgment or guess.

Second, the budgeting and forecasting of payrolls and unit costs is far more accurate, and the requirements for departmental performance are more realistic. Budgets follow the trend of increased productivity instead of poor past performance.

Third, the company now has a control of production costs that can be used with accuracy. Production records are kept on a daily basis and all work performed is recorded on each individual's "time and production record." The plan therefore gives employees an opportunity to increase their earnings for any extra effort they put forth. Signouts, or a constant number of units of work are assigned to each individual to maintain an even flow of work through all activities. These units are recorded in regular 10- or 20-minute intervals so that the productivity of each individual is maintained, and so that this productivity can be checked by the supervisor at any time of the day. The need for further training of individuals is quickly determined and corrective action taken. Those people who are not suited to a particular job, and who cannot improve efficiency to increase their earnings, are transferred to other jobs or dismissed. A weekly production efficiency report shows individual and departmental efficiency.

Productivity increased from 31% efficiency to a high of 97% efficiency in the first 10 years after the plan was installed, and payroll costs decreased in proportion. About 73% of all jobs, including 83% of all office clerical jobs, are "on incentives." Excluded are secretaries, receptionists, accounting and advertising personnel, merchandisers, and executives.

This has been a historical review to tell you why a company started a wage control plan, and it indicated some of the benefits gained. It is important to describe the "tools" for control and explain how they are used.

Incentive Payment Plan

A wage control plan which involves a system for work measurement requires some form of incentive payment in order to realize the full benefits of the plan. The benefits of a plan must work two ways to be effective: for the employees, and for the company. Management reduces operating costs by establishing good procedures and controls; but at the same time the employees must have the opportunity to increase their earnings when they exert extra effort and increase their efficiency.

The Incentive Plan the company installed in 1926 was a modified version of the Emerson Plan—a plan where bonus increments are paid for increases in efficiency, and based on percentages of their base earnings. The bonus payment was an amount added to their regular earnings (hours worked times their hourly base rate). Efficiency was calculated by dividing *standard minutes* for work produced by *actual minutes* worked.

The plan started bonus payments at 60% efficiency, with a graduated scale of payments up to 20% of their base earnings at 100% efficiency. During World War II, the starting point for bonus payment was dropped to the 40% level—at which point a bonus of 2½% of the base rate was paid. The rate of payment was then scaled up to a payment of 25% at 100% efficiency. Over the 100% level, payments were made at an additional 1/2% for each 1% increase in efficiency. The theory behind lowering the starting point was that the new employee would have a chance for bonus earnings at an earlier time and would therefore be encouraged to reach a higher and more satisfactory efficiency much sooner.

Although the plan worked effectively for many years, it was difficult for some employees, especially the new hires, to understand and to calculate their bonus earnings. During contract negotiations with a union, for example, a request was made for some new simplified plan for bonus payment. A new plan, called a *"Performance Rating Plan"* which is a version of the *"Standard Hour"* plan was developed. Like its predecessor plans, the Performance Rating Plan was *established under standards of work measurement then in effect.* Earnings were calculated as the product of hours worked times a rate level based on production efficiency. The efficiency was determined by dividing *standard minutes* produced (units X standard) by the *actual minutes* on standard. The hourly rate increased as the level of efficiency increased. When an employee increases production to a new performance level, and can hold that level for three consecutive weeks, the hourly rate is increased to a higher rate level. By the same measurement, an employee who reduces production for three consecutive weeks will be reduced to a lower rate level. A change in either direction must be maintained for three consecutive weeks before a change in rate is made. When the upward direction is maintained for three weeks the new hourly Performance Rate is based on the lowest efficiency of the three weeks. When the downward direction is maintained for three weeks the new hourly Performance Rate is based on the highest efficiency of the three weeks. With a steadily rising efficiency, or a steadily lowering efficiency, it is possible for an employee to have his hourly rate changed each week.

Thirty rate grades were established with the PR Plan, and all jobs are classified by rate grade—based on job evaluation.

Objections have often been raised against the use of work measurement and incentive plans for office work. Most common is the claim that these plans work for factory jobs, but that they will not work in office operations where the flow of work is different; or that the type of help used for office operations will not tolerate the supposed driving methods used with a work measurement plan. But if you really give this some thought you must admit that this is not true. While it is possible that some types of office work may not be measured with the same degree of accuracy as factory jobs, you can establish satisfactory standards that will produce a good workable plan. Regarding the second objection that the office help will not work with a plan, the company can vouch that this has not been true. It has received no objections from employees once the plan was understood, and it is the responsibility of the supervisory and managerial staff to make sure that it is understood.

To work properly it is necessary that practical goals or standards be set. That means that the standards must be fair and possible to attain—neither tight nor loose. *It is important that the job be measurable,* for there are some which are not. Finally, there must be a sufficient volume on any particular operation to make it practical to establish and apply a standard.

What about the responsibilities for maintaining a work measurement and incentive plan? You will notice that the plural is used for responsibility. It is the responsibility of the entire management group to maintain a plan. This includes management at all levels, starting with the supervisor of an activity. In too many companies the responsibility for maintaining a plan is fixed entirely in the industrial engineering department. This results in a large engineering staff with high fixed payroll costs, but which cannot give the same results as when the responsibility is shared by all levels of management. There must however be a final or overall responsibility, and in this case this was given to the methods and standards section. They are the "watch dogs" of the plan. They set up good work procedures, establish standards for each operation, provide managers and supervisors with job specifications and controls to perform their job satisfactorily, approve changes in the rate when these are to be made, and finally make periodic audits to provide a check on all the controls established.

The activity supervisor is probably the key in the maintenance of the plan. He is in constant and direct contact with the workers of a unit—the first step in the management level. It is his job to sell the plan to people and to achieve acceptance of the standards that have been established. To do this, the supervisor must be sold on the soundness of the plan. He must be able to explain the method by which the standards have been set, and how the rate levels are set at the different levels of efficiency. Further, he must followup to see that workers follow the procedures established for any job. Any variations that either add to or take away from the established time allowance must be reported to the time study group so that corrected standards and work procedures can be set. He must also see that the reporting of production is accurate and that standards are not being misused. Finally, he must make certain that people are shifted to other jobs or activities when insufficient work is available for his people. If he fails in this, the possiblity for increased earnings for the employees, and for the savings in cost available to management, will not materialize.

The assistant section manager is the first executive level of management. Her job is one of overall supervision of all the activities in the section. She must work constantly with her supervisors to sell, train, and followup to see that all jobs are being performed as established. She uses the same controls as are available to the supervisor. She keeps the lines of communication working in both directions—workers and management. Most important of all she must keep in daily contact with all supervisors to review the production in each activity, to review costs, and to listen and offer guidance in the solutions of any problems which might arise in connection with the plan.

Establishing Standards

When the plan was first put into effect, there was, of course, a mass study of all operations by the consulting firm in order to establish the standards needed for the plan. Thereafter new or revised standards were also set by time study in order to keep the system updated.

Briefly, what is a time study? It is a method whereby each element of a given operation is subjected to a thorough analysis in order to determine the quickest and best way to perform each step; to standardize equipment, methods, and working conditions; and finally to determine by accurate measurement the amount of time required for an average person to do the job. Please note that the actual measurement of the time value came last.

The study begins with a thorough analysis of the job, methods used, conditions, equipment, and anything else that might effect the final standard. Factors such as amount of inspection required, the materials used, and work layouts are all considered in order to discover any means for improvement. Standardization of these factors helps in the application and administration of the final standard. Motion study is required in the analysis of the job so that the number of motions can be reduced, if possible, and that only those which are best suited will be retained. The proper sequence of these motions is also important.

After the job has been properly analyzed, it is further subdivided into "elements." These elements are recorded in their proper sequence and the operation is timed with a stop watch in order to obtain an accurate reading for each element. A sufficient number of readings is taken for each element so that a time value can be determined for each, and a total time arrived at for the whole operation. After this the engineer "levels" the operation. This requires a considerable amount of judgment on the part of the engineer, and is a somewhat controversial point with those who are opposed to work measurement plans. It is a process by which the engineer evaluates the performance of the operator for the factors of skill, effort, and consistency, which in his judgment he felt the operator indicated at the time of the study. The leveling process is an equalizing factor and results in a standard which is attainable by the average operator. The total of all these steps is a standard for an operation that will not only give the best method for doing the job, but also provide an accurate time value to be used in measuring output.

A time study starts with a request received from a section manager. The request indicates the job or operation to be studied and the reason for requesting the study. Thereafter an engineer is assigned to the study and performs the various steps already indicated.

After this has been completed the company issues a "top sheet," which is a Standard Time Allowance Record for that operation. This sheet identifies the section and activity, the operation, the sequence of the elements performed—as set up by the engineer, the rating of the operator, the code number for identifying the operation, and the final standard. Three copies are made of this top sheet—one for the standards section file, another for the department, and a third copy is sent to the union. The union involved maintains a complete file of these top sheets.

Finally, the necessary information for the approved standard is added to a "Standard Time Allowance List" which is prepared for each activity of a section. This is the authorized list of standards which is to be used by the activity when reporting the employees' production. The list identifies the department, activity, each standard by code number and description, the unit of work, the time standard, and the date when established.

Control of Wage Rates

The company keeps an accurate record of the units of work produced in all operating activities. These units are recorded on Individual Production and Time Records which are called "signout" sheets. The entire operation is operated on a 10-minute schedule, that is, a complete turnover of orders is processed in shipping activity each 10-minute period. Work is signed out in all activities, including order clerical, in 10-minute periods in order to keep an orderly flow of work. The signout sheet shows name, activity, department, and has spaces for listing signouts for each period. It also identifies by standard code and standard time the units of work produced. On this sheet is recorded all activity for the individual for the entire day. The signout function is performed by a signout clerk in each activity. (Time card are used to record actual hours for each individual—which is used for payroll purposes.)

On the following workday the signout sheets are processed by record clerks who report to the section manager in each operating section. The record clerk totals the number of units of work for each standard code and posts that total, by standard, to a Weekly Production and Time Record. The two pass periods per day are entered at at standard time of 10 minutes each. On this sheet the company can accumulate all actual and standard hours for the week so that the individual's efficiency can be calculated.

(PE, for past efficiency, indicates that the worker is paid at his or her established rate level for unavoidable idle time, or for work performed which is not on standard. This must be authorized by the manager and is reviewed by the methods section to avoid payment when not warranted.)

The weekly efficiency is posted to the worker's performance record card. This is a three year record of the individual's weekly efficiency performance. The record clerk also notates these performance cards whenever a new base efficiency or level has been established—and which requires a rate change. (The three consecutive week formula for changing rates was previously mentioned.) If rate change is to be made, the individual's salary card is notated with the new rate, it is initialed by the manager, and the salary card and performance card is sent to the I.R. Section for review and approval. All Weekly Production and Time Records are sent to Methods for a sampling review. The salary cards and performance record cards *are not* sent to I.R. if no rate change is to be made.

The I.R. Section reviews the salary and performance record cards and initials approval on the salary card, which is sent to payroll for authority to make the rate change to the individual's master salary card. This new rate is used for the next payroll week. The performance record card is returned to the operating section. (The Weekly Production and Time Records kept in I.E. and the time card are also forwarded to payroll and stored in their personnel archives where they are available for periodic audits by Methods or by the Auditing Department.)

All of this covers the mechanics for controlling wage rates and incentive earnings, based on the work measurement plan.

APPLICATION OF JOB ENRICHMENT

Job enrichment, or enlargement, is a fairly recent concept based on the personal satisfaction an employee needs to increase his motivation. These needs are centered in the work itself. *Dr. Frederick Herzberg,* of Ohio State University, is the leading exponent of this theory. He identifies achievement, recognition, work interest, responsibility and advancement as prime motivators that should be incorporated into the work. These five motivators will be discussed in the light of what wage and salary administration can do to maximize their effectiveness.

The job description should be structured to emphasize functions which the worker can perform in the broadest sense possible. For example, some firms encourage employees to plan and set their daily production, perform necessary operations, and inspect the product. The emphasis is on responsibility; as the employee becomes more involved, his work becomes more interesting and challenging.

The pay structure, competively set, emphasizes meaningful motivating pay increases which the employee earns and doesn't have to ask for. A job hierarchy is established which serves as a ladder for the promotable. Job evaluation data provide necessary information on educational and experience requirements which the trainee must master. Advancement is stressed.

Pay policies are communicated to all employees so that each knows where he stands. Pay responsibilities are spelled out for each supervisor, so that consistency and control are maintained.

The performance ratings on each employee should emphasize goal-setting by supervisor and subordinate so that the achievement motivator is enhanced. Feedback is furnished the employee as help in achieving the goals. The supervisor becomes the motivating coach, responding to the employee's needs.

DEVELOPING AN EFFECTIVE PERFORMANCE REVIEW PROGRAM

Like the weather—everyone talks about performance review but few do anything about it. To be sure, many companies have developed (and use) performance review forms and interviews on a regular basis. The concept has moved from the production and clerical areas to the management and sales areas in rapid order. But on the whole, too many firms tend to let review procedures slip, especially in the *exempt* or *salaried* personnel area.

A review of individual employee performance is necessary if an employee is to progress according to a stated company plan. A plan that has been used successfully for some years by a leading utilities organization is described in its office manual as follows:

INTRODUCTION

The management of a company has no choice as to whether it will have a program of performance appraisal or not. Judging people, whether it be done formally or informally, skillfully or ineptly is inevitable. Not only is the evaluation of people as employees inevitable, but such judgments are necessary, and good, bad or indifferent, are used on a continuous basis and in a variety of important ways.

In any business organization each employee is assigned tasks, given responsibilities, trained, promoted, transferred on the basis of someone's estimate of his ability and potential. In any business organization, so far as groups of employees are concerned, there are continuous efforts to improve the quality of performance of employees—to improve motivation. These efforts, too, depend upon someone answering such questions as:

"What *should* Employee Y be doing?"

"What is he *actually* doing?"

"How is he falling short of expected results?"

"Why?"

"What could he do *beyond* his current assignment?"

The question then, is not whether an organization should have an appraisal program. No firm has this choice. More importantly, every firm *does* have a choice as to the *kind* of program it will follow and every member of the management team *does* have a choice as to *how well* it will be accomplished.

This Manual introduces an Appraisal Program and the new *Performance Review* form. Together these constitute a standardized and workable way for supervisory and managerial personnel to think about the past and current performance of career employees, to assess their future prospects and to communicate these judgments clearly against the background of the total work situation.

It should be noted at the outset that a fair and objective appraisal of an employee's performance is impossible unless there is a mutual understanding and agreement between the employee and his supervisor concerning important elements of the job, expected results and the standards of performance which will apply. Such an understanding can only be achieved if there are periodic discussions between job incumbent and his senior in which priorities are established, goals are set and expectations are agreed upon.

Completing the *Performance Review* form, therefore, is well along in a cycle which has its beginning in a firm mutual understanding of *what* is required, *when* and in accordance with *what* criteria.

Equally important, letting the employee know how well his performance has "measured up," is in a sense both the end of this cycle and the beginning of a new one.

Together, these elements are not only the essence of "management by objectives" but key ingredients of the total Appraisal Program.

The *Performance Review* form itself is therefore designed to provide a regular periodic and systematic appraisal of an employee's excellence in matters pertaining to his present job and his potentialities for a bigger and better job. It is also designed to appraise the abilities of key employees in terms of their readiness to assume new, different or greater responsibilities and to provide management with a picture of the Company's present resources for filling important positions at all levels in the organization. When carefully and accurately completed, it will also indicate steps that must be taken by the Company and the department to develop career employees for positions of greater technical or managerial responsibility. The *Performance Review* is therefore, an important element in corporate, divisional and departmental manpower planning.

The *Performance Review* form or any well designed system to appraise employees is therefore a vital management tool. Nonetheless, it is important that its limitations, too, be recognized. Its use cannot be a substitute for the day to day responsibilities of all members of management to know their people and to employ them to the fullest mutual advantage. Appraisals cannot be considered a magic cure for previous errors and omissions. A manager must manage *every day;* a supervisor must supervise *every day.* An Appraisal

Program cannot be desperately sought out in emergencies, condemned for deficiencies and then casually ignored until "next time."

STATEMENT OF PURPOSE

The Appraisal Program is designed to provide a practical and efficient Company-wide system to enable managers at all levels to assess individual employees and groups of employees in terms of their recent performance, current effectiveness and probable future prospects. The *Performance Review* form is designed specifically to reflect these things in respect to career employees who have completed their basic training and are functioning in a promising manner in an established permanent position. (See page 287)

The *Performance Review* should serve the following purposes:

1. As a means to inspire "total performance of the total individual" in the interest of "total performance of the total system"—to help each individual do better in his present position.

2. As a stimulant to each employee not only to perform his assigned duties to the best of his ability, but to stretch himself and participate in the attainment of unit, department, division and corporate objectives.

3. As an aid to developing people to the full extent of their innate potential.

4. As a vital tool for "management by objectives"—knowing who's doing what and how well.

5. As an essential ingredient of sound salary administration.

6. As an assurance of thoroughness, objectivity and uniformity in the consideration of individual employees as candidates for new responsibilities. To provide relevant information in advance of when it might be needed and avoid spot judgments.

7. As a basis for manpower planning at successive levels in the corporate hierarchy.

8. As valid and comprehensive information for corporate personnel records in a form and degree of detail necessary for manpower inventories, talent searches, etc.

9. As a means to perceive and identify training needs.

10. As an aid in telling employees how well they are doing and suggesting needed changes in their behavior, attitudes, skills or knowledge. As a basis for coaching and counseling of individual employees by supervisors.

Responsibility

Each department head or manager is directly responsible for the operation and success of the Performance Appraisal program in his own office or department. The *Performance Review* should be completed by the employee's immediate supervisor, reviewed and signed by the responsible manager or department head and sent, via appropriate administrative channels, to the Personnel Services Department.

The *Performance Review* form will do the job it is designed to do only if it is used objectively, systematically and with care. How effective it is depends to a large extent on how well it is used. It can only be used well when there is a complete and common understanding of its contents and purpose. This requires that each appraiser be continually alert to those aspects of performance upon which his evaluation will be based. His skill and enthusiasm are keys to a good performance appraisal system. He must be thoroughly indoctrinated in the importance and value of the program.

Conversely, a program is weakened by lack of understanding or intermittent and casual attention to it. A program cannot be carried out successfully if its priority is low or if it is used as a means to diminish the "troublesome business" of working with and worrying about people.

A *Performance Review* is required yearly, after the first year, on each career employee. The following schedule applies:

First Year Employment	Trainee Review	Between 4th and 9th month (Prior to Head Office School or equivalent)
Second Year of Employment	First Performance Review	3rd month or later birth-month in second year of Employment.
Third Year of Employment Etc.	Second Performance Review Etc.	Birthmonth in third year of Employment. Etc.

THE PERFORMANCE REVIEW FORM

Identifying Information

The first section of the *Performance Review* form (shown opposite) is designed so that you can record the factual information that

MERIT RATING/INCENTIVES AND PERFORMANCE REVIEW

PERFORMANCE REVIEW

NAME		REVIEW DATE	
PRESENT POSITION	HOW LONG	EMPLOYMENT DATE	
LOCATION	DEPARTMENT	UNIT	
REVIEWER	MANAGER OR DEPT. HEAD		

MAJOR DUTIES AND RESPONSIBILITIES

List the major duties and responsibilities of this employee's present position. Evaluate how well he is performing each of them in terms of actual results achieved:

	OUTSTANDING	SUPERIOR	AVERAGE	ACCEPTABLE	INADEQUATE
1.					
2.					
3.					
4.					

OVERALL PERFORMANCE

Based on the above ratings, how do you evaluate this employee's overall performance:

PROMOTIONAL POTENTIAL

Indicate below to what level, type or specific position this employee could be promoted in the light of present performance and estimated potential.

	NOW	WITHIN 2 YEARS	LONG RANGE		NOW	WITHIN 2 YEARS	LONG RANGE	Other Specific Division or Dept. Job Titles.
Senior Officer				Superintendent				NOW
Junior Officer				Senior Supervisor				
Resident Manager				Supervisor				WITHIN 2 YRS.
Manager or Dept. Head..				Professional or				
Assistant Manager				Technical Specialist ..				LONG RANGE

In my opinion this employee's potential can best be applied to responsibilities of the following type:

☐ Administrative   ☐ Administrative-Technical   ☐ Technical

Comments:_____

C-2104   1/67   PERFORMANCE REVIEW   Printed in U.S.A.

is needed for individual and group identification and record keeping. Because of this, completeness and accuracy are important. The definitions given below should help to assure this.

NAME—Employee whose performance is being reviewed, last name first.

REVIEW DATE—Date on which Review is completed.

PRESENT POSITION—Use official Job Family Title.

HOW LONG?—Answer in terms of years and months individual has been in his current position.

EMPLOYMENT DATE—Use original employment date; indicate if there has been interruption in Company service.

LOCATION—If Head Office, indicate Division; if field, indicate name of specific Regional Processing Center, Service Office or Field Office.

DEPARTMENT—Use recognized official designation.

UNIT—Use as applicable.

REVIEWER—Name of individual completing Review.

MANAGER OR DEPARTMENT HEAD—Signature indicating Review has been seen and noted by appraiser's superior.

Major Duties and Responsibilities

This is the key element of the *Performance Review*. People are employed to implement and accomplish corporate objectives. How well they handle the most important elements of their individual job responsibilities is the most meaningful measure of their contribution to corporate objectives and the effectivess with which they share and participate in them.

The major duties and responsibilities listed should be those which represent the essential functions of the employee's present position. They should represent the principal reasons the job exists. They should represent the most important and critical elements of the job.

The official Job Description should be a primary source of information in identifying major duties and responsibilities. If possible list them in the order of their importance.

In evaluating the *Major Duties and Responsibilities* in each instance consider them in light of results:

Volume—such things as progress toward attainment of objectives or completion of projects or assignments that are related to a specific aspect of the job; units processed, produced or handled; services given; contributions made.

Quality—such things as thoroughness, accuracy and timeliness compared with standards, established principles, policies, procedures, plans and objectives which bear on a specific aspect of the job.

Economy—such things as efficient use, handling and coordination of people, equipment, facilities and material; proper assignment of personnel; savings through control of cost; budgets and cost reduction plans.

In evaluating *Major Duties and Responsibilities* compare the results this employee has achieved in respect to each major job element with the results achieved by others in the same or similar positions.

Having described at least three and no more than four *Major Duties and Responsibilities* make a check-mark in the space on the scale which best represents your evaluation of each. In each instance consider objectives set, results expected, achievements desired, etc.

OUTSTANDING—Performance is exceptional; consistently at a level greater than expected—in terms of targets and goals.

SUPERIOR—Definitely and consistently exceeds overall performance requirements.

AVERAGE—Performance satisfactory; consistently meets overall performance requirements; weaknesses offset by strengths. The spacing on this scale permits high and low ratings within the AVERAGE level. Goals achieved as planned in terms of completeness, timing, etc.

ACCEPTABLE—Making satisfactory progress but doesn't do all that is expected for competent performance.

INADEQUATE—Performance at a level much less than expected and needs considerable improvement. May be due to newness in position or definite weakness.

Overall Effectiveness

Using the descriptions given above as a guide, make a check-mark on the scale where overall performance is best represented. Do *not* attempt to average the ratings given for *Major Duties and Responsibilities*. Consider *ALL* factors carefully giving the most weight to those factors most important to this position.

Promotion Potential

Indicate in the spaces provided your best judgment as to this employee's capacity to meet specific job requirements at the time intervals given. Your answers should be in terms of the levels, types or specific positions listed. Also give an indication of the nature of the responsibility you envision.

The two parts of this section of the *Performance Review* should reflect what you think the individual can *become*. In determining your response, refer to the foregoing section—*Major Duties and Responsibilities*.

The soundest basis for judging an individual's ability to handle a higher level job is how well he is dealing with similar problems in his present job. Past and present performance is the most reliable key to future performance.

QUALITATIVE PERFORMANCE FACTORS

In following the instructions printed at the top of the second page of the Form you should consider how each of these factors is manifested in the performance of the employee's job. In combination, your comments here should provide support for the job-centered appraisal you have made on the first page. In each instance give two or three brief and representative examples or evidences of the trait or quality under consideration. (See page 292)

Knowledge—Technical know-how, on-the-job.

How well is the employee equipped with the information and "expertise" he needs to do his job? How well does he understand required policies and procedures? How much does he know about other jobs? other functions? other departments? the Company?

Managerial Proficiency

A. Planning (Setting objectives, foreseeing contingencies, etc.)
    How effective is he in establishing short and long range objectives? How well does he provide clear, specific plans for accomplishing these objectives? Does she arrange the most effective use of use of her own and her subordinates' time in a manner consistent with the relative importance of the work to be accomplished? Does she meet time commitments, budgets, forecasts, etc.?

B. Organizing work (Making assignments, schedules, establishing priorities, etc.)
    Does he clearly define subordinates' responsibilities, make appropriate work assignments, establish clear relationships between positions and eliminate overlaps and unnecessary activities? Doe she arrange work for most effective handling of assignments?

C. Personnel Management (Finding, placing, directing, motivating, developing staff.)
    Degree of effectiveness in selecting, training and motivating subordinates. How well appropriate assignments and reasonable performance standards are established and communicated. How well she appraises subordinates' performance and provides constructive guidance for improvement and development. How well he develops subordinates for greater responsibilities.

D. Control (Reports, records, expenses, measuring results.)
    How well does this employee establish the procedures, standards and policies necessary for proper control? Is he effective in reviewing and following through on activities, assignments and reports to assure timely completion and conformity with established policies, plans and procedures?

E. Communications (Written, oral; timeliness, appropriateness, feedback.)
    Accuracy, clarity and timeliness of written and verbal reports; keeping appropriate individuals informed on current operation changes and problems which may affect their discretion in handling and use of confidential information. Communicates in a way others understand and accept. Conserves time in communications. Conducts worthwhile meetings. Comes to the point quickly in discussions, etc.

F. Problem Solving (Investigation, analysis, decision-making, "business sense," etc.)
    Thoroughness in obtaining and providing facts and information pertinent to his responsibilities. Readily recognizes essentials of problems and arriving at sound solutions based on available facts without "hedging" or procrastinating. Anticipates and recognizes changing circumstances and conditions affecting his function. Is willing to make decisions and take timely, positive action; willing to take calculated risks, and to face up to unpleasant decisions. Able to arrive at independent conclusions and know when to refer a problem to others.

PERSONAL QUALITIES

A. Appearance (Dress, manner, poise, self-assurance.)
    Do her personal habits of grooming, her poise and presence in the company of other people create a positive first impression? Does she have mannerisms or idiosyncrasies of behavior or appearance that might be distracting or elicit unfavorable reactions from others?

B. Energy (Drive, ambition.)
    Industriousness? Physical energy? Persistence in getting job done? Persistence in self-improvement?

C. Adaptability (Flexibility, versatility, mobility.)
    How open-minded or single-minded? Is he consistent and steady in thought and action? How flexible is he in adapting to unusual or difficult situations? Can he tactfully adjust to personalities and circumstances? Is he willing to transfer; take on new assignments, etc.?

IN THE LIGHT OF THE MAJOR DUTIES AND RESPONSIBILITIES YOU HAVE EVALUATED, DESCRIBE HOW YOU WOULD RATE THIS EMPLOYEE IN TERMS OF THE FOLLOWING FACTORS:

I. KNOWLEDGE

    A. Technical know-how, on-the-job.

II. MANAGERIAL PROFICIENCY

    A. Planning (Setting objectives, foreseeing contingencies, etc.)

    B. Organizing work (Making assignments, schedules, establishing priorities, etc.)

    C. Personnel Management (Finding, placing, directing, motivating, developing staff)

    D. Control (Reports, records, expenses, measuring results, etc.)

D. Initiative (Ingenuity, self-reliance, self-starting.)
How alert is she to better ways of doing things? Does she assume responsibility, initiate action, originate ideas? Does she recognize situations which need improvement and correct them? Does she make the most of a promising idea or plan?

SUMMARY FACTORS

The three questions on the last page of the *Performance Review* form require comprehensive statements about the employee's principal assets, his or her inadequacies and how the reviewer plans to deal with the latter in a development program. (See page 294)

MERIT RATING/INCENTIVES AND PERFORMANCE REVIEW

E. Communications (Written, oral; timeliness, appropriateness, feedback)

_____
_____
_____
_____

F. Problem-Solving (Investigation, analysis, decision-making, "business sense," etc.)

_____
_____
_____
_____

III. PERSONAL QUALITIES (Habits)

A. Appearance (Dress, manner, poise, self-assurance)

_____
_____
_____

B. Energy (Drive, ambition)

_____
_____
_____

C. Adaptability (Flexibility, versatility, mobility)

_____
_____
_____

D. Initiative (Ingenuity, self-reliance, self-starting)

_____
_____
_____

In describing the individual's major assets, strengths, and abilities, relate them to examples of effective performance in the present position and to the supporting evidences of Knowledge, Managerial Proficiency and Personal Qualities.

In discussing areas requiring improvement, confine your remarks to the most important of them. Anything you list here you should be able to back up with specific examples or instances in which the deficiency or inadequacy was demonstrated.

In outlining _developmental plans,_ be specific; be practical. Check specific areas of subject matter and plans by which development can

IV. MAJOR STRENGTHS: Describe this employee's major assets, strengths and abilities in the light of their relationship to the foregoing and to the requirements of his present position:

_____

_____

_____

_____

_____

V. AREAS REQUIRING IMPROVEMENT: Describe the areas requiring improvement in this employee's performance in his present position:

_____

_____

_____

_____

_____

VI. DEVELOPMENT PLANS: Indicate below your plans to bring about improvement in those areas indicated above. For each **subject**, indicate by **priority**, the **type of plan or plans**, that you intend to employ and the tentative timetable for action. Use the appropriate numbers provided below.

PRIORITY	SUBJECT AND TYPE OF PLAN(S)	TENTATIVE TIME TABLE	
		BEGIN: MO. — YEAR	END: MO. — YEAR
1			
2			
3			

SUBJECT

1.—MANAGERIAL TECHNIQUES
2.—SUPERVISORY TECHNIQUES
3.—COMPANY INFORMATION
4.—PERSONAL FACTS OR HABITS
5.—COMMUNICATION SKILLS
6.—TECHNICAL KNOWLEDGE OR SUBJECT MATTER (SPECIFY TYPE)
7.—OTHER (SPECIFY)

TYPE OF PLAN

1.—DIRECTED SELF-DEVELOPMENT (READING, SELF STUDY, ETC.)
2.—INA FORMAL TRAINING—(ED. DEPT. COURSE)
3.—OUTSIDE EDUCATIONAL PROGRAMS (SEMINARS, COURSES)
4.—COUNSELLING, COACHING
5.—ON-THE-JOB TRAINING
6.—NO PLAN AT PRESENT

Comments:_____

_____

_____

_____

VII. Date discussed with Employee: | By Whom:

best be accomplished. Here you are essentially saying what you think an individual must do to achieve the level of performance desired and to fulfill the potential of which you estimate he is capable. Your answers will also indicate what programs or facilities must be provided.

As indicated in the *Introduction* to this Manual, completing this Form is only part of your role in the *Appraisal Program*. If the *Performance Review* is to fulfill an important element of its purpose, its content must be communicated to the employee concerned in a meaningful way. The post appraisal discussion requires sensitivity and skill of the highest order. It is particularly important that you seek advice and guidance in this area if it is an activity in which you feel ill-prepared. Personnel managers are ready, willing and able to work with any supervisors who may need special help. It is anticipated that special training and printed guidelines will be available in the near future.

GENERAL GUIDELINES

Many volumes of profound advice have been written about performance appraisal; there are an even greater number of courses, seminars and all manner of educational programs on the subject. Some of these books are good and useful and practical; others are long, esoteric and difficult. The range of value of training programs and instructional materials is equally broad. Withal there is no "easy" way; there are no short-cuts.

Gleaned from the lessons others have learned and the principles others have proven to be valid, the following list of some important "do's and don'ts" may be of help to you.

1. Remember, when we judge people we are really judging situations and circumstances. We can only estimate on the basis of what can be seen and observed. Confine attention to job behavior.

2. It is not within the power of the person being appraised to control all of the many factors that influence ability to work effectively.

3. For the reasons of the foregoing, it is imperative that a reviewer *know the job*. The image an incumbent has of the job and the ideas the boss has may be worlds apart.

4. It is wishful thinking—indeed downright harmful—to measure a person against a mythical ideal such as "the perfect person for the job."

5. Avoid the tendency to force judgments into predetermined categories or "pet" theories.

6. Avoid the tendency to "lump" traits—such as the assumption "He's young" (therefore he must be immature). Don't permit one aspect of an employee's behavior to influence appraisal in other areas.

7. Remember, not may people are actually qualified to assess personality. Human personality is complex and highly abstract. There are over 18,000 different terms that can be used to describe an individual. Contrary to popular belief, no one trait or group of qualities has been discovered to account for

success except in specific situations. Avoid the confusion between causes and results of behavior.

Review Conferences

According to employees, an "appreciation of work done" is the most important motivator, whereas compensation is ranked fifth in importance. However, there is a connecting link, *communication*, which if tied into a job description and merit compensation program helps to achieve the following employee motivators:

1. Appreciation of work done.
2. Feeling "in" on things.
3. Sympathetic help on personal problems.
4. Good wages.
5. Promotion and growth in the company.
6. Personal loyalty to employees.

Employees should know what to expect when they start. Though it is not always advisable to publish a full position and rate table and make everyone's earnings common knowledge, an employee should be made aware of the merit increase structure and next probable promotion salary level. Where there are vacancies in other departments, these positions and their salaries should be advertised internally. In all cases, the job skills required for promotion should be clearly defined. Promotion from within is a great motivator and employees should be encouraged to train for advanced positions.

The semiannual merit review should serve to assist both the employee and management in continuing and improving relations. Therefore, it must be two-sided and constructive. Management should be represented by a respected representative who has a "feel" for this type of conference. Frequently, this is conducted by the personnel manager, or sometimes an administrative supervisor such as the office manager. The conferences should be conducted privately.

Line supervisors should be required to prepare semiannual merit review forms for each employee under their jurisdiction. This form will serve as the basis of the merit review.

At the outset the reviewer should explain the purpose of the conference and make the reviewee feel at ease. The conference should start with a review of performance and be compared to past performance. If the employee's performance has slipped, then he or she should be allowed to comment thereon. Much can be learned by management from these interviews concerning the quality of supervision, the status of morale, suggestions for improved procedures and working conditions, the personal ambitions of the employee and his or her personal problems. It is vital that the employee be made aware that these conferences are as important for management as for the reviewee. It is also important to emphasize that the semiannual interview is not the only time the employee can talk to management, but that the doors are always open to each employee. Two important concepts should be carried away by the employee:

1. The review process is intended to assist each employee in bettering his or her performance.
2. Management can gain from the employee by his or her criticism. In that way it is a review process for management too.

When an employee's performance has slipped, this should be discussed frankly. If there are no openings for promotions, indicate that. It is far better to be truthful than to mislead employees about nonexistent opportunities.

CHAPTER 13

HOW TO PREPARE
A PERSONNEL POLICY MANUAL

THE purpose of a personnel policy manual is to provide employers, personnel directors, industrial relations directors and supervisors with a systematic approach to administering company policies and practices.

A company policy manual should be designed as a fundamental communications tool for these members of management to help clarify policies and practices and thus prevent morale problems, complaints, and grievances before they arise.

Your policy manual should serve its purpose by preventing difficulties due to lack of understanding of personnel policies and practices which have resulted from unwritten policy, inconsistent policy, and lack of proper communications.

Above all, your personnel policy manual should be a working tool designed to help you and your company provide equal employment opportunities to everyone in your organization regardless of race, religion, creed, sex, or national origin, since this is now the law of the land.

How You Benefit from a Policy Manual

There are many tangible and intangible benefits that can be claimed by companies which prepare a policy manual. Not the least of these benefits is the peace of mind which takes the place of headaches and indecision which usually result when management must continuously meet to discuss and reach decisions concerning given personnel policies and practices.

A major benefit is that a written manual of policy provides everyone in management with a clear explanation of all existing company policies and practices. This in itself is an invaluable asset to communications. In many respects it literally speaks for itself.

A third benefit is that it provides excellent material that can be used in conducting supervisory training courses for new supervisors and refreshing their understanding of past company policy. There are hundreds of companies spending endless hours and a great deal of money trying to decide what to teach supervisors. There is a desire to make the company more efficient and to promote better employee morale. If these companies would develop a company policy manual and use it as a basis for supervisory training programs, they will reach this goal.

For years, hundreds of companies, small and large, union and non-union have attempted to build more effective personnel programs for their supervisors and employees. They have made every effort to achieve the desired goal of industrial peace and good employee relations within their organizations. But many have frequently found, to their dismay, that the programs which top management felt were best for everyone were poorly received.

Why? Such hopes and aspirations of management toward improvements in bettering their personnel relations program were doomed from the very conception of the idea. The employees were not to blame; the front and middle-line supervisors were not to blame. But the responsibility can be laid at the door of top management for failing to properly clarify and document personnel policy and practice in writing and then train the supervisors and department heads to administer the policy.

A fourth benefit of a policy manual is that it serves as written documentation of a company's good faith in providing fair employment practices and equal employment opportunity for present employees and future job applicants. The enactment of Title VII of the Civil Rights Act has once again placed great importance on the personnel tool of communications. Frankly, a manual should be the beginning of good faith efforts to prove nondiscrimination and to provide equal employment opportunity to everyone in all phases of personnel action. In communicating your equal employment opportunity policy, you may find it necessary to simply reaffirm your past policy. On the other hand, many companies today are faced with the responsibility of establishing fair employment practices for the first time.

Needless to say that the development of a company policy manual will not in itself provide a guarantee of complying with Title VII. To comply effectively, company personnel policies must result in a program of active, good faith effort. This implies, of course, following the contents of the manual to be sure that everyone who should know of policy sincerely believes it and sees the policy working.

Since the enactment of Title VII and other federal and state nondiscrimination laws many firms throughout the United States have found that one of the weakest, most potential areas of vulnerability under Fair Employment Practice Laws has been front and middle-line supervision. In interviewing supervisors, we find a great lack of understanding of company personnel policies and practices. Certainly, without understanding, they cannot be expected to know how to protect the company's interest in what they do and say to job applicants and employees under their supervision.

We all know that management's greatest asset is a well-trained, qualified foreman or supervisor who is capable of administering company policy in a fair and consistent manner. It is even more important today for your foremen and supervisors to know how to interpret company policy effectively, clearly and properly in order to avoid any possible unfair employment practice charge which could come about as a result of the Title VII requirements.

Whether we want to admit it or not, management has placed added responsibilities in the hands of foremen and supervisors with little or no authority and no definite policy to guide them in their performance of these new responsibilities. Thus, your company policy manual is highly important since it can be used as a training manual for all ranks of supervision and key personnel officers in clearly understanding your personnel policy and practices so that they can administer these policies fairly, firmly, and equally to all employees regardless of their race, color, religion, sex or national origin. Members of management can support your personnel policies and practices toward providing equal employment opportunities only to the degree of understanding such policies and practices. Your policy manual can provide you with this desirable benefit.

Who in Your Company Should Use a Policy Manual

Policy manuals are used by different individuals from company to company. Generally speaking, it is designed for those individuals whose primary responsibility is to carry out and administer company policies and practices. Thus, most companies provide company policy manuals for the industrial relations director, personnel director, employment manager, administrative manager, department heads, and supervisors.

A realistic answer to the question of who should receive a policy manual depends largely on the nature of the contents. If the contents of the manual pertain to ways and means of communicating, getting the service performed or the product manufactured at the least cost in the smallest amount of time with the goal of maintaining job satisfaction and high employee morale, then anyone responsible for these functions in the company should have a copy of the manual.

There are certain dangers in limiting the distribution of the manual to only one particular level of management. For example, if you distribute the manual to *only* middle-line supervisors, they may feel that they are being singled out as a group that needs to be given rules to work under, while front-line supervisors have more freedom. In another case, if you limit the policy manual to production foremen and exclude office supervisors, the office supervisors may feel that plant foremen are given more authority and status than themselves.

We recommend, that unless your company has sound, specific reasons for excluding the distribution of the manual to certain ranks of supervision that you issue the same policy manual to all managerial employees from the top corporate officer to the assistant foreman.

Where a company organization is so large that to provide every supervisor with a manual would be an impractical goal, it may be necessary to limit distribution to middle and upper ranks of management. For example, if your organization has 4,000 supervisors, it would be rather impractical and extremely expensive to publish and distribute 4,000 copies of your company policy manual.

The Decision to Produce a Manual

If you are convinced that your company is in need of a policy manual, or if it is obvious that your present manual is in need of revision, the first decision reached is a clear-cut go-ahead for the project. Topmost management is charged with making this decision.

The chief executive or the chief governing body of the company (board of directors, management committee) must:

1. Choose the person who will have the authority and responsibility for preparing the manual.
2. Outline the major sources of information for the manual.
3. Be responsible for the ground rules covering what should and what should not go into the manual.
4. Put the final OK on the format and organization of the manual.

In most cases policies do exist in some form. The production of a new manual will probably entail the revision of an old manual or the writing of previously unwritten policies.

Some of the basic reasons given for revision, by many sources, point out why this should be undertaken. For example:

1. Your organization has been unionized since your last manual was written or revised.
2. You have moved your company to an entirely different labor community.

3. You haven't made changes in your policies and practices to comply with all the fair employment practices requirements of Title VII of the Civil Rights Law of 1964 and its later revisions.

4. Your current written policies and practices have not been revised to conform to the latest minimum wage and overtime requirements of the Federal Wage-Hour Law.

5. Your present written policies or practices are in conflict with recent state or federal laws (labor) which might affect a particular classification of your employees.

6. Your organizational structure has changed in size (grown) substantially or your products and methods of manufacture or distribution have changed.

The above guidelines for a revision cover obvious contingencies. The most obvious reason for revision is when your manual is old or out-of-date.

Authority and Responsibility for Preparing the Manual

Following the decision that a manual is to be produced, it is up to top management to decide *who* is going to be in charge of the production. It is highly recommended that *one person* should have the responsibility, and he should be a member of the management team.

This person should have the authority to set up a small committee which will assist in gathering the data necessary for a complete and comprehensive manual. The committee should, in effect, do some of the legwork required in bringing the necessary information to this committee chairman.

In every company, there are several persons available who know current policy and perhaps formulate it on a date-to-day basis. One of these people should have enough background to take charge of the project. This person, then, can be aided by a committee of individuals who have working knowledge of the various departments of the company. Someone from personnel has background on employee relations, someone from accounting may have access to wage and salary administration, an industrial relations man knows all about the union.

As stated before, this committee should be small to be functional. It serves to reduce the effort that the chairman-writer must put forth to produce a comprehensive manual. The committee's initial task is to gather data from individual departments. Individual members can make recommendations, and finally each member should carefully appraise the area of policy within his or her realm. It would be wise to set a time limit for each report.

The Role of the Supervisor

The committee should utilize the ideas and observations of supervisors to the fullest extent possible. The supervisors are on the firing line daily and are primarily responsible for administering company policies and practices. They know how past unwritten personnel policies or past written policies have affected employee morale and productivity.

The supervisors should be interviewed for the purpose of learning what is going on in the company now. They will be a great help in finding out where present policies, written or unwritten, are working and where they are not working. For example, the supervisors may be able to point out certain policies which have proved unworkable or which are unnecessary and should be revised or abolished. They may also be able to recommend new policies which are necessary in order to attain greater efficiency and more desirable job satisfaction for the employees. The supervisors will be the best informed source on where present policy and practices are being administered inconsistently, or unequally among their subordinates. Thus, the role of the supervisors will prove of great benefit to the policy manual committee by helping them determine what the policy and practice should be concerning various subjects.

An indirect benefit of using supervisors as a source of information for the proposed policy manual or revision is that it gives the supervisors the opportunity to participate in its development or revision. In fact, by participating, the supervisors are helping to "create" the new or revised manual. In so doing, you will find that there will be greater effort on the part of supervisors to support company policies and practices because they have helped create them.

For the supervisors to be effective in helping the policy manual committee, the committee itself must be systematic and practical in approaching the supervisors. Above all, they must be specific in their questioning. They should ask every supervisor to tell them what he or she thinks company policies actually are on a given subject. If a given company policy is silent or ambiguous on various subjects, the supervisors should be asked to express themselves on how they actually handle a problem that arises in a particular area. The supervisors should also be asked what changes need to be made on existing company policies and practices.

For companies developing a policy manual for the first time, the following questionnaire can be extremely helpful to members of the policy manual committee in working with supervisors. The following set of questions can be applied to any given subject dealing with personnel policies:

1. Are you familiar with our policy on _____?
2. Do you think this policy is working out to the best interests of both the company and the employees?
3. Do you feel that this policy meets our present needs?
4. Do you feel that you know and understand this policy well enough to interpret and administer it correctly? Are you aware of any improper understanding or adminstration of this policy?
5. Do you feel that we need a new policy on the subject of _____?
6. What do you think the new policy should be?

The above recommended questionnaire approach in interviewing supervisors has practical value. It can help clarify both past and potential personnel problem areas that have resulted in complaints, grievances and misunderstandings. It can assist in developing new policies to prevent additional problems from arising in the future.

It can be of great value as an aid in reviewing overall personnel policies and procedures periodically. We recommend this be done at least once every year. Furthermore, the interviewing and questioning of supervisors can provide many good ideas on where present training programs need to be revised or improved for the benefit of new supervisors, new managers, and staff personnel.

Finally, the questionnaire approach, through in-depth interviewing of supervisors, can help to keep present supervisors up-to-date on current policy and practice. Thus, it can prevent misunderstandings and incorrect interpretation and administration of your company's policies.

Sources of Information for the Manual

Company policies which are already written form the main base for a new or revised manual. All of these should be brought together with three things in mind:

1. **Comparison**—if the existing policies conflict or vary from area to area or department to department, they should be checked and unified. If written policy conflicts with present practice, the changes should be incorporated.
2. **Review**—past and current policies should be examined in the light of new developments. Changes may be contemplated, and it is wise to make them part of written policy now.

3. **Authenticity**—practices currently in use, if not written in a policy manual, may be without basis. Perhaps managers or supervisors have inaugurated *their own* policy without formal submission to top management.

Comparing the existing policy manuals, employee handbooks and even bulletin board notices will provide the bulk of information necessary to build the basic policy areas.

As an example, the company's vacation allowance policy is probably in writing or certainly well understood. A new employee usually is told exactly what his vacation allowance will be. On the other hand, holidays may be determined on a year-to-year basis or even on a month-to-month basis. Company files might produce a series of bulletin board announcements giving experience through the years.

If this area (holidays) is becoming a part of policy for the first time, it might be wise to collect as much information as possible about the present practices within the company's industry. Surveys are valuable guides. Industry organizations and management groups (Chamber of Commerce) also make continuous surveys in this area.

Wage and salary administration policies may not be as clear-cut within your organization as vacation allowances or holidays. If there is a definite policy (written or unwritten), you should make every effort to incorporate this policy into the policy manual. If top management is not sure about expressing this area in writing, it would be of value to collect policy statements from other companies in similar industries to show top management what is being said.

Reviewing past policies, manuals and guidebooks differs from comparing policy statements in the respect that change is the guide. It is normally estimated that policies go out-of-date in about five years. This does not mean all policies, but it does cover a good many areas—especially those involving fringe benefits and employee benefits. Initiating a new manual is obviously the time designated to consider all present policies. Making changes at this point will eliminate the need for constant revision during the next period of use.

Authenticating known policies is a vital task. All department managers, supervisors and even division heads should be requested to submit any information they have on policy. This may necessitate an extensive job of research, but it should provide the greatest amount of information available. Part of the job here will be to trace the present policy to its source, if this is possible. This can be revealing to the extent that top management might wish to make sure that in the future, policy comes from only one source. It may also disclose excellent procedures in some areas that will work well for all areas of the company.

What Should and Should Not Go Into a Policy Manual

A working policy manual must be a usable tool for supervision. The emphasis on clarity reflects the necessity for careful editing of the available material. Many rules, regulations and procedures will be compiled during the initial materials search. This is one area where the working committee can be called upon to make decisions.

If the manual is to have general distribution, the bulk of the written material should cover all the policy areas which affect all personnel. If, for example, the rules governing maternity leave are the same for all departments or operations (plant and office), they can be stated in general terms with or without procedures.

If there are certain conditions which affect office help as compared to plant help, these may or may not be spelled out specifically in the single manual. They might be basically included in a departmental or operational manual designed specifically for the area involved.

Certainly, the specific holidays a company grants would be included in the policy manual by name—Independence Day, Washington's Birthday—but it wouldn't be practical to try and use the exact date of the year. The manual, as conceived, must be of value for at least three years and perhaps as long as five years.

Union Agreements

A big area for consideration is the presentation of a policy manual in conjunction with a union agreement. In most cases the union agreement represents policy on seniority, on holidays, on remuneration, and job descriptions.

If the *entire* company is not within union ranks, then there will be a separate policy for the nonunion personnel. For the sake of clarity, it is wisest to include both statements in the policy manual. The union agreement can stand as an appendix item and an entity, or the two areas can be ranked side by side within the sections designated. This is where management must make the final decisions.

Sources of Outside Help

With the help of this publication, you should be able to produce an effective working policy manual. However, under certain circumstances, it is not out of line to recommend the use of competent, professional outside assistance.

If the amount of time available is limited, there are specialists who will do the basic legwork, draft, compose and edit a policy manual. There are also professional consultants who will act in an advisory capacity, providing suggestions and recommendations at various stages of the project.

A major consideration might be the use of a management consultant to analyze and audit your entire organization *before you write a manual* on policy.

This is a valid consideration if your company has never actually committed policy to writing before. Many areas of policy might not be presently covered in writing or practice. The suggested move here is to obtain guidance in formulating such policies or practices which will then become part of your organization.

A final thought in this area is the use of the corporate lawyer and/or industrial relations specialist to check out all possible legal questions and to affirm (if a union is involved) that union agreements are not violated.

If such fringe benefits as a corporate pension plan or annual bonuses are included in a policy statement, they had better be worded in a manner that protects all parties involved.

Format and Organization of the Manual

While the choice of format and organization is pretty much up to the individual in charge of preparing a policy manual, it is obvious that some type of outline should be developed and followed throughout.

An immediate suggestion is to make sufficient copies of each outline for committee members and for key executives. These lists can be combined for an overall look at the requisites for a written policy. They can also serve as a springboard leading to a singular type of checklist for your particular organization.

Early discussion can center around differences discovered in the outlining of policy areas. This point is the best for resolving these questions. When a master copy is completed, the writer-chairman has a completely developed picture of *what he needs*. This, however, does not give him a picture of the order of the material or of what the material consists.

After it is determined that the various areas of policy *will* be included in the manual, it is the job of the chairman-writer and committee to come up with the material (handbooks, previous policies, etc.) that will form the policy.

Organizing the policy material—Once the research is completed and the information is at hand, it is necessary to establish the organization or arrangement of the manual. The primary requirement here is that the material be organized in a logical manner. One or a combination of several techniques have been used extensively. Recommendations for each are universal. One of the simplest methods is to arrange the subjects in an alphabetical order according to the name of the policy area. An example of this technique is as follows:

A
ABSENTEEISM
ABSENTEEISM REPORT

B
BONUSES
BULLETIN BOARDS

C
CHANGES IN PERSONNEL STATUS
CHRISTMAS PARTIES
COMPANY BENEFITS

D
DEPARTMENT HEADS MANUAL
DEPARTMENTAL SENIORITY

E
EMPLOYEE BENEFITS
EMPLOYEE DISCIPLINE
EMPLOYEE HANDBOOK

F
FAIR LABOR STANDARDS ACT
FALSIFYING RECORDS
FIGHTING ON COMPANY PREMISES
FIRST AID

Alphabetical Code—With an alphabetical code, each main classification of policy statements is given a key letter. These major classifications are then broken down into smaller subdivisions which are also given alphabetical letters. An example of such an arrangement is the following:

A
EMPLOYEE BENEFITS

AA—
PAID HOLIDAYS

AB—
NUMBER AND NAME OF HOLIDAYS OBSERVED

AC—
ARRANGEMENTS FOR CHRISTMAS, ELECTION
DAYS AND RELIGIOUS HOLIDAYS

AD—
HOLIDAYS FALLING ON NONWORKING DAYS

B
EMPLOYEE RELATIONS

BA—
POLICY OF COMPANY ON UNIONS

BB—
EMPLOYEE RELATIONS PHILOSOPHY

BC—
POSITION OF THE COMPANY ON EQUAL
EMPLOYMENT OPPORTUNITY

C
HIRING

CA—
TYPE OF JOB APPLICANTS TO LOOK FOR

CB—
PHYSICAL EXAMINATIONS

The above technique of organizing the company policy manual is very simple. *However, it has some disadvantages.* For example, it is often troublesome to locate a specific policy statement under such a system when the subject of the policy statement could be listed under several alphabetical words. If your policy manual is to be finalized into a looseleaf format, it is often impractical to number the pages consecutively. Thus, it is often desirable to use a different technique of arranging the policy statement material through the use of a coding system. The coding technique is often used alphabetically or numerically, and sometimes, as a combination of the alphabet and by numbers.

There is one primary disadvantage in using the alphabetical code technique in that it is often difficult to identify the code letters with the subject of the policy statement in any logical manner. If this system is used, it will be desirable to use an alphabetical code letter which is identical with the first letter of the subject of the policy statement. However, this is not always practical.

Numerical Code Technique—The technique of arranging your policy manual contents by numerical code is very similar to the alphabetical code system. With this technique, you use numbers instead of alphabetical letters to identify the major classifications and subclassifications. An example of this organization technique is as follows:

1. *EMPLOYEE BENEFITS*
   1.1 PAID HOLIDAYS
   1.2 NUMBER OBSERVED
   1.3 ELIGIBILITY
   1.4 HOLIDAYS FALLING ON NONWORKING DAYS
2. *SAFETY RULES*
   2.1 EQUIPMENT AND WORK AREA
   2.2 EMPLOYEE RESPONSIBILITY
3. *TERMINATION OF EMPLOYMENT*
   3.1 HOW TO HANDLE RESIGNATIONS
   3.2 HOW TO HANDLE TERMINATIONS FOR CAUSE
   3.3 UNEMPLOYMENT COMPENSATION
   3.4 REFERENCES

The numerical code technique can also be modified by organizing the major classifications of policy statements and begin a page on a major section with 100 with the more detailed subject matter pertaining to the major classification on pages numbered consecutively from 100, i.e., 101, 102, 103. Once the major classification has been coded by page number according to this variation, the next major policy statement classification would begin on page 200.

Alphabetical and Numerical Combination—Under a combination of the two coding techniques, the major policy statement subjects are arranged alphabetically and the subdivisions or more detailed aspects of the major policy subject are identified numerically. For example, an illustration of this combination technique is the following:

SECTION 1—ACCIDENTS ON THE JOB
  SAFETY RULES   —1.1
  GOOD HOUSEKEEPING   —1.2
  PREVENTATIVE MAINTENANCE   —1.3

SECTION 2—BONUSES
  ATTENDANCE BONUSES   —2.1
  DISCRETIONARY BONUSES   —2.2
  PRODUCTION BONUSES   —2.3

Whatever technique is used to organize and arrange the subject matter of your policy manual should be explained in your manual.

The Index or Table of Contents—It is desirable to have a table of contents and an index for a policy manual. It is particularly desirable to have both if your company policy manual has a large number of pages.

The type of subjects listed in the table of contents vary according to the particular organization. Many factors account for this. The size and type of the organization involved, the purpose of the policy manual, the types of personnel who are to receive and use the manual are all factors influencing the subjects listed in the table of contents. However, general subject headings such as those on the next pages may prove helpful.

The table of contents may consist of the short form as illustrated above—which is arranged by major subject headings in order of their appearance—or it may be a more detailed format with both major headings and subheadings for each key topic. The table of contents should, of course, be placed at the very beginning of the manual where it can be located quickly.

It is recommended that the manual also be indexed alphabetically by page number. A general exception to this recommendation is whenever your policy manual is arranged by alphabetical order according to tabs dividing the major subjects.

The index cannot be undertaken until the final draft of the manual has been read and approved.

In indexing the manual, you should read through your final draft. Have available a package of 3- by 5-inch cards while reading through the manual, and write the key subject of each policy on a card. After you have finished writing out the subjects of all policy statements and practices, arrange them in alphabetical order. Then begin editing these cards. You may find that you have identified a given subject using different words on two different cards. Decide on the most logical word or words which identify the policy statement and discard the other word. If, for example, you have made references to "paid holidays" and "holidays," use the more common usage in your organization.

Once you have edited the cards, you are now ready to combine all page references to the same key word in ascending order. Thus, your index should look something like the following:

A
Absence, 3, 20
Accidents, 64, 68
Applicants, 8, 10, 14, 25
Attendance, 30, 41, 50
Attendance Records, 40, 38

B
Bidding, 40, 42, 52
Buddy System, 19, 22, 37

C
Complaints, 20, 28
Cost Control, 28

Writing the Drafts of the Policy Manual

If you have reviewed the recommended steps on how to prepare and revise your policy manual, you should now be ready to begin writing the first draft. You can review sample policy statements in this manual which are included in this chapter, and adapt examples of policy on various other subjects in use in different companies, as described in other chapters.

In drafting the first copy of your manual you can use 8½-by 11-inch sheets that will fit into this three-ring binder, or you can use an index card system (3- by 5-inch cards) that can be kept in a file. If you wish to put the actual policy statements on cards, it is suggested that you use a larger size.

This guide can be adapted quickly to fit your basic need for a manual draft. Keeping the section guides, the checklists and policy statements you wish to use, you can develop your own manual. Add your policy statements within the sections. When all the topics have been covered, the manual can be alphabetized to fit your needs.

Keep Language Clear

At this point, it should be emphasized that a policy statement requires the utmost in clarity. Nothing can be more damaging to organization or morale than a policy which is not understood or which is not clear to the reader.

Writing experts Robert Gunning and Douglas Mueller in the book "*How to Take the Fog Out of Writing*," offered excellent suggestions that could be considered before the first attempt is made:

HOW TO PREPARE A PERSONNEL POLICY MANUAL

Break Up Long Sentences—If you want to keep your meaning clear, keep the length of the sentences used as short as possible. Express *one idea* at a time in a sentence.

Prefer the Simple to the Complex—Many complex terms are unnecessary. When there is a simpler way of saying a thing, use it. Avoid complex sentences.

Avoid Unneeded Words—Nothing weakens writing so much as extra words. Be critical of your own writing and make every word carry its weight.

Put Action into Your Verbs—The heaviness of much business writing results from overworking the passive verbs. Prose can usually be kept impersonal and remain in the active tense.

Use Terms Your Reader Can Picture—Abstract terms make writing dull and foggy. Choose short, concrete words that the reader can visualize.

Tie In With Your Reader's Experience—The reader will not get your new idea unless you link it with some old idea he already has.

Write the Way You Talk—As much as you can, use a tone that you would normally use in expressing the same thought orally.

Write to Express, Not to Impress—Present your ideas simply and directly. The writer who makes the best impression is the one who can express complex ideas simply.

This final point reiterates the beginning statement—the policy statements must be absolutely clear. A policy manual is no place for displaying your rhetorical ability.

Here are some other suggestions to keep in mind:

1. *Keep your first draft flexible and open to additions and changes.* Make your point as clear as possible and find out if others agree that it is clear.

2. *Tables and charts are always good when explaining a difficult area.* Even breaking up a section into a table-like grouping can get the message across.

Complete Shift Cycle

12:00 (midnight) to 8:00 a.m.

8:00 a.m.   to 4:00 p.m.

4:00 p.m.   to 12:00 (midnight)

Incomplete Shift Cycle

7:00 a.m. to 3:00 p.m.

or 8:00 a.m. to 4:00 p.m.

and 3:00 p.m. to 11:00 p.m.

or 4:00 p.m. to 12:00 (midnight)

3. *Be your own first critic.* Don't be hesitant about rewriting something two or three times. Try to have the first draft as complete as it can be. This may eliminate extensive corrections at the review and cut down the number of times the manual will be subjected to review.

4. *Make enough copies of your first draft to be sure that all who need to review it will be able to do so.* Keep track of these copies to avoid missing key corrections suggested by some member of the management team.

Get the First Draft Proofed and Reviewed. Once the policy statements have been selected, written to order, and checked for presentation, the first draft can be typed. This is the point at which the manual should be put into order, with the organization technique you have chosen. It is a good idea to retain the master copy and produce sufficient copies for distribution to key personnel who must help in the review.

Each of the copies should have the name of the individual who receives it *written on the cover or first page.* This will keep your record clear when it comes to checking on any revisions. Besides making changes or suggestions, some of the executives will read the copy closely enough to catch possible typographical errors. These should be caught in proofreading, but experience shows that many manuals such as this do contain some errors.

After all the review copies have been returned, it probably will fall on the shoulders of the chairman-writer to check each revision. A meeting of the committee (hopefully the final meeting) can resolve the possible differences or conflicts that might arise. This is the final chance to make revisions within the existing body of policy, and since the subject is a current one, some management ideas (changes for the future) might be included now.

Each committee member should OK his or her particular area of administration. As an example, it is very important that personnel administration puts the final OK on the company's employment practices statement. It is also necessary, perhaps, to have legal counsel on the statement. It is important that financial officers OK the pension plan statement, again with legal concurrence.

Check with Supervisors. Since it is primarily the supervisor who will work with the policy manual, it is a good practice to have certain key people read over the entire presentation. After they have studied the policies and policy statements, they might join with the committee for a brief question and answer session. Do they understand the policy? Do they know how to explain the policy to an employee? Do they feel the policy, as it is written, will be understood by the employee?

If there is serious doubt in the mind of a supervisor, or if he or she is unable to interpret a policy statement, there is no better time to change it. This doesn't mean the supervisors have the final say, but policy is going to be hard to enforce if this group doesn't comprehend the meaning. It will further result in a widespread problem of control if supervisors in one department are interpreting policy one way and supervisors in another department are interpreting it another way. Besides avoiding confusion, this meeting will help to eventually cut time and money from the program.

Production of the Manual

With all corrections incorporated into a master copy, the next step is to have the manual printed or reproduced. Cost could be a factor here. It is up to management to set some ground rules. Company size will probably determine the number of copies needed. This also has had an effect on the actual page count of the manual. It pretty much follows that the larger the company, the larger the manual, but this is not a hard and fast rule.

If you have been following the step-by-step procedures in this handbook, you have already determined who will get a copy of the manual. The next step is to determine how many extra copies you will need (for replacement, etc.) and how long this particular manual will be in use. If you are producing a looseleaf manual, you can make additions and changes on a periodic basis without too much difficulty. This means the initial run can be a little larger than normal.

What Type of Manual? The choice here is wide. If your company has a printing facility, the man in charge will be your best source of information. If you have offset facilities, your shop can reduce an 8½- by 11-inch typed page to half the size and produce a compact little booklet. This may be harder to read, but it will fit conveniently in a desk drawer.

Remember, however, if you decide on a printed and bound edition, there is really no opportunity to make a simple change without running the entire job through again.

It is recommended that the company policy manual be bound in a looseleaf format. The pages can be printed, run on a mimeograph or duplicator or, for that matter, copied and punched. The looseleaf binder allows for updating and changing of pages with a minimum of difficulty. A new fringe benefit can be quickly added to the policy manual by distributing new pages to the manual holders.

For a large manual (in pages) the three-ring binder is probably the best bet, but for smaller manuals, the Duo-tang binder is adequate. Both of these allow for flexibility. Both can have printed covers, or both can have simple labels on the covers. Both plastic and paper covers are available from many sources of supply (including the local stationery store), and the choice should be made on the basis of use.

If the aim is to keep the manual for at least five years, a substantial cover is best, but keep in mind that people dealing in policy matters are technically supposed to be fully aware of the policy, so reference to the manual is not that frequent. It will spend a great deal of time in a desk drawer or in a file cabinet.

How to Keep Your Policy Manual Up-to-Date

As stated before, a policy manual can function for as long as five years, but it is recommended practice to consider updating at least every two years.

Many companies have found it rather expensive and impractical to revise a manual every time a single policy change is necessary. Instead they keep management and supervisors informed of policy changes by issuing "Policy Bulletins" or other types of memoranda to the recipients of the manual. Such bulletins can be retained in the front or rear of the manual, or if it is a looseleaf publication, inserted in place of the former statement.

One area where this change could be considered almost constant is that of vacation and holiday benefits. If policy is explicit, then it is probably subject to biennial or even annual change.

Another technique that has been helpful for some companies in handling policy changes before revising the manual is to set up a section in the manual entitled *"New and Revised Policies and Practices."* If this area gets extensive, however, it becomes a chore to maintain a manual in usable condition. Secretaries, as well as managers, dislike filing pages into existing booklets or manuals. They are apt to drop them in anywhere, insisting they will get to proper placement at some time in the near future.

Getting Ready for Revision. The time will come when a policy manual needs revision. Most of the steps outlined in this section will have to be followed again, but the time utilized can be cut dramatically.

A policy file should be retained by the current writer of the manual. If the assignment is given up, this file will be valuable to a replacement. If the title of chairman-writer is assumed again, there will be much of the information at hand.

This does not mean that he or she won't have to form the committee again. Each item of policy must be rechecked if this is a true revision. Each item must be approved again. At this point, suggestions can be sought for improvement of the manual—format, organization, presentation, etc.

This is also an excellent time for a *critical evaluation of policy itself*. Is the current policy up-to-date? Does the company operate the same way it did five or two years ago? Have employees thrived under current policy, or has there been dissension?

The same type of evaluations should be conducted for the format of the manual. Has the manual held together? Has it been easy to use? Has it been criticized by members of the management team or employees?

Making the Revision. With the experience of producing one manual under her belt, the writer can proceed with confidence on the revision. She will probably be given less time for the effort, but it is wise to remind management that the job still must be thorough. A mistake in a revision is just as bad as a mistake in the original publication.

By retracing the steps in this section, the manual can be brought into being with a minimum of effort. Copies of the current policy statements can be made for the individuals concerned and directed to their attention. They can be asked to OK the current policy statement or make a recommended revision.

Do not ask them to use their own copy for this revision. Until the new manual is produced, they may need to refer to their own copy. Photocopies of the specific manual pages will do the job best.

As a final word, when the new manual is released, be sure that old copies are collected and destroyed—except for record copies. This is the best way to prevent a serious problem, especially when both new and old manuals look pretty much the same.

We all tend to gravitate toward responsibility rather than away from it when we know there is written policy on which to rely. Furthermore, the ever-present tendency to pass-the-buck is reduced to a great extent.

Specifically speaking, this Personnel Policy Manual is designed to provide us with the following advantages:

> **UNDERSTANDING**—Written company policy is one of the best antidotes in the personnel medicine chest for the troubles a company grapevine can cause. Even though everything is subject to interpretation, the odds overwhelmingly favor the written word as against the oral. It's incredible how a single fact can become so distorted by the word-of-mouth avenue.
>
> **LINE OF AUTHORITY**—Top management cannot make all decisions that need to be made within our company. But so often they try to, simply because they are afraid to release authority to subordinates.

Naturally, it follows that if top management felt that subordinates could make decisions like top management would, the reluctance would be relieved. This Personnel Policy Manual achieves this desired relationship. It thus results in a solid delineation of authority.

CONSISTENCY—The idea of consistent application of our company policies is coveted simply because it means employees will be treated equally. It prevents, to a great extent, the seepage of prejudice and bias in the decisions of supervision. The achievement of this one personnel virtue is to take a colossal step in your maintenance of satisfactory employer-employee harmony.

PLANNING—Many times we have found deficient policies which urgently needed changing. However, since all policy was orally transmitted, the need for change never seemed to achieve attention. Then, in preparing a policy manual, where all policy is together and coordinated, the need for change became quite apparent. Likewise, other existing policies which suddenly seemed out of place were deleted, changed, or amended. In short, we find that when developing our policy manual, we are more often than not made aware of incongruities in our present policies which heretofore might have seemed quite sufficient.

We feel that no company is too small to make unnecessary the need for a Personnel Policy Manual. In short, no company is invulnerable to the fallacies of human nature.

Policy Statement:

This manual contains statements of personnel policies and procedures. It is designed to be a working guide for supervisory and staff personnel in the day-to-day administration of our company personnel program.

These written policies should increase understanding, eliminate the need for personal decisions on matters of company-wide policy, and help to assure uniformity throughout the organization. It is the responsibility of each and every member of management to administer these policies in a consistent and impartial manner.

Procedures and practices in the field of personnel relations are subject to modification and further development in the light of experience. Each member of management can assist in keeping our personnel program up-to-date by notifying the personnel department whenever problems are encountered or improvements can be made in the administration of our personnel policies.

Policy Statement:

Many of us are aware of the great need for leadership in government, churches and schools, but, unfortunately, we have neglected some phases of industrial leadership. Much of our conscious time is spent at work. If we are to have daily satisfaction, it must come from our jobs as well as from our community and family activities. Therefore, it is our earnest hope that this manual will enable you to better understand your management duties and the responsibility of establishing leadership in the field of human relations. We know that if you understand the philosophy of management, you will furnish the present and future industrial leadership that is so sorely needed to continut the traditions that mean so much to each of us.

Policy Statement:

This manual brings together in a convenient form personnel policies and procedures having general application throughout the company.

It is designed to serve as a ready reference for members of department management and supervision in everyday personnel administration.

This manual is in looseleaf form to allow for changes and additions. New pages will be sent to holders of manuals with instructions to remove any sheets that are superseded.

For purposes of this manual, a *policy* is the general statement of a company goal. *Procedures* are specific steps for reaching that company goal.

Nothing in this manual should be construed to be in conflict with the current Agreement between the Company and the Employees' Union.

Where references are made to the Union Agreement in the policies and procedures contained herein, the provisions of the Agreement shall apply to exempt employees as well as to those covered by the Agreement unless indicated otherwise.

Policy Statement:

To All Who Supervise:

The management of our most valuable resource, the people who work for the Company, is a constant and continuing challenge. As a supervisor your task is to achieve our common goal—the highest caliber of trust and investment service—through those who work with you and for you.

Set forth in this manual are standards of human conduct which are designed to help you achieve this common purpose. It is a tool designed specifically for your daily use.

It is the function of the Personnel Department to codify and clarify the policies of management. In this revised and updated edition, personnel was assisted by many supervisors who made valuable suggestions for the implementation and clarification of these policies.

It is your responsibility to apply these policies in a consistent manner to assure the staff of our common purpose. In the meantime, personnel stands ready to assist at any time in interpretation.

AUTHORITY AND DISTRIBUTION OF POLICY MANUAL

Policy Statement:

The attached manual is being assigned to all positions which entail supervisory responsibilities of any magnitude. Please notice that the manual is assigned to the *position* and not the *incumbent* of the position, and should remain with the position if the incumbent moves on.

We also ask your cooperation in keeping the manual up-to-date when page changes are sent to you in the future. With more than 100 copies in circulation, a great deal of confusion could arise if changes are not made. The manual can be a reliable and effective tool for good management if carefully maintained.

To avoid confusion, if you should have a copy of any previous manual in your possession, please return it to Personnel.

Policy Statement:

This manual contains statements of personnel policies and procedures. It is designed to be a working guide for supervisory and staff personnel in the day-to-day administration of our company personnel program.

These written policies should increase understanding, eliminate the need for personal decisions on matters of company-wide policy, and help to assure uniformity throughout the organization. It is the responsibility of each and every member of management to administer these policies in a consistent and impartial manner.

Procedures and practices in the field of personnel relations are subject to modification and further development in the light of experience. Each member of management can assist in keeping our personnel program up-to-date by notifying the personnel department whenever problems are encountered or improvements can be made in the administration of our personnel policies.

Policy Statement:

This Personnel Policy Manual is issued to you as a means of providing you and your job with a very important personnel tool. It is designed to serve as a source of information you can look to for authority and completeness. If for some reason you leave your present supervisory position, please return this Policy Manual to the personnel department.

Policy Statement

Every salaried supervisor of the Company is to receive a copy of this Policy Manual upon entering the supervisory position. This present Policy Manual is up-to-date and contains the complete and accurate policies of our company as of this date. It is to be carefully preserved in your desk at all times. We ask that this Policy Manual remain on the premises at all times in your department. Should you, for any reason, be transferred within our company, upgraded, or change your status for any other reason, please contact your immediate supervisor and return the Policy Manual. If your supervisor is not immediately available, please turn the Policy Manual over to the Office Administration.

Policy Statement:

This Policy Manual is the result of a great deal of study, planning and dedicated work of many members in our management and supervisory family. The group was composed of _____, _____, and _____. After the initial drafting was completed, the manuscript was reviewed by representatives of all departments and divisions throughout our organization. The complete Personnel Manual can, therefore, be said to have been prepared by _____ people for the use of _____ people. Your company gratefully acknowledges the important contribution of those who collaborated in the drafting and editing of this Policy Manual.

You are receiving a copy of this Policy manual which I sincerely believe you will find useful in increasing your understanding of company-wide personnel policies and practices. It will tell you how our personnel program should operate. The manual is designed primarily for use by all supervisory staff members at all levels of authority and to whom are delegated responsibility for the operation of their personnel program and for the evaluation of its effectiveness.

We believe that the policies and practices of our personnel program presented in this Policy Manual will produce information essential to carry out our personnel program and to determine how well our program is meeting our company and employee needs, in carrying out the basic personnel policies of our company.

Our aim in issuing this Policy Manual is to assist each supervisor in making certain that his supervisory techniques further the personnel program of our company. We sincerely hope the Personnel Policy Manual will prove to be of material help to you and will thereby contribute to a general strengthening of our overall employer-employee relationship.

Policy Statement:

Our Personnel Policy Manual is being made available to all supervisory personnel in our organization. Its purpose is to: (1) provide a basis for and objectives of our personnel program; (2) assign responsibility for carrying out the principles and practices of our personnel program; (3) provide recognized authority, consistent with applicable laws, and which action is to be taken and to minimize the possibility of unauthorized personnel action; (4) to bring about understanding of our personnel policies and practices; (5) facilitate decisions and promote consistency of interpretation and application of cross organizational lines and over a period of time; (6) provide a record to guide future policy and serve as a framework for the revisions that appear to be desirable on the basis of experience.

SUPPLEMENTS TO THE POLICY MANUAL

Policy Statement:

The personnel policies, practices and guidelines in this Policy Manual will remain in effect until changes are considered necessary as a result of internal growth, competitive forces, or as a result of general economic conditions pertaining to our particular industry. However, any such change to be made in any personnel policy or practice will be made only after we give due consideration to the mutual advantages, benefits, and responsibilities of such changes on you as a supervisor and on other employees of the company. Should such changes be warranted and approved by the future Policy Manual committee, you will be notified immediately and given revised policy changes which are to be placed where indicated in the Policy Manual.

Should you have any question as to the interpretation or understanding of any revised policy or practice, please visit with your immediate supervisor immediately. It is most important that we all continue to have full and complete understanding of all our personnel policies and practices.

Policy Statement:

From time to time, you will receive additional supplements to our Personnel Policy Manual. These new supplements will update and revise present policy and practice whenever deemed necessary. You will want to study the revised supplements carefully prior to placing them in your Policy Manual. Please be sure to remove old policy statements and procedures when recommended to do so in the memorandum attached to revised supplements. Should you have any question concerning the intent or procedure to follow in the supplements to your Policy Manual, please see your immediate supervisor.

ESTABLISHING NEW OR REVISED POLICY

Policy Statement:

Standard Policies and Procedures concerning the relationship between the company and its employees will be reproduced in writing and made available to all concerned.

When the need for a new or revised Standard Policy and Procedure is indicated, it will be referred to the Policy Board for consideration.

If it is decided by the Policy Board that such a policy or revision is desirable, the Board will outline or suggest the principal points which should be covered.

The Industrial Relations Department will prepare a preliminary draft of the policy and distribute this to the members of the Board.

The Policy Board will review the preliminary draft and provide the appropriate direction for preparation of a tentative draft.

The Policy Board will be responsible for the final draft of the proposed policy. A copy of the proposed policy in its final form will be sent to members of the Policy Board for their signatures of approval.

> To assure coordination with Corporate policies, copies of the proposed policy will be sent to the Corporate Director of Industrial Relations before it is issued.

Standard Policies and Procedures become effective upon approval by the Division Manager.

The Industrial Relations Department will mail sufficient copies of the approved Standard Policy and Procedure to each Policy Board member for distribution and discussion to those supervisors having a copy of the Policy and Procedures Manual. Supervisors will be responsible for placing the new policy in the manual and destroying any superseded policy.

SUPERVISOR'S RESPONSIBILITIES TO THE COMPANY

Policy Statement:

In simple and brief terms, the task of a foreman is to produce through the combined use of people and machines. Probably the most complicated of these two tools are the people. Therefore, this factor demands the greatest ingenuity of the foreman.

In your effort to produce our product in an efficient manner, you will encounter many obstacles. Some of these obstacles will be created unconsciously by ourselves. Others will be created by outsiders, or by some employees for selfish reasons. The efforts of the Industrial Relations Program should be to anticipate the obstacles and make the atmosphere of our plant unfertile for their creation. Some of these obstacles can be lack of incentive by the employees, union organization attempts, conflict between employees and management, between the employees themselves, poor employee attitudes, lack of concern for the welfare of our jobs, etc.

WORKING THROUGH PEOPLE

1. Your employees will normally respond best to fair and equitable treatment. You should apply the policies which are established for our plant so that the results are as fair and equitable as possible.

2. You should acquaint yourself as thoroughly as possible with all policies of the company so that your decisions affecting your people are educated decisions. The "standard practice instructions" are the backbone of this policy. You will receive new "instructions" as they are issued and when they apply to your job.

3. It is the responsibility of the Industrial Relations office to furnish assistance whenever a foreman has a problem that requires more than normal consideration.

4. The policies or instructions that will be furnished you will *not* be nearly as valuable to you as your own good judgment.

5. The attitudes of your people will often reflect your attitude. If you are unhappy with your job or your company, chances are they will be too. Keep a good attitude and let them see that attitude. If you have a personal problem, talk it out with your boss, not your people.

6. There are matters that you as a foreman will know of or need to discuss that are not the business of others. Do not discuss such matters in the presence of employees or with them.

7. It is always dangerous to become involved in other people's private affairs. This is also true in regard to the private lives of your employees. Although you should be sincerely interested in the welfare and personal lives of your employees, be

wise enough not to involve yourself to the extent it interferes with our primary responsibility. Be helpful, but not a "busybody." If a problem is affecting their work, then it may be best to direct them to professional assistance or you may ask for guidance from Industrial Relations.

8. Having both male and female employees can create potential problems that can destroy your departmental morale. You should speak and act in only the best moral manner so as to provide the best influence for all your people.

9. You should review the performance of your employees constantly, but to ensure regular reviews, you are required to complete a "Performance Appraisal" at least once every six months. This will aid you and the employees.

10. All instances of absence or tardiness must be reported on the "Absentee Report" form No._____. These forms must be completed and turned in to the Industrial Relations office for each department once a week. The green "Request for Leave of Absence" form No._____ must be completed and signed by the employee for any advance request for leave or when funeral pay is involved.

11. Any insurance claim on group insurance must be relayed to the Industrial Relations Office as soon as possible.

12. An employee requesting a visit in the Industrial Relations office should be encouraged to make the visit during breaks, lunch, or after hours. However, if such times seem impractical, call and make an appointment for the employee as soon as possible.

13. Holiday, vacation pay and all other employee benefits shall be granted in the manner set out in the Employees' Handbook.

14. On-the-job injuries should be investigated by the foreman and reported in detail to the plant manager and the Industrial Relations office on Form No._____—Report of Accident.

15. Sick or injured employees should be removed to their homes, their doctor or hospital as soon as possible. If the seriousness of an employee's injury or illness is in doubt always assume the worst and take appropriate steps.

THE JOB

Each manager should check out on the following list before trying to lead people:

1. Know the names and positions of the people you work for and those with whom you work on the same level.
2. Recognize that a manager's greatest resources are the people who work for you so learn your profession well.
3. Develop your work group to be confident and resourceful.
4. Acquaint yourself with all aspects of your job.
5. Understand your specific responsibilities and authority.

Policy Statement:

A supervisor is an employee to whom authority has been delegated to direct the work of others, and who has responsibility for their work output. You are a person in a job that has been established and defined by our organization, and which is located at a particular place in our company. You may be at the first level of management, directly overseeing a group of workers; or you may be at the middle management level with subordinate supervisors under you; or you may be a manager with executive rank.

All supervisory positions are not alike. There are differences not only in the technical aspects of the work, but in the way supervision is exercised, as, for example, a route supervisor for a bottling company, the production line supervisor for a cabinet manufacturer, chief engineer of an engineering design group, or the manager of an office task force.

All this means that we have to think of supervision, not in terms of one definite kind of job, but in terms of a broad category of positions occupied by a wide variety of people. We cannot outline to all of our supervisors a formula to control the way you work. Rather, we must seek to promote the development of your subordinates so that they may realize in their work the maximum productive usefulness and their greatest personal satisfaction.

SUPERVISOR'S RESPONSIBILITIES FOR COST CONTROL

Policy Statement:

As a department head for this dealership, it is your duty and responsibility to help us control our operating expense at a minimum. We can accomplish this goal by following these important steps:

1. Carefully analyze every possible area of waste in your department. Try to decide how wasted materials or wasted effort

can be corrected. Delegate the responsibility to somebody to correct these areas, and then follow through to see that the corrections are made.

2. Continually analyze ways and means of improving work performed in your department. Take each job and look for possible ways that it can be performed more efficiently. At the same time, look for possible way to save materials.

3. Make every effort to study and use any cost data pertaining to your department that you presently have or can obtain. You will want to maintain your own record of your department's operating costs, cost savings, and other improvements. This will serve as an incentive to you to further cost saving in your department.

4. Inspire your staff members to be cost-conscious with regard to materials and equipment we use in our operations.

5. Make every effort to eliminate any working condition in your department which could cause an accident.

6. Make every effort to arrange the work in your department so that your people can perform their service with as little wasted effort and backtracking as possible.

7. Constantly keep informed of the present condition of the tools and equipment in your department to be sure they are in proper working condition to turn out satisfactory work.

8. Keep a sharp eye out on ways to reduce waste and rework jobs in an effort to overcome losses in materials and to keep from having work go out which will be rejected by the customer.

9. Constantly review new employees to be sure they are properly trained for the job at hand so that they can turn out the highest quality and quantity of service and work for our customers.

10. Look for better ways to utilize our present equipment, machines and floor space.

11. Be sure that each employee is on the job at the proper starting times.

12. Make every effort to settle employee complaints or grievances at the earliest possible moment. We must make every effort to keep employee morale on a high level and create teamwork within your department.

13. Always seek suggestions from your workers on ways to reduce waste and costs in your department.

Policy Statement:

From all appearances, our company is on the threshold of one of the busiest periods yet experienced. While our company continues to expand and progress, we cannot maintain this progress unless we continue to watch our cost and to cut expenses to absolute minimum whenever possible.

With this policy in mind, we ask every supervisor to try very hard to completely eliminate time wasted by employees, needless time spent away from the job and other wasted effort. It becomes even more imperative that we work together to eliminate those things that are time-consuming and unnecessary on the part of employees because we will have more essential work to do this year than ever before, and it will not be possible to add anyone to any department.

Let's be on the lookout for time wasted by ourselves or by the employees under our supervision in such areas of carelessness, waste, mistakes, loafing, poor quality, poor attitude, absenteeism and tardiness. All these things add up to thousands of lost payroll dollars every year.

Policy Statement:

One of the most difficult problems you as a supervisor have is that of creating a genuine interest in cost reduction on the part of your subordinates, to correct the mistaken idea that a little wasted material here or wasted effort won't make any difference. In order to gain the cooperation of your employees in this important area of cost control, we recommend that you daily follow these five important guidelines:

1. Create in your employees a feeling of being important and of being "in" on things. Try to make them feel they are really part of the department and of the company rather than "I just work here."

2. Make every effort to show new employees as you introduce them to their jobs during the orientation process how company costs are directly related to their long-range job security and direct income. Show new employees how our customer, the real boss, won't buy from us unless our costs are competitive, our quality is superior and our service is excellent.

3. Make every effort to look out for wasted utilities such as light, heat, water, etc. and other costly services when they are not in use or being needed.

4. Constantly search for ways to eliminate wasted materials in your department. By all means, set an example daily for your employees to follow.

5. When possible, explain to your employees the reasons for our large expenditures for new equipment, supplies and materials so that they will understand the reason for this spending by the company. It all results in our continuing efforts to make our company the best possible place to work for everyone so that we can have excellent, safe and pleasant working conditions and make their work easier.

SUPERVISOR'S RESPONSIBILITY TO IMMEDIATE SUPERIOR

Policy Statement:

Every supervisor and foreman within our organization must assume several responsibilities. One important area of this responsibility is to your immediate superior or supervisor in top management. It is the policy of our corporation that every supervisor and foreman fulfill the following duties and obligations to his immediate superior on a regular, recurring basis:

1. Cooperate with immediate superior.
2. Obey orders and execute instructions in detail. Inform your superior of all changes in working conditions and other phases of production. Responsibility should be taken to ensure that job instruction and day-to-day orders to subordinates are clearly understood.
3. Prepare yourself for greater responsibility by training your subordinate to become a back-up man.
4. Report the outcome of any important phase of the production service operation fully, simply and accurately to the immediate supervisor when requested.
5. Show courtesy and respect to immediate superior at all times.
6. Look for better ways of doing things and offer ideas and suggestions for improvements to immediate superior.
7. Make every effort to relieve the immediate superior of job details whenever possible.
8. Always assume full responsibility for work assigned to you and your subordinates.

SUPERVISOR'S RESPONSIBILITY TO OTHER SUPERVISORS ON THE SAME MANAGEMENT LEVEL

Policy Statement:

The purpose of this policy is to outline the responsibilities of each supervisor to his fellow supervisors on the same management level within our organization.

OFFICE ADMINISTRATION HANDBOOK

It is continually important that we must have a strong team effort among our supervisors in order to progress as a strong, unified company. To have a strong company, we must have the cooperation and team effort of each supervisor. Therefore, each supervisor in our corporation should daily assume the following responsibilities to fellow supervisors:

1. Cooperate with each other.
2. Exchange ideas for improvements in all areas of company policy which can be for the good of all concerned.
3. Always show courtesy, respect, understanding and tolerance to the other supervisors at all times.
4. Try to help a fellow supervisor with personal problems if invited to do so.
5. Make every effort to set a good example with the helpful cooperation of other supervisors.
6. Never belittle a fellow supervisor in front of subordinates for any reason whatsoever.
7. Always show confidence and respect for fellow supervisors in the presence of subordinates.
8. Be fair, patient, understanding and helpful to all fellow supervisors at all times.

SUPERVISOR'S RESPONSIBILITY TO SUBORDINATES

Policy Statement:

We all know that good, sound leadership is important in our company. You might say that it is an absolute necessity. You, as a supervisor, must be a leader and not a boss or a driver. Effective, sound leadership requires that you handle your subordinates in a way that you can get the job done by them in the safest, least expensive and most effective way and still achieve the quantity and quality of production we desire. To do this, you must be ever mindful of the importance of trying to meet the individual, personal needs of your subordinates on a daily basis.

We must realize, as supervisors, that subordinates will follow you if you prove to them that you understand their needs, and you try to help them meet their needs better than anyone else. Therefore every supervisor in our company must recognize this obligation to subordinates, as well as responsibilities for them in order that the supervisor can gain respect, cooperation and team effort from these subordinates. To achieve this goal, you, as a supervisor, must meet the following responsibilities to the employees under your supervision:

1. Consider your employees as individual, important human beings at all times and respect them.

2. Do a good job of representing your employees to top management.

3. Make every effort to interpret and explain company policies accurately to your subordinates at all times.

4. Be an example to your subordinates both at work and at play.

5. Go out of your way to pat an employee on the back when he does a job exceptionally well. When necessary, reprimand in private. Always remember, "Praise in public and reprimand in private."

6. Let your employees know that you are giving them every opportunity to develop and improve their skills and earnings.

7. Always evaluate your people carefuly and objectively. Judge them honestly. Never permit individual personalities or prejudices to cloud your objective opinion of any employee.

8. Always try to improve your confidence in dealing with your subordinates by being considerate, firm and fair in your individual dealings with employees under your supervision.

9. Always place an employee on a job according to his or her present skill, ability and attitude.

10. Never pass the buck if something goes wrong in your department. Always assume the responsibility for the action or the job done by the employees under your supervision.

11. Learn to know your subordinates individually. Learn as much as you can about their individual interests, likes and dislikes.

12. Always take time to give proper and adequate instruction to new job applicants and make them feel at home through proper job induction and orientation.

13. Always be alert to keeping your work area safe and clean. Be ever mindful of the importance of good, clean and safe working conditions.

Policy Statement:

1. It is the policy of this organization that each employee is to have the opportunity to earn a fair day's pay for a fair day's work, and that each employee will have the opportunity to grow and be advanced to better jobs according to his or her effort and ability.

2. Supervisors are to study each subordinate and each job so that every employee can be given job duties according to his

or her qualifications and present ability. Supervisors should always make every effort to place their subordinates in congenial work groups whenever possible.

3. Every supervisor is responsible for giving the best possible training on the job to every job applicant. To accomplish this goal, the supervisor must be skilled in the techniques of job instruction. The supervisor must also be able to supervise job instruction given by an assistant.

4. Supervisors are to be sure that each employee is trained to do the job as efficiently and as satisfactorily as possible. Each employee is to be provided with suitable tools, equipment and materials at all times.

5. The supervisor is to take the necessary steps to be sure that each employee thoroughly understands job duties, responsibilities and authority. The employee must know how to perform them and have the incentive to constantly improve performance.

6. It is the supervisor's responsibility to properly indoctrinate all employees with present and future company rules and personnel policies which affect them. The supervisor must know these rules and policies well enough to interpret them clearly and simply to the employees so that they will understand them.

7. Every supervisor is responsible for letting each worker know how he or she stands on the job. Supervisors are to be liberal in giving praise and credit where due. The supervisor is to be sure that each employee's skill and ability are being used to the fullest at all times.

8. Supervisors are to know how to correct the employee's work performance and personal conduct without giving personal offense to the employee. The supervisor is to know when to be friendly and easygoing and when to get fair and firm. Above all, the supervisor is to be consistent in disciplinary action with employees at all times.

9. The supervisors are to be alert to potential sources of friction within their departments at all times.

10. The supervisors are to be responsible to the employees in seeing that their working areas are kept as clean and safe as possible at all times under present plant facilities.

11. Supervisors are to provide the fullest possible protection for the employees' personal safety and welfare. Supervisors are to be responsible for eliminating and correcting all potential hazards, and to make full use of all present and future safety

equipment, first-aid techniques and the fundamentals of good safety practices.

12. Every supervisor is responsible for seeing that each employee has a clear and correct understanding of how the method of payment is computed on the payroll.

13. Supervisors are responsible for communicating the correct feelings and attitudes of employees to top management. In the same manner, supervisors are primarily responsible for conveying to the employees plans, intentions and expressions of top management to the extent necessary to build continued team spirit and high employee morale and job satisfaction.

EMPLOYEE RELATIONS PRINCIPLES

Policy Statement:

We believe that the mutual interests of supervision and employees can best be served by living under the following principles each day:

1. It should be recognized by both employees and supervision that compensation due any of us is in direct proportion to the quality of service and work which we are able to perform.

2. The company will maintain wage rates on a level equal to or slightly higher than the average of the community for comparable types of work under similar working conditions.

3. The company will maintain a staff of competent, permanent employees by following the best possible screening techniques.

4. By carefully observing the individual progress of employees, the company will be able to pay employees according to their merit and length of service for their jobs in the organization.

5. Should a vacancy occur in the company, every effort will be made to fill the position with someone from within the organization with due regard for ability, qualifications, experience and length of service.

6. We will avoid discrimination with regard to race, religion, color, sex, or national origin in hiring and in all future phases of the employee-employer relationship through termination.

7. We will observe and follow the established grievance procedure.

8. We will maintain reasonable hours of work, good employee benefits and the best possible working conditions for everyone.

9. Through these and other practices, the company will encourage employees to increase their longevity with the company.

Policy Statement:

We realize that our strength and future growth depend directly upon the contribution made by every supervisor and employee of our organization. We also know that high productivity and efficiency result from your individual job satisfaction and happiness.

Our policy is to be frank, fair and honest with the personnel always and to respect their rights as employees. We shall continue to strive to achieve mutual respect in our working relationship. We will always insist that our supervisors do all in their power to carry out such a policy.

To continue working together successfully, each employee and each supervisor must realize that harmonious relationships are not entirely a matter of rules but are the outgrowth of daily decisions and friendly attitudes of team spirit.

POSITION TOWARD PRESENT COLLECTIVE BARGAINING REPRESENTATIVE

Policy Statement:

It is our objective to establish a consistent labor relations policy in this corporation. The purpose of this policy is to develop a sound working relationship with the union without surrendering our rights to manage the organization. The foundation of our labor relations policy is a reputation of consistency, credibility, and fairness with the union representative and to our employees in the bargaining unit.

Therefore, in order to make this policy work for the benefit of the employees, the union and management, the following personnel policies and practices must be followed and administered on a daily basis:

LABOR RELATIONS POLICY AND PRACTICE NO. 1: We shall accept union representation of our employees in good faith so long as the union represents a true majority of our employees in the bargaining unit.

LABOR RELATIONS POLICY AND PRACTICE NO. 2: We shall maintain management's right to manage.

LABOR RELATIONS POLICY AND PRACTICE NO. 3: Management representatives must use caution in dealing with union representatives socially.

LABOR RELATIONS POLICY AND PRACTICE NO. 4: The top management of this corporation must continually support its own representatives in carrying out and administering our industrial relations policies and practices.

THE DISCIPLINARY POLICIES IN THE CORPORATION WILL BE ENFORCED IN A FAIR, FIRM AND CONSISTENT MANNER DAILY.

LABOR RELATIONS POLICY AND PRACTICE NO. 5: Our employee union representatives will be subject to all company rules except those that they are specifically exempted from as spelled out in the present labor agreement.

LABOR RELATIONS POLICY AND PRACTICE NO. 6: A wildcat strike will never be condoned or accepted on the part of management.

LABOR RELATIONS POLICY AND PRACTICE NO. 7: Supervision will handle fairly, firmly and without discrimination all employee complaints as efficiently and rapidly as possible.

LABOR RELATIONS POLICY AND PRACTICE NO. 8: Every single representative of management down to the lead man level must exercise extreme caution on a daily basis to avoid establishing "past practices" in administering company policy that is inconsistent with prior policy and practice.

LABOR RELATIONS POLICY AND PRACTICE NO. 9: Document all decisions, side agreements, and enforcement adminstration of the present labor agreement in writing.

Policy Statement:

Since our company policy is to give our employees all the advantages they could get by union affiliation, without the many disadvantages and expense to them that union membership would entail, following are suggestions that will support such a policy.

EMPLOYEE ATTITUDES

1. Learn what your employees really think about the company, their job and their supervisors.
2. Keep constantly alert to possible conditions of employee unrest. Carefully check and analyze gripes and complaints.
3. Alert supervision to keep top management informed of any changes in employee attitudes.
4. Make an immediate study of employee attitudes and general morale.

5. Give attention and consideration of industrial recreation as a means of building employee satisfaction and higher morale.

WORKING CONDITIONS

1. Make work areas as pleasant, clean and attractive as possible.
2. Check on adequacy of summer ventilation, lighting and equipment arrangements.
3. Take steps to correct unusual heat, noise, dust and odor.
4. Eliminate hazardous conditions at work stations.
5. Compare working conditions with other companies in your area.
6. Provide employees with convenient and adequate washrooms, drinking fountains, eating facilities and parking areas.
7. Provide employees with equipment and supplies that are adequate for safe and efficient work.

LISTEN TO AND TALK WITH YOUR EMPLOYEES

1. Keep them regularly informed of company plans, policies and "news" verbally and by written communications. Send a letter to their homes now and then.
2. Personalize your employee communications so that every worker feels that you are interested in each of them.
3. Make regular tours of your plant or store and smile sincerely.
4. Give careful consideration to *all* employees' suggestions and complaints. Provide answers.
5. Review the effectiveness of your present communications program.

EMPLOYEE BENEFITS

1. Find out if employees know what benefits they are now receiving. Communicate sufficient benefit information in order to maintain understanding and appreciation at a high degree.
2. Consider carefully the needs of employees before offering or considering a new benefit.

PERSONNEL POLICIES

1. Put policies in writing—(A policy manual and employee handbook are recommended.)
2. Review policies periodically and keep them up-to-date.

3. Keep policies sound, fair and in line with area practice. Administer policies consistently.

4. Indoctrinate new employees through a systematic induction program. Make orientation personal so that the new employee feels "at home."

5. Be sure that every employee understands clearly his or her job, responsibilities and privileges.

FAVORITISM

1. Remind supervision to assign work in a fair, equal manner. Remind them to be impartial in their dealings with subordinates. They must not play favorites.

2. Develop a written procedure to provide fair administration of discipline. Follow this consistently. (We recommend a written grievance procedure.)

SENIORITY

1. If length of service is recognized, communicate how seniority is acquired, retained and works in regard to layoffs, recalls, promotions and transfers.

2. *Be certain* employees know how your system works and how it affects them individually.

If you are now wearing the "silver spurs of freedom" you are very fortunate. You can continue having this privilege only by taking action now in the above recommended areas.

EQUAL EMPLOYMENT OPPORTUNITY

Policy Statement:

The company's employment policy shall provide for its employees the quality of opportunity, regardless of race, color, sex, creed, political affiliation, or marital status, and shall not show partiality or grant any special favors to any employee or group of employees.

Policy Statement:

There shall be no discrimination on the part of either the company or the union on account of the race, color, sex, national origin, or political or religious belief of any employee.

Policy Statement:

It is the policy of _____ Corp. of Tennessee to grant equal employment opportunity to all qualified persons without regard to race, color, sex, religion or national origin. To deny one's contribution to our efforts because he is a member of a minority group is an injustice, not only to the individual, but to the company and the nation as well. It is the intent and desire of the company that equal employment opportunity will be provided in employment, promotion, wages, benefits, and all other privileges, terms and conditions of employment.

Policy Statement:

The progress of our organization requires that we utilize all available manpower to the fullest, regardless of race, color, religion, sex or national origin. To deny one's contribution to our efforts because he is a member of a minority group is an injustice, not only to the individual, but to the company and to the nation as well. The continuing pressure to find sufficiently qualified people makes it necessary that discriminatory practices, if they exist, be eliminated and that individuals with talent be recognized and encouraged through equitable personnel policies. It is the policy of this company to grant equal employment opportunity to all qualified persons without regard to race, color, religion, sex or national origin. This policy is based on the same philosophy as the Equal Employment Opportunity Act of 1966, that discriminatory employment practices are unjust and economically wasteful.

In the past it has been the practice of this company to show no discrimination to employees with respect to race, color, religion, sex, or national origin. We feel it best to announce again this practice.

Policy Statement:

The company believes that all persons are entitled to equal employment opportunity and does not discriminate against its employees, or applicants for employment, because of race, creed, color, national origin, age or sex, provided they are qualified and meet the physical requirements established by the company for the job.

PURPOSE

The purpose of this policy is to reaffirm the company's position regarding nondiscrimination in all matters relating to employment throughout the organization.

RESPONSIBILITY

The Industrial Relations Division has been assigned the responsibility of seeing that all phases of personnel administration are in harmony with this policy. The responsibility for administering and in complying with this policy has been delegated to the operating heads of the various divisions, plants, sales offices, warehouses, and departments with respect to employees within their jurisdiction.

SCOPE OF EMPLOYMENT RELATIONSHIP

As an indication of our affirmative action, the company policy of nondiscrimination must prevail throughout every aspect of the employment relationship, including recruitment, selection, placement, training, compensation, promotion, transfer, layoff, recall and termination.

PROCEDURE FOR COMPLIANCE

1. Notify all recruitment sources of our equal employment opportunity policy.
2. Include the phrase "an equal employment opportunity employer, M. and F." in all "Help Wanted" advertising.
3. Include equal employment opportunity clause in all purchase orders and subcontracts.
4. Notify all labor units with whom we have collective bargaining agreements of our policy of nondiscrimination and make every effort to have same incorporated in future labor agreements.
5. Maintain common facilities, such as lunchrooms, restrooms, and drinking fountains on a nonsegregated basis.

Policy Statement:

The firm policy of this company, and our deep belief, continues to be that applicants for employment, and employees, should receive fair and equal treatment regardless of their race, color, religion, sex or national origin. The policy not to discriminate includes, but is not limited to, help wanted advertising, recruiting, hiring, placement, upgrading, transfer, rates of pay and termination.

As in the past, we will not lower our standards in any way for employment or promotion. the *most qualified* individuals will be hired or promoted regardless of their race, color, religion, sex or national origin.

SCOPE OF NONDISCRIMINATION POLICY

Our nondiscrimination policy shall be issued, along with appropriate executive directives for all management personnel to implement this policy. Management and supervisory meetings will be held for the purpose of discussing this policy and methods of expediting its objectives.

All employees shall be informed of the increased emphasis on nondiscrimination by means of our corporate brochure, employee newspaper, meetings and bulletin boards.

Labor unions shall be informed of the policy on nondiscrimination. Further labor agreements will contain nondiscrimination clauses.

All public news media shall be given information concerning our efforts toward nondiscrimination.

RESPONSIBILITIES FOR NONDISCRIMINATION

The Industrial Relations Director shall be the overall director of our nondiscrimination policy.

The General Manager in each Division shall advise, assist and monitor line management in their daily compliance with this policy.

Each supervisor shall carry out the policy within his department or work group.

Each Division shall review, at least annually, the status of this program of expanding and re-emphasizing nondiscrimination.

RECRUITING AND PLACEMENT OF JOB APPLICANTS

We will inform all applicants of our equal employment opportunities. All applications for employment will be printed with the term, "Equal Opportunity Employer."

We will inform all recruitment sources of our desire to consider all qualified job applicants regardless of race, color, religion, sex or national origin.

We will review the status of current minority group employees to determine if their services are being fully utilized.

TRANSFER, PROMOTION AND LAYOFF OF EMPLOYEES

During work force reductions, down-gradings or layoffs and subsequent recall will be accomplished based on our seniority plan.

All employee transfers will be based solely on qualifications, corporate needs and our transfer policy.

TRAINING OF EMPLOYEES

All minority group employees shall have equal opportunity for all training programs, including supervisory-development.

Scholarships, grants, gifts to educational institutions shall follow a nondiscriminatory policy.

SOCIAL ASPECTS OF
NONDISCRIMINATION POLICY

We will re-emphasize the nonsegregation of all facilities including work areas, restrooms and cafeterias. Memberships in management and recreation clubs will be available on a non-segregated basis. Corporation-sponsored sports activities and social functions shall be open to all employees regardless of race, color, religion, sex or national origin.

DEFINITION OF EMPLOYEE STATUS
(A Midwest Company)

Policy Statement:

Applicants who meet qualifications for employment according to the foregoing eligibility and other requirements, will be offered employment as vacanies become available, according to the definition and procedures in the following paragraphs.

Probationary employees are those:

    a. Who are employed on a full-time schedule for not more than 90 calendar days and

    b. Who are former employees who were rehired after a separation of more than one year, or

    c. Who are newly employed people who never have worked for the company.

Regular employees are those:

    a. Recalled from layoff within one year of layoff, and who were in a regular employee status immediately prior to their last layoff.

    b. Full-time employees who have completed 90 calendar days of uninterrupted full-time employment, or part-time employees who have worked 480 hours uninterrupted by layoffs of more than 30 days.

Relief employees are those employed as vacation or other relief for a limited period of time during peak employee absences.

Part-time employees are those working a part-time schedule such as parts of days or weeks. A part-time employee when assigned a full-time work schedule, will take the probationary or regular status, according to definitions for these.

All new hourly rate full-time employees will be hired into the Transfer Pool as probationary employees.

Probationary employees will be paid the probationary high competitive rate, will not accumulate seniority and will not be eligible for other benefits during the 90-day probationary period.

If employment continues uninterrupted beyond 90 days, the employee will be:

> Considered qualified.
>
> Reclassified as a regular employee.
>
> Given mill seniority retroactive to his probationary starting date.
>
> Eligible to receive the higher of the Transfer Pool High Competitive rate or the High Competitive rate to which he is classified or assigned, as provided in Standard Policy and Procedure W-2.
>
> Enrolled in the company Benefit Plan.
>
> Informed of the above changes by the Personnel Services Section.

Relief employees will be hired into the Transfer Pool, will be paid the probationary High Competitive Rate, will not have seniority, and will not be eligible for employee benefits.

> Relief employees must agree to work as required during the entire period for which they are employed.

Part-time employees will be hired as needed and assigned to the work for which they were employed. They will be paid at the rate mutually agreed to upon employment.

> Part-time employees will be considered probationary until they actually work 480 hours uninterrupted by layoffs of more than 30 days.

Policy Statement:

Employment Status

A. *Probation*

The probationary period for new employees is three months, unless reduced by Management in special instances. During this period, the employee has an opportunity to demonstrate proper attitudes and abilities for the postion for which employed. He may be dismissed without prior notice or obligation during this period. Upon satisfactory completion of 90 days of service, he is given permanent status and granted life insurance and health insurance benefits.

B. *Part-time*

Anyone employed less than 35 hours a week is considered part-time. A part-time employee is eligible for fringe benefits depending upon the regularity of employment and the number of scheduled hours.

C. *Temporary*

Anyone employed for a specific period (such as summer) or for a specific purpose (to replace a sick employee) is considered temporary. A temporary employee is not eligible for fringe benefits.

D. *Outside Employment*

Holding of a second job elsewhere is subject to critical appraisal only if it conflicts with the full performance of the employee and the interests of our company.

College Cooperative Program

The Company from time to time employs college students who work less than the normal 37½ hour week during the academic year, while attending college on a full-time basis. Work programs and benefits for college co-ops are modified as follows:

1. *Working Hours*
   a. Normal Academic Year-25 hours weekly.
   b. Summer and Mid-Year Vacation Periods—37½ hours weekly.
   c. Specific starting and quitting times will be determined by the department head directly involved.

2. *Salary*
   a. One standard rate for all clerical work performed by college co-ops is determined by market conditions.
   b. Hours in excess of 25 per week will be reimbursed at the rate of $3.35 an hour.
   c. Hours in excess of 37½ (when performing a full workweek schedule) shall be at 1½ times the employee's current base pay.

3. *Leaves of Absence*
   a. Leaves of Absence will not be granted for the sole purpose of study.

4. *Benefits*
   a. College Co-ops are eligible for all fringe benefits, except tuition refund provided they are employed on a permanent part-time basis for a workweek of no less than 20 hours.

HIRING FORMER EMPLOYEES, FRIENDS, RELATIVES AND HANDICAPPED

Policy Statement:

All vacancies are filled by promotion from within the Company whenever possible. If a suitable candidate is not already available on the staff, a new employee is secured in accordance with the following policies:

1. *Recruitment*
   a. Preference is given to employees who are recommended by present employees and friends of the Company, provided they meet all job requirements.
   b. No employee shall solicit applicants from among employees of another company.

2. *Selection*
   Employees are selected on the basis of character, intelligence, aptitude and physical fitness. Qualifications for the job at hand as well as for future advancement are given prime consideration.

3. *Age*
   Applicants under 16 years of age and over 65 will not be considered. Age is not a factor in employment except for those openings in which long-range considerations are paramount.

4. *Education*
   Applicants without a high school diploma or equivalent business experience can be considered only for a relatively small number of positions.

5. *Former Employees*
   Employees who have left the Company voluntarily or through no fault of their own and who make application for re-employment will be given consideration. It is our policy not to reemploy those who were discharged for cause. A reemployed person must waive all rights accruing from prior service.

6. *Nondiscrimination*
   There shall be no discrimination in employment because of race, religion or membership or nonmembership in any lawful organization.

7. *Physical Handicap*
   Persons with physical handicaps shall be considered for employment on the basis of their capability for a particular job. Handicaps which do not interfere with performance shall not

disqualify if they do not constitute a hazard to the Company or its employees.

8. *Relatives*

The employment of close relatives is not permitted. Close relatives are defined as:

a. Blood relatives of direct lineage only.

b. Relatives by marriage—spouse and the employee's in-laws *only*.

c. Exceptions:

    1. Female relatives of female employees.

    2. Employees who marry each other.

CORPORATE PRE-EMPLOYMENT PHYSICAL EXAMINATION

Policy Statement:

I. *PURPOSE*

This policy is intended to protect the company against unwarranted claims for illness or injury, to reduce absenteeism, and to assist in the proper placement of employees in jobs which they can perform effectively without endangering health and safety. It will also standardize the pre-employment physical examinations throughout the company regardless of the location involved.

II. *POLICY*

The company requires that all qualified applicants undergo a pre-employment physical examination, prior to temporary or permanent employment, in order to ensure that they are physically fit to perform the job for which they are being considered.

III. *PROCEDURE*

A. Upon determination that an applicant is qualified for a certain job, the Personnel Manager, or the person responsible for employment, shall make arrangements for the pre-employment physical examination with a physician selected by and at the expense of the company.

B. The physician shall be advised of the specific nature of the job for which applicant is being considered.

C. The Medical History Questionnaire shall be completed by the physician and signed by the applicant at the time of the examination.

D. The Medical Examination Report, which should also be completed by the physician, must contain his recommendation as to whether or not the applicant is qualified for the specific job opening.

E. The completed Medical History Questionnaire and Medical Examination Report shall be enclosed by the physician in a sealed envelope and turned over to the applicant for delivery to the company. This information shall be kept confidential by the company and these completed forms will then become a part of the employee's permanent personnel file, wherever it is maintained.

F. Bills for the pre-employment physical examinations shall be approved at the locations where incurred and forwarded to the Headquarters Accounting Department for payment. Examination expenses will be charged to the location involved.

IV. *SCOPE OF EXAMINATION*

All qualified applicants shall be given a general physical examination as indicated on the Medical Examination Report.

Policy Statement:

Before an applicant may be employed, it is necessary that the applicant pass a physical examination according to prescribed medical standards.

Each new propective employee will be given a physical examination to assure that the individual is physically capable of performing the specific work.

The examination will be conducted by the Medical Department. If further examination is necessary, the individual may be referred to other medical specialists.

To be considered for employment, each individual must meet the physical requirements that have been established by the company.

A list of established reasons for medical rejection is on file in the Medical Department. While some reasons will automatically cause medical rejection, acceptance or rejection for other reasons will depend on the individual case.

Each individual examined will be classified by the company physician according to the results of the examination. This classification will be forwarded to the Employment Section for final acceptance or rejection of the applicant. If the applicant is rejected for physical reasons and a further explanation is desired, he will be referred to the company physician or, in some cases, to his family physician for this explanation.

STRAIGHT TIME

Policy Statement:

A. *The normal workweek consists of 37½ hours*

1. For recordkeeping purposes the workweek starts at 12:01 a.m. Monday, and ends at midnight Sunday, and consists of 5 working days of 7½ hours each.

2. The pay period covers two workweeks. It consists of 10 working days.

B. *The normal workday consists of 7½ hours*

1. Normal office hours are from 9:00 a.m. to 5:00 p.m.—an elapsed time of 8 hours. While the normal lunch period is 45 minutes, only 30 minutes should be deducted from total elapsed time providing that not more than 45 minutes is consumed, for a net total of 7½ hours daily.

2. The workday commences at 12:01 a.m. and ends at midnight.

C. *What constitutes hours worked*

All elapsed time, from the moment an individual actually commences work for the Company until the work is finished for the day, except for the deduction of time spent at lunch or dinner, constitutes a day's work. Arriving early or leaving late for the employee's own convenience is not to be included in working time, provided that the employee performs no duties for the Company during such intervals.

OVERTIME

Policy Statement:

The Company compensates employees for overtime in accordance with federal and state legislations; making every effort to carefully plan required overtime with due regard for its impact on employees and the service needs of customers, subject to the following conditions:

A. *Nonexempt Employees*

1. Will not work beyond 37½ hours per week *without official authorization.*

2. Will be compensated for all authorized hours worked in excess of 37½ hours per week.

3. Will not be compensated for unauthorized hours worked between 37½ hours and 40 hours per week.

WORK INTERRUPTIONS

Policy Statement:

I. *Lunch Hour*

The lunch period is 45 minutes. On pay days the period is extended to one hour to permit the cashing of salary checks.

Variations from the policy are subject to the following restrictions:

A. *Shorter lunch hour*

1. The department head may not arrange for a lunch period shorter than 45 minutes.
2. Employees may not forego the lunch period in order to shorten the workday.

B. *Longer lunch hour*

1. The department head may at his discretion, arrange for a longer period on occasion but not as a regular matter.

II. *Supper Period*

A. *Overtime Workers*

1. A supper period of not less than 20 minutes to be taken between 5 and 7 p.m. must be granted to all employees whose work period commences before 12 noon and continues after 7 p.m.

B. *Second Shift Workers*

1. A meal period of not less than 45 minutes to be taken midway in the shift must be granted to all employees beginning work between 1 p.m. and 6 a.m.

COFFEE BREAKS

Policy Statement:

III. *Other Work Interruptions*

There is an official coffee break of no more than 15 minutes' duration once a day. There are no other official breaks.

Employees may not leave the building during normal working hours without consent except for business purposes.

GUIDE SERVICE

Policy Statement:

Company will pay hourly rate and nonexempt salary employees who volunteer to serve as guides to conduct visitors through the plant.

A roster of men who have volunteered to serve as guides during the hours when they are not working will be maintained by the Industrial and Community Relations Department.

In unusual circumstances supervisors may be requested to release employees off the job to serve as guides.

Substitute supervisors will be solicited and encouraged to volunteer to serve as guides.

Employees serving as guides on company scheduled tours will be required to ring their time cards both in and out for timekeeping purposes.

When an employee serves as a guide at a time other than his working hours, he will be paid for a minimum of 2½ hours or his actual hours served, whichever is greater.

When guide service continues beyond his regular working hours, the employee will be paid for the hours actually worked in guide service.

When an employee serves as a guide during his regular working hours, he will be paid his regular pay, except incentive bonus.

WAGE PAYMENT FOR TIME SPENT AT COMPANY-SPONSORED AFFAIRS

Policy Statement:

Company will encourage and assist employees to take an active part in civic and approved company-sponsored affairs, but expects such participation to be secondary to job duties.

The intent of this policy is to provide a plan whereby employees may participate in approved civic and approved company-sponsored affairs:

With the least interruption to production.

With the least disruption of work schedules.

At a minimum of expense to the company.

Company-sponsored affairs will include:

Meetings of standing committees of the company, as approved by the Vice-President and Division Manager.

Special recreational activities as approved by the Vice-President and Division Manager.

Special company affairs for which wage payment has been approved by the Vice-President and Division Manager.

Approved civic affairs will include:

Meetings of general community interest in which the company desires representation by delegates as approved by the Personnel Administration Manager.

The employee will be paid for attendance to the functions listed above according to the following conditions, and his time deviated to the proper Personnel Administration burden charge.

A written request for an employee to be away from his job will be made to the foreman by an authorized representative of the organization or activity with the approval of the Personnel Administration Manager.

The written request must be in the hands of the foreman at least 48 hours prior to the requested day of absence.

The written request will be required both for re-arrangement of schedule and/or receipt of payment for time off.

Payments will not be made to an employee for attendance or participation in the above-mentioned functions during scheduled time off from his job.

CHAPTER 14

DAY-TO-DAY ADMINISTRATIVE PROBLEMS/SOLUTIONS

EMPLOYEE relations has been defined as the communications aspects of sound human relations. The communications always have a specific goal: to get employees to listen to the company's story, and to listen with such effect that employees immediately or eventually associate with the company's purposes. Where this happens, the company has gained the confidence and trust of its people and can proceed to the business at hand—the task of satisfying the customer.

Good employee relations always show up on the profit and loss statement. They provide an imponderable element whose importance cannot be overestimated. In the office setting, they are not only compatible with pursuit of the company's main goal of business success; they are essential if that goal is to be achieved. People and profit-making have to meet half-way or neither will survive.

Much research has been carried out to find out why some employees are highly motivated and other are not. For example, the *Engineering and Management Institute of Iowa State University* once studied general and basic needs that most people share. The Institute then related these needs to a number of things that people seem to want to obtain from work. Because these factors are basic and virtually universal, and because they set the parameters and goals of a good employee relations program, they are worth listening:

1. *Recognition as an individual.* No one wants to be "just a face in the crowd."

2. *Job security.* Employees need to know what is expected of them and where they stand with respect to others in the department or section and the company in general.

3. *Freedom from arbitrary action.* People in any work situation need to know that promotions and personal advancement depend on accomplishment and not on prejudice or favoritism.

4. *Opportunity for advancement.* Anyone who feels that he is at a "dead end," or that he is frozen in his present spot, will probably do just enough to avoid being fired.

5. *A meaningful task.* A person doing a job needs to know where his or her job fits into the big company picture.

6. *Congenial associates.* Most normal people like to work in a friendly atmosphere, a place where they can develop new friendships and have a chance for at least *some* social contact with other employees.

7. *Satisfactory working conditions.* A competent office administrator will try to keep working conditions at a high level by good housekeeping, setting a good example, and seriously considering all subordinates' ideas and suggestions for improvement of the working environment.

8. *Fair wages.* The concept of a fair wage differs from area to area and from year to year, but it is usually regarded as that wage that is generally paid for the same type of work in the same geographic area.

9. *A voice in matters concerning him.* Employees likes to feel that they have some say in things that concern them on the job—even to the point of participation in setting up a project and carrying it through.

The Personal Letter

One direct, effective, and economical medium of communication with employees is the personal letter. Employees, especially in a large company, are usually pleased to hear the voice of their company president addressing them as individuals, talking about matters of mutual interest. Next best to hearing the president's voice—say, on a recording or in person at a meeting—the most direct way to reach the employee is by sending a letter, preferably addressed to the home. There the employee can read it in relaxed privacy and give it the calm and thoughtful consideration it should have if it is to accomplish its purpose.

It may seem like a small matter, but one secret of effective letters to employees is to have them individually typed—perhaps on electronic typewriters—and, if possible, signed personally. When an employee gets a letter at home, written personally by the president of company, he or she feels a special sense of importance and identification with this place of employment. This feeling is often shared with family and friends.

International Harvester Company started using letters years ago as a primary medium in its communications program. The letters would go to employees in their homes. They might be written by the company president or by works managers. Subjects covered included the company's side of a labor dispute or the reasons behind increased prices or lowered prices. The letters even discussed impending layoffs.

A weakness of such communications is that they may become "automatic." Employees in such a case may see the letter simply as a device to "pep them up." Thus, it is better not to send the letter at all unless it carries a message of real importance.

Advantages of Letters to Employees

There are, of course, limitations to the value of a personal letter written to an employee, but there are at least four major advantages:

1. *Letters are personal.* Even though an employee knows fellow employees will get the same letter, there is a feeling that the message is more personal than a notice on the bulletin board or a printed circular.

2. *The letter is important.* A letter sent to the employee's home says that the subject of the letter is important, and that management wants to be sure that the information is received.

3. *Letter are flexible and timely.* A letter can be written on a moment's notice, or it can be written in advance and held for mailing at an opportune time.

4. *The letter is offical.* Whatever the message, the boss says it's so and signs it. It becomes an official record of the company's position.

There is good evidence that employees are impressed when they receive a letter from the head of their company. They may not remember reading an article in the company publication, but they do remember a letter from the boss.

What to Say—When

The average employee wants to know what's happening in the company and wants to know about his or her job. However, there is a need for specific information that is easily understood and that can be identified with the job. Letters on "bread and butter" subjects tend to be the best ones. Such subjects include: the general outlook for the business, improvements in wages and hours, state of the competition, job security, company benefits, and new products.

Personnel man Jerome C. Okonski of Chicago has offered a list of 10 special occasions when a letter to employees is well worth sending:

1. *To report the news of a special instance of company progress.*
2. *To give a brief summary of the company's financial report.*
3. *To offer congratulations on a job well done.*

4. *To thank an employee for a valuable suggestion.*

5. *To announce and explain a new company policy.*

6. *To share bad or disturbing news. Keeping the employees informed is essential even if you know that some news will be upsetting to them.*

7. *To announce a new or improved program of employee benefits, such as expansion of insurance coverage.*

8. *To express seasonal greetings such as at Christmas or Thanksgiving holidays.*

9. *To welcome new employees, to announce an important new assignment or appointment, to honor a long-service anniversary, or to recognize someone's retirement.*

10. *To issue an invitation to a special employee event such as the company picnic or golf outing.*

Do's and Don'ts

One way to alienate employees is to write letters in which the style is pompous and stuffy. Equally bad is the letter which is "all sweetness and light," or the letter telling the employees, for example, how lucky they are to live in this country. The patronizing letter is another to avoid—the "from me way up here to you way down there" type of letter.

Such letters are by no means rare. In fact, the interesting letter, written in good taste, has been found to be the exception rather than the rule.

The main problem is that, too often, the letter is not carefully planned in advance. The writer is expected to write a letter. So he gropes around for a subject and comes up with something on free enterprise, or loyalty, or teamwork—full of platitudes but without much real interest for employees.

When employees begin to look forward to receiving letters from management, you have accomplished your main purpose. As the letters gain in importance, they become more useful to you. They begin to be effective in correcting misinformation and stopping harmful rumors. When you know the letters will be read, they can be used in dealing with all types of situations—good or bad—such as emergencies, meeting production deadlines, and labor difficulties.

Although what you say in a letter to employees may be of primary importance, the readers must feel that the subject affects them somehow; otherwise they probably will not be interested.

DAY-TO-DAY ADMINISTRATIVE PROBLEMS/SOLUTIONS

The Employee Newsletter

A well written newsletter sent to your employees on a regular basis—say, weekly or monthly—can give you a powerful mechanism for communicating with employees. Newsletters say what you want to say, exactly as you want to say it, to as many people as you wish, and as often as you like. They have value in small offices and large, serving as basic tools for rounding out the company communications program.

Your newsletter can be a single sheet, run off on the office reproducing equipment, or it can be a 4-, 6-, or 8-page magazine-type newsletter using color, photographs, and commercial typesetting and printing. Where the company letter deals normally with one subject, a newsletter contains information on a number of different subjects. The goal should be to make the newsletter as personal as possible without allowing it to become gossipy. Subject coverage is usually brief and to the point.

Many of the benefits of communicating with employees by means of a newsletter were demonstrated in a quality-control program carried out by Moore Business Forms, Inc. Reduction of human error and the need for consistently high product quality presented continuing problems at Moore, as in almost any manufacturing company. How Moore tackled this problem should be instructive to concerns facing similar quality-maintenance problems among their employees.

The program introduced by Moore was called "PRIDE/ZERO DEFECTS," with PRIDE standing for *Personal Responsibility in Daily Effect.* Carried out among 2,200 employees in eight plants and 45 sales offices, the program was planned to encourage employees to:

- Progressively improve product quality
- Achieve personal quality goals
- Identify and eliminate causes of defects

The program involved a variety of communications techniques. One of the most important was a special four-page newsletter, issued to keep employees informed of progress. A feature of the newsletter was the great amount of space given to photographs of winners of the *General Manager's Award.* Accomplishments of plants, departments, and individuals were featured so that all employees had a sense of participation.

The newsletter is a bread-and-butter item, usually on two or four or (at the most) eight pages. It is frequently nothing more than a string of paragraphs, often with typography resembling the words typed by a typewriter. It is hardly ever illustrated. (*"Kiplinger's Letter"* was an external forerunner of many successful newsletters. This service out of Washington, D.C., to which many businessmen have subscribed for many years, was cast in a newsletter/typewritten style for the purpose of moving fast and economically.)

A large company will have newsletters distributed on both a "vertical" basis and a "horizontal" basis. A "Manufacturing Newsletter" will be a "vertical" medium; it will go to everyone in manufacturing from the general manager to the janitor who sweeps up in the smallest plant. A "vertical" medium digs deeply within a given function—like manufacturing or marketing or research. Thus, "vertical" is an accurately descriptive adjective.

The Management Newsletter is a so-called "horizontal" publication. It will go to all general managers and sales directors and manufacturing directors and research directors. That's a "horizontal" group, with distribution sweeping across various functions but sticking to essentially the same managerial echelons. Consequently, "horizontal" is an accurately descriptive adjective.

Newsletters are often distributed on a selective basis. As a result, information which goes in them is quite selective.

Many companies use management newsletters effectively, restricting their receipt to the top 50 or 100 or 200 employees. Sometimes such newsletters are marked "confidential."

Some companies send newsletters to selected upper management echelons with the hope and prayer the readership will consistently "pass along" selected highlights, as occasions permit to their subordinates. Normally, this doesn't work out too well. A few companies which hope for "pass-along" benefits caution against making photocopies.

The big objective of newspapers, magazines and newsletters is to keep the information flowing for employees, to educate, to instruct, to explain—to motivate.

And don't forget that word motivate.

Employees can be "turned on" or "turned off" by a wide variety of factors. By working conditions. By compensation practices. By what they perceive to be an element of "fairness" or "unfairness." By policies and practices. By the way their supervisors treat them. *And by the information they do or do not get.*

TIPS ON PREPARING YOUR NEWSLETTER

All stories should answer the traditional newspaper reporter's questions: Who? What? Where? When? Why? How?

All stories should be:

Newsworthy	Timely
Complete	Novel
Accurate	Interesting

Suggested story topics are:

Engagements	Sympathy in injuries or death
Marriages	Classified ads
Births	Special hobbies
Retirements	Contests
New employees	Company-sponsored sports
Anniversaries	General news about a department
Promotions	
Travels	Human interest stories

EFFECTIVE BULLETIN BOARDS

Although the bulletin board has been around for a long time, it remains an essential part of the communications system of any company. A Dartnell survey of 223 companies indicated that 98% of industrial concerns relied on the bulletin board as one of the best single methods of keeping employees informed.

Commenting on boards in general, one respondent said, "The only thing that has changed about the use of bulletin boards is the fact that they are getting fancier and sharper in appearance." The truth of this is evidenced by the growing number of companies whose sole business is to supply posters, photographs and other bulletin board materials to industry.

When you post an important notice that you want read by all your employees, what can you expect in the way of percentage of readership? A survey showed that estimates of numbers of employee readers ranged from as low as 30% to "almost 95%." Median average of the estimates was almost 75%. This does not take into consideration the word-of-mouth reaction that sets in once a vital notice is posted.

It could be noted at this point that *Professor Leonard N. Persson* of *Sacred Heart University,* Bridgeport, Connecticut, offered two warnings concerning the use of bulletin boards.

In one case, he noted that "it is quite possible that items placed on a bulletin board can be construed to have some effect as a pseudolegalistic document. Intentions, policies and commitments made by a company on its bulletin board may be referred to by employees in situations relating to grievances, EEO charges, and so on."

"For this reason," he continued, "copies of any document, even one as simplistic as a vacation schedule, that are placed on the bulletin board should be held in a separate file for future reference, including the dates of posting and removal. This could prove quite handy if a company has to establish that it did, in fact, state its position or policy on a certain matter."

He also pointed out that the bulletin board is probably the proper place for the various "required" postings deemed necessary by governmental agencies.

A food supply house ran a series of notices as an experiment. It found that a favorable notice—one that pleased the employees—received high readership in a hurry. But it also found that notices that were displeasing to the employees had a peculiar way of going unnoticed by a large segment of the group. For instance, 90% of the employees knew within three hours after the announcement was posted that the Monday before Christmas was a paid holiday. On the other hand only 35% knew that the Monday before New Year's was to be "work as usual," though it was posted at the same time.

Many companies believe that the most effective announcements are those accompanied by pictures or cartoons. "They are easy to understand," said one executive, "and employees catch the meaning quickly when the idea is visualized."

Types of Boards and Locations

Three types to bulletin boards are in common use: "major" or company boards, departmental boards, and separate boards for safety information.

Major boards should be divided into three parts—one for posting current items (up to ten days), the second for semi-permanent items (up to six months), and a third part for what could be called permanent postings, that is, up to one year. Permanent postings, however, should be kept to a minimum. The effectiveness of bulletin boards

DAY-TO-DAY ADMINISTRATIVE PROBLEMS/SOLUTIONS

depends on the company's skill at keeping their contents as interesting and up-to-date as possible.

Departmental boards are frequently used at the discretion of department managers or supervisors to post work and vacation schedules, and items of interest only to people within the department.

Since safety is a vital factor in nearly all manufacturing and industrial companies, it is generally a good idea to maintain separate *safety boards* for such information.

Who Maintains the Board?

If the percentage of readership of materials posted on the bulletin board is low, one of the chief causes will certainly be poor maintenance. The poorly maintained board is usually sloppy and unattractive. It may be poorly lighted so that postings are difficult to read. Notices tend to stay posted long after they have become obsolete. Another characteristic of the poorly kept board is that it may be cluttered with miscellaneous items posted by anyone.

One key to keeping the board up-to-date and attractive is to centralize the responsibility for maintaining the board. According to 85% of the companies contributing to the Dartnell survey, one person or a designated group is responsible for bulletin board upkeep. In 65% of the cases, the personnel department is responsible for the boards. In larger companies, the industrial relations department maintains the boards. Department heads do the posting in 10% of the companies and various other departments are responsible in 8% of the cases.

How 200 Companies Control Bulletin Boards

Most firms—almost 95%—have a system for keeping their boards current. Whoever is responsible for maintenance of the board and the notices posted on it follows a definite system of service and inspection. Here are the methods used by companies responding to a Dartnell survey:

Weekly inspection	40%
Biweekly inspection	22%
Monthly inspection	10%
Outside service	5%
Announcements dated for posting and withdrawal	15%
No set system	8%

Suggesting ways to make the board more effective, a personnel director said:

BULLETIN BOARD CONTROL

Glassed-in plant and office bulletin boards:

Announcements of company-wide or plant-wide interest; i.e., major personnel appointments; company earnings and sales; new plants; acquisitions; diversification; union notices from union headquarters; safety posters; advertising reproductions; employee blood bank and United Fund programs and promotions; employee activities.

Posting is done once a week on a day best suited to the plant's operations. There are nine plants, as well as corporate headquarters. The plant boards are posted by that plant's industrial relations staff. The corporate boards are posted by the corporate industrial relations staff.

Glassed-in permanent boards:

Permanent notices, either company or government.

Postings are placed on these boards whenever it is necessary either for updating or providing previously unposted information. These boards are the responsibility of the industrial relations staff, corporate or plant, depending on the board's location.

Open plant and office department boards:

Department announcements, both permanent and those requiring immediate attention; personal thank-you notes, or whatever else the department head deems feasible.

Postings are made at the discretion of the department head in consideration of the department's needs.

Timeclock boards:

Flash notices regarding working hours, overtime or changes. Postings are made at the discretion of the department head whenever necessary.

"Careful consideration should be given to the location of each board, placement of materials, and frequent changes of materials; furthermore, some light matter, such as cartoons, should be interspersed with regular announcements to attract readers."

Another office executive reports, "Some boards are like some people: they talk too much and say nothing." He adds, "A little personality in your office bulletin board will make it individual and interesting—there is a definite art to administering a bulletin board effectively."

As a third executive commented, "Bulletin boards are now accepted as the very backbone of effective office and plant communication by most companies, and, as such, they should be handled seriously and methodically, not as catch-alls for scraps of paper."

THE EMPLOYEE HANDBOOK

The effective employee handbook should be designed to serve the dual purpose of telling employees what they need to know and imparting information on what the employer wants them to know. Although *it will not replace personal contacts,* the handbook can help in getting vital information to the employees. Thought should be given to issuing a handbook if you want your employees, old or new, to understand:

1. What you expect of them and what they can expect of you.
2. What your policies on wages, working conditions, and benefits are.
3. How much time, thought, and money go into making their jobs secure.
4. What your company's service to customers is.
5. What place your company has in the community and the industry.
6. What makes a job in your company good and permanent employment.

An employee handbook can cover many subjects under these general headings. The sample table of contents that follows, reproduced from a *Small Business Administration Management Aid,* lists the more common items.

The handbook should speak to the point. Employees are not interested in unnecessary details. Be brief but explicit.

The Handbook and the New Employee

The handbook is especially adapted to the task of passing on to the new employee basic information about the company or plant. He will have many questions on his mind. Most of these can best be answered by the employee's immediate supervisor. Others must be answered in the employee handbook—and answered correctly and simply, so that he can understand them. The answers may have a decisive bearing on whether or not the newcomer stays with the

---

EMPLOYEE HANDBOOK

SAMPLE TABLE OF CONTENTS

---

company or leaves after a short term, becoming a statistic in the "turnover" reports.

Should an employee handbook be geared *primarily* to the new employee and his informational needs? Most definitely, says *Edward L. Adams,* vice president and director of personnel for *Maynard Plastics, Inc.,* of Salem, Massachusetts. "The employee handbook is the document that introduces the company to the new employee and the new employee to the company," Adams notes.

Should the handbook include rules on fighting on company premises, theft and similar offenses and misdemeanors? Opinion varies on this score. Where one company believes such rules belong in a separate listing of work rules, to be posted on bulletin boards or elsewhere, other company handbooks include such listings. Officials of firms whose handbooks include these basic rules believe the new employee should know and understand company regulations on the day he starts work.

Should an employee handbook be issued to a job applicant *before* he is accepted for work—while he is still under consideration? A consensus of 20 companies canvassed by Action Research Institute of Chicago provides a negative answer. "The handbook is for employees only, for people *on the job*"—this is the general feeling. "The handbook should contain information of a more specific nature than that given to *prospective* employees," said one executive in a typical comment.

COMPANY PUBLICATIONS

Company publications today come in a wide variety of sizes, styles and format; they cover the gamut from the old-fashioned multilithed sheets to commercial type magazines, produced as a four color slick magazine with a professional format. American firms publish an estimated 11,000 employee publications with a combined cost publication estimated at more than $12 million annually. Total monthly circulation is over 70 million and total readership is believed to exceed 100 million.

At one time, certan internal/external publications such as *Think* magazine (produced by *IBM*) and *Kaiser Aluminum News* (produced by *Kaiser Aluminum and Chemical Corporation*) became so popular that the circulation ran to large numbers of "outsiders." In the case of both of these publications, the cost of distribution rose to the point that negated the value of wide circulation.

Today, these employee magazines are internally (primarily) distributed, but they are still produced with the same care and excellence. Other companies which have such publications are *Western Electric Company* (publishing *WE*), and *Southwestern Bell's Scene*.

The normal role of a company publication is to inform employees. This function is exceptionally well done by *United States Steel Corporation*, which produces a daily *News Report*, prepared by its public relations department for selective distribution at New York headquarters. The report is generally a single page mimeographed sheet, written for employees, which quotes AP, UPI and Dow Jones news highlights as well as articles from other sources.

Using Audio Tapes

Imperial Life Insurance Company of Canada, for one example, had a program of information distribution through the use of audio tapes. When new information is available, the message is taped at headquarters in Toronto and distributed to the field. One cassette features a company vice president explaining how a prospective employee can develop a sales career with the company. There are more than 100 tapes in the audio tape "library" which provide basic information about insurance programs and insurance selling.

The company is also urging branch managers to prepare audio "newsletters" on cassettes for distribution to the superintendent of agency operations.

What Employees Want To Read

To be effective, an employee publication, regardless of its format, must be editorially well balanced. It should give the reader information of value and interest to him. In an effort to find the proper balance between news and educational material in an employee publication, a reader survey was conducted some years ago among workers in several industrial plants of The National Cash Register Company. The survey showed employees were more interested in news about the company than they were in news about other employees.

An exception to this rule might be the small organization having less than 300 employees, most of whom know one another. Another exception would be a publication for members of a specific department. Even in such cases, however, the balance should still be tipped in favor of company news.

Employee publications are designed to influence employee attitudes and opinions, and to do so they must maintain a reasonable stance. Extremism of one form or another can defeat the key purpose, according to authorities on the subject. Once the employee family begins to feel that management is using a publication to force opinions on them, executives feel, they cease to trust the publication and its continued appearance may do more harm than good. But if the publication wins the trust and confidence of its employee readership, it will be accepted as a legitimate effort to inform; it can become a meaningful factor in the never-ending process of winning employee cooperation in the attainment of the company's goals.

Another pitfall has been pointed out in studies. It appears where the material carried in an employee publication is above the level of comprehension of the employee audience. Almost any worker—whether in office, mill or plant—becomes disenchanted with what he is reading if he finds it difficult or impossible to understand. In such cases, studies of work forces show, the employee group may actively resent the publication because they feel it gives them a feeling of inferiority.

Well worth remembering is a list of 10 objectives for employee publications. These were originally compiled by the *Chamber of Commerce of the United States.*

TEN OBJECTIVES FOR EMPLOYEE PUBLICATIONS

1. Interpret company policies to employees.
2. Keep employees informed about new company plans and developments.
3. Promote employee cooperation and loyalty through better understanding of company problems.
4. Explain the financial structure and operation of the company.
5. Expose rumors that breed misunderstanding.
6. Nullify harmful propaganda from antibusiness sources.
7. Promote an employee-company family concept of mutual aims and interests.
8. Build a favorable attitude toward the company on the part of wives and children of employees.
9. Foster friendly press relations.
10. Build community goodwill for the company.

To sum up: to do its job an employee publication should improve employer-employee relations, contribute to industrial peace, encourage productivity, foster ambition, build morale, provide public recognition of accomplishment, and keep employees well posted.

What Is the Editor's Job?

Every business has a story to tell, and it is the job of the editor of any publication sponsored by a company for its employees to tell that story well. That does not mean filling the publication with "puffs," or articles that sound like a page from the company catalog. But there is a philosophy that motivates a business which an editor must understand and interpret in an interesting and readable way.

William G. Caples, former president of *Inland Steel Container Company,* made some key points in an address to a meeting of industrial editors in Chicago: "Anyone charged with the responsibility of running a business will have figured out the place of that business in the economy and society; what he wants the business to be, now and in the future; and how he intends to accomplish those objectives. Whether you agree or disagree with that philosophy, it is the philosophy of the management that employs you. It is your obligation to present that philosophy as effectively as you know how.

"If the philosophy has not been formalized or put in writing, one of an editor's first duties is to go to the men who run the business and find out from them what their philosophy is. For instance, I have seen many employee publications issued by companies in which I knew there was considerable controversy with a union. And yet, to read the company publication you would not know that any such thing existed.

"There is a company side to any union controversy and one of the places in which that side can be most clearly stated is in the company publication. Certainly, the workers who read that publication know that it is written with bias from the standpoint of management, but the employees are entitled to know that view, just as they are entitled to know the union view. In this regard, let me quote the *Labor Relations Advisory Letter:*

" 'If management does not undertake to tell its story to employees, no one else will. The employees will, in all probability, be told a story by someone or some organization, but . . . it will *not* be management's story and it will not be designed to do management any good. The effectiveness of management's story will, however, depend on: (a) How sound the story actually is; (b) how well it is told; and (c) whether it is told over the course of the year or saved for an "emergency." You can't blame employees for being a little suspicious of management communications that appear only in times of tension or friction.'

"To my mind, a company publication should meet company problems, deal with them and report accurately and fairly the management's viewpoint toward these problems and their probable solutions. An employee publication must be specific and straightforward. Following a 'head-in-the-sand' policy is unrealistic."

Types of Employee Publications

Most companies issue at least one employee publication on a regular basis. While this category of communication is read by all employees, it is usually used primarily to reach nonsupervisory personnel. In some instances the publications are departmental, but in most instances an overall publication is used, with sections devoted to the various departments. A common roster of publications by type is as follows:

1. **The employee bulletin.**
2. **The employee newspaper.**

3. The monthly house organ.
4. The daily news digest.
5. Letters to employees' homes.
6. Pay envelope inserts.
7. Reading racks, booklets.
8. The annual financial report.
9. Individualized benefits report to employees.

Each of the major classifications may be broken down according to the needs of the business. Where a company has more than one plant it is customary to issue a publication for the workers of each plant. General articles may be carried over from one publication to the other.

The Employee Bulletin

This is usually an informal multicopied sheet for bringing urgent spot news or information to employees within a short period of time. It is usually distributed by supervisors or posted on bulletin boards as the situation dictates.

The Employee Newspaper

Many companies regard the employee newspaper as the backbone of their written communications program. These periodicals, published in a tabloid newspaper format, generally strive to accomplish four primary objectives:

1. To inform on company regulations, practices, and policies, and on management's objectives, plans, problems, success and failures.
2. To help employees understand their jobs, the end products of their endeavors, and the reasons for the demands made upon them during the work day.
3. To keep employees up to date on economic, social and political matters which might affect them and their jobs, thereby making them better qualified to make sound decisions in those areas.
4. To give employees social news so that they become better acquainted and feel more at home in the company.

The newspaper format permits deadlines as late as one day prior to issuing and, since speed is essential in handling the news, this makes the newspaper an ideal format. In addition, the familiar daily newspaper resemblance seems to enhance readership and credibility.

According to *Willard V. Merrihue,* former manager of community and business relations, General Electric Company: "When the employee newspaper is soundly integrated into the complete communications program and when it is edited to achieve its primary objectives, it is invaluable. Unfortunately, too many companies still consider it an employee benefit or an entertainment medium which in some way is supposed to build morale."

The Monthly House Organ

The monthly house organ is usually issued in the familiar magazine format with cover, color, and often slick paper. The layout may be skillfully designed. Large audiences long used to the mass-circulation magazines found in homes find a certain appeal in this type of publication. The magazine also serves as a perfect home for company prestige-building articles.

One problem with the monthly magazine is that it reduces the flexibility of a communications program. Immediacy and primacy of information are essential in today's competitive communications arena, according to Mr. Merrihue, and "if the monthly issue, with its long advance deadlines, is the only medium for mass communication, the entire communications program is no more flexible than the dinosaurs of a bygone age."

The Daily News Digest

If maximum speed in the dissemination of news and management messages is the goal, the best method is the daily news digest. Short news items, easily garnered from a local radio station, are sometimes interspersed with the company messages. Since many workers do not have time to read a morning newspaper, the news digest is read, especially during lunch and snack breaks, by almost all workers. The digest is unmatched as a means of dispelling rumors and refuting untrue charges that may be making the rounds of the plant. The news digest, thus, is a quick, flexible, low-cost medium of printed communication.

Letters to Employees' Homes

This is one of the most effective of all communication methods. As often as it suits the purpose of management, the chief executive of the company may write a letter sent to the homes of all employees. The letters can cover an almost infinite range of subjects and in emergency situations they are particularly effective in keeping employees and their families well informed; they can effectively combat the volumes of misinformation that surround negotiations, strike threats, strikes, representation elections and disasters.

DAY-TO-DAY ADMINISTRATIVE PROBLEMS/SOLUTIONS

Pay Envelope Inserts

Pay envelope inserts are widely used to supplement bulletin board notices, items in the company newspaper, and other basic information modes. For the most part, pay envelope stuffers relate to the nitty-gritty facts of life on the job: changes in working hours, pay schedules or pay rates, new or revised rules on paycheck deductions, and the like. But inserts have also been used in union election campaigns and other situations where management is trying to get across the message that each employee's paycheck may be affected by what is taking place in the conference room or in the company parking lot.

Some companies take advantage of prepared inserts such as Dartnell's publication: *Earl Nightingale's Step-up-to-Success Series*. This is an inexpensive, colorful and inspirational addition for a paycheck envelope.

Reading Rack Booklets

Reading racks carrying informational booklets and placed at convenient locations throughout offices or a plant can be both attractive and useful. The racks may be filled with up to 50 copies of about a dozen or so booklets covering a wide range of interests; cooking and gardening hints, hobbies, wood working, vacationing, income tax preparation help and so on. Scattered among these booklets may be some that management would like its employees to read so as to increase individual productivity or develop greater understanding of company problems and aims.

The booklets are replaced as fast as they are taken. Maintaining a reading rack is not inexpensive and results are difficult to prove, but hundreds of companies use this device. The limited research conducted so far in this area suggests that if proper care is taken in the selection of materials for the reading rack, it can achieve a high carry-over of ideas.

The Annual Financial Report

In today's mood of increasing awareness on the part of employees, the annual financial report offers one of the prime opportunities for explaining the problems of the business to employees. The report, reduced to simplified figures and easily understandable summaries, is, in many cases, mailed to all employees; in still others, management conducts meetings with groups of employees for a dramatized presentation of the report.

Individualized Benefits Reports

Individualized benefits reports have proved spectacularly success-ful for some companies. One method is to send each employee a letter every one or two years to report on current equity in each of the company's benefit plans. The report indicates how much both employee and the company have contributed to the pension plan, provides a formula for calculating ultimate retirement income, in-cluding Social Security, and concludes with a review of all the other plans that belong to the total benefits package.

Other companies use other techniques in putting together the benefits report. Many list all the benefit plans of the firm and the cost of each to the company, appending a figure at the bottom to show the total annual value to the employee of the company's con-tribution. That figure may be identified by a notation indicating that the total can be added to the individual's take-home wages to show how much he is actually earning at both the "front end" and the "back end" of the paycheck.

How to Get "Live" News

News has long been utilized as a means of building goodwill among employees and loyalty and enthusiasm among those who carry a company's message to the buyer. No plant is too large, no business too small, to use it.

The trick to getting "live" news for publication in your employee publications is to develop a "nose for news." While it is possible to create a certain amount of news, the best news comes out of the daily activities of a business. The alert employer keeps a weather eye open for any unusual development that can be passed along. It may be a story about a person: a closeup of someone who has performed outstandingly. It may be news about a shipment of mer-chandise received from abroad, or the experience of a man in the shop. But it must be interesting or it will not be worth printing.

Formats for Employee Publications

One popular type of employee publication is the small-sized news-paper, printed inexpensively on newspaper stock. Even though coat-ed paper reproduces halftones better than newsprint, the more ex-pensive coated stock may give the publication an atmosphere of extravagance that is not always desirable.

If the number of copies to be printed is relatively small, the publication is usually produced on the office duplicating machine. The intimacy of the office-processed news bulletin produces a sense of community that pleases employee readers.

If the size of the company warrants, a magazine format may be acceptable as a format. The magazine allows a certain amount of editorial makeup and a diversity that can attract the reader's eye. Picture stories are especially adaptable to the magazine format. But it should be remembered that the magazine costs substantially more than the newspaper. Often, bulletins are issued daily or weekly, supplementing the magazine by carrying shorter news items. In such a case, the magazine tells the company's long-range story in words and pictures, while more immediate news is given more timely airing.

Maintaining Interest in Your Publication

A cardinal sin of industrial journalism is to let a publication "go stale." Even the best publications need a change of pace once in a while. An imaginative editor will conceive new ideas and features to keep his readers interested. Good journalism involves not only writing and editing the news, but also creating news to get the publication talked about and read—much in the style of the daily newspaper that is always searching for new material and presenting that material in different ways.

For some years, the Jewel Tea Company, of Barrington, Illinois, used a one-page form carrying the title, "Fill it out! Send it in!" to secure news for its employee magazine. In time this form was discontinued in favor of personal letters in which employees are encouraged to write to the editor of the magazine.

The company discontinued the printed form because (1) familiarity with the form led to its being neglected, and (2) the standardized form led to a stereotyped type of reporting. The letter method was found to produce a greater variety of material.

How far the daily bulletin or newspaper should deviate from strict business news depends wholly upon the organization and the viewpoint of the men at its head. Should personal news, such as information on births, deaths and marriages, be included? Where there is an employee house organ, such news may be saved for it. But if there is no employee house organ it may be advisable to include at least the most important items of this kind.

Uses of Contests in Employee Publications

An employee publication must try to inform—but at the same time it should try to be exciting. One method of arousing reader interest and achieving a sense of excitement is that surefire feature, the contest: not just a contest among the sales personnel, for these are the rule rather than the exception, but contests open to all employees. Suggestion contests provide a good example. Prizes are awarded to those employees submitting the best suggestions—and judging is usually done by an employee-management committee that often includes one outsider who is not an employee at all.

As an offshoot of the contest idea, the employee publication may stimulate a competitive spirit among units, sections and departments by publishing production figures, attendance records and data on deadlines met, or shipments delivered in record time. All such items are published with an eye to instilling pride and desire in employees.

A Chicago mail-order firm prepared a series of bulletins concerning its employee relations policies. To be certain employees had read the policies outlined in the bulletins, a series of contests, to be held every six months, was launched. Fifty prizes were awarded in each contest, the amounts ranging from $15 for the first prize to $1 for the last 47 prizes. All hourly employees could enter the contest.

The first contest consisted of 40 questions of the fill-in-the-blank type, with considerable weight being carried by the answer to the last question: "Tell us in 25 to 50 words which personnel policy you like best."

Is Your Publication Read?

Sooner or later, economy minded people in top management begin to question whether or not the employee publication is worth its cost. The accepted method of ascertaining the readership of a publication is the employee questionnaire, which asks pertinent questions: who in the family reads the publication, what they think of it, what features they like best, and others. However, the number of readers who will bother to return such questionnaires is usually small. The important thing: how many readers say they read the publication in relation to the number of questionnaires returned.

Getting Publications Into the Home

An analysis of more than 100 bulletins, house organs, and other publications showed that three out of 10 still overlook the importance of the employees' families.

Since it is impossible for management executives to visit personally the families of all employees and talk over the problems that the company and its workers have in common, the next best thing is the printed word. An employee publication which is oriented in part toward the family, and especially the spouse, is a must for any business employing substantial numbers of workers.

While a company publication is essentially a medium for company news, it is also important to remember that the employee's family is a part of the company family. The company publication should be able to interest the worker's spouse as well as children. With many married couples working at two *different* companies, there is even a small rivalry in some cases. If one publication is bright and attractive and informative, it will show up a poor job done by the spouse's firm. The company newspaper is a very definite reflection of the company.

A Useful List of "Don'ts"

Years ago, one of the outstanding papers in the field of employee relations was *Wright at the Moment (Wright Engineering)*. As a guide for the information of associates who contribute to the publication, the editor prepared an interesting list of "don'ts" that still make sense for editors of employee publications. The list was widely reprinted and has helped many editors to make their publications more effective:

Don't "salute" anyone. The mere fact that a story or picture appears is in itself a bow and repeated salutes makes the expression meaningless.

Don't "Mr." unless you "Mr." everybody from floor sweeper up.

Don't recommend. It's only the editor (one more baldish guy on the payroll) who says it.

Don't reveal the mechanics of news reporting unless that's part of the story. Only cub reporters and pretenders to Broadway-columnizing say, "Your reporter called on Mr. Frud . . ."

Don't poke fun. A fellow's hobby of collecting old trolley car transfers is probably more important to historians than your collection of orchids.

Don't fill a page, even a back page, with dry copy and no pictures. Try to treat each page as a show window for its own wares.

Don't misquote—not even if it makes it sound smarter. On the other hand, don't quote if you know it may make the quoter look foolish. Just leave it out.

Don't play up an executive's favorite subject because he's your favorite brass hat and might give you a promotion some day. If it's not a story, be polite but firm. Leave it out.

Don't call everybody "genial," "amiable," "lovable" . . . And don't call every buck-toothed, shiny-nosed, bulgy-eyed girl on the assembly line "pretty." Skillfully handled, the pictures and the facts will prove it—if it's so.

Don't print general copy about events or anything else, if you can fight your way out of it. Keep it local. Find an angle. The hometown newspaper, reporting a train wreck on the other side of the county, will always headline "Local Man Killed in Train Wreck," then will tell about the senator who also died.

Don't shake hands with yourself. Even if you did have to stalk somebody for three weeks to get a story, the company paper is supposed to be ubiquitous and omniscient and to get the story if it's to be gotten. Unlike the city papers, company papers have no scoops.

Don't generalize if you can particularize. On the other hand . . .

Don't give all the gruesome details. Unless it's the Holy Grail, a baseball trophy is a baseball trophy, not "an 18-inch-high brass figure of a ball player standing ready to strike, with inscription underneath." The audience knows the company buys these things ready-made by the dozen.

Don't begin all score-reporting stories with the same corny lead, even if it is the same corny stuff each time.

Don't let a dull subject stay dull if you can help it. Lighten the spread on safety, for example, with a shot of some safety proponent hanging a "For Rent" sign on the first-aid room of a no-accident department.

Don't subordinate people to things. Maybe a lot of them never saw the inside of your plant before Tuesday, but to the company paper, the plant would fold up without them.

Don't "Don't" if you can help it. Company papers must report rules and restrictions, but they can be put in terms of Do just as easily as in terms of Don't.

Don't make a Santa Claus out of the company. It's more fitting to let workers feel sports, prizes, and conveniences are their just due than it is to try to make them think the company is a warm-hearted prince who lives on the hill. They all know that the total spent for sports and such is a tiny fraction of net income anyway!

Don't follow a practice of not letting your external public relations hand know what your internal relations hand is doing. What you tell the outside world should not be contradicted by what's in the company paper. And employees read about the company in local papers.

Don't "slop over" in calling affairs "successful" when they were actually short of success. Nothing undermines an editor so much as being overlavish with praise. Strive to win a reputation for accurate reporting, even if it hurts at times. Nothing succeeds like accuracy in journalism.

Don't reject a good story because of one single reason for not using it. The reason why it should be used may be better.

Finally, don't have to many don'ts. *Let policies be the slave, not the master.*

VIDEO COMMUNICATIONS

If a company is large enough, it can use television for communicating with employees. Many business firms and industrial plants geared up for closed circuit TV in the early 1970's, especially if the equipment could be used for training as well as employee communications.

The corporate communications department of Niagara Mohawk Power Corporation, for only one example, calls its regular TV program "NEWSCOPE" and broadcasts are scheduled on a daily basis. Western Electric Company has used TV for many years. In Allentown, PA, it ran "Look-In" on a monthly basis starting in the 70's.

It is obvious that a company must be big enough in terms of employees before considering TV as a communications medium unless there is a heavy video training program. A good system would run $250,000, and this expenditure would most certainly have to be cost-effective.

Magnetic Tape

In the sixties, magnetic tape, which had become popular in the fifties for recording and playing back strictly audio material, began to carry a larger load. It began to record and play back both sight and sound—initially only black and white sight, but, before long, color.

Videotape has revolutionized communications within companies, between companies, and between companies and their constituencies—and it has particularly revolutionized communications with employees.

Slide presentations have withstood the onslaught mainly because of the Eastman Kodak Carousel system of storing and projecting 35-mm. transparencies from rotating crowns atop semi-automatic projectors. Motion pictures, mainly 16-mm., have had to face, and overcome, new challenges within the business community. They will survive, of course, for there is a proper role for industrial films, just as there is a very big place for slide presentations. But the newest hero in audio-visual communications is, beyond doubt, the videocassette in this wide and wonderful new world of communications for employees.

Case Histories

Ford Motor Company has sent videocassettes to its dealers everywhere with instructions about the best way to play back the sight and sounds of its new line of automobiles. Customers in dealer showrooms saw the cars zoom up a mountain road in the Rockies, to be followed by a demonstration of a modern service department using the instant tuneup machine, computer-controlled. And all of this showed up at dealerships from coast to coast, thanks to a cassette almost as easy to put into place as dropping a piece of bread in your kitchen toaster.

Exxon crewmen aboard a super-tanker in the South Atlantic can watch a 25-minute video program in the ship's lounge. The show is part of a growing library of cassette programs which Exxon furnishes for use aboard the 75 vessels whose routes take them to the waters off Africa and into the Mediterranean Sea. Produced with English, Spanish and Italian soundtracks, the cassettes dealt with subjects such as pollution prevention methods and general safety practices relevent to life aboard ship. Cassettes for shipboard use were issued monthly out of New York. Many were specially-created to cover subjects unique to mariners. Knowing that all work and no play makes long voyages dull, the company also provides entertainment cassettes—including full-length features.

When Parke-Davis wanted to introduce a new pharmaceutical product and have a staff meeting with more than 1,000 salesmen in 11 cities, it could see the cost of bringing everyone into headquarters would be staggering. An electronic staff meeting worked almost as effectively, considering it contained the following elements: (1) the "introduction" by cassettes played onto video tubes in the various cities, (2) a two-way, back-and-forth discussion, involving closed circuit "live" television, and (3) a follow-up "live" question and answer session, audio only.

Illinois Bell executives in Springfield, Ill., are almost a thousand miles away from a meeting at AT&T headquarters in New York— but thanks to a cassette, "they're there." And Illinois Bell installers and repairmen can meet in the corner of a garage in Springfield, Ill., to watch and hear their president in Chicago explain the company's efficiency objectives for the new year—via cassette.

Monsanto employees in Brussels can gather in a conference room to see and hear the annual meeting of shareowners which took place a few days before in St. Louis.

Job Training

IBM production workers got a first-hand look at simplified methods which resulted in saving time and maintaining quality. They found it easy to follow the new technique through close-ups, repeated explanations and step-by-step superimposed titles. "What an easy way to learn; what painless training" summed up their reaction. Again—it's on a cassette.

U.S. Gypsum held a sales-incentive meeting. Its marketing people saw a new cassette program dealing with construction systems. Printed texts were distributed as soon as the 30-minute program had been completed on the TV tubes.

A Hewlett-Packard salesman has just put a playback machine in the back of his car. Very shortly he can be "tuning in" a cassette at a customer location, doing a more graphic job of demonstration—via cassette—then he could ever do on his own. He knows his line of electronic products as well as anyone in the company. But he can show his line best with a friendly assist from a cassette.

At Smith, Kline & French, employees in high traffic areas can catch a few glimpses of things they'd not ordinarily see—photography awards presented to their co-workers, an intramural basketball game, a product introduction in another city—via cassette.

Aetna Life & Casualty, Caterpillar Tractor, Eastern Airlines, Citibank, J. C. Penney, Lord & Taylor, Merrill Lynch, Pfizer, Time, Inc., and Travelers Insurance—are all using videocassettes for an A to Z variety of internal communications in today's busy, information-hungry world.

Did these companies "see the light" early—in the late sixties, for example—when videotape for business organizations became available? In a few cases yes but in most cases no.

Significant Advance

The significant advance occurred in 1971 when the Sony Corporation of Japan shipped in its first videocassette recorders and playbacks into the U.S. IBM acquired part of that first shipment.

The videocassette system was so much "the solution" that it turned many apprehensive corporations into willing customers almost overnight. It made complicated technology "look simple" by the expedient of "putting the whole show in a foolproof package" and making the recording and playback hardware easy enough for a child to operate, push-button style.

Divisional offices are now "producing" their own TV programs for internal use. Plants are now making their own safety and training films.

Cassette Libraries

Several thousand U.S. companies now have libraries of cassette programs for employees, embracing a wide variety of subjects. It has been commonly accepted for years that "audio visuals are excellent for training purposes." That slogan was traditionally the song sung by manufacturers of motion picture projectors, and by companies specializing in producing 16mm. motion pictures for business organizations.

Many programs are available on both motion picture film and cassette. If the audience is likely to be small, the cassette is the way to go. If the program is to be seen by 150 people, a large motion picture screen is still ideal.

Closed Circuit TV

Some companies have gone beyond making cassette programs available for "our people" and have established budgets, staff and hardware to engage in regular programs involving closed circuit television, generally referred to as CCTV.

CCTV programs have some distinct advantages and some distinct disadvantages. Their big plus is the element of immediacy. "There's Mr. Big 1,000 miles away, reading the riot act *right now*" is a particular piece of clout which is not carried quite as effectively by the same program on cassette TV a few days later. CCTV can even be two-way or—considering multiple locations—three-way, four-way, five-way, etc. The big disadvantage is "time inflexibility." In order to see a CCTV program "live," all concerned—principals and audiences—have to gather promptly at the appointed hour.

John H. Barwick of Westport, Conn., president of Barwick Kranz, Incorporated, emerged in the mid-seventies as somewhat of an encyclopedic authority on the subject of "business use of video-communications." He was most helpful in this author's roundup of different uses of the still-emerging medium.

Business Week magazine's administrative and publishing staff took an early interest in the subject—and even went so far as to develop "deskside conference" programs which permitted businessmen to rent videocassette programs and hardware for a broad spectrum of programs. Want to hear and see Raleigh Warner Sr., chairman of Mobil Oil Corporation, give his views on the energy problem? He'll be at your desk-side via what *Business Week* calls its "Playback" series for businessmen. Want to hear and see C. Peter McCullough Jr., Xerox chairman, or ex-astronaut Frank Borman, president of Eastern Airlines? Want the latest comment from experts in accounting, insurance, taxes? The magic carpet ready to carry it into your office is the videocassette.

Many companies have developed a substantial expertise in producing their own video programs. some have their own TV studios, writers, cameramen, editors. Programs are quite often made for external use (TV clips for the local station are ideal) but there is an increasing amount of programming being planned for "internal use only."

Companies are finding, more and more, that TV has most of the advantages of motion pictures plus many new and singular plusses on its own with respect to production, editing, use—and economy.

Visuals within an organization are normally mounted for four principal purposes: to train, to inform, to motivate, to entertain. All echelons of employees can become involved, upwardly and downwardly.

At Exxon

The following information was supplied by Andrew T. Purcell of Exxon U.S.A., New York, concerning an early experimental series of video interviews for employees, entitled "Exxon Conversations":

"A principal reason for using the medium of television was our assessment that we needed greater credibility in communicating about such heavyweight issues as taxes, profits and the environment. We felt that TV, which offers the faces and voices of visible, recognizable people, would be more believable than printed messages which might be, in the minds of the readers, ghost-written and 'laundered.'

"We have chosen the in-depth interview approach, as opposed to the newscast approach, because it seems to be a better way to meet our twofold objectives: to explain the company's operations and to explain public issues which affect Exxon.

"One particular difficulty relates to that old nemesis called clearances. A TV editor can't rewrite, delete a paragraph or add a paragraph as simply as with a manuscript. This fact required us to set up a new approach for clearances. When we arrange the time and date for the videotaping, we alert appropriate departments (law, public affairs, employee relations, etc.) concerning our production schedule and ask them to be prepared on a short notice to come to our TV studio to review the unedited tape as soon as shooting is completed. If there is any part of the program which has to be changed, we reshoot the offending portion immediately. We do this because it is exceedingly difficult to recreate the exact sound and lighting conditions, not to mention the talent's skin tones, voice and appearance, a day or a week later.

"Another discovery made early in our TV effort was the invaluable assistance a professional in the field can provide. We retained for our pilot programs a free-lance TV producer and would flatly state such a person is a must."

THE EMPLOYEE OPINION SURVEY

Since employee relations are generally thought to be the foundation of good *public* relations, it is highly important to determine as accurately as possible the effectiveness of management and supervision, the training program, and other matters affecting worker-management relations. To do this, many companies survey employee attitudes regularly. Attitude trends can thus be spotlighted and the results of management programs measured from one year to the next.

A basic fact of business life is that employees form the foundation and backbone of any company. As the workers perform, so goes the company. For this reason alone, maintaining the best possible employer-employee relations requires management awareness of those factors in employee thinking that could affect performance. How can such awareness be achieved? The first step is to keep a finger on the attitude and opinion pulse of the work force; the opinion poll has been held up as one of the best ways of doing so. The second step is to seriously consider any matter that the polls show to be important to workers.

The second step ranks as high in importance as the first. The theory that opinion polls conducted too often lead to a "familiarity breeds contempt" attitude among workers has validity only if the polls produce no results. Where polls do lead to improvement in the areas considered important to workers, employees have been found to be more than happy to cooperate in each and every survey.

Purposes of Employee Opinion Surveys

Before undertaking an opinion poll, the employer should understand both the purposes of a survey and the various kinds of surveys. The employer should know initially that in polling employee attitudes he is utilizing only one of three fundamental types of survey, each geared to a different audience:

Financial (Shareholders, market analysts, etc.)

Marketing (Users, consumers of specific products)

Employee (in reference to company policy, organization, etc.)

"Each type of survey has importance in its own right." J. B. Strenski stresses. "Each group surveyed can include employees, but each is surveyed for a different purpose. Each has proved appropriate for us in given circumstances."

Surveys are costly enough to warrant careful planning and definition of purposes. When directed toward employees, specific areas under question or scrutiny must be emphasized, and those areas about which no question has arisen may be ignored. For example, if management knows that company washroom facilities are modern and well kept, it may not be necessary to survey workers on that point. It has been found to be the part of wisdom, however, for management to obtain the opinions of workers regarding the company cafeteria even though the company may have tried to make the eating facility as acceptable and attractive as possible. Food quality in particular may vary from time to time, a fact that management may not understand unless it asks questions of those who use the cafeteria.

The following outline of purposes should prove useful in the initial planning stage:

A. To measure in *general* the level of employee morale.

B. To measure *specifically* in what ways and to what degree employees are satisfied or dissatisfied with the following:

1. Physical working conditions, such as temperature, ventilation, noise, restrooms, equipment, etc.

2. Job security.

3. Qualifications of the supervisors in matters of technical competence and human relations.

4. Opportunities for advancement, specific reasons for dissatisfaction with promotion policies.

5. Compensation, both direct and through fringe benefits, fairness of wage and salary scales between jobs in the employer organization and compared with other employers in the community.

6. Relations with fellow employees, working with them as a team, ways in which they are most satisfied or dissatisfied.

7. Other specific policies, practices, and factors that affect employee attitudes.

C. To evaluate more exactly both general morale and specific job attitudes by comparisons in each respect with averages or norms established in other employee surveys.

D. To determine where specific job dissatisfaction of each type is most concentrated—in which divisions, departments, plants, or smaller work groups in the organizations.
Regarding each type of dissatisfaction, this analysis helps to determine what the need is for corrective action, training or information—whether to apply it uniformly throughout the organization or only in certain employee groups.

E. To test how well employees are informed and their interest in becoming better informed. This refers to subjects of two general types:

1. Matters relating to their jobs, particularly those in which accurate information will contribute to job satisfaction.

2. Company or industry problems in which it is desirable to build greater public support—an aim to which employees can contribute if they are well informed.

F. To provide employees with an organized opportunity for full expression of their attitudes, and to do so through a form of upward communication which they are assured will reach the top echelon. This in itself will have a healthy effect on morale.

G. Looking beyond the first survey and its benefits, another result will be to establish a benchmark for measuring progress in improving employee relations.

Which Employees to Survey

In some types of surveys it is sufficient to "sample" the opinions of employees instead of taking the opinions of all of them. In such cases a cross section of the employees can be used, with proportional representation given to each division, department, plant or other classification. It may be desirable to further sub-divide the poll by work groups, employee levels, length of service, and so forth. These surveys are only valid when the questions apply to each employee on an equal basis, such as cafeteria service, insurance programs, the retirement plan, or a company publication to which everyone has equal access.

In a survey that seeks employee attitudes and opinions over a wide range of subjects, some of which will pertain only to particular sections or groups, all workers should be surveyed. If management personnel are to be polled, a special questionnaire is usually prepared for them. The point that must be noted is that "sampling" of a portion of a work force is seldom adequate when the survey calls for opinions that may vary widely from one work group to another. Examples are opinions about supervision and, in some cases, working conditions.

Good reasons exist why employees in certain classifications or types of work should be excluded. Most often, these are employees who are doing temporary work such as construction. But many companies also give separate and different survey questionnaires to plant and office employees; such managements are acting on the theory—often a correct one—that the problems of plant and office differ so basically that different approaches should be taken to each group.

Too often the objects of management's immediate concern are those groups that are farthest removed from it by background and work level. It is certainly advisable to seek to learn how these groups feel on key questions, but management should not uniformly exclude groups closer to it. Top management may be surprised by the opinions of those closest to it.

The Best Time for a Survey

In one sense, the conditions for conducting a survey may never be "ideal" throughout a business organization at any given time. A survey tries to obtain the truest possible measurement of employee opinion, without the distortion that may result from any temporary situation that appears either more favorable or less favorable than "normal" conditions. But is it ever possible to rule out distortion entirely? Possibly not. A poor supervisor may create special—and unfavorable—conditions through a department. A particular group may have had an unusual amount of overtime in the period prior to the survey.

"Most organizations are in a continual state of flux" notes *Science Research Associates*. "This month a paid vacation plan is inaugurated; next month layoffs will be necessary; the following month a new administrator will join the company; a consolidation of several departments is planned . . . Changes such as these do not invalidate a survey. Seldom, then, is there a better time than *the present* in which to conduct a survey."

Some strictures are logical, however. A survey immediately following a general wage increase probably would not reflect the attitudes about wages that customarily prevail. On the other hand, a survey taken during a strike, or even in a period of wage negotiation, might indicate less favorable attitudes than actually exist under more usual conditions.

In general, surveys should be timed to take place when they will interfere least with necessary work. Vacation seasons should be avoided because many employees will be away and cannot be included in the poll without special effort—if at all.

How Surveys are Conducted

Most of the attitude or opinion surveys conducted in 55 companies polled by Dartnell utilized printed questionnaires that employees filled in themselves. Only a few involved personal questioning of employees by interviewers, a more expensive method.

The surveys were quite comprehensive regarding subject matter. All but three included at least 20 questions, and about half covered more than 50 points. Subject matter in most surveys included the following, as a minimum:

General attitudes toward job	Wages or salaries
Attitude toward management	Employee benefits
Supervisors	Promotions
Working conditions	Job security

Most of the surveys included all employees (except, of course, the 5 to 10% absent for normal reasons: vacations, illness, etc.), rather than a cross-section sampling. The surveys usually covered supervisory personnel as well as rank-and-file workers, and in some cases the questionnaires were also filled out by all top-level executives.

The majority of the surveys were conducted on company time and on company premises. Very few companies mailed the questionnaires or let employees take them home to complete.

Forty-five of the 55 firms had some help from outside consultants—especially in planning the survey and questionnaire, and in analyzing or interpreting the results.

The advantages cited in the use of outside consultants included objectiveness, impartial approach, greater confidence among employees that they would not be singled out or identified, and general skill and experience in the conduct of such surveys. Only three firms mentioned any disadvantage in using consultants—citing the cost and the consultant's lack of specific knowledge about the company's operations.

Results Obtained

In most cases answers were analyzed by departments, divisions or other work groupings to pinpoint the information from the survey. Several of them stated that these analyses by separate work groups yielded the most valuable information obtained.

Practically all companies said they obtained new information about employee attitudes, and that results were helpful in giving a more exact measurement of attitudes that were known or expected prior to the survey of employees.

All of the replying companies stated that their employees answered frankly and honestly in most respects, and took the survey seriously.

Benefits from the surveys covered a wide range. Most typical results reported were these:

Improved morale

Located poor morale areas

Disclosed strong and weak points in company policies and administration

Constructive criticism obtained

Attitude toward supervisors revealed

Learned things employees needed to know but did not know

Showed management weakness in communication

Bettered understanding of supervisors' attitudes

Provided facts instead of guesswork as a basis for planning and appraisal

Improved communications

Yielded material for supervisory development

Cleared up general misunderstandings

Showed need for emphasis on human relations in supervisory conferences

Fewer than one-third of the reporting companies indicated any dissatisfaction with their surveys or the use made of the results. Most of these referred to weaknesses or delays in executive follow-through rather than to flaws in the conduct of the surveys themselves. Other complaints, voiced by a very few, included:

"Too small a return—too few employees." (These answers were by firms who mailed questionnaires to employees rather than follow the usual practice of distributing questionnaires on company time at the place of work.)

"Difficulty in ascertaining general source of complaints." (This problem can be overcome by the use of outside consultants whose surveys are coded for identification purposes in any area or group desired.)

"Not enough learned about the 'why' behind certain complaints."

"Inconclusive nature of some of the analyses."

Reporting Survey Results to Employees

Reporting survey results represented one specific use of surveys: such use was indicated by all but 10 of the reporting companies. Almost half reported the complete general results (not detailed breakdowns) to all employees. Most of the others did this in a more limited way—only to supervisors or only selected results rather than a complete summary.

Passing along the results of surveys to employees, in whatever way management might think advisable, serves a dual positive purpose. Making the results public reassures the employees that the survey was not merely an instrument of appeasement, a method of making the worker think his opinions are important, after which the surveys end up in the nearest waste basket. Obviously, if management takes the time to compile the results, it must be interested. Making known the results also serves to inform the employees that they can compare the results with their own answers, which in turn might be influenced. For example, if a man gave as his opinion that the company cafeteria was inadequate while 97% of his co-workers thought it was excellent, he might well review his stand.

In addition, if the management is sincerely interested in taking action on valid complaints, publishing the survey results will give the employees a check-list against which they can compare results. If a company has no intention of correcting areas that need it, the company's management should not make public the results of surveys, or better yet, should not take a survey in the first place.

Twenty of the reporting firms had unions representing their employees, and answered four additional questions about union acceptance of their employee surveys.

Twelve of these discussed the survey in advance with union representatives. None of them reported opposition to the surveys by unions, although some unions were neutral or noncommittal on the subject. In general, it has been seen to be desirable to work with the union when possible. If this is not done, trouble may follow. Walter Reuther, for instance, once complained bitterly that a survey made among union members in the auto industry prior to negotiating for a guaranteed annual wage (GAW) was purposely slanted to prove that workers were against the union's stand. He charged that the questions were loaded. The matter came up before the American Association for Public Opinion Research, but no action was taken.

The techniques of pollsters who use small sample populations in taking surveys have on occasion come under criticism. The charge has been that the samples are inadequate as bases from which to project findings applying sometimes to huge groupings. But Opinion Research Corporation of Princeton, New Jersey has long believed that most persons accept the validity of the small-sample technique.

Acting on the Results

To act on the results of employee opinion polls is usually not a difficult or costly problem. Charles N. Parker, former chairman of Central Surveys, Inc., a firm with extensive experience in employee opinion polls, says, "Not all employee complaints call for correction. Most of them call for information." The action called for by employee surveys has led to results of three general types:

- Taking corrective action when complaints are justified and something can be done about them without delay. Companies report many such types of action as the result of surveys. These range from minor changes to revisions of company policy in different respects.

- Recognizing the need for corrective action and explaining fully why it cannot be taken immediately.

  This may occur most frequently in regard to complaints about physical working conditions. When a major rebuilding or remodeling program is planned, for example, it is not feasible to undertake some minor repair jobs that would more quickly stop complaints about working conditions.

  It may have to be explained why corrective action in other respects is necessarily planned as a long- rather than a short-range activity. For example, certain complaints about supervision may call for a training program that cannot be started immediately.

- Answering complaints, in appropriate instances, by giving information rather than taking corrective action.

  Complaints often result from lack of information or from misinformation. An example would be the mistaken idea that wages in a certain plant are below average for the community.

"When corrective action is taken or is planned, as the result of a survey, it is usually best to let the employees know it was their survey answers that stimulated this action," states Parker. "It will be most satisfying to employees to know that management has shown this regard for their opinions."

The Carnation Company's Opinion Poll

Some time back the Carnation Company wanted to poll its sales organization, so it retained the California Institute of Technology to conduct the survey. This case history is explained in detail because it was so well planned, and it can stand alone now, or in the future, as a good example of "how to do it."

The Carnation sales organization was scattered across the United States and Canada, with no large numbers of people at any single location. Group meetings were impractical. Carnation decided to conduct a mail survey with the confidential returns going directly to Cal Tech.

Prior to beginning the poll all top sales management people were advised of the nature of the poll. This group included division sales managers. They were given advance copies of the questionnaire draft for their suggestions or criticism.

Cal Tech personnel also contributed to the construction of the questionnaire from their experience with previous polls for Carnation and other companies. Questions about certain items, such as pay, were stated in such a way as to draw written comments that would be more meaningful than a simple "Yes" or "No" answer.

The survey forms mailed to each member of the sales force were, of course, blank in the spaces provided for answers. Instructions included the statement, "Please do not sign your name," at the beginning and end. The request for general information was prefaced with the explanation:

At the beginning of this questionnaire, we are asking some information about you. Answers to the following questions will assist in the study of whether or not opinions are affected by age, length of service, or department. (Note: The numbers preceding the answers will be used in tabulating the replies.)

Over 50% of the questionnaires came back almost immediately. A follow-up postcard from Cal Tech brought the total up to 72.9%. The follow-up was sent to the full list and said simply: "If you haven't sent in your questionnaire, please do so."

The fact that some salesmen had doubts was indicated by the note Cal Tech received from one man after the follow-up. It read:

"If you aren't identifying the replies, how did you know I hadn't sent mine in?"

The surveyors promptly explained that the card had been sent to the entire list!

Note the particular care that was taken in the letter below to make it clear to all concerned that the follow-up did in fact go to the full list; and there was no intent to identify replies of the opinion sampling at any stage or for any purpose.

The results of the opinion poll of the Carnation Company sales organization given in this pamphlet are the exact figures which we compiled and submitted to your company.

The summary includes 557 questionnaires which we received on or before April 20. This represents 72.9% of the questionnaires which we mailed to you, a phenomenally high rate on any survey by mail. We are vey much indebted to the 50% who returned their questionnaires immediately and to the others who mailed their questionnaires after we sent a reminder to everybody.

The quality and quantity of your write-in comments exceeded those we have received from other parts of the Carnation Company. Actually, 481 of you (86.4%) took the time to tell us some of the things you liked best and least about working for your company and to make many constructive suggestions. Since most of you gave more than one idea, we received well over 2,600 separate comments.

To facilitate the tabulation of the questionnaires, we transferred the information you supplied us to punched cards. The original questions have now been destroyed. No tabulation has been or will be made that will reveal the identity of any employee or indicate how a specific person answered any question or what comments he made.

On behalf of Cal Tech's industrial relations section, I wish to thank everyone who participated for the cooperation which was given to us in completing the poll.

The Cal Tech staff was surprised by the more than 2,600 written comments. Compared with other surveys they had conducted on non-sales groups, it was obvious that salesmen, as a group, are inclined to express themselves in writing.

The Results

Cal Tech coded each questionnaire on an IBM card. Analyses and summaries of those cards have made possible studies by areas, employee groups, types of supervision, and so forth. For instance, the company wondered how supervision and morale in areas where it operates through brokers compared with that in areas where it maintains its own district offices. Such studies were easy to make.

Reviewing the steps taken to achieve management benefits from the results, the company reported:

> Immediately after the overall results were available, a mineographed copy went to the entire top sales group, including this time the district sales managers, who are the next level of supervision below the division sales managers.
>
> This was followed by a special meeting of our top company management people, at which Cal Tech presented a summary of the results, including some comparative data. The booklet summarizing the results was then prepared and distributed to all participating sales personnel.
>
> We then had a meeting of the original top sales management group that had first been informed of the opinion poll to present detailed results to them. We made many comparisons and discussed in some detail both the problems and good points as highlighted by the opinion poll. Each division sales manager was supplied at the meeting with additional material giving detailed percentage results for his division and, where possible, districts within his division. He was also supplied with the written comments made by people within his division, broken down into various subject matter classifications. All of this material was made available to him for his confidential use within his own organizaiton.

Making the Results Known

The booklet which reported the results of the poll, *The Company You Keep,* was prepared as quickly as possible and sent to all those who had received the original questionnaire. It was felt that this rapidity in sharing the results promptly was an important morale factor in itself—one important to the success of any future polls.

The booklet listed all the percentages of answers, question by question. It also included a cross section of written comments. Every effort was made to produce a representative selection, including what might be termed both the "good" and the "bad." There was enough of the "bad," constructive and otherwise, to provide plenty of material for review and discussion and, in certain areas, action.

Summarizing the Survey Project

The sales personnel manager for Carnation commented on the major values of this opinion poll as follows:

1. The very fact that we made the survey was evidence of our interest in our people and their opinions. This brought an immediate improvement in morale. Turnover in our sales organization was down 18% for the three months following the poll, compared with the three months prior to the poll.

2. The poll gave us facts and figures to use in talking with top management. It was no longer a case of what we "thought" our people liked and disliked—we had proof, the "voice of the people."

3. Some local situations were pointed up, and it was possible to take corrective action before serious trouble developed.

4. The favorable nature of the results improved the stature of the sales operation within the company and our public relations outside the company.

The survey disclosed that Carnation salesmen showed a higher degree of loyalty to the company and a comparatively better morale index than was found in any other Carnation operation. Cal Tech observed that these factors appeared to be higher than it had found similar factors to be in any other industrial survey.

A majority of opinion surveys have a specific focus; they are designed to test group opinions on a particular problem or situation. They are usually confined to questioning—either through trained interviewers or by mail—a single, well defined population or group, such as employees, stockholders, suppliers or customers. There are occasions, however, when it is necessary for effective management planning to obtain facts on a broad subject—for instance, to determine public opinion regarding a labor dispute, or a political situation that might affect the company's operations, or to determine in advance the public's reactions to a proposed decision in the public relations or other areas.

It is advisable to engage the services of an organization specializing in this type of general opinion poll. The size and composition of the sample may be determined according to the extent and urgency of the poll and the funds available.

How big a sample you need depends on your purposes in conducting the survey. If you wish to test a campaign theme or sound out the main ideas on an issue, then 100 or 200 participants may be enough. But if trends are to be measured, or differences between employee or other groups, or if you plan to publish the findings as a broad measure of public opinion, then a sample in the thousands may be necessary.

A common idea is that a large sample or population guarantees reliability. It is not that simple. Though a large sampling may well contribute to reliability, other factors can be even more important. Opinion Research Corporation, a leading authority on opinion polls, offers these guidelines:

1. Determine the desired degree of accuracy. A 750 probability sample of the general public will produce findings fairly certainly within 4 percentage points, plus or minus. You can cut the range of possible error to 2 points by taking 3,000 interviews—if the added cost is justified.

2. Set up a sampling plan that assures a representative cross section of the population group you are studying.

3. Shoot for a high completion rate on the interviews assigned. The hard-to-reach are busy people; they may differ in their views from the stay-at-homes.

4. Validate the field work to make sure each interviewer's work is honest and thorough.

5. Errors can occur in processing. Check each person's work for accuracy, from coding through report typing.

In short, the smart research buyer does not depend solely on sample size but insists on quality performance in each step of the project.

How to Take Your Own Poll

The first step toward taking your own opinion survey is to plan the questionnaire, deciding exactly what you want to know and how to obtain that knowledge with as few questions as possible. Don't try to cover too much ground. An experienced interviewer who is skilled in drawing people out in conversation can take a multisheet questionnaire and get answers quickly to most of the questions. But a novice may encounter resistance. The result may be that the frustrated interviewer supplies his or her own answers to most questions. You end with a poll that simply tells you what the interviewers think or favor.

In preparing a questionnaire for use by either personal interviewers or by mail—or on company premises on company time—it is important to decide at the outset what type of reaction you want. Do you want offhand reactions so that you can evaluate the existing state of mind concerning a given proposition or situation—or set of situations? Or do you want deliberate reactions: what the person being polled thinks about a situation or question after being given both sides of the question? The former seeks to give a picture of public opinion as it exists; the latter concerns itself not so much with existing attitudes or opinions as with what general opinion will be on completion of an educational program.

Above all, make sure that the survey is honest. Otherwise it will be a liability rather than an asset; the results will mislead rather than inform. "Loaded" questions designed to support a pet theory always give a picture that can lead to costly mistakes and poor strategy. The poll-taker is more interested in proving his own theories than in finding out what those he is polling really think.

Making the Survey Objective

In setting up a survey that is both dependable and objective, the following suggestions may be helpful:

1. Start Off with a "Know-Nothing" Attitude. This will give you a clear, fresh approach, and such an approach is necessary in order to avoid biased results.

2. Conduct Survey to Learn—Not Prove. If the basic idea behind your survey is to produce sales material, it is best that you forget the whole thing. You will get plenty of good sales material as a by-product, and it will be pure and untainted by obsessions of selfishness.

3. Avoid Preconceived Ideas of Results. If you already know the answers, wy make the survey? No honest survey will perfectly follow the pattern you think it will take, so don't warp the results by striving to have them parallel your unwarranted conclusions.

4. Strive for Absolute Accuracy. You won't achieve it—no one ever did, but the only way to approach perfection is to make perfection your aim. Errors come too easy for us to court such disaster by carelessly inviting them.

5. Apply Stiff Accuracy Tests to Both Desirable and Undesirable Results. It is just as easy to go wrong in one direction as another, so either test everything from all angles or let the chips fall where they may. The law of averages is a great leveler, but not if you strangle it on one side.

6. Don't Hide Unpleasant Results—Tell the Whole Truth. It is surprising how much will be added to the believability of your report if you include those few embarassing results. There will probably be some answers that will embarrass the recipient, so include yours so you may blush together.

7. Use a Scientifically Accurate Sample—There's No Safety in Numbers. Certainly, get an ample number of reports, but most important, the people interviewed must be typically representative of the whole.

8. Include Questions to Check Against Known Facts. This is the best method of testing the accuracy of your sample.

9. Avoid Complicated, Unexplainable Methods. If the basic problem behind your survey is so complex that a complicated method is necessary, call in an outside organization to do the job. This is just as important as calling in a doctor to look after your physical complications.

10. Explain Method Fully in All Published Reports. Make certain that you cover the five "W's"—who, what, when, where, and why. Who made the survey, what it's about, when it was made, where it was made, and why it was made. These five things are just as important as your general statements of how it was made.

11. Point Out Any Weakness or Limitations in Your Method. There is no perfect method, so be sure you enumerate those imperfections. The recipient is just as likely to jump to conclusions as you, so prevent such suicidal leaps by plainly stating all limitations.

12. State Sources Clearly for All Outside Information Used. Some answers can be better qualified if correlated with outside statistical material. Label every item of this type so it won't be confused with survey results.

13. Don't Extend Results Unless You Definitely State the Size of Your Sample. Preferably, don't extend results at all, but if you do, make certain that everyone understands how the projection was made.

From the standpoint of top management, the best polls are so well planned that the required information is quickly obtained. Questions should be framed to get honest opinions and reactions; answers should be analyzed intelligently and not simply "totted up." Moreover, the results should be conclusive. A survey that does not produce conclusive results is of little value. Reports of polls should be brief and to the point. Executives have little time to digest masses of statistics; they want summaries of poll results in the most concise form possible.

A GOOD SUGGESTION SYSTEM

Using a suggestion system as one more means of improving employee morale, and with it productivity, has been standard practice in some companies for many decades. The practice, in fact, dates back to the coming of assembly-line production—when in the face of sharper competition the boss decided to turn to the rank-and-file worker for ideas. Earlier, the boss *was* the boss; he did all the thinking and gave all the orders. The worker was not supposed to have ideas—he was hired to work, not to think. As things changed, Eaton, Yale & Towne Manufacturing Company installed a suggestion plan—one of the first to do so. Others began to follow suit.

It is fairly obvious that plans that have survived for 40, 50 years and more have had three things in common: (1) they were properly set up in the beginning; (2) management played an active part in selling the program to the supervisory group and to the rank-

and-file worker, and (3) they were intelligently and consistently administered.

During World War II, when every man and woman had to have a vital interest in high production levels, the suggestion plan really came into its own. To encourage the installation of suggestion systems, a special governmental department called the National Suggestion Program went into operation. It was conservatively estimated that production suggestions during the war period saved more than 200 million man-hours of work per year. This is equivalent to the full-time annual labor input of about 800,000 workers.

A National Association of Suggestion Systems functions today as a source of information on suggestion plans. This organization, headquartered in Chicago, has an imposing membership list, an organized program of idea exchange, including publications, and an annual meeting. Among its members are Ford Motor Company, Du Pont, Eastman Kodak, General Motors, and others. Many smaller companies also belong to the NASS, which can supply any organization with adequate data on which to base a good, effective suggestion system. Among the types of information offered: what awards are prevalent today.

Why Do Suggestion Programs Fail?

A tremendous number of suggestion programs have failed. Some estimates put the figure as high as 90% of all the plans inaugurated in the past several decades. The Small Business Administration of the Federal Government gives what may be a more realistic estimate: ". . . Of a group of 222 companies which had set up suggestion systems, 166, or more than half, had discontinued them."

What were the reasons for so many failures? In many instances they were the result of poor planning and still poorer execution. Lack of publicity in the employee magazine and on the bulletin boards was another factor. Many companies set up their plans without sufficient funds to carry on, and some of the monetary awards for intangible benefits were so small that the employee felt he was being cheated. Intelligent managements have avoided such problems by setting up minimum awards of reasonable amounts. In earlier years the minimum was $2; today it is up to $5 to $10 or more.

Another reason for the failure of many suggestion programs was a letdown on the part of management after the first burst of enthusiasm. Too often those who set the plan in operation leaned back and considered the job completed. Like all other employee campaigns, drives, or contests, enthusiasm must be maintained for the entire duration of the program if it is to have a chance of success. The main reasons for failure:

1. Insufficient time spent training the supervisory group to handle employee suggestions.
2. Lack of supervisory enthusiasm for the program.
3. Indifference on the part of employees.
4. Insufficient number of suggestion boxes or poorly placed boxes.
5. Lack of advertising and publicity material in the plant to motivate the employees.
6. Too long a delay between the submission and the acknowledgment.
7. Unsatisfactory explanation for rejections.
8. Awards too small to interest employees.

If a suggestion plan does not come up to par, it is a good idea to make a list of the things needing change before management scraps the program. Once the weak spots are uncovered and corrected, the plan is likely to start paying off at once. Most programs that do not work are weak at the supervisory level, and it is here that management should look first.

Elements of a Good Suggestion Program

While a suggestion program cannot cure all employee motivation problems, such a plan should help to improve employee morale. A good plan can result in close and mutually rewarding contact between management and worker.

Suggestion plans not only keep management alert; they also provide a creative outlet for the average employee. If, for example, the employee is working on a routine job that follows a regular pattern each day, any effort he may put into a suggestion identifies him more closely with the company. Other benefits of a good suggestion program will include the following to one degree or another:

1. A SAFETY VALVE—Constructive suggestions may take the place of gripes.
2. SELF-IMPROVEMENT—The employee is encouraged to develop himself beyond and above the requirements of his job.
3. TEAMWORK—A suggestion to management helps build esprit de corps.
4. RECOGNITION—The development of pride is an accomplishment itself.
5. CASH AWARD—Last but not least, the award the worker receives for his suggestion.

Clearly, dollar return to the person making the suggestion ranks high among the advantages of a suggestion plan. But companies can find other advantages. According to the findings of one Senior Management Committee, the suggestion plan:

— *Gave management two-way channels of communication for encouraging self-expression, individuality, and recognition;*

— *Enabled management, in its answers to suggestion, to inform employees who might not be knowledgeable about a particular function;*

— *Provided the stimulus to examine many long-standing procedures, policies, and practices, and*

— *Afforded an opportunity to equate extra effort with reward.*

Management has three types of programs to choose from: (1) a company planned and adminstered program; (2) a plan organized and operated by an outside organization, and (3) use of a management engineer to study conditions and suggest a plan best suited to the requirements of the company. Regardless of which type is selected, the program must be tailor-made. Even if a packaged plan is chosen, it should be studied and so reorganized that it will fit the company's needs.

Basic policies regarding the suggestion program should be determined by management and put in writing before any steps are taken to install the plan. Without this preparation, contradictory statements may be made to workers and their supervisors, with the result that the program gets off to a limping start. One company issued a booklet summarizing all basic information on its suggestion plan. The handsome, 12-page booklet went into such questions as, *Who may make suggestions? What kind of suggestions will be considered for awards? What kind of suggestions will not be considered for awards?* and *What are the cash awards? How to submit a suggestion* was another subject covered, along with *general regulations.*

The main policies that must be put in writing can be specified on the basis of such examples: (1) organization; (2) general routine; (3) eligibility, and (4) awards. These policies should be so carefully and clearly set up that workers will have no trouble understanding them. In addition to establishing such policies, management should be sure to sell every supervisor on the plan—or it will almost certainly lose effectiveness or break down completely.

What Is a Suggestion?

This is one of the important questions to answer before the plan goes into operation. Unless the answer is clearly understood, endless confusion will result and the plan will never get off the ground.

SUGGESTION BLANK

● Hammermill Paper Company

NO. _____

DATE RECD. _____

BOX NO. _____

DATE _____

I suggest _____

_____

_____

_____

_____

_____

_____

_____

_____

_____

I BELIEVE THE ADOPTION OF THIS SUGGESTION WILL ACCOMPLISH OR RESULT IN _____

_____

_____

_____

_____

_____

_____

_____

_____

_____

BACK SIDE OF THIS FORM MAY BE USED FOR SKETCHES OR FLOW DIAGRAMS.
IF YOU WANT HELP, CONTACT YOUR SUPERVISOR. WHEN COMPLETED, DROP IN SUGGESTION BOX.

Signature_____ Dept._____ Clock No._____

A good suggestion form, like this one is simple in design. The reverse of this form is gridded to facilitate the making of illustrative sketches.

A bulletin may be circulated, or a poster hung on bulletin boards to indicate what suggestions will be acceptable. A statement such as this may be helpful:

A suggestion is a constructive idea to improve methods, equipment, and procedures, to reduce operational time or costs, or to make working conditions better or safer.

Such a definition eliminates from consideration ideas concerning repairs, housekeeping, maintenance work or other routine matters. But even though a proper suggestion has been clearly defined, many an employee will still use the suggestion blanks to air gripes or grouches—especially when the program is new. What is more, he may expect to receive an award for his gripes! Management should not be deterred by such deviations from the normal. Eventually the employee will settle down to the real business of thinking about his job, and when that happens his gripes will become suggestions. Management has continually tried to impress every employee with the idea that it is his suggestions that are sought, not his gripes.

Many companies examine any and all gripes for constructive content. Often the employee not only voices a gripe but may include a suggestion for eliminating a problem situation. In such cases the employee should definitely figure in the awards.

At the start of many programs, as experience has shown, many suggestions may land in the suggestion box. After a couple of weeks, however, the number may drop off considerably. Management should not be concerned with the decrease in number; a natural letdown often takes place after the first rush of enthusiasm to enter ideas. The questions that no longer appear as time goes on are usually those that management can do without.

QUALITY should remain the goal of any continuing suggestion plan. It is better to have only a half-dozen suggestions, each of them of real value, than to have hundreds of half-baked ideas or gripes.

Eligibility of Suggestions

Some basic principles have been isolated as the key ones governing the question of eligibility of suggestions. These principles include:

1. The suggestion must be adopted or scheduled for adoption.
2. The suggestion must not be under active consideration by the management.
3. The suggestion must not be based on an idea to which another employee has priority.

4. The assignment must not be developed as an assignment from management.

A company in the Midwest that has definite policies regarding the eligibility of suggestions tells the employee that to be eligible for an award the suggestion must accomplish at least one of the following:

1. Conserve material, energy, or time over and above that ordinarily used in his work.

2. Eliminate or improve an existing operation or method.

3. Eliminate or improve a tool, die, jig, fixture, or other equipment.

4. Eliminate an existing safety hazard, improve working conditions or improve housekeeping.

5. Increase the present output of a machine over and above his responsibility to do so.

6. Improve the quality of the company's products.

The same company considers the following suggestions ineligible for awards:

1. A suggestion pertaining to an integral part of the regular or assigned work.

2. Any suggestion that duplicates one previously submitted or pertaining to a project already under consideration.

3. A suggestion on a routine function, or a job still in the developmental stage.

4. Any suggestion not submitted on a standard employee suggestion blank.

5. An idea whose implementation will not justify the cost involved.

6. A suggestion that covers an obvious error that should have been the subject of a routine report and correction.

Training the Supervisors

The cooperation of supervisors is absolutely necessary to a successful suggestion system. Supervisors should be trained in the rules, policies, and procedures essential to the smooth operation of the system.

This training is generally informal and takes only a small amount of time. In addition to informal meetings, a number of companies either add a section to the supervisor's policy manual which provides the basic information, or they issue a special booklet to cover the operation of the program. The subjects included in the booklets may be broken down into two parts: (1) purpose of the program and (2) procedures or operation of the plan. The main subjects are usually listed as follows:

Purpose of the plan	*Investigations*
Organization of the plan	*Awards*
Procedure	*Method of payment*
Routine maintenance	*Forms used*
Eligibility of employees	*Rejections*

One of the supervisor's major concerns is the matter of rejections. The supervisor must be trained to handle rejections, for it is especially important that in his personal contact with the rejected suggester he prevent discouragement and keep the employee in the mood to participate again. The supervisor's main function is not to do any of the detail work of the program, but rather to encourage and inspire.

Because some supervisors complain about the additional work the suggestion system makes, management should see to it that he is fully aware of the importance of the work. He should be made to understand that his efforts to cooperate in the program will be a matter of record so that when he comes up for promotion, that record will count in his favor. In addition, when the supervisor's promotion is given space in the employee publication—as it should be—his achievements with regard to the suggestion system should receive publicity at the same time. Other supervisors who may not have taken the suggestion system seriously then see what such cooperation can mean.

Acknowledging Suggestions Promptly

Suggestions should be acknowledged as promptly as possible. "The acknowledgment of receipt of suggestions . . . contributes to the employee's reaction to the program," notes a booklet issued by the National Association of Suggestion Systems. "A prompt, courteous notice or, even better, a personal contact, makes an excellent impression." To be remembered in this regard: the employee is in a state of "white heat" when he enters his suggestion. Since it is HIS suggestion, he expects to get an immediate answer from the suggestion committee. If time drags, his interest wanes; his disappointment may be so great as to affect the morale of others in his department; and he may become actually embittered.

On the following page is a reproduction of a type of blank originally developed by the Allis-Chalmers Manufacturing Company—a

ALLIS-CHALMERS MANUFACTURING COMPANY

SUGGESTION ACKNOWLEDGMENT

Sugg. No...

Date:..

To..Clock No...........................Dept.:.................

Address..City...Zone...............

We acknowledge with thanks your suggestion covering..

....

....

....

....

Your suggestion will be investigated and a report given to the Suggestion Committee as soon as possible. We will try to keep you informed if any unusual delay occurs, and will notify you promptly of any final decision of the Committee.

Please use the Suggestion number above for reference if further inquiry is necessary.

Sincerely,

HOWARD GABLE
Coordinator, Suggestion Committee

Allis-Chalmers' acknowledgment form illustrated a way of handling one of the important aspects of the suggestion system.

form that can be used to acknowledge the suggestions easily and without delay.

In large offices where hundreds of suggestions may be received, suggestion committees have also found it helps to post a daily notice on the bulletin board, listing by numbers the suggestions received by the committee during the preceding 24 hours. Quick action such as this encourages other employees to take part in the program.

No specific time limitation can be set on the process of determining the value of a suggestion. However, if the investigation of the suggestion committee must continue more than two weeks, the employee should be contacted again. He should be told that the committee is still deliberating.

The suggestion committee should operate on the premise that every suggestion should be investigated promptly, completely, and impartially. No deviation from this rule should be permitted.

Compensation for Suggestions

A continuing problem for all companies that install suggestion systems is the amount and type of the awards to be given. No absolute standards can be set, and the amounts vary so much it is up to the individual company to determine what it can afford and what it thinks is fair.

Most companies use a percentage of savings system for those suggestions which actually save the company money in an area where that saving can be computed. A poll of industry revealed that the awards in this category ranged generally from 10% to 20% of the company savings for the first year. This formula gives the employee and almost limitless potential for cash rewards.

Many valuable ideas, however, cannot be measured in terms of savings to the company. These suggestions·must be rewarded on a fixed basis set by the company according to its policies and economic structure. In addition, one means of stimulating intangible suggestions is to set up special quarterly and yearly awards for the best suggestion of that type.

While it is generally conceded that there should be a minimum award and that the minimum usually runs about $10, opinions differ on the question whether a maximum limit should be set. Those who favor a maximum believe it keeps a suggestion plan within certain bounds. On the other hand, executives who approve of having no maximum believe that employees become more enthusiastic about a plan under which they can achieve great awards.

The proponents of no-maximum would seem to have the right idea if the 3.88-to-1 ratio of one year's cost-savings to expense incurred in bringing in ideas is correct. This median ratio was derived in a poll of industrial firms; it simply means that for every dollar spent for a suggestion system in maintenance and awards, the companies enjoyed a return of $3.88. Suggestion systems, thus, appear as a profitable concept, and in some cases may have a greater profit margin than the company's products.

Handling Rejections

One of the most difficult problems connected with a suggestion system is encouraging those whose suggestions have been rejected to try again. Some companies use a printed notice to inform the employee that his suggestion has been turned down. A better way to do the job is to write a letter signed by the administrator of the suggestion program. Such a letter should be brief, but it must give the reason or reasons for the rejection. It should also be written in such a way that the suggester will not lose interest in the program.

The disappointed employee should be told that most suggesters do not succeed in having an idea accepted on the first try. As a rule, only one out of every five suggestions submitted will win an award.

Maintaining interest in a suggestion system has presented many managements with a problem parallel to that of tactfully passing on word concerning a rejection. While most large companies keep their suggestion programs in operation year in and year out, others have found that special suggestion programs at various times during the year enjoy greater success. Aside from stimulating employee interest as a "special contest," such periodic programs serve to give an employee an immediate goal toward which to work.

The best results from special contests have been obtained by timing the program or contest to coincide with the average employee's need for money. The three best times are: (1) just before Christmas—to provide extra spending money; (2) just after Christmas when the bills must be paid, and (3) just before the summer begins, when employees need to put away money for vacation spending.

Organizing the Suggestion System

Only when a suggestion program has the active, continuing support of the president or top management representative on the scene can an employee be assured that his suggestions will be properly received and handled. An important by-product of such top-level involvement is the stimulation of interest in the program among department heads, supervisors, and other executives and managers.

No top official needs to spend more than a minimal amount of time on the program. It is important to emphasize this point, for the top executive may be reluctant to become involved at all if he believes the time input will be prohibitive. He should understand that his participation may be required primarily at the beginning—at an initial meeting with the executives or managers will be running the program, for example. That meeting may include a brief talk by the top executive and an introduction of the administrator of the plan. Another brief talk may become necessary or advisable when some outstanding award has been given to an employee—if the award warrants a special ceremony.

In addition, the president's approval of several other features of the program will be essential as proof of continuing interest. For example, he may sign his name to letters or bulletins announcing the program; or a special suggestion plan leaflet or booklet may be issued with his signature under the foreword. Whatever else the top executive can do to indicate his continuing interest in the program will increase its chances of success.

The Administrator

The administrator does the actual work of running the suggestion plan. He or she should be carefully chosen. Not only should he be "research minded," he must also be receptive to new ideas—have imagination. Furthermore, he must be tactful and able to secure the confidence of the workers whose ideas are rejected. He should have the confidence of supervisors who may be reluctant to consider new methods and procedures. He must be an enthusiastic salesman for the system. His ability to pledge complete protection of all ideas received must be beyond question. In the words of a booklet issued by the National Association of Suggestion Systems:

> "The Suggestion Administrator's job should be assigned to a person who, in addition to being personable and articulate, has a flair for promotion. While the investigation of suggestions and all other aspects of processing must be handled with care and dispatch, it is necessary also to keep interest in the program alive. A person whose interests are limited to the clerical aspects of the activity might inadvertently let the program die on the vine."

In large companies, the administrator—or secretary or chairman—may be assigned to run the suggestion program on a full-time basis. In smaller companies, the administrator may be a regular staff member with other duties.

The Committee's Job

Because suggestions should be considered promptly, the suggestion committee should meet on a regularly scheduled basis—usually once a week on a specified day. The agenda will generally follow an established pattern:

1. A report on the suggestions received since the previous meeting.
2. A report on the suggestions reported on at the previous meeting which will require further investigation.
3. A report on pending suggestions for the consideration of their acceptability.
4. A committee discussion and determination of pending awards.

If the committee is to function smoothly and without waste of time, adequate preparation for each meeting is a must. This is particularly true when a large number of suggestions is to be processed.

One manfacturing company supplies its investigators and suggestion committee with these instructions:

> The suggestions are collected from locked suggestion boxes each Monday morning. In the office, the date of collection is written on the face, an acknowledgment form is sent to the suggester, and the date of acknowledgment noted on the face. The suggestion is then recorded on the suggester's individual file card and on a card which shows suggestions received, rejected, and awarded each month. An investigation form is attached to the file card and identified by number.

> The investigator studies the suggestion, then seeks out the suggester and through discussion gains a full understanding of the meaning of the suggestion. The supervisor is then asked his opinion of the suggestion without, if possible, revealing the identity of the suggester. Since the supervisor usually knows who it is (many workers talk over their suggestions with their supervisors) this is not of the utmost importance. If further information is necessary, the investigator turns to whichever other departments are likely to be helpful.

> When the story is ready to be told, the suggestion is presented verbally to the consultation committee. This committee considers the acceptability, eligibility, and practicability of the idea. It may reject the suggestion, approve it for trial, ask for further information of a specific nature, or various members may decide they want to look at the operation themselves and report back to the committee.

> The committee meets every Tuesday afternoon. Results of each meeting are reported by form to the general manager and employee relations manager.

> Upon acceptance, the suggestion is turned over to the award committee. This group authorizes awards for all suggestions. It may also reject a suggestion despite the recommendation of the consulting committee or it may ask for further specific information.

Identifying the Suggester

There are two schools of thought on whether or not the suggester's name should appear on the suggestion form. For this reason there are two basic types of forms in use—the coupon form and the open form. The coupon form has a detachable perforated coupon with either one or two stubs. Both the form and the stubs bear a matched serial number and the employee may write his or her name on each stub, one of which is kept. The other is sent to the suggestion administrator. His or her name does not appear on the form proper and he or she can be identified only by means of the stub. On some forms only one stub is provided and the worker's identity is not revealed to the committee. This makes it certain that those who pass on the suggestions submitted are not influenced by the name of the suggester.

Companies using the coupon type of form believe such confidential handling encourages many worthwhile suggestions which might otherwise never reach the suggestion committee.

The open form is designed on the theory that not only should there be no concealment of the identity of the suggester, but there should be no implication that secrecy is necessary. Those in favor of this type of form believe that if there is any suspicion on the part of the employee that his supervisor or the suggestion program cannot be trusted to play fair with him, it is obvious that he cannot depend on getting a square deal in anything else. Proper training of the supervisory group, it is felt, makes the anonymous suggestion unnecessary. Such training emphasizes the importance of getting supervisors to understand that an essential part of their jobs is to develop good ideas from the employees in their department. In addition, they must have the assurance of management that good ideas developed through cooperation with employees are a credit to themselves and their departments.

Investigating the Suggestion

As a rule, the supervisor of the department to which a new suggestion or idea may apply is assigned to the investigation of that suggestion. What points should the investigation cover? The following is a list prepared by one company to help investigators to prepare a complete and detailed reply to the suggestion committee:

INSTRUCTIONS TO INVESTIGATORS

Your reply should be courteous and complete, giving detailed reasons for your recommendations. If previous consideration has been given to this idea, include reference to specific correspondence, drawings, shop orders, etc.

PLEASE REPLY TO ALL QUESTIONS AS EXPLICITLY AS POSSIBLE

1. Is the idea now in our practice?
2. Is it already under consideration from another source?
3. If so, who has the matter in hand?
4. Adoption? (Answer "Yes," "In part," or "No.")
5. Improvement in quality of product? Estimated value?
6. Reduction of material? Yearly saving?
7. Saving of labor? Yearly saving?
8. Other savings?
9. Total yearly saving?

10. Show in moderate detail how savings are figured.
11. If suggestion is adopted, when will it be put into effect?
12. Who will be responsible for putting it into effect?
13. Have instructions been issued to put it into effect?
14. Estimated cost of putting it into effect?
15. Other information of interest.

When the Program Bogs Down

When the flow of suggestions from employees shows signs of slowing down perceptibly, the suggestion committee should look for the answers to these ten questions:

1. Is it possible to reduce the length of time between the receipt of a suggestion and its acknowledgment?
2. Is the length of time between the receipt of a suggestion and its acceptance or rejection over a month? (This does not apply to technical ideas which may take longer to process.)
3. Is the employee notified promptly if his suggestion is held up because of the time required for investigation of the idea?
4. Is the acceptance letter or memo friendly or just a cut-and-dried proposition? Does it sell the worker on submitting other suggestions in the future?
5. Is the rejection of an employee's suggestion handled tactfully? Is the employee given adequate and logical reasons for the rejection? Is an effort made to sell him on another try?
6. Are workers given sufficient help by their supervisors in the preparation of their ideas?
7. Has the supervisor been sold on the idea that getting his workers to turn in suggestions is part of his job?
8. Has the style of the suggestion posters been monotonous? Should they be completely changed?
9. How long has the suggestion form been in use? Should a new style be considered?
10. Has a short suggestion program been tried for a change of pace?

Unless thought and action are applied to such questions from time to time, a suggestion program can easily become static. If it is to be a continuous means of encouraging employee thinking, it needs continuous attention. Necessary changes and innovations must be undertaken to keep it fresh and stimulating.

CHAPTER 15

WORKING WITH A
UNIONIZED OFFICE

ALTHOUGH major unions have been interested in organizing the massive American office-worker force for many years, the inroads have still not been impressive. One important reasons is the variety of jobs performed. Another is the gap in educational and training requirements for the people who work side-by-side. Only eight percent of the offices in the U.S. have union affiliation, while 10 percent of the offices are unionized in Canada.

It is understood in the majority of offices that various tasks command various grades in salary. The opportunity to move from one task to another and from one salary level to another exists in most business operations. The "people in accounting" do not have the same opinions on work as the stenographic pool or the word processing department people. The receptionists are normally far less trained than the computer programmers.

But this has not stopped unionization in its tracks. The basic successes have come in the large office operations where the plant (blue-collar) workers have strong, established bargaining units.

The union/company agreement which follows provides insight into the areas which are covered for office workers, including salaries, job postings, benefits, regulations, etc.

UNION WORKING AGREEMENT

The _____ COMPANY, hereinafter referred to as the Company, and Local _____ of the _____ UNION, hereinafter referred to as the Union, agree as follows:

ARTICLE I—Recognition and Purpose

Section 1

The Company recognizes the Union as the sole and exclusive bargaining agent for all employees employed in the Company's General Office except employees classified as confidential, professional, or supervisory; and except employees in the following classifications: Carpenters, electricians, elevator operators and starters, operating engineers, painters, plumbers, secretarial trainees, administrative car chauffeurs, engineering assistants, and senior engineering assistants.

The Company agrees that confidential, professional and supervisory classifications will be made with the intention of complying with the overall objective of governmental regulations applicable to the making of such classifications.

Section 2

The term "employee" as used in this Agreement means any person covered by this Agreement as stated in Section 1, above.

Section 3

The Company agrees that it will not discriminate in any manner against any employee because of membership in, or activities on behalf of, the Union, or interfere in any manner with the internal administration of the Union or the selection of its representatives for the purpose of collective bargaining with the Company.

The Company agrees to furnish to the Union the names and positions of new employees of the Company placed on jobs within the bargaining unit defined in Section 1 of this Article I.

The Company agrees further that all new employees eligible for membership in the Union shall, at the time of employment, be informed of the existence of the Union.

Section 4

The Union agrees that there shall be no intimidation or any coercion of employees by the Union or any of its members or representatives.

The Union agrees that there will be no solicitation of members, or performance of Union activities, during the working hours of any employee engaged therein or affected thereby, except as otherwise provided in this Agreement.

ARTICLE II—Payroll Deductions

Section 1

The Company will make deductions from the wages of an employee who is a member of the Union upon authorization of such employee. The amount so deducted will be the amount of the employee's dues in the Union and the amount of the deduction from each employee's monthly earnings will be that certified by the Secretary of the Union as the amount of the Union's monthly membership dues. The money so deducted will be paid to the Treasurer of the Union.

It is agreed further that the authorization for the deductions will be signed by the employee concerned and will be in the following form:

Date _____

I hereby request that _____ *Company deduct from my wages the amount of my dues in the* _____ *Union, Local* _____, *the amount of $*_____ *each month, or such amount as may hereafter be established by the Union. The money so deducted will be paid to the* _____ *Union, Local* _____.

It is understood that the above-stated payroll deduction will be discontinued at any time at my request made in writing and presented to the _____ *Company.*

_____

Section 2

The Union hereby agrees to save and hold the Company harmless from any and all liability and to indemnify it against loss arising out of or in connection with the Company compliance with the foregoing provisions of this Article.

ARTICE III—Grievance Procedure

Section 1

A grievance is defined as any question involving application or interpretation of this Agreement or any written side agreement(s).

Section 2

Any employee or group of employees have the right to present a grievance through channels of the Company's administrative organization and to have the grievance adjusted without intervention of the Union. The adjustment must comply with the contract and any written side agreement(s) and the Union given the opportunity to be present at such adjustment.

Section 3

Any grievance presented in writing will be answered in writing.

Section 4

An employee may present a grievance to his immediate supervisor, who will call for a Union representative if requested by the employee.

If the grievance is not satisfactorily settled in three (3) workdays after presentation, the Union may bargain with the department head.

Section 5

If a grievance involves more than one supervisor, the Union may bargain directly with the department head.

If a grievance brought to a department head under Section 4 or this Section 5 is not satisfactorily settled in ten (10) workdays after presentation, the Union may bargain with the Manager, Employee Relations Services—General Office, or with the person or persons designated by him.

Section 6

If a grievance involves all employees, the Union may bargain directly with the Manager, Employee Relations Services—General Office, or with the person or persons designated by him.

Section 7

No grievance will be considered unless it is presented in accordance with this Article III within thirty-one (31) calendar days from the date on which the incident occurred. Any grievance not carried to the next higher step of this procedure within thirty-one (31) calendar days will be considered closed.

Section 8

Any time limits set forth above in this Article III may be extended by mutual consent of the parties.

Section 9

The Company agrees to notify the Union in writing within one (1) working day (excluding Saturdays, Sundays and Holidays) following discharge or disciplinary action resulting in loss of wages of any employee covered by this agreement. The Union will make no grievance on discharges or disciplinary actions after five (5) working days have elapsed from the date of discharge or disciplinary action.

Section 10

The Company shall make available to the Union information, as mutually agreed, as being essential for investigation and consideration of a grievance.

ARTICLE IV—Arbitration

Section 1

Cases which may be referred to arbitration shall be limited to:
  (1) Questions of application, interpretation or alleged violation of this agreement, arbitration awards or written side agreements or,
  (2) Disputes concerning disciplinary action resulting in the loss of pay or the discharge of employees.

Section 2

If the question is one which may be referred to arbitration as provided in Section 1 of this Article IV and it is not settled as the result of negotiations between the Manager, Employee Relations Services—General Office, or those designated by him, and the Union within a period of ten (10) workdays, or within an extension of time mutually agreed upon, the Company or the Union may refer the subject to arbitration provided written notice of intention to do so has first been served by the Union on the Manager, Employee Relations Services—General Office or by the Company on the Secretary of the Union. If the party on whom such notice is served does not indicate the desire to negotiate further on the question within ten (10) workdays after service of such notice, the subject will be eligible for referral to arbitration. Should notice of the desire to negotiate further be served, then such negotiations shall be considered as starting as of the date of the service of such notice, and if agreement is not reached within ten (10) workdays thereafter, or an extension of time mutually agreed upon, the subject will be eligible for referral to arbitration for settlement.

Section 3

The Union and the Company shall select an arbitrator from a panel of five (5) arbitrators designated by the Federal Mediation and Conciliation Service for each arbitration session. Such selection shall be made by the Company and Union alternately striking out the names of the panel until only one name remains. It is understood that an arbitration session shall not be limited to a single arbitration case. The decision of the arbitrator shall be final and binding on both the Union and the Company. The Union and the Company shall bear equally the expense and fees of the arbitrator.

Section 4

Questions concerning any liability or obligation of the Company, which require the application of any statue or law, for example, but not by way of limitation, Fair Labor Standards Act, Workmen's Compensation Laws, National Labor Relations Act, Social Security Law, and amendments thereto, shall not be eligible for arbitration. The provisions of this section will in no way affect the arbitration rights of the parties as set forth in Sections 1, 2 and 3 of this Article IV.

ARTICLE V—Bargaining Meetings

Section 1

For the purpose of bargaining between the Union and the Manager, Employee Relations Services—General Office or his designated representative, on terms of a new Agreement or changes in terms of an existing agreement, meetings shall be held at any place and date mutually agreed upon. At such meetings, the Union may be represented by not more than five (5) accredited representatives. Likewise, the Company may be represented at these meetings by not more than five (5) accredited representatives.

Section 2

For the purpose of bargaining between the Union and the Manager, Employee Relations Services—General Office or his designated representative, for reasons other than those referred to in Section 1 of this Article V, meetings shall be held after a lapse of not more than three (3) workdays from receipt by either party of notice from the other party that a meeting is desired. Such notice shall state the nature of the question or questions to be considered at the meetings. At such meetings, the Union may be represented by not more than three (3) accredited representatives and the Company, likewise, be represented by not more than three (3) representatives.

Section 3

The Union representatives and the Company representatives to any meeting referred to in this Article V shall have the privilege of appointing a stenographer to take accurate records of all proceedings.

ARTICLE VI—Wages

Section 1

The current salary settlement and salary ranges for employees represented by the Union are listed in attached (not pictured here).

Section 2

The Company through its designated supervisors in the General Office will, as nearly as possible, on an annual basis, review the salary status and counsel with employees under their supervision in an appropriate manner and may grant such individual merit increases in compensation as said designated supervisors consider to be warranted, based upon merit, of which the Company and said designated supervisors shall be the judge; and in consideration thereof, the Union agrees that it will not request the Company to bargain on the subject of merit increases for any employees represented by it. It is understood, however, that employees and/or Union representatives will retain the right to discuss with the immediate supervisor, or the appropriate department head after having had a discussion with the immediate supervisor, individual cases where they feel that an injustice has been done or a serious inequity exists.

ARTICLE VII—Hours of Work

Section 1

The regular workweek will be five (5) consecutive days in any one calendar week, excluding Sunday. The normal workweek will be Monday through Friday. However, if it becomes necessary to change any workweek schedules in effect during the term of this Agreement, such changes will be effective for a period of two (2) or more consecutive weeks and the employees affected thereby will be given at least three (3) workdays notice of such change in their workweek schedule. Changes of workweek schedules for periods of less than two (2) weeks duration will not be made.

The Company will notify the Union at least three (3) workdays in advance of any changes in workweek schedules affecting an entire department or a majority of the employees in any department.

Thirty-eight and three quarters (38¾) hours of working time shall constitute a normal workweek for all employees covered by this Agreement.

Section 2

The normal workday for employees covered by this Agreement shall be 8:15 A.M. to 4:45 P.M. with a 45 minute luncheon period.

The starting, lunch and closing times may be varied from the basic schedule as may be required to provide the best possible elevator service at peak periods of operation.

The Company agrees to notify the Union at least seven (7) days in advance of any major change in the regularly scheduled hours of work.

ARTICLE VIII—Overtime

Section 1

The hours of work of an employee classified as "exempt" under the Fair Labor Standards Act, as amended, shall not be restricted by the provisions of ARTICLES VII and VIII of this Agreement.

An employee classified as "non-exempt" under the provision of the Fair Labor Standards Act, as amended, who is required to work overtime will be compensated for such overtime work as follows:

(1) Time worked in excess of forty (40) hours in a workweek or in excess of eight (8) hours on a scheduled workday shall be compensated at the rate of one and one-half (1½) times his regular straight-time rate of pay.

(2) Time worked in excess of thirty-eight and three quarters (38¾) hours in a workweek but not in excess of forty (40) hours, and time worked in excess of seven and three-quarters (7¾) hours for a scheduled workday but not in excess of eight (8) hours, shall be compensated at his regular straight-time rate of pay. This provision does not apply to any represented employee whose normal workweek shall consist of forty (40) hours per week and whose workday schedule shall consist of eight (8) hours per day.

Any employee who is required to work more than his regularly scheduled hours in any work day shall not be required to take time off to limit the time worked by such employee in the workweek. There shall be no duplication in pay for overtime work or pyramiding of rates for overtime work. Any time paid for on one overtime basis shall not be counted again for any other overtime payment.

Section 2

The Company will schedule overtime work and give employees notice of overtime work required of them as far in advance as possible.

WORKING WITH A UNIONIZED OFFICE

Section 3

Any employee who is off duty and is required to report for work outside his regular schedule, shall receive not less than three (3) hours' pay at one and one-half (1½) times his regular rate.

ARTICLE IX—Shift Differential

Section 1

The following shift differential provisions shall apply to employees represented by the Union:

(1) For work performed between the hours of 4:30 P.M. and 12 midnight by employees regularly assigned to a shift other than the normal workday shift set forth in Article VII of the Working Agreement between the parties, a differential of 15 cents per hour will be paid. No such differential will be paid to employees who are regularly assigned to said normal work day shift. Effective March 11, _____, the differential will be 20 cents per hour under this provision.

(2) For work performed between the hours of 12 midnight and 8:20 A.M. by employees regularly assigned to a shift other than the normal workday shift set forth in Article VII of the Working Agreement between the parties, a differential of 30 cents per hour will be paid. No such differential will be paid to employees who are regularly assigned to said normal workday shift. Effective March 11, _____, the differential will be 40 cents per hour under this provision.

(3) Any overtime payment due employees regularly assigned to a scheduled shift other than said normal workday shift set forth in Article VII of the Working Agreement between the parties shall be computed on the basis of the regular rate plus the applicable differential.

ARTICLE X—Holidays

Section 1

Recognized holidays are New Year's Day, Good Friday, Memorial Day, Independence Day, Labor Day, Thanksgiving Day, the day after Thanksgiving Day, Christmas Day, and a Christmas holiday to be observed as follows:

When Christmas Falls On	Holiday Will Be Observed
Monday and Thursday	December 26
Tuesday and Wednesday and Friday	December 24
Saturday and Sunday	December 23

419

In the event a designated holiday occurs on an employee's scheduled day off, the employee will be given a scheduled workday off with pay. Such day off with pay will be the employee's last workday preceding the holiday, when the holiday falls on the first of the employee's weekly days off. If the holiday falls on the second of the employee's weekly days off, the day off with pay will be taken on the day next following such holiday.

Section 2

An employee who does not work on a holiday shall receive holiday pay equivalent to his regular rate of pay provided that on his nearest scheduled workday preceding or following the holiday he actually works or is on vacation in accordance with the Policy Concerning Vacations. If a holiday falls on an employee's regularly scheduled workday, the workweek in which such holiday occurs shall be reduced by the number of hours which the employee would normally have been scheduled to work on that day except for the holiday. If the employee works on the holiday, he shall receive in addition to his regular pay, one and one-half (1½) hours' pay for each hour worked on such holiday.

If an employee works other than on the holiday in excess of scheduled hours in the workweek, reduced as indicated in this Section 2, he shall be paid overtime for such hours worked in accordance with the provisions of ARTICLE VIII giving recognition to such adjusted workweek schedule. This Section 2 applies only to employees working on a non-exempt basis.

Section 3

If an employee is entitled to a day of vacation in lieu of a holiday which occurred during his vacation, the workweek in which he takes the remaining vacation day shall be reduced by the number of hours which the employee would normally have been scheduled to work on the day of vacation. If such an employee works in excess of the scheduled hours in the workweek, so reduced, he shall be paid overtime for such hours worked in accordance with the provisions of ARTICLE VIII. This Section 3 applies only to employees working on a non-exempt basis.

ARTICLE XI—Seniority

Section 1

Seniority of any employee in the General Office of the Company where applicable under this Agreement shall be by department and based on the length of his continuous service with the Company and shall be determined in accordance with the rules of the Company governing continuity of service.

Section 2

Promotions, demotions, transfers, and filling of newly created permanent positions within the classification of employees covered by this Agreement will be made on the basis of ability of an employee to best meet all requirements of the position in the judgment of management's representatives. Seniority, as defined in Section 1 of this Article XI, shall be given consideration along with regard for experience and performance on previous assignments in all departments of the Company. Seniority shall be the governing factor with respect to such changes of positions, as between two or more employees judged to have equal ability for performing the work satisfactorily.

Section 3

Seniority shall be given full consideration, along with ability, when determining layoffs of employees. When, in the judgment of management's representatives, ability of employees is substantially equal, seniority shall be the governing factor in determining the order in which layoffs are to be made. Returns from layoff will be in the reverse order to the laying off.

Section 4

In arranging vacations within a department, seniority will be given consideration, and those employees with greatest seniority will have preference as to time of vacation to the extent possible in keeping with proper work requirement schedules.

ARTICLE XII—Job Postings

Section 1

When a permanent opening occurs due to either a vacancy in an existing job or the establishment of a new job, an announcement of the vacancy shall be placed on all bulletin boards in the Company's General Office for at least forty-eight (48) hours before filling the vacancy, except as provided in Section 3 of this Article XII.

Section 2

A supervisor designated by management shall interview and discuss with any applicants for the job, the functions, duties and other details concerning the job and the qualifications which a person would need in order to satisfactorily fill the job. In addition, the supervisor will notify all unsuccessful applicants with respect to the filling of the vacancy. Present employees shall be given due consideration for such openings. The Company shall be the judge of the ability of any applicant.

Section 3

Any permanent opening occurring on a represented job in a posting unit listed below, which the Company elects to fill from within said posting unit, need not be posted. Any such permanent opening which cannot be filled from within the posting unit concerned, must be posted according to the provisions of Section 1 above.

ARTICLE XIII—Benefit Plans

Section 1

This Agreement shall in no way affect the status of employees under employee benefit plans such as Retirement Plan, Sickness and Disability Benefits Plan, Occupational Illness and Injury Plan, Employee Savings Plan, Military Leave of Absense and Job Restoration Plan, Group Life and Long Term Disability Plan, Comprehensive Medical Expense Plan, and Medicare Supplemental Plan for Annuitants. The policy concerning vacations is made a part of this Agreement. The Severance Allowance Policy is made a part of this Agreement subject to cancellation by each party upon twenty-four (24) hours written notice.

It is agreed that issues pertaining to said plans may be bargained upon through the procedure set fourth in Article III, except that neither party shall have the right to have any such issues arbitrated. If any such issue is not settled as a result of negotiations between the parties, either party shall have the right to refer such issue to the Vice President—Employee Relations of the Company whose decision shall be final and binding upon both parties.

Effective March 11, _____, the Company will contribute up to $30 per month toward the cost of Comprehensive Medical Expense Plan family coverage for employees represented by the Union; effective March 11, _____, for the balance of the term of the Working Agreement, the Company will contribute up to $35 per month toward the cost of Comprehensive Medical Expense Plan family coverage for employees represented by the Union. Any change in total premiums during the period may result in a change in rates paid by the employee.

An employee who retires at or after age 62 under the provisions of the Retirement Plan will not have his annuity reduced by reason of having retired prior to age 65, the normal retirement age. For early retirement below age 62, there will be a 5% reduction in annuity each year down to age 55.

The Retirement Plan is non-contributory on the part of the employees. The Social Security offset to the terminal earnings minimum will be 50% of the statutory benefit under the law in effect at the time of retirement.

Retirement Plan changes are subject to approval by the Board of Directors and the Internal Revenue Service.

Section 2

The Company agrees to notify the Union in writing of any proposed change in any such plans, or the adoption of any new plan, and to designate in said notice, the date upon which such change or such new plan will become effective, such date to be not less than thirty (30) days after the date of such notice. If questions with respect to any such change or new plan become the subject of negotiations between the parties before said effective date and have not been settled by negotiations before said date, the Company shall nevertheless have the right, at their option, to make such change or new plan effective on or after said date; and in the event the Company does make such change or new plan effective, any bargaining then pending between the parties shall be continued, as provided in this Article XIII.

ARTICLE XIV—Miscellaneous

Section 1

This Agreement shall be subject to all present and future applicable laws, orders, rules and regulations of Governmental authority.

Section 2

In the event that any provisions of this Agreement shall at any time be declared invalid by any court of competent jurisdiction, such decision shall not invalidate the entire agreement, it being the express intention of the parties hereto that all provisions not declared invalid shall remain in full force and effect.

Section 3

Representatives of the Union or any member of the bargaining unit who are employees of the Company shall not be subject to loss of time or pay for such time as they spend during their working hours conferring with the General Office Management or when representatives of the Union, as limited by Article V of this Agreement, attend arbitration hearings.

Section 4

If an officer or director of the Union desires a leave of absence in order to engage in any work pertaining to the business of the Union, said leave without pay will be granted by the Company and the granting of said leave shall not cause such employee to suffer loss of seniority. Such leaves of absence shall not exceed a total of thirteen (13) weeks per calendar year.

Section 5

When an employee serves on a jury or as judge or clerk for a general or primary election, he will receive in addition to any remuneration which he may receive for such service his straight-time rate for the regularly scheduled hours he would have worked had he not been serving on the jury or as a judge or clerk. Such time shall not be considered as time worked for purposes of computing overtime.

Section 6

The Company and the Union agree jointly and separately that they will not discriminate in any manner against any employee because of race, color, religion, sex, age or national origin. Furthermore, in response to the requirements of the Federal Equal Employment Opportunity Commission, and Office of Federal Contract Compliance, the Union firmly supports the Company in Affirmative Action Programs to recruit, train and promote members of minority groups.

Section 7

This Agreement may be modified or amended by mutual consent of the parties hereto. The modification(s) or amendment(s) will be written and signed by both parties.

Section 8

The Union agrees not to strike and the Company agrees not to lock out employees during the period of this Agreement.

Section 9

Any person newly employed shall be so employed for a probationary period of thirty (30) work days. Any discharge or layoff during the probationary period shall not be made the subject of a grievance or subject to arbitration under the terms of this Agreement. This section is not intended to limit the rights of the Union to enroll any employees otherwise covered by this Agreement.

ARTICLE XV: Effective Date, Termination, Amendment or Renewal

Section 1

This agreement shall continue in full force and effect until March 11, _____, and thereafter unless either party notifies the other in writing of its desire to amend or terminate the agreement by serving a written notice on the other party not earlier than sixty (60) days prior to March 11, _____.

If notice to amend is given, the entire Agreement shall continue in full force and effect until negotiations are completed or until a sixty (60) day prior written notice of termination is served by the party desiring to terminate the Agreement.

If such notification of termination is given the entire Agreement shall terminate on the date sixty (60) days subsequent to the date on which notice of termination is given.

Section 2

Issues arising out of negotiations will not be referred to arbitration. Executed this _____ day of _____, 19____.

CHAPTER 16

MANPOWER PLANNING TODAY FOR TOMORROW'S NEEDS

IF material resources can be systematically programmed why can't the same approach be applied to human resources? That's what manpower planning attempts to do.

In a more formal sense, manpower planning is a process to assure that essential manpower will be available and ready, in both numbers and disciplines, as needed. The definition of manpower planning adopted by Towers, Perrin, Forster & Crosby, Inc. is:

"Manpower planning is the process by which management prepares to have the needed types and numbers of people in the right places, at the right time, in order to fulfill both corporate and individual objectives."

Manpower planning is necessary for every company that expects normal growth, rapid expansion, diversification of product lines, even cutbacks.

The primary purpose of manpower planning, as with any other aspect of planning, is to prepare for the future by reducing its uncertainty. It has as a basic goal the reduction of the uncertainty as related to the acquisition, placement, and development of employees for future needs.

How much more sensible to attack the problem before it gets out of bounds than to simply continue to react as needs arise. When future needs are not "felt" in advance, the results are hiring delays, desperation placements, inadequately trained workers, and the filling of positions without consideration of qualifications and preparation.

Manpower planning, on the other hand, is a systematic effort that comprises three key elements:

1. **Workforce forecast:** what kind and how many employees will be needed—and when.
2. **Workforce inventory:** what talents and abilities are already "on board" to fill many of the critical forecasted needs.

3. **Placement programming:** what outside recruiting schedules or inside assistance for promising and promotable employees is called for to have people ready.

Forecasting

Workforce forecasting consists of estimating the numbers and kinds of employees required to acquire, deliver and retain the ongoing and also the changing business at a pre-determined date in the future.

There are many different factors to be considered in making a workforce forecast including:

1. Looking at the composition of all the jobs in the present organization.
2. Listing the vacant positions.
3. Estimating losses through normal attrition.
4. Noting possible surpluses of skills or people.
5. Expressing any extension of productivity in terms of jobs.
6. Taking into account new projects and their requirements.
7. Making allowance for anticipated changes in systems.

Underlying the methodology is the contention that information about the past workforce and its productivity provides a springboard from which to project future workforce needs. Along this line of reasoning, forecasting is a three-phase effort requiring management to:

1. Examine the historical record of past workforce productivity.
2. Make a projection of the workforce needed against a specific future target date on anticipated business volume.
3. Refine the projection for expected changes in volume, markets, products, technology, and environment.

Once the overall forecast is completed, it can be separated into the applicable divisions and departments. A bottoms-up procedure may be easier, with each functional division making its own analysis. Approaching the forecast from both directions (as is often done in budgeting) offers a checks-and-balances way of making the forecast more accurate and practical.

When using the yardstick of productivity, which seems only natural, the method of expression is in terms of work loads. Properly gauged work loads are in turn translated into jobs. This is necessary for "pricing" the job needs. The price of staffing includes direct and indirect (fringe benefits) wages for the periods of time specified, as well as acquisition, training, housekeeping, and other hidden charges.

The procedure for conducting a workforce forecast varies with size and type of business but generally includes the following steps:

Prepare data base (past productivity and present structure)

Estimate future needs (ongoing and new)

Adjust for assumed changes

Translate work loads into specific jobs

Consolidate the forecasts, if done fractionally

Cost out the total forecast

Review with top management

Approve as submitted or modified

Prepare the timetables and schedules

Proceed to develop the manpower plan.

For this purpose, simple manpower forecasting methods are widely used. The more advanced techniques such as computer modeling are rarely employed even while interest in them is high.

Much of the information derived from manpower forecasting is used subjectively for designing broad corporate strategy, arranging for facilities, and identifying replacements for management positions.

Inventory

After the forecast has been made and the assortment of jobs listed, employees should be evaluated to establish who are ready or could be made ready for assignments elsewhere. What is critical to manpower planning is that job needs, as specified through the forecast, be systematically reviewed against all employees who may be qualified or qualifiable for these new opportunities.

There are a number of ways of doing this. Some companies already have performance and/or potential appraisal programs for identifying the good employees and for bringing promising talent to light. In companies with relatively small numbers of employees, especially managerial personnel, each employee's experience and background is probably well known to the decision makers. In these cases, earmarking certain individuals for special consideration does not require any sophisticated technique.

The danger, however, is that as companies grow larger, top management may mistakenly believe they still know all about their employees. They may know about some employees, particularly oldtimers, but it is doubtful that they know everything about everybody. The tragic consequence is that some talent is innocently

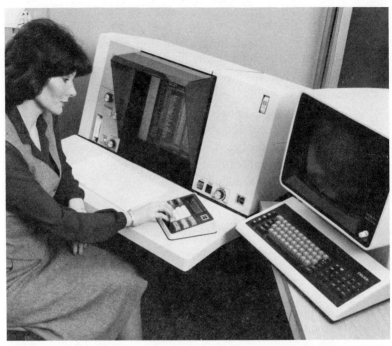

Manpower planning today includes the ability to forecast the need for many highly-trained people or people who can be trained for the new office jobs. Here the operator is using both a computer terminal and a microimage terminal to find and work with specific documents. Courtesy Kodak Company

overlooked. To avoid such mistakes an objective procedure should be followed.

An impersonal method should be designed to assure equitable consideration for all. Some employees, because of their duties or personalities, are not as visible as others and their good qualities are likely to go unrecognized. Inadvertently overlooking anyone is unfair to the individual and costly to the company.

Taking an inventory periodically is merely a mechanical procedure. Its purpose is to:

1. Identify employees who can possibly fill critical positions included in the forecast.
2. Assure that deserving employees are not overlooked.
3. Establish what skill requirements can be met by training and development—and which cannot.
4. Determine what shortages of skills exist that make it necessary to recruit on the outside to fill certain positions.

5. Avoid any needless recruitment expense.

6. Decide to what extent the forecast has to be altered because the number and types of employees required may not be available either internally or through an economically feasible outside effort.

The inventory should be more than a documentation of historical data. It should also include an appraisal of past and present performance as well as future potential from which a sound judgment can be made.

The assessment of employees is simply to compare individual employees with the stated requirements of jobs, present and future. It is very likely that few will automatically qualify for bigger assignments, but at least the gap between an employee's present qualifications and the qualifications needed to fill a higher or different job will be identified. What to do to narrow the gap is the next question. Ideally no one should be asked to perform a job for which he is underqualified.

The assessment of present employees for manpower planning is not easy. Many supervisors are willing to express opinions, but making valid judgments about an employee's potential for more responsibilities or for other kinds of work is difficult. Managers feel inadequate in their ability to evaluate subordinates in this respect. They feel more comfortable accepting the recommendations of outsiders who, they rationalize, are expert in the field; hence, they resort to external recruitment.

Appraisal of performance is mostly a post mortem review based on factors that can be seen. Appraisal of potential is a rating "out front" and calls for judgment based on factors that cannot be seen.

The purpose of the combined assessment is to permit management to make a rational choice between filling a job from internal or external sources.

Programming

In any case, programs must be developed for meeting future manpower needs. The most common manpower programming applications are:

1. Recruiting for present and future needs.
2. Filling job vacancies internally.
3. Designating replacements for management positions.
4. Identifying promotable talent.
5. Encouraging individual development.
6. Training to fill qualifications gaps.

Manpower planning means more than matching estimated number needs with corresponding recruitment drives. For better results it is advisable to develop talent ahead of the need, particularly for upper level positions. Still better yet, is career development in which capabilities and ambitions of employees are meshed with the goals of the company.

There is a lot to be said for career planning, especially in connection with manpower planning. This is a process of individual choice, guided by management, among alternative jobs and types of work which represent changes in responsibility. The focus is on the individual—his or her abilities, interests, and aspirations—within the context of the organization's future manpower needs.

This area encompasses career pathing, career guidance, managerial succession, and "fast track" progression.

A by-product of manpower planning is the avoidance of the danger of obsolescence. In times of change, mechanization, or other technological advancements, some jobs may be abolished, reduced, or altered. Then the people in these jobs become "leftover employees" unless they are salvaged and helped in efforts to change with the jobs or change into different lines of work. Career planning anticipates these problems and helps employees get ready for the next step instead of letting them become victims of technological unemployment.

This is no idle threat. It is easy enough to understand in the parlance of office and shop jobs where the introduction of modern machines or new systems eliminates or rearranges jobs. But it exists and is far more serious in the management ranks. The American Management Association calls this "middlescence" which is described as a traumatic and sometimes debilitating change of life that hits career men and women between ages 35 and 55. It is a crisis period that won't go away by itself; it calls for special handling and understanding.

Once the people who are prone to middlescence were called bureaucrats, but now they are likely to be called technocrats, a word popularized by *John Kenneth Galbraith,* the Harvard economist. A technocrat is the product of technology and specialization and he is a member of the technocracy, the amalgam of specialists, scientists, engineers, and technicians found in most large corporations.

In this technological environment the individual is subordinated, which is frustrating. He or she starts out full of hope, gets on a promising career track, enjoys his ascendancy prospects, finds he cannot move the corporation, becomes disillusioned and dispirited, possibly even derailed, and by middle age no longer looks ahead but, instead, reflects wistfully on life.

MANPOWER PLANNING TODAY FOR TOMORROW'S NEEDS

The tragedy of middlescence is that, apart from what this does to capable and high-spirited individuals, it drains corporations of crucial managerial resources.

Assessing Labor Market

While the in-house search is going on, the personnel office, or at the very least, the employment interviewer, should be assessing the outside market. It is always desirable to reward deserving employees with preferential consideration before going on the outside, but this should be the policy only when present employees qualify or can be made to qualify. Every position should be filled by the best qualified candidate who is available, no matter where she comes from; anything less is a compromise that could adversely affect production and efficiency.

The personnel office or the employment interviewer should be surveying the labor market on the availability and cost of acquiring the number and types of people necessary to fill the positions.

In the study the recruiter should be trying to learn information for each position as it relates to:

1. The best applicant source.
2. The prevailing starting salary.
3. The availability of qualified candidates.
4. The lead time needed to acquire acceptable applicants.
5. The cost of acquisition.

It is usually necessary to go outside to fill jobs calling for special skills or where the "get ready" time is too short to prepare someone. The decision in each case is whether to train an individual internally for the job or recruit an individual already possessing the necessary skills. Training time for individuals will vary because some jobs are more difficult than others and some employees may be closer to being ready than others.

An assessment of the workforce and an assessment of the labor market will determine what route to follow to fill certain jobs by a given time—from internal transfer or external recruitment.

Employees obviously unfit or unqualified for any positions other than their own are screened out. Over-qualified employees should be marked for quick consideration. Others who can be made ready should be counseled, a career path established, and assistance given.

While this may seem expensive, and it is, it may be less than an exorbitant agency fee or search firm retainer. Besides, every new employee, no matter how well qualified in a specialty, still must be trained in company policies and practices and this takes time and money.

The question is not only which route is less costly but also which will deliver the better, well-rounded employee.

Staffing

There is a tendency sometimes to assume that the manpower planning program is completed once the workforce forecast is made, the inventory updated, and the assessments set in motion. These subactivities involve work and time and after they have been accomplished there may be a relaxation of the effort as managers sit back and admire their handiwork.

The subfunctions are not ends in themselves but means designed to serve the main objective of manpower planning. They will quickly fall into disrepair unless they are tied together in support of each other for staffing purposes. The plan for staffing the company as old and new jobs must be filled has to be implemented and controlled. This is done by evaluating progress and modifying the plan as appropriate.

It is common practice to cost out the staffing requirements annually through normal budgeting procedures. This is fine since it commits financial resources to complement manpower plans. When manpower requirements are considered beyond one year—and this is a likelihood—then cost estimates must be made and tacit approval given to aid in subsequent budgeting.

Staffing is concerned with the total task of keeping all jobs, existing and anticipated, properly filled. As a concept it relates to numbers as much as skills. In reality, however, it emphasizes managerial, supervisory, professional, and technical positions.

Use of Coordinator

Quite often manpower planning is mistakenly treated as an activity that stands alone. In some companies it is looked upon as little more than "busy work," a kind of numbers game, for the Personnel office. But like any other operational planning it should be tied to corporate planning and overall objectives. Unless this is done, it becomes an academic exercise and destined to failure.

As in any other company planning programs, the endorsement, support, and participation of top management is vital. The "heart and soul" of manpower planning lies with the line management. These operating managers provide the data on which the manpower forecast is made. They decide on the content of the jobs. They are involved in assessing the skills of employees, determining their training needs, and evaluating their progress. They make the final hiring and placement decisions.

While the responsibility for manpower planning is vested in a number of different line managers, success of the effort depends on the designation of one person to serve in a staff capacity as coordinator. Working with and through the operations managers, this person's direction, guidance, and follow-through will influence its ultimate value.

The qualifications of the coordinator to perform this function are in three related but distinct areas. You must have the type of person who possesses:

1. **An unquestioned rapport with top management that makes it easy to comprehend instinctively what they want and will accept.**

2. **An innate ability to influence others and guide them toward a common perspective that will help them and also serve the company's interests.**

3. **A knowledge of corporate objectives to understand how they impact on manpower and vice versa.**

Once the manpower planning effort has settled down into an approved staffing schedule and the necessary parts of it such as recruiting, training, and the like set in motion, it becomes the responsibility of the manpower planning coordinator to monitor progress, evaluate the program, check the costs, and recommend modifications if these seem necessary. Certainly all observations should be reported to people directly involved and possibly issue periodic written reports to top management.

The coordinator could logically be someone from the Personnel office, for there is where the work of implementing the manpower plan will utimately be centered.

Employee Information System

Some kind of employee information system, whether manual or computerized, is also essential to support the manpower planning program.

An employee information system is a storage, manipulation, and retrieval system for one or more types of employee data. It may gather the data through manual procedures or mechanization programs. It makes any or all of the data immediately available and thereby provides faster and better ways of access to information about employees for decision-making purposes.

For planning purposes it would include a skills bank that would yield information about each employee's background, experience, training, specialties, interests, and job preferences. In addition it would show progress in the company, with job progression, wage history, and appraisal scores.

The employee information system will merely produce data as valuable and accurate in its output as it was carefully collected and entered into the system. It will make selection preferences, matching its answers to the questions it is asked, but it will not make decisions. These must still be made subjectively by management on the basis of information supplied.

Control

Ultimately manpower planning leads to manpower budgets and manpower controls. Procedures must be established for keeping track of what is going on.

Because of the scope of manpower planning, it is important to develop a timetable of action that reflects the pressures of the company. Without the discipline of a detailed schedule with deadlines there can be a tendency to sidetrack planning in favor of the more urgent everyday demands.

Equally critical is the need to equip line managers with base knowledge of overall corporate planning and objectives. Without this information the managers would be working in the dark.

As a control mechanism is designed and set up, it is necessary to check to see that:

1. Necessary monies are properly allocated.
2. Monies are available.
3. Recruitment is underway with time, money, contacts, and staff.
4. Appraisal programs produce correct assessments.
5. Appraisal of potential is effective.
6. Training activities have been developed.
7. Qualified trainers are assigned.
8. Facilities and equipment have been provided.
9. Schedules have been prepared.
10. Everybody involved is cooperating.

As manpower planning systems become more advanced, companies are demanding analysis and audits to determine the value of the technique. Manpower planning practices, employee information systems (especially those computerized), and development of human resources require major corporate investments of time, talent, and money.

Some Pointers on Using Temporary-Help Services

Almost every business needs extra help at one time or another. A rush order comes in; the workload suddenly zooms, and as suddenly drops back to normal when the rush order is finished. More employees than usual are absent because of illness or vacations. A special project has to have attention right away. Seasonal demands must be met or inventories must be taken without disrupting your usual business. The extra-heavy workload puts a strain on you, on your employees, and your budget because of the overtime it requires.

These temporary shortages of help are especially hard for the owner-manager of a small business to handle. The staff is small, and there is little leeway for shifting schedules. Yet you can't afford to keep on your payroll workers that you need only when the workload peaks.

If unexpected or uneven workloads are a serious trouble spot in your business, you have two choices. You can hire extra workers—either recruiting them yourself or going to a public or private employment agency. Or you can call on a temporary-help service. More and more businesses, large and small, are turning to these specialized personnel services.

What Is a Temporary-Help Service?

A temporary-help service is not an employment agency. Like many service firms, it hires people *as its own employees* and sends them out to companies requesting help. This means that when you use such a service, you're not hiring an employee; you're buying the use of his *time*. The temporary-help firm is responsible for payroll, bookkeeping, tax deductions, insurance, fringe benefits, and so on in connection with the employee. You are relieved of the burden of recruiting, interviewing, screening, and even testing and training if these are necessary. Some national temporary-help companies also offer performance guarantees and fidelity bonding at no added cost to their clients.

You may contract for a typist, a truck driver, a machinist, a lathe operator, a switchboard operator, or any of many other types of office, professional, and industrial workers. You may need help for a day or for a much longer time.

Whatever help you need, a temporary-personnel service will try to provide the right person for the job. Some temporary-help agencies specialize in only one type of help, such as office workers.

Others can supply a broad range of personnel from unskilled labor to executives and professionals.

Why Not Hire Your Own Temporary Help?

Hiring temporary workers on your own has several important disadvantages. For one thing, it may hamper your efforts to attract good permanent employees—layoffs when an emergency has passed can lower morale among the regular employees and, if it happens too often, give your firm a reputation for instability.

Another disadvantage is that you may not be able to get help when you need it. There may be times when the labor market is tight and the skills you need not readily available. Also, you may feel that the time you spend in orienting new people for short-term employment is largely wasted.

Advantages of Using a Temporary-Help Service

Workers supplied by a temporary-help service are quickly available. Experienced and well-qualified, they need little, if any, breaking in—they can usually walk in and begin to function right away. By using workers from this source, you can adjust to fast-breaking opportunities or problems without interrupting your regular production schedule.

Some companies need temporary help every week for a few hours, for example, for payroll computation. Others need temporary workers for full days at various times—regularly or occasionally.

The hourly rate you pay a temporary-help firm may be higher than you would pay an employee you hired yourself, but the total cost of getting the work done will probably be less. Using a temporary-help service does away with many personnel and recordkeeping operations that are costly and time consuming. You don't have to advertise for help, screen responses, interview and test applicants, check references—perhaps without producing a single qualified worker. You save the cost of training, of overtime and idle periods, of paid employee absences and other fringe benefits.

Many services pay bonding fees when these are required and the premiums for workmen's compensation, unemployment, and other insurances. They handle the reporting and deductions for Social Security and income taxes.

Disadvantages of Using a Temporary-Help Service

In considering whether to use a temporary-help service, list the disadvantages to your company as well as the advantages. In some instances, the disadvantages may involve answering the complaints of regular employees who lose overtime pay because of temporary workers.

It is entirely possible that through circumstances beyond the control of the temporary-help service firm with which you are doing business that a change of personnel may occur during the assignment. If this should occur it may require that you go through the orientation procedure again.

In still other cases, the work itself may mean that temporary help cannot be used as effectively as regular employees. For example, the job may be complex and require a great deal of supervision for a worker who is unfamiliar with your way of doing it. In some instances, it may be more economical to pay overtime to a regular employee than to use a temporary worker.

What Will It Cost?

Rates charged by service firms differ with the type of help you contract for. Obviously, rates will be higher for a secretary than for a typist, higher for skilled labor than for unskilled.

You pay one service charge to the temporary-help firm. That firm in turn, pays the employee for the hours worked and takes care of such costs as payroll taxes, Social Security payments, workmen's compensation, and so on. Charges are based on hourly rates comparable to the rates for similar work in your area, and you are billed only for the hours actually worked.

Most reputable services don't charge you for the hours worked by an unsatisfactory worker if you let them know promptly that you are dissatisfied. Generally, you must notify them within 4 hours after the employee reports for work, but this provision varies with the individual firms.

What you save by using temporary-help services depends on your situation. If you are to get the most for your dollar, however, you must analyze your needs and plan carefully to make the best possible use of the time and skills of the employees supplied by the firm. The guidelines that follow will be helpful.

How To Select a Temporary-Help Firm

There are about 1,000 firms in the temporary-help industry in the United States. Many are located in large population centers. Some of them operate regionally; others, nationally. If you are likely to need temporary workers, it's a good idea to do some exploring in advance.

Check with your local chamber of commerce, your attorney, your accountant, your banker. Look in the Yellow Pages of the telephone directory under "Employment, Temporary." (Some directories use the classification "Employment Contractors—Temporary Help.")

Try to meet in person with the executive of the firm you select. A give-and-take discussion at the executive level will help the firm understand your operations and problems. You, in turn, can gain an understanding of just what services the company provides. For instance, temporary-personnel services vary considerably in the types and amount of insurance and bonding coverage they carry. Discuss this with the representative of the firm you select. Ask for the details in writing so that you'll know just how much coverage they have on employees they will providing you.

If possible, visit the offices of the firm or have your personnel director do so. You may want to invite one of its people to vist your business and learn about your operation. Look on this company as one of your suppliers—because that's exactly what it is. You wouldn't buy materials from an unknown source. Neither should you deal with a supplier of people without knowing what sort of firm you're dealing with.

Plan Early

The key to the successful use of a temporary-help service is in planning what type of help you'll need how much, and when. You need answers to questions such as these.

How seasonal is my business?

Do any of my regular employees have to work overtime to meet peak overloads? If so, what does the overtime cost?

If an extensive amount of overtime is needed, will there be a performance lag and possible morale problems during regular working hours?

With better planning, could I spread any of the peak workloads through the year?

Are my deliveries made on schedule?

Do customers often come up with rush jobs? If so, can I get them to plan their needs farther ahead?

Are my employees' vacations scheduled so as not to interfere with peak seasons?

What extra help do I need to cope with these problems and reduce costs?

MANPOWER PLANNING TODAY FOR TOMORROW'S NEEDS

Sit down with your key personnel—those involved in planning day-to-day operations. Study your production schedules. Note peak periods. Compare this year with previous years. A pattern will begin to emerge, and you'll be able to see where some extra help would have avoided problems and kept your costs down. Many temporary-help firms will supply trained personnel to advise you in this regard.

If you decide that the best way to meet your schedule is to use part-time or temporary help, don't wait until you are in the midst of a crisis. Get in touch with a temporary-help service right away. An advisor there will help you plan ahead so that you'll be ready for emergencies when they arise.

What To Do When the Time Comes

When the time comes that you need extra help and you want to place an order with a temporary-help service, take these steps:

One—Estimate your needs.

Decide what the specific requirements of the job are. Exactly what talents do you need? How long will you need the employee? Don't ask for someone with higher qualifications than this work calls for—the cost will be unnecessarily high. On the other hand, don't try to economize by getting underqualified help and then expecting the worker to carry out tasks that he or she isn't prepared to handle.

Two—Give the temporary-help service full information.

If the temporary-personnel firm is to help you get the best results at the lowest possible cost, you must give its people detailed information about the work to be done. Tell them the nature of your business, the working hours, when and how long you'll need help, the skills required, the types of equipment to be operated. You may want to send samples of the work to be done, if it is feasible, for example, with various clerical tasks. Be sure to give the exact location of your business, transportation available, parking information, and the name and title of the person to whom the temporary employee is to report.

Preparing for the Temporary Employee.

A few steps taken before the temporary employee reports for work will do much to make the association a success, both for the employee and for you.

One—Arrange for supervision.

Appoint one of your permanent employees to supervise the temporary employee and check on the progress of the work from time to time. Be sure this supervisor understands the job to be done and just what his own responsibility is.

Two—Tell your permanent employees.

It's a good idea to let your staff know that you are taking on extra help and that it will be temporary. Explain why the extra help is needed and ask them to cooperate with the new employees in any way possible.

Three—Prepare the physical facilities.

Have everything ready before the temporary worker arrives. The work to be done should be organized and laid out so that the employee can begin producing with a minimum of time spent in adjusting to the job and the surroundings. See that the materials needed are available and the equipment is in place and in good working order.

Four—Plan the workload.

Don't set up schedules that are impossible to complete within the time you allot. Try to stay within the time limits you gave the temporary-help service, but plan to extend the time period, if necessary, rather than crowd the employee. Rushing and over-work can result in costly mistakes.

Five—Prepare detailed instructions.

Describe your type of business, the products you manufacture or the services you offer. Be specific in outlining the procedures your company follows. Most employees of temporary-help services adjust quickly to the methods of an individual firm because of their varied experience.

The Work Begins

You've made all the preparations. The employee has arrived and is ready to start work. What now? How do you get a temporary worker started? What should you expect? What if you're not satisfied?

This is the crucial stage of the relation between your company and the temporary employee. Get off to a good start and the rest will go smoothly.

MANPOWER PLANNING TODAY FOR TOMORROW'S NEEDS

One—Help the employee settle in.

Receive the temporary employee as you would receive one hired on a permanent basis. Make him or her feel like a member of your team. Explain where to hang coats, the location of the washroom, the lunch hour, coffee breaks, and so on.

Introduce the temporary employee to the permanent employee who will supervise the work.

Introduce the temporary employee also to permanent employees in the same department. Explain that "Miss Jones will be here for a few days to help out." Or, "John will be here this week to help get out the rush job."

Two—Explain the job.

Go over the work assignment and the instructions. Explain company routines. Make your directions as simple as possible and provide samples of the work to be done. If the work is complex, explain it clearly and make certain that your explanation is understood. Assure the temporary employee of your staff's cooperation and willingness to help, and show your own interest and concern.

Three—Don't expect the impossible.

How much can you expect from a temporary employee? Fully as much as you contracted for with the service firm. Most employees of temporary-personnel services perform well. They are experienced and versatile. Because they have worked for a variety of businesses, they have learned to adapt quickly to a new situation, and they know that future assignments depend on their doing satisfactory work.

But don't expect the impossible. Don't overload temporary employees—make a slight allowance for the fact that they are not familiar with your business and its operations. Check the work occasionally, ask for any questions, never leave the employee feeling stranded or left out. At the same time, don't make him nervous by hovering over him. And don't push or prod too much.

How Does the Employee Measure Up?

Within a few hours after the worker has reported, you'll be able to judge how the work is going. If you aren't satisfied, don't hesitate to call the temporary-service firm. A replacement will be sent as quickly as possible.

443

A good temporary-help service will ask you to evaluate the employee's work. If you are pleased and would like to have the services of the same employee in the future, say so. The service firm will try to send him when you need him. It will depend, of course, on whether he is available at the time.

Judging the Overall Results

The employee's time sheets must be filled out properly to make sure that you are charged only for the services you receive. But you should also keep a complete record for your own use of the times you use temporary services. In making your records, keep these points in mind to help you plan for future needs:

How much did the temporary employee cost?

How much work was done?

What was the overall impact on your operations?

What specific benefits were there?

Were there any disadvantages?

If so, did the advantages outweigh the disadvantages?

Discuss the pros and cons with your key people. Confer again with the temporary-help service, and correlate the results of this evaluation with the study of your needs made at the planning stage. You may be able to work out a program for hiring personnel throughout the year, so that you will be fully covered for workloads at all times.

PART 4

Guides through the Paperwork Jungle

CHAPTER 17

PAPERWORK SIMPLIFICATION

By Dennis J. Zaiden

ANYONE who thinks that the paperwork problem was blown away by the coming of sophisticated electronic office equipment hasn't waited in line for a turn on the copying machine.

Much has been done to cut back on the amount of paper being stored in office files, thanks to microfilm and microfiche. Much more information is now retained on disks and magnetic tapes. But the continuous creation of office "paper" remains a major problem. We can't get along without it.

A rapidly increasing population has expanded the needs for business and government activities, and the rapid pace of technology has also added to the paperwork burden. The computer was once regarded as the answer to the ever-mounting problem. But since the computer has the capability of producing many more times the amount of paperwork than humans, this has proved to be too much of a temptation and has often been used to exaggeration. Very few firms have used an economical approach to its production capabilities.

Each new product, each new method, each new employee and each new government requirement gives rise to a new form and procedure. Multiply this by the number of new business transactions and one can begin to see the consequences of the paperwork explosion.

What is Paperwork?

Paperwork is the recording, analysis, transmission and storage of information in business. Paperwork is some form of communication to be delivered or received, and can be recorded on any form of media. It therefore not only includes pieces of paper, but such media as a blackboard, a recording, telephone and telegraph communications, computer tapes and disks and punched cards. Communication need not only be from one person to another, but can involve a message to one's self, such as a calendar notation.

The *primary purposes of paperwork* should be: (1) to help someone do his or her job better, and (2) to meet the requirements of various governmental agencies. Paperwork improves the performance of work since it is far more substantial than memory or impressions. However, today's mass of paperwork includes many procedures and forms which are not required by government, nor do they improve work performance. Therefore, they are unnecessary.

Another vital factor of paperwork is *work performance.* Even if the work is limited to only that which is essential (an ideal seldom achieved), the performance may be far less than satisfactory. This involves methods, supervision and motivation. The methods may be inefficient, or an employee's performance may be poor, or supervision may be inadequate. Paperwork not only involves the media, but performance, methods and supervision as well.

Paperwork has developed into a serious problem for business and government. The technology to meet this problem has increased the capability of producing paperwork, but has not made its production more "efficient." By "efficient," we mean a savings of waste by eliminating unnecessary work. Simplification can be accomplished only by eliminating data or by decreasing the effort essential to the work.

All unnecessary paperwork costs dollars. In order to gain management's support for a paperwork simplification program, one must first demonstrate how unnecessary paperwork affects the pocketbook. Without management's support, simplification will fail.

Work simplification can only be accomplished by the use of the "scientific" techniques; such as, defined purpose, careful observation, experimentation and exhaustive analysis. When these techniques were first employed, the pioneer analysts detected another nonmechanical or human element in the consideration of the problem. They found that happy and well-adjusted employees performed better, regardless of the procedural aspects.

FUNDAMENTALS OF PAPERWORK SIMPLIFICATION

The four fundamental objectives of paperwork simplification are:

1. **To simplify**
2. **To eliminate**
3. **To combine**
4. **To improve**

The *simplest* way of doing the work is normally the easiest and most practical. Methods can be simplified by changing the sequence of operations, rearranging the work place, redesigning the forms, and applying modern means. Everything that is *not* absolutely essential should be *eliminated*. If the entire project can't be eliminated, then any portion or details that *are not required* should be eliminated.

If you can't eliminate, *combine*. Combining eliminates some details and simplifies and improves at the same time. Webster's first definition of *improve* is: "1. To turn to profit or good account; to use to advantage; as, to *improve* one's time."

Improve means to use a more thorough or modern method and discard the old one. However, the word signifies a lot more, for here lies the entire area of employee relations. Improve means to *stimulate* employees to do better work. It also involves improving working conditions. Improve is a key word and may suggest a better name for this entire subject: *work improvement* instead of *work simplification*. Sometimes simplification and improvement may conflict where a proposed work simplification change interferes with employee relations, so this field is not strictly a scientific endeavor but an "art" as well since human relations are involved. Understanding can be developed by experience, but not everyone can gain understanding through experience.

The fundamental factors involved in paperwork are as follows:

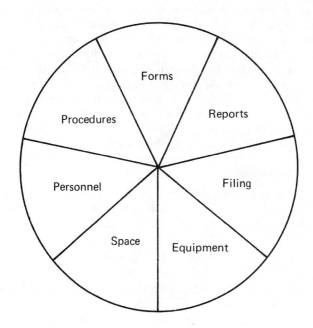

The four fundamental results should be as follows:

1. Get the most practical result.
2. In the shortest time period.
3. With the least amount of effort.
4. At the lowest cost.

The "Total Systems Approach"

Piecemeal solutions usually fail. A fragmented approach is wasted energy, and often adds to the confusion. The paperwork problem normally can be traced to a common cause or causes, which evolve with the growth of the company and the compounding of work at each new desk and department. When systems are not analyzed in total, the interrelationships and their coordination can be overlooked and duplication is obscured. Therefore, without total systems in perspective, the source problems cannot be effectively analyzed.

The *total systems approach* is a difficult one to sell to top management. The author has encountered difficulty in doing this during the many years he has been a systems consultant. Being an outsider he can qualify all his partial engagements by stating that the full benefits of efficiency cannot be realized from a limited engagement. However, he usually goes one step further in the interest of quality. Being an experienced and rapid surveyor of systems, he usually manages to sneak in a "quickie" review of all systems. This at least gives him a "feel" of the overall, and aids him in avoiding the designing of conflicting or duplicating procedures.

How does one handle these limitations if he or she is an employee? First—try to sell management on the need for a total approach. Explain the cause of complexity—the evolvement of fragments. If this doesn't work, don't ignore the overall. Try to include input and output considerations for all "outside" connecting links—but do it discreetly if you are without authority.

Basic Considerations

Paperwork simplification can best be accomplished by an organized approach. This approach is called the "scientific method" and is the technique employed in many disciplines. It involves the following:

1. Defining the problem. (However, sometimes this initial definition requires redefinition after Step 2 or 3.)
2. A study of the conditions and environment under which the problem exists.
3. An analysis of the data collected in Step 2.

4. The development of alternative solutions.

5. Testing the alternatives.

6. Development of the most feasible solution(s).

Step 2 is a *systems study or survey.* The basic product of the systems survey will be *documentation.* Documentation can be defined as a description of the organization, functions, policies, decisions, procedures, and essential transactions of the business. This documentation is usually called a *systems and procedures manual.* The product resulting from this effort should be *recommendations for improvement.* Without documentation, effective improvements cannot be determined. The recommendations are supported by the defects in the old procedures evidenced by the documentation collected and compared to the newly recommended procedures.

The adoption of recommendations is followed by *implementation of the new procedures.* Recommendations are meaningless unless the new systems are made to work. New procedures, of course, require revision of the systems and procedures manual. After all the effort it takes to create the documentation, it would be a waste to obsolete it by not *updating the manuals* to reflect the new procedures.

In order to simplify, we must analyze. Webster defines analysis as "*a separation of anything into constituent parts or elements; also, an examination of anything to distinguish its component parts, separately, or in their relation to the whole.*" So that we can analyze paperwork with the purpose of simplifying it, we must document the current forms, procedures and work flow.

This program should include some vital questions:

1. *Valid or logical purpose?* What business are you really in? This question may lead to some interesting observations. Has the business or certain facets of it evolved into a paperwork generation business? Is the paperwork directly related to current business affairs, or is it something continued from the past? Is it necessary to conduct current business? Are the reasons surrounding its purpose obscure?

2. *Currently useful?* Is the information still required? You'd be surprised at the number of activities which attend ancient history.

3. *How is it used?* Does the information help you to reach the goals of the business? Purpose and direction often are lost sight of.

4. *Cost vs. value?* This information cost $X to produce. Is its value worth its cost?

5. *Timeliness?* Is the information provided timely? If it's obsolete by the time it reaches its goal, why generate it?

Earlier we talked about the total systems approach. Let's not lose sight of that. But we must get started by focusing on a single area; for, obviously we can't get started everywhere. So now we'll move on from underlying principles to practical application.

Step 1 is to *select an area*—an area to attack first. This can be approached in one of several ways.

1. *By desk.* If several individuals perform the same tasks, then only one of these desks or employee job functions need be considered in obtaining the procedures or routines. For example, incoming telephone order desks or invoice coding clerks. However, if performance is to be measured, then the output of each desk need be considered.

2. *By department.* For example, the order department or customer correspondence. This is actually an expanded version of the desk approach.

3. *By system.* For example, order-invoice or inventory control. If a particular desk function involves several systems, then the desk will be revisited when each system is considered.

The author uses the technique of attempting to visit a desk only once and collect data on all the routines, regardless of the systems involved. However, in collecting this information, he immediately classifies it by system. He uses folders which he labels with the system identification the name of the individual interviewed and his or her job title. Therefore a single employee may have several folders, one for each system he or she works on. *The key to an organized approach is to classify data as soon as it is received.*

This method provides for the orderly collection of all of the routines, desk by desk, and for all of the systems by the time the study has been completed. It is vital that you identify the sources of input for a given desk and also the destinations of the output. Without this information, you will not be able to trace the flow of paperwork.

Step 2 is to obtain all the facts. This is the *data collection phase.* Only practice will make you proficient. In the beginning, you will be doing plenty of backtracking. In time, experience will enable you to refine your techniques so that you won't miss too much.

How do you collect data?

1. By interviews.
2. By collecting blank forms:
   a. All of the copies
   b. Showing the complete routings.

452

3. By collecting filled-in specimens of forms and determining:

   a. The work performed at each desk.

   b. The source of the document.

   c. Where the form goes when it leaves that desk—all copies.

4. By observation—observe what is going on at a desk during the interview.

5. By collecting organization charts.

6. By collecting job descriptions.

7. By collecting written procedures, policies, etc.

8. By requesting that each employee prepare a chronological record of work performed for a week, month, etc.

9. By obtaining quantities of work performed.

All the foregoing are tools for collecting data. Vary the techniques to fit the circumstances.

Step 3 is to *organize the data* into a logical arrangement. Earlier, we mentioned that the author collects the data by desk and by system. The next logical step is to organize the data by the chronological sequence of system functions for each specific system. This may involve a rearrangement of the data. If this is done, you must be careful to retain a record of the specific desk functions.

Start by labeling the forms and specimens collected. You can do this by noting on each—Exhibit 1, Exhibit 2, etc. On the back of each form, the author writes the name of the person from whom he received it. Prepare an index of the exhibits, listing the exhibit number, title or name of the form and the name of the employee who gave you the form.

Next list the operations performed for each exhibit and where performed. You can start with this narrative form or flowchart the exhibit, indicating the operations and the desk performing each. The narrative version is a rough draft for the preparation of the procedures manual. Once you have the desk operations documented, you can physically move the exhibits into a systems sequence.

You have collected and organized much data. What is done in the office? What pieces of paper move through the office? What is their route? You can present this in narrative form or graphically with *flowcharts*. A flowchart is an excellent way to illustrate a procedure, or group of procedures, or system.

What else are you doing while organizing the data? You should be *analyzing and evaluating* the material. Note observations in this preliminary review for later use in the formal evaluation stage.

Organization charts are also very helpful. They graphically present the organizational structure and lines of authority, and without them it can be difficult to understand the paperwork flow. Sometimes it is not so much the paperwork itself which needs to be revised but the organizational structure. These organization charts list departments and subdepartments. Organization charts may also be presented by job functions; such as Chairman of the Board, President, V.P.-Finance, V.P.-Manufacturing, V.P.-Sales. Or, the organization chart may show both in the boxes. Sometimes these charts contain boxes big enough to give brief descriptions of departmental functions.

Challenging Every Detail

When you have your facts collected and organized, you are ready to analyze and evaluate. This involves challenging every detail. Everything the analysis disclosed about the problem should be questioned with an open mind:

1. What is done and why?
2. Where is it done?
3. Why is it done there?
4. Where should it be done?
5. When is it done?
6. Who does it?
7. Why does this person do it?
8. Who should do it?
9. How is it done?
10. Why is it done this way?
11. How should it be done?
12. Opportunities should be sought to:
    Eliminate
    Combine
    Rearrange
    Simplify.

Desirably, work should flow in one direction. If the flowchart reveals long transportation and storages, a regrouping of equipment and activities can often reduce excess travel.

Developing a Better Method

The analysis and evaluation are aimed at developing a better method. Review the situation with all those who can contribute to improvements. This includes the employees who do the work, their supervisors, department heads, and sometimes the representatives of forms and equipment manufacturers.

Well designed forms, simple office devices, and motion economy are the chief means of making the work easier and faster. An awareness of some principles of motion economy can be very helpful in:

1. Eliminating hesitation in movement.
2. Prepositioning tools and supplies.
3. Placing work within the normal working area.
4. Minimizing movements, distance of movements, operations.
5. Batching work to save make-ready time.
6. Using fixed work stations.
7. Shortening distances.

Applying the New Method

Applying the new method is the last step. To ensure success, first make a dry run—but before doing this, document the new procedures and review them with the employees involved. Hopefully, the new procedures will not be a surprise to those who will be working with them. These employees should have been involved as early as it was practicable. All people resist change; that is natural. But if the office staff can be made to realize that the change is the result of their own thinking, resistance, if any, will be short-lived. Follow-ups and reappraisals will ensure a healthy climate to maintain the new method, and perhaps will even stimulate suggestions for future improvements.

Implementing a Paperwork Simplification Program

Where do you start? How can the simplification program be built upon a solid foundation of mutual confidence and understanding? Obviously it is difficult to generate much enthusiasm at the lower levels if people there have not seen evidence of activity at the higher levels first. An excellent initial approach in tackling problems of paperwork is to start with top management forms and reports.

The paperwork simplification program must be led by someone who has the qualities of leadership. The leader of a paperwork simplification program must like people, be firm and just but not domineering or overbearing, be a good listener, and have developed a capacity to analyze situations and people. This individual should receive special training in systems and procedures, work analysis, personnel and training.

If an inside employee is selected to lead the program, the initial thrust should be in a pilot program where experience can be gained without upsetting "outsiders." Therefore, the program should be started in the project leader's own department, starting with his or her own desk. No greater objectivity lesson can be gained than analyzing one's own performance. Next, the leader should tackle the next desk, finally ending up with a project for the whole department. However, he or she should keep the results of those efforts confidential.

If others are to be used in the project, they should be requested to analyze their own and the surrounding desks too, under the guidance of the project leader. Finally, the project team should compare their findings and develop a program for their own department.

This practice in individual and team effort will enable the members of the project team to expand the program, in coordinated effort, to other departments.

CHAPTER 18

HOW TO PRODUCE A COMPANY OPERATIONS MANUAL

By David D. Seltz, noted author and consultant, and Marvin J. Radlauer, author and communications consultant*

WHEN visualizing a Company Operations Manual, most people think of a big, fat book crammed full of small type and complex charts. They usually identify such company manuals with giant corporations. Sadly, they are usually correct.

Practically every large corporation today has a company manual. Many have whole series of manuals covering every aspect of their operations broken down by department and, still further, by individual job functions. Entire departments are devoted to continually analyzing systems and procedures with the objective of eliminating wasteful steps, simplifying methods and improving communications and controls.

At what point does a company achieve the level of development that an operations manual is needed? It's never too soon if it is a business that should be manualized—but contrary to the big, fat manuals we visualize for large corporations, the smaller company can get along with a manual that is proportionate to its relative size and complexity.

Some companies are in more complicated business than others. This alone may force a relatively small company to produce a manual that is considerably larger than might be indicated by mere size alone.

As an illustration of why companies with equal volume might have entirely different needs for manuals, consider the contrast between these two companies grossing $500,000 annually. The first is an importer of various grades of rope and twine. Each year the owner of the business makes a trip to visit his overseas sources to

---

*Authors of the Dartnell Management Guide: "*How to Prepare an Effective Company Operations Manual.*"

place orders, obtain samples and get a firm commitment on prices. Upon returning home he prepares an offering letter which is mailed along with small samples to some two thousand customers and prospects—all known to be large users of rope and twine. Within weeks, orders with shipping schedules arrive that pretty much clean out the rope and twine to which he is committed for the year. In addition to himself, the company employs a bookkeeper, who doubles as typist, and a warehouse man who takes care of receiving, inventory control and shipping.

Although this business achieves a level of profitability that many larger companies could only hope for, it would be difficult indeed to convince Mr. Rope Importer that he needs a Company Operations Manual. Obviously, since he is not interested in further growth, as long as he's around he really doesn't need a manual. The two employees do nothing but simple, routine work for which he can easily train replacements whenever needed.

His strength, however, is also his greatest weakness. He is the only one who knows his sources; how to deal with them; how to arrange for timely shipments to his warehouse; how to get through the maze of customs; how to arrange for letters of credit; how to evaluate product quality; and how to project the amount of merchandise to order.

While Mr. Rope Importer is alive and well his business, with net profits exceeding $150,000 annually, is worth a fortune. Without him it is nothing but an empty warehouse with a useless set of records of past events.

Would a company operations manual have value? Of course it would! In the event of his death or incapacity, it could mean the difference between his family's inheriting an asset worth many hundreds of thousands of dollars or winding up with little or nothing. The manual for this business could be written completely by the owner and could probably be done in just ten or twelve pages.

On the other side of the coin, let's look at the second company grossing $500,000 annually. This firm happens to be in the residential burglar alarm business which means right off that there are four relatively complex business activities to contend with: marketing, installation, administration and service.

The average job the company does bills for $1,250; therefore, to achieve the $500,000 level, some four hundred systems must be sold and installed annually. Achieving this volume level necessitates the employment of at least three commissioned sales representatives, four installation crews of three each, a crew manager, an advertising manager, a bookkeeper, clerk/typist and a purchasing manager who also maintains control of inventory. The owner of the business functions as sales manager, credit manager, personnel manager and chief trouble-shooter.

He is young, energetic, highly motivated and anxious to expand to other cities and eventually to other states. No question about it—this company not only needs an operations manual, but despite its modest volume, a suitable manual will probably run at least 100 single-spaced typed pages and most likely 150 or more.

The answer to the question, "What is a company operations manual?" then is quite simple. It is a written study of the philosophy, systems, procedures, techniques and concepts under which a given business is operating—set forth in such a manner and style as to be easily referenced and fully understood.

WHO DOESN'T NEED A COMPANY OPERATIONS MANUAL?

Although the rope importer's manual could be done in 10 to 12 pages and the burglar alarm company's might require 150 pages or more, they both illustrate reasons, however different, for needing a company operations manual. Yet there are many types of business that do not need a company manual of any size or fashion.

Generally, the businesses that have little reason for a company manual are those which either depend on an individual's skill or are so straightforward as to be obvious to almost anyone. Businesses of the former type are usually difficult to transfer and might include such specialties as shoe repair, radio and TV service, auto mechanics, electrical installation and repair, plumbing, commercial art, photography and, of course, all of the degreed professions.

This is not to imply that all of these categories are impossible to transfer. As going businesses, even doctors' offices and practices are often sold. The same holds true with accounting practices and others. The relevant factor is that a medical practice must be sold to a doctor and a shoe repair business must be sold to a qualified shoemaker. In either case, the continuity of the business depends upon the skills and knowledge of the individual rather than the incidental systems and procedures under which the business functions.

As with any rule, there are exceptions. There is today at least one chain of shoe repair shops which operates under quite unique systems and procedures. Without a doubt their operation should be manualized. The same holds true with any other specialty business that is operating under a unique concept that can, and might, be duplicated in several locations.

In the realm of particularly straightforward businesses that are so obvious as to preclude the need for a manual might be included, with qualifications, such businesses as: manufacturer's representative, lawn trimming, house painting, refuse removal, package delivery, and other businesses that deal with a single, uncomplicated product or a relatively unskilled service.

By way of qualification, we'd have to eliminate from the category of "not needing a company manual" any business for which the owners have plans to branch out. This might include opening company branch operatons or appointing franchisees, licensees, agents, or representatives.

Types of Manuals

Depending upon objectives and planned utilization, there is a wide variety of types of company manuals. These are described below:

1. **Internal Manuals**—those needed for personnel and departments to clarify and control work "flow." Within the scope of internal manuals are:

   A. *Administrative*
      a. manuals codifying overall company policies and objectives
      b. those explaining the functions and procedures of specific departments
      c. those setting forth personnel policies and company benefits

   B. *Technical*—comprises manuals that spell out technical working procedures as, for example:
      a. research and development
      b. manufacturing techniques
      c. installation procedures
      d. servicing

   C. *Marketing*—these are manuals that develop the company's concepts regarding:
      a. public image to be projected
      b. introduction of new products
      c. methods for evaluating relative market position and opportunities
      d. selling philosophy and procedures

2. **External Manuals**—These comprise manuals that go outside the organization. For example:

   A. Manuals that go to customers to help them assemble, install, use and maintain the company's products

B. Manuals that go to affiliates such as:
   a. affiliated or associated companies
   b. jobbers and distributors
   c. outside service organizations and installers
   d. representatives
   e. retailers to help them sell the line
   f. franchisees and licensees

C. Manuals that instruct outside consulting organizations on how to handle the company's graphics with regard to style and trademark usage and other pertinent policies:
   a. advertising agencies
   b. public relations counselors
   c. industrial film producers
   d. printers and signage suppliers

Manuals can be done in virtually an unlimited variety of shapes and sizes depending upon the complexity of the business, individuals to whom directed, anticipated frequency of changes and additions, security considerations and overall purpose.

Let's take a look at these one at a time:

A. *Complexity of the business*—to a great degree, would dictate the size of the manual in terms of overall bulk. This is determined by the number of subjects to be covered, how many departments have to be explained, the number of systems and procedures and their interlocking relationships that must be detailed. When a business reaches the degree of complexity that might cause its manual to become unwieldy, it is advisable to break it up into separate books; i.e.: Personnel Procedures; Purchasing Manual; Sales Manual; Accounting and Administration Manual; Manager's Guide; Forms and Systems Manual; Installation Manual; Manufacturing and Quality Control Manual; etc.

B. *Individuals to whom directed*—if the person supposed to use the manual is expected to carry it around in his pocket, then without a doubt it should be pocket sized. This means length, width, bulk and weight—for you can rest assured that if you exceed any one of these dimensions, the manual, which you nurtured so carefully and in which you invested so much time, effort and money, will be out in the car or in the closet at home at the critical moment for which you so carefully had planned its use.

A manual directed to typists and secretaries explaining the company's policies regarding letter format, filing systems, interoffice communications and telephone policy need not, and probably should not, contain scads of non-relevant information about purchasing procedures or how to handle marketing problems. On the other hand, the office manager who is doubling in brass as personnel manager should certainly be provided with manuals covering all of the functions, systems, procedures and job titles encompassed by his or her responsibilities. Since portability is not a consideration in this case, size and bulk are not important factors.

C. *Anticipated frequency of changes and additions*—is the major point that dictates the method of binding to be used. Obviously, any permanent type of binding makes it rather difficult (not impossible) to make changes, additions and deletions. For this reason, although there are several disadvantages, most companies use loose-leaf binders which are available in a variety of sizes and capacities.

If frequent revisions are expected, a page numbering and indexing system should be incorporated that permits the user to know whether or not his manual is up to date. A subsequent section will suggest and detail various methods that have been used successfully.

Anticipated frequency of changes might also influence the choice of copy preparation method, reproduction process and quantity of manuals to be run. If substantial changes are expected, reproduction-quality typing (electric typewriter with carbon ribbon) would probably be used rather than considerably more expensive printer's type. Further, if changes are inevitable, it would be poor judgment to reproduce many more manuals than are immediately needed. These subjects are also fully covered in a subsequent section of this book.

D. *Security considerations*—this is a most difficult subject to discuss since there is no doubt that any competitor would love to get his hands on your company operations manual—especially if you have a reputation for running a smooth, profitable, well-organized operation. The other person you must be concerned with is the ambitious, highly motivated employee who might borrow your manual for purposes of going into competition with you. Of course, any size manual can be appropriated; however, if the various departmental and functional sections are bound separately and are distributed on a "need-to-know" basis, the chance of someone walking off with the whole store is somewhat lessened. Actually, the principal means of protecting yourself against unauthorized use of your materials by an employee, or former employee, is through a properly drafted restrictive covenant and trade secrets clause in a valid employment agreement.

E. *Overall purpose*—a company operations manual can serve many purposes and should, therefore, be designed accordingly. Primarily, it will be used as a reference source when there is a question as to the proper procedure or policy that might affect a given transaction. For this reason, it must be divided, sub-divided and indexed for ease in finding the answers to specific questions.

Company manuals are also used as planning guides. For this reason, there must be a smooth and logical flow of information so that top management can be sure that new programs and procedures blend well without upsetting ongoing activities. All of the checks and balances built into the systems must be focused upon so they are not ignored or weakened when instituting changes.

Company manuals are also used as text books in the training of new employees and in re-training old employees for new or added responsibilities. Further, they are used extensively in the training of franchisees, licensees, agents, dealers and independent representatives. It is important, therefore, that in addition to excellence of content, the overall impression projected by a company's manual is one of efficiency and solidity. No one wants to be associated with a company whose direction seems confused and whose substance appears questionable.

The following questionnaire is designed to help you objectively ascertain whether or not your business should have a company operations manual and just how extensive it should be.

DOES MY COMPANY NEED AN
OPERATIONS MANUAL?

If your answer to any one of these questions is "yes," then chances are your company should have at least a modest operations manual. If there are two or more "yes" answers, there is no chance about it, you need one.

	YES	NO
1. Does management wish to accelerate the current rate of growth?	( )	( )
2. At the current rate of growth, or at a desired accelerated rate of growth, would the number of employees requiring training rise proportionately?	( )	( )

OFFICE ADMINISTRATION HANDBOOK

3. Do you now have branch operations* or do you contemplate having such branch operations in the foreseeable future?   ( ) ( )

4. If any executive, key employee or group of employees were to leave the company or unexpectedly become unavailable, would the loss of such personnel's knowledge make the uninterrupted continuation of the business difficult?   ( ) ( )

5. Is it the owner's desire that the business continue without interruption after his retirement or demise?   ( ) ( )

HOW EXTENSIVE A MANUAL DO WE NEED?

Assuming you've already determined you need a manual, a rating totaling 10 or more indicates you need more than just a minimum, basic manual (10 to 12 typed pages explaining systems and procedures). If your total is 15 to 20, you probably need a manual detailing the functions of each department. A total of 20 to 25 indicates the addition of separate job descriptions and responsibilities. A rating over 25 indicates that a full manual is needed, probably requiring separate volumes for each department and each major function.

1. Through attrition, turnover, growth or other reasons, we must hire and train at least five new employees a month.

2. We open branches†, or are planning to open branches, at the rate of at least two a year.

3. Resulting from changing technology, new products, mergers, acquisitions or other major business changes, we must introduce our procedures and concepts to groups of new associates or employees.

NEVER (0 Points)
SOMETIMES (5 Points)
FREQUENTLY (10 Point)
ALWAYS (25 Points)

4. Our gross volume is:
   a. Under $1 million (0 points)
   b. $1 to $5 million (5 points)
   c. $5 to $10 million (10 points)
   c. $10 to $25 million (15 points)
   e. $25 to $50 million (20 points)
   f. Over $50 million (25 points)

---

*Includes company-owned branches, franchisees, licensees, agents, independent representatives.
†Includes company-owned branches, franchisees, licensees, agents, independent representatives.

464

HOW TO PRODUCE A COMPANY OPERATIONS MANUAL

PREPARATION PROCEDURES

Once the decision to produce a company manual has been made, it is wise for management to see that a careful job of *delegating, planning* and *scheduling* is done before any work is actually begun. It is most important that these be given thoughtful consideration since the quality of the finished product will depend heavily upon the skills of the coordinator and how well the initial planning has been done.

Delegating

A large company will usually have a Systems and Procedures Department, which, naturally, is charged with the responsibility of developing and revising systems and procedures, as well as their implementation and manualization. Smaller companies, which do not have such departments, must delegate the work to individuals or groups who are competent to analyze what is going on and present it in readable, understandable language.

In many cases there is at least one person in the company who has the broad perspective and ability to quarterback the job. He or she will be an individual who thinks logically, is inquisitive, and who expresses thoughts well in writing. If no such individual is available, or if one cannot be relieved from other duties, then it may be necessary to seek outside assistance.

The type of talent needed is generally found in one of several different types of management consultants. If the company's activities are financially or commercially oriented, then the assistance of one of the larger accounting firms might be solicited—they often have management consulting groups available for various types of assignments.

If branch expansion through franchising or licensing is, or is planned to be, important in the future of the company, then the best source for talent is probably a franchise marketing consulting organization.

Any, or all, of the aforementioned, as well as any of the reputable management consulting firms, may very well have the person or persons needed to accumulate information and be responsible for writing the manual, no matter what the company's main activity might be. In most cases it will be found that a generalist with wide business experience and good graphic communications skills will do the best job.

Planning

The first step in planning the company manual is to agree upon objectives. What is the purpose of this particular manual? What should it accomplish? To whom and for whom should it be directed? How will it be used and what format should it have?

After everyone involved in the decision-making process has agreed upon the objectives, and they have been committed to writing in the form of a brief statement of objectives, the next step is to prepare a broad outline of the major topics to be covered. This step is relatively simple and merely requires the application of logic to the problems that have been defined and objectives that have been spelled out. In your planning, bear in mind that it is always good to do a bit of merchandising of the manual and PR for the company by providing prospective readers with a certain amount of background information and reasons why as well as how to.

Assuming that the following is the statement of objectives, here is a typical broad outline of a proposed company manual:

PURPOSE AND SCOPE
OF PROPOSED COMPANY MANUAL

The purpose of the proposed company manual is to provide a working tool for all departments and employees of the company. It shall contain all current operating systems and procedures with separate volumes for line and staff personnel. The manual shall be so designed that it may be easily revised and separated by department. Further, it shall be designed to be broken down by job category wherever possible. The style and format shall permit usage as a working reference guide and as a training textbook for new employees and others being retrained or upgraded.

TYPICAL BROAD OUTLINE OF
COMPANY MANUAL

   I. Introduction
      A. Brief company history
      B. Company philosophy
      C. How to use and update this manual
  II. Organization of Company
      A. Explanation of chain of command
      B. Table of organization
 III. Operating Policies
 IV. Personnel Policies
  V. Purchasing Policies
 VI. Housekeeping and Maintenance

After the broad outline has been thoroughly reviewed and accepted by all of the concerned executives, the next step is to expand and detail the outline. To accomplish this, there is a choice between two techniques that may be employed.

The first technique is for the person who is coordinating the project to conduct interviews with executives and key personnel in each department. During these interviews the objective is to extract enough information to gain a general understanding of the functions of each department and its interlocking relationships with other departments. This should provide enough knowledge to expand the broad outline into the fully detailed outline.

The alternate technique that might be employed is to assign each departmental manager the task of detailing the outline for the department. In all cases there should be a general format to follow so there is a certain amount of uniformity and cohesiveness to the submissions from each department. Additionally, each manager should be given a due date to have completed and submitted the outline.

Below is a suggested form that might be used for guiding department managers in preparing their detailed outlines. After receiving the completed outlines from the department managers, the coordinator will create the fully detailed outline by editing them and arranging everything into a logical sequence and format for management's approval prior to proceeding with the first draft.

Scheduling

In any project as complex, and involving as many people, as developing a company manual, establishing and adhering to a schedule is

---

SUGGESTED MANUAL OUTLINE FOR
_____ DEPARTMENT

The following is a guide to the general content and format of your department's manual outline. Do not confine yourself to this if you feel another approach might be better. Expand your outline to any degree you deem necessary to cover all systems, procedures, functions, objectives and activities. Since other parts of the company manual will depend upon timely completion of this portion, please adhere strictly to the schedule noted below. Many thanks for your help.

    I. Primary Departmental Function
       A. B. C, etc. for secondary functions

   II. Table of Organization

  III. Job Titles, Descriptions, Functions and Responsibilities
       A. B. C. etc.

  IV. Forms Instituted, Negotiated and Disposition
       A. B. C. etc.

   V. Departmental Systems and Procedures
       A. B. C. etc.

  VI. Departmental Files and Retention Schedule
       A. B. C. etc.

VIII. Inter-departmental Flow and Relationships
       A, B, C, etc.

PLEASE COMPLETE AND SUBMIT BEFORE
_____

---

of paramount importance. Not only is it necessary for obtaining the input when it is needed, but proper establishment of a segmented schedule exposes all of the many pieces that must fit together while focusing on the sequential steps that are necessary.

Many parts of the project can be undertaken simultaneously while others will have to wait for preceding portions to be completed. For this reason, the type of scheduling we have found to be most efficient is a modification of the "P-E-R-T" system.

PERT is the acronym for "Program Evaluation and Review Technique," which was developed early in the Space Age as a system for scheduling and supervising highly complex missile development programs. Since then, the term has come into general use to define a system of diagramming the steps of any relatively complex program. Parallel and interconnecting lines are used to indicate the sequential flow of actions as well as the steps that may be performed concurrently or parallel. For each step a box is used to set forth the activity or "milestone" and the estimated time for its accomplishment.

Finally, after the steps have all been diagrammed, and the connecting and parallel lines have been drawn, we can identify the "Critical Path." This is done by following the line from start to finish that allows for completion of all steps that cannot be completed before preceding steps are done. In essence then, the Critical Path, indicated by a heavier line, is the shortest time in which the project can be expected to be completed if all schedules are maintained.

Below is a very much simplified version of a PERT diagram which shows all of the basic elements.

SIMPLE PERT CHART

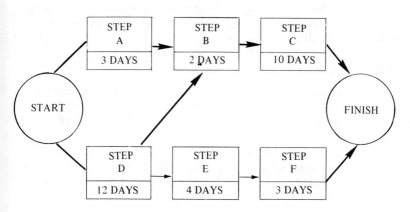

The simple PERT chart shows that Steps A and D commence after the completion of the starting step. In preparing a company manual, this starting step might be the appointment of the person who will be responsible for coordinating the project. It further indicates that Steps A and D can be completed concurrently while Step B cannot be accomplished until both A and D are completed. Step C cannot be completed until after Step B is done and Steps E and F must be done sequentially after Step D is finished. The Critical Path, indicated by the heavy line, is the shortest time in which the project can be completed.

STEP D	12 Days
STEP B	2 Days
STEP C	10 Days
CRITICAL PATH	24 Days

Although any unit of time may be used in a PERT chart, for a project like preparing a company manual, we generally figure time in working days. Holidays and weekends are added at the end to project a calender date or calender time frame for completion.

The principal reason management might have decided to prepare a company manual at this time is that some of the new products are nearly ready for production and marketing. This will necessitate the hiring of additional people for manufacturing, marketing, order processing, warehousing and shipping. Another probable reason for producing a company manual at this time is that management suddenly realized that the flow of paper had been steadily increasing. They felt that a thorough review might simplify some of the systems and procedures. A further reason was the noticeable, and costly, increase in employee turnover in white collar as well as manufacturing classifications. It was agreed that an operations manual would serve as a valuable training tool for new employees while helping to instill job satisfaction through understanding of the importance and function of each work category.

What do we learn from the PERT Chart?

First, of course, we see a graphic representation of the many steps it takes to produce a company manual, and the time it takes for completion of each step. The Critical Path tells us how long it will take from start to finish.

If thoughtfully developed and properly executed, a PERT Chart is an extremely valuable management tool. But, frankly, the person who prepares the PERT Chart can, either deliberately or unintentionally, distort the scheduling and time estimates. This may cause the completion time to appear grossly exaggerated or unrealistically short.

It is management's responsibility to study the PERT Chart to be certain that no steps have been overlooked and that time estimates are realistic. If the Critical Path indicates a completion date that is too far distant for planned need, then it may be necessary to take one of these directions: 1) assign additional manpower to the project; 2) establish completion priorities to meet needs by department or function, 3) revise the company planning regarding activities requiring usage by the unattainable time.

PROBLEMS YOU MAY UNCOVER

When analyzing forms, systems and fling procedures, you will have a unique opportunity to focus on weaknesses in the company's systems. Among the problems you may uncover are:

1. Redundancy of effort by various departments and/or the individuals.
2. No means of catching or correcting errors (improper checks and balances).
3. No system for keeping transactions moving through departments (possible dead-ends).
4. Unnecessary forms.
5. Poorly designed forms making extra work.
6. Antiquated forms (not being used as originally designed).
7. Separate forms that should be combined.
8. People unnecessarily receiving parts of forms (needlessly adding to paper flow).
9. No standardization of filing systems, unlimited access to files, and no method of keeping track of items taken from files.
10. Sloppy filing, making it difficult to file or to find filed items.
11. No forms retention and disposal system. (Various types of forms should be retained for differing lengths of time for legal as well as procedural reasons. Those of a highly confidential nature may require more stringent means of disposal than others.)
12. Badly designed external forms (from the esthetic viewpoint) providing a poor image of the company to customers and vendors.
13. Poor intra- and inter-department communications (causing confusion, errors and unnecessary delays).

Since our primary purpose is to manualize the company's current operations, it is not recommended that you try to solve all of the problems as they are brought to light. If you are charged with the responsibility of improving forms and systems, unless you are starting from scratch, it is best to work on them after the manual is completed and in use. In this way, you can be more sure you have the best operational answer to each problem and will be better able to mesh revisions into existing systems.

Our suggestion is to write up explanations of the problems that become obvious to you as they are exposed. Maintain a file of these explanations so that after the manual is operational, you can review them for action or pass them on to the party who will be responsible for the systems and forms improvement program.

Getting into the Draft

Everything you have done up to now has been leading you to this step in the preparation of the company manual—writing the draft.

Here is where you first become concerned with presentation style.

Will writing be narrative—terse—technical? Will you use graphs, charts, illustrations liberally or only where absolutely necessary, as in depicting Tables of Organization?

Obviously, the principal factor dictating writing style should be the audience for whom the company manual, or its parts, is targeted. That portion intended for clerical and production workers should, as much as possible, avoid technical language. If graphs and charts are used in these sections, they should be clear and uncomplicated—designed to quickly clarify a point that might be more difficult to explain verbally. Here illustration might come in handy to emphasize important points, perhaps with the judicious use of humor. For instance, you might make a strong point of discouraging the use of company phones for personal calls by illustrating an important customer fuming and fussing, becoming angry, while phones are tied up on obvious nonsense calls.

Semihumorous illustrations are also valuable for emphasizing points relative to safety, promptness, quality standards, courtesy, time wasting, unnecessary absences, wasting supplies, care of tools and equipment, and many others.

The portions of the manual that are aimed toward engineers, technicians and degreed professionals will be the most difficult to write, unless you are educated in the specific discipline with which you are dealing. For these portions of the manual it is recommended that you circumvent the most technical areas by leaning upon the concerned department heads for technical writing assistance. Use

472

your own talent to weave these sections together into a smooth-flowing, logical presentation.

Caution—don't be completely hoodwinked by the technicians. You will find that much of their gobbledygook is unnecessary and often is not even clear to other professionals of a like calling. In other words, except for chemical, mathematical and scientific formulas, and technical matters of the highest order, you should be able to make sense out of the language of most of the writing, whether it be legal, financial, electronic data processing, scientific, or whatever.

Before "freezing" any of the more technical sections of the manual, be sure they are read by qualified individuals, other than those providing the input or having done the actual writing.

How To Get It Down On Paper

How any writer gets his thoughts down on paper is a very personal matter involved with personal preferences, capabilities and psyche. Some are adept at dictating into a voice recording machine—which is probably the fastest way to work. Others cannot sufficiently organize their thoughts working this way and must either write or type it out. Still others may prefer to dictate to a stenographer who will then transcribe her shorthand notes or to a fast typist who can type directly from dictation.

In any case, it a good idea to have the typist do the first typing as a rough draft. This means that typing will be double spaced (allowing room to note corrections and changes) and little effort will be made to produce a perfect typing job—even "X"ing out of errors is permitted.

If you are a good enough typist to be creative while you are typing, then of course you can do your own rough draft while you are writing.

Most of us find that the type of writing necessary for company manuals is best done first by hand on "foolscap" paper (yellow-lined). If your handwriting is legible, and you do not have too many complications with cross-outs and insertions, the typist can work directly from your notes. If this is difficult, then you can work the way this writer does, by dictating your rough notes into a voice recording machine. This allows you to give the typist smooth-flowing input—often resulting in a rough draft that is amazingly clean.

The Draft You Submit

When deeply immersed in writing and creating, it is often difficult to judge the product of your efforts as objectively as you should. It is usually best to re-read at least one last time after you have put your work aside for a day or two.

After you have read, re-read and corrected the rough draft, re-type the first draft for submission to department heads and company executives. As with any other type of creative work, the quality of the presentation will have an important bearing on the critical response it generates. For this reason, do not penalize the product of your work with shoddy "packaging."

If your facilities include word processing equipment, of course you will be able to develop a very attractive first draft as well as a professional finished product. If you have access to a typewriter with executive typeface, try to use it, even for the rough draft. If you must use regular office equipment, make sure that the draft is neatly presented. It should be complete with headlines and sub-heads and underlining where needed.

Double-spacing is a necessity for the draft. If you think there will be many, you could consider triple-spacing, but this might lead to a bulky draft copy.

The authors have always found it a good practice to submit drafts in an attractive binder of some kind. This is not only for the purpose of keeping the work together, but is a form of merchandising— packaging, if you will. It gives the reader the feeling of a more finished product and it enhances the importance of the work being submitted. There are several types of looseleaf "report" binders available at any commercial stationer that do a very satisfactory job.

If illustrations and charts are to be utilized, you can handle them in the draft in any one of several ways:

1. When finished art is available, paste photo copies into the correct position in the draft.
2. If art has not been done yet, allow space and type in a parenthetical explanation of the proposed art.
3. Prepare rough renditions of the proposed art and insert in the correct positions.

Basically, the more complete your draft is, the better others will be able to visualize and judge your work. You are asking too much if you expect people to use their imaginations.

Writing Style

The objective of the manual writer must be to present facts and ideas to readers in such fashion that they are easily and agreeably understood.

In no instance should writing style overpower the substance of the subject matter. The reader's attention should be directed to *what* is being said rather than to *how* it is said. The style of manual writing should never be obtrusive. It should be guided by the objectives of the company and the needs of the readers.

Unlike writing for general audiences, each part of a company manual is directed to people engaged in similar activities. This homogeneity of readership rather simplifies the task of establishing the tone and writing style to be used. Here are a few general guidelines that, if followed, will save you hours of rewriting:

Have Direction. Don't wander, keep on track. Each chapter, each section, each paragraph, each sentence should have a central purpose and everything in it should contribute to its development and achievement.

Keep a Balance. The relative importance of subject matter is often indicated by the amount of space devoted to it. Usually, the more important the topic, the more thoroughly it is explained. Besides the amount of space, positioning of the parts helps to strike a balance, with more important matters usually appearing at the beginning.

Strive for Clarity. If the reader does not understand what is written, he cannot use it. Worse, if he gets the wrong meaning out of it, it could be more harmful than getting no meaning.

What may be clear to one reader may be completely incomprehensible to another. The first consideration, then, is to determine the intelligence, the educational and cultural level of the prospective audience.

Professional categories and technical experts can be expected to understand terminology commonly used in their respective fields. Business executives should be able to fully comprehend language that is common to the educated. Lastly, there are those who will be using parts of the manual who are relatively uneducated and have culturally limited backgrounds. For these, the language must be simple and untechnical without sacrificing accuracy. When it is expected that there will be a mixed readership of professionals, technicians, executives and laymen, the writer will have a particularly difficult time in balancing the writing style. One must satisfy the specialist yet must not overwhelm the general reader.

For the sake of clarity, it may be necessary to define certain terms that are used in the manual. However, try to avoid using too many definitions because they will interrupt the flow of the subject matter and reduce clarity.

OFFICE ADMINISTRATION HANDBOOK

Be sure you are saying what you mean since nothing will confuse the reader more than incorrect usage of words and phrases. As a simple illustration, consider the change in the meaning of a phrase if the writer said, "including all salaried employees" when he meant to say, "excluding all salaried employees."

Writing clearly depends on many factors: careful choice of words, proper sentence structure, good punctuation, and thoughtful paragraphing all contribute. Most importantly, the writer should be thoroughly familiar with the subject matter to avoid vagueness and uncertainty as to what she means to say.

Be Concise. Do not leave anything out but say what you have to say in the fewest number of words possible. One way to accomplish this is to eliminate masses of detail that most probably will never be read. Often, much detail can be relegated to the appendix or exhibit section of the manual.

GRAPHS, CHARTS AND ILLUSTRATIONS

The purpose of graphs, charts and illustrations in a company manual should never be merely decorative—they should each be used to illustrate or emphasize a given set of facts, an idea or a message . . . in a way that words alone cannot do satisfactorily.

Graphs

Graphs are most effective when used to show the quantitative or size proportions between related factors, especially when such proportions are difficult to visualize in stated numbers and verbal description.

There are many forms of graphs, including the familiar line graph which illustrates peaks and valleys in a linear, or analogue, fashion. Other forms of analogue graphs include curved line graphs which are used to illustrate changing factors, quantities and relationships in a continuous curve rather than from point to point. Then there are bar graphs—both horizontal and vertical—which are used to show the comparisons between two, three or more values by the relative length or bulk of the bars. These are digital, rather than analogue, because they show the quantitative relationships at fixed intervals instead of continuously as line graphs.

Bar graphs can be most interestingly designed in that the bars do not necessarily have to be bars. They can be people, shown in different sizes, stacks of coins, factory buildings, or any variety of commodities, products or objects shown either in different sizes or in different quantities.

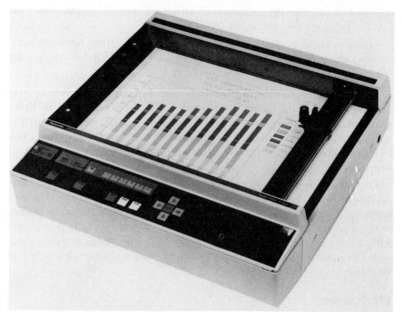

Graphs, today, can be produced in color or in black and white on digital units run by computers. This unit, which works with up to eight colors, can generate a wide range of business graphics, including charts, diagrams and computer-assisted design graphics.
Courtesy Panasonic Industrial Company.

Pie graphs are effectively used to illustrate the relative sizes of the several parts of a whole. Although usually done in the familiar flat pie format, interest and appearance is enhanced by using a sectioned coin, wheel, food can, or some other round object that may be pertinent to the subject being presented. A variation of the pie graph is the "salami" graph in which a symbolic object is used with the proportionate shares shown as slices of varying thicknesses.

Charts

Charts are used for several purposes, among which are:

1. Sequential checklists (see the PERT Chart on page 469).
2. Cross references (typical are mileage charts showing distances between cities, or multiplication tables).
3. Consequential results of measurable actions or factors (work yield from specified horsepower).
4. Illustrating flow of processing (used extensively in Electronic Data Processing as well as in many industrial and office procedures).

5. Illustrating organizational structure (most commonly, the Table of Organization chart).
6. Conversion charts (illustrating the relationship between various standards of measurement as Fahrenheit to centigrade, inches to decimals, pounds to dollars).

Of course, there are many other uses for charts which you may discover as you are writing the manual. Be especially alert to those situations where repeated reference must be made to the information you are presenting. If a chart will save the reader time, will help prevent errors, then by all means have an appropriate chart prepared.

Organization charts indicate reporting channels and authority levels along with titles and responsibilities. When a large, complex corporate structure is depicted, the relationships between authority levels can be extremely difficult to chart. If not carefully done, and fully cleared with top authority prior to publication, a new or revised organization chart can be very upsetting to those who may feel slighted.

Illustrations

There are two basic types of illustrations which encompass the entire spectrum of single color illustration—line and continuous tone. As the designations imply, line art is made up of solid lines against clean paper while continuous tone art has the capability of depicting all gradations of shading between the solid color and the clean paper (or white).

Photographs are, of course, continuous tone. Also continuous tone are wash drawings and any other type of art that contains a variety of tonal qualities.

In reproducing continuous tone art, halftones, which break up the gradations of tone into a screen of dots of varying sizes, are required. Continuous tone art, unless it has been "screened" beforehand, adds somewhat to reproduction expense since it has to be photographed separately and then combined with the film of the text matter by a hand process called "stripping."

Line drawings, on the other hand, if combined in the art with text matter, can be shot at the same time with no addition to reproduction costs. This assumes that the line drawing appears in its finished size (or proportion) and position in the reproduction copy of the page.

In recent years, new techniques have been developed whereby photographs are photomechanically converted to line art. This is not done to save money, but to achieve desired artistic effects.

Conversely, it is possible to achieve tonal gradations in line art by having the artist apply screened tonal overlays to the art, or by having the printer "lay" tones or "benday" tints to specified portions of the art. Even in single color printing, the possibilities are limited only by the creativity of the artist or designer.

SOURCES OF REPRODUCIBLE
STOCK ILLUSTRATIONS

Line Illustrations
Harry Volk Jr. Art Studio
1401 N. Main Street
Pleasantville, NJ 08232

Publishes a variety of "clip books" each printed on high-quality kromekote paper and containing a somewhat related set of line drawings in a variety of styles.

Idea Art
740 Broadway
New York, NY 10003

Publishes a wide variety of top quality reproducible art presented in several loose-leaf binders. Pages are printed on one side of kromekote paper.

Dover Publications, Inc.
180 Varick Street
New York, NY 10014

Publishes many books containing reproducible art of an old-fashioned nature in many specialized subject areas—for instance, transportation, machines, animals, people in costumes, trade cuts, cartouches, etc.

Stock Photographs

There are many companies in the stock photograph business, generally concentrated in the major advertising centers throughout the country. These companies maintain extensive libraries of various types of photographs and have them categorized in such a way that they can usually offer a selection of photographs for any specification you may provide. Some of these companies charge for the search as well as for the eventual use of the photograph. Rates are often determined by proposed one-time usage and potential circulation. Available are black and white photographs, color transparencies and movie stills. Some of the better known sources are:

Bettmann Archive, Inc.
136 East 57th Street
New York, NY 10022

Ewing Galloway
342 Madison Avenue
New York, NY 10017

H. Armstrong Roberts
4203 Locust Street
Philadelphia, PA 19104

Underwood and Underwood
30 S. Michigan Avenue
Chicago, IL 60603

CHAPTER 19

HOW TO DEVELOP
A COMPANY HANDBOOK

BY way of definition, a handbook is a compact reference book. It has become an increasingly popular management aid for building and preserving good employer-employee relations.

The use of handbooks is becoming increasingly widespread because they perform a most useful service: employee communications. Workers from the largest to the smallest business concerns thirst for information about their companies and their jobs. A handbook can spell out the details by providing data on company objectives, its financial status, its community standing and the employee benefits program. The worker is clearly told what is expected of him or her, and what he or she can expect from the company.

If there is such a thing as a typical employee handbook, it would probably contain from eight to 32 pages, and would be reproduced by any means from mimeograph to full-color lithography. To be effective, however, it must be carefully organized and thoughtfully written to convey the intended message.

Following are several subject categories that might be included. Use them as a guide for structuring a useful company handbook:

> *Greeting from Management:* Since company handbooks are usually given to new employees, they should commence with an informal welcome message signed by the chief executive officer. This greeting should welcome the newcomer and emphasize how important are the company's people to its success.
>
> *Background:* To help new employees develop pride in the company, include a brief history of the firm and highlights of its accomplishments. People like to be associated with a highly regarded concern having a background of which they can be proud.
>
> *Current Operations:* New employees often know little or nothing about the company's activities. Include a section in the handbook, therefore, for general information, location of facilities, number of employees, detailing of products and services, profiles of customers, and names and title of principal executives.
>
> *Growth Potential:* Since this section relates directly to the employee's prospects for income enhancement and career advancement, it probably will be the most thoroughly read portion of the handbook.

Explain the general criteria by which the company rates performance and provide information on wage policies, salary reviews and promotion policy.

Company Rules: Set forth the regulations governing hours, coffee breaks, safety rules, registering of complaints, absences, tardiness and smoking. Laying it on the line leads to a clear understanding and a happier relationship.

Benefits Program: The employee handbook should fully list and detail the benefits provided to employees by the company. Additionally, the mandatory government benefits should be listed and explained so that employees have an overall view of what they can expect under various circumstances. This also serves as a reminder that the company bears the major burden of the cost of Social Security, Unemployment Insurance and Disability Insurance (where applicable). Vacations, holidays, sick leave, bonus programs, insurance, training programs, stock purchase plans, and all other facets of the benefits program should be spelled out.

If properly handled, the company handbook can be an effective tool for engendering company loyalty and building morale. By creating a sense of involvement, employees are motivated to contribute more than the minimum necessary to get by. An understanding of the direct relationship between their personal advancement and company profitability helps eliminate waste and improves productivity.

Other Types of Handbooks

Vendor's Guide—Many firms use these to welcome representatives of companies wishing to offer their services and products. Their principal function is to direct representatives to the departments and individuals they should solicit and to explain purchasing policies and objectives. These handbooks often outline the company's background and current operations.

Handbook for Prospective Franchisees—A specialized booklet designed to respond to inquiries from those seeking information about the company's franchise program. Included should be the following major topics: greeting from the president, company history, explanation of the business, earning potential, corroboration of claims (testimonials), and request for further action.

Company Style Book—Sets forth the company's standards for use of its trade names and trademarks, the specifications for company colors and its preferences concerning typographic style, signs, decor and other points of taste. Probably not as widely used today as formerly, but can be a valuable guide for advertising agencies, public relations counsels, advertising department, purchasing department, reproduction department, sign makers, etc.

Business Conduct Handbook—Often given minor space in company manuals, many larger companies have seen fit to present this vital subject matter in separate, highly detailed handbooks. IBM, for one, publishes a 76-page booklet entitled, "Business Conduct Guidelines" and, as a matter of policy, requires certain classifications of employees to read or review it each year. These employees are further required to certify that they understand their responsibility to comply with the guidelines set forth and to recognize that any violation may be reason for termination of employment.

The IBM handbook attempted to state in clear and understandable language some guidelines that apply to all IBM employees. These guidelines reflected IBM's policy of conducting itself within the letter and spirit of antitrust laws and of adhering to the highest standards of business ethics.

MECHANICAL PREPARATION, REPRODUCTION AND BINDING

Because of the limitation on distribution and the probability of revisions, most company handbooks are reproduced in relatively small quantities, seldom exceeding 200 to 300 copies. As a result, a high percentage of the total preparation cost must be apportioned to each manual produced. For this reason it is usually necessary to keep a tight lid on mechanical preparation costs.

In terms of economy, the least expensive means of preparing text matter is the office typewriter. When setting up pages, remember always to allow room for binding—right-hand pages (odd numbers) should be off-centered to the right. Left-hand pages (even numbers) should be off-centered to the left.

Although justified text matter (squared both left and right) is more finished looking, people have become quite accustomed to reading text with an uneven, or ragged, right-hand margin. Reproduction typing with a ragged right-hand margin can be done in a single typing, while squared margins require two typings.

Automatic typewriters have letters that are most like printer's type in that wider letters, such as, "W" or "M," are given more space than thinner letters, such as, "i" or "j." Also, the space bar is divided into two parts, one having a two-unit value and the other having a three-unit value. Since the back-space key has a single-unit value, you are able to vary between-word spacing from a single-unit space to any wider space. This capability permits you, in two typings, to achieve perfectly justified text matter that most laypeople cannot distinguish from printer's type.

Any typewriter can produce squared margins, although not as professional looking as a word processing unit, by merely using the following system:

1. Decide how wide a column you wish to compose, set the left-hand margin and note number on the unit scale on the typewriter that corresponds to the desired width. (The unit scale usually appears on the bail-bar that holds paper to the platen (roller) or on a stationary scale a bit lower down on the machine.)

2. Start typing but do not go past the scale number you have selected as your desired width. At the end of each line of typing note the number of additional spaces needed to reach the selected scale number. Type this number beyond the selected width on the right.

3. Continue the first typing in this fashion as far as you wish to go. Although strike-overs are permissible, and corrections do not have to be made perfectly, all corrections affecting spacing must be made accurately in this first typing.

4. In the second typing (for reproduction), divide the number of units of space needed to "space out" each line to the selected scale number by the number of between-word spaces in the line and add extra spaces between words accordingly. In most cases, the number of additional spaces required to fill a line will not correspond to the exact number of spaces available between words. For best appearance, add extra spaces between words that end and/or begin with letters having ascenders or descenders, such as, "d," "y," "g," "b," etc.

Using a word processing unit permits the use of a variety of type faces—light, medium, bold, italics, script, as well as different sizes for headlines.

Making Corrections On Reproduction Copy

If errors are caught while the work is still in the regular typewriter, satisfactory corrections can usually be made with Ko-Rec-Type or by smoothly blocking out the error with opaque white correction fluid and typing over.

When errors are found after work has been removed from the typewriter, it is often difficult to strike corrections into the exact position. If corrections will fit into the same space as the error, then the word, or words, can be retyped on a separate sheet of blank paper and "cut in" using the following procedure:

1. If a light-table is available, lay the reproduction copy face down on the ground glass and tape the edges to the glass in two or three places with transparent or masking tape (folding over the ends of the pieces of tape will make subsequent removal easier). When a light-table is unavailable, the writer

has often found that taping the copy to a convenient window works quite well.

2. Lay the separate sheet with the typed corrections face down on top of the reproduction copy and adjust its position so that the correction is matched identically to the error which it is to replace. Tape down the correction sheet in two or three spots.

3. Using a sharp, single-edged razor blade, cut through both sheets simultaneously closely around the correction.

4. Remove the excess paper of the correction sheet.

5. Keeping the correction patch in the exact position on top of the error, cover the correction patch and the now exposed back of the reproduction copy around it with piece of thin, transparent tape.

6. Remove the reproduction copy from the light-table and brush away the patch of paper with the error (if properly cut through in step number 3, it will just fall away and the correction patch will have taken its exact place).

NOTE: When whole lines or paragraphs have to be replaced, it is best to work face up on the light-table by just cutting around the correction patch with a scissors and pasting the correction exactly on top of the section containing the error. Cellophane tape with sticky surface on both sides (Scotch-Double Coated) is handy to use for this purpose. Removal of the error, since it is covered over in this case, is not necessary.

Other Means of Preparing Text Matter for Reproduction

Printer's Type—Expensive, but results in superior reproduction of copy and is available in the widest assortment of type scales. Corrections are relatively simple because type is set in lines. The line, or lines, with errors are removed and corrected lines are inserted. It is most important to proofread carefully after corrections are made (as well as before) because it is not uncommon for the printer to remove the wrong line or to insert the correction in the wrong place or even upside down. Since it is unwieldy and expensive to keep type-matter "standing" (type metal is remelted and used over and over), future revisions are usually made by resetting affected portions and pasting corrections into the old reproduction proofs. If there are large insertions of additional copy, or many changes, a complete reset may be necessary.

Automatic Typing—There are several systems currently being used. Some use a punched tape or card input while others use magnetic tape. The main advantages of using automatic typewriters are: (1) proofreading and correcting can be accomplished on the tape or cards after the first typing without necessitating complete retyping or complex artwork; (2) justifying, on most types of machines, is done automatically when input is run through for the reproduction copy; and (3) tapes (or cards) may easily be retained for future revisions and re-use. This last feature can be a most important advantage when it is known that a handbook being prepared will be subject to frequent revisions of the type that require many small insertions, changes or deletions.

Computer Composition—A relatively new and fast growing means of setting type that embraces all of the advantages of automatic typing, with the added advantage of looking as good as printer's type—and reproducing even better. Input is magnetic tape that is fed into specially designed computers that produce finished film negatives of the text copy. Justifying (squared margins), leading (space between lines), paging, indentions, changes to italics, bold face and other variations, can all be programmed for automatic accomplishment in the computer. Tapes are prepared on a machine having a keyboard similar to a typewriter. The computer can convert tapes to page negatives at an extremely rapid rate, perhaps a minute or two per page. Computer composition, although coming down in price, is still more expensive than copy prepared on an office typewriter or automatic typewriter. It is the preferred method when top quality reproduction is desired, and retention of input for future revisions is required.

Preparing Headlines

When using a typewriter to prepare text copy, the simplest and least expensive way to do headlines is to use all-caps, with or without underlining. When a more finished, professional looking job is preferred, there are several alternate methods available:

1. Type a group of headlines on one sheet of paper with allowance for cutting space between. Order a reproduction quality glossy photostat enlarged to the size desired. Cut the photostat apart and, squaring carefully, paste into position on the typed page.

2. Use one of the several brands of transfer lettering available in art supply stores and some commercial stationers. These come in a wide variety of type styles and sizes and do an extremely fine job. They are very easy to work with—just follow the manufacturer's instructions.

3. Photographic headline machines are made by several manufacturers and they afford the user many benefits. First, the reproduction quality is excellent. Secondly, there is a wide selection of type styles available which can, on some of the machines, be reproduced in different weights, slants, and degrees of condensation or expansion.

4. There is at least one pantograph lettering machine that has been promoted in communications trade media. With the use of a single master, this machine can produce headline lettering in many sizes, and with any degree of forward or back slant. It can also be controlled to expand or condense the lettering.

   NOTE: With the exception of transfer lettering, which can be applied directly to the reproduction typed copy, all of the other methods must be trimmed and pasted into position with the text matter.

Combining Illustrations with Text

Drawings can be done right on the same paper as the text; however, this is usually impractical because artists prefer to work on different textures and weights of illustration board.

Most often, in the case of line drawings, it will be necessary to make reproduction glossy photostats to the required sizes and paste them into position in the text.

Since photostats do not reproduce tone gradations well, for wash drawings and photographs it is usually best to indicate size and position on the text art (in red outline) and have the printer shoot originals to required sizes and "strip" into position.

Captions and Footnotes

Captions and footnotes are usually done in a smaller size than text matter. When reproducing from typewritten copy, as with enlargements for headlines, reductions can be made with reproduction quality photostats. These, of course, are then pasted into position with the text copy.

Printer's type, Varitype and computer type can be set in the desired sizes without going through the step of making photostats.

When typing matter that will eventually be reduced (or enlarged) adjust width of typing proportionate to the subsequent change of size. It is well to bear in mind that when copy is reduced, the weight of the letters is also reduced making them lighter than might be desirable. It is suggested that this can be compensated for somewhat by over-typing each line two or three times.

Proofreading

After copy for reproduction has been completed, it must be carefully proofread by persons other than the author or typist.

· In addition to having an uninvolved individual proofread, the directly concerned executives (department heads) will want to proofread sections that pertain to them. The author should certainly proofread the finished copy at least once.

With all of this handling, it is necessary to protect the reproduction copy from smearing and smudging. Usually this is done by attaching a tissue paper covering sheet to the face of the copy with two pieces of transparent tape at the head. By using an artist's grade of thin, translucent tissue paper (available from commercial art supply stores), those who do the proofreading can mark their corrections and suggestions on the tissue, rather than damaging the reproduction copy. Another way that is frequently used to circulate copy for proofreading is to use office copies of originals.

Paper

The determination of the type of paper to use for handbooks depends upon the amount of abuse you expect pages to endure during their active life. Most such work is done on either 20 lb. sulphite bond or 50 lb. offset paper which, for our purposes, can be considered interchangeable. These papers have acceptable opacity for one or two-side reproduction and the right amount of bulk— neither being too thin nor too heavy.

If more durability is required, consider using 24 lb. ledger paper or 60 lb. offset paper. For still more durability, switch to 24 or 28 lb. rag content ledger paper, which has excellent strength and a fine reproduction surface.

For maximum strength at the binding edge, paper can be purchased with Mylar reinforcing on the punched side. This, of course, is rather expensive and is more difficult to feed on automatic machinery because of the added bulk of the Mylar on one side of the pile of sheets.

Best results in electrostatic copying are obtained with papers having a smooth surface. A toothy, or vellum finish will result in reading matter having unpleasant, ragged edges. Photo-offset, on the other hand, since it transfers images to the paper from a pliable rubber blanket, can print sharp and clean on practically any paper surface.

Tabbed Index Pages

Properly planned and used generously, tabbed index pages are most valuable to the person referring to a manual frequently. By making it easy to locate the information being sought, not only is time saved, but greater utilization of the manual is encouraged.

Insertable celluloid tabbed index pages are made commercially in several grades and are generally available with either five or eight clear or colored tabs to the set. The cost of the different grades depends upon the weight and quality of the base paper, which is usually a buff-colored ledger stock. The insertable blanks are provided in perforated strips so they can be handled in the typewriter. The cost per tabbed index page ranges between 6 cents and 15 cents a sheet according to size and quality. Standard sizes are: 8½ by 5½ inches, 9½ by 6 inches, 11 by 8½ inches, 11 by 17 inches. They are usually Mylar reinforced at the binding edge and have fused plastic tabs.

If your run of books is relatively large, and you have many tabbed index pages, it might pay to have them custom printed and die-cut— either with or without the tabs protected with plastic or Mylar lamination. There are companies that specialize in this type of work. Consult your reproduction manager or local printer—they should know the sources in your area.

Binding

The type of binding to use for your handbook is best determined by considering several factors that should influence the choice:

1. *Bulk*—number of total pages and whether they will be divided into separate manuals or not.

2. *Updating*—a manual that will require frequent updating of individual pages or small sections should have some type of looseleaf binding. The more frequent the changes, the easier it should be to remove and replace pages. If revisions will be major, and on a predetermined schedule, it may be better to use a more permanent binding and just replace the entire manual periodically.

3. *Quantity*—If your quantity is small, you will probably not want to use a custom made binder but will, instead, want to use a stock item. These can be customized by hot stamping, silk screening or by the attachment of labels. Decorating the spine (backbone) can be a problem. Stock looseleaf binders are now available with the entire front cover forming a transparent vinyl pocket in which can be inserted a page-sized cover design sheet.

In larger quantities, all kinds of custom designing can be done. If a looseleaf format is to be used, be sure your size and planned bulk conforms to available standard metals. If the looseleaf format is not required, you might consider using a plastic comb binding or a spiral metal binding. These are both practical for small or larger quantities. Plastic combs can be imprinted on the spine (backbone) which, in use, can be an advantage in selecting the correct manual from the shelf.

4. *Usage*—If the manual is to be carried around by a sales rep or serviceman, the size, bulk and weight should be kept within reasonable bounds. Certain types of bindings do not open flat; e.g.: side-wire stapled, post screw, Acco, etc. These are not recommended when the user of the manual will need both hands to work with while referring to the manual. Plastic comb bindings, although they are attractive, lie flat and bindings, although they are attractive, lie flat and are rather inexpensive, will not stand up to hard usage. Spiral bindings will stand up better but they tend to cut through unreinforced pages if used continually. Saddle-wire stitching lies flat and is probably the least expensive, nonlooseleaf method of binding.

Descriptions of Most Commonly Used Types of Bindings

Saddle-Wire Stitched—Staples go through from the spine of the cover to the center of the book. Pages must be printed in four page folios so one sheet can be folded in half to make four pages (two leaves). This low-cost type of binding lies flat but should not be used for books having more than 96 pages (48 leaves) plus cover.

Side-Wire Stitched—A low cost, nonlooseleaf method of binding thicker books whereby wire staples are driven from the front to the back of the book ¼ inch from the binding edge. Books as thick as ½ inch (or a bit more) can be done in this way. The staples can be driven through the front and back covers as well as the inside of the book, or staples can be concealed by pasting the cover on the back-bone after stitching the inside. Revisions can be made with correction labels. This type of binding will not readily lie flat and plenty of backbone margin should be allowed in laying out pages.

Plastic Comb—An attractive type of flat-opening binding that is so named because the plastic piece that serves as the binding medium has a row of "teeth." These are curled to secure pages by locking under the solid portion that forms the backbone. Combs, of which the backbone can be hot-stamped or silk screened, come in a variety of capacities from ⅛ to 1½ inches. In practice, the covers (front and back are separate pieces) and assembled inside pages are slot-punched in a special punching machine. The teeth of the comb are then opened on another machine where they are inserted into the holes in the pages. When released from the machine the teeth automatically curl up again and lock behind the backbone portion. Although not considered looseleaf, pages may easily be removed by tearing them out. New pages can be inserted by having them specially punched with slotted holes that have slit openings on the backbone side. A small, comb-like device is used to snap these pages into the binding. The disadvantage is that such replacement pages are too easily pulled out of the binding. Revisions can, of course, be made with labels.

Spiral Wire—Pages and two-piece covers are prepared similarly to plastic comb binding except that punching is a line of small round holes rather than slots. The spiral metal is driven through the series of holes by being spun on a machine that simultaneously holds everything in place while the wire winds its way through. Wire ends are crimped to prevent unwinding. Pages lie perfectly flat but are not looseleaf. Spiral wire is available in capacities from ¼ inch to 1 inch. It is a very strong binding but under hard use there may be a tendency for the pages to cut through at the holes. The only practical way to make revisions is to provide correction labels.

Loose-leaf—Metals for loose-leaf bindings come in many sizes and quality grades. Sizes run from ¼ inch capacity to as much as 3 inches; however, in the smallest sizes it is difficult to turn pages (unless punching is very close to the edge of pager), and in the largest sizes it is difficult to keep the rings closing properly. Ring metals are made with anywhere from two to eight rings—perhaps more, for special purposes. Less expensive metals are opened by pulling and pressing directly on the rings. Better metals have opening boosters on the ends. Still better metals have opening and closing boosters. Covers can be made either flexible or rigid and in any desired thickness. Backbones are done either flat or curved to conform to the shape of the metal. Curved is more attractive and more expensive. Metals are usually riveted to the backbone, with rivets being exposed on the less expensive binder and concealed in the better binder.

Stock binders are available in a wide assortment of colors and covering materials—cloth, vinyl, leatherette, embossed paper, plastic, etc. Some are made with insertable frames for titling on front covers and backbones. Others are made with the front cover having an overall clear vinyl pocket in which a title sheet can be inserted. All stock binders can be personalized by hot stamping or silk screening the front and back covers. Backbones are difficult to decorate on stock binders.

Custom covers for looseleaf binders can be obtained directly from manufacturers in relatively small quantities—as few as 100 binders. If you want a unique design, it is best to engage your own artist. In addition to the cost of the design, you will be required to pay for finished art and the dies or screens needed for the job. New heat-sealing techniques make it possible to laminate a preprinted design, permitting extreme latitude in creating your cover.

It is inadvisable to overload a looseleaf binder because it will be difficult to turn pages and messy to make changes in any part of the book other than the center. Also, overloading will place an undue strain on the metal causing it to misalign where the rings join.

Updating

As pages are revised, or new pages are added, the page numbering system is employed to locate the spot for the new or revised page. A revised page that merely replaces an old page will bear the same page number as the one it replaces.

To avoid the confusion that might arise from having page numbers repeated, code letters or numbers delineating each section should be combined with the page number. To illustrate:

A. Using a number code, sections would be numbered consecutively starting with "1." The page numbering of the first section would look like this: 1-1, 1-2, 1-3, 1-4, 1-5 . . . and so on; the second section: 2-1, 2-2, 2-3, 2-4, 2-5 . . . with each succeeding section handled similarly.

B. If preferred, an alphabetic code could be substituted for the numeric code. In this case the pages of the first section would be numbered: A-1, A-2, A-3, A-4, A-5 . . . the second section: B-1, B-2, B-3, B-4, B-5 . . . and so on.

To differentiate the replacement page from the old page, it is recommended that the replacement page be coded with its effective date on the bottom, in the corner closest to the binding edge.

When a revision requires more pages than the portion it replaces, ordinary consecutive numbering of the replacement pages would upset the pagination of the following pages of the section. To solve this problem, add a decimal to the extra pages being inserted. For instance, you have to insert four pages between pages 2-8 and 2-9—the new pages would be numbered 2-8.1, 2-8.2, 2-8.3, 2-8.4.

CHAPTER 20

FORMS DESIGN
AND CONTROL PRINCIPLES

CORRECTLY designed forms are a major factor contributing the *success* of office methods, systems and procedures. The prime objective of a forms control program is to effect economies in office operating procedures through proper design, construction, and application, and economical purchase or reproduction of business forms. Centralized control is essential to achieve these objectives. All new or revised forms should clear through a centralized forms control unit; and this unit should make periodic reviews to determine which forms are obsolescent, which should be discontinued and which should be revised.

The company should actually maintain a catalog of forms for control purposes. Forms should be assigned numbers and titles, and the catalogs should be maintained in alphabetic and numeric sequence. This catalog or manual should explain the use, routing and procedures related to the form. The forms should be indexed, and the index should contain the reference to the text, the form name and number.

The purposes of forms design are as follows:

1. Simplify

2. Standardize

3. Reduce paperwork involved in:
   Preparing
   Reading
   Analyzing
   Distributing
   Filing

4. Effect economies in:
   Printing
   Paper costs

5. Provide effective management control

The general principles of forms design are standard design as far as practicable for:

1. Lines
2. Spaces
3. Columns
4. Type styles
5. Sizes
6. Placement of specific items.

Forms Design Principles

Before attempting to design a form, the data should be considered logically. Every form can be broken down into its major categories of data. Usually, the form can be organized into this sequence of data, as follows:

Now, it is possible to consider each requirement in terms of category and location.

Top of Form

Form Identification (Title and form number)
Introduction (Origin, addressee, date)
Body (Main section of form)
Instructions (Use and routing)
Conclusion (Signatures, approvals)

Bottom of Form

1. Make the form easy to follow:

   a. The sequence of data should be logical. The top-to-bottom analysis format above facilitates this.

   b. The sequence of the items should correspond to the source and subsequent transcription records. However, where this is not compatible with "a" above, determine the sequence which reduces the clerical effort the most and use it.

   c. Make the important items stand out by using larger or heavier printing, or emphasis lines.

   d. Make the data locations uniform on all forms. (For example, the form number should always appear in the same corner.)

   e. Group items, to permit user concentration on only one small area at a time.

   f. Don't crowd data. The exhibits discussed earlier are good illustrations of crowded and confused forms.

   g. The sequence should facilitate totalling and summarization.

2. *Plan for a continuous writing flow:*

   a. The sequence of items should provide for the continuous writing (and reading) from left to right and from the top to the bottom of the form.

   b. Group the items so that if there is more than one writing required, there can be a continuous writing of each set of items.

   c. Start each writing line at a common left-hand margin wherever possible.

   d. Arrange printed captions so as not to obstruct the line of writing.

   e. Locate the most frequently used items first.

3. *Sufficient and proper spacing:*

   a. Always allow ample space to accommodate the data.

   b. Vertical spacing:

     1) Manual spacing—usually ¼ inch for manual writing.

     2) Typewriter—usually ⅙ inch for a typewriter.

     3) Computer—Use forms layout paper provided by the manufacturer.

   c. Horizontal spacing:

     1) Manual spacing—Provide space to accommodate the average writer.

     2) Typewriter or other machine—10, 8 or 6 characters to the inch, depending upon the machine.

     3) Computer—Use the forms layout paper of the manufacturer.

4. *Minimize writing and space:*

   a. If sufficient space has been allowed and there are large areas of blank space, then the form may be too large.

   b. Maximize the use of preprinting and consequently reduce the amount of writing.

    c. Use a window envelope if mailing is involved.

    d. Use abbreviations, codes and contactions where their meaning will be clear to whoever must read the form.

5. *Facilitate routing and use of each part:*

    a. Identify each copy on its face. For example:

Sales Invoice

Copy 6—Shipping Copy

    b. Where subsequent writing is required:

      1) Arrange that part of the set together (example: first five copies).

      2) Provide carbons or NCR paper for duplicating subsequent writing.

    c. Eliminate written information from any copy on which it is not desired.

6. *Employ the most economical form size:*

    a. Eliminate unused areas of "dead" space.

    b. Limit length and width to a practical minimum.

    c. Use a standard size.

Chart of Form Sizes

3×5 inches	=	standard index card size
$3\frac{5}{8} \times 8\frac{5}{8}$ inches	=	standard size of bank checks
4×6 inches	=	large index card size
$4\frac{1}{4} \times 4\frac{1}{4}$ inches	=	standard size of production cards
5×8 inches	=	standard visible file size
$8\frac{1}{2} \times 7$ inches	=	short invoice size
$8\frac{1}{2} \times 11$ inches	=	standard letter size
$8\frac{1}{2} \times 14$ inches	=	standard legal size
$8\frac{1}{2} \times 17$ inches		

Standard printers' sheet = $17'' \times 22''$

Economical cutting sizes: two sheets = $11'' \times 17''$, four sheets = $8\frac{1}{2}'' \times 11''$. There is no waste.

7. *Identify the form:*

    a. The most logical initial requirement is forms identification. This includes the name and number of the form, which should be at the top, as follows:

SALES INVOICE   NO.

    b. Please note the serial number in the upper right-hand corner. This is the invoice number which will be used for filing (see next page) and is not a part of the forms identification.

8. Make judicious use of prenumbering:

   a. Prenumbering is an element of good internal control and allows for an accounting of the documents used. This is an excellent device, but should not be applied universally. (Should it be used for telephone messages?)

   b. Prenumbering requires an additional printing charge.

   c. Prenumbering should,conform to filing requirements.

9. Placement of filing information:

   a. If the form is to be filed and later looked for by name, date, etc., place that key information in a position on the form where it can be easily found.

   b. The best position is usually the upper right-hand corner since this is the most customary spot to look for that data. However, the filing device may be the controlling factor. (Visible index forms usually have controlling information on the bottom.)

   c. Carefully consider the filing data:

     1) Suppose there is a different requirement for active and inactive files. Employees' earnings cards may be used in department and employee number order for payroll preparation. However, terminated employees are most frequently referred to by name and Social Security Number. Even though there are more terminated employees, the active employees' records will be used more frequently for payroll preparation. Therefore, the employee number and department can be located in the upper right-hand corner:

Name	Soc. Sec. No.	Emp. No.	Dept.

Please note that all key items are contained on the top line.

10. Horizontal lines:

   a. ..... Light, single-dotted lines are the most desirable for general use.

   b. _____ Light, single, solid lines are generally used as guides.

   c. _____ Medium weight lines are used to break up sections of light lines.

   d. _____ Heavy weight lines are used for major breaks.

   e. ===== Double lines are used to break up a form into distinct sections. They are used to distinguish between major breaks and section breaks where the use of one kind or the other would be confusing. Also used for totals.

11. Vertical lines:

a. ┊ Light, single dash lines are used for minor segregations of columns, such as dollars and cents.

b. │ Light, single, solid lines are used for general vertical separations.

c. │ Heavy single lines are used as major column divisions.

d. ‖ Two vertical lines indicate a sectional break.

e. ‖‖ Three vertical lines indicate a major sectional break; where there are pairs of sections, each is separated by a double line.

12. Headings:

a. Examples

Poor Form

Employer	From	To	Title	Salary
Employer	From	To	Title	Salary
Employer	From	To	Title	Salary

Good Form

Employer	From	To	Job Title	Salary

Please note that there is less printing in the second format. Not only is the "box heading" more economical, but it facilitates forms preparation.

b. The ballot box saves on clerical effort where there is standard repetitive information.

☐ Single ☐ Married ☐ Divorced ☐ Widowed
☐ Children ☐ Number ☐ Number of dependent children

☐ Rent ☐ Own home ☐ Other_____

13. *Margins:*

   a. Binding margin—The marginal requirements for forms to be housed in binders affect only the binding side. The size of the margin depends upon the type of binder and the size, weight and number of sheets it will hold.

   1) Ring binder—Minimum of ⅝″ on binding side.

   2) Post binder—Minimum of 1¼″ on binding side.

   3) Binding fasteners—Minimum of 1¼″ on binding side.

   b. Reproduction margin—The marginal requirements vary with the method of reproduction. Seek the advice of the prospective printers; or if you are going to reproduce the forms on your own equipment, consult the manufacturer.

14. *Hole-punching:*

   a. For post binders:

   1) $\frac{5}{16}$″ diameter posts:
   Distance from center to center of each post:

   > 6⅜″
   > 7⅛″
   > 8¼″

   2) ⅜″ diameter posts:
   Distance from center to center of each post:

   > 2¾″
   > 4¼″
   > 7″
   > 9″

   3) $\frac{3}{16}$″ diameter posts:
   Distance from center to center of each post:

   > 2¾″
   > 4¼″
   > 7″

   b. For ring binders:

   1) 2-ring binders:

Sheet Size	Distance Between Posts
8½ × 5½″	4¼″
9 × 6″	8½″

    2) 3-ring binders:

Sheet Size	Distance Between Posts
8½ × 5½"	5½"
9½ × 6"	7"
11 × 8½"	8½"

    3) 4-ring binders:

       14½ × 8½" sheets, with 10½" distance between posts.

  c. Prong-type fasteners:

Sheet Size	Distance Between Posts
	End Fasteners
5½ × 8½"	2¾"
7 × 8½"	4¼"
6 × 9½"	2¾"
8½ × 11"	2¾"
8½ × 11"	4¼"
8½ × 14"	2¾"
8½ × 14"	4¼"
9½ × 12"	4¼"
11 × 14"	8½"
11 × 17"	8½"

Sheet Size	Distance Between Posts
	Side Fasteners
5½ × 8½"	5½"
9½ × 6"	7"
11 × 8½"	8½"
12 × 9½"	8½"
14 × 8½"	8½"
17 × 14"	8½"

15. *Choice of paper qualities:*

  a. Sixteen-pound white sulphite paper can be considered the average weight and quality paper for most forms. The range of paper qualities as compared to this standard is as follows:

Content and Quality	Weight	Relative Cost to Standard
25% rag, durable high quality	20 lbs.	150% of Standard

Content and Quality	Weight	Relative Cost to Standard
25% rag	16 lbs.	137% of Standard
Sulphite, heavier than average	20 lbs.	120% of Standard
Sulphite, tissue paper weight	11 lbs.	80% of Standard

b. Number of carbon copies available:

Weight	Pencil	Business Machine	Electric Typewriter
5 lbs.	-	12–14	16–18
7 lbs.	5–6	8–10	12–14
9 lbs.	4–5	6–8	9–12
12 lbs.	4	6–7	7–9
13 lbs.	3	4–5	6–8
16 lbs.	2	3–4	5–7
20 lbs.	1	2–3	4–5

(For computers, consult the manufacturer.)

16. Reverse printing:

   a. Reverse printing is negative copy (opposite to normal) with white characters against a dark background of solid color. It is used in forms design to attract attention. Text and characters having a dark background stand out over the rest of the copy on a sheet. It can be used as a substitute for two-color ink printing, which will reduce the printing cost.

Printing

Knowledge of the method of printing may save money. Some large printers have two prices for the same form. There is one price if it is a custom job. There may be 15% to 18% savings if the job conforms to printer's standards of color, size, construction, etc. The reason for this is that a printer can combine in one run unrelated forms for different customers if all conform to the same standards.

Price discounts are usually allowed for increased quantities up to a certain maximum. However, one must be careful not to overstock. A six-month supply generally is adequate.

There are large and small printers. Some of the large national printers have design assistance specialists, national forms libraries, large research and development efforts and a variety of quality papers and carbons. They can provide assistance in forms design and in the selection of papers and carbons. Three of the large national companies which provide these services are UARCO, Moore Business Forms and Standard Register. However, some of the small printers may also provide excellent service and can be very competitive on price. It is a good idea to seek out three printers for bids and compare their prices, services and quality.

One should keep in mind that the primary goal is to save on clerical work. This may be identical with saving on printing costs: but where it is not, there is usually a far greater return in clerical work savings than on savings on printing costs.

Forms Management

The initial step in a *forms control program* is to appoint someone to direct it. The next step is to give this person real authority and top management support.

How do you select someone for this job? If you are not large enough to be able to afford hiring an experienced individual, you can select someone from your own ranks. This will be a "part-time" job for this person, but certain qualifications are worth considering:

1. Familiarity with office paperwork routines.
2. Possession of good common sense.
3. Capable of commanding respect.
4. Willing to learn.
5. Some measure of "tough-mindedness."

What benefits are provided by such forms control?

1. Elimination of duplication of forms currently in use and avoidance of such duplication in the future. Sometimes, without central control, "the right hand doesn't know what the left hand is doing." Now, the forms coordinator is equipped with the tools to eliminate or avoid costly duplications.
2. There is now a source reference which shows all permanent and temporary locations of each form. One benefit is that it is now possible to determine which copies and routes are essential. Another benefit is that it is now possible to determine what is required to secure the maximum standardization of form sizes to minimize the variety of storage devices.
3. Another benefit is that it is now possible to evaluate record retention practices, seek legal advice on outside requirements and minimize storage space requirements.
4. The forms analysis sheets also show the relationships between forms (records, etc.) which can be used as a basis for simplification.

FORMS DESIGN AND CONTROL PRINCIPLES

Form No. 157

FORMS ANALYSIS SHEET
(Attach Form)

Title of form _____ No. _____

System used in _____

Purpose _____

_____

What department originates? _____

Source for preparation (give form nos.) _____

_____

This form is transcribed to (give form nos.):

_____   _____

_____   _____

_____   _____

Form size _____   Used per month _____   Per year _____

Used: Internal ____   External ____   Standard form? ____   Designed _____

How prepared? (Manual, kind of machine, etc.) _____

_____

Prepared daily _____   Weekly _____   Monthly _____

Routing (briefly describe how department uses - Use more than one line if req.)

Copy	Department	Where filed
____	_____	_____
____	_____	_____
____	_____	_____
____	_____	_____
____	_____	_____
____	_____	_____
____	_____	_____
____	_____	_____
____	_____	_____
____	_____	_____
____	_____	_____
____	_____	_____

Interrelated forms or reports? _____

_____

Have the actual users been consulted for suggested improvements, additional
requirements and possible eliminations? _____

Are the copies reproduced clearly? _____

Are there written instructions for preparing this form? _____

Comments: _____

_____

_____

Prepared by_____ Date_____ Approved by_____ Date_____

171

503

OFFICE ADMINISTRATION HANDBOOK

At this point, he or she should check the forms catalog for possible duplications or for the possibility of consolidation with existing forms. This is the focal point of control and at this time it is essential to determine:

1. The degree of need.
2. Economy in and simplicity of design.
3. Number of copies required.
4. Does the form satisfy all parties which will be involved with it?

This same control should be exercised over the reorder of existing forms. A requisition form should be used for this purpose. Any standard requisition form can be employed.

Computer Reports

A computer can generate reams of paper every day. There is a continuous need to determine what reports are required and/or being used. Therefore, forms management should include computer reports. The control functions should be exercised outside of the jurisdiction of the computer department.

It is not only essential to consider these reports when they are introduced, but their utility should be evaluated at least every six months.

The same principles of paperwork simplification apply to computer generated reports as for manual ones.

CHAPTER 21

HOW TO ORGANIZE
AN EXECUTIVE FILE

WELL-organized executive files—the recorded memory of the executive's activities—stand as an all-important source of reference which contains information on when, what, and why actions took place. Even though an executive secretary can spend more time on the preparation of correspondence than on filing, the letters are of little value unless they can be found when needed—along with all related material.

Poorly-organized files assure that time will be wasted, and that both executive and secretary will endure frustration at a time when there is a job to be done by both. Some secretaries rely on their memories as the foundation for a filing system, but this is a hazardous practice not only because a person's memory is not infallible, but because a secretary can be, and is, absent at one time or another. Retrieving information under this circumstance may be practically impossible.

An executive's file can be defined as the records made or received in the performance of various duties. This is a formal, not a practical, definition, since it does not cover all the material in the file. In many cases the files contain personal material such as insurance data, tax data, and even some social or organizational activities. Since this material does exist, it must be provided for just as correspondence and records are maintained.

Executive files can be considered as personalized in that they serve an individual with a specific position. When the person leaves or is promoted, the files stay to serve a successor. Much of what is in the files are definitely a part of the records of the company and do not belong to the executive (except for personal papers). This means they are a part of any records management program. The fact that such files are of comparatively small volume and accessible to only a few people does not preclude the need for using the same basic principles and sound practices in organizing them as for files generally. In a well-operated records program there are standard practices for executive files as well as for others. Records programs of any kind, let alone well-operated ones are rare, however, and more often than not it is up to the office administrator to organize executive files.

The basic plan which is presented here can be adapted to serve practically any executive, even those in a special or technical field. In fact, the activity of an executive is usually in a specialized area of work—accounting, personnel, sales, etc.—and the file will reflect this specialty.

Sometimes there is a problem about what records should be kept and what should be sent to the central files. The general rule is that what concerns the company as a whole—dealings with vendors, customers, etc.—belong in central or department general files. *Only those records created and received by an executive which relate to the specific work and position should be kept in the office.* No hard and fast rules can be set that will be suitable for all companies, but there should be an understanding as to what is, or is not, to be kept in the executive files. Once this is established, the next task is to review the file material and organize it according to the plan presented.

FILE SERIES

The first step in organizing a file is to gain an understanding of what kind of material it contains. The contents of an executive file usually is of three main types—correspondence, reference material, and extra copies. Sometimes there are other items such as reports, laboratory tests, etc. but these are the exception rather than the rule.

The three types mentioned—correspondence, reference material, and extra copies—are usually used separately and for different purposes, nor do they fit into the same filing arrangement. Each type should be filed in a way which will make it readily available. The initial task then, is to separate the file material into these three categories and work out a filing plan for each one.

Correspondence File

The heart of an executive's file is the correspondence which consists of memorandums and letters written both to other members of the company and outsiders. Included is a variety of material from trivia—luncheon dates, hotel reservations, requests for a copy of something etc.,—to very important matters.

A unique (and troublesome) factor is that some of the material is nearly always asked for by the name of the correspondent and some by subject. The filing plan recommended provides for this dual reference. It is a combination of subject and name filing which is easy to operate both for filing and finding.

Encyclopedic Plan

Filing plans recommended for executive files are usually based on an encyclopedic arrangement starting with general subjects and sub-dividing them into more specific ones. Sometimes numbers are also used. A brief example of an encyclopedic plan is as follows:

100	Accounting
101	Budget
107	Travel
200	Administrative Services
202	Files
205	Mail
207	Office Supplies
209	Typewriters
300	Personnel
307	Vacations
308	Work Hours
400	Production
403	Formulae
406	Marketing
408	Time Studies
500	Sales
502	Distribution

For an encyclopedic arrangement an index is needed, such as:

Accounting	100
Administrative Services	200
Budget	101
Distribution	502
Files	202
Formulae	403
Mail	205
Marketing	406
Office Supplies	207
Personnel	300
Production	400
Sales	500
Time Studies	408
Travel	107
Typewriters	209
Vacations	307
Work Hours	308

This system is difficult to set up both in determining the main subjects and their subdivisions. It is also difficult to make it flexible enough to allow for growth and change.

A file should never be more complicated than is necessary to provide for the organization of material for retrieval. In the suggested encyclopedic plan, the numbers serve no real purpose and there is nothing to be gained by grouping the material into large divisions and then breaking it down into smaller subjects. This, in effect, constitutes an indirect filing system because either one must use the index to find a specific item, or memorize the file pattern. A file should never be set up which *requires* the use of memory. Use does cause the person to remember where items are, but it should not be a requirement. An efficient file plan provides direct access to material.

Dictionary Plan

Another plan is known as the dictionary plan which is an alphabetic arrangement of small subjects with no regard for their relationships. The index to the encyclopedic plan (minus the numbers) is an example of a dictionary arrangement. If carried too far it can lead to fragmentation, overlapping subjects and synonyms causing the same kind of material to be filed in more than one place and sometimes causing related material to be separated. A list of the subject headings used is necessary to have some kind of control in any subject file, but this plan still leaves a good deal to be desired.

Combination Plan

It is possible to combine the best features of both the encyclopedic and dictionary plans and create one which is more flexible and practical than either alone. No plan can be perfect, but it can be designed so that it provides a suitable place for all the material and is flexible enough to allow for both expansion and change. The combination plan also provides direct access without the use of memory because the headings will be filed in alphabetic sequence and the user can go directly to the item wanted. It is well to note that most references to a file are for specific items. The Reference file may be used for browsing, but not the Correspondence file. The simple alphabetic arrangement of subjects and names provides for speedy retrieval. The items are those used in the regular course of the work and there is no need to remember the arrangement because the alphabet is so well known that the knowledge of where to look is practically automatic.

Too much stress cannot be laid upon the need for flexibility. No business or organization is static; rather, they are dynamic and changes occur constantly. A filing plan to be successful must take this factor of change into consideration.

Codes

Some people feel that a subject file is not complete unless a numeric code is used, and that such codes make the records easier to file and find. The common mistake is to forget that the subjects must be worked out in words first. Numbers by themselves can do nothing to make the file any more logical.

The use of a numeric code is not recommended because the subjects which are in words must be translated into numbers and this adds to the work. Besides, a numeric code flexible enough to allow for changes and expansion is not easy to work out, and using it will add to the operating cost of the executive file.

Filing Plan for Correspondence

This series contains both internal and external correspondence. For correspondence with other departments, the preferred arrangement is by the name of the department or unit with no regard for the organizational structure. To set it up according to the organization chart requires more effort to learn the sequence and also more care to maintain because the names of departments are changed, divisions are dropped or combined which cause changes in the arrangement of the folders as well as the labels. A minimum of change is required in an alphabetic arrangement.

It is a general rule that names of persons are not used as file headings. People change more frequently than position titles or names of companies.

It is advisable to have some general alphabetic folders for single items. When there are five pieces of correspondence for a company, an individual folder should be made. How many general folders are made will depend upon the volume. The number can be increased as required. If the volume of correspondence is small, some letters can be combined, e.g., A–E, F–L, M–R, S–Z.

Correspondence with outside companies and individuals with whom the executive has dealings should be set up in a separate section in alphabetic sequence by the name of the company if the volume is great enough. Otherwise it could be filed together under "Correspondence Outside." Some individual's names might be included such as lawyers, consultants, etc. As in other sections there should be one of more alphabetic folders to take care of the single items, e.g., CORRESPONDENCE OUTSIDE A–E, M–Z.

Subject Heading List for a Correspondence File

A–B

Accounting Department

Advertising Department

Applications: Also see Personnel Applications

Associations and Societies, General Alphabetically by name

Board of Directors

Branch Offices—General

    Boston General

      Budget

      Expense Accounts

      Monthly Reports

(A set of folders like this for each branch office).

Budget

Buildings and Grounds

C–E

Committees General Alphabetically by name

Conferences and Conventions: Also see Name of sponsoring group under Associations and Societies

Contracts and Agreements

Correspondence Outside A–L M–Z

Credit Department

Data Processing Department

Duplicating Section, General Requisitions

Expense Accounts

F–L

Foreign Trade Division

Forms

Furniture and Fixtures

Insurance: Also see Personnel, Health and Medical Insurance

Investments

Leases, General

    Property

    Vehicles

Legal Department

Licenses and Permits

M–R

Mailing Lists

Memberships: Also see Associations and Societies

Offices Services Department—General

    File Dept.

    Mail Sect.

    Telephone Serv.

Organization Charts

Patents and Trademarks

Permits: Also see Licenses and Permits

Personal Matters

Personnel—General

Applications (If there is enough material, break it down by positions)

    Health and Medical Insurance

    Labor Relations

    Leaves and Vacations

    Pensions

    Profit Sharing

    Unemployment Compensation

    Wages and Salaries

President's Office

Price Lists

Publications

Purchasing Department—General

    Purchase Orders

    Requisitions

Reports—General

    Annual

S–Z

Safety Section

Sales Department

Secretary's Office

Seminars and Workshops

Suggestion System

Taxes—General

    City

    Federal

    State

Workshops: Also see Seminars and Workshops

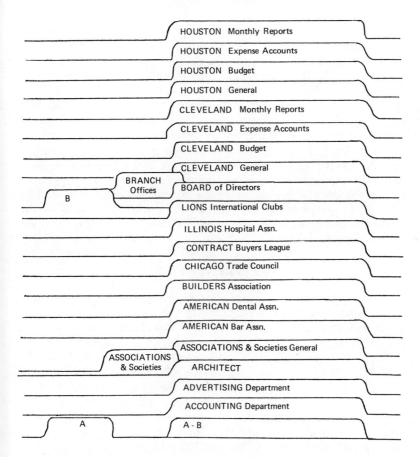

HOUSTON Monthly Reports

HOUSTON Expense Accounts

HOUSTON Budget

HOUSTON General

CLEVELAND Monthly Reports

CLEVELAND Expense Accounts

CLEVELAND Budget

CLEVELAND General

BRANCH Offices

B

BOARD of Directors

LIONS International Clubs

ILLINOIS Hospital Assn.

CONTRACT Buyers League

CHICAGO Trade Council

BUILDERS Association

AMERICAN Dental Assn.

AMERICAN Bar Assn.

ASSOCIATIONS & Societies General

ASSOCIATIONS & Societies

ARCHITECT

ADVERTISING Department

ACCOUNTING Department

A

A - B

No attempt has been made to provide a comprehensive list of subject headings. Rather, a sample list has been given which contains most of the common terms and which can be enlarged or adapted to the special needs of the file.

EXTRA COPY FILE

In working with an executive, it is not unusual for a secretary to have a supply of extra copies of reports, pamphlets, speeches, directives, etc., to fill requests. This material is apt to be bulky and vary in size from small leaflets to oversize reports so that a legal size file is best to house them. The drawers should be equipped with some kind of additional support such as dividers attached to the bottom of the drawer, pressboard or hanging folders, etc., to keep the material upright and in good condition. Generally these items will not take more than a drawer or two.

The best way for the secretary to arrange this material is first by size—small leaflets and booklets, letter size items, legal size—and then alphabetically by title. In the case of reports, it may be necessary to arrange them by date if they are issued periodically, e.g., Sales Reports Jan. 19—, Feb. 19—, etc. How fine the breakdown will be will depend upon their frequency and volume. It is rare that there would be a supply for computer printouts, but if so, special equipment would be required to house them.

An Extra Copy file can easily become a collection of obsolete items unless it is systematically cleaned out. One way is to have your secretary check the file every six months and remove obsolete material. Another way is to indicate the period the material should be kept either on the folder or the first copy and weed it out as the file is used. An occasional check would remove any items which had been overlooked.

REFERENCE FILE

Reference material is information received primarily from outside the company on subjects pertinent to the work or interests of the executive. It is usually composed of a miscellany of leaflets, pamphlets, magazine articles, newspaper clippings, and reports. Since its use and content are different from correspondence, it should be kept separately.

Some guide lines should be set on the kind of material which should go into the file. Too many times the Reference file is a conglomeration of items the secretary does not know what to do with and is afraid to throw out. The executive may be helpful in making such decisions, but frequently he or she is too busy, or does not want to be bothered. Nevertheless some decision must be made and it is wise to record the guidelines or criteria for retaining items in the manual.

In setting up the file it is necessary to become acquainted with their content. While scanning them, it would be advisable to jot down tentative subject headings. At this time it also should be possible to weed out extra copies, obsolete items and those obviously of little value. The subjects will be derived from the material, itself, and the same principles will apply as in choosing headings for the other file series. (See Mechanics, Subject Headings)

Just how much effort should be expended on setting up and maintaining the file will depend on: •

1. The content of the items; whether they are technical, general, etc.
2. The physical form of the items, such as leaflets or articles on one subject or larger items covering several subjects.
3. How much they are used and by whom. If not only the executive but also associates and other people refer to them frequently, it may be necessary to have an index or a finer breakdown of subjects. If they are referred to only occasionally, then broader subjects will suffice.

Whatever, it will require a list of the subject headings used with provision for expansion and change.

FOLLOW-UP FILE

Every secretary needs some way of reminding the boss of things to be done at a future date. In some cases a notation on a calendar is sufficient. In others, a more elaborate arrangement is required.

Making an extra copy of a letter in a distinctive color and filing it chronologically by the future date of consideration is one way of establishing a Follow-Up file. If the volume is not great, an Everyday file kept on the desk is sufficient to file such copies in. If the volume is greater, then a series of date folders set up in a file drawer would be better.

It is not advisable to put the supporting correspondence in the Follow-Up file as it may be needed for some other purpose. The better practice is to leave it in its proper place in the file and put a notation on the follow up copy as to where it is. After the copy has served its purpose, it can be discarded.

Still another way to handle follow up material is to set up a card file chronologically with the necessary information on the cards to identify it. This is a good system when the supporting records are kept in the central files and must be requested by using a charge slip. The charge slip, itself, can be used as the follow up form.

The Follow-Up file can become a valuable means of adding to the efficiency of an executive office. What form it will take is up to the secretary who should be able to determine whether a card, charge slip, extra copy, or just a notation on the calendar will serve best.

OTHER FILES

Sometimes an executive has a special responsibility, such as issuing quotations or a special kind of report and the volume is large enough to warrant setting up a separate file series. Segregating such material allows for it to be arranged in a sequence best suited for its use without interfering with any other part of the file.

Today an executive may receive computer print outs which are bulky and of an odd size. The first requirement is to determine if they should be kept long enough for filing. Frequently the print outs contain current information and can be discarded in a short time. Usually a Reference copy is available elsewhere which can be consulted if necessary. If they must be kept, however, suitable space must be provided. Exactly what this will be is dependent on their size and volume.

Although in general it is best not to establish too many separate file series, still usage and volume dictate that different types of material should be segregated for better control and reference. What is important is to define each file series so that it does not overlap another one. Many times one kind of material is filed with two or three others for no particular reason except that no plan for the files has ever been thought out. They have "just grown."

Some extra copies are found filed with correspondence and reference material as well as some being filed separately. Reference items and correspondence are sometimes filed together under a vague heading, such as "Planning" and other reference items lumped together under "Resource Material." Such practices lead to inefficient files with memory playing the major role in retrieval. By the establishment of separate and clearly defined file series for each basic type of material, these practices which foster confusion can be eliminated.

FILE MECHANICS

Subject Headings

In describing both the Correspondence and Reference files, it was stated that material would be asked for by subject. Choosing suitable subjects as file headings requires a knowledge of the principles of word arrangement which are applicable to all types of material.

Subjects should be chosen which are concise, accurately descriptive, technically correct, and of as few words as possible. The most suitable term is a concrete plural noun—Vacations, Unions, etc.—but not all items can be described so simply.

Compound nouns or combined terms are useful headings for keeping all material in an area of information together, e.g.

Timekeeping and Payroll
Licenses and Permits

Sometimes a noun and adjective or even a short phrase is the most accurately descriptive, e.g.

Office Machines
Crossing Guards
Cost Accounting
Estimating Formulae for Maintenance

A sentence or long phrase should never be used because it is difficult to read and file, and usually too limited in scope.

If there are several aspects of a subject, it is preferable to put the noun first and follow it with an adjective, e.g.

Taxes: General
County
Federal
Municipal
State

Such an arrangement will keep all tax matters together. If they were written with the adjective first—County Taxes, Federal Taxes, etc., the information on taxes would be fragmented and filed in different places. The term "General" is used on the first folder when a subject is subdivided. It is for the purpose of providing a place for material which does not fit into any of the subdivisions of the subject.

It takes practice to choose suitable headings. Some thought must be given to finding exact terms and also to put them in the proper sequence for filing. The first word should be the one the folder will be filed under. For example, if a folder headed "Unsold Type B Cars" were filed under "Unsold," it probably never would be found. Examination would show that "Cars" is really the subject. The heading should be rearranged to read: "Cars Type B Unsold."

Nothing should be put into a folder that is not on that subject. Sometimes an item is filed under a related heading and then is forgotten. Even if a folder is made for one sheet of paper, it is preferable to do that to ensure its retrieval. If there are too many instances of a single sheet in a folder, something is wrong with the choice of headings.

Another factor to consider in choosing headings is the point of view. It should be consistent. For example, if headings were being assigned to describe information on furniture, they could be grouped by function:

Bedroom	by item:	Beds
Dining Room		Chairs
Kitchen		Tables

or by material:
    metal
    plastic
    wood

Mixing these points of view would cause an overlapping and no clear cut headings:

Wrong:	Wrong:
Chairs	Chairs, Plastic
Dining Room	Metal
Living Room	Tables
Sofa Beds	Wood

Correct:	Correct:
Beds:	Sofas
Metal	
Wood	Tables:
Chairs:	Metal
Metal	Plastic
	Wood

These are obvious errors. Some changes in point of view are more subtle and harder to detect, e.g.

    Safety Driving Rules
        Goggles
        Hats
        in Shop Work
        Shoes

In this list of headings both practices and items are included. A more logical grouping would be:

Safety Equipment	Safety Practices
General	General
Goggles	Driving Rules
Hats	Shop Work
Shoes	

If there are similar headings for a group of subjects, a pattern of subdivisions can be used. e.g. If there are branch offices, the same headings should be used for each one for the same kind of material.

Name of Office

General	Expense Accounts
Budget	Monthly Reports

Subjects may also be divided by: Date: Sales Reports General

Jan.–June

July–Dec.

Name: Associations General

American Management Association

Chicago Bar Association

National Dairy Council

or other suitable groupings.

If necessary, terms should be defined so that they will be clearly understood as was done in the sample list for the Correspondence File.

The choice of subjects also depends upon how the material is asked for. Terms commonly used in the business can be used, but trick or nicknames should be avoided.

Example: DoubleTruck Orders. Double Truck is an advertising term used for a center double page spread in newspapers, and is a suitable heading.

Big Mary Repairs. "Big Mary" is the nickname for the Statue of the Republic in Jackson Park, Chicago, Illinois, and is an unsuitable heading.

Although executive files usually do not include technical material, if there are such items and a choice has to be made between technical and common terms, the common ones are preferred unless the file is used exclusively by professional people, and they insist on their own jargon, or the executive does.

Control of Subject Headings

No subject file can operate successfully without a list of subject headings, for a control. The list will help avoid using synonyms, overlapping subjects, and more than one folder for the same subject. An active file is constantly growing and so must be controlled.

As the subjects are chosen, they should be written on a list, two columns to a page, so that as many subjects can be seen as possible at one time. This makes it easier to spot irregularities. When the list has been completed, it should be typed double spaced so that there is room to add new headings. If the file includes a section of names, such as associations, it is not necessary to list each name, but the section should be indicated, e.g.

Correspondence Outside—See this section for companies and organizations on which there is correspondence.

One thing to remember is that the list is for use and notations, definitions, or any other information which will aid in using the file should be added to it. To be of the greatest value, the list should be kept up to date and no new subject folder added without the heading being entered on the list. From time to time the list should be scrutinized for inconsistencies. They will occur even though care is used to avoid them. The only way to correct them is to spend some time looking for them. The list should also be retyped to keep it easy to read whenever it becomes cluttered with additions and changes.

Cross References

Since the English language abounds in synonyms, there are choices to be made of subjects. Sometimes more than one term is used to refer to the same thing, therefore, cross references should be included on the list to show under which term the records are filed. A "See" reference means "Nothing here, look under the subject indicated." A cross reference can be used to indicate:

Change of name or terms—Human Relations See: Community Relations.

The heading used when there is a choice: Automobiles See: Motor Vehicles.

Which form of a subject is used: Income Taxes See: Taxes Income.

Referencing part of a heading to the full one: Valves See: Pumps & Valves.

The cross references should be included in the list of subject headings and if properly used, will eliminate the need to remember a lot of details besides making retrieval easier.

Sometimes the records are filed under two subjects which are related—not enough to be put together, but enough so that it would be helpful to know that the other records exist, e.g.

Traffic Accident Prevention Also See: Safety Practices Driving

This type of cross reference means "Something here, something under the other subject also." It is put both on the list and on the folder label as a direction.

If only a single item is involved and related items are filed in different folders because of other considerations, a notation can be made on the item itself, referring to an item in another folder. With the current easy access to copy machines, a copy can be made and filed under another heading. The danger in this practice is in filling up the file with extra papers. It can become an expensive use of space.

If an item is filed in a folder other than the one where one would expect to find it, a cross reference sheet can be made out as follows:

CROSS REFERENCE SHEET

File: Heading under which this sheet will be filed.
See: Folder heading where the item, itself, is filed.
Re: Brief description and date of item.

Examples

File: Duplicating Section
See: Office Services
Re: Budget for 19— Dec. 14, 19—
File: Adamson, James B.
See: Johnson, Robert R. (Lawyer)
Re: Accident at 35th and Racine on June 10, 19—

This form would be on a letter size sheet usually of a distinctive color.

PREPARING MATERIAL FOR FILE

If a few things are done in preparing material for file, the filing will be faster and retrieval easier.

An accumulation of file material should be checked through and:

1. Paper clips removed and replaced with staples. Clips add to the bulk of the file, slip off, and catch on other papers. If there is a need to separate the papers later, they can be stapled "open end."

2. Letters and replies as well as related items stapled together.

3. File headings underlined, checked, or written out so that they are easily seen. This will ensure that if an item is pulled, it will be refiled in the same folder. It is here that the subject heading list is of value because it is possible to settle the questions of where an item is to be filed by referring to the

list and finding a suitable heading without going to the file. Also, if it is decided to add a new heading, it can be done in the context of those already in existence. This will avoid creating duplicate or overlapping headings.

4. Cross reference headings marked and cross reference sheets prepared.
5. The material sorted into the different file series and fine sorted into the sequence of the headings within the series.
6. Items for the Follow-Up file checked for the come-up date.

The manual should be kept handy for reference to settle questions. This is when the manual will prove its worth.

FILING RULES

The best results in filing can be obtained by following a few rules consistently.

1. File the most recent papers in the front of the folder. Requests usually are for the latest material and it will be easier to find if it is in front.
2. In removing papers from the file, pull the folder up, but do not remove it. Folders are easily misfiled and sometimes are misplaced.
3. Charge out any material that is taken out of the office. Do not try to remember such details.
4. Follow these rules of alphabetic arrangement:
    a. Each part of a name or heading is considered as a separate unit. The last name is considered first, then the first name, and then the middle initial or name.
    b. All the letters of the first unit should be considered before going to the next one, e.g.
        1. Adam John R
        2. Adam Joseph
        3. Adam Joseph B
        4. Adam Joseph Bert
        5. Adams Anthony
    c. One of the best general rules to follow is "nothing before something." This is illustrated by the sequence of names, 2, 3, and 4 in the example given above.
    d. The same rules apply to filing subjects. There is one difference though, and that is, if a subject is subdivided, the

first folder is the "General" one even though the headings which follow it may start with a letter which precedes G alphabetically, e.g.

Furniture General, Design, Display

5. Type the folder labels in a uniform manner which will make the filing and finding easier because the eye quickly learns to seek the units and match them with the mental image you have of the heading you are looking for.
6. Use a different color label for the alphabetic folders so that they will stand out.
7. File *behind* the guides placing the folders in back of the proper guide.
8. Label the file drawers accurately.
9. In the manual list the filing rules you follow so that you will be consistent in your practices.

DRAWER ARRANGEMENT

The arrangement of guides and folders in a drawer or shelf can be clear, easy to read, and facilitate finding a specific item, or it can be cluttered, hard to read and make retrieval a laborious process.

Generally one guide for every ten folders is adequate. The guides should be in one or two positions and the folders all in the same position with a two-fifths or one-third cut.

A set of alphabetic guides purchased from a stationer is usually in five staggered positions which are hard to read. Besides, the material for some letters is heavier than for others. Because of the individualized plan of using both names and subjects, it is best to use blank guides with insertable tabs and label them to fit the file. Special headings can be made for certain subjects and as the file changes or enlarges, guides can be added or labels changed as needed.

The fewer positions used, the faster the file can be read because the eye will not have to zigzag from one side of the drawer to another. The unused space allows the eye to glance at the drawer and immediately see the section wanted; then to read down the tabs in a straight line.

It is possible to type directly on the folder or use folder labels. In either case, a standardized pattern of typing the labels should be established, i.e. The first word of the folder label should be typed in upper case starting three spaces from the left hand edge and one space from the top no matter how long or short the heading. The edge of the folder should be considered the same as the margin on a sheet of paper. Following this practice means that the eye can always focus on the same spot to read a label. The first word, which is in caps, will stand out. The rest of the heading should be in upper and lower case for contrast.

If labels are used, a different color can be used each year. Color can also be used to indicate different types of material. If color is used, however, it should mean something to add to the efficiency of the file.

EQUIPMENT

Cabinets

The standard four drawer file has dominated the market for so long that it is usually the first type that comes to mind. Today, however, there are other types which are more suitable for an executive office. Lateral files which open from the side frequently have roll-out drawers and come in a variety of colors. They fit into any office decor and are becoming increasingly popular. Usually they fit better into the space of a private office or secretarial area taking less space to use and providing greater accessibility.

In purchasing a file there are several things to look for:

1. Sturdy construction—can the cabinet be moved and still stay rigid?
2. Do the drawers move easily? Are they on rollers or a track?
3. What kind of supports are there to hold the material erect—compressors which slide or vertical dividers which hook into slots? Can they be moved easily and do they provide sufficient support to keep the folders from sliding?
4. Is the finish baked on and thick enough to withstand ordinary wear without chipping or scratching?

Such matters should be considered if new equipment is being purchased. If what is on hand is to be used, then particular attention should be paid to the use of guides and folders to provide easy access.

Certain rules to safety should be followed:

1. Always allow three to four inches of work space in the drawer of a vertical file to avoid tugging at the folders.
2. Do not overcrowd the drawer or shelf. Trying to file or retrieve from an overstuffed one is fatiguing and often causes broken fingernails and paper cuts.

3. Never pull out more than one drawer at a time from a vertical file. It can tip over.

Guides and Folders

Conventional guides and folders will give good service if properly set up as discussed under "Drawer Arrangement." There are also hanging folders which will fit into a standard file drawer. They hang on rails and the natural force of gravity pulls them down so no compressors or other mechanisms are necessary to hold them erect. They move easily on the rails and the movement of papers in and out of the folders is accomplished with little difficulty. Their disadvantage is that they take up more space than conventional folders. Tabs can be affixed in any position. They can be purchased blank or with ready made inserts and in color.

Sometimes an executive file is so active that manila folders will not stand up under the wear. A heavier duty paper-kraft—will give this service. Another type of folder is pressboard which is rigid and has a reinforced linen gusset at the bottom for expansion. The pressboard folders will keep bulky items in good condition and they will hold more than other folders.

It is surprising how many people do not notice the lines scoring the bottom of a manila or Kraft folder. They can be creased to allow for expansion so that the bottom of the folder is flat and it will remain upright. A folder should not contain more than one inch of material which is the width allowed by the last scored line.

Good equipment properly used adds to the ease of filing, but it does not solve the problems of classification and arrangement. Their solution requires the application of the principles previously discussed.

RETENTION

Not every company has a records management program which means that there is no plan for the regular disposal of records. If this is the case, then the individual secretary should be asked to set up her own schedule in collaboration with the executive she serves. An annual purging is necessary to get rid of the trivia and retain those records needed for reference.

If there is sufficient drawer space, a two period transfer is suitable. With this plan the current year's correspondence is kept in the two middle drawers or shelves, and the previous year's in the bottom or top ones so that the most recent records are the most accessible.

There are three kinds of records included in the correspondence—namely:

1. Trivia—correspondence of ephemeral nature, such as luncheon dates, meetings, hotel reservations, requests for copies of reports, etc. which should be discarded. Weeding is expensive because of the time it takes and unless the items for destruction are marked so that they are easily recognized, it is better to retain them as long as the rest. For example, if "trivia" records were marked with a red "T" at the time of filing, they could be purged toward the end of the year at the same time that the regular filing was being done.

2. Records of a business nature which are ordinarily needed for another year for reference and are considered to be semi-active. Whether they should be retained longer is dependent upon the needs of the executive. If the retention period is being set for the first time, it is wise to allow extra storage time and decrease it as experience indicates how long a period the records are referred to frequently enough to warrant keeping them. The time should be watched closely, however, and records should not be kept an unreasonable period "just in case." One way to make a decision is to consider what problems would ensue if the records were not available. How badly would you be hurt? It is also probable that copies are being kept elsewhere which would be available, or that the information may be available from another source. The point is not to accumulate unnecessary records just because a decision must be made to discard them. A retention program can be considered to provide an opportunity to rid the files of "excess baggage."

3. Historical records which should be segregated so that they can be kept permanently. (This will be discussed more in detail under "Historical Records.")

When the transfer of records is actually made, the guides should be retained for the current file. The alphabetic folders can serve as guides for the transferred ones. Guides are expensive and it is extravagant to use them for transferred records.

A new set of individual and miscellaneous folders should be made for the current files. This is also the time to check on the charge outs to be sure that all borrowed records have been returned.

The Extra Copy file is self-clearing so that it will not have a retention period. This is also true of the Follow-Up file. The Reference file should not contain items for storage. Either the material is used for reference, or it is obsolete or of no value for other reasons and should be discarded. It is advisable to set a special time to check the Reference file for obsolete material so that it will be done as a routine task.

HISTORICAL RECORDS

Probably the most neglected area of record keeping is that of historical records—information which shows the history and development of the company. Few companies have an archivist, but that does not preclude the need for keeping historical records. "Many executives still depend entirely upon memory for a knowledge of their firm's experience with the result that mistakes are repeated, significant long-time developments escape notice, and rich opportunities are overlooked."*

How high the executive is in the company ranks will determine how important his or her correspondence is. All correspondence of senior executives with the exception of trivia should be kept permanently. "From no other source can be found the day to day problems and decisions, the formulation of policies and procedures, the clash of personalities, the ceaseless press of people and affairs demanding attention, the exercise of business judgment, and the opinions and reasons influencing business administration."

If the executive is of a lower rank and only selected items are to be kept, a separate series should be set up using the same headings as in the current files. As the historical records are transferred, a record of them should be kept in the manual. Either a separate list should be made, or there should be an indication on the regular list, e.g. PERSONNEL Union Matters (H1970–72 tr. 1/31/73).

As the file is used, historical items should be recognized and clearly marked. An "H" is sufficient. When transfer takes place, the items are easily recognized and can be added to the historical series.

The following guidelines are useful in determining those records which are of historical value. Those which:

1. Show a change in organization (creation of a new department, change in the name or function of a department, combination of some sections, etc.).
2. Describe the introduction of a new product or change in the design of a present one.
3. Tell of change in personnel. This will be important only in the top executive level.
4. Delineate changes in corporate structure—mergers, selling or closing part of the company's operation with resultant changes in organization, personnel, place of operation, or financing.
5. Record policy statements and goals.

---

*The Preservation of Business Records, Ralph M. Hower.

In addition the records kept should include:

- Biographical information on the executive and his or her employment record with the company, filed under the name of the position, i.e. SALES Manager, PERSONNEL Director, etc., with a cross reference from the name.
- Speeches given and articles written.
- Special reports prepared for top management or the Board of Directors.

An executive's files are an integral part of a firm's history, and some consideration should be given for their preservation.

MANUAL

Many problems of executive files exist not only because there is no filing plan, but also because day to day decisions are made on an individual basis as to where to file records without regards to the rest of the file. This practice frequently results in records on the same subject being filed in different places. For example, in a certain file union matters were considered a function of the Personnel Department and such material was filed: Personnel Department Unions. Later a new division, Labor Relations, was created which became responsible for union matters. A new folder was made without any reference to the previous one. A manual would have provided a place to record the name of the new division and a list of headings which could have been checked for related folders.

A manual helps to ensure consistent practices because, among other things, it provides a source of reference for previous decisions and as stated before, no filing plan should be based on memory.

The fact that a file is small does not preclude the need for a manual. Decisions must be made on file headings and how to handle special items in a small file as well as a large one. It helps to have these decisions in writing because it is surprising how quickly one can forget why a certain decision was made or that it was made at all.

Format

A manual is for use, not show, so its format should be practical. It should be typed double spaced with wide margins to allow room for notes and changes. It is best kept in a looseleaf binder so that new information can be added and individual sections revised. Each revision should be dated and the fact that it has been revised indicated.

The best practice for numbering is to divide the manual into sections and to number each section in a separate series so that when one is revised, it will not disturb the numbering of the others.

A letter prefacing the page numbers is sufficient to identify the different sections, i.e. A1, A2, B1, B2, etc.

An outline form is preferred for instructions because it encourages the use of short sentences which makes it easier for reference and readability.

Example:
1. FILES
    A. In the file there is a folder for each district office arranged in alphabetic sequence. The folder label bears the name and number of the district.
    B. The folder should contain:
        1. A copy of each audit made at that office.
        2. Correspondence with that district or about it.
        3. The original of the memo received from the Director assigning the audit.

Content of Manual

Any information pertinent to the operation of the files and useful to the person operating it should be included in the manual. There are no rules as to what the information should be, but the following is recommended:

1. A brief statement giving the title of the executive and the area of work responsibility.
2. A description of the files. It is best to indicate the different series and to describe each one by giving the content, arrangement, size, volume and retention. Using these headings the files could be described as follows:

The files are composed of the following series:

Correspondence

Content:	Correspondence reports and related material created or received by *title* in the performance of his or her duties.
Arrangement:	Alphabetic by subject (see list of headings)
Size of Volume:	Letter size—3 drs.
Retention	Current plus 2 years for historical material which is retained permanently.

Extra Copy File

Content:	Extra copies of sales reports, speeches, and miscellaneous reports.

Arrangement:	Sales reports—chronologically miscellaneous reports, speeches—alphabetically by title.
Size of Volume:	Legal size—2 drs.
Retention:	Sales reports—current plus previous year then destroy.
	Speeches—3 years then destroy.
	Miscellaneous reports—current plus previous year then destroy.

Reference File

Content:	Clippings, articles, booklets, etc.
Arrangement:	Alphabetically by subject (See List of Headings)
Size of Volume:	Legal size—2 drs.
Retention:	Indefinite—should be weeded out periodically.

Follow Up File

Content:	The pink copy of letters on matters to be considered at a future date.
Arrangement:	Chronologically by the date to be considered.
Size of Volume:	Letter—½ dr.
Retention:	Self clearing—destroy when no longer needed for follow-up purposes.

3. The list of file headings for the correspondence and reference sections.
4. Instruction on preparing material for file.
5. File maintenance items such as instructions for typing folder labels.
6. Instructions for charging out material.
7. When to use and how to fill out cross reference sheets.
8. When and how to transfer the files.
9. Any other useful information.

CHAPTER 22

RECORDS MANAGEMENT— FILING AND RETENTION

WHAT happens to forms once they reach the files can be very important to records design and redesign. If a record copy lands in a departmental file after being completed and is rarely if ever consulted thereafter, it is probable that this copy could be dispensed with and that any future revision of the form should embody one less copy.

Also, the collation of forms with a file folder can supply an important clue. It may be noted that certain consistent groupings occur; perhaps several forms could be combined into one form, thereby avoiding the collating operation. Whenever papers are assembled, there is a grave possibility of the loss of a component paper. Besides, the labor of file attendants who must gather several forms together for each folder can be curtailed if the material can be supplied with less documents.

Of course, not every seemingly unimportant copy of a record can be eliminated, nor can every group of forms be consolidated. Sometimes, the material presented is given in a special way by the forms as filed, and any change would slow down more important operations. The most intelligent way to appraise this condition, the main method to evaluate economies in record structure, is to analyze the files and the use to which the housed material is put.

Starting Promptly

The creation and revision of records need not be deferred until the completion of a file survey. The study of the files will, in practice, progress along with the designing and revision of forms in deference to the need the company may have for records improvement, which usually cannot await the completion of a full-scale file study. The time element must be considered, and the need for records improvement may be too great to ignore.

Observation of the files will reveal much valuable information for the records management program beyond the clues given for adequate records creation and revision. Chief among the discoveries that can be made are faults which can exist within the filing system that can render ineffective all other efforts of the program. It must be remembered that record data, to be worth its keep, must be recallable quickly and with *full* information to be given to those who need it. Any departure from these two requirements will bog down any system, no matter how carefully other parts of the program have been worked out and applied.

This is not a treatise on filing. There are many such books available that give details of methods to keep records available for instant recall. The books that deal with filing techniques, however, do not approach this subject from the viewpoint of records management. They are simply guides to those who do the filing. There are certain filing faults which are detrimental to the records management program and which should be watched for in the course of file study.

TWELVE FILING FAULTS

There may be more, but we have been able to isolate a dozen basic errors in filing. The first five of these are easily discoverable, the last seven take a bit of sleuthing to find. All twelve, however, are serious, and even though they may have been countenanced with a smile by management for many years, they should be remedied as quickly as possible after detection.

1. *A very active file which is located too far from those who must consult it is inefficient.*

Centralized files are excellent—if the material in them is not in constant departmental use. When a file is transplanted bodily from where it is in great use, the service to those who request it in order to get records in quantity and in a hurry, cannot be good. The departmental file, accessible to those who need the records, is much more likely to give good service when the volume of consultations is high. There are many people who will dispute this statement, who believe that centralized files are a cure-all for the ills so frequently found in departmental files. The cure for the laxity inherent in departmental files (for records consulted frequently) is the imposition of controls.

Cure: Move Files to Point of Use

There can be little if any dispute with the statement that departmental files should be located so that the least clerical effort and consequent time waste are occasioned when they are used. The segregation of files in order to squeeze in as many people as possible into as small a space as conceivable is false economy if, in using the

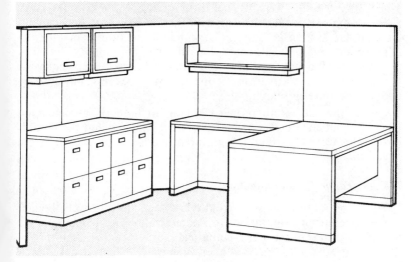

In the modern open offices, much of the filing is done at the workstation, where either administrators or secretaries have direct access. The picture at the top is a drawing of an administrative area, showing storage for files and other materials. The picture below is a drawing of a secretarial area, showing extensive filing capacity in two, 5-foot high lateral files.

Courtesy All-Steel Company

files, personnel must take long, circuitous trips. The time and energy to consult filed papers makes this process such a chore that, frequently, consultations are reduced through inertia. This, too, can be costly. It is much more economical to have frequently handled material filed as close to the point of use as possible, based on a motion study of those who use the files.

The records administrator will note the long trips that could result from too-distant files or the block-up that centralized files suffer when excessively active material is being called for constantly. The remedy takes just a grain of common sense.

> **2.** *A file which is not designed to fit the needs of the department it serves, because the material is not filed in the order it is used or properly collated, is faulty.*

There are filing supervisors and "experts" who hold preconceived ideas of how a file should be constructed—and impose those ideas on the files they attempt to manage or reconstruct. They do not try to ascertain the manner in which a specific department will utilize the records once they are filed. The imposition of a system, a favored one, without due concern for the requirements of the users is thus often encountered.

The users of the files struggle with the filing system, never thinking that the system is faulty. The simple correction of making the filing order geographical, chronological, or in any other way than it is now arranged never occurs to anyone. "It was set up that way, therefore it is up to us to use it the way it is—even if our answers take a long time to search out."

Often, the files were properly set up to function at maximum efficiency but the needs of the department changed and the records in the files were consulted in a different manner—yet the files were never changed.

Cure: Tailor Files to Situation

The filing method may be good in general, but not well thought out for the specific operation. If a numerical file is obviously called for, should it be "straight numerical" or "terminal digit"? The former type is good for infrequently consulted material; the very busy numerical file is difficult to operate unless misfilings can be quickly determined and rectified. The terminal digit method, in which the last three (or more) numbers determine filing order (all numbers ending in 346 being filed together from No. 346 to No. 999346 and beyond, in numerical sequence) points up a filing mistake promptly.

Operational ease is often sacrificed to expediency. Correction of the files is usually postponed indefinitely because of the necessity of closing down service and consequent jamming of business operations. There are concerns that can be engaged to make the required change at night or on weekends with well-trained personnel. The records administrator should supervise this effort to assure its proper, prompt execution.

    3. *A file must give complete information; folders full of irrelevant material or with incomplete data are wasteful of effort.*

In observing the files it may be noted that huge folders must be handled to find information on one or two sheets. The question of why this is necessary may find answer in that much extraneous material must be sifted to get at a few necessary papers. Or, if a clerk must go from one file to another, possibly distant, to get full information, it is obvious that a costly waste of clerical time is going on.

Cure: Segregate Permanent Records

In curing this fault, the necessity of segregation of permanent material must be remembered. If reference to such records is heavy, it may be necessary to originate a non-permanent copy for inclusion in the active folders.

    4. *A file which contains a grouping of subjects without proper headings or wherein folders contain assorted subjects, is disorderly.*

The piling up of folders behind certain file divisions and the absence of material behind others is a sure indication of poor file organization. Either too many dividers were "sold" to the company (or too few, if records are too solidly packed to get at easily) or a system is in use that badly needs review and revision. There is a system of forms control in which forms are filed according to their function, based on a glossary of subjects. A huge collection gathers behind a classification such as "payments," while other topical headings have few or any forms behind them.

Cure: Better Organization

Of course, the problem could be one of poor supervision of the files or of incapable personnel. A mixture of subjects which is flagrantly ridiculous, a predominance of "miscellaneous" material which should have been cataloged, are indicative of a personnel problem. The correction lies in making file workers advance *in their jobs,* not *out* of them through promotions to other departments when they show ability. Adequate standards of hiring and retaining files, supervisors and attendants should be suggested by the administrator.

5. *A file that is out of sequence is virtually unworkable.*

This fault stems from the previous one and is mainly attributable to the same causes. When every secretary is also a file clerk, the case for centralized files is strengthened: Departmental files get out of order when everybody gets access to them. Papers become misplaced when they are hastily returned by users or when files are tended by persons unskilled in this type of work. Searching through files for an important paper which has been misfiled is a miserable job and can be expensive both in time consumed and in the loss sustained if the records remain missing.

When records are heavily used, they will be found readily even if misfiled. The file that does not do as much business suffers more from misfiling. Once a record has been put away out of sequence and no one looks for it for a long time, the additions to the file cover up the misfiling and the record is presumed lost. More active records are rarely presumed lost for they are too "hot" to be assumed as having been discarded. Thus, search for a misfiled active folder will be more intensive before anyone gives up. Not so in the instance of the less active record, especially if it is relatively old.

Cure: Designate One to Replace Files

This in no way condones the practice of sloppy use of active files. The supervision of such files should be entrusted to someone who can look out for this situation and refile material which has been carelessly returned or, preferably, this person can be entrusted with all returned folders, to put them back where they belong.

We now approach some of the less obvious filing faults. The five discussed above are ordinary enough, even in files of large organizations, and recognition of the condition is often prevalent among the companies' own management who deplore the faults but do nothing to remedy them. The filing errors next discussed are usually not realized by the management of the companies afflicted. This makes the next seven faults even more insidious.

6. *A file which does not have adequate supervision to assure the proper handling of its contents is dangerous.*

We must assume that records are very valuable things. If not properly supervised, they can become lost or destroyed. In either case, the information which the record possessed is irretrievably lost. It may not matter or it may be a very serious loss, depending on how grave the need for the information may be. It could be a source of business catastrophe if records are lost.

What constitutes "adequate supervision"? We have mentioned that supervision of an active file is not as urgent as that of a less active one, for activity protects a record to a certain extent. The less active files, especially those harboring inactive material, are often left to spend their last days without capable attendants. Either such files should be protected through sufficient personnel efforts at recall and orderly maintenance, or the contents should be destroyed. There is no sense in preserving records which cannot be counted on to be recallable if needed. And supervision of the less active records is urgently necessary to assure that files are usable. Any records which repose in a clerk's desk and which are active enough for someone else to demand them will be flushed out quickly. But if those records in the desk are not needed for several weeks or months, the chance of finding them diminishes to the vanishing point.

Cure: Keep Track of Files

Supervision requires service to distant points as well as continual check of outstanding records, demanding them to be returned. Otherwise, the normal tendency is to postpone the return of forms and folders—until they are forgotten. Supervision ensures the integrity of the files.

7. *A file of executive records subject to removal when the executive leaves the company or dies, can be a source of great loss.*

Certain papers of a company executive must, of necessity, be personal. This fault of commingling company business with personal data means that the entire file can become lost when the executive leaves. The records administrator must be a diplomat to make executives understand this problem and do something about it. What should be done is to separate the personal material from that which is of interest to the company.

Cure: Separate Personal and Business Material

Of course, this job is a touchy one. The executive instinctively dislikes any idea which gives the impression that he or she may be "on the way out" or may die. One hardly ever feels dispensable, very rarely thinks that he or she may leave the company, and virtually never believes that he may die. The job of putting the papers in order to assure their proper transfer to the company at an executive's severance is a formidable one to sell, best to be proposed and guided by the president. Incidentally, *he* should establish a good example by being the first one to have his own file set up for the removal of this filing fault.

8. *"Pet files," amassed through sequestering data otherwise unavailable, is a form of mania.*

Companies have been known to experience the same difficulties over and over again, because the information about a previous experience had been taken out of files and hidden somewhere else where the information was promptly lost. As one executive said, "We have to invent the wheel over again every year." Data respecting past errors and achievements cannot be placed in private files so that trial and error has to be repeated indefinitely.

These segregated files generally are given a sacred aura which protects them from violation. There is no objection to locked files containing data not to be made generally available, but other files should contain cross references to the material thus filed in order to assure that qualified persons will have access to the impounded information. Just to ignore any mention of what is in secret files defeats the purpose of record preservation.

Sometimes the blame for a private file cannot be directly levied upon the executive who has it. This is the product of giving an "extra copy" to certain executives who may or may not request any. The reasoning is: "It costs so little to make an extra copy—let's give Mr. Smith one." This logic does not take into consideration that Mr. Smith has to look at this copy, perhaps read it, and have it filed.

This is expensive. Mr. Smith's time costs money, and whatever portion of it he must give to the reading or study of a form which can only slightly interest him is a waste of money. The salary of those who must file these copies and keep them orderly adds to the expense. The accrual builds up, generally unimpeded for the simple reason that no one either dare concern himself with Mr. Smith's "special copies" or for an equally important reason—nobody thinks about Mr. Smith's accrual when the forms' other copies are scheduled for elimination.

Automation cannot fail to make this situation more acute. The huge initial cost of computers and their installation makes it almost obligatory to produce reports in multiple copies for the study of as many executives as possible—and possibility can, in this case, be stretched beyond normal limits. The data that can only remotely interest Mr. Smith will get into his files and, because of the immense cost of automation, or for the reason that he would hardly wish to be "left out" when reports are distributed, he will let them grow, and grow, and grow.

Cure: Cross References or Dismantling

There is another reason for the accrual of data, set up in a file which nobody knows about. That reason is the squirrel instinct of some executive who feels that he, alone, should know about this material. Either he does this to make his own stock of company knowledge greater or to keep his position secure by the key that he thereby holds to administrative information. Whatever his purposes, he must be induced to relinquish the exclusive use of his files to those who should have access. And the maintenance of the separate file should be permitted only if the material is cross indexed in other files to which the data pertains.

When the "pet" files are found to contain nothing more than assorted copies of worthless value, already assembled in other files, the "pets" should be dismantled and the data which can be used filed elsewhere.

9. *A file containing records of mixed quality could be difficult to use or could cause the loss of essential documents.*

We must recognize that some papers are more valuable than others. A valuable record can be destroyed by mistake when a folder full of worthless papers is destroyed. The one or two records which should have been kept should not be mixed with records that will be thrown away after maximum utility has passed. Cross reference to another file should be provided in such cases to avoid premature discard of records of further value.

This solution smacks of violation of a previous fault's correction in which we stated that two files should not have to be consulted when one is all that should be needed. This is true only in general practice, but when a permanent record must be consulted, a permanent file installed near the temporary one will give good service and prevent indiscriminate destruction of records which should be kept permanently.

"Mixed quality" could also mean that some records are active, and others combined in folders or files with it are either semi-active or inactive. This is not as spectacular a fault as the other interpretation, for it is not likely that any record will be lost if active and semi-active or inactive forms are in the same file.

Nevertheless, this is as serious an aspect of the filing fault, for file workability suffers when active material must be selected from a mass of less used records. The degree to which this condition can deteriorate can bring grave consequences. Search becomes lengthy and difficult, making looking for an active record costly and unpleasant.

Cure: Time Study

It is suggested that a time study be made of any file suspected of harboring material of different activity, even though some of the records in the file may not be old, but may be less active than others. Some forms or copies of them may be rarely referred to after they are filed, and may swell the mass of paper, rendering the files unworkable. If file clerks have to wade through a lot of less-active or inactive records in order to find active records which are needed often and badly, the fact should be noted and a remedy imposed. The cure can be either the removal of the less-active records to files containing just that quality of records or the discontinuance of the form or copy which no one ever consults.

10. *Master tabulating card or tape files which permit withdrawal of masters for departmental use can be destructive of any data-processing program.*

A copy should be made of any master summoned from a master tabulating card or tape file, and that copy should be circulated, the original promptly being replaced in the file. When the processing or inspection of the copy has been done, it may be returned to the master file and the master replaced by the amended copy.

The loss of a master, through its being held for some change, inspection, or awaiting action, can render all efforts of balancing accounts impossible. The truly efficient tabulating or tape file should live in the realm of a perpetual inventory, never closing up at the end of the day without all its charges safe at home.

11. *A file that is heavily used may be too expensive in clerical effort and operational personnel for its efficiency. Mechanization of such files should be considered.*

Employees bending over, rushing to and from an extremely busy file get in each other's way. They become tired, which results in poor work; too many people are needed for operation. A mechanized file, of adequate dimensions, with convenient working area, will save on both space and personnel requirements. It should pay for itself in a reasonably short time.

There may be reluctance to convert from standard equipment, apart from the money involved; employees may fear the motor and the motion of the conveyers, which, of course, will be strange to them. Safety devices can prevent injury to hands or arms, and ingenious ones have been incorporated to eliminate hazards and to stop action if hands are in danger.

12. *A file housed in containers or premises that do not give it maximum protection can be very expensive.*

If a record is worth keeping, it is worth safe preservation for as long as it has value. Saving money on poor containers which will not protect contents from fire, water, dirt, rodents, and other types of damage is as risky as keeping records in a ramshackle firetrap.

Active files are subjects to fire hazards while the records are in use—not all fires are obliging enough to start at night when records are carefully tucked away. Let us consider what would happen in the computer room if someone should holler, "Fire!" Seeing the smoke and a few tongues of flame, would any employee carefully round up all the tapes in use, run—not walk—to the "vault floor" which may be two floors down, put the invaluable tapes away, and finally shut the door?

Cure: Fireproof Containers

More likely, the shout of "Fire!" would find the employee out the nearest exit and the valuable records right where they were. Perhaps, with proper training drilled into all employers who work with valuable records, a handy fire-resistant file container with a four-hour rating for fire would get the scooped-up records. If every department that handles vital tapes or papers had enough file container space allocated *within the department* in highly rated safes or other housing equipment, the chances that the records would be saved would be vastly increased—and well worth the money.

Some companies feel that safety is better afforded by keeping duplicate tapes, microfilm, or paper records in remote premises, adequately safeguarded. This is good practice only in respect to inactive records. Active records, especially those which are constantly being updated such as tabulating cards and computer tapes, present a problem of maintaining a continuous stream of records back and forth from the distant repository. If such duplicating is done once a month, a disaster one day before the "duplicating day" catches the company with virtually a whole month's business unaccounted for. Any more frequent duplicating would make the traffic in records burdensome.

Vaults Can Be Funeral Pyres

The security of a vault is rarely open to question, yet as already pointed out, these structures are often inaccessible when danger arises. Also, elaborate vaults—air-conditioned, water-sprinklered and all—are the funeral pyres of innumerable records. Whatever duct leads into a vault permits the entry of fire or water. Air conditioning can furnish such a duct; the sprinkler system, especially if no drain is provided (and a drain is an admirable duct for the entry of fire or searing heat), can ruin valuable records in the eventual flooding of the vault.

Fireproof safes, vaults, and files must close with a tongue over closing edges to prevent the seeping in of heat or flame. The contents do not have to be enveloped in flame to be rendered worthless, for about 300 degrees of heat is quite enough to do the job.

Water damage, resulting from efforts in controlling fire, will also be reduced by closing of containers with tongued overlaps. Carbon dioxide is a better fire-controlling agent than water, and contents of a vault equipped with this type of extinguisher will not drown.

22 FILING PROBLEMS AND SOLUTIONS

Do you have any of these typical filing problems? If so, here are some solutions offered by the National Office Products Association.

TROUBLE	SOLUTION
Too many filing places	Centralize filing of records of common interest in one location under one supervisor. File specialized records in departments where handled, but follow handling procedure.
Everybody a file clerk	Centralize authority with responsibility. Allow only designated persons to use files except in emergencies.
Files didn't keep pace with firm's progress	Check size of alphabetic breakdown to see if it is adequate. Check type of alphabetic breakdown to see if it fits customer name patterns.
Files disordered; show no particular plan or arrangement	Pick a ready-made engineered system that best fits your needs. Adjust it if necessary as time goes on. Your office products dealer carries several systems and can suggest one to suit your needs. No charge beyond regular cost of folders and guides without a system.
System doesn't fit the way material is called for	Study the possibilities of using subject, geographic, or numeric, as well as alphabetic filing for certain specialized materials.

RECORDS MANAGEMENT—FILING AND RETENTION

TROUBLE	SOLUTION
Filing decisions erratic	Start a filing procedure manual and then USE it! Don't depend on snap judgment or the opinions of others. Whan a problem arises, make a ruling, then write it down.
Takes too long to find a folder	Have an index guide for each inch of active drawer space for each 6–8 folders. This averages out about 25 guides per drawer for best efficiency.
Same trouble with card files	Have not more than 30 cards to a guide in an average reference file; not more than 20 in an active or growing one, and definitely not more than 10–15 to a guide in a posted record file, such as a ledger.
Drawers jammed too tight	Allow 3 to 4 inches of working space in letter files, 1 to 2 inches in card files.
Bulging folders slow down filing speed.	Have not over 25 sheets per folder for best efficiency, not over 50 maximum.
Papers pile up in the Miscellaneous folder	Give a person or firm his own folder after his 6th letter to you. If that doesn't work, you need a larger number of divisions in your index.
Individual folders too full	Make a special name guide for the individual then put a set of period or chronological folders back of the guide.
Guides in bad condition	Replace broken guides. Use reinforced tabs in the active file, use angular tabs for easier reading. Use tab inserts for greater versatility and less expansion expense. Use edges of guide and not the tab when pushing contents of file.
Folder tabs difficult to read	Use gummed labels; they strengthen and beautify as well as add legibility. Use reinforced tabs when reference is frequent. Use a good grade of material for active files—it pays.
Folders out of sight	Check compressor. Use stiffer folders. Use scored or bellows folders for better expansion. Investigate use of suspended folders.

TROUBLE	SOLUTION
Folders wear out too soon	Use at least an 11 point folder for frequent usage out of the file. 14 point or pressboard for heavy use. Save space yet add strength with double tabbed folders.
Old correspondence slowing up filing of current papers	Transfer old material at least once a year, oftener if necessary. See if some types of correspondence need to be filed at all.
File storage using up valuable floor space	Check use of 5-drawer cabinets. Check shelf filing for certain records. Establish a definite destruction plan for all types of papers you file. Consolidation of files might help.
Trouble finding material called for before it is filed	Use sorting devices and sort immediately on arrival. Keep in the sorter until ready to index.
Getting papers into the folders takes too long	Use sorting devices to completely arrange the papers. Saves walking and fumbling time and reduces errors.
Work is tiring	Use filing shelf to free both hands for filing. The stool is another handy device to ease fatigue.
Trouble finding missing papers or cards	Keep track of removed papers and cards with out-guides or folders. You are always responsible unless you can point the finger of blame with facts to back you up.

16 STEPS FOR FILING AND FINDING CORRESPONDENCE

The files of a business concern are its *memory*. Since the success of any business is in direct relation to the complete and accurate utilization of facts from its *memory*, it is highly important that the files be thoroughly under control at all times. Filing without control is dangerous for any firm.

Filing control involves two basic jobs; getting *all* the worthwhile material into the files by proper classification, and retrieving *all* that is required quickly whenever called for.

Obviously, each office will vary to some degree in the exact method for controlling its records—its filing plan. Whims of the executives, volume of materials, skill of filing clerk personnel, knowledge of good procedure, willingness to invest in better supplies and equipment, all contribute to the choice of filing procedure.

The National Office Products Association offers a 16-step procedure for handling the filing and retrieval of company correspondence which embodies the typical controls found in a well-organized records management system. The filing procedures for other types of company records will have similar controls but will naturally be modified to fit the operation.

1. Time Stamp. Whoever first receives the correspondence should time stamp or at least date stamp it. This serves as a check or when it was received and the time elapsing before reply.

2. Release Mark. The person responsible for answering the correspondence or his secretary, initials the original to give the files operator authority to file the letter. A carbon copy of the reply is attached to the original correspondence but need not be initialed. It is wise to include the date of answering as well as the initialed release mark. Before sending the letter to the file, the executive or his secretary will indicate the need for follow-up and cross-reference. By agreement, the request for follow-up could be simply by writing in the date in the lower right hand corner. Cross-reference may be indicated by drawing a line underneath the name or subject. (See points 9 and 10)

3. Collection of Material. A junior file clerk or messenger collects the material to be filed from letter trays on executives' desks and from one central point in the various departments at least twice a day. The collection bag should be made so that material from each collection point is kept separate. In that way any irregularities can be traced.

4. Time Stamp. Time stamp all records entering the filing section to show the date it assumes responsibility.

5. Inspect. Check for proper release or authorization to file. Send back if every department indicated on the letter has not been checked off. Mend and straighten out, trim and fold to fit folders. Check every paper attached—some may go to a different file. Remove all clips and pins. Staple with latest date on top.

6. Segregate for Files. Segregate papers which go into whatever different files are kept, like customer file, invoice file, catalogs, credit, sales department, applications, etc. Sometimes a count is made at this stage to keep track of volume. Stamp or otherwise mark the papers with the name of the file to speed identification for return to files if borrowed later.

7. Read to Determine Key Title. Read to determine the title under which the material should be filed. In some procedures, the person sending the material to the file marks the key title. Here are some suggestions for selecting the key title:

    a. The name of the firm.

    b. For carbons of outgoing letters, the name of the company on the inside address. If no company is given, then the name of the individual.

    c. Where an incoming letter has no letterhead, the name of the person signing unless the firm name appears elsewhere. Inappropriate letterheads, like that of a hotel where the writer is staying, should be ignored.

    d. Subject or a name within the body of the letter if this is more important for filing and finding.

    e. Special file section title where maintained, like *Job application*.

    f. The name of the person for letters of a personal nature regardless of the firm to which he belongs.

8. Code. Mark the key title with a code so it need not be determined again. Underscore with colored pencil the name or word under which the material is to be filed. If the firm name has several words, a good plan is to underscore only the key word and place numbers above the remaining words in the order in which they are to be considered in filing. Circle the subject if it is used or write it down. Write the name of the special file if used.

9. Cross-Reference. It often happens that a single letter might be called for under several headings. One of the headaches of filing is outguessing the possibilities. By means of cross-referencing, the material can be located quickly even if called for under different headings.

If the executive or his secretary on releasing the record for the files sees the need for cross-referencing, they should code it. Otherwise, the file operator will code the material for filing under the name most likely to be called for, and look for possibilities of other headings. Typically cross-reference is indicated by writing a cross or wavy line under the secondary name or names. To be safe, a cross can be written in the margin, too.

The file operator fills out a *Cross-reference card*, sheet, or folder immediately after coding. These are filed in the alternate filing spots the same as though they were original documents, referring filing personnel to the exact location. This reduces the number of tries at finding a record to a maximum of two if the cross reference is complete.

While cross-reference is safer than risking a lost important paper, it is expensive in extra filing time and materials, and doubles the amount of papers in the file. So it should not be overdone as a practice. Sometimes an extra carbon made at the source or a facsimile copy of the original can be used instead to file under the alternate title.

10. Follow-up. Many papers require attention at some future time, such as papers on prospective customers, delinquent customers, expiring subscriptions, expiring life insurance, orders, etc. Too common is the practice of having the papers stack up on the executive's desk awaiting future action, thereby running the risk of loss and keeping other persons from referring to the correspondence.

A better method is to have the executive indicate in a selected corner the date on which he wishes to refer to the letter again. The indexer turns the letter over to an assistant who makes out a follow-up slip then files the letter in the usual manner. The slip goes into a *chronological file* under the date required. When that date rolls around, the file clerk removes the letter and sends it to the executive. The follow-up slip is then used as a *charge-out-card.* On outgoing letters, an alternate plan is to make an extra carbon copy on a special colored paper which, when given a follow-up date by the originator, goes into a chronological file and is then handled the same as a follow-up slip.

Correspondence follow-up should be the job of the file section. Other office sections, however, have occasion to use *tickler files* or *joggers* for remembering actions not involving correspondence.

Following are examples of need for cross referencing:

Material Filed Under:	Cross Reference Under:
International Business Equipment	I. B. E. (Abbreviated name)
Foster and Lukens Company	Charles Foster (Officials of firms)
Denver Office Products	Western Stationers (Former firm name)
Fuller, George	Fuller, (Mrs.) Jane (Wives)
Atchison, Topeka, Santa Fe, R.R.	Santa Fe R.R. (Common or incomplete name)
Eaton Paper Corp.	Paper (Product)

These may take the form of cards filed behind date guides, folders behind date guides, folders with signal devices that slide along the top edge exposing the follow-up date, or folders with dated tabs along the top edge which can be cut off except for the tab representing the follow-up date. Each day the clerk removes the cards, folders, or materials from behind the guide for that day and takes whatever action is needed. When the action is taken, the cards or other reminders can be replaced in the tickler file behind the next date required.

11. Sorting. When the materials are ready for filing, they are given a preliminary rough sort to speed up the final filing. It is important that this be done immediately after the coding and cross referencing even if the actual filing has to wait. A letter needed in a hurry can be found without much trouble from the sorter whereas it could be quite a job finding it in a pile of unsorted material. The preliminary sort also reduces the danger of loss and damage while awaiting final filing.

There are a number of commercial sorters available to make the job easier and faster. A sorter with 25 guides or compartments is sufficient for a file of 320 alphabetic subdivisions. For larger subdivisions, use about one-tenth as many guides in the sorter as there are in the file.

When ready for filing, additional refinements can be made in the sorting so that the final filing can be made in consecutive order without unnecessary walking or reopening of drawers. Remove the papers from the sorter one section at a time and put into proper sequence. File one section at a time or wait until the complete sorting is done.

12. Filing. Filing completes the cycle for getting the material into the files. The exact resting place of the paper is determined by the system used, but most systems follow this general plan:

a. *Back of the guide.* The eye finds the right guide, then continues forward to the right folder. This is the natural movement, according to time and motion studies.

b. *Into a folder.* All papers go into a folder for protection and ease of handling. Technically, it is the folder that is filed rather than the papers in it.

c. *Latest letter on top.* The latest letter is usually referred to most frequently, hence in correspondence filing, it should be on top or in front of all previous correspondence from or to the same person or firm. Place the heading to the left.

d. *Use Miscellaneous Folder*—for "Not-so-active" names. File papers of each firm in alphabetic order first, then chronologically with the latest letter of each individual to the front of his section in the Miscellaneous folder.

e. *Individual folders for five or more letters.* When five or more letters of an individual or firm are accumulated in the Miscellaneous folder, prepare an individual folder and remove the papers to it.

13. Charge-Out. Only those persons *responsible* for the files should remove materials from them. This just follows good management principles of assigning authority with responsibility. Those persons for whom materials are withdrawn from the files should be charged in some manner for the papers' safety while in their possession.

The charge-out system keeps track of materials removed from the file, helps locate them quickly, and assures that all data, even that temporarily out of the file, will be considered when making decisions important to the firm. This is one of the important keys to records control—*being able to account for any desired record.*

Persons requesting material from the files may telephone, send a messenger, or come personally to the files. A simple requisition form is filled out for each item desired usually in duplicate. It tells what was taken, by whom, and when. One copy goes into the file as a replacement for the material and the other is filed by due-date for follow-up.

When the requisition calls for one piece or a few related pieces, an *Out-card* or *Out-sheet* is substituted in the folder. The requisition card is attached to the *Out-card* to save rewriting. The *Out-sheet* is actually a duplicate of the requisition and thus saves rewriting.

When the requisition calls for an entire folder, the operator replaces the original material with an *Out-guide* or *Out-folder*. The out-folder method allows additional filing to be made while the original folder is out of the file.

A third method is the Carrier-folder, actually a substitute folder. The contents of the original folder are transferred to the carrier so that the original folder remains in the file drawer to receive additional materials. It is protected from damage that might otherwise occur while out of the file. The carrier folder is a distinctive color to remind the user to return it promptly.

The *Out-sheets, Out-guides* and *Carrier-folders* are available ready-made from the office products suppliers.

Charge-out should be rigidly observed. It takes less than 30 seconds, can save hours of search, and can prevent costly losses which might occur if someone acts without knowledge of missing data, or if important data is lost.

When material is passed from one party to another without returning to the files, a *Transfer slip* or *Recharge form* should be used to keep the file section informed. Both file personnel and guilty executives can be embarrassed when a top man calls for a letter that can't be found. Forms are sometimes attached to the material to aid the user in following this procedure. Some offices require the material be recharged through the file section to pick up any recent material.

14. Cancel Charge-Out. It is important that the charge-out records show that the borrowed material has been returned to the files. The procedure is usually a simple removal of the charge-out card, sheet, or folder. On reusable charge-out cards and folders, the last entry is scratched out when they are removed from the file. Requisitions can be removed and discarded along with duplicates, including the copy used for follow-up.

15. Follow-up. A follow-up plan is a double check against loss. A log or tickler serves the purpose. A carbon copy of the requisition placed in a tickler file is perhaps the simplest and most accurate method. After a given number of days, the borrowed materials are collected or the time is extended.

16. Or Make Copies Instead. Modern copying machines can make copies in seconds from the original, so when only a few pieces of material are requested, it might be better to furnish facsimile copies and return the originals to the files immediately. The cost of the copy could be less than the labor involved in getting the material out and back to the files, and it obviously prevents the danger of loss. Some firms have strict rules on the removal of material from a folder, sometimes requesting that the reference be made in the file room or that facsimile copies be made.

16 RULES FOR ALPHABETIZING

Alphabetizing names for filing involves more than a knowledge of the alphabet. Even though alphabetizing is based upon the sequence of the letters of the alphabet, the variety of names is so great that knowing the A-B-Cs is not enough.

Names of individuals are of many national origins. Some have prefixes, some are made up of two words, and in others, abbreviations are used. Business names are even more complicated, since coined words, single letters, numbers, names of individuals, and all manner of combinations are used.

To add to the difficulty, people are inconsistent. No one thinks about the same things in the same way everyday. That is really fortunate, for there would be no inventions, new products, or art if people did not consider things differently on occasion. In alphabetizing, however, consistent practices must be followed, so that whatever is filed today by "Anne" can be found next month by "Betty." This requires that rules be established to provide guidance.

Although there are rules for both ordinary and unusual names, they cannot cover the individual problems of every file. Frequently an adaptation or change in the rules is required. For example, the practice of filing a bank under its location and then its name is not practical if the file contains the names of just a few banks in the same city as the company which has the file. Filing each of them under its name would be more suitable. If there are a great many numerical names, arranging them in a separate series in numerical sequence may be a better way to handle them rather than filing them as spelled.

When Rules May Be Changed

A decision to change or vary a rule should based upon the number of names and their use. The change should apply to a category of names, never to an individual one. It also should be made in relation to the file as a whole, so that a change that solves a problem in one part of the file does not create one in another part. Any variation in the rules should be fully documented so that the "why" is understood. Exceptions should be few, however, because the more exceptions there are to learn and remember, the more opportunity there will be for inconsistent practices to develop.

Some filers use the telephone directory as an authority in alphabetizing names. It can serve as a convenient reference, to see how someone else handles some specific problem of arrangement, but it should not be considered as an authority, because its primary purpose is to serve its customers. The rules used for filing in the phone directory are based upon the way the average user is apt to look for the name; this is not always in accordance with generally accepted filing rules; e.g., the 's is considered as part of the name in the directory, but this is not standard filing practice. A phone subscriber is allowed to choose how he or she wishes to be listed. This accounts for some company names, which are names of individuals, being listed under the first name, a dubious practice at best and not followed consistently even in the directory.

Numeric names are arranged in numeric sequence, with some exceptions when they are written in words. In the directory, Eight Forty East Cosmetics comes before 8 Track Recording Company, while 840 N. Michigan Bldg. is in the numeric group of 8's.

In general the rules will be learned almost automatically with constant use and occasional reference, and by knowing them, alphabetizing will become a routine task. The use of rules will help ensure the accuracy of the files and make retrieval faster.

RULES FOR FILING

The first step in alphabetizing is to consider the alphabet inviolate. *DO NOT TAMPER WITH IT!* Do not consider Mc as a twenty-seventh letter and file names beginning with *Mc* out of the alphabetic sequence, or lump the *MAC*'s and *Mc*'s together. Whatever its deficiencies, the alphabet has been around for a long while and has withstood the test of time very well. Its sequence is commonly known, and introducing even slight changes will make alphabetizing more difficult.

There are three basic principles to be used for guidance in alphabetizing:

I. Separate each name or file caption into units.

II. Consider the sequence of all the letters in the first unit before paying attention to the next unit.

III. Apply the principle of "nothing before something."

First Unit	Second Unit	Third Unit
1. Brown	A.	
2. Brown	A.	S.
3. Brown	Adam	
4. Brown	Adam	R.
5. Brown	Adam	Roy
6. Brownar	Aaron	
7. Browne	Albert	
8. Browne	Arnold	
9. Browne	Arnold	B.

In this arrangement, each name or single letter has been considered as a separate unit. The first unit of the first five names is BROWN, and in these names it is the initial or given name that determines the sequence within the group. The first name has only one initial or only one filing unit beyond the surname; therefore it precedes the second name which has a third unit, illustrating the principle, *NOTHING BEFORE SOMETHING.*

In the third name, the second unit is a full name, Adam or A plus something and, consequently, it must follow all the names in which the first unit is only the initial A. The same reasoning applies to the third unit of the fourth and fifth names and governs their position. Principle II is illustrated by the position of the sixth, seventh, eighth, and ninth names in the list.

The principles apply to all names and filing captions, while the rules cover the problems presented by their variety. Regardless of whether the name is of a person, a business, a government department, or an institution, rules in the following list apply to their proper alphabetizing.

Rule 1 Names of individuals are transposed as follows: Last name, first name or initial, then middle name or initial.

As Written	As Filed
John W. Clark	Clark John W.
James A. Collum	Collum James A.

Rule 2 Surnames with prefixes such as De, La, Le, Mc, Mac, O', Van, Von, etc. are filed as one word in alphabetic order.

As Written	As Filed
D'Amico	Damico
de Hopper	deHopper
Mc Andrew	McAndrew

Rule 3 When it is impossible to distinguish the first or last name in a foreign name, it is filed as written.

As Written	As Filed
Chow Hung	Chow Hung
Vi-Sen Lin	Vi-Sen Lin

Rule 4 Hyphenated and compound last names are treated as one unit.

As Written	As Filed
Paul Allen-Smith	Allen-Smith Paul
Ann St. John	St. John Ann
Fidel Hinojosa-Flores	Hinojose-Flores Fidel

Rule 5 Consideration of titles.

    a. Titles that are an intrinsic part of the name are considered as the first unit, whether in personal names or shops, etc.

As Written	As Filed
Prince Henry Theatre	Prince Henry Theatre
Sister Mary Theresa	Sister Mary Theresa
Madame Carlotta	Madame Carlotta
Madame Gralli's Restaurant	Madame Gralli's Restaurant

b. **This rule also applies to company names (but see also Rule 7).**

As Written	As Filed
Prince Edward Hotel	Prince Edward Hotel
Captain Nemo's Pub	Captain Nemo's Pub
Miss Nettie's Lounge	Miss Nettie's Lounge
Dr. Pepper Co.	Doctor Pepper Company

c. **When a title is added to a full name, it is considered as the last unit.**

As Written	As Filed
Father Hugh Stacy	Stacy Hugh, Father
Captain John Akers	Akers John, Captain

d. **Other titles and appendages, such as Sr., Jr., II, Mrs., Ph.D., are also considered as the last unit.**

As Written	As Filed
Seth Edward Brown, M.D.	Brown Seth Edward, M.D.
James M. Holland, II	Holland James M., II
Samuel R. Clark, Jr.	Clark Samuel R., Jr.
Robert G. Lamb, Ph.D.	Lamb Robert G., Ph.D.

Rule 6 Abbreviations are alphabetized as though they were spelled out.

As Written	As Filed
Herbert St. John	Saint John Herbert
Geo. Brown	Brown George
Ft. Knox Post	Fort Knox Post
Bates Mgmt. Co.	Bates Management Company
Dr. Piso's Remedies	Doctor Piso's Remedies

Rule 7 Business and organization names are filed as written unless they are the name of an individual; then the name is transposed.

As Written	As Filed
American Bar Association	American Bar Association
James Brown Coal Co.	Brown James Coal Co.
University of Chicago	University (of) Chicago
Louis A. Weiss Hospital	Weiss Louis A. Hospital

Rule 8 When a business name is made up of two or more surnames, it is filed as written, considering each name as a separate unit.

As Written	As Filed
Grossett-Dunlap Co.	Grossett Dunlap Co.
Pierre, Smith & Richards	Pierre Smith Richards

Rule 9 Hyphenated words and names of firms.

a. A hyphenated name is filed as one unit.

As Written	As Filed
Bind-O-Matic Corp.	Bind-O-Matic Corp.
Nu-Way Binding Co.	Nu-Way Binding Co.

b. A hyphenated word is considered as one unit.

As Written	As Filed
Anti-Tuberculosis Society	Anti-Tuberculosis Society
Pre-School Nursery	Pre-School Nursery

Rule 10 When letters are used as a name, each letter is considered as a separate unit.

As Written	As Filed
A A Accounting Service	A A Accounting Service
A B C School	A B C School
W O R Radio Station	W O R Radio Station

Rule 11 Consideration of the apostrophe.

a. When used to designate a possessive, the 's is disregarded, since it denotes possession but is not part of the name.

As Written	As Filed
Jane's Pet Store	Jane Pet Store

b. The apostrophe designating the possessive following a plural is disregarded. The "s" is part of the word and is considered.

As Written	As Filed
Boys' Club	Boys Club

c. The apostrophe in an elision is disregarded.

As Written	As Filed
It's-Unique Gift Shop	Its Unique Gift Shop

Rule 12 Articles, conjunctions, and prepositions are generally not considered.

a. An article that begins a name is disregarded.

As Written	As Filed
The Red Star Inn	Red Star Inn The
A Sweet Shop	Sweet Shop A
The Wisconsin Dells	Wisconsin Dells The

Exception: The article is considered when it is an intrinsic part of a geographic name.

As Written	As Filed
The Dells	The Dells
The Dalles, Oregon	The Dalles, Oregon
The Hollow, Virginia	The Hollow, Virginia

b. Conjunctions, articles, and prepositions that are part of the name are disregarded.

As Written	As Filed
Top-of-the Rock Lounge	Top (of the) Rock Lounge
Society for the Blind	Society (for the) Blind
Candy & Cracker Shop	Candy (&) Cracker Shop

c. Prepositions that begin a name are considered.

As Written	As Filed
For-Men Furnishings	For Men Furnishings
In-the-Round Playhouse	In (the) Round Playhouse

Rule 13 Numeric Names

a. Numeric names are filed as though spelled out.

b. Numbers of more than two digits are given their proper numeric value unless they are spoken otherwise.

As Written	As Filed
400 Club	Four Hundred Club
50th Floor Shop	Fiftieth Floor Shop
A-1 Repair Service	A- One Repair Service
5000 Elm Apts.	Five Thousand Elm Apartments
5623 Building	Fifty-six Twenty-three Building*
333 Building	Three Thirty-three Building*

*This is the way the name is spoken.

RECORDS MANAGEMENT—FILING AND RETENTION

Rule 14 In geographic names of more than one word, each word is considered as a separate unit. Names with a prefix are considered as one unit, the same as an individual's name (Rule 2).

As Written	As Filed
New Haven Railroad	New Haven Railroad
Des Plaines Coal Co.	Des Plaines Coal Co.
Forest Park Country Club	Forest Park Country Club

Rule 15 Names containing compass terms should be filed as written.

As Written	As Filed
North East Bank	North East Bank
North West Publishers	North West Publishers
Northeast Transit Co.	Northeast Transit Co.
North Eastern Coach Line	North Eastern Coach Line

Note: Cross references can be used for clarification.

North East	Also See:	Northeast
Northeast	Also See:	North East

Rule 16 Names of governmental units are filed under the name of the location or political division followed by the significant word or title. The name of the political entity (state, county, city) is understood but is not considered in filing unless it is part of the name.

As Written	As Filed
City Collector of St. Paul	Saint Paul City Collector
Saint Paul Dept. of Welfare	Saint Paul Welfare Dept.
Illinois State Highway Police	Illinois State Highway Police

RETENTION AND STORAGE OF RECORDS

One section of this handbook deals with 12 common filing faults and how to cure them. Once a records-management program has been initiated or brought up-to-date, setting a record retention schedule is important to ensure its effectiveness.

Every company should build and maintain a Forms Manual. The manual should be directed to division heads, who are thereby appointed to see that all further efforts in effecting the program will be carried out.

The benefits of a reorganization in the records department do not become evident until the first batch of records is tossed out. This

555

EXAMPLES

The best understanding of the rules of alphabetizing can be secured from actual observation. The following list, therefore, is designed to illustrate the practical application of these rules. The principles apply to every entry and the numbers in the last column refer to a specific rule. Only enough rules have been given to indicate their application and to clarify the alphabetizing of unusual names.

NAME			FILED AS		RULE
	1st Unit	2nd Unit	3rd Unit	Other Units	
A A A Electric Co.	A	A	A	Electric Co.	10
A A Advertising Agency	A	A	Advertising Agency		
A M S Manufacturing Co.	A	M	S	Manufacturing Co.	6
A No. 1 Cartage Co.	A	Number	One	Cartage Co.	13a
A-1 Adding Machine Co.	A	One	Adding	Machine Co.	1
Arthur A. Aagard	Aagard	Arthur	A		
Aagard Laundry Co.	Aagard	Laundry	Company		9a
Ace-High Exterminating Co.	Ace-High	Exterminating	Company		8
Allan-Baker Corp.	Allan	Baker	Corporation		
George B. Allan	Allan	George	B.		
Anticosti Shipping Corp.	Anticosti	Shipping			
Anti-Cruelty Society	Anti-Cruelty	Society			9b
The Big Dipper Ice Cream Shop	Big	Dipper	Ice	Cream Shop, The	12a
Big Sisters Association	Big	Sisters	Association		
Capt. Thomas H. Braun	Braun	Thomas	H.	Captain	5c
Harold J. Burr Co.	Burr	Harold	J.	Company	7
Dominion of Canada	Canada	Dominion (Of)			
Chicago Boys' Club	Chicago	Boys	Club		11b
City of Chicago Fire Dept.	Chicago (City)	Fire	Department		16
Chicago Police Dept.	Chicago (City)	Police	Department		
The Committee to Aid Dependent Children	Committee (to)	Aid	Dependent	Children	12a, b
Dang Nu Shin	Dang	Nu	Shin		3

556

NAME	1st Unit	2nd Unit	3rd Unit	Other Units	RULE
Road Commissioners of Des Plaines County	Des Plaines (County)	Road	Commissioners		16
Dennis T. Devries	Devries	Dennis	T.		2
Dwyer's Pastry Shop	Dwyer	Pastry	Shop		11a
Robert Saunders Dwyer	Dwyer	Robert	Saunders		
Ever-Nu Auto Top Shop	Ever-Nu	Auto	Top	Shop	
51st Street Florist	Fifty-first	Street	Florist		13a
First National Bank of Florida	First	National	Bank	(of) Florida	
Ft. Henry Grain Exchange	Fort	Henry	Grain	Exchange	14
Fort Hill Electric Co.	Fort	Hill	Electric	Company	
Here's How Beer Co.	Heres	How	Beer	Company	11c
Hotel Innesbrook	Hotel	Innesbrook			
Martin Johns-Miller	Johns-Miller	Martin			4
LeHarra & Lewis	LeHarra	(&) Lewis			
Charles T. Leonard, M.D.	Leonard	Charles	T.	M.D.	5d
LePage Glue Co.	LePage	Glue	Company		
Francis T. Macauley	Macauley	Francis	T.		
Richard T. Mack	Mack	Richard	T.		
Charles Robert MacLaine	MacLaine	Charles	Robert		
Mary J. McAulay	McAulay	Mary	J.		2
McNab Bros. Co.	McNab	Brothers	Company		
Hugh L. M'Whinney	M'Whinney	Hugh	L.		
North Carolina State College	North	Carolina	State	College	15
Northwest Coal & Coke Co.	Northwest	Coal	& Coke	Company	
Princess Pat, Ltd.	Princess	Pat	Limited		5b
St. Anne's Hospital	Saint	Anne	Hospital		6
Sister Collette	Sister	Collette			5a

557

should not take place until the records have been inventoried and the findings of the inventory have been analyzed. Many companies have developed forms for better control over record disposition.

There are, of course, other dispositions to be made of inventoried material besides destroying it. What happens to this remaining material should be decided by the legal and operating needs of the individual company.

The problem of establishing retention dates based on legal requirements is not a difficult one: Check the state and federal laws and examine your records with these in mind. For companies in interstate commerce there is one more step: Determine the statutes of limitation for the states in which you do business.

Retention information based on these legal requirements is a fairly clear-cut matter; the influence of operating needs on the retention schedule is not. The following paragraphs outline one company's approach to the problem of retention dates; it is typical of the methods used by many others:

A. A records retention system to be workable should be:
    1. Simple.
    2. Flexible—decisions are made on a variety of factors requiring judgment and appraisal, rather than on the basis of sharply drawn definition.

B. The important elements affecting records preservation policies and the periods for records retention are:
    1. The statute of limitations.
    2. Governmental regulations.
    3. Historical value.
    4. Business judgment.

C. The following are four classifications often applied in grouping records for retention purposes:
    1. *Class 1 or Vital Records*—These records are irreplaceable and include records which offer direct evidence of ownership, franchises, minute books, deeds, journals, and ledgers.
    2. *Class 2 or Important Records*—These are administrative instruments and include reports, statistical and cost studies, and the great bulk of accounting records supporting current operating routines.
    3. *Class 3 or Useful Records*—These are records frequently used and currently available, but their loss will not seriously handicap business operations.

4. *Class 4 or Nonessential Records*—These records have no long-term value and are eligible for immediate destruction.

D. In classifying records into retention groups consideration should be given to:
1. Possible future value.
2. Legal value.
3. Possible interference with operations.
4. Relations with the public or customers.
5. Relations with governmental agencies.
6. The problem and expense of replacement in case of loss.
7. Availability elsewhere of identical copies.
8. The extent to which the same data summarizes or is summarized by other records.
9. The degree to which the record provides essential details.

E. Records may be further classified into file groups for reference purposes as follows:
1. *Active Files*—These files should include only records to which relatively frequent reference is made.
2. *Semiactive Files*—These are files which contain records no longer in the "Active" group but which should be retained within the office premises area for occasional reference.
3. *Inactive Files*—Records included in these files are to be retained permanently or for a specified period and are seldom used for reference purposes. Inactive files would be placed in the Records Storage Warehouse.

It is often unwise to rely entirely upon one department head's judgment when establishing retention and destruction schedules. He or she sometimes has distorted ideas of the importance and frequency of use of certain records. An accurate check can be made of the frequency of reference to records by having file clerks tabulate the requests. An earlier Dartnell study of this problem disclosed that when one company compiled such a tabulation for several months and analyzed the data, it discovered that 91% of the requests were for material less than six months old; only 1% was for material older than a year. Some companies take what they call a "calculated risk" in destroying some records; they get rid of records whose lack in the years to come may cost the company money. This decision is, of course, not made until all the facts, pro and con, are tallied up, and until the cost of retaining the particular record far outweighs all possible losses which could result from not having it.

Disposition schedules should function continuously and as automatically as possible. Companies that delay disposition until file cabinets are overflowing often discover to their sorrow that the job is too big to be handled without a major effort on everyone's part.

Retention schedules should be characterized by a flexibility that will allow them to conform to the changes that experience indicates necessary from time to time. It is important that some device be set up for recording this experience—to show that some records will have to be kept for a longer time, others for a shorter time.

Unfortunately, establishing a well-coordinated retention schedule does not in itself ensure that a company will have safe, economical, accessible, and efficient records. The program has to be policed. As an official of the General Tire & Rubber Company said a few years ago:

> Our main experience with our retention schedule is that it must be constantly policed. Two years ago when this function of our company was placed under my supervision, I started a house-cleaning campaign and disposed of over 50 tons of old records which could have been thrown away had our manual been followed. We again reviewed our old files this spring and secured approval from our Legal Department to shorten our requirements on some items and were able to dispose of a great many more old records.

Specific Record Groups

The following summary of typical record groups includes an explanation of the factors to watch in setting a retention period for each type of record. The list was prepared by the president of The National Records Management Council as a management aid for small manufacturers.

Accounting, General. (journals, ledgers, trial balance) Journals and ledgers mean different things to different companies. The general ledger, as the basic summary accounting record, is usually retained permanently. The subsidiary journals and ledgers are required only for internal administration and need be retained only through periods of actual use by the accounting department, auditors, or top management. Trial balances are working papers that need be retained only through final audit.

Accounts Payable. (general canceled checks, canceled payroll checks, vouchers) While canceled general checks may be retained for the number of years defined in each state's statute of limitations (average of six years), some companies keep payroll checks for only two years. Canceled payroll checks can create a volume problem. The greatest activity is in the first few weeks after issuance, and usually falls to next to nothing after the first year. Vouchers are always a bulk problem. Rather than keep them all for six to 20 years, breaks can be made between plant vouchers (retained permanently), operating vouchers (retained for an average of six years), and petty cash vouchers (retained for an average of one to two years). This holds for originals only. Further breaks might be made by dollar value. It pays to limit retaining copies of these vouchers for a minimum number of weeks or months.

Accounts Receivable. (billing copies of invoices, credit-memo invoices, accounts receivable ledger) Management's chief concern is in the unpaid invoices. Paid invoices—particularly large-volume, small-dollar-value items—may often be disposed of within six months to two years. Most complaints on payment or amount of payment are received within this period. Equally important is minimum retention of any invoice files that duplicate the basic record (arranged by customer or by invoice number). Only those invoices connected with items of new design or the first item of a patentable product require long indefinite retention. The accounts receivable ledger, as a basic summary of credit sales, need be kept only so long as it is a ready index to invoices or total daily sales. Where there is no other summary of sales, it may be useful to retain it indefinitely for historical purposes.

Legal. (contracts, copyrights, patents, trademarks, suits) Copyrights, patents and trademarks are usually retained permanently. Contracts are more often kept for six years after expiration, but when renewed annually are generally kept for shorter periods. Records on lawsuits are typically kept for six to 10 years after settlement. Bulky work papers and routine notes connected with contracts and suits should be cleaned out as soon as the matter is legally completed.

Payroll. (earnings records, payrolls, pension records) The basic legal requirements are: (1) Internal Revenue Service—four years for earnings records (Federal Insurance Contributions Act and Federal Unemployment Tax); (2) Department of Labor, Wage and Hour Division—three years for payrolls, two years for earnings records; and (3) The Department of Labor, Division of Public Contracts—four years for wage and hour records. Pension records are usually retained permanently and may often serve as the earnings record as well.

Personnel. (applications for employment, attendance records, time clock cards, employee history records, personnel folders) Where a company maintains both employee history cards and personnel folders, the history cards may be destroyed within one year after termination of employment. An exception to the latter might be the top executive personnel data. Employment applications

should be kept only for jobs or persons where the company anticipates action in the near future. Attendance records, time clock
cards, and related data should be handled as a package: where this
information is summarized on project or payroll records, the bulky
initial records may be discarded within one to six months.

Production. (job tickets, maintenance records, operating reports,
production orders) Job tickets and production orders are really only
of value in processing the order through the factory or when the
customer raises questions on delivery or quality. These points come
up in the initial months after shipping. Actual production orders are
the only ones that warrant retention beyond one year. And of all
the records for one order (e.g., job ticket, shipping ticket, bill of
lading) only one need be retained in the original. Most information
is repeated from one form to the next. Maintenance records are
usually retained for the life of the equipment on which the data are
compiled. Monthly operating reports on production are valuable up
to two years. Annual operating reports should be kept permanently
for historical and management purposes.

Purchasing. (bids, purchase orders, receiving reports, purchase
requisition) Purchase orders should be broken down into categories
for retention purposes: major equipment, expendable supplies and
materials, and the like. Major purchase records, particularly where
specifications are included, might be kept for six years. Routine
items may be cut to three years and still stay within legal requirements on proof of local purchase and on records of use for tax
purposes. Purchase requisitions need be retained only until the
items are received—since the data are covered on the purchase
order. Receiving reports are usually supporting documents for the
accounts payable vouchers and are retained accordingly. Bids are
kept after a contract is let out only so long as management wants
them for post-audit purposes, and so long as purchasing agents may
need them as references for the next contract where the services or
items may be identical, or nearly so, for the same service or items.

Real Estate. (deeds, leases) Deeds, rights-of-way, and easements
are usually retained permanently; leases for six years after expiration. If leases are renewed annually, they may be kept only for the
current year plus one.

Sales. (correspondence, customer orders, salesmen's reports)
Sales correspondence on deliveries, acknowledgments, bids, and so
on, need only be kept at the most 30 to 60 days for possible answer
and followup. Policy letters should be segregated and retained permanently. Customer orders in sales departments are only copies of
accounts receivable files and should be kept, if at all, for minimum
periods. Salesmen's reports on individual sales, and expenses, are

important only for immediate review. They warrant keeping for only a few months.

Secretary. (annual reports, by-laws, minutes of stockholders' meetings, canceled stock certificates) The first three items are usually kept permanently. Canceled stock certificates are not governed by any federal legal requirement (except for regulated companies) and may be destroyed at the discretion of the company. However, most firms keep a formal certificate of destruction.

Tax. (purchase-and-use tax returns, state and federal tax returns) Regulations on purchase-and-use taxes usually state that a city must announce its intentions to act on a company's returns within three years. There is no limitation, however, in case of fraud. The same holds true of state and federal returns. The purchase-and-use tax statements are usually retained for three years. State and federal returns, being more involved, are retained at least six years, often permanently. Work papers may be destroyed within the minimum periods.

Traffic. (bills of lading, freight bills, packing lists) The only legal requirement on these items is on "order, shipping, and billing records"—Department of Labor, Wage and Hour Division—for two years. However, there is rarely need for more than one official record to cover any one shipment (see also preceding section on "Production").

Preparing Records for Storage

Some companies, particularly larger ones and those located in expensive office buildings, have established outlying records centers in low-cost buildings or areas. One consideration here is the possible historical use of the records to be stored. Company rules and policies, for example, that were in effect during World War II will provide valuable guides to follow in the event of another war. Then too, it sometimes happens that a company must revive a practice which has not been in use for a number of years; the memory of some office "old-timer" is all the company can lean on.

Many companies retain historical material by sampling a certain part according to some established plan. Some save 10 percent by selecting every tenth record, destroying the rest. Others use certain key days of the month or letters of the alphabet. Following is one system used by a major corporation for many years. The description is directed to employees preparing records for storage. Here is how the procedure was explained:

1. Records shall be reviewed to determine whether they belong in the group classified "General" for which mandatory periods

of preservation are established by the secretary, or whether they belong in the group classified "Routine" for which retention is determined by organizations having jurisdiction.

2. Papers having no value as records such as extra copies shall be removed and destroyed, and records for which prescribed periods of preservation have expired shall be removed and authorized for destruction.

3. For most economical storage heavy binders, folders, index sheets, fasteners (including paper clips) which constitute unnecessary bulk shall be removed or replaced with less bulky items which can be made to serve the same purpose (i.e., heavy binders may be replaced by kraft folders; many thin folders may be combined into a single folder; contents may be removed from folders and filed loosely in stapled sets; Acco or other bulky fasteners may be replaced by wire staples).

4. Rubber bands deteriorate in storage and shall be replaced by paper bands to eliminate risk of confusion which may be caused by physical breakdown of files.

5. Papers constituting a file or subject segregated by means of paper bands, or folders, or fastened together in stapled sets shall be plainly labeled to indicate the divisional file reference number and other description of records, including date or period covered.

Card records expected to be used infrequently for reference shall be arranged in banded sets in such a way that they can be conveniently placed in storage boxes. Custodian of the record room shall be consulted for method of packing and labeling since these vary with the size and nature of the records.

6. Records so prepared shall be placed in kraft storage envelopes (9 inches high, 12 or 15 inches long, 4 inches expansion), and the filled envelopes shall then be placed in storage boxes approximately the same size as the envelopes. (The boxes, which are marked with temporary numbers on the outside, are used for convenience in transporting records to storage.)

Upon arrival in the record room, the envelopes and their contents are removed from boxes and placed in metal transfer cases. Pressboard tabbed guides are used to mark the beginning of each storage unit (see Par. 7d) which may consist of one envelope or many envelopes of related records. All records contained in one storage unit shall be scheduled for destruction at the same time.

In order to facilitate the handling, storage, withdrawal and refiling of inactive records, the subdivisions within a storage unit (i.e., folders, binders, banded sets, etc.) shall be arranged in organizational file sequence and each of the subdivisions shall be assigned a number in sequence beginning with the numeral 1 for the first subdivision at the front of the first envelope in the storage unit, and continuing through the last subdivision in the last envelope of the storage unit.

7. For each storage unit four copies of a form entitled, "Index to Records in Secretary's Organization Storage at General Headquarters" shall be prepared in typewritten form showing:

    a. Subdivision number, with complete description of records contained in each subdivision, including period covered;

    b. Records Schedule—i.e., information indicating whether records are classified "General" with applicable paragraph number of Secretary's Direction which covers such records and which specifies period of preservation established for them, or "Routine" with period of preservation established by organization having jurisdiction over the records involved;

    c. Name of organization having jurisdiction, and name of person responsible for sending records to storage;

    d. Date period of preservation expires as computed from date of records (see item a, above) on basis of records schedule (see item b, above);

    Custodian of the record room examines all records reviewed for storage to ascertain that all instructions regarding preparation for storage have been complied with, and then assigns a storage unit number which is a combination of (1) prefix letter indicating size and type of container in which records are to be stored; (2) year records are consigned to storage; (3) accession number in series beginning with 1 for each storage container group; (4) suffix letter combination indicating name of general division having jurisdiction over records sent to storage.

    Example: C-56-1236-GA—indicates the 1236th unit filed in correspondence size transfer case for the year 1956—sent by Comptroller's Organization.

    This method of assigning storage unit numbers enables the custodian of the record room to fill up transfer cases (and shelves where used for oversize records) solidly without regard to kind of records or sending organization, thus eliminating guesswork and wasted facilities which ordinarily result when storage space is allocated to the various organizations or according to type of record involved.

8. Storage unit members are stamped on pressboard guide tab (see item 6), on each subdivision within the unit, and on all copies of the Index form referred to in Par. 7. One copy of the form is filed by the records clerk in a centralized file according to divisions sending records to storage, arranged by unit number within the divisional groups, and one copy is returned to organization sending records to storage. Other copies used for followup.

9. Requests for records from storage are made on special salmon tabbed requisitions which serve as "Out Guide." The only information required for locating records in storage is storage unit number and subdivision number. (By using this method records clerk avoids the necessity of familiarizing herself with labeling idiosyncrasies and filing systems of a hundred or more file clerks in the various organizations—theoretically she doesn't even have to know what has been sent to her for storage.)

Storage Costs

A specific area of dollar savings is reduction of high rent space necessary to store unnecessary records. Very probably a company's file rooms are bulging and chewing up dollars of cost. It is almost a foregone conclusion that if a company decides how long it should keep a specific record (based on the need to keep) that it will discover that it keeps that record considerably in excess of the needed time. Therefore, if these records are destroyed, space is liberated intelligently with a minimum risk to the company and with a resultant saving. Any reduction in the amount of records kept must also result in a savings in filing equipment used.

In some cases the space and equipment savings have been of sufficient size to justify the entire expense of a records retention program and the reference and protection needs of a company have been bonus achievements.

A record retention program will satisfy these sometimes conflicting requirements and needs. Any record should have a reference or protective use or it should not be kept.

It will be remembered that the subject of record retention is not an "attention getter." The motivation of various levels of supervision is not nearly as great for this subject as it is for others with more appeal for personal advancement.

Nevertheless, without cooperation at all levels the program will probably not succeed. But experience has shown that when supervision has become familiar with the program and its objectives, and when the program has become routine, then the program receives the cooperation it needs to survive and it will become better and better.

Therefore, the education of supervision, including department heads, becomes something to which the committee should direct considerable attention.

The level of personnel to which some program of explanation should be directed is that level immediately under the management level which is fostering the program. It is this level which usually is sensitive about someone else "sticking their nose into my records." It is to this level that top management must communicate their feelings about the program and the need for a centralized control.

In each company this will be handled differently. In some companies it will be practical to accomplish this communication directly through a combined meeting. In others, particularly the larger companies, this is impractical and the usual means of a directive letter may be used. However, a letter can only cover the directive part of the communication and can rarely carry sufficient explanation to produce the degree of cooperation wanted. In this case, some form of visual presentation such as a slide-tape talk may be justified. Experience has shown that a reasonably complete explanation at the very outset of the program can avoid quite unpleasant misunderstandings. Said bluntly, it is difficult for this level of authority to realize that management really wants or needs centralized control on this rather unimportant (in their minds) area of records or that management is really "behind the program."

Whatever form of communication is developed for the higher levels of supervision can usually be used with little or no change for all levels of supervision down to and including department heads.

CHAPTER 23

MICROFILM
AND MICROFICHE

THE STORAGE AND RETRIEVAL of information are greatly facilitated by the use of micrographics—reducing the size of the original document to very small (micro) form. Popularly, this process has been called "microfilming." Today, however, this labeling is hardly adequate due to the continuous expansion of the field of microrecords and the invention and marketing of new methods and equipment. Today, there are not only rolls of film, but also film cartridges, aperture cards, microfiche, and the strip holder—a 14-inch-long, molded plastic channel into which are inserted from one to 10 strips of microfilm. Owing to the many new "faces" of microrecords, the term "microforms" is more adequate in referring to the entire process of reducing the size of original documents for easier and prolonged handling.

Usage of microfilms can effectively contribute to the control of records management costs. The rather inexpensive photographic and storage methods today enable any company, large and small, to take advantage of the substantial savings in space, personnel and hard cash. The narrowing cost-profit picture has a lot to do with the popularity of microforms. Executives and records management supervisors have found in microforms a very good alternative to the more costly information handling and storage methods.

A Dartnell Institute of Business Research survey indicated that about one-third of the respondents had microform equipment. Of this number, approximately three-quarters had microfilm capability, 50 percent had microfiche, and nearly 20 percent had COM (Computer Output Microfilm) ability. Of the total number of respondents indicating some kind of microform equipment, nearly half had only microfilm capability.

We also asked respondents how long the microform equipment had been in use (any units). The response was *a median of six years* with 5½ years as an average. This represented a range from one month to 20 years.

Large volume users of microfilmed documents can take advantage of today's technology by using this Kodak KAR-4000 information system designed for the storage and retrieval of computer data and source document images on microfilm. The central processing unit supports a printer and up to eight information consoles consisting of a CRT and a Kodak IMT-150 microimage terminal.

Offices with microfilm capability have a range from one month to 10 years of operation. Those with microfiche alone had a range of from one month to eight years.

This information, compiled on length of time microforms have been in these offices, indicates that many of the respondents have had a substantial period of operation, apparently successful. On the other hand, the large number of new installations would seem to point to a growing use, with many decisions to convert having taken place in 1976. It might also be noted that companies which have microfilm capability (only) have had the capability between two and 10 years in 5 percent of the reports submitted.

Filming Capability

It probably would be no surprise to learn that offices with more than one microform capability also have more filming capacity (cameras). Some 52 percent (still only half) of the offices reported that they prepared their own films within this group. Some 35 percent of the firms with microfilm capability have only camera equipment, and only 16 percent of the companies with microfiche capability have only the cameras for doing this job.

Actually, the large majority of offices rely on service bureaus, suppliers and the home office to get the microforms into their system. At the same time, a strong number of offices reported the use of *both* the rotary and planetary cameras to accomplish the job.

Comments

About 5 percent of the total group responding to the records management survey said they had either looked into the potential use of microforms, were planning to use some system or wished they had the capability. Here are a few comments to round out the picture:

> "I know that by using microfilm or microfiche to copy old but important records, we could save floor space as well as storage space. Right now, we have boxes of old membership application forms that could easily be converted to microfilm or microfiche. But, the expense of conversion has been our drawback."

> "We are in a study process to determine the best system for fiche in our central files. We estimate a one-time expenditure at $10,000 to achieve annual savings of $6,000."

> "We checked into the possibility of microfilm, but it was too expensive for our use."

> "We are trying to determine if microfilm can be used cheaply enough for our work."

> "By not having micrographics in operation, our storage of 'live' and 'active' files has become cumbersome. We are rapidly approaching a critical shortage in storage space."

These comments, perhaps, sum up the basics of current records management. Many people are fast running out of space for file drawers and shelves, others are concerned about the costs and operations of microforms. The individual reports proved, at least, that money can be saved in many ways, not least of which is file reorganization and the dumping of old and useless records.

Questions to Ask

Any company can benefit from the use of microforms to record, preserve and retrieve business information. Transformed into microfilms are purchase orders and the documents they generate: shipping tickets, invoices, bills of lading, receiving reports and others. Other records that are easily kept on microfilm are waybills, sales slips, personnel files, requisitions, check vouchers, canceled checks, warranty data, stockholder lists, medical records, suggestion files and correspondence. To find out which of your operations can be enhanced by microfilming, answer the following questions:

1. On a monthly basis, what is the paper volume involved?
2. What is the filing method, and how often are documents retrieved?
3. How many employees are retrieving documents from these files, where are the files and the employees located, and how frequently are searches unsuccessful due to "out-of-file"?
4. How long does it take to make an average retrieval?
5. What is the average retention time of the documents?

Careful answers to these questions will indicate whether or not microfilm can be used with considerable advantage in your firm. However, these are only preliminary incentives, and when a microform system is seriously contemplated, consultations with a microform consultant is highly recommended, as the pros and cons of any such systems will be expertly laid out for your final judgment.

However, the following general criteria should be evaluated carefully to determine if it is feasible from the standpoint of cost and systems efficiency to convert the original documents to microform.

- Can considerable space be saved by converting to microrecords?
  Consider the facts:
  Savings in space of 99 percent are reported when microrecording is used. For instance, as many as 3,000 standard-size 8½" × 11" letters or 30,000 bank checks can be placed on 100 feet of 16mm film with obvious savings in floor space and filing equipment, ease of handling, and freeing of space for more productive use.

- Can the paperwork system be rendered more efficient by using microrecords?
  Consider the facts:
  Commercial banking check-return systems are facilitated by microfilming in that both sides of a customer's check are microrecorded after the check is charged against the customer's account and before the check is returned to the customer. Retail stores use microrecording in connection with monthly billing of customers. The beginning balance, monthly charges and payments, and the final balance are recorded on the statement form, and the statement is microrecorded, after which the original of the statement and the sales slips are mailed to the customer. In case of error or dispute, a full-size print (hard copy) can be made. Other bulky materials, such as engineering drawings and university research papers, which are difficult to store and transport through the mails, are now microrecorded. Duplicate copies of the film can be made on other film or

transferred to aperture cards for use by engineers (in the case of drawings) or scholars, and are easily mailed.

- Will microrecording properly protect and preserve the records?
  Consider the facts:
  Microrecords may last as long as the best rag-content paper—100 to 300 years—but careful atmospheric conditions must be maintained. Copies of important documents can be microrecorded and stored in a safe place away from the original storage location to protect the records against fire, theft and other mishaps. Equipment is available for double filming, in which case one copy can be made for storage and one for active use.

- Is a large quantity of records to be stored for a long period?
  Consider these rules of thumb:
  If a record is to be retained only three years, or for a shorter period of time, it costs less to keep the record than to photograph it. If a record may be retained from four to seven years, it may be less expensive to keep the record than to microrecord it. Records kept from seven to 15 years should be considered for microrecording if the accessibility of the record and the cost of the "saved" storage space warrant it. Records kept on a permanent basis should be converted to microform unless they are frequently used in their original form.

- Can the cost of the microrecording operation be justified?
  Consider the facts:
  Each of the preceding four criteria must be carefully weighed before a decision on microfilming can be made. Since the use of microrecords cannot be considered solely on a dollars-and-cents basis, the convenience of the system to the office personnel and to management must be given priority.

Specific Criteria

In addition to the general criteria just discussed, many specific criteria must be considered before a decision is made to convert to microrecords. The following are key points:

- Are microrecords acceptable as evidence in courts of law?
  Consider the facts:
  Microrecords are largely accepted in courts of law, but care must be taken to ensure that

  —all governmental regulations concerning records have been observed;

  —all microrecords have been properly certified as to their authenticity with certification "targets," which are included as a part of the microfilmed copy, showing the reason for microrecording and method of record disposal;

— microrecording is a regular, standard procedure and not a sudden "coverup" to falsify or "manufacture" new filmed records.

Records such as government securities, licenses, citizenship papers, passports, and draft cards—along with others specified by the federal government—may not be microrecorded because of government prohibitions. The original of these documents should be kept.

- Are the specific costs involved low enough to permit microrecording?
Consider the facts:
Microrecording is rather expensive and time consuming. The following specific costs are involved:
1. Cameras. To photograph the original documents.
2. Readers. To enlarge the miniature record for viewing.
3. Film. For photographing and storing the records.
4. Special storage files. For storing the microforms.
5. Labor. For preparing documents for microfilming (straightening out documents that are folded, removing staples or clips, etc.).
6. Labor. For operating camera equipment.
7. Labor. For managing the microrecords, such as:
Inspecting the record for filming.
Indexing the record.
Editing the record.
Labeling containers, files, etc.
Supervision in training workers, and developing any new procedures.

- Are security and protection of the records adequate in microrecording?
Consider the facts:
1. Has the original document been destroyed?
2. Can a dispersal system be developed for storing two microimages of a record in two safe but different locations?
3. Are all contingencies, such as fire, flood, temperature, theft, provided for? (Extreme heat, cold, dryness or moisture subject a film to irreparable deterioration.)

- Will the characteristics of the document to be microfilmed permit it to be photographed successfully?
Consider the facts:

1. Blurred carbon copies on white paper do not photograph well.
2. Color problems frequently found include trying to photograph faint hectographed or mimeographed material, negative photostats, deep shades of colored paper and blurred carbon copies with "trees" of carbon on the sheets.

The Elements

MICROFILM. The microrecording operation involves photographing the documents, usually on 16- or 35-millimeter film. Film sizes may range from 8 to 70 or 105mm, and records microphotographed may be reduced in size to varying degrees. If a record 10 inches by 10 inches were reduced to a microimage 1 inch by 1 inch, the reduction ratio would be 10:1. If this same original size record were reduced to one-half inch, the reduction ratio would then become 20:1. The reduction ratios may vary from 5:1 to more than 50:1. The tiny microimages, of course, are actual pictures of the original documents; but specialized equipment is required before they can be either photographed or later used. Although there is considerable variety in the type of this equipment, depending on specific needs, generally the microfilming operation includes these basic items of equipment:

1. The camera and film processor.
2. The reader (either a reader-viewer or reader-printer) for magnifying the filmed image and projecting it for viewing.
3. Photoprinting attachments.
4. Special cabinets for microrecorded storage.

Several recent variations in this basic procedure should be noted. Usually when someone wishes to use a microrecord (the original of which has been destroyed or stored elsewhere), the microform on which the document appears is placed on a reader-viewer which magnifies the image to its original readable size. A reader-printer enables the user to obtain a copy of any document existing on the microform.

APERTURE CARD. Although the most widespread use of microrecords is on reels of film, individual pictures (frames) are frequently clipped from the film roll and mounted on a special card that contains an opening (aperture) that fits the size of the frame. These aperture cards can then be handled manually or mechanically in a manner similar to the method of processing or of sorting punched cards. Retrieval, therefore, can be mechanically performed on aperture cards just as the punched card sorter is able to select out of a deck of cards those cards with prescribed identification on them. The microrecording operation then becomes an integral part of a mechanized data processing system. The most common use of aperture cards is for storing microimages of engineering drawings.

MICROFICHE. While the most common microimages appear on rolls of film and aperture cards, another microfilm—the microfiche—is achieving widespread popularity. "Fiche" (pronounced "feesh") is a French word meaning "card." Microfiche, therefore, represents a sheet of film the size of a standard index card on which microimages (microsize negatives of photographed records) are arranged in an orderly fashion. Such microfiche sheets are usually produced in one of the popular standard card sizes, 3×5, 4×6 or 5×8, with either positive or negative images. The negative image serves as a master for photographing the images onto plates for offset printing where large quantities of hard copies (prints) are desired.

A microfiche card, therefore, represents a set of microimages of related documents. The images are easy to find, easy to read or reproduce in reader-printers, and can be mailed quickly and economically. This microform, too, is easily adaptable to coding signals. Since it is usually standard-card size, it can be manually indexed, filed and retrieved as are cards. Usually microfiche carries eye-legible indexing data above the microfilmed frames at the top of the card, showing in a coded or abbreviated form the contents of the microfiche.

The largest user of microfiche is the Federal Government in the National Aeronautics and Space Administration and the Atomic Energy Commission. As a result, the Government and the National Microfilm Association have adopted the 105×148mm (or 4×6 card size) as the microfiche standard. Since one such microfiche may contain a maximum of 98 pages of records (originally 8½×11 in size) reduced to microimages, common applications tend to be collections of related documents such as automotive service and parts data and the Thomas Micro-Catalog—a seven-inch stack of 4×6 microfiche in which 60,000 industrial catalog pages are recorded and held ready for reference.

System Affordability

A small company can get into microforms without investing a large sum of money. As a matter of fact, a highly functional microfilm system can be had for less than it would take to lease a medium-size office copier—only a reader and camera are needed.

In its simplest form, a secretary uses a microfilm camera to photograph original documents, and produces two rolls of 16mm film at one time. The exposed film is sent to a film laboratory for processing and inspection. When the processed films return to the office, one roll goes to an off-premises storage vault as a security copy, the other is cut into strips and loaded into coded or indexed film jackets. A desk-top reader is used to view the filmed information. Records which are not frequently searched can also be kept, filmed and stored on 16mm roll film.

To reference a document, the microfilm is placed in the reader and the operator manually locates the desired information by following document sequencing. If paper copies are required, they can be quickly reproduced with a reader-printer—which is more expensive than a plain reader.

A more elaborate system would start with a larger rotary (roll film) micro camera which offers indexing capabilities. Indexing is done by recording a retrieval code right onto the film, thus facilitating faster accessibility to requested information by pinpointing the location of such information. In case documents usage is frequent, special indexes can be created for each document at the filming stage. Using equipment such as Kodak's image control, an external index can be created for direct access referencing, and the master index can be retained in the computer. The appropriate code can be pressed into the keyboard on the microfilm reader. The average search time is 10–15 seconds. In the most sophisticated combination, documents are retrieved by description rather than by location code. Descriptors are put onto the film during the filming and the information is retrieved by keying descriptions into the reader keyboard. Individual documents can be electronically retrieved at the rate of 170 per second.

THE EQUIPMENT

Microfilm Cameras

Microfilming begins with a camera, and choosing the proper one requires careful planning and foresight. If you are considering in-house filming (as there are facilities for outside filming of documents and records), the following guidelines should help you in evaluating the many systems available.

Types of Cameras

Microfilm cameras are divided into four categories:

ROTARY. These cameras feature simple, largely automatic operation and rapid throughput. Documents to be filed are hand-fed one at a time by an operator or are automatically fed into the unit on a transport mechanism connected to a film transport. The movement of both the document and the film is precisely synchronized so that they move past the lens at the same time as the exposure is made.

Rotary cameras will microfilm in any of three formats or modes—standard, duo or duplex. Most of them offer a choice of film units and packages that determine the reduction ratio and mode. The major disadvantages of these units are the size restrictions of source documents that can be filmed and the inability to accept bound documents.

PLANETARY. When photographing with a planetary camera, the document remains stationary on a flat surface while the camera shoots it. The film, too, remains in a stationary position and is intermittently advanced, much like conventional cameras. Different reductions are obtained by raising or lowering the camera. The primary advantages of planetary cameras include lower equipment cost, the variety of size and type of documents which can be microfilmed and the fine quality of reproduction produced. However, these units involve the slow manual operation of placing each source document on a flatbed.

STEP-AND-REPEAT. These cameras are highly-specialized planetary microfilmers. They create a series of separate images on rows and columns on an area of film according to a predetermined design, producing microfiche rather than roll film. Step-and-repeat cameras are known for fast turnaround time.

COMPUTER OUTPUT MICROFILM (COM). These units eliminate the computer printout stage by converting the data stored on a computer's magnetic tape directly to microfilm. Although there are several ways to convert mag tapes to microfilm, a commonly-used method is for the tape to be read and the image displayed on a cathode ray tube. A camera, which is part of the COM recorder, then photographs the image. COM units are also capable of producing microfiche directly.

Type of Document is Important

Before purchasing a microfilm system, carefully investigate the various types of source documents that will be filmed. How do the documents vary in size? Will the camera accommodate them all? Some cameras, for instance, will not accept legal-size documents. Generally, planetary cameras accept a greater variety of size and type of documents than rotary cameras. The quantity of documents to be filmed is also important, so determine how much microfilming you will be doing and if your volume warrants a high-speed unit.

This new Kodak microimage processor utilizes laser technology and a heat-processed film to produce computer output microfilm.

Another decision you must make is the type of microform that will best satisfy your needs. Microforms are available in many formats, each having a range of applications designed to fulfill certain requirements. Thus, in choosing between roll microfilm, microfiche, cartridges, aperture cards, cassettes, jackets, or others (as new forms are constantly being patented and marketed), be sure you select the form that matches your needs. In making your decision, keep in mind the type of input, the nature of the information to be stored, how it is to be used, frequency of updating and retrieval, storage density and means of reading and duplication. If you will be using applications where both roll microfilm and microfiche will be used, choose a conventional roll microfilmer since roll film can be

579

cut into strips to produce fiche, but fiche cannot be converted into roll film.

Also be sure that the camera can facilitate the storage and retrieval method that will save you the most time since retrieval indexing begins in the camera. Many film indexing systems are available, including sequential numbering of documents, use of a code line, image control marks, and a retrieval blip encoder. A binary code that describes the contents of the document, as opposed to its location, is also available.

Image Quality

What kind of image quality do you require in the microfilm? Is legibility of data sufficient or must fine lines be reproduced? A high degree of image quality is dependent on a good optical system and a low reduction level. The reduction ratio, as defined by the National Micrographics Association (NMA), is a "measure of the number of times a linear dimension of an object is reduced when photographed, expressed as 16X, 24X, etc." Basically, the lower the reduction level, the clearer the image. This is not to say, however, that a high reduction and a sharp lens will not provide a sharp image. Deciding which reduction ratio is best for you also depends on such factors as storage space, since the reduction level will affect storage density.

In general, planetary cameras produce the fine-line reproduction and image quality needed for such technical applications as the microfilming of engineering drawings. In addition, they provide a greater variety of reduction ratios than rotary units without changing the film unit. However, since they are slower than rotary cameras, production throughput will not be as great. Considering these factors, you must therefore determine if a high-speed rotary camera will deliver sufficient image quality for your application or if a slower, more precise planetary camera is required.

Resolution (the measure of sharpness of an image) also affects the image quality. Resolution is usually expressed in terms of the number of lines per millimeter that are discernible. This measurement is important for the readability of the microfilm duplicate, and printability when a hard copy is required. According to the NMA, resolution in processed microfilm is affected by film emulsion, exposure, camera lens, camera adjustment, camera vibration and film processing. Therefore, to make sure that you will obtain the resolution you desire, it is worthwhile to test the resolution of the camera you are considering purchasing. This can be done by examining a microfilmed resolution test chart under a microscope to determine the smallest pattern in which horizontal and vertical lines can be seen.

Normally, the lowest resolution considered acceptable is 90 lines per millimeter. A measurement of 120 or higher is considered excellent for reduction ratios below 30X. Again, remember that as reduction ratios increase, resolutions must reach higher values to provide a sharp image.

Compatibility

Be sure the camera you choose will be compatible with existing or proposed microfilm equipment in your company. For instance, there may be other microfilm users in other departments in your firm or among agencies with whom you deal. If your program is compatible with theirs, fewer problems are likely to occur. Thus, if you do source document filming, and COM is being used or considered, the reduction ratio should be compatible to enable the same readers to be used for both applications. The microfilms should also meet the same standards for quality, mode or archival quality others in the company may have. Also, be sure that the indexing code used by the camera is acceptable to the readers.

Costs

Measure equipment costs in relation to factors other than the initial capital cost. For instance, planetary cameras are generally less expensive than high-speed rotary cameras. However, the savings resulting from increased productivity and a reduction in labor by using a rotary unit might save you more money in the long run. However, if your volume is so small that high-speed automated equipment might save you only a few minutes each day, the extra cost cannot be justified. Similarly, the advantages in reduced labor in fiche production from step-and-repeat cameras should also be weighed against higher capital costs. Other than speed, the quality of optics affects the price of a camera. Added accessories designed to make the camera more rapid or versatile also add to its price. You must decide which of these features are essential enough to warrant the extra cost.

Some of the leading manufacturers of microform cameras are: Bruning Division of Addressograph-Multigraph Corp.; Bell & Howell; Eastman Kodak Co.; GAF Corp.; Information International; 3M Co.; NCR Corp. and Zytron Corp.

Microfilm Processor

In a complete in-house micrographic system, the film processor provides an important link between film exposure and duplication. Processing is necessary to visibly form and fix the latent image on the microform. Determining the exact combination of features necessary to meet your needs is complicated and should be done only after investigating all possibilities and discussing options with qualified vendors. However, an analysis of some of the elements involved in processing and points to consider in choosing a processor should be beneficial in making this decision.

In-House Processing

One of the most important decisions about microfilm processing concerns whether the film should be processed in-house or sent to a service bureau. This will depend largely on whether your volume is large enough to cost justify purchasing a microfilm processor and the necessary supplies.

To calculate the cost of an in-house processing system consider the following: A small in-house processor can be obtained for $2,500. However, the cost of film and chemicals should also be included. Ideally, the camera operator would also process the film, eliminating additional labor costs. To further evaluate the costs involved, multiply the service bureau's charge for processing one roll of film by the average number of rolls per day. If you now send out five rolls per day at $2.20 per roll (a reasonable average cost for processing of 16mm x 100 ft.), your daily cost is $11 and your annual cost is $2,200. In such a case, you would be able to amortize the $3,000 cost of the processor, film and chemicals in a little over 18 months. You would also maintain complete control over the film, providing quality control, file security and confidentiality. In addition, you could ensure fast turnaround on priority items.

Input to Processor

Choose a processor that is suitable for the film you are using and your workload. Establish your needs, taking into consideration the amount of film being processed, the size or sizes of film being processed, and the thickness of the film being processed. Volume, normally expressed in the number of feet of film width per month, should also be considered. Short runs should use a leaderless processor while longer runs usually require leaders. Throughput time in processors can vary from immediate processing to 10 or more minutes, so choose one that can run fast enough to handle your peak load. In addition, try to determine any growth in processing volume that might occur in the foreseeable future.

Kinds of Processing

The processor should be able to prepare the film for the stage that will follow. One of the most important decisions you must make concerns the polarity of the processed film, a term used to indicate the change or retention of the dark to light relationship of an image. To make this decision, it is helpful to know the kinds of processing operations and the types of film involved.

Standard processing, also known as direct, negative or nonreversal processing, develops the film to the polarity opposite the original document. In source document microfilming, standard processing produces a negative-appearing image — one with light characters and images on a dark background. In COM, it produces a positive-appearing image — one with dark characters and images on a light background. Standard processing includes develop, wash, fix and dry stages.

Full-reversal processing, on the other hand, is a polarity maintaining process. This procedure creates a positive-appearing image in source document microfilming. In COM, it produces a negative-appearing image. Stages involved in this process include develop, bleach, clear, re-expose, develop, fix, wash and dry.

Types of Film

Different types of film are used in microfilming, each designed for a specific application and each demanding a specific type of processing. Diazo duplicating film, for instance, is exposed by strong ultraviolet light to form an image which is developed with ammonia. Diazo retains image polarity and requires use of chemicals. Its strength lies in its retention of image throughout duplication.

With vesicular duplicating film, the image is exposed by ultraviolet light and developed by heat. The exposed elements in the film form light-scattering centers upon development. Duplication reverses polarity and requires no chemicals. Silver halide film, which is used for original camera exposure and occasionally for duplication, is composed of silver compounds that produce a white image from black, and a black image from white. Silver film reverses or maintains polarity. Archival film is used for archival records due to its high resistance to deterioration during use and storage.

Facilities

Most processors require electricity, a drain of sufficient diameter and noncorrosive material, and hot and cold water plumbing. Running wash water is necessary to process large quantities of archival film. These processors are designed for medium or long runs. Other processors, however, are designed as self-contained plumbingless units. These have the advantage of requiring only electricity, allowing processing in many settings. And even though the absence of running wash water restricts the possibility for archival quality film, it does not completely eliminate it. Plumbingless processors are usually built with small capacity tanks and are mainly designed for short runs.

Some processors require a darkroom while others can be operated in normal office light. Similarly, standard room ventilation may be adequate for certain units, while added ventilation is required for others.

Camera/Processor

Although stand-alone cameras and processors are very popular today, combination camera/processor units are gaining wide acceptance. In determining whether your requirements warrant such a unit, evaluate your needs based on the demand for immediate availability of film, security, quality control and cost.

Costs

Most processors on the market today will provide the user with a comparable high level of quality output. The difference in price is mainly due to the various features and capacities of each processor. When comparing processors, a cost and time analysis should be performed on chemical consumption, cost of chemicals required, width of film, speed and volume. In weighing the initial capital cost, keep in mind that a small processor may be more expensive to run when it is frequently overloaded. And, of course, be sure that your volume warrants the purchase of an in-house processor and that the cost can be justified.

Some of the leading manufacturers of processors are: Bruning Division of Addressograph-Multigraph Corp., Cordell Engineering, 3M Co., Stromberg DatagraphiX and Zytron Corp.

Readers and Reader/Printers

One of the first decisions to make is whether to buy a reader, a reader/printer or a mix of both types of equipment. Microform readers display the image on the screen; reader/printers also have a display, but they can produce paper copies of a microfilmed image when desired. Most firms will need at least one reader/printer, but since they are considerably more expensive than a reader, the cost should be justified by usage. How often is a hard copy printout of a microimage needed? That should be the main determining factor in deciding for or against a reader/printer.

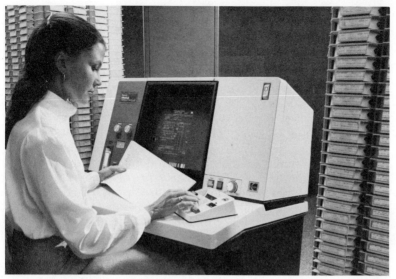

This modern microimage terminal provides users with an automated retrieval capability in a stand-alone configuration that does not require the terminal to interface with a computer.   *Courtesy Kodak Company*

Type of Microform

One of the first factors to consider is the film format that will be used by the organization. The most popular types for office use are roll film (in reels, cassettes or cartridges), jackets and microfiche. For very high reduction ratios ultrafiche, a condensed form of microfiche, is used. Aperture cards are utilized mainly in engineering applications. Many readers and printers are designed to handle only one microform, but an increasing number of models can accommodate, or can be adapted to accommodate, two or more different types of microforms. Some models, for instance, can change from fiche to a roll or cartridge in seconds. The hardware chosen should be capable of handling the film formats which are used by the firm.

The size of the equipment is also an important factor. Readers are available in portable, desktop and large console sizes; printers come in desktop and console models. Portable readers are ideal for low volume office applications, as well as for use by traveling executives. The most commonly-used readers and printers in the office, however, are desktop models. They are durable, compact and provide the user with a number of important features and options. Reproduction (blow-back) size on desktop models usually falls between 75 percent and 100 percent of original size, although some models produce images that are larger than the original. Console models are best utilized in high-volume applications or when a very large screen size is required.

Readers range in price from $100 for a portable model to over $1,000 for a heavy-duty console unit. Printers start at under $1,000 and may cost several thousand dollars, depending on the sophistication of the unit. Models with automated retrieval of film images are generally the most expensive, but the time saved in the retrieval process may more than compensate for the initial high cost.

Emerging now are microcomputer controlled readers. Indexing information is stored in the computer for automatic retrieval of randomly-filed documents. Today, this type of system is being used extensively to retrieve and display directory listings. Static information is stored on microfilm; changes to the listing are shown on a display terminal that is on-line to a minicomputer.

Screen Quality

Whether a reader or printer is purchased, the unit's screen is an essential element of the system. Its size, color, mode, viewing angle and clarity of image should be carefully studied. The choice of screen size should be based upon the size of the original documents filmed and whether or not full document viewing is a requirement. If originals are standard letter size, an 8½ × 11 inch screen is suitable. For viewing slightly larger documents or COM (computer output microfilm), and 11×11 inch screen may be chosen. For full viewing of computer printouts, and 11×14 inch screen is required, and an 18×24 inch size is recommended for engineering drawings.

Green, blue and gray are the most commonly-used screen colors, but a black-and-white combination is also available. Color is largely a matter of personal preference; however, tinted screens lessen eye fatigue, while a neutral or gray screen is essential for viewing color microforms. Screen modes may be either vertical or horizontal. Vertical screens are used mainly for source documents, but COM requires a horizontal screen. Square screens are also available.

Two other screen features, viewing angle and clarity of image, have a great impact on operator performance. The screen should be tilted, or be able to be tilted to a viewing angle that is comfortable for the operator. The image should be sharp and clear across the entire screen, and the illumination of the magnified image should be uniform between the center and the edges of the display. Illumination should be neither too dim nor too bright. Focusing of the image should be adjusted as the microform advances from one frame to the next. All of these factors will influence operator performance by relieving eye strain and fatigue. And that results in increased productivity.

Two other elements involved in viewing microforms are projection and image rotation. Projection of microform image may be either on the front or from the rear of the screen. The image rotation feature gives the unit the capability to handle both vertical and horizontal images. Image rotations of 90, 180 or 360 degrees are common.

Enlarging Capabilities

One of the main factors influencing the flexibility of a reader or reader/printer is the magnification capability. Some units have a fixed lens with only one magnification mode, while others can accommodate a number of interchangeable drop-in lenses with several different magnifications. Machines with dual or triple lens mount assemblies have, respectively, two or three lenses built into the unit. This gives the user the ability to change lenses easily by pushing a switch or rotating a floating turret. A variable zoom lens is used to zero in on one particular portion of an image. Magnifications range from under 20X for aperture cards and X-ray microfiche, to 24X for source documents, to 42X or 48X for COM (48X is the government standard), to 60X and up for ultrafiche. The most commonly-used magnifications are 24X, 42X and 48X, but the machine chosen should be able to handle whatever magnification modes are required by the company.

Film Carriers

Another element that affects the flexibility of the system is the carrier. Film carriers or holders consist of two glass plates which open to accept fiche, jackets and/or aperture cards, depending on the unity. Some units handly only one film size—a 4×6 inch fiche, for instance—while others will accept two different sizes, such as fiche and aperture cards. Similarly, a number of carriers can handle only one fiche at a time, while dual carriers are large enough to accommodate two fiches. Four-fiche carriers and double-deck, eight-fiche carriers are also available.

Other questions to ask about a film carrier include: Is it easy to load? Does it travel smoothly from one image to another? Is it sturdy enough for heavy use? What type of indexing is used?

Indexing of fiche and jackets is most often accomplished by referencing specific positions on the carrier's index grid. Models with a variety of interchangeable grids are available. An X-Y dial or manual positioning is used on some readers to index a specific image on the fiche. At the other end of the spectrum are automated fiche readers, which provide indexing from a keyboard control.

Finding a specific frame on roll film—whether it be in a reel, cartridge or cassette—can be done in several ways:

- Flash cards identifying separate files or groups of documents are filmed on the roll along with the files.
- Sequential numbers are filmed at the top of each image during the microfilming process.
- Code lines are used to separate each frame.
- An odometer is used to register the length of each image as the film advances through the reader. When a number that corresponds to the desired frame appears on the counter, the operator stops the film.
- Marks or blips on the film by a microfilm recorder are sensed by the reader, which counts the blip marks and stops the film at the desired frame. Pushbutton retrieval is also possible with some of these units. The desired document number is entered through the keyboard, and the machine automatically searches for it. This capability can also be linked to a minicomputer, which stores the film file index. This makes it possible to automatically retrieve a randomly-filed document without extensive coding on the film.
- Binary code patterns, which designate index terms or document numbers, enable a reader to present search questions by subject area. The complex readers that are designed for this type of indexing can scan the codes and stop at all frames that come under that classification.

Hard Copies

Where paper copies of microfilmed images are required, a reader/printer is essential. The main factors to consider about the copy-making process are print quality and size, cycle times, process used and cost per copy.

The quality of the print will vary somewhat from model to model, but the copies produced should be easily readable. Copy size will also vary—from 4×5½ inches to 8½×11–12 inches. Some models make both vertical and horizontal prints and others produce reduced-size copies. Continuous copies up to 18 feet long can be made on one model, while another unit offers snap-in cassettes for different paper sizes. A multiple-copy option is available on a few models. Print cycle time—the amount of time required to produce a copy—averages seven to 10 seconds. The process used to make copies may be either wet or dry. The wet electrostatic process requires a liquid toner; the dry silver or thermographic process does not. Cost of wet copies is about 5¢ apiece; dry copies cost about 10¢. A few printers produce copies on plain bond paper for about 10¢ per copy.

Before making a final decision on any reader or reader/printer, be sure it is durable, well constructed and safe. Ease of maintenance and operator convenience features should also be considered. Buy from a reputable vendor who will back up his product with prompt, local service. Read over the warranty carefully. Does it cover both parts and labor? For how long? Consider the variety of options available. Don't buy options you won't use. On the other hand, it is good to know that those options are available if you should need them sometime in the future.

Some of the leading manufacturers of readers and reader/printers are: Bell & Howell, Addressograph Multigraph Corp., Canon U.S.A., A. B. Dick, Eastman Kodak, GAF and NCR.

There Are Limitations

There are limitations and drawbacks that should be known and weighed against the potential cost and operational advantages of a systems microfilm operation before any decision is made to implement it. Some of the disadvantages are:

- Microform records are subject to deterioration that paper records are not. Because microfilm utilizes a gelatin emulsion, it is extremely vulnerable to deterioration due to excessive humidity and temperature variations, as well as the presence of such acidic gasses as sulphur dioxide. Microfilm must therefore be stored in an environmentally-controlled area in which relative humidity remains between 35 and 40%; temperatures between 60 and 72 degrees Fahrenheit; and the air is either free of acidic gases or is filtered to remove them.

- Microfilm is also subject to decay due to improper processing that leaves too much residual hypo on the film's emulsion.

- Microfilm records cannot be annotated. And this is an important thing to consider because report recipients cannot make notations in the margins, nor can they update between its issues, nor correct mistakes.

- It is difficult to compare two microfilm reports or forms simultaneously. Usually, unless the user works with multiple viewers placed side-by-side, he or she must resort to the creation of enlarged reproductions of the microimages.

- Microfilm is panchromatic (sensitive to light of all colors in the visible spectrum), and will not reproduce colors. Therefore, if records are color-coded, either more expensive microfilm must be used or alternative coding must be developed.

- Microfilm must be better indexed than paper records because, due to the many thousands of images contained in the more popular microfilm formats, "browsability" is rarely feasible. This in-depth indexing often necessitates the use of computers, leading to higher preparation costs than would be necessary with a paper-based system.
- Updating of a microfilm-based file through the addition of a new record, or the revision of an existing one, requires the remicrofilming of the entire file with all formats other than micro-jackets or the use of "trailer" microforms, since only the micro-jacket has an add-on capability. The first alternative is generally undesirable since it requires the retention of at least one complete hard copy file and replaces only the duplicates with microfilm. The second alternative is bad since it complicates the retrieval process by introducing multiple microfilm rolls or fiche that must be searched before a retrieval can be completed.

PART 5

Office Practices and Procedures

CHAPTER 24

ORGANIZING FOR OFFICE AUTOMATION

(The following report was prepared for Dartnell by L. Welson. Mr. Welson was with INA Service Company, INA Corporation, at the time. The report is an excellent example of how a large company prepared for the total intergration of office operations in a positive manner.)

THROUGHOUT the 1970's and throughout the business world, study after study was made of the office environment. Generally, these studies concluded that the traditional office required a major overhaul if it was to respond to the increasing workloads and cost pressures that were being imposed by a variety of factors and forces.

INA Corporation, one of the nation's largest diversified financial services companies, was neither immune to nor unaware of these office problems. In the mid-1970's, INA mounted a research-and-technology-oriented effort that was designed to realize the benefits of the "Office of the Future," while minimizing the trauma usually associated with the arrival of new or drastically changed ways of doing things.

Elements of a Problem

Despite impressive figures for assets, revenues and earnings, there existed at INA in the late 1970s the basic elements of a major problem, which may be summarized as follows:

- Workloads were increasing rapidly.
- Costs—particularly labor costs—were rising.
- The environment was labor-intensive.
- Yet there was little or no increase in productivity.

These factors, separately and in combination, had the potential to affect adversely the profit-making capabilities of the various INA lines of businesses. A detailed examination of each factor was therefore undertaken, with the following results:

Increasing Workloads: In INA, revenues adjusted for inflation provide a fairly good measure of workloads. Using 1967 as a base and accounting for inflation, it was found that Corporate revenues—and therefore the workloads—had doubled in the 10 year period, 1967–76.

This internal business growth was the major internal factor directly affecting workloads. In addition, however, it was found that there were external factors exerting a strong impact on the growing workloads at INA.

Rising Costs: At INA, in the 1972–76 period, it was found that the average clerical salary increased from $5,800 to $7,500. This increase did not include the cost of benefits, which were rising at a rate even faster than salaries.

When benefits were taken into account, the average yearly clerical compensation at INA had reached $8,700 by 1977. At the same time, communications and costs at INA were also trending upward, with no relief foreseen.

These trends were of course not unique to INA. Most labor-intensive businesses have experienced these same trends, which are still present in the standard office environment.

Static Productivity: INA revenues doubled in the 10-year period. In the same period the total number of employees also doubled. The number of employees tracked remarkably close to the workloads, as indicated by revenues.

The result was that revenue per employee was constant, indicating no productivity increase. Yet, as was just shown, the costs per employee were increasing.

It was easy to see the continuation of a trend toward an increasing complexity in the way INA was doing business. In addition to the increased workloads related to direct business growth, there were increased workloads arising from external pressures. These pressures resulted in more information to process, more paper to handle, more records to keep. The result was the INA version of the well-documented "information explosion." Among the major external pressures were:

- Growing demands from Federal agencies (such as OSHA, ERISA, and the EEOC) for increased record-keeping. There were also similar demands from state and local governments.
- The need to meet the challenges posed by the competition.
- Pressures from the public sector in the form of consumerism and calls to "meet social responsibilities."
- Last but not least, there were the pressures—and opportunities—arising from technological innovation.

The Electronic Deluge

INA, like other companies, seemed about to be inundated by an electronic or technological deluge. Semiconductor miniaturization techniques were promising reduced costs for almost anything to which the new technology could be applied. The huge drop in cost of the hand-held calculator (from $1,600 to less than $10 in less than a decade) is an often-cited example of the economic effects of this technology. With such dramatic cost reductions always a possibility, the application of technology became an attractive option.

In fact, there were many technologies to be considered. These technologies—new and renewed—were accompanied by a small army of vendors and a bewildering array of products, as well as the possibility of the integration of data processing and word processing (DP and WP).

The most visible technology back in 1977 at INA was word processing, which was then (as it is now) difficult to define. That is, word processing can range from simply buying a few fancy machines to installing a comprehensive system of office processing.
Other technologies included:

Dictation—providing the capability to dictate at any time and place—in the office, at home, or while traveling.

Optical character readers (OCR)—holding the promise of reducing keyboarding, and hence reducing proofing and correcting processes.

Reprographics—including "smart copiers," photocomposition, and electronic distribution.

Micrographics—offering improved records management through computer-assisted location and retrieval techniques. A 100-year-old technology, microfilming, allied with computer techniques, gained a new lease on life as a records management tool.

Minicomputers and microprocessors ("minis" and "micros")—offering sophisticated on-site data processing capabilities approaching those of large central computers, and thus making possible distributed processing.

New communications equipment and techniques, including "intelligent" PBX's and satellite transmission, with a relaxed regulatory environment contributing to the potential for change.

Overall, there was "office automation" or "the office of the future," which included and was impacted by all of the above.

Adding to the turmoil was the proliferation of vendors. New vendors were appearing so rapidly that it was difficult to catalog them, let alone stay current with their offerings. The vast potential office market attracted companies of all sizes and of all levels of expertise and reliability. Many small firms (particularly the technological pioneers) were absorbed by larger firms seeking to expand their product range. Some very large companies, not formerly factors in the office technology field, opted to create or acquire a strong market presence. Exxon, for example, established a new division devoted to developing and exploiting new business technologies. Division products include Vydec word processors, Qwip facsimile equipment and Qyx intelligent typewriters. Xerox, besides its copier offerings, developed a full line of communicating word processors marketed under the Xerox name, and also acquired Daconics, a leader in word processing technology.

Because each vendor generally offered a number of products or product-lines, the total number of products bordered on the astronomical. The products varied widely in cost and capability, but they shared two characteristics: they were new and they were untested. Some of the major classes of products included:

- Word Processing Equipment
  —Standalone
  —Shared logic
  —Time Sharing
  —Communicating Word Processors
- Non-Impact Printers
- Intelligent Copiers
- Graphic Analyzers
- OCR Equipment
- Facsimile Machines

It seemed inevitable that the new technology of office automation would come to INA. In fact, an advance guard was already on the scene, in the form of scattered, and mostly incompatible, equipment and services. Since some of the word processing equipment and services were connected to data processing equipment, and since the WP equipment was so heavily dependent on DP technology, a major topic of interest was the possibility and desirability—indeed, the inevitability—of merging data processing and word processing. One attractive possibility of such a merger would be the expanded availability of data base information. It should be noted that the INA view of DP/WP convergence stressed that the convergence is a matter of planning, and not an organizational problem.

To sum up the office environment at INA in the late 1970s, it can be said that as a result of a variety of internal and external forces, there was a potential for serious problems. At the same time technological innovations offered ways to counteract these problems. What was needed, it seemed, was a plan that would apply the benefits of technology to the office environment.

Genesis of SCOPE

INA's examination of the problems and possibilities inherent in the office environment led to the development of a comprehensive plan for all office processing at INA. This plan is known as SCOPE, and acronym for **S**ystem for a **C**orporate **O**ffice **P**rocessing **E**nvironment.

SCOPE's formal definition is as follows:

> A **system** of interrelated technologies implemented across the Corporation to improve the **office** environment, using advanced technology and techniques to help minimize labor-intensive processing, and specifically designed for the user environment.

SCOPE was developed in the context of the continuing research and technology effort that is central to the planning function of INA's data processing operations. Initially, a four-year DP plan, called the Long Range Processing Plan (LRPP), was developed to provide the DP services needed by the various Corporate operating elements to implement their four-year business plans. In order to create a viable LRPP, it was found necessary to consider communications and office systems as well as data processing.

The SCOPE project expanded on the office systems material developed for the LRPP. SCOPE paid particular attention to the changing technical and business environments.

A key attribute of SCOPE was its modularity. That is, SCOPE consisted of a number of related elements, or modules, each of which could stand alone on technical and cost-benefits bases. Yet each element could be combined with any or all of the others to create an integrated structure.

SCOPE personnel provided advice to other INA organizations who were considering office automation. The SCOPE project had approval power over all purchases of office automation equipment.

SCOPE Goals and Approach

The SCOPE goals reflected what had to be achieved if office automation was to be applied efficiently and effectively within INA Corporation. Specifically, SCOPE was designed to:

Control Costs and Proliferation. Despite the declining cost curve of the new technology, the equipment was—and is—expensive. And vendors were aggressively marketing the wide variety of equipment and services.

Increase Productivity. Even with the descending technological cost curve, the key to cost-effectiveness was still more output per unit of time.

Improve Quality of Service. It was expected that the new equipment and techniques would provide, for example, error-free letters and better telephone service.

Improve Work Environment. It was felt that such things as a quieter work area and a more attractive office layout would contribute to employee satisfaction and productivity.

Accommodate Growth, Change and Increased Complexity. The modularity of SCOPE, coupled with the capabilities and flexibility of the emerging technology, was designed to provide the ability to expand and/or reconfigure as INA's business grew and changed.

Although SCOPE consisted of a number of discrete modules, a single, straightforward developmental approach was to be used for all the modules:

- A study methodology would be created for the given module, i.e., a set of techniques and procedures for data collection, analysis, design and implementation.
- A target area would be selected, with the selection based on such factors as cost-benefits, receptiveness of personnel, and applicability of technology.
- Users in the target area would be involved in the project.
- The study methodology would be applied to gathering data about the user area and to creating an appropriate design.
- The design would be then tested under pilot conditions.

Once debugged, the design would be available for installation throughout the Corporation. Post-installation follow-ups were to be conducted to confirm that the design was operating smoothly. Any problems that developed were to be analyzed, and the design was adjusted accordingly.

Secretarial Support—The First SCOPE Target

Secretarial support was selected as the first SCOPE module. This choice was dictated by the following considerations:

- Although secretarial support was (and is) basic to almost every office function, the support being provided by the existing system at INA was not uniform. Top-level managers with personal secretaries were usually well satisfied, but staff members often had to queue up, with expensive professional time spent waiting.

- Some secretaries seemed to be always busy, while others were idle for half or more of their working day. And there was usually no way to level the workloads among the secretaries.

- The technology of word processing was available, and its introduction was inevitable. It was preferable to control its use and its costs, rather than have it proliferate in an uncontrolled helter-skelter fashion.

- Because secretarial support was so basic, it provided a firm baseline system for other SCOPE modules.

- There was a significant target of opportunity, which in 1976 at INA consisted of over 5,000 secretarial/clerical personnel and over $36 million in secretarial costs.

Since study after study showed that the average secretary spent about 20 percent of the time waiting for work, it was felt that potentially millions of dollars could be saved annually by making secretarial services more productive and cost-effective.

INA's approach to office processing emphasized creating the proper mix of people, equipment, organization and procedures. Though people always received the primary consideration, the other factors were heavily screened.

Methodology for Office Systems

The basic methodology used to create and install the SCOPE office administration system in the selected areas was as follows:

- The project was introduced through briefings or meetings, to which were invited all personnel in the area . . . managers and professional staff (called *principals*), as well as secretaries and clerks.

- Each person was asked to fill out a questionnaire about the existing office support arrangement—what it was like, what was good, what was bad, what could be changed, what should not be changed, and so forth.

- The questionnaires were collected and analyzed. Interviews were held in which the questionnaire data was validated. Work distribution charts then were prepared showing the activities performed, and the percentage of time people estimated was involved for each activity.

- Formal tools were used to collect detailed data on the office environment, functions and requirements. This data was compared against the users' evaluation of what was required to meet the office processing needs of the given area. The various design possibilities were analyzed and the optimum design for the area was selected, with user concurrence.

- Procedures specifically tailored to the area needs were developed. The local office management personnel, the secretarial supervisory personnel and the secretaries themselves received formal training in the new procedures.

- If the design called for the use of new equipment, arrangements were made to order the equipment and to ensure that the required equipment training was scheduled. Any needed facility modifications were carried out.

- With training completed, the equipment in place and the facility modifications made, the system was formally installed. After installation, system operation was monitored and any needed refinements were made.

A typical SCOPE office system design was the organization put in place at the INA Corporate Processing Center (CPC). This design was geared to provide better services to the professional/managerial staff, tangible savings, and job enrichment to the secretarial staff.

The hierarchy consisted of a manager and three supervisors, with each supervisor directing two support clusters which were headed by a coordinator. A cluster consisted of from six to nine secretaries.

This organization was designed to help the people do their jobs more efficiently. That is, it was designed to be service-oriented. Principals (both managers and staff) received improved support—support that was continuous, and uninterrupted by vacations or sickness. In most cases the existing manager/secretary relationships were maintained.

At the same time the organization provided a career path for secretarial personnel. This helped increase job satisfaction and reduce personnel turnover.

Another source of increased job satisfaction was the assumption by secretarial personnel of "para-professional" duties—tasks that formerly were performed only by professional personnel.

Design Goals

As noted previously, the specific design of each office system was tailored to the user needs in the given area. However, each design had to meet a number of general goals that addressed the desired level of support that was to be provided for the area's professional/managerial personnel. The general P/M goals were as follows:

- Secretarial support was to be continuously available to all of the principals.

- Turnaround times were to be negotiated initially and then guaranteed. For example, some installations had to provide four-hour turnaround for letter typing. Other areas had longer or shorter turnaround times. In any case, the principal could count on having his work completed within the guaranteed period.

- Phone coverage was to be provided as the managers decreed. Some managers wanted their phones answered; others did not. In case of the manager's absence, however, phone coverage was always provided.

- Wherever possible, existing manager-secretary relationships were to be maintained. This meant that if Secretary A had been Manager A's secretary previously, Secretary A still did Manager A's typing, filing, and so forth. But when Secretary A was sick or on vacation there was always a backup to fill in—someone who knew both Manager A's *and* Secretary A's routine.

- At the same time Manager A would no longer have to be concerned with "managing" Secretary A. Secretarial reviews, salary actions and so forth were to be taken care of by the office system supervisory personnel.

- If Manager A had a very large job—an overload, in effect—that Secretary A could not handle alone, the other secretaries in the cluster would be called on by the Coordinator to help out.

The secretarial design goals were in many cases the reverse side of the P/M goals. Like the P/M goals, the secretarial goals provided general criteria to which the specific office system designs had to conform. The general design goals for secretarial personnel were as follows:

- A career path was to be provided, assuring the possibility of upward mobility to all those who wanted such mobility. (It was found that many secretaries wanted to remain secretaries.)

- Secretarial personnel were to be promoted on the basis of what they did—not on what their bosses did.

- The performance of secretarial personnel was to be judged by office system supervisors who themselves had been secretaries.

- Work was to be distributed equitably. No longer would one secretary be always busy while a neighbor sat idle a good part of the time.
- The opportunity to acquire new skills was to be made available to secretarial personnel. (Some would learn to operate WP equipment, others learned how to prepare budgets, some learned supervisory skills.)
- Secretarial personnel were also to be provided with the opportunity to cross over to professional areas, such as programming and budget analysis, if they demonstrated aptitude and desire.
- Wherever possible the existing secretary/manager relationships were to be maintained.

Vendor Controls

One of the most important actions of the SCOPE office automation effort was to implement the corporate policy of advice and consent with regard to the acquisition of WP equipment and services.

This policy kept INA from being vendor-driven, i.e., from making decisions based solely on vendor information and hence related more to vendor needs than to INA requirements. The first step in implementing this policy was to develop vendor selection criteria to facilitate the choice of vendors and equipment. The key selection criteria included cost, performance and reliability.

The next step was to create a preferred vendor list, based on the established selection criteria. This list helped provide leverage in the area of costs, delivery schedules, and development of special features or equipment wanted by INA.

A continuing activity of the vendor control program was the monitoring of technological developments. This helped ensure that INA was getting the most suitable equipment, at competitive costs.

This vendor control policy was instrumental in reducing the proliferation of vendors and products.

Office Automation Can Work

The INA office automation concept worked. There are some caveats attached to this statement. The system worked well in certain areas, and not as well in others.

Overall, however, it was found that there were significant benefits:

"Productivity" improved, with larger workloads handled by fewer secretaries.

Career paths were developed. Over half of the original secretarial group at the CPC moved upward in the first 15 months of operation.

The WP equipment proved out. Corrections were easier, reducing workloads for both the WP operator (who had only to push keys to make changes) and the professional staff (who now spent less time checking corrections).

Besides helping productivity and making it easier to get a perfectly typed letter, the SCOPE office automation effort had some less immediate but very important benefits:

- INA people at all levels were exposed to the "Office of the Future." The secretaries, the principals and the designers learned a great deal about what could and could not be expected from the new technology. The secretaries in particular learned that the machines could help them, and that people were not going to become robots. Overall, INA benefited from bringing what had been "pie in the sky" down to ground-level reality. WP equipment and the related new procedures became relatively commonplace. This helped create a climate of acceptance in which people are more likely to try out—and in fact sometimes seek out—additional technologies like electronic mail and automated phone systems.

- Another benefit, one which stemmed primarily from the analysis and design effort, was that the content of the secretarial function was clarified. Where most previous studies and installations had divided the secretarial job into two basic functions, namely, typing and administrative duties (such as filing, answering the telephone, and keeping the manager's calendar up-to-date), SCOPE found that there was a third function, which at INA is called *processing*. Processing is para-professional in nature and involves judgmental activity by the secretary. In many cases these activities are unique to the area or to the support required by a given manager. Often the manager spends weeks or even months personally training the secretary in how to perform a specific processing task. Creating a generalized procedure for such tasks is extremely difficult and time consuming.

Some Reservations

Although the SCOPE office system overall can be said to have worked, there are some reservations to be made:

Users need to be deeply involved in the analysis, design and installation. They want to feel they control their own resources and environment.

There was no consensus on how to define, let alone how to measure productivity. It is true that, for WP equipment, line counts can be made. However, these counts can be interpreted as measures of utilization, rather than of productivity. SCOPE took the pragmatic approach of saying that if the same work was being done with fewer people than previously, then productivity had increased.

Many users felt that talk of increasing their productivity implied that they were not already highly productive, and they resented this implication. Again, this points up the fact that users must be totally involved.

Most users initially opposed in very strong terms any change in the manager/secretary relationship. This is not surprising, since the response to the introduction of any new system is usually negative. Depending on how well the concept is marketed, this response can range from neutrality to guerilla warfare to a pitched battle.

The professional staff and the lowest level of management generally offered the most positive support for SCOPE. This too is not surprising, since they were the ones who were experiencing the longest response times in the old arrangement. On the other hand, upper-level managers, who had been receiving good support, usually on a one-to-one basis, generally felt that there was no need for a change.

The resistance to change was usually (but not always) strongest in groups that had a history of good business performance. The general opinion in such situations was that a change might have a negative impact on this performance.

Senior INA management was highly interested in increased productivity. High-level personnel managers stressed career paths.

Secretaries, however, were interested in what their salaries and levels would be in the new arrangement. For the most part they felt they had been as productive as conditions allowed under the old system. However, they were not opposed to increased productivity, which was achieved through use of new equipment or streamlined procedures. Still, they were more interested in job satisfaction than in career paths or productivity gains.

Training Essential

Installing a new and technologically advanced office system was complicated by the fact that the quality of available people is declining. In this context, it was found at INA that training is essential. Training increases acceptance of the system and improves performance. Conversely, lack of training had strong adverse affects on acceptance and performance.

Everyone who was in any way affected by the system needed some kind of training or orientation. This included managers at all levels, the professional staff, the secretaries and the secretarial supervisors. Procedures and standards were needed to make sure that everyone was operating on the same wavelength. The procedures had to be developed prior to the training sessions, and they were thoroughly explained in these sessions.

To ensure proper utilization of word processing equipment, it was imperative that operators were not only intelligent and motivated, but also well-trained. In this connection it should be noted that it proved unwise to depend heavily on vendor training. This training was cursory and had to be supplemented by in-house training to ensure that operators achieved proficiency on the equipment. This was especially true with regard to the more sophisticated equipment functions, which were addressed only superficially (if at all) in vendor training programs.

Personnel Department Heavily Impacted

The personnel department had a critical role to play in ensuring the success of the office automation system. In most companies, however, the personnel department generally does not understand office automation and has not come to grips with the effort needed on its part to help make office automation a success within the company. It is therefore imperative to get the personnel department involved early on in the office automation effort.

The personnel department must create or revise job descriptions and compensation levels and help create paths for office systems personnel.

The personnel selection process must take into account new or upgraded skills, such as WP operators, needed in the new office system.

The training function (usually associated with the personnel department) must be able to provide instruction in the new skills, equipment and procedures. Remedial training is often necessary to bring under-qualified applicants up to acceptable standards.

Technology Highly Volatile

It is generally agreed that office technology will continue its explosive development pace. New products are being introduced at such a rapid pace that the potential user seems to be on a fast treadmill. He has to run full speed simply to stay in place. If anything, the rate of change is accelerating, with new vendors entering the field and new products being announced almost daily. The relaxed regulation environment, particularly with regard to communications, heightens the potential for change.

With all this activity, there is the distinct possibility that people who are seeking ways to improve office processing may overlook obvious and available but unglamorous solutions simply because they want to keep up with the Jones' by having the latest "space-age" equipment. This kind of mentality is especially susceptible to being vendor-driven—that is, to being sold overly sophisticated or even inappropriate equipment or services.

Implementation a Huge Job

Implementing office automation in any company is a very big job, since the system will potentially affect almost every employee. At INA, the challenge was to install a system to service over 37,000 employees. This system would drastically change the procedures and work environment for over 5,000 secretarial personnel.

With the number of people and geographical dispersion involved, it was found that corporate-wide installation of SCOPE would require an enormous staff to complete the job in a reasonable period of time (say three to five years), or a lengthly schedule if the installation was to be performed by a relatively small staff on hand.

The installation process was complicated by the need to create "one-of-a-kind" or custom designs in some areas, "production" designs stressing high output in other areas, and combined "custom-production" designs in still other areas.

An intensive and continuing marketing effort was required to "sell" the office automation concept. Specific presentations had to be created for almost every level of activity in the corporation, from senior management to operating management to professional staff to the secretaries themselves. In some cases the concept had to be sold a number of times.

A Recapitulation

- The SCOPE office automation concept worked—under certain conditions.
- Office automation was—and still is—a very new area.
- Detailed operating knowledge of the specific office environment is essential.

- Experimentation or "taking a chance" is a valid step. Even negative results are positive, as long as one learns from them what not to do next time.

- Offices are run by people. Each office is different and bears the stamp of the local management. Alternatives must be provided to suit the local management, the different sizes of office, the different functions.

- The user must be deeply involved in all phases of the office automation effort.

Research and Technology Orientation

Office Systems was clearly defined as a research and technology function. Implementation activity was transferred to line organizations, in part to take advantage of their detailed understanding of their own processing methods and requirements.

The role of Office Systems thus changed from "advice and consent" to "advice and guidance." Office Systems provided alternatives, including but going beyond the original office automation concept. A major concern was investigating ways of increasing the productivity of the INA professional/managerial staff.

The basic aim of the Office Systems research and technology efforts was to light the fires of interest throughout the corporation with regard to the possibilities inherent in office automation technologies and techniques.

As a prerequisite to achieving this aim, Office Systems kept current with the state of the art. A key part of this effort involved establishing and maintaining contact with a wide range of vendors.

Systems and technologies that appeared promising were investigated. "Promising" in this context refers to a system or technology that offered attainable results for INA users in the short and near term. Possible applications of these advanced systems and technologies were brought to the attention of the appropriate INA senior management and line organizations through presentations or pilot demonstrations.

SCOPE—Vanguard of a New Era

The SCOPE office automation effort resulted in the development of a corporate climate that was far more receptive to the introduction of new technology in the office. SCOPE has provided a better understanding of the office environment, its problems, and its opportunities. More specifically, SCOPE served as the forerunner of a new era by:

- Showing the need for a precise definition of productivity. This would include the development of productivity measurement criteria and the associated measurement tools and techniques.
- Introducing the office automation concept to the INA corporate community.
- Helping to create an awareness of the need to improve office processing methods.
- Sparking interest in utilizing office automation technology to achieve the needed office processing improvements.
- Causing the establishment of a formal research and technology function for office systems and technologies.

CHAPTER 25

THE CHANGING OFFICE

By Vincent J. Byrne

A GLIMPSE at some futuristic writing over the past few decades gives insight into the relationship between man and technology—a relationship with potential for both conflict and harmony.

- A vivid scene from the earliest of three works to be cited, *1984*, describes the character Everyman as he is monitored during his early morning wakeup exercises in his home by an advanced communications system known as Big Brother.
- Another scene, this one from the film classic *2001*, depicts a huge computer which has become so advanced that it has programmed itself to take over its human creators.
- The third and final allusion is a series of scenes from the smash-hit trilogy *Star Wars*. Two lovable, memorable characters by the names of R2D2 and C3PO dominate these scenes. Ironically, the characters in question are not humans but computerized robots who—or which—do the bidding of man in a friendly, compatible way.

The first two allusions to futuristic writings—the oppressive monitoring system known as Big Brother and the computer take-over of the world in the year 2001—give examples of technology permitted to run roughshod over the knowledge, values and self-respect of its creators. Contrast these two examples with the last of likable, lovable robots who captured the hearts of audiences viewing *Star Wars*. R2D2 and C3PO demonstrate technological creations not only *of* and *by* man but *for* man. The exemplify the potential for creating technology and applying it in ways that are compatible not only with the needs of man, but also with his highest interests.

This potential for meeting man's needs and interests is the opportunity office technology can provide for *Employees* and *Organizations*. Office automation systems can be programmed for increased user friendliness and decreased user apprehension. The responsibility for doing so is a collective one that challenges the knowledge and wit of systems engineers. These systems will, however, need mold-ing, shaping and forging that only trial and error over lengthy periods of time can evolve. Since users will have access to limitless opportunities for hands-on experience, they are destined to carry the brunt of this burden through the 80's.

Let me say at the outset, I believe that the power to capitalize on technology and systems, and the way they are employed in the office environment is in the hands of managers like ourselves. *If a*

"The Ultimate Chair," designed by Luigi Colani on a commission from Comforto Incorporated, is an "integrated mobile module" which allows its user to sit upright, slump or practically recline while typing or operating a data processing terminal. The cradle-like device aims to support almost every part of the person operating modern office equipment. Actually, Comforto is using this prototype to adapt its new seating systems.

paperless office is too threatening or simply uncomfortable, a *less-paper* office can be shaped. *If* systems designed to monitor the performance of employees challenge rights to privacy, then the same systems can be programmed for employees to monitor their own performance for purposes of self-development. *If* electronic technology drastically reduces the need for workers, jobs can be redesigned and upgraded rather than eliminated, and workers can be retrained and redeployed to other types of jobs. *If* employee morale plunges after a particular system is installed, it can be turned around by managers provided with attitude survey feedback on specific problems. *If* workers' needs for social interaction are stymied by new work-at-home trends made possible by distributed data processing, flexible work time and office schedules can be implemented.

The challenge of learning from early success/failures and building on that knowledge is our responsibility. My purpose is to share my personal work experience with Xerox and other companies. This report—*"A Blueprint for Progress in Information Management"*—consists of three parts:

1. Assessing the *forces of change* pressing technology forward at ever-increasing rates and the barriers restraining that forward progress.
2. Developing a blueprint for effectively implementing office automation systems in the 80's.
3. Taking that soul-searching step back to assess how we can capture the potential for organizational improvement that technology offers.

Driving and Restraining Forces To Office Administration

We often discuss in conferences like this the powerful forces driving office automation. Yet for each force that propels movement forward, there is another that restrains it. Each of the following 10 items (Exhibit I) combines a force *for* automation with a force that *counters* it. In combination, they constitute the environment we face in making the "1980s Office" a reality in our organizations.

1. INCREASED PRODUCTIVITY . . . SOCIAL RESISTANCE: *Industrial productivity* climbed 90 percent during the 1970s. This contrasts sharply with the four percent figure reported for *office productivity* during the same period. The conclusion that the introduction of automation to the office would bring about comparable productivity increases was, unfortunately, not totally valid. The major reason the

Exhibit I

```
FORCES OF CHANGE
```

DRIVING	RESTRAINING
Increased Productivity	Social Resistance
Rushed Implementation	High Failure Rate
Focus on Support Component	Lost Leverage
DP Analogies	Differences in Systems & Environment
Information Volume	Causes and Value
Organizational Complexity	Coping with Change
Information Society	Confusion on Priorities
Young People	Today's Establishment
Cost-Effective Technology	User Resource & Responsibility
Improved Information Management	Quantification of Benefits

situations are not analogous is the *sociological* complexity of today's office as compared with yesterday's factory. The human tendency to resist change of any kind has been strengthened by continuous bombardment of the individual with change in all arenas of life. The office family of today often clings "to the status quo" with the same closeness, trust and mutual dependency of the family at home, with bonds too strong for television, the pill—or even office automation—to shake loose. Not only interpersonal relationships but also old ways of structuring organizations and getting work done is the fabric that provides security *against*—and resistance *to*—office automation that can dehumanize or unsocialize.

2. RUSHED IMPLEMENTATIONS . . . HIGH FAILURE RATE: *Office operating costs* have doubled over the past ten years, with overhead accounting for 30% to 50% of overall costs of U.S corporations. And labor costs rose at a steady rate of 6% to 8% each year. The resulting pressure exerted on managers at all levels to reduce headcounts, increase productivity and lower costs gave impetus to *rushed systems implementations* designed to get quick bottom-line results. The inadequate planning, communication and training inevitable in such fast-track installations often resulted in high failure rates. These, in turn, produced fallout in the form of extreme morale and motivation problems that made follow-up implementations significantly more difficult and challenging.

3. FOCUS ON SUPPORT COMPONENT . . . LOST LEV-
ERAGE: Internal administrative costs of our companies
have been increasing much faster than manufacturing costs.
The *administrative* work of managers and professionals as
well as the *typing* or *copying* work of support staff, should
be questioned. Yet our tendency has been to focus on the
creation and manipulation of information through word processing. True, short-range productivity increases in typing
and copying work are easier to measure through headcount
reductions, line-counts and support ratios than longer-
range, less tangible improvements in the way administrative
work gets done. But we should carefully assess the trade-
offs of this limited orientation on support vs. a broader
focus on applications and level of service. That includes
both direct and indirect people and spending.

4. DP ANALOGIES . . . DIFFERENCES IN SYSTEMS
AND ENVIRONMENT: Management has looked to data
processing to exemplify the endless range of possibilities for
office technology to increase productivity and lower costs.
But analogies between data processing and other forms of
office automation are frequently invalid because office information systems are less tangible, less formal and less
precise than data processing systems. This makes the conversion from paper to electronic processing more difficult
because it makes the monitoring of systems, the gathering
of statistics and the conducting of studies more difficult. In
addition, differences exist between data structures, and information processing in the areas of job structures, work
relationships and organizational accountabilities.

5. INFORMATION VOLUME . . . CAUSES AND VALUE:
Recent studies reveal that the average manufacturing organization maintains *two* file cabinets per employee. This contrasts sharply with the rapidly-growing service-based organization which maintains *four* file cabinets per employee.
The figures on the flow of paper to floodlevel proportions
double those of only 10 years ago—and are expected to
double again in only *five* year's time. Still most managers and
organizations continue to question only the *what, who* and
how of information processing, leaving out the most crucial
question of *all—why*, in terms of value and purpose. The very
existence of any given pieces of paperwork and the function
of the workers who create them needs questioning and a
constant challenge process.

6. ORGANIZATIONAL COMPLEXITY . . . COPING WITH CHANGE: *Organizational complexity* has mushroomed along with the complexity of information processing. As corporations get larger and more diversified, getting tasks accomplished in them becomes more and more difficult. And information required to complete these tasks magnifies in proportion. (For example, General Electric with its 128 operating divisions has to coordinate at high levels the application of OSHA regulations. The resulting information processing problem is tremendously more complex than any accounting problem likely ever to occur.)

7. INFORMATION SOCIETY . . . CONFUSION ON PRIORITIES: More workers today are employed in activities related to the manipulation of information than are employed in mining, growing crops, raising cattle, manufacturing goods or in providing personal services. Analyzing *how* the so-called *knowledge workers* of this *information society* spend their time in exchanging information—both verbally and in writing—is crucial. On the other hand, many companies have set precedents in initiating systems that focus only on the way information is created and manipulated, to the exclusion of the ways it is stored, retrieved, reproduced and transmitted. This limited concentration often misses the drivers of information management costs.

8. YOUNG PEOPLE . . . TODAY'S ESTABLISHMENT: Younger generations of Americans greet technology with less apprehension and more fascination than ever before. Nurtured on TV—and some on TV dinners—the youngsters handle pocket calculators, CB radios, terminals, minicomputers and push-button banking all with equal finesse. This phenomenon is bound to mold positive attitudes toward automation among the office workers of the future. But what of older generations of workers still around who view automation as a natural enemy of mankind? As companies herald the approach of automation in the office, secretaries and clerical workers fear for their jobs; managers are apprehensive over prospects of closer monitoring of their performance; and executives are concerned with the potential development of absenteeism, turnover and low employee morale.

9. COST-EFFECTIVE TECHNOLOGY . . . USER RESOURCES AND RESPONSIBILITY: Cost-effective technology is entering and will penetrate our offices in the 80's simply because it is here and will become more productive

on a unit/cost basis: mini- and micro-computers, satellite communication, shared logic systems, networking of work stations, voice recognition, micrographics, TV conferencing, electronic mail. And when you add the fact that its cost has been falling at a rate of 10 percent to 20 percent each year, its impact will be further magnified. But rapidly developing technology, frequently changing organization structures and emerging communications systems are taxing the user decision and approval process. Organizational responsibilities are no longer clear! Because of these complexities and pace of change, vendors will continue over the next 3–4 years to emphasize equipment rather than systems in their marketing strategies. And pressure will continue to be exerted on marketing staffs to increase current equipment sales necessary to fund aggressive product development efforts that will lead to the integrated systems environment of the late 80's. That leaves us and our organizations with the challenges of implementation, evaluation, expansion and integration.

10. IMPROVED INFORMATION MANAGEMENT . . . QUANTIFICATION OF BENEFITS: Greater demands than ever before are being placed on managers *not only* to make decisions, but also to make *accurate* ones. The resulting decrease in their willingness to take risks creates a pressure for better quality information. Inexperienced in approaches to information management, they are forced to break entirely new ground. One reason for the absence of prototypes is the newness of the field; the other reason is the uniqueness of each organization and its operating procedures. We must, through conferences like this and through strong user groups, develop continuing communications and a forum for information exchange.

All of these opposing forces cause friction that is not easily coped with. Yet all of these conditions are creations of man in the office environment. If they were created by us, we can surely alter them to complement changing needs, interests and priorities. But it will take determined, disciplined effort for solid, long-term success.

These forces set the stage for developing the blueprint for emerging office information systems. The action plan that follows consists of three parts:

1. **Analyzing the key systems components.**
2. **Plotting organizational progress.**
3. **Devising a game plan keyed to our organization's needs.**

615

The first step, an analysis of components, segments the complex problem of automated office systems into interrelated parts. These appear in the column to the far left of Exhibit II, entitled "FIRST STEP . . . Analysis of Components": facilities, hardware, communications, data processing, personnel, financing, accountability, pacing focus, and, lastly, information management.

For each component, there are three stages of progress, which comprise the remaining three columns of the chart. The key words describe levels of sophistication. They progress left to right from least to most advanced, known to unknown, present to the future. Our job is to plot our organization's current position and build action plans for progress. The outcome should be a line graph that profiles highs, lows and gaps. Ten systems components are listed on the vertical axis (top to bottom). The three stages of progress are listed across the page. When you've completed your profile, I think you'll see we all have strong job security well into the 80's.

Let's now take a look at each component and the stages of development we can expect in the future.

Facilities: Deal with the work environment and the smooth interfacing of furniture, equipment, systems and people in that environment. Perhaps more than any other component, facilities demonstrate management's basic convictions about the importance of people, their role and their morale.

Stage 1. Management provides sufficient space for new equipment and ways of working. In some instances, the wiring and cabling for new equipment influences space needs.

Stage 2. Management provides the furniture, design and layout that integrates new equipment and systems into the office environment. Such coordination permits aesthetics to be improved, people-motivated and work-facilitated.

Stage 3. Management plans work spaces based on optimum interfacing of furniture, systems procedures, equipment and people. This basic perspective on facilities is known as *ergonomics.* Here are some concrete ways ergonomics is applied to assist people in performing tasks: work surfaces the worker can tilt, raise or lower; furniture equipped with individual heating, cooling and lighting systems to suit personal needs; and task ambient lighting in place of general lighting to reduce glare, eliminate eyestrain and conserve energy.

Exhibit 2

FIRST STEP . . . ANALYSIS OF COMPONENTS

COMPONENTS	STAGE 1	STAGE 2	STAGE 3
FACILITIES	SPACE	FURNITURE DESIGN	ERGONOMICS
HARDWARE	STANDALONE	MULTI-PURPOSE WORKSTATION	INTEGRATED COMPANY-WIDE SYSTEMS
COMMUNI-CATIONS	TERMINALS EXTERNALLY-DIRECTED	NETWORKS/INTRA-COMPANY	HIGH-SPEED INTERCONNECTED NETWORKS
DATA PROCESSING	DISCRETE APPLICATIONS	MULTIPLE APPLICATIONS	INFORMATION SERVICE
PERSONNEL	SELECTION	DEVELOPMENT/REDEVELOPMENT	HUMAN RESOURCES
FINANCING	EXPENSES	INVESTMENTS	ROI
ACCOUNT-ABILITY	TASK FORCE	REVIEW BOARD	TOP ORGANIZATION OFFICE
PACING	REVOLUTION	SHORT-TERM EVOLUTION	LONG-TERM EVOLUTION
FOCUS	SUPPORT STAFF/SINGLE USER	MANAGERIAL STAFF/CROSS FUNCTIONAL	EXECUTIVE STAFF/TOTAL ORGANIZATION
INFORMATION MANAGEMENT	ASKS: WHAT/WHO?	ASKS: HOW?	ASKS: WHY?

617

Hardware: Includes the function, type, size and make of equipment, its capability for integration with other systems, and company standards and policies for purchasing it.

Stage 1. Standalone equipment replaces human labor in isolated tasks such as data entry, storage, retrieval and documentation creation. Managers at the departmental level make purchasing decisions on the basis of individual needs.

Stage 2. Equipment combines to form multi-purpose workstations. Individual in-house efforts and software development frequently defines unique interfaces, typically with input/output commands written for specific components. Managers at the divisional level make purchasing decisions.

Stage 3. Hardware elements begin to function as a system through the power of software supplied by vendors who specialize in total workstation systems. Multifunction commands are implemented through rich software systems, part of which are micro-coated. Systems at this stage are designed to facilitate information management at its highest level. The possibilities created are all-prevading, limitless and beyond our exact comprehension at this time. Top management makes purchasing decisions with consistency applied to company-wide standards.

Communications: Concerns the technological sophistication of individual equipment, its integration with network systems and the type of messages transmitted, both verbal and written, intra-company and externally-directed.

Stage 1. Individual terminals at individual workstations are used for externally-directed applications. These messages are sent via the telephone, facsimile, teletypewriter, mailgram and communicating word processor.

Stage 2. Individual terminals are connected to formal networks. They are used to send intra-company messages presently sent through internal messenger-service systems and teleconferences.

Stage 3. Interconnected networks focus on high-speed communication via wideband circuits. They are used for computer-to-computer data transmission, electronic mail (including many messages now carried by voice) and interactive management workstations.

Data processing: Deals not only with sophistication of equipment, facilities and applications, but also with theories of cost justification, administrative ease and availability throughout the organization.

Stage 1. Discreet applications aimed at reducing the cost of labor and material are introduced. Data processing resources are incremented on a per project basis with costs justified through offsets resulting from each application.

Stage 2. Careful planning projects into the distant future. Focus is placed on the development of more complex facilities and the wide range of applications in the functional areas they make possible. These applications are justified not by immediate labor savings, but by contribution to the business function. Frequently, during this stage, the process of delivering large software packages becomes strained. More explicit definition of responsibilities, project management and functional area budgeting becomes necessary.

Stage 3. An information service environment is created, with multifunctional data bases brought under control and put on line for access by a wide spectrum of users. Stabilization of data center facilities is a must with investments being made for contingency, reliability and security provisions. Most new applications are communications-based, providing for interactive query and transaction processing. A significant amount of the processing is provided through a distribution processor at the user's sites.

Most systems managers are well-grounded in the present and future potentiality of the first four components. Yet, smooth transition into the office of the future requires that an additional six components be included.

Personnel: All levels, functions and categories of employees need to be considered as integral a part of developing systems as hardware and facilities. Personnel need consideration as a forethought rather than an afterthought.

Stage 1. Employees are selected and placed in positions after careful consideration of their knowledge, experience, aptitudes and preferences.

Stage 2. Workers are trained in the skills and behaviors necessary for adapting to the equipment, procedures and work relationships of new systems. They are developed, trained and redeployed when jobs are eliminated or redesigned. If automation eliminates upward of 20% of all office jobs, unions and worker councils can be expected to protest, advocating guaranteed re-training, shorter work hours, longer vacations and earlier retirements.

Stage 3. Human resources are finally accorded top priority. Their resource value is computed on the basis of the cost of hiring, training, developing and replacing them when they leave. All personnel actions and activities are based on this concept.

Financing: Differences here range from single project cost savings to measures of employee investment timeframes, accounting practices and measures of playback.

Stage 1. Initial expenses are the focal point with an eye toward immediate bottomline returns.

Stage 2. Planning is done on long-term investments, calling for spending X amount of dollars for Y returns over Z years.

Stage 3. Planning is done over even longer periods of time with primary focus on ROI (Return on Investment) that is constantly and rigorously evaluated over project/program life.

Accountability: The issues here concern who reports to whom, at what level and with what responsibilities. Jobs are positioned for clout . . . measuring success or failures in performance.

Stage 1. Task forces are created consisting of members from a variety of fields, for example, personnel, data processing, marketing, finance and so on. One major disadvantage of them is their transient nature. Operators of new systems are usually accountable only to themselves for success and failures.

Stage 2. Permanent review boards, committees and program offices are created to oversee a task force and interpret their progress to senior management. Operators become accountable to office managers.

Stage 3. A truly permanent entity in the corporate structure is created which reports directly to senior management and has explicit, full-time responsibility for informations systems management. Office managers of new, developing systems become accountable to an adminstrative vice president.

Pacing: The rate at which a company converts systems to integrate developing technology needs to be determined by individual organizations in light of their unique structures, operations and priorities. Conversations that are too rapid—or too slow—ignore the need for the trial and error process that is always essential to the overall transition.

Stage 1. Change can be likened to a revolution. The questions asked are: What are our goals, and how quickly can we get there? Focus is clearly short term . . . "bruises will heal over time" philosophy. Workers make little difference; productivity is the only major concern.

Stage 2. Change can be likened to a short-term evolution. Questions asked are: If this is our eventual goal, what intermediate steps are necessary to get there? If workers are not receptive, how can the course be directed?

Stage 3. Change can be likened to a long-term evolution. The same questions are asked as in Stage 2, except forethought, planning and follow-up are greater in comprehension and scope.

Focus: Perspective on organizational change can be monitored in three areas: hierarchical level of usage, range of activities and intra-company utilization.

Stage 1. Changes in systems mainly affect administrative support staff. Emphasis is on the creation and manipulation of information. The system is utilized by a single department.

Stage 2. Changes affect managerial and professional staffs as well as support staffs. Emphasis extends to the storage, retrieval, reproduction and transmission of information. The system is utilized cross-functionally, that is, by two or more departments.

Stage 3. Changes permeate up to the highest executive levels of the organization. The very existence of information is questioned through total information management. Systems are utilized in senior management decision-making.

All of these components lead up to the final one, which is total *information management*. It encompasses all of the preceding elements of systems change that comprise the office of the future.

Information management: Information is valued in the same way that other resources, such as cash, personnel, material and facilities are valued. The accuracy level of the decisions made by managers at all levels depends on the quality, not the quantity, of information at their disposal. And greater demands for better, faster decisions are placed upon managers all the time.

Stage 1. Systems prove *what* information is produced and *who* produced it, in conjunction with possible reassignments of information tasks to other workers.

Stage 2. Systems probe *how* information is produced and whether it can be produced more effectively with the use of

Exhibit 3

THE 1980s OFFICE PROGRESS PROFILE

COMPONENTS PRESENT IN ALL SYSTEMS	THE THREE LEVELS OF PROGRESS		
	STAGE 1	STAGE 2	STAGE 3
FACILITIES			
HARDWARE			
COMMUNICATIONS			
DATA PROCESSING			
PERSONNEL			
FINANCING			
ACCOUNTABILITY			
PACING			
FOCUS			
INFORMATION MANAGEMENT			

different approaches and work methods. It analyzes the way particular workers function in their jobs in reaching end results.

Stage 3. Systems probe *why* any piece of paperwork has been produced, questioning whether its production was even necessary.

At this point the level of your organization's progress toward achieving the office of the future is likely to be plotted (Exhibit III). Once you have assessed where you are, the next steps are to decide where you want to go and how to engineer the course that will take you there.

Charting Your Organization's Course

Any examination of potential systems needs must be tempered by an analysis of your organization and operations. Your plan needs to be business driven rather than systems-driven; it must arise out of needs rather than ambitions.

In setting your organization's course, I believe these questions will help provide consistent focus:

What are the basic business opportunities offered by technology? (Remember that *technology* is the *enabler; management makes it happen.*)

What *basic business processes* need improvement when compared with competitors?

Where will quality information improve decision-making?

Exactly what is your primary goal: cutting labor costs and/or increasing output?

What are the relative priorities of these goals?

What are the most promising *applications* for initial projects that have high success probability?

Where is there high potential receptiveness to new systems?

What performance and success criteria will be applied?

How can I keep new systems simple and manageable in the key early stages?

Finally, how can I leverage lessons learned . . . successes and failures?

Keeping the Faith

The blueprint and charting I described may appear to be somewhat complex and overly complicated. I want you to know that I strongly believe that a solid game plan can only be established after all facets of our automation opportunities are clearly in focus.

Here are some vital guidelines to insure that the office of the future becomes a reality for your organization:

1. Senior management must lend its unqualified endorsement to your activities in a solid, visible, consistent way. (Participation and action not verbal endorsement.)
2. General managers must demonstrate their willingness to deal with the issue of information management by positioning the same high quality of people in information systems as in manufacturing and marketing.
3. Management must be willing to invest heavily in human factors that insure man/machine synchronization. (Proactive planning, not reactive fixes.)
4. Company long range plans must include information management as a business priority.
5. Broad-gauged individuals with thorough understanding of technology must be responsible for managing office automation systems. Future information systems will transcend functional organizational lines.

The overall challenge for us is difficult, but possesses potential for rich personal and professional development. Failures should be expected when we break new ground. I believe that the mark of the outstanding professional is an ability to draw on knowledge from current failures to insure future successes.

This, of course, is *not always possible* and is *never easy*. Yet, its critical nature is described by Santayana in his quote: "Those who cannot remember the past are condemned to repeat it." And also by the wit and guile of the cartoon character Pogo: "We have met the enemy, and he is us."

Our systems successes may not always fall on fertile ground. The impact of our work may not today be fully appreciated by professional colleagues impacted by the changes we are recommending. The ability to maintain perspective is, therefore, crucial. I believe that progress in the coming decades will be measured *not* by man's ability to produce sophisticated technology, but by his ability to adapt it to the institutional, social and human needs of his contemporaries. Some words from Havelock Ellis, which, although written earlier in this century, apply directly to the issue at hand: "The greatest task before civilization at present is to make machines what they ought to be, the slaves, instead of the masters of men." Our challenge is to see that the future of technology and its potential use will enrich rather than enslave.

In summary, I believe the future looks positive and very challenging. The Orwellian social projections into the future have not come to pass. Computers have not turned on their creators as they did in the film *2001*. The film *Star Wars* depicts machines as facilitators *for* man rather than dictators *over* him. This offers great encouragement. Perhaps the same harmonious relationship between R2D2 and C3PO and their human contemporaries in the film is also demonstrated by our children and the electronic computers they now use as toys.

In conclusion, I would say that history has shown that the way systems are installed reflects the basic values and beliefs of any institution or organization about its function, purpose and role in society. Our work in the coming years will to a great extent determine the success of these office systems—and our organizations. We can, in a very real sense, make a difference. In today's world where so many are searching for personal contribution on important issues, that's an opportunity we should not hesitate to seize.

CHAPTER 26

WORD PROCESSING/
INFORMATION PROCESSING

PRODUCTIVITY in the office, a long-sought and somewhat elusive goal, was the major factor contributing to the wildfire growth of the word processing/information concept during the past two decades.

The history of the concept is interesting in as much as it centered on the development of the IBM MT/ST, a magnetic tape *Selectric* typewriter that offered new capabilities in typing or text editing. The new unit was a text processor, capable of producing error-free typing at speeds of 150 words a minute. It was far more efficient than the automatic typing equipment introduced years before, and IBM hinted at an immediate improvement in business communications.

Early seminars provided office administrators with new ideas about "power typing" being separated from the function of the secretary as an administrative assistant. In some of the larger, early operations, departments were organized on this basis. Typing was left to typists (much like the old typing pool concept) and secretaries were there to function as assistants. This worked in some cases and was not particularly successful in others. Often, the implication was made that the only genuine word processing installation was one comprised of a battery of sophisticated, magnetic-media typewriters fed by a complex wed by telephone lines and specialized cables connected to dictating stations.

The concept of "bigness" kept many administrators away from the WP equipment, although many were intrigued by the advantages of text editing and storing in a single unit. Most small firms shied away from the equipment as too complicated and much too costly. (It is still costly.) But persistent advertising, persistent sales personnel and growing interest pushed more and more people into further investigation of the potential.

Groups Formed

By 1970, the Administrative Management Society, among others, began sponsoring conferences on the subject of word processing. In

1972, the AMS founded the International Word Processing Association as a non-profit, separate organization. In 1977, the IWP became an independent association with a growing membership and chapters in 20 countries throughout the world. By the time the 1980's rolled around the IWP had changed its name to International Information/Word Processing Association, and there was a basic change in the approach to word processing management underway.

What Is Word Processing?

Walter A. Kleinschrod, author of the Dartnell management guide entitled *Management's Guide to Word Processing,* takes the view that "the systems outreach of WP is potentially so sweeping and its ability to interact with other office systems so strong that by the end of the 1980s, true 'intergrated office systems' could well be working realities in many American offices. They would fuse word processing, data processing, reprographics, microfilm, facsimile and other telecommunications technology into one *information support center.*"

Wang Laboratories offers an Office Information Systems series of equipment to cover many information needs. Various units can be combined to offer advanced text manipulation (including spelling verification and list processing, to networking and data communications).

He takes what is perhaps a more pragmatic view by stating: "Today this much can be said without equivocation: that whatever else it is, WP is a system. It involves remote dictation. It involves typing. It depends heavily on the electronic logics and automated actions of new generations of typing equipment.

"But it is a system—and it is noticeably different from the system it replaces. The difference is the crux, the source of WP's payouts and most of its start-up difficulties. For WP goes to the very heart of traditional office operations. It alters many 'social office' relationships—most often the boss-secretary relationships which have endured, comfortable, unquestioned, and inefficient, for decades. It rearranges them along more controlled and purposeful lines."

Another picture was offered by Thomas Holmes, writing in *Output* magazine. He said: "A word processor employs computer elec-

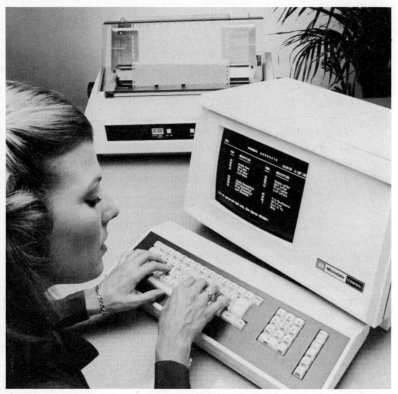

This WORDMATE Word Processing System by Microdata utilizes a multipurpose computer terminal which does both word processing and data processing. The system offers information storage, fast processing speeds and more versatility than a standalone WP unit.

tronics to assist its operator in preparing typed documents. It is designed to handle at least three interrelated tasks: entering text information by way of a keyboard and a visual display screen; manipulating this information through the use of application instructions, and printing the text on paper. The key to all this is the ability of the word processor to store information for future reference, revision and reprinting."

As a wrap-up statement, there is the following quote from *"An Introduction to Information Management,"* published by Clapp & Poliak, Inc., sponsors of the annual Information Management Exposition and Conference:

> "Some businesspeople have avoided thinking about word processing because of the terminology associated with it. Although a word processing system can be elaborate and expensive if your needs are great, there are applications in which all you need is an electronic typewriter.

"There are many applications for word processing systems, particularly when joined with a computer, but four obvious advantages of word processing systems may be noted to start:

- Revisions of lengthy documents are simplified because the entire document does not have to be retyped. This not only saves time but avoids the possibility of new errors creeping in during a retyping.

- Typing errors are easily corrected without erasures and without the need to retype an entire document when a correction is substantial.

- Form letters may be individualized so that each looks like (and is) an original.

- Avoids repetitive typing of frequently-used phrases, specifications, price quotations, shipping instructions and the like.

"Electronic typewriters are capable of storing a number of frequently-used paragraphs, or a few pages, and additional memories extend this capacity. But the ability of electronic typewriters to freely manipulate text is limited, particularly in comparison with sophisticated word processing systems in which a typewriter keyboard is linked to a cathode ray tube, and the CRT is linked to a computer. The potential of these computer-based systems is almost limitless.

"Dictation by executives is closely associated with the word processing system. The executive may substitute numbers for lengthy paragraphs or call upon the computer to provide long mathematical calculations if the company has a modern word processing system that is also capable of data processing.

Standard equipment on this electronic typewriter from EXXON includes multi-line correction memory, automatic column layout, three storeable page formats, one default format and expanded printing.

"Lists of addresses may be stored in the computer and used for a large group of letters without specifying each by name.

"Secretaries, of course, find that correcting errors (either their own or those which the executive finds in reading the letter for signature) is easy because the secretary simply replays the original until reaching the error, makes the correction, and replays the remainder. Simple corrections are made easily on either an electronic typewriter or a computer-based system.

"If, however, your own business requires the flexibility to rearrange paragraphs, make unlimited additions and deletions quickly and employ an extensive memory, then a sophisticated, computer-based word processing sysem should be examined.

"In these computer-based systems, whatever is being typed appears on the CRT screen. Just by typing over a particular letter, the correction is made, and by striking a key you may delete a letter, a word, a line or an entire paragraph. Strike another key and you can insert as much copy as you wish. Push a series of buttons and you move the fourth paragraph up to be the second and the second to be the eighth.

"A 'standalone' unit is available when only the secretary will be involved with the system. Such units consist of a CRT with a built-in microcomputer and printer. The next step up is a system involving multiple CRTs tied to a central processing unit (CPU) that will enable people to use the system simultaneously and to review each other's work.

"With any computerized system, you need a separate printer to transfer the words on the screen onto paper, or 'hard copy.' If you need only one copy of the page, you may choose an impact printer. These work with a jet-stream of ink which forms the letters on the page at high speed and with virtually no noise. Copies may be made with a copier. Impact printers, which work as a typewriter does with a key striking a ribbon to leave the impression on the page, are noisier, but they may be essential if you need carbon copies.

"Word processing is only one aspect of the Information Management System. Word processing makes life easier for your secretary—and secretaries will be extemely difficult to find in a few years. But more important, it can dramatically improve communications with your customers and within your company."

Information Processing

In the minds of many closely associated with the functions of word processing, the concept has been changed to or joined with information processing. This is more quickly accepted if one agrees that information processing is what people *do* in offices. Word processing, however, is more concerned with the physical documentation of the information being processing.

To achieve required speed and efficiency, sophisticated equipment, new systems and even new office layouts were obvious needs, and within a few years there were myriad suppliers offering varying systems. Office layouts were changed, radically in some cases, to provide the proper environment. As was the case (and still is) with data processing, some installations were very successful and some were much less than successful.

To meet the need for increased production and/or productivity, there was IBM in the beginning—offering its MT/ST units. In the early 1970s, IBM had about 95% of the market for what could be called word processing equipment. Within a few years, smaller, technically-oriented companies, with single product concepts, began to sell systems that had immediate appeal to administrators looking for versatility. Virtually unknown companies such as Wang Laboratories in Lowell, Massachusetts, showed technical expertise in high form by developing what is now called shared-logic systems.

Companies such as Lanier Business Products, Inc., a leading distributor of dictating systems, tied in with firms such as Wordplex, Inc., a California-based firm making shared-logic units, and 3M, to distribute copiers and microfilming equipment. Other new names came into view—Micom, for example, founded in 1975 to produce word processing systems. Within five years, the firm was selling $100 million in products and had entered a partnership with Philips Electronics of Canada.

By the early 1980s, the industry had grown to achieve $1 billion in sales. This effort was helped by such well-known names as Xerox, Digital Equipment Corporation, AM International, Burroughs Corporation, A. B. Dick and Dictaphone. New names included Basic Four Corporation, CPT Corporation, Jacquard Systems and NBI of Boulder, Colorado. You can get your word processing system, or at least stand alone units, from Exxon Office Systems, from Olivetti, from Olympia or even from Radio Shack. A strange but familiar group of names.

The movement toward the integration of word processing with data processing and other office systems will continue throughout the 1980s. In most cases, the hardware will blend into single systems; i.e., units capable of word processing functions and data processing functions (the desktop computers). According to a study by Venture Development Corporation, shipments of word processing equipment will grow at a steady rate through this decade. The predicted sales figure for 1986 was set at $8.6 billion. The research firm expects that shared resources (connected) systems will experience the greatest growth in terms of dollar shipments, but standalone units will still lead the way in numbers.

For still another view of word processing and computers, we turn to Nicholas Rosa and Merl Miller, authors of the Dartnell management guide entitled "Management's Guide to Desktop Computers."

As they so simply express it, "Word processing is a powerful technique for writing, rewriting, editing, correcting, modifying and formatting documents of any size and nature *at high speed,* with relaxed operators, and *without paper* save for the final approved copy or copies."

This statement implies that your office *has a need* for this kind of capability. If many letters sent out each day are the same in format and content, there is an obvious advantage to using WP equipment.

The advantage grows if your office produces reports, contracts, proposals, promotional letters or even press releases. Law offices were among the first to see the advantage of storing repetitive data for repeat printing upon demand. Assembling a 100-page or even a 300-page proposal is not unheard of in some companies. Obviously, getting this out in a single pass could speed up operations.

The authors of this book, however, were not interested in the word processing "department" operation where skilled operators pour out reams of finished copy. They are computer-oriented and see word processing as a function of the modern desk-top computer. The small computer, with a suitable word processing program, can provide the user with all of the features of a word processing system. A companion printer is needed for the finished product.

Not Always Needed

Talking about word processing systems, Dan Dawson of Nelma Electronics said: "Word processors are not a magic wand for all companies. For some they may not be a feasible investment at all.

"It would not, for example, be worthwhile for a company to reduce typing time from six hours to three hours with a processor if there is no other work to occupy the saved time."

There are many, even within the WP industry, who will be quick to agree. The office, according to reoccuring reports by consultants, is a place where time is always wasted and productivity is always low. This spurs office administrators to dwell on the time-saving potential of new equipment. If the office personnel have better things to do and more productive things to accomplish, then automation will be an advantage. The decision must be based on what is currently being done and what is supposed to be done.

Where Is Word Processing Needed?

The obvious initial answer is any office overwhelmed by volumes of paperwork. With that assumption out of the way, other applications include:

Single Entry Typing (one-time keyboarding): Typist inputs a copy at rough-draft speed, correcting her typographic errors as she detects them. Error-free finished copy is played back from the medium at the full speed of the automatic typewriter. If any typos are caught during proofreading prior to playout, they are corrected by stopping playback and making the necessary insertions and deletions.

Examples:

Transcription typing

Any one-time letter

Difficult or correction-free forms (legal and insurance)

Any very difficult typing job where revisions are light or non-existent

Final document typing

Partial Retrieval: This includes all editing or revision typing applications where author changes are made. Not all of the document is reused, but any keystrokes not changed by the author are retrieved from tape or card for automatic error-free playback. Only the editing changes are from new typist keystrokes.

Examples:

Any authorized documents (the more recipients the more revisions)

Manuals

Training Guides

Reports (including statistical)

Briefs

Proposals

Minutes

Multiple Use: This includes all applications where documents, or parts of them, once recorded and revised, are stored for reuse, once or repeatedly.

Examples:

Directories and lists

Contracts and Agreements

Publications

Repetitive letters

Specifications

A Flexible Approach

Word processing is designed for people. It is not a rigid matrix of rules but rather a program to enable management-support personnel to meet the administrative needs of an organization.

Different word processing systems offer different advantages. When designing a system, the following elements should be kept in mind:

- PRODUCTIVITY, the amount of work a given management-support group should be able to perform in a given time.
- RESPONSIVENESS, how quickly work should be performed in meeting management needs.
- CONVENIENCE, how easy the system is to use and how much direction a principal must give support personnel to secure the support services required.

- JOB SATISFACTION, how well a job is designed to match certain skills and how well personnel practices are designed to provide job satisfaction over a period of time.
- QUALITY, the proficiency, initiative and judgment of people as well as the appearance and accuracy of the completed work.

The final system, of course, should emphasize the performance requirements of the users.

In designing a system, each component should be weighed against specific performance criteria. For example, under a decentralized approach, a support person outside the principal's office can provide

DICTATION AND TYPING CYCLE COMPARISON

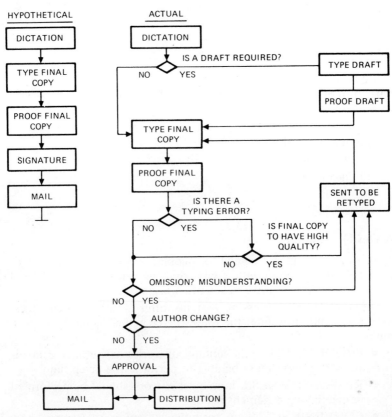

Actual usable production time of a typist is 9 to 14 words per minute, as depicted in the comparison of a hypothetical versus actual dictation/typing cycle; this shows the fallacy of the usual criterion of 50 to 75 wpm as "acceptable." Courtesy, Raytheon

responsive, convenient support for that principal. But productivity can be low because of interruptions, an imbalance in workloads, or intermittent secretarial coverage. The support job must be defined.

If mass productivity were to be emphasized, then the clustering and supervision of secretaries would allow work to be more evenly distributed. Jobs can be designed to match secretarial skills and realistic priorities can be established for principals.

Feasibility Study

If the decision is made to go into a word processing operation, it will still be necessary to conduct a WP feasibility study. The study is no less important than one which would be made for the purchase of small computers (See Chapter 28), or for that matter for the purchase of copying equipment, microfilm units, or electronic mail machines.

To begin with, you or someone has made the suggestion that word processing equipment might help with the current "bottlenecks" in the office. A starting point is to find the bottlenecks and identify the problems. This will entail a study of the office operations and the role of typing or paper production in the office. Remember that word processing is still viewed as a *means to an end* in most cases. It means faster typing of letters, speedier production of reports, more accurate proposals, etc.

Step One, then, is to identify the problem as it appears to exist.

As most people know now, all problems in offices are not solved by the introduction of automation. The "way things are done," or the work flow in an office must be understood before a problem can really be defined.

Step Two is the study of how this office or department works. Who does what and why?

It's always possible that Step Two will provide the solution to Step One, the problem. If not, the administrator has to begin a study to find alternative methods. This calls for an involvement of the people in the office. Their input is vital to any study of a problem, and again something in this input might trigger a solution. If nothing appears possible without new systems or equipment, you then begin the search for the system that will help you.

The rest of the activity is pretty much understood. You try to match up equipment to your needs; you try to match up cost with your budget, and you sell the idea to management and to your fellow workers.

The administrator can set up an elaborate feasibility study for any new program. Step by step, the study can examine every aspect of the problem. It can take weeks or even months and entail visits to vendors and from vendors as well as proposals from vendors. In truth, none of these steps can be totally avoided, but they can be cut down. You go back to the three questions which must always be asked:

What is being accomplished in the department now?

What would we like to be accomplished?

Is there cost-effective equipment available to accomplish the goal?

Making Decisions

The size of the word processing installation is the most important consideration to be faced. The amount of work produced is probably based on the size. This means that if you are looking for three to five to 50 units to meet the needs of 10 to 1,000 people, you are getting involved in shared-logic systems, distributed office systems or even multifunction office systems. On the other hand, your immediate need may be for two or more electronic typewriters in two or more locations. In between these you have stand-alone units that function independently either as word processing units (dedicated) or as microcomputers.

Surveys conducted by the Dartnell Institute of Business Research indicated that respondents (especially in the smaller or medium-sized category) were using electronic typewriters even if there were small computers or a mainframe computer available. You can find WP units in the office of the president, the field engineering department, the district office, the advertising department and the company operations department. You will usually find shared logic and/ or DOS (Distributed Office System) units in departments dedicated to the word processing function.

The survey also revealed that there were substantial numbers of microcomputer units being used as word processors, often with the new software programming such as *Wordstar©*. These units usually show up in the office of the manager or the office administrator, and they are usually under different management than the word processing systems. One large office operation (under 1,000, however) had a mainframe computer, three mini computers, 750 electronic typewriters, one standalone unit in the R&D department, 8 shared-logic systems and 10 standalone display systems. There were also 10 microcomputers in this operation. Apples, TRS 80s and IBM were included.

If you think you want one or more standalone systems (which might be formatted as a microcomputer as well), you know you will be getting a system that operates under its own power and uses its own logic (commands) in the operating system or software. You will not be connected (interfaced) with any other pieces of equipment unless you have a micro. If you want a shared logic system, you will have several terminals of varying ability that are driven by a central processor. There are varying abilities to store, edit and print. Usually, there is a central processing unit and a central storage unit with peripheral printers involved. If you opt for distributive word processing, you have standalone stations with local printers and storage but you have access to a shared resource controller and shared storage.

The Dartnell Survey

Approximately 375 companies in the United States and Canada responded to a Dartnell Institute of Business Research Target Survey in 1982 which covered automated equipment in offices of every size. Nearly half of the U.S. respondents were reporting on offices with less than 50 employees. The operation of equipment other than word processing units will be covered in the next few chapters, but there were results in the WP areas.

For example, 79 percent of the U.S. companies (all companies) and 79 percent of all Canadian companies in the survey reported using word processing equipment. The majority of the units described in the survey *were not* specifically located in word processing departments nor were the units managed by persons with word processing titles. In other words, the equipment is being used in departments where it is needed.

Within the group of respondents with less than 50 office employees, 75 percent of the companies reported word processing equipment. Approximately 92 percent reported the *kind* of equipment used in the small offices: 35 percent had electronic typewriters, 17 percent had standalone systems, 22 percent had standalone display systems, and 18 percent had shared-logic systems.

Electronic typewriters could be found in the personnel department, administration, operations, accounting, mail room, sales, bookkeeping department, marketing, legal department and a few in a word processing department.

The standalone word processing units were found in the sales departments of many of the companies as well as in administration and editorial departments. The standalone display units (with CRT display) are primarily used in administrative departments, but they are also found in word processing departments, accounting, personnel and marketing. The shared-logic systems were described in word processing departments, administration, sales, marketing, office services, computer services departments and data processing departments.

Word processing operations in small offices are supervised by people with several titles. The bulk of replies indicated office administrators, office managers, business managers and "supervisors" as the most popular titles. There were word processing supervisors named in a few instances, but at this level of office size, the department head; i.e., marketing manager or director of operational services, was the person in charge.

Offices with over 50 Employees

In the size category 50 to 99 employees, the name percentage (75 percent) reported word processing equipment in operation. Electronic typewriters were reported by 53 percent, standalone systems by 28 percent, standalone display systems by 43 percent and shared logic systems by 16 percent.

Electronic office typewriters like this model from Swintec have a full line of correcting memory, a relocation key, express key, independent repeat key, automatic paper feed, electronic indexing, reverse indexing, L.E.D. displays, 11-character programmed buffer, electronic margin setting, half-space key, automatic indentation, centering, decimal tabulation, automatic return and automatic underscore. You still must find the keys on the board.

Within the survey, this particular group of offices showed more word processing departments than any other group (on a percentage basis). The WP departments included all types of equipment. Other locations for units included secretarial offices, administration, the business office and the controller's office.

The same people who had administrative control over the computers in these offices also were in charge of the WP functions. There were some word processing supervisors named, but titles were varied. Systems people and the data processing chief were also named as department heads.

100 to 499 Office Employees

Over 80 percent of the companies with offices of this size reported word processing equipment within their locations. Here, however, only 36 percent reported the use of electronic typewriters while 30 percent reported standalone units and a majority 57 percent reported using standalone display systems. A significant 35 percent also indicated the use of shared-logic systems.

Less than one-third of the companies reported a "word processing" department as such, and many simply said "various" departments. There were specific mentions of administrative offices, the office services department and the accounting department on a regular basis.

For the word processing functions in offices of this size, there were few word processing supervisors or managers by title. More data processing managers were in charge, but there were also administrative managers and office services managers named as well.

For larger word processing operations, one can use a word-input center like this Norelco 260T which provides 24-hour-a-day, seven-day-a-week dictation. It can be accessed by telephone and it has six-hours of unattended dictation time available. Visual and electronic indexing are also possible.

The Largest Offices

In offices with more than 500 employees, 93 percent of the respondents said that WP equipment was in use. While only 40 percent of this group reported the use of electronic typewriters, 61 percent reported standalone units and 61 percent also reported standalone display units in action. More than half (54 percent) indicated the use of shared-logic systems. The latter were located in various departments and were most often a part of a microcomputer setup or working through the mainframe computer.

In the word processing segment (equipment) the people in charge included managers of administrative services, office automation managers, systems people and vice presidents. The latter group included a vice president of administrative services. Only a handful of firms reported a word processing manager or supervisor in charge of the area. In this size category, it was found that only 17 percent of the firms reported the person in charge of data processing as the head of word processing.

Who Uses Word Processing?

Thousands of large and small companies across the U.S. and Canada now have word processing equipment in use. Many of these offices have microcomputer-based systems which are used for computer operations as well as word processing. To accomplish this, you need a word processing program package of some kind. You also will need a printer with a daisywheel element or something similar to obtain neat copies of your reports or correspondence. There are almost as many printers as there are word processing systems to choose from, so you have to decide what you want that will go with your particular system.

For an example of a large operation, there is the New York City Department of General Services. It has set up a sophisticated information tracking system using a Wang OIS word processing network. Most tasks that involve extensive text processing or large data bases are done using the word processors. The systems, along with three optional 10-megabyte disk drives (high-capacity storage units) are distributed at 36 different locations throughout two buildings. The three central processors (computers) support 57 CRT display terminals, including 27 archiving workstations. Also tied into the system are 28 printers, four of them equipped with twin sheet feeders. In other words, this is a big, centralized, sophisticated system which is even used by other city agencies for text printing applications.

Word processing is also used by Analytical Systems Engineering Corporation in its Burlington, Massachusetts headquarters and

Washington, D.C. office. The company provides systems engineering and technical support services to government and public service agencies. The main activity of the operation is proposal writing. It is the nature of the business that clients must be demanding because of the high priority and top security services and programs they offer. Timely and accurate proposal preparation is critical so that deliveries may be made on schedule.

Using a Wang System 25, Model 3 with seven video display workstations, two 40-character/second printers and a wide carriage printer at the headquarters office, the department can generate some 2,500 pages of accurate proposals a month.

The brief reports above indicate word processing on a large scale. There are thousands of single units used throughout offices of every kind. The memory capability and the speed capability of the final copy makes the use of the equipment worthwhile, even for personal letters.

Word processors, however, are not a magic wand for any company. For some they may not even be a feasible investment unless sufficient work can be produced. For example, it would hardly be worthwhile for a company to reduce typing time from six hours to three hours with a processor if there is no other work to occupy the time saved. On the other hand, a word procesor should be a profitable investment for any company producing documentation. Even if the company deals entirely in printed forms, a word processor can eliminate pre-printing costs by blocking the forms and then filling them out.

Even Legal Forms

One of the earliest markets for word processing equipment with memory capability was the law office. Here, affidavits, pleadings, contracts, briefs and other lengthy typing jobs were quickly brought under control. Every time a brief was revised, for examples, it had to be retyped by a secretary. Today, the revisions are made, edited, reread and okayed before the final copy is produced.

Today, it is possible to even obtain automated legal forms. Lanier Business Products, Inc. and Callaghan & Company marketed a series of such forms a few years ago. The forms come in two formats: a printed version of the information contained on each storage disk is provided in a set of loose leaf binders. The second version is contained on the memory disk. Each form can be recalled on the screen so that the secretary can edit, alter and fill in the document needed. The standard forms made available include lease agreements, employment agreements, stock purchase agreements, wills, trusts and the like.

Some Problems

Because administrators consistantly are reminded that the modern office is not as "productive" as it should should be, they turn to automated systems as a way of "improving productivity." There are many who would turn the office into a production line through automation because the factory production line is considered efficient.

The introduction of word processing equipment or a word processing department will, in truth, offer the potential for more production and sometimes more trouble. There are problems with location, with machine noise (printers, not word processors) and with screen fatigue. Sometimes a manager will cause a problem because he or she knows that it takes only a few minutes on the system to make a change in a document. The typing of the change may be very quick, but the time spent by the manager on making the change (especially a minimal change requiring maximum effort) may not be worth it.

In a recently released book entitled *"A Practical Guide to Word Processing and Office Management Systems,"* the authors from Digital Equipment Corporation provide this insight:

"Sometimes the application of word proccessing equipment is referred to as 'office automation' or 'office of the future.' Both these terms, regrettably, appear in the literature with such increasing frequency that they are almost impossible to avoid. The problem is that the former term is threatening, and the latter misleading.

"Office automation is an inherently unpleasant term since it implies that office work can be standardized and performed by a machine—in other words, *automated.* When an auto plant stamps out fenders each fender is exactly identical to the one before it. If you can teach a machine to stamp out *one* fender, you can teach it to stamp out *thousands* of fenders. Office work, on the other hand, may involve some dull or repetitive tasks, but it also demands *creativity, originality,* and *judgment.*

"Office automation makes it sound as if people will wind up serving the machines. In reality, word processors and Office Management Systems are machines which were designed to help people.

"The problem with the term *office of the future* (oft abbreviated OOTF) is that it fails to tell you *whose* future. If you look around, you may find that the office of *your* future is installed and running in someone else's office *today.* By the same token, you may find that the office where you are working today is someone else's concept of the office of the future.

"The term *office of the future* is so vague that the same issue of a popular office magazine featured two articles entitled 'Office of the Future—Close But Still Elusive' and 'Office of the Future?—It's Here Right Now.' What's more, both authors were absolutely right.

"Amy Wohl, a widely read expert in office systems, states, 'The limiting factor is no longer the technology; we already have more technology available than any of us is ready to use. The limiting factor will be our ability to absorb this technology and use it in meaningful ways to increase the productivity in our offices and make the working place more pleasant for those who toil therein.'

"Word processing can help office personnel to be more efficient and more effective by relieving them of most repetitive, frustrating, and unrewarding tasks. This leaves them free to concentrate on the interesting and creative tasks which, fortunately, are the most important and rewarding tasks in any organization."

The Future of the Office

In a very real sense, word processing *is* the future of the office. What's more, the economic pressures are building to a point where many offices may have no future at all without word processing. In the future the office will be an even pleasanter place in which to work because of word processing and office management systems, according to Digital.

The major thrust of office systems development in the future will be in communications—communications between machines and communications between machines and you. Your word processor will continue to play an increasingly important role as the information center of your office. The trend will continue towards personal word processing/office information workstations. Your word processor, file cabinet, computer terminal, electronic post office, calendar, and memo pad will all be combined into a single personal workstation.

Complementing and accelerating the trend towards personal workstations are several factors. Word processors are becoming increasingly *friendly* and easy for you to use. This trend will culminate in the development of word processors that understand and respond to your voice. Although it's too early to mourn the demise of the keyboard, if you look carefully, you can see the writing on the screen. There are systems today that can talk to you. It's just a matter of time before we have systems that can listen to you and accept verbal orders as well.

The development of voice recognition systems will certainly be dramatic, but several other developments will have a more *immediate* effect on your daily office work. The development of local-area comunication networks will greatly facilitate communications between the various machines in your office. Wide-area networks will let your word processors communicate with both word processing and computer systems anywhere in the world.

As a result of these developments, your word processor will become increasingly important to you as your personal window into a world of information. Much of the information you will need is in information banks or commercial databases. These are electronic libraries of information which are stored in central computers. There are as many kinds of information banks as there are kinds of information. They range from stock prices, sports scores, and newspaper articles to sophisticated financial forecasting models and other computer programs you can *rent* when you need them. Users of information banks can press a few buttons and, within seconds, get information that used to take months to gather. In the future, these information banks will become even easier to use, with sophisticated aids to help you quickly find the information you want.

Word processors, which started out as modified typewriters, have evolved into versatile office management systems that not only help with clerical tasks but also add important new information management capabilities to your office. In the future, this trend will continue with office management systems growing into personal workstations communicating with other devices in your office and with other word processors and computers throughout the world.

Some Word Processing Terms

Word Processing is a growing influence in the business world. If your firm doesn't have a word processing unit now, it might in the future. If it has one now, perhaps you deal with these people from time to time—yet are confused by the terminology that surrounds this specialty.

To help in your dealings with these people on their own terms (no pun intended), Dartnell has compiled this WP glossary, drawn from many industry and user sources. Special acknowledgments must go to the International Information/Word Processing Association, Willow Grove, PA, and Word Processing Innovators Inc., Milwaukee,

WI. Thanks, too, to the various WP-oriented subcommittees of computer and office machine committees of the American National Standards Institute, for their help.

A

AGC Automatic gain control.

ALC Automatic level control.

AM 1) Administrative management; administrative manager.

2) Amplitude modulation.

APS Alphanumeric photocomposer system.

ASCII American Standard Code for Information Interchange, a standard machine code.

ATS Administrative Terminal System.

Access time Time required to "get" and "move" recorded material stored in a DP or WP system to a point where it is available for transfer, playout, or new storage.

Acoustic coupler A device which converts recorded data into signals for transmission, over telephone lines, from an I/O (input/output) unit to a computer.

Active documents Documents requiring original thought. Research, organization, proofreading, and revision are generally required. Error-free copy is often needed.

Activity list A department's main operations as defined by its manager.

Activity-oriented Term used to define an AS operation in which aides are specialized by task, as distinct from one in which aides are "principal-oriented" and do many tasks for specific executives.

Address 1) n. Name given to a specific location of encoded material on a recording medium. An address could be designated by a line number. 2) v. The act of finding such a location, usually through machine instruction, and usually for purposes of making an editing change.

Adjust Playback position which permits the operator to add or delete material, and which instructs the machine to ignore the originally recorded carrier-return signals and to establish new margins.

Administrative aide A job title also sometimes designated as "administrative support aide" or "administrative secretary" (which see).

Administrative center An area where secretarial specialists perform activities other than typing, such as mail handling, filing, phoning, and special projects.

Administrative manager A general executive responsible for numerous information and support operations, including word processing, data processing, recordkeeping, in-plant repro, mail systems, telecommunications, and office furnishings.

Administrative secretary A specialist who supports principals with activities other than typing, such as mail handling, filing, phoning, and special projects.

Administrative study A study into nontyping secretarial activities which identifies the levels of support and measures their adequacy.

Administrative supervisor The person in charge of an administrative center; one who supervises administrative secretaries.

Administrative support One of the two broad areas of specialization under WP (the other being typing). In general, it comprises all the non-typing tasks associated with traditional secretarial work carried out under administrative supervision.

Administrative Terminal System IBM's term for a software package which programs a computer for WP work, with text being entered and retrieved through interactive typewriter terminals.

Allowances Time which is computed into a work standard for fatigue, rest time, activity reporting, and other normal delays.

Allowed time The time fixed as a standard for performing a given task. Also sometimes designated as "standard time" or "standard allowed hours."

Amplitude modulation One of the three ways of altering a radio signal in order to make it "carry" information. The sig-

nal called a *sine wave,* has its amplitude modified in accordance with the information being sent.

Analog transmission In telecommunications, a transmission technique of varying (rising and falling) magnitudes or frequencies. Distinct from "digital transmission" in which discrete, encoded, bits of data are sent from point to point.

Attendant phone In a central dictation system, a phone which allows the word originator to communicate with an aide in the WP center or other remote recorder location.

Augmented mode; augmented system An administrative support arrangement which introduces some WP/AS principles into a traditional secretarial environment with little or no change in the office layout.

Author The person who originated the document.

Automated typewriter A general term covering all types of WP keyboard equipment.

Automatic forward reset In telephone dictation, a feature which enables the recorder to continue in playback mode to the end of recorded dictation, even though the person reviewing the dictation has disconnected. The next dictator thus begins recording on an unused part of the medium.

Automatic pagination Once the chosen number of lines per page are met, the page numbers are inserted automatically.

Automatic repeat key A typewriter key, such as the underscore, which continues operating as long as the key is depressed.

Automatic selector In telephone dication, a connection method which automatically links the handset to the first free recording unit available for input.

Automatic typewriter The simplest of the automated typewriters, used mainly for straight, repetitive output involving little or no text editing.

Automatic word recall In dictation systems, an adjustable feature which enables the word originator or the transcriptionist to replay a measured portion of the previous dictation.

Availability The time, or percentage of time in a certain period, during which a piece of equipment functions properly.

Average letter According to IWP, a letter in the range of 92 to 115 words with from 18 to 23 lines of 12-pitch typing. This is not a widely recognized standard.

Azimuth loss The loss of signal due to misalignment between a playback-head gap and the recorded signal on a medium.

B

BCD Binary coded decimal.

Backspace code A key-operated instruction which backspaces the carriage or carrier of a WP typewriter without backspacing the recording medium. It is used, for example, in underscoring.

Baseplate A device attached to the underside of certain non-automated typewriters, enabling performance of various automated typing functions, including text editing and playback.

Basket Term applied to the typing mechanism of a standard typewriter in which each character, as a capital and lowercase pair, is conveyed on a separate typebar—the entire set of typebars being "basketed" in a curved array in front of the platen. See also "single-element," "typing element," and "typing mechanism."

Batch A collection of similar work which can be processed at one operation.

Batch control A way of apportioning predetermined quantities of work to employees at regular intervals.

Baud In telecommunications, a unit of signaling speed. The speed in bauds is the number of discrete conditions or signal events per second. Where each signal event represents one bit condition, baud is the same as bits per second. Where each event involves several bit conditions, baud is less than bits per second.

Baudot code A standard five-channel teletypewriter code in which five equal-length bits represent one character.

Beating the shift A typewriter action in which a very fast or erratic typist causes a character to malprint following or preceding a shift.

Bi-directional printer A device capable of printing from right to left as well as from left to right, thus reducing "waste motion" during playout. Also called "reverse printer."

Binary code A system for representing decimal numbers in various combinations of 1's and 0's, pluses and minuses, or other on/off states. Typically BCD's are made up of four such "bits."

Bit 1) The smallest unit of information in a binary system.
2) The smallest unit of information recognized by a computer and its associated I/O terminals and telecommunications interfaces.
3) Contraction for "binary digit."

Black box Slang term for a central processor unit.

Bleeding 1) The "splashing" of carbon material from a typewriter ribbon onto the paper or into the machinery.
2) Intermingling of the differently colored inks in a red/black typewriter ribbon.

Breakage The difference between equivalent manpower and actual manpower.

British thermal unit (BTU) A unit of heat often applied in office temperature considerations; specifically the quantity of heat required to raise the temperature of one pound of water 1°F. at or near its point of maximum density.

Buffer 1) A device that reconciles the different speeds at which various electronic and mechanical units of a system operate.
2) An isolating circuit or system used to avoid or delay reaction between a driven circuit and the corresponding driving circuit.

Buffer storage A device in which information ready for transfer is assembled and stored.

Bundling The lump-sum pricing of DP or WP equipment along with associated systems analysis and support services, in contrast to an "unbundled" arrangement in which each of these products or services is priced separately.

Byte A sequence of adjacent binary digits operated upon as a unit and usually shorter than a word.

C

cpi characters per inch.

CPM Critical path method.

cps cycles per second.

CPS Certified Professional Secretary.

CPU Central processor unit.

CRT Cathode ray tube, a TV-like display screen for text.

Calendar of conversation A schedule prepared for the implementation of a WP system.

Capstan The driven shaft in a tape dictation recorder, usually the motor shaft, which rotates against the reel or cassette hub, pulling the tape through the machine during input and playback.

Cartridge A container of magnetic tape, usually associated in WP with MT/ST equipment.

Cassette A container of magnetic tape, often of the standard Philips variety, used with certain dictation equipment as well as with certain WP typing equipment.

Center 1) To position typing with a given measurement equidistant from the margins. 2) Command to a WP typewriter that it automatically center lines during playout.

Central processing unit The main controlling "box" of a DP system or computerized WP system, containing the necessary circuits to interpret and execute instructions for multiple I/O devices.

Centrex A telephone switching system allowing direct dialing to an extension phone without going through a manned switchboard.

Chad The small pieces of paper tape or card removed when a hole is punched.

Clean line A circuit supplying power to only one unit.

Clipping A condition in dictation when the first part of a word is not recorded because the mechanism does not engage fast enough.

Code 1) The pattern or system of signals, recorded on media, which stand for alphanumeric characters or machine actions. 2) Name given to the specified

instruction or action required of a typing unit in playback; a command—i.e., "center," "indent," "justify," "stop."

Cold type 1) Text, usually intended for offset reproduction, produced by a direct-impression typewriter mechanism or through photocomposition.
2) Term applied to systems which produce cold-type text, as distinguished from "hot type" or "hot metal" systems such as Linotype.

Command An instruction to a machine, such as a WP typewriter, to perform a certain action.

Command key A key which, when hit, enters a particular command into a system.

Communicating typewriter A WP typewriter which can send text to, and receive text from, another communicating typewriter or in exchange with a computer, over phone lines or via other telecommunications hook-ups.

Connect time The time during which an ATS or other I/O terminal is connected to a computer.

Console The unit housing the record and playback mechanism and related controls of a text-editing typewriter.

Continuous loop See "endless loop."

Control Card A magnetic card containing basic instructions for the processing unit.

Converter A machine which makes information recorded

for use in one DP or WP system compatible for use in another DP or WP system. It does this by changing the electronic coding of the material as it transfers it from the original recording media to new media.

Copy Textual input; the basic material or manuscript from which final documents are prepared.

Correct In WP, to fix errors or otherwise replace "wrong" copy with "right" copy, usually by backspacing (to remove the unwanted material) and rekeying (to insert the desired material).

Correcting typewriter A typewriter with the special capability of removing errors directly from the paper being typed, either by masking them over or directly lifting them off the sheet.

Correspondence center 1) A WP center.
2) A secretarial group performing typing activities.

Correspondence secretary A secretary responsible for typing activities and assigned to a correspondence center: a WP operator.

Correspondence study A survey which identifies typing activities, including sources of input, and measures the volume of typing in an organization.

Critical path method A procedure for planning and scheduling each part of a complex project so that successive steps can be accomplished on time.

Cursor The movable dot on a CRT screen which shows the place, on a displayed document, for entering new text or making editing changes.

D

dB Decibel, the unit of measure for the strength of sound.

DC Direct current (of electricity).

DE Dictation equipment.

DP Data Processing.

DSK Dvorak Simplified Keyboard (which see).

Data 1) Plural form of "datum." 2) The basic ingredients of "information," often expressed factually in words, but more commonly as numerical quantities.

Data base A collection of tape disks by libraries used by an organization and made up of files of information.

Daisy wheel A print element available in several styles for typesetting equipment.

Dead key A typewriter key which does not automatically advance the machine to the next character position when struck.

Decimal tabulation A WP typewriter function which provides for automatic vertical alignment of decimal points at predetermined locations.

Dedicated A machine systems term meaning reserved for one user or type of application. A "dedicated recorder," for example, is reserved for specific individuals or types of dictation.

Degauser A device which neutralizes magnetic charges; in WP, a device used to erase magnetic tape without removing it from the reel.

Delete A non-embedded command which permits removal of previously recorded material from the recording medium.

Diablo Trade name of a typing mechanism employing a high-speed, interchangeable printwheel.

Dial seizure The gaining access to, and control of, a recording unit by dialing assigned telephone numbers.

Direct impression Term applied to text-production techniques in which each character is struck onto the paper, as in conventional typing.

Discrete media Term applied to recording media that are individually distinct—that can be filed, mailed, moved, and otherwise separately handled. In DE, for example, belt, disk, cartridge, and cassette media are "discrete;" endless loop media are not.

Diskette See "floppy disk."

Display 1) n. Term applied to the screen of a CRT-equipped WP typing system, as well as the textual images appearing on that screen.
2) v. The act of commanding a CRT-equipped WP system to produce specified text on its screen.

Distortion Any difference between an audio input signal and that played back by the recording device.

Document 1) In general, any paper, book, or other instrument conveying information.
2) A collection of information pertaining to a subject or related subjects.

Dot leader A WP typing command which automatically places a series of periods between two items of copy, as an index work.

Double voicing An echo effect produced on out-of-tune belt transcribers where the sound head and recording track are not in proper alignment.

Dropout During playback, the brief loss of a recorded signal due to imperfection of the medium.

Dual media Term applied to WP equipment capable of utilizing two different types of media—i.e., cards and tape, or cards and diskette.

Dual-pitch printer A unit capable of producing text at increments of both 10 and 12 characters per inch.

Duplex A method of operating a communication channel whereby both ends can send and receive simultaneously. More properly called "full duplex."

Duplicate To reproduce material from one medium to another with or without printout. See also "transfer."

Dump Placing memory contents onto the storage medium.

Dvorak Simplified Keyboard (DSK) A rearranged typewriter keyboard whose advocates claim permits 35 percent faster output than conventional keyboards. First patented in 1932 by Dr. August Dvorak of the University of Washington, Seattle.

Dynamic range In DE, the span between the softest and loudest sounds that can be reproduced without distortion.

E

EDP Electronic data processing; in general, computer operations. Also referred to as DP.

Editing 1) The act of revising and correcting text or a manuscript prior to its production as a final document or publication.
2) The act of operating the function and alphanumeric keys of a WP typewriter to alter the recorded text it will eventually play out automatically.

Electrostatic printer A non-impact printer which forms images on paper by means of electronic charges, which either burn them in or create the characters through minute changes in a jet-stream of flying ink particles.

Element In WP, usually a reference to the typing component on an automated typewriter, such as the Diablo or Qume printwheel or the Selectric "golfball."

Embedded command A WP program instruction generally affecting the format of text, and not its content.

Embedded hyphen See "required hyphen."

Embossed media In DE, belt or disk media whose sound tracks are grooved like a phonograph record by an embossing needle, in contrast to magnetic media (which see).

Endless loop Term applied to a family of DE systems which employ sealed, continuous loops of magnetic tape as a recording media. The tapes are kept in containers called "tanks."

Equivalent manpower Weekly hours of secretarial work expressed as manpower.

F

FM Frequency modulation.

Facsimile The process of transmitting textual and illustrative copy electronically, sometimes by radio but in office operations more typically by telephone. Documents scanned on a rotating drum at the sending site are recreated on a comparable drum at the receiving site.

Feed code A "no action" code recorded to block out any unwanted character.

Fidelity The degree to which an electronic system accurately reproduces sound.

Final copy A correct finished document.

Firmware A permanent program stored on chips (on the read-only memory) that speeds up operation.

Floppy disk A circular recording medium providing fast random-access when used in certain WP typing systems, and called "floppy" to distinguish it from the rigid version often employed in computer memories.

Flowchart A graphic representation of the sequence of work from origin to completion, in which symbols stand for operations and equipment.

Flutter A recurring variation in tape speed which causes pitch and volume distortions.

Font An assortment of type of one size and style.

Frequency modulation One of three ways of altering a radio signal in order to make it "carry" information. The frequency function of the sine wave so modulated may be continuous or discontinuous.

Full duplex See "duplex."

Full equity lease Type of lease in which the purchaser becomes owner of the equipment at the end of the lease term.

Function 1) An identifiable operation or segment of ongoing work.
2) The operational unit, line or staff, responsible for such work.
3) A performance feature of a WP typewriter, such as an editing capability or automatic action.

G

Gap The effective distance between opposite poles on a magnetic recorder head.

Glide time A timekeeping principle where, within limits, an employee can set his/her own starting and stopping times.

Glitch A pulse or burst of noise that causes drop-out, etc. What happens when you don't need a crashout!

Global change The ability of a WP system to change a word or other text element everywhere it appears in a document, with one instruction. Also called "global search" and "repetitive correct."

Goof sheet An interoffice form in which word originators and WP personnel can note down suggestions to one another for improving service and avoiding problems.

Graphics 1) As used in business, a broad range of fare designed and prepared to be seen, including printed matter, signs, diagrams, and transparent media for projection on screens. 2) The pictures and diagrams that accompany text in typed or printed material, or that can be computer-generated on a CRT.

Grouping The combining of secretarial or typing workstations to facilitate supervision and improve support for principals.

H

Hz Hertz; a measure of bandwidth or frequency. The same as "cycles per second."

Handshake The electronic process whereby communicating units—transmitter and receiver—query one another to insure that each is ready for message transmission.

Hard copy Written, typed, or printed matter; a document.

Hardware The machinery of which a system consists, as distinct from the "software" of programs, instructions, and training.

Headliner A photolettering machine which produces headlines and other large "display" copy.

Highlighting Brightening or blinking certain portions of CRT.

Historical data Information concerning past production in a department; any data that have been accumulated from prior periods.

Hot zone The area, adjustable in width, for controlling the right-hand margin of text. When a line of typing is played out under reset margin conditions, the WP typewriter, having reached the "hot zone," will either "decide" to start a new line, or pause so the operator can make a hyphenation decision.

Hybrid Term applied to certain jobs in a WP/AS system where the worker is a typing specialist for part of the time and an administrative aide the rest of the time.

Hyphen drop A feature of WP typewriters, whereby a hyphen which originally appears at the end-of-line word-break is automatically dropped if the word later appears in the middle of a line.

I

I/O Input/output, as in "I/O terminal."

IPN Information processing network.

ips Inches per second; usually a reference to tape speed.

IWP Abbreviation for International Word Processing Association, a WP user group affiliate of the Administrative Management Society (AMS). The seemingly proper abbreviation "IPWA" is never used.

Impact printer A device in which the typing element directly strikes the paper to produce a character or symbol.

Impedance A form of power loss, or resistance to the flow of alternating current, often caused in DE by the improper connection of microphones, recorders, and the like.

Insert A WP machine function which allows for the introduction of new material within previously recorded text.

Interactive Term applied to WP typing systems that communicate with computers or other WP terminals, in contrast to "standalone" systems which are self-contained.

Interface The point at which two systems, or two devices, or a person and a device (the "man-machine interface") come into contact with each other.

J

Job enrichment The opportunity for an employee to exercise more independence in his/her work through task assignments or delegation of authority.

Job levels The steps in a career path.

Justify To type with flush margins on both sides of the text.

K

k Abbreviation for "kilo,' prefix meaning 1,000. As used in DP, a term such as "12k memory" would indicate a memory with a capacity for 12,000 units of storage.

kHz Kilohertz, 1,000 cycles per second.

Keybar Term applied to typewriters having conventional typebar or "basket" typing mechanisms.

L

lph Lines per hour.

LSI Large scale integration, i.e., miniaturization (of computer circuitry).

Landscape See "office landscape."

Leading Amount of space between lines of type, usually referred to in terms of "point" size. The notation "10/12" or "10 on 12" means 10-point type in a 12 point space, or, expressed another way, 10-point type with 2 points of "leading" between lines.

Level A paper or magnetic tape term referring to the vertical rows of holes or electronic impulses on the tape.

Line A row of typing often used as a unit in work measurement. There is no universal standard, but one common definition fixes a "line" at 6 inches of elite type, 72 keystrokes.

Line number access A means of "addressing" points within prerecorded text through codes which generally correspond to lines of the document, numbered sequentially.

Line switching In telecommunications, an arrangement whereby a circuit path is set up between the incoming and outgoing lines, in contrast to "message switching" (which see).

Load transfer A method of re-recording material from a continuous loop tape onto a different medium.

Lockout A DE feature which insures that users will not be able to intrude on, or review, another person's dictation.

Log sheet A document prepared and maintained by supervisors or WP operators to keep track of incoming and outgoing work, turnaround times, and the like.

Logging A method of recording incoming and outgoing work to assist in monitoring it and controlling its flow.

M

MCD Master Clerical Data.

MOS Metal oxide semiconductor, a class of components used in computers.

MS, Ms Manuscript.

Ms. An alternative to the use of "Miss" or "Mrs." when neither of these is known or desired.

MTM Methods-time measurement.

MT/ST Magnetic Tape Selectric Typewriter, an IBM product.

mag Short form of the word "magnetic."

Magnetic card A card coated with a magnetic substance on which approximately one page of typewritten material is recorded.

Magnetic cassette Magnetic-coated tape in a cassette on which approximately 20 pages of typewritten material is recorded.

Magnetic keyboard A device, commonly a WP typewriter, which records keystrokes and editing changes on a magnetic medium.

Magnetic media Any of a wide variety of belts, cards, disks, or tapes coated or impregnated with magnetic material, for use with appropriate WP equipment and on which dictation or keystrokes are recorded and stored.

Make ready/do/put away According to work analysts, the basic components that make up any job: preparation, doing the job, and putting away materials afterwards.

Manpower factor The statistical expression of secretarial manpower used to convert secretarial administrative hours into equivalent manpower.

Manual selector In telephone dictation, a connection method by which the handset is linked to an available recorder. The switching is done manually, in contrast to the "automatic selector" method.

Margin adjust zone See "hot zone."

Master clerical data In work measurement, a special body of predetermined time standards.

Measure 1) A line standard usually expressed in terms of character units.
2) The unit value of line length.

Measured backspace In DE, a transcriber feature which provides a controlled repeat of recorded dictation each time the foot pedal is depressed.

Media In general, the recording supplies, commonly magnetic-coated or of paper, used with WP equipment (see "magnetic media"). Common forms include paper tape, and magnetic belts, cards, disks, and tapes in cassettes or cartridges.

Medium 1) Singular form of the plural word "media."
2) A paper or magnetic entity for recording used with a WP device.

Memory As used in DP and WP, the (usually) electromagnetic component(s) in which data are stored. Memories may be resident in hardware (in core arrays or rigid disks, for example), or on removable media (cards, tapes, etc.), or, as is generally the case, in both the internal and external parts of the system.

Memory typewriter A kind of WP typewriter with limited powers and capacities, suitable as much to conventional larger-volume typing areas as to truer WP environments.

Merge To combine, as in the automatic bringing together of information on two tapes into one tape, or onto a document.

Message switching The technique of receiving a message, storing it until the proper outgoing line is available, and then retransmitting. No direct connection between the incoming and outgoing lines is set up as in "line switching" (which see).

Methods-time measurement A work measurement technique which recognizes that certain motions, or combinations of motions, occur repeatedly in work, and which assigns time standards to these operations for purposes of evaluating performance.

Mil One one-thousandth of an inch, a unit in measuring tape thickness.

Mini-Computer A small computer; in word processing, a computer designed specifically for the word processing function.

Mode The operating states of an automated unit. In WP typewriters, modes include "record" and "playback."

Modem 1) A contraction for "modulator-demodulator." 2) A device which converts data into signals for telephone transmission and then (at the receiving end) back again into data.

Module An interchangeable plug-in item or other "building block" for expanding capacity.

N

Net lines Finished lines of typing on final documents. Also called "net output."

Nixie tube A glowing tube which diplays changeable alphanumeric characters, commonly in a multi-tube array on an instrument panel or machine console.

Non-embedded command A program instruction which effects an immediate change in the material to be processed, such as to delete a given line.

Non-impact printer A mechanism which produces textual output on plain or special paper without contact between the printing mechanism and the paper, in contrast to an "impact" printer. See also "electrostatic printer," "ink-jet printer," and "photocomposition."

Nonselector In telephone dictation, a connection method which links various handsets to only one recorder. Thus, only one handset may access the recorder at any one time.

Non-volatile storage Recorded material which is not lost when the power source is removed.

O

OCP Optional character printing.

OCR Optical character recognition, a form of data input employing optical scanning equipment.

Off line A DP or WP mode or operation performed on peripheral equipment independent of the central processor.

Office landscape A form of open-plan layout in which desks, files, screens, and plants are arrayed in non-rectilinear, free-standing clusters for reasons of better communication and easier rearrangement.

On line A DP or WP operation directly accessing the CPU.

One-to-one A traditional office staffing ratio, one secretary to one executive.

Open plan A form of wall-less interior office layout, analagous to "office landscape," but with a tendency to more formal alignment of desks, files, and other components.

Originator The person who created the written material to be processed.

Output 1) The final results after recorded "input" is processed, revised, and printed out.
2) The final documents or other information produced by an automated system.

Output WP equipment Automated typing systems.

P

Patching A method of transferring previously recorded material onto another medium.

Pause control A feature on some dictation recorders which enables the tape to be stopped temporarily without switching from the "play" or "record" settings.

Peripheral equipment 1) In DP and WP, accessory units which

work in conjunction with a large central unit, but are not part of it.
2) Units, such as I/O terminals, which work in conjunction with a major systems component, such as a CPU.

Photocomposition A form of "cold type" text production in which each character is exposed photographically on light-sensitive paper, which is then developed to become a reproduction-quality proof.

Pin feed Term applied to typewriter platens having sprocket-like ends pieces which help convey continuous forms through the unit.

Playback The process of listening to recorded dictation.

PBX dictation system A centralized dictation system using telephone company wiring and dial or Touch-Tone controls.

Page control A WP typewriter feature that causes pages to be numbered and ejected automatically during playout, thus reducing the need for human monitoring.

Paper tape A recording medium used by certain WP typewriters and photocomposition systems. Punched perforations carry the coding.

Paragraph indent A program instruction which enables a WP typewriter to indent automatically the first word of a paragraph by a pre-set number of spaces.

Parity check A method of detecting errors in recorded data by adding a noninformational bit to the coding for each character. The number of 1's in each binary grouping should always then be even or always odd, making it possible to identify groupings that contain a single error.

Patch cord A wire or cable for connecting two pieces of audio equipment.

Playback, playout The automatic typing of recorded text.

Power keyboard Loosely, the keyboard of any automated typewriter.

Power typing 1) Automatic typing that is essentially repetitive and involving only minimal text editing.
2) Loosely, any WP typing application.

Pre-con A prerecorded tape which "pre-conditions" the memory of a WP typewriter to accept certain codes which control the format of final copy.

Predetermined time A time standard for a routine work operation, established through time studies.

Prefix A coded signal to a WP typewriter console to accept a subsequent coded signal.

Preparation In WP, a task definition which includes paper handling, media loading, and margin tab, and console adjustments, prior to typing.

Prerecorded Term applied to material stored on media for repetitive use, such as programmed instructions or the standard paragraphs of form letters.

Principal An individual within an organization who originates paperwork and requires secretarial support. An executive; a word originator.

Principal-oriented Term applied to AS operations in which aides perform many tasks for a few specific individuals, as distinct from an "activity-oriented" arrangement in which aides handle a few specific tasks for many individuals.

Principal-to-secretary ratio A numerical expression of the number of principals served by one secretary. A 4:1 ratio means one secretary serves four principals.

Printer In WP generally, a device which produces text from recorded material. In some WP systems, the printer is a separate device wired to the keyboard unit; in others, it is an integral part of the typewriter. See also "Diablo," "Qume," and "typing mechanism."

Printwheel A typing element, daisy-like or cylindrical in shape, used on certain WP typewriters and printer units.

Private wire In telephone dictation, a system which does not use telephone company lines.

Program A set of machine instructions for the operation of automated equipment such as computers and WP typing systems.

Programmed search The automatic finding of various segments of prerecorded material, on media, for playout in some predetermined sequence.

PERT Project evaluation and review technique.

Proportional spacing A typewriter feature whereby alphanumeric characters are given horizontal spacing proportionate to their shape.

Punch A device which cuts holes into paper tape or cards in accord with a machine code.

Q

Quad tabulation A function which provides for automatic alignment of a character or group of characters within a column.

Quality control A more or less formal check on output to assure that the work meets established standards.

Queuing theory A mathematical procedure useful in predicting how a service with a known capacity will be able to handle various demands made upon it.

Quickcharting A flowcharting technique which does not require knowledge of standard flowchart symbols.

Qume Trade name for a typing mechanism employing a high-speed, interchangeable printwheel.

Qwerty Keyboard. The standard typewriter keyboard, so named for the arrangement of its first six letters.

R

RAM Random access memory.

ROM Read-only memory.

Random access In DP and WP, a storage technique in which the time required to obtain information in memory is relatively independent of the location of the information most recently obtained. Disks are generally regarded as randomly accessible media, in contrast to tape, which is "serial" (which see).

Random assembly A WP typewriter feature which eases the production of documents by automatically putting together parts from separately recorded material. Also called "programmed search."

Reactive document A routine document which is rarely revised and infrequently proofread.

Read As applied to DP and WP machinery, the ability to interpret material encoded on recording media.

Reader A device, or component part of a device, which converts material encoded on media into machine instructions, including instructions to produce the designated alphanumeric characters or symbols.

Ready tone In telephone dictation, the tone which tells a user that he has "seized" a recorder, and it is ready to accept his dictation. Also called "talk-down tone."

Record v. 1) To capture on a medium such things as the speech of dictation or the keystrokes entered into a WP typing system.

2) To log data or other notations on a document, such as a business form, for purposes of

control and evaluation.

n.3) That which is written to perpetuate a knowledge of events.

4) A document, form, or other paper containing information for the control of business operations.

5) In general, any of the encoded media used in WP, such as belts, cards, and cassettes.

Recorder In a dictation system, the unit which transfers the dictation onto a medium.

Recorder coupler A type of interface unit which links a centralized dictation system to phone-company telephone equipment. Unlike "trunk links," recorder couplers cannot directly interpret dial or Touch-Tone signals.

Reel-to-reel In audio equipment, a type of tape recorder that does not use cartridges or cassettes.

Reference code 1) An electronically recorded indexing point on a magnetic tape.

2) Loosely, any indexing signal, regardless of medium.

Repetitive correct Another term for "global change" (which see).

Required hyphen A program instruction entered to insure that the hyphen is not omitted during playout, in contrast to "hyphen drop" (which see). Also known as "embedded hyphen."

Response time The time a system takes to react to a given input.

Reverse printer Another term for "bi-directional printer" (which see).

Reverse search The searching, in a nonplay direction, for reference points on a magnetic tape.

Revision cycle The path of a typed document through a series of corrections after its initial keyboarding.

Revision work The typing of corrections and editing changes at some point after the original keyboarding of a document, and also (usually) the final playout of that document.

S

SAH Standard allowed hours.

Satellite A station, terminal, or other unit of equipment connected to, but at some distance from, a centralized DP or WP system.

Scanning 1) The rapid listening to recorded dictation to locate a specific part.

2) Optical scanning; "OCR;" a form of data input in which an electronic device "reads" the marks or characters on a document.

Search The function of a WP typewriter in which specific material is located on a magnetic tape.

Secretarial activity A composite of tasks involving basic support activities such as mail handling, filing, telephone answering, and typing.

Secretarial support center 1) A secretarial group performing all secretarial activities, including typing.

2) In some contexts, an administrative center (which see).

Secretary 1) Traditionally, one employed to handle correspondence, records, errands, and other tasks for a superior. 2) In WP/AS systems, a title sometimes assigned, along with prefixes such as "WP" or "administrative," to the typing and AS specialists within the system.

Secretary, administrative A specialist who supports principals with activities other than typing, such as mail handling, filing, phoning, and special projects. An AS aide.

Secretary, correspondence An individual primarily responsible for transcribing dictation and producing documents on a WP typewriter; a WP operator.

Seize To electronically gain control of a recorder in a centralized dictation system.

Selector In private-wire DE systems, a device which connects the user's handset to the centralized recording equipment. See also "automatic selector," "manual selector," and "nonselector."

Selectric An IBM trademark applied both to the company's interchangeable "golfball" typing elements and to the entire mechanical subassembly which activates the typing elements.

Self-logging The activity whereby an employee keeps a record of his or her own tasks and the time required to do them.

Serial storage Term applied to technique in which bits, words, or other units are stored one after another in sequence, as, for example, on magnetic tape. Since searches can involve considerable back and forth movement of the medium, the time required to obtain stored data is relatively dependent on the location of the information most recently obtained, in contrast to "random access" storage (which see).

Shared logic Term applied to a type of text editing system in which several keyboard terminals simultaneously use the memory and processing powers of a single CPU.

Shift A typewriter key which activates the typing mechanism to print either in capitals or lower-case characters.

Short interval scheduling The assignment of predetermined segments of work, and the systematic follow-up for completion on a planned, predictable basis.

Signal-to-signal ratio The voltage ratio in dB between the loudest undistorted tone recorded and played back by a recorder, and the noise reproduced when the audio signal is reduced to zero.

Simulation 1) A management assessment technique in which mathematical "models" or formulas are used as test substitutes for real-life situations. 2) In the testing of DP programs, a technique in which specific software substitutes for the actual use of terminals and lines.

Single element Term applied to a typing mechanism in which all print characters are contained on a single unit, such as a printwheel or Selectric "golfball."

Skip A WP typewriter feature used in playback mode to avoid or delete the printout of a specific character, word, or line.

Slave An output unit, such as a printer, operating in parallel with, and controlled by, a master unit.

Software All materials needed to control and operate the "hardware" of an automated system, such as flowcharts, manuals, programs, and the like.

Split keyboarding A production technique in which material is keyboarded and edited on one WP unit and played out on another.

Stand-alone Term applied to a WP typewriter or typing system that is self-contained, i.e., not connected to other systems or system components.

Standard allowed hours Term applied to a concept, and the data supporting it, in which certain fixed amounts of time are set as standards for the normal completion of recurring tasks. Analogous to "methods-time measurement."

Standard data The predetermined lengths of time accepted as the norms for accomplishing various common, recurring tasks.

Stat typing Priority typing.

Station 1) The receptacle of a magnetic tape WP typewriter in which cartridges or cassettes are placed for recording and playback. More precisely, the record/playback drive mechanism on an editing typewriter.

2) In telecommunications, any of the input/output points in a system, such as an individual telephone extension or a teletypewriter terminal.

Stenographer A writer of shorthand; one employed chiefly to take and transcribe dictation.

Stop 1) A code recorded on a medium which instructs a WP typewriter to halt at some point during playback.

2) A WP typewriter key which, when hit, encodes stop instructions or halts action directly.

Storable Term applied to the portion of a pre-recorded document that is not subject to change.

Stroke counter A device fitted on a typewriter that counts every key depression that is made.

Stroke storage Capacity of a machine to receive and store impulses faster than the unit can print them.

Study team Group which surveys the needs and working conditions in an organization as a basis for deciding on the feasibility of converting to WP.

Subjective tone In telephone dictation, a "talk-down" tone signal which indicates to the user that he has "seized" a recorder and it is waiting to accept his dictation.

Supervisor's console In DE, usually a reference to the panel from which endless loop tanks can be monitored and dictation distributed.

Support requirements The secretarial assistance required by a principal.

Switch, switch code An instruction to a two-station WP typewriter console to selectively play material from one medium and then switch to the second one and play.

System 1) An assembly of components united by some form of regulated interaction to form an organized whole.
2) A network of procedures designed to carry out an overall major activity.
3) The operations, procedures, personnel, and equipment through which a business activity is carried on.

Systems approach The examination of an overall situation or problem with the aim of devising a total solution, as opposed to dealing with the separate functions which constitute the whole.

T

TMC Telephone message coupler.

TMU Time measurement unit, basis for many work measurement standards, equalling 1/100,000 of an hour.

TRC Telephone relay coupler.

T/W Typewriter.

Tab 1) Short for "tabulator," the typewriter key which controls space indentation.
2) The act of operating the tab key.
3) Term applied to typing work involving heavy tabulation, such as statistical work or multi-columned text.
4) In DE sometimes a reference to the indexing slip on a recorder.

Talk-down tone In telephone dictation, a whistle-like tone which tells the user that he has "seized" a recorder and it is ready to take his dictation. A "subjective" tone.

Tank recorder An endless loop dictation system.

Task An assigned piece of work.

Task data sheet A record of jobs by time period, usually for a single day.

Task list A record of each type of work performed by each employee, and the average number of hours spent performing it per week.

Telecommunication Generally, the transmission of voice or encoded material by way of telephone or direct wiring.

Telephone message coupler Interface equipment which connects DE to telephone lines and allows recording from any telephone in the world. The term is loosely interchangeable with "recorder coupler" and "trunk link" (both of which see).

Teleprocessing A form of information handling in which a WP or DP system utilizes communications facilities.

Teletype Trademark of Teletype Corp., usually applied to a series of different teleprinter units such as tape punchers, reperforators, page printers, and keyboard terminals used in hard-copy communication systems.

Teletypewriter Generic term for teleprinters and keyboard terminals used in hard-copy communication systems, but distinct from communicating WP typewriters, which possess a wide range of text-editing capabilities not found in teletypewriters.

Teletypewriter exchange service A public, switched service of Western Union in which suitably arranged teletypewriter stations are provided with lines to a central office for access to other such stations throughout the United States, Canada, and Mexico. Abbreviation: "TWX."

Telex A dial-up teleprinter service of Western Union comparable to TWX, but with separate rates and certain operating differences, which enables subscribers to communicate directly and temporarily among themselves, and also with TWX users, throughout the United States, Canada, and Mexico.

Ten-pitch Term applied to typewriter spacing of 10 characters per horizontal inch. Also known as "pica" spacing.

Terminal 1) Any device capable of sending and/or receiving information over a communications channel.

2) In DP and WP, an I/O device.

3) In WP, often a reference to a communicating typewriter.

Text 1) The actual matter of an author's work.

2) The main body of matter on a typed or printed page, as distinct from illustrations and marginal matter.

3) Broadly, the output of a WP system.

Text-editing typewriter A WP typewriter; one that records or "captures" keystrokes on a medium, and that has the ability to make additions, deletions, corrections, and format changes in the recorded text prior to automatic playout of finished documents. Text-editing typewriters may be either "interactive" or "stand-alone" (both of which see).

Text processing A term generally synonymous with WP, though often applied specifically to applications dealing with lengthy documents, such as articles for publication, which go through several editing cycles.

Text string search A machine function which allows a user to access a point or points within a document by keying in a set of unique characters identifying the desired point(s).

Thermographic printer A non-impact printer which creates images through heat impressions.

Third party lease An arrangement whereby a vendor sells equipment to a buyer, often a leasing company, who in turn leases it to a user.

Throughput The volume of work processed by the word processor.

Time ladder A form for logging the time spent at various tasks in a work measurement study, on which lines are marked off in five-minute segments for bracketing or other notation by the person making the study.

Time-measurement unit See "TMU."

Time sharing 1) A computer technique which permits many users to work with a large DP system for different purposes at the same time.
2) A commercial service in which access to a time-sharing computer is offered to subscribers through terminals placed in their offices.

Tone control A DE feature to vary treble and bass response during playback.

Touch control A device which adjusts the pressure of a typewriter keyboard to suit the operator.

Touch-tone A Bell System trademark applied to the 10-key panel on a pushbutton phone.

Track The path on a magnetic tape or card along which a single channel of sound or codes is recorded.

Traditional secretary A pre-WP

secretary; one employed as a general-purpose servant to an executive, to handle his correspondence, phone calls, errands and other random tasks, in contrast to an "administrative" or "correspondence secretary" (both of which see).

Transcribe To convert recorded dictation into a typed document or other form of hard copy.

Transcriptionist One who transcribes; a correspondence secretary or WP operator.

Transfer In a two-station WP typewriter, the automatic copying of material from one medium onto another.

Transport The mechanism that moves or "drives" a recording medium in DE or WP equipment.

Trunk link A type of interface system which permits phone-company telephones to "give instructions" to centralized dictation equipment, by converting rotary (dial) or Touch-Tone signals into commands such as "record" and "play back." See also "recorder coupler."

Tuning Alignment of a dictation sound head with the track of a recording medium.

Turnaround time The elapsed time between the dispatch of a task and its completion.

Twelve-pitch Term applied to typewriter spacing of 12 characters per horizontal inch. Also known as "elite" spacing.

Typebar 1) Term applied to typewriters having conventional "basket" typing mechanisms, with one capital and lower-case character-pair per key-bar.

2) An individual typing element in the basketed set.

Typeface A synonym for "font" (which see), though often used loosely to designate the specific hardware component, such as a typing element or printing chain, which produces text in a given font.

Typing element The unit which produces a character or characters of typing by striking on paper through an inked ribbon. Individual typebars, printwheels, and Selectric "golfballs" are all typing elements.

Typing mechanism Generally the subassembly within a typewriter that includes both the typing element (or elements) and the linkages which position and power its (their) strike.

Typing station An individual workstation at which documents are typed.

U

Unaffected correspondence Correspondence, expressed in hours of work, which is not processed by a text-editing typewriter. For WP/AS recordkeeping purposes, such hours are considered AS hours.

Unattended playback A feature allowing documents to be printed without operator intervention.

Unbundling The pricing sepa-rately by DP or WP equipment suppliers of systems analysis and other support services, in contrast to lump-sum "bundling" in which these items appear to be offered at no charge.

Underscoring In WP typewriters, the automatic underlining of designated words and phrases.

Unit In proportionally spaced typing, an arbitrary size value assigned to every character.

Unloading The act of rewinding a magnetic tape and removing it from a WP typewriter.

Uppercase 1) The capital letters of type, in contrast to small letters or "lower case."

2) Typing done in all capital letters.

User's manual A book of instructions issued to word originators outlining procedures for proper dictation, and setting forth other documents, style, and WP standards used in the organization.

Utility typing Short, out-of-the-ordinary typing tasks not sent to the WP center, but handled more or less informally by AS personnel.

V

VDT Visual display terminal; a "CRT" (which see). In general, the printing trades prefer VDT, while office-oriented WP users say CRT.

Variable Segment of a prerecorded document, such as a form letter, that is subject to change.

Velocity In typing, the speed and force at which the typing element strikes the platen.

Visual display 1) A CRT or VDT.

2) The textual or graphic image shown on such a screen.

Voice bank Term applied to recorder systems in which dictation can be stored and easily accessed for reference.

Voice grade A telephone line service suitable for transmission of speech, facsimile, and other digital or analog data, having a frequency range of about 300 to 3,400 Hz.

Voice guard A DE feature which sends a loud, steady tone over the phone if the recording medium is not moving.

Voice operated relay (VOR) A device used in central dictation systems which activates the recorder when it senses that voice sounds are coming over the line, and stops the process when only silence fills the line. The "VOR" thus eliminates long pauses during playback and transcription.

Volatile storage Recorded content which is lost when electrical power is interrupted.

W

WATS Wide Area Telephone Service; a U.S. telephone company service which permits a customer to dial an unlimited number of calls in a specific area for a flat monthly charge.

WP Word processing.

WP AS Word processing and administrative support.

WP typewriter A text-editing typewriter; one that records or "captures" keystrokes on a medium, and that has the ability to make additions, deletions, corrections, and format changes in the recorded text prior to automatic playout of finished documents. WP typewriters may be either "interactive" or "standalone"(both of which see).

wpm Words per minute.

Word In DP, a sequence of bits or characters longer than a byte (which see) treated as a unit and capable of being stored in one computer location.

Word originator 1) A principal; an executive.

2) A person who dictates "copy" for transcription into final documents.

3) In general, an individual within an organization who originates paperwork and requires secretarial support.

Word processing Broadly, the automation of document production. Among other definitions:

1) An automated system designed to cut the cost and time of the originate/dictate, check/type/retype, sign/mail/distribute cycle of producing business documents.

2) A concept for improving the efficiency of business communications.

3) The combination of people,

procedures, and equipment that transforms ideas into printed communications and helps facilitate the flow of related office work.

4) A systems approach to hard-copy communications flow.

5) The automation of secretarial work.

Word processing center 1) The room or area housing equipment and personnel for the production of typed documents.

2) The centralized location in which WP operations take place.

Word processing system A combination of equipment and personnel working in an environment of job specialization and supervisory controls for the purpose of producing typed documents in a routinized, cost-effective manner.

Work count A tally of the volume of work accomplished by an employee.

Work distribution chart A consolidation of "task lists" and "activity lists" which shows what a department does, and how each worker fits into the department's overall activities.

Work group A unit of personnel engaged in a specific function useful to, or necessary for, or ganizational operations. A work group may consist of an entire establishment, a department, or a section within a department, but it is always an entity unto itself.

Work measurement A process for determining the reasonable time required to do a given amount of work.

Work sampling A work measurement process which assays actual work situations, through random selection, to determine the average and reasonable times required to do given tasks.

Work simplification A planned way of modifying a job through the combination or elimination of its parts to increase production per employee hour.

Work standard The time fixed as reasonable for completion of a task, as determined by work measurement studies.

Workstation 1) An identifiable work area for one person.

2) In an office, desk and the associated furnishings required for a worker to accomplish his or her assigned responsibilities.

Wow In DE, a relatively slow, periodic variation in tape speed affecting pitch.

CHAPTER 27

WORKING WITH SMALL COMPUTERS

ONE SEMICONDUCTOR CHIP about the size of a thumbnail, a flake of silicon with a mass of microcircuitry, holds the key to computing power for the modern office. The chip is called a microprocessor, and this integrated circuit device is capable of performing arithmetic and logical operations needed to get a computing job done. One microprocessor serves as the central processing unit (CPU) for today's microcomputers. It also runs a digital watch, controls ignition in an automobile and keeps an eye on a thermostat.

Needless to say, there are more complicated aspects to a micro or minicomputer, and it takes different circuits for different functions. At this writing, scientists are packing one million or more tiny transistors on that little wafer of silicon to really power things along. Others are working on chips made of gallium arsenide because electrons can race through this GaA chip as much as six times faster than through silicon. The office administrator, working with, or planning to acquire, a microcomputer, need not worry too much about these developments. The micro, in operation today, will do the job just fine.

Computers Proliferate

The Dartnell Institute of Business Research, in a survey on automation in the office, received information from 375 administrators and executives that conclusively indicates the presence of small computers in offices of all sizes and companies of all sizes.

Approximately two-thirds of the U.S. respondents and nearly 60% of the Canadian executives reported that the mainframe computer, or central processor, was located within their office facilities. This should be coupled with the fact that well over one-half of the respondents were representing companies with office staffs of 50 or less people and the majority of this group were companies with less than $5 million a year.

Some 39 percent of the companies also reported that they work with a computer service bureau, bringing automation/computerization up to about 100 percent. At the same time, another two-thirds (66%) reported the presence of small (mini and micro) computers within their office areas. Most of the micros which were identified by manufacturer were the Radio Shack TRS 80s and the Apple IIs, although there were actually a large number of manufacturers named in all. Within the mini category, the IBM units, Digital Equipment Corporation systems and Hewlett Packard computers were named most frequently.

A Look at Desktops

In the Dartnell publication, *"Management's Guide to Desktop Computers,"* authors Merl Miller and Nicholas Rosa offer an excel-

In the beginning, or close to it, there was the Apple, which was fruitful and multiplied. Apple computers were actually designed as a home and hobby computer but demand grew to the point where the power had to be increased. This is an Apple II plus, a forerunner of many things to come. The Apple III put the system all-in-one, and the Apple IIs have been known as workhorse units, thanks to the utilization of Visicalc.®

lent insight into "The Advantages of Computerization." The following is one section of a lucid and fascinating guide to microcomputers, minicomputers and the software that makes them go.

MANAGERIAL USES OF COMPUTERS

By Merl Miller and Nicholas Rosa

The first, and most important, managerial use of a small computer is as a "drudgery machine". A computer allows your staff to be real assistants, rather than just secretaries and clerks. Most of the repetitive aspects of clerical work can be taken over by the computer. This will free the human staff for more meaningful tasks. No matter your real intention, the staff, not you, will ultimately make the heaviest use of the computer or computers. This is all for the best.

The computer enables the staff to complete more work in less time. This obviously means that a department can do with a smaller staff for a given volume of work—or, as the work expands with company or departmental growth, fewer new people will have to be hired.

Some things are not done, because the practical means of doing them are not present. At least, the practical means of doing them quickly are not available. Any manager has objectives and goals. Not only must you be able to plan for the future, but you must be able to forecast with some degree of accuracy. It is supremely useful to project current trends—in production, production costs, sales volume, inventory, inflation rates, interest rates, and so on—for reasonable periods into the future. It can be career-enhancing to be able to relate several of those trends to an actual model of a future situation, and to have firm data for supporting proposals. It can be lifesaving to have plenty of advance warning if the department goes over budget.

Technically, forecasting and trend-tracking can be done with a pencil and a pocket calculator as the only tools. Every manager has tried it, more than once. Every manager has succeeded with it more than once. But the time involved usually was phenomenal and the effort exhausting. The more complex the operation for which forecasts had to be made, the more sketchy the basis of the forecast had to be—and the more sketchy and unreliable the forecast itself. It is not something you can do manually any time you choose. You may have submitted something really exciting to top management, but then "J.B." himself brought it back to you with a "What if—?" question. You were stuck. To give J.B. a hard and fast answer to his question, you would have had to run the entire forecasting exercise

The IBM PC (Personal Computer) hit the market with a resounding bang, forcing many microcomputer companies to meet the challenge. Here the PC is shown on an ergonomically-designed terminal stand, another development stemming from the new micro age. The stand is adjustable to meet the needs of the operator.

Courtesy Howe Furniture Corp.

again. And it was plain he didn't want you to take the time just for an "interesting" idea he wasn't yet sold on. But a small computer could have changed that.

True Forecasting Capabilities

Today's small computer system gives you forecasting capabilities. It holds all the relevant data and keeps it on tap for you. Its programs can manipulate the data faster than you and your calculator can manipulate it. Since so many of the figures that you would punch into that calculator are already sitting there in the computer's memory, even your key-poking time is cut drastically. You can repeat a forecast or a complex analysis, in hours instead of days, or in minutes instead of hours. You can even do *spread-sheet analysis.**

A spread-sheet analysis is fruitful, tiresome, fun, worthwhile, worrisome and draining. Just setting it up is tedious; that is, if you are doing it manually. You can avoid much of this tedium by using a computer. Several inexpensive spread-sheet analysis programs are available for small computers. They go by names like *VisiCalc, SuperCalc,* and *Execuplan.* If you change one variable in doing an analysis or forecast manually, you have to work through and make relevant changes everywhere on the sheet. You might make up to 20 recalculations in a row. With the VisiCalc-type programs, you specify what is relevant to what. When you change one variable, the recalculation is automatic across the sheet. Analyses that once took days of your time boils down to a few hours.

A small, independent businessman in San Jose, California, spent several hours doing his payroll (16 employees) and then updating his general ledger to reflect the payroll disbursements. Using a *VisiCalc*-type program on a rather rudimentary desktop computer, he cut the entire process down to minutes. The automatic linking and updating features of the program relieved him of tedium and time drain. His accounting is now less error-prone because it involves fewer human steps and much less of the human fatigue factor.

Of course a mistake made in using such a program is still a mistake—and the mistake may "update" its way through, or across a ledger—but now all the San Jose executive has to check and verify are starting figures.

Over and Over

What any computer does best is repetitive and exacting tasks. These are tasks that human beings do grudgingly at best and usually poorly, as compared to the tireless machine. The drudgery aspects of work are seen by most people as "getting in the way of the work." This is especially true of managers, assistant managers, section superintendents, and talented people who know the purpose and function of the department. These are the people who want to help fulfill the purpose and function.

Endless shuffling of pieces of paper, endlessly reading and writing long columns of figures, repeatedly performing the same petty calculations, endlessly opening and closing file cabinet drawers to with-

---

*SPREAD-SHEET ANALYSIS—A multicolumn work sheet used by accountants and auditors for analysis of transactions, aging of accounts receivable, summarization of appreciation for several time periods and similar purposes. Source: *Dictionary of Accounting,* 1981.

The Atari 800 system pictured here was a latecomer (1981) in the microcomputer field, but the company had a well-established name in arcade and home video games, and it came on strong. The 800 system, pictured here, is a very management-oriented working tool supplied with excellent software packages.

draw and restore file folders are anathema to your best, most worthwhile people. These tasks do not make the best use of anyone's time. It's cheaper to let a machine do them—or do the machine equivalents.

As a manager you need a constant stream of information from many sources. Floods of paper wash across your desk. You may have subordinates capable of predigesting much of the information into concise reports—or you may not. And they, too, tend to get swamped. Important details often get lost in the welter. Key subordinates frequently keep much of the operation in their heads, and this generates crisis situations when any such person is sick, on vacation or quits. You may have to keep too much information in your own head for the department's (or your own) good, because any other person probably can implement only a part of that information. What's going well? What's going poorly? It can be difficult to keep up and to institute remedial actions.

Information Must Flow

Departments that operate efficiently and smoothly normally have finely tuned information flow. The information is well-processed and unpolluted by irrelevant or obsolete detail. Everyone routinely receives the information he or she needs to carry out the next phase of an assigned task. All files are sufficiently updated and complete. On the other hand, departments that are floundering, or at least making frequent ordeals for the manager, have poorly organized information flow. In modern business practice, the computer is looked upon as a solution to managerial information problems.

This computer may be the corporate giant, located at that remote computer center. Or, you may have time-sharing—access to the computer by means of a terminal installed in the department. Regardless of which you use, you are still at the mercy of the corporate DP setup, using whatever software the DP experts think you need. In many recent instances, managers have lugged in an Apple or Atari or TRS-80 they bought for the kids to play games on, just to try to tackle some specific problems. (Playing games yourself, by the way, is a good way to learn how to use a computer. Many games originated on those big, *serious* computers as a way to teach neophytes and help remove their fears of the system.) That *home* computer turns out to be a powerful programmable calculator.

It can become a powerful administrative assistant if its memory is expandable and if sophisticated software is available. It also makes an excellent, drudging, robot clerk, taking the load off human hands whenever told to. And, it does this job without protest. It has no ego that can be crimped and cannot remember having held a more exalted position.

Bringing in the home computer on an *ad hoc* basis can help with spot problems, but those "spot" problems turn up all over the department—just about everybody could use a small computer from time to time. A bottleneck-ridden department has less than optimum information flow or downright poor information flow.

Poor information flow reflects chaos. A computer can be used as a device to alleviate chaos, if you implement it correctly. However, it can cause more problems than it solves, if you implement it incorrectly. You can't computerize chaos. The computer operates in an orderly fashion, which is the only way it knows how to operate, and it's much worse in dealing with chaos than human beings. It has no intuition, no inspirations. There is an old saying in Computerdom, "garbage in, garbage out." This can mean chaos in, chaos out. The computer can keep enormous volumes of information flowing in an organized manner, divided into dozens of fast rivulets running accurately where they are supposed to go, *only* after human beings have organized the flow of this information.

Where the information flow is good (the department is efficient if overloaded), trying to impose a computer on it may generate chaos. There's another old saying: "If it works, don't fix it." The computer system must fit the existing flow. The role of the computer is to speed up the flow and speed up the *results*. A computer system implemented before that flow is known *and* clearly understood will clog and dam it.

You Get "Organized"

A computer always forces "organization." A ready-made computer system forces you to organize your data flow to suit the available software. Humans wind up doing "what the computer wants them to do." Actually, they are conforming to the plan envisioned by the person who wrote the program. If you buy a ready made system, you have to deal with a programmer who is not a part of your organization and does not understand your operation.

This is why acquiring a computer and casting about for ways to put it to work is not a desirable solution. Many times it has not even been a viable solution. Computers have been acquired by business entities of all sizes, installed, wrestled with for months and then abandoned. Any computer can become an expensive white elephant.

Your information flow must be organized before you get a computer. Your computer tool must be planned for and carefully acquired like any other tool. You must develop a clear idea of how a computer might help you streamline your operation. You need to become acquainted with the requirements of a computer, too; know its limitations. You start out with the knowledge that *all* computers must be meticulously instructed. You should also know that a human programmer, not directly acquainted with your operation, cannot write a program precisely tailored to it without some clear guidance from you.

Department Analysis Needed

To accomplish this, a thorough analysis of the departmental operation is required. This can be a tedious task, the kind that everyone naturally shrinks from, but it *must* be done. The most efficient strategy is to do it before any part of the computer system is acquired, or even specified. If it is done last, or even *during* the computer installation process, it will be both less effective and less efficient. If the computer is to work at all, even poorly, the operation must be analyzed. For the computer system to work well, this must be done first.

The analysis of the departmental operation defines everything the department does. The analysis further determines whether it is doing it all and whether it is doing it according to plan and intention. The basic questions are: What's going on? Is this supposed to be going on? How do we do what we do? Should we be doing it this way? Who's doing what? There are corollary questions: What ought to go on? How might we better do this or that? This analysis spotlights what kinds of information are needed, and how much, by whom, for what purpose, at what times, and so on. It also spotlights who has or generates the information, where it ought to go and what happens once information is delivered. It distinguishes between archival and "metabolic" details; the latter includes the details needed for day-to-day or even momentary decisions.

Flow Charts Help

The analysis, itself, has to be kept organized and annotated. For this, you and your key subordinates should develop informal but detailed *flow charts* of what actually goes on in the department. Depending on the size and complexity of the department, these charts can become quite large and complex. So, every effort should be made to keep them clear and readily informative. From these charts, you and your key subordinates should then generate a second set of charts showing what *ought* to be going on. While the first set of charts is being generated, ideas for minor and major reorganization, or at least adjustment, should keep occurring to everyone involved.

The first result of this is that some improvements can be made while the computer is still a long way down the road. Is it possible to learn more about your operation than you had ever known before? It certainly is. Managers who carry out this analysis have the same experience as the small independent businessmen who carry it out. Everyone has blind spots; everyone has unconscious assumptions about his or her own enterprise. Analysis, description, and charting of what is going on suddenly unveils blind spots and illuminates hidden assumptions. Often, what is really going on comes into focus, unsettling complacency about what is supposed to be going on.

You Feel Achievement

The departmental analysis recommended here is tedious at first and then gets heady, almost intoxicating, because of the opportunities it brings to light. It will prompt you to make changes, to improve the department's ways of doing things well in advance of acquiring a computer. It will be the new ways, not the old, that you will want to "computerize", so you may as well hold off on any part of the acquisition until you have your new ways well established.

Once you have the computer, you will leave your old manual system intact, and in place, for several months. Manual and "computerized" methods should be used in parallel until you are truly confident that the computer is doing what you want it to do. Therefore it should be a new manual routine you "computerize". You also need repeated checks on the accuracy of what the computer is doing. Suppose it was misprogrammed? Suppose operators are feeding information in wrong? Either way, results will be erroneous. There is only one way of checking computer results, and that is against "hand-calculated" results you know are correct. Once you have confirmed that the computer is consistently correct, you can let go of the slower manual methods.

In the course of your analysis you will develop clear ideas of what kinds of reports you and your subordinates need, and which ones should be daily, weekly, monthly, quarterly, or on demand. You will know the depth of detail required for each kind of report. You will develop the ability to know whether a particular matter can be handled in a standard accounting-type report (for which computer software undoubtedly exists already), whether the matter requires something special (difficult to find in the existing software), or whether it is unique (you will have to have it custom programmed). You will start developing ideas about what your computer's data base should be like.

Your Data Base

A data base is a way of organizing information in a computer's data storage (disks, etc.) so that several, or all, programs can have access to virtually any item. Yet a particular item need be keyed into the computer system only once. "Data base management system" software is more expensive than conventional, program-by-program software, but can be well worth its cost for complex operations. Otherwise, much the same items of data have to be keyed in repeatedly for each program. In a total accounting sequence this would include accounts payable, accounts receivable, general ledger and profit-and-loss sheet.

The spread-sheet analysis programs mentioned earlier provide a sort of "instant data base." Once the "sheet" is set up, most input data need only be entered once. But such a "data base" is limited in its data capacity, and it is ephemeral. Essentially, it disappears once you exit from the program, or replace the program in the computer's memory with some other program. Still, the spread-sheet analysis programs are powerful tools, and they are inexpensive in terms of what they do. Since their inception, some have had recent add-ons, including graphics auxiliaries that will convert numerical data into bar or line graphs, and so on.

Your Operation Defined

The departmental analysis closely defines your operation. Defining it produces an important by-product: refinement and amplification of your own job description—what it is *you* do. There are myriad places in the operations where you are plugged in, yet many of those places were not mentioned by the job description the company showed you when you were courting each other. Nor were they visible when you were first promoted upwards or sideways into your present job. Some of those places "just grew". Under your leadership, the department and its functions have grown. Everything you are doing is more important to the company. You are doing more than anyone expected. Now you have a way to bring that to the attention of top management, and you have documented facts to back your claim.

Even though we recommend that you analyze your entire operation before you computerize it, we also recommend that you start small, with one desktop computer system, preferably single-user, and "computerize" the operation a step at a time. Just the enormous convenience of programs like *VisiCalc* or *Wordstar* is a reason for buying a computer to run them on. A few, or several, of these inexpensive packaged programs will streamline many aspects of your operation early—*and the staff will learn how to apply a computer to the operation's needs*. Thus, going step-by-step, you and your staff will be trained informally and painlessly without morale problems.

It would not be "unprofessional" to encourage the staff to play games on the computer for the first week or two, before it gets too busy doing substantive work. That's how children learn to operate computers. By playing games, they never learn that operating a computer is supposed to be difficult.

True portability in a business computer came with the Osborne 1, which weighed in at 24 pounds and has its own carrying case. It also has a five-inch screen, two disk drives, 64K memory and a built-in modem. This unit was a reflection of the "possible" when it was introduced.

Must Be Expandable!

Just make sure the system is *expandable*. You will start with a minimum memory capacity. Make sure the system's memory is *inherently* expandable to at least 48K, and further expandable through the bank-switching technique to even bigger sizes. Make sure the system will accept either 5¼ or 8-inch floppy diskette drives, *and* hard-disk drive add-ons if you do not start with a hard disk drive. Your system will probably have a minimum of two diskette drives at the outset. Its hardware and software should be capable of driving up to four diskette drives plus some reasonable number of hard disk drives, for example, up to four. Make sure the systems will later accept more terminals if you start with a single-user system.

Your single-user "starter" system should have, then, one terminal (a keyboard and CRT-type display screen), two floppy diskette drives, a small hard-disk drive (optional), a printer, and a memory size of 32 to 64 kilobytes (very fast, and low cost) or a letter-quality printer (a bit slower, and usually higher cost).

Strange as it may seem, a versatile, expandable system like this one will *not* cost much more (exclusive of printer) than a system that forever limits you to one terminal, two diskette drives, one printer and a memory of 32 to 48 thousand bytes. Also, the expandable systems are likely to meet certain industrywide standard design, connection, and intercommunication protocols. The limited systems are usually nonstandard, by design. As explained earlier, the makers of limited systems had hoped to capture their customers, making them dependent on said companies for all hardware and software. With a standard, expandable system, you are not limited to "one brand" for peripherals, accessories, software, and improvements.

Time-Sharing Possible

When you expand that system to several terminals, the operator at each terminal will have the illusion of having the computer to himself or herself. This is called time-sharing or multiplexing. The computer not only switches between terminals, it even switches between programs, if the different terminals are using different programs. The computer constantly queries each terminal as to whether it is ready for work. This occurs thousands of times a second, so that any time an operator strikes a key on the keyboard, the computer either has just "inquired" or will be inquiring during the keystroke.

In point of fact, time-sharing can slow some things down, especially if the computer has to keep re-accessing a program or relevant data from disk storage. This is one reason for having a large internal memory. Even without time-sharing, the larger the memory, the larger and more versatile a program it can store, and the larger the chunk of data the computer can work on at one time. With time-sharing, the computer needs more memory space for storing separate programs (or program segments) for separate terminals. Some systems get around the limited-memory problem by providing *each* terminal with *additional* memory of its own. (A caution is in order; all terminals have some memory, but not enough for this trick unless they have been modified for conflict-free time-sharing.)

You Can Network

Two or more complete computer systems can be networked (joined) together, to share each other's memory, storage, and peripherals. Ultimately all the computers in your department, and probably in the entire firm, will be networked together.

Your computer can also be connected to any one of a number of existing external information and communications networks. It is

Another idea of portability is this DEC VT18X kit which includes a z80-based micro-processor module, dual 5½-inch floppy disk drives, and associated hardware and documentation. It allows the DEC VT100 video terminal to act as either a terminal to a larger system or as a standalone personal computer.

Courtesy Digital Equipment Corp.

necessary to subscribe to the network (they have names like *Ethernet,* or *The Source*). Your corporation may already have its own *local network*. Computers, or computer terminals, are given access to a network—actually, to the network's "host" computer—through telephone lines. The device used to connect your computer to the phone line is called a *modem*. Through a modem, a computer may be connected with any computer, anywhere, that has a compatible modem. If you wanted to connect your departmental computer system to your firm's main computer, it would be through a modem; you or the computer would simply dial up the mainframe. If you have two or more desktop computers in different locations in the department, you might use modems to connect them together, even if you had wiring installed for that purpose. (Small computers can be linked together directly by the same kind of multiwire cable that connects a computer to its printer or other peripheral.) However, losses and electrical noise usually become problems at cable lengths greater than sixteen feet.

Tapping Into the Mainframe

Your desktop computer can serve as an "intelligent terminal" for connection with your company's big mainframe at the DP center. If they have already given you an intelligent terminal for a direct link with the big computer, they have really given you a microcomputer. It can probably accept a couple of diskette drives and act as a stand-alone local computer. In theory, at least, any intelligent terminal should be able to do this.

If your start-off budget can afford more than the "simple" single-user systems already described, it is probably better to go for two similar small systems than for a very complex one (having several terminals, many soft and hard disk drives, several printers, vast memory, etc.). Remember, both of those systems are expandable (aren't they?). Meanwhile, for either of them you have a set of spares, and a rough diagnostic tool. You also have separate data processing and word processing systems, if your departmental word processing load is heavy. Yet either system can assume either role; either can pinch-hit for the other. Early on, while only part of your operation has been computerized, you have a working system and a training system.

You have a diagnostic tool in the sense that, if either of the small systems seems to break down, you can substitute components to help isolate the trouble. For example, was "computer failure" really a terminal failure? Try plugging in the terminal from the other system. If the once-stricken system now works, you know what to report to the dealer's service shop, what to have ready for them to pick up and what loaner module they should bring. More commonly, has one of your diskettes really gone bad? (You keep getting a "Bad Sector" message, instead of your program or your data.) Try the diskette in the other machine. If it works all right in that one, you know you are developing disk drive trouble. (Perhaps it's only a need to clean the read-write head, but consult the service shop right away.)

One System Should Keep Running

With two systems, you know you'll always have one working, no matter what. You don't lose time. You can make decisions concerning priorities: bump the word processing, the budgeting must go through—or bump the budgeting, that contract must get finished, printed out, and mailed.

Don't forget complete sets of connection cables as spares. Cables can get damaged, especially when systems are moved from one room to another, or even across the same room. They get crimped—they even get stepped on. Their connection plugs may have 24 or more pins, and anybody who yanks a connection plug may snap a wire from its pin.

Since either system is expandable, you can start adding more floppy disk drives, hard disks, more terminals, additional printers, a graphics plotter, etc., to either or both of them as the extent of your "computerizing" increases. A corollary of Parkinson's Law will have your computerizing growing to fit the system capacity as time goes by. However, trying to start with an oversized system that "does everything" is usually expensive, chaotic, and traumatic for the staff. (More about the real problems of staff morale in later sections.)

Standing in Line

Who gets to use the system or systems? You may be eager to use it yourself. If you have run *VisiCalc* or *SuperCalc* into the kids' Star Trek computer and run a spread-sheet analysis, you are probably hooked. Yet, a computer system is inherently a "staff" tool unless *you* want to take on the chore of keying in all the data and running all the routine programs.

Managerial resistance is notorious. Many managers don't want to be seen using anything that has a keyboard, which has been a real obstacle for firms that have tried to "futurize" their offices by networking everybody into a computerized communications-and-data-processing system. A keyboard, after all, suggests "typewriter," and typewriters are for secretaries. Only in publishing companies will you find typewriters in the offices of high executives (and these are often battered old Underwoods there for effect, for nostalgia— everybody is supposed to remember that the publisher was once a working reporter, or even a war correspondent). This resistance to keyboards will probably erode, provided that the keyboards are always plainly associated with computers, not typewriters.

In some firms, on the other hand, the terminal in the manager's office is a prestige item, even as the pocket calculator was only a few years ago. (In the days of clunky, noisy mechanical calculators, managers shunned calculators.) However, new kinds of keyboards have appeared, just for executives.

Different Keyboards

These managerial keyboards lack the QWERTY typewriter set, but have instead a handful of function keys and perhaps a numerical keypad. Battery operated and entirely wireless, radio-linked with the secretary's computer terminal, the "executive keyboard" or "executive terminal" give the executive access to the computer. Perhaps he or she wants to see the updated Dow Jones averages from the external network. The secretary sets up the function the executive wants, but then he pushes his chosen button, and the desired data appears on a TV screen in his office. Of course the gadget is encased in mahogany, teak, or other luxury wood. (This is an expensive gadget you will probably forego, at least while you are starting off with one "simple" desktop system in the department.)

Very likely, full QWERTY keyboards, mounted in desk slides perhaps, will begin to appear in managers' offices. There are things you want to tackle yourself, and the keyboard is a must for that. (One of the authors of this book is working on the design of a compact non-QWERTY keyboard, amenable to executive hunt and peck, and mountable in a decorator case. Yes, it will be expensive in early production runs. You would be better off just taking over a staff terminal after hours, which is when you probably perform your greatest feats anyway.)

A desktop is *not really* the ideal place for a desktop computer. The vendor of your system will probably offer a "computer desk" designed to hold a system.

The Advantages of Computerization

It is a truism in the small-computer industry that you can now have "all the computing power of the giant mainframe computers of the 1960's and 1970's for the price of a new car." This price includes the computer proper, common peripherals, and adequate software for most office tasks. The price is usually more like the price of a medium- to large-sized sedan than of a Honda Civic, but remarkable minimum systems are available well below the Honda price.

It is possible—in fact advisable—to begin a process of "computerization" with a minimum system that will do some desired portion of the total data processing job. (More about this later.) It is easy to expand and upgrade a microcomputer system in stages, something like expanding or upgrading a system of stereo components. Because the cost is low, the departmental manager can usually find a way to finance a microcomputer system even if higher management refuses an appropriation for a "computer".

The pioneer "managerial desktop computer" was probably a home computer that some manager brought in to help with a problem that was beyond the practical capabilities of a pencil and calculator. "I bought it for the kids to play games and learn math on," said one real estate executive, "and I just borrowed it temporarily. If any software existed for the projections I was trying to do, I didn't know about it. So I programmed the formulas myself in

BASIC, and went from there. The kids were yelling to have the machine back, so as soon as I finished with my immediate problem I bought another one to use in the office." This was in 1979. Not long afterward his need to program the special application himself disappeared. By 1980, packaged programs which could do various real estate costs, interest, and value-of-money projections were commercially available. By mid-1981, several flexible, versatile and inexpensive program packages for doing whatever kinds of analyses and projections the user wanted to set up were on the market. (Nevertheless, the ability to handle BASIC or any other computer language is a valuable tool for any manager.)

A High-Level Language

BASIC, by the way, is a "high level" (human oriented) computer language. The language follows human thought processes and thought conventions. It involves English words, and with a little familiarity BASIC even seems "English-like." High level languages were designed to be easy for humans to use, and this is especially true of BASIC. The name is an acronym for "Beginners' All-Purpose Symbolic Instruction Code." It was first devised to give the untutored, or inexpert, access to large computers. It was immediately adopted as the first language of the microcomputer family.

When microcomputers first appeared, *only* BASIC was available for them. Today many business microcomputers offer BASIC, FORTRAN, PASCAL, or COBOL as an option. Each of these languages has special characteristics suiting it to particular applications. (FORTRAN was originally written for scientific and engineering purposes; COBOL is an acronym for "Common Business-Oriented Language," PASCAL is a more powerful, figuratively more eloquent, "BASIC-type" language, and so on.) There is now an enormous library of business programs written in BASIC, and libraries are available in the other languages as well.

Low-level Language

A "low-level" language is expert-oriented and the lowest-level languages are machine-oriented (these are called machine languages). Expert programmers work in these languages. They have their advantages. Programs written in the lower-level languages require less memory space in the computer and run much faster than programs written in high-level languages. The high-level languages suit human convenience, while the low-level languages suit machine convenience. (If you need machine-language programs for your microcomputer, libraries of these exist, and so do programmers who write custom machine-language programs for you.)

The microcomputer, like its common languages, is human-oriented, and microcomputer techniques are modernized and streamlined. There is no need for card-punching or wrestling through voluminous printouts of meaningless numbers to find a desired item of data. With a desktop microcomputer, there is no need to wait for an immense pile of paper to arrive from a remote computer site. Your input information is keyed directly into the microcomputer memory. Desired output information is then displayed on the television-like CRT screen, or is printed out as a concise paper report.

An Office Tool

The microcomputer is an office tool, literally "just another office machine," once people have learned to use it. Its price is within the bounds of an office budget, and since it is just an office machine, it is not likely to provoke serious opposition from higher up. It should not provoke invincible objections, suspicion, and jealousy from the corporate computer center. The DP center has its corporate processes and goals, and you have yours. There should be no conflict, and the corporate DP center can still get your inputs, and you will still receive their archival printouts. Meanwhile, you and your staff will have the rapid local data processing you need.

The first thing to computerize are those little things that deal with lots of paper or numbers. These are repetitive, time-consuming tasks when done manually, and they are tedious and therefore vulnerable to error. Updating the data in one function because of changes in some other function is also time-consuming and error-vulnerable. The amounts of data handled in these operations tend to be massive. Since a computer is ideally suited to handle large volumes of endlessly repetitive data and tedious tasks, these functions are naturally prime candidates for computerization. Perhaps the most important reason for computerizing these operations is that they are probably handled in some standardized way and will be amenable to standardized treatment. Therefore, the software required probably exists somewhere, or it can be generated by custom programmers in a straightforward, economical way.

Familiar Functions

Most important, these functions are familiar to the staff. This makes them desirable for training the staff to use the computer. Learning to use a new technique for less familiar functions is bound to be difficult for anyone. However, whatever has you thinking about computerizing is usually not a standard function like budgeting, but some bottleneck peculiar to your department's operation.

This is called the Hewlett-Packard HP 125 Computer System. It is used as a business system for manipulating words, numbers and pictures. It also communicates with the larger Series 3000 computers by HP.

The idea of having a computer help you eliminate the bottleneck is very appealing.

Trying to apply a computer to the bottleneck, as it exists, means trying to "computerize the bottleneck." The more practical solution is to dissect the bottleneck, straighten out the information flow, and thus devise a solution to the bottleneck. The solution should be computerized, not the bottleneck itself. With the standard accounting functions running on the computer, human time and talent become available for dealing with the bottleneck.

Of course, there may be some bottleneck aspects to the data flow in the "ordinary" accounting operations, but these are usually due to excessive workloads. Adding more people tends to cause confusion, so with the computer taking over most of the workload delays and confusion are lessened and can ultimately be eliminated.

An automated system provides up-to-date and even up-to-the-minute reports, so that the operation can be monitored by the manager or his key subordinates. This enables you to identify problem areas and initiate corrective action. Areas in which problems commonly occur are in inventory maintenance, cash flow, and personnel turnover. Properly shaped and interpreted computer reports can keep you informed of, and can help you anticipate, trouble spots.

What Are the Trouble Spots?

Trouble spots tend to involve tasks that people do not like to do. Whether this is "moral" or not, it is real, and has to be taken into account. The boring aspects of bookkeeping, order entry, file updating, inventory control, and repetitive manual calculation are all perceived as peripheral to "the job," which is whatever the department, and its people, are supposed to be doing. The department's reason for existence is more interesting and challenging to most people than is the continual entry of thousands of tedious numbers on different pieces of paper. In an automated system, most of the paper disappears since computation and manipulation of data are accomplished within the machine, and the results are stored for concise printout when desired.

Given a properly designed data base, virtually all the tedium can be removed. When a shipment goes out, the computer can note this fact in every file that needs to be updated because of the shipment. These include inventory lists, shipping schedules, and general ledger. An audit trial can be automatically maintained on every thing that has to do with that shipment. When an item is sold off the sales floor, the punching of the "Enter" key on the point-of-sale terminal updates inventory, registers new cash or a new amount for accounts receivable, and indicates a new asset in the general ledger. It can also update a comparable sales file which, by the end of the day, week, or month, will show the manager which items are moving and which are not. Not only can inventory be updated, but the particular item can be flagged for reorder with lead time for delivery stated and allowed for. All this is done instantly (from the point of view of human response time), where it could take minutes or hours of concerted work by several people to accomplish the same things manually.

The manager has the advantage that all files are continuously and automatically updated, so it is easy to determine the status of anything at any moment, on demand. With the proper projecting or forecasting programs, it is possible to generate reliable estimates of where everything will be in a month, a quarter, six months or a year from now. Several excellent inexpensive programs for spread-sheet analysis and projections are available.

There are also advantages that can be gained in retrieving information. This is especially true when the clerks may not understand quite what is wanted or where something might be in the manual filing system. The desired information item is still part of a file, but the file is on a computer storage disk—and can be retrieved by use of keywords. There can be a primary keyword for retrieving the file itself, and secondary and tertiary keywords for finding specific items within the file. (In some systems, any of the keywords will put the user somewhere in the file, even if it is not to the exact record wanted.) The file can always be subjected to an automatic global search to find any item in the file, even a single word. Whatever is retrieved is displayed immediately on the CRT screen.

There can be some waiting, while the computer scans the spinning disk to find the item, but waits are usually shorter than the time it takes to locate and retrieve a paper record from a filing cabinet. Paper handling is minimized, so this encourages economies in an age of ever-rising paper prices. The only paper required is for the hard copies the computer prints out, and it prints them out only on command.

Time Is Saved

The savings in time should free the staff to do things that only humans can do (or at least, things humans can do better than computers can). Suppose a misunderstanding has arisen with some customer, or with another department. Human beings can work to resolve the matter and even store the resolution in the computer. Suppose an employee has married and changed her name. She is registered in the computer's personnel and payroll files by her social security number, so the name change causes no complications. Her records can be instantly retrieved. Her payroll record will be complete. When her W-2 Form is automatically written, it will reflect a continuous record.

In another example, a customer has moved and is being billed incorrectly. A human can spot and diagnose the trouble and have the computer file altered. Past names, addresses, or other historical information can be retained as notes in any file.

Managers tend to be victims of many work interruptions because of problems that can be traced to clogged or confused information flow. The manager is called upon to intervene in petty situations that others could handle if the available information were complete and sure. The manager's discretionary powers substitute for the clear-cut information that is needed if a subordinate is to make a decision "safely". Anything that improves the precision, speed, and certainty of information flow relieves the manager of time-usurping demands on his or her attention.

Personal Systems Persist

Some things run smoothly because subordinates have worked out systems for accomplishing certain tasks or making certain decisions, but these systems exist in their heads. If Marie the bookkeeper or Arthur from the stockroom is out sick for a day or two, or goes off on vacation, their part of the operation can be thrown into chaos. Getting what Marie and Arthur know, and the way in which they do things, down into computer files and converted into computer program routines can keep things running smoothly. (It also dethrones Marie and Art, and they may resist sharing their magic secrets "with a computer," but in actuality with you. Some people's inner security depends on their being "indispensable" or on their being king or queen of their own little bailiwick. Marie and Art are valuable people but what if they got hit by a truck?)

The physical manifestation of administrative work is stacks of paper, still much paper work doesn't get done because people are too busy to attend to it and don't like to do it. At least it doesn't get done on time and in the right way. "Computerizing" paper work makes it easier to complete. The essential information is keyed into the computer, and the program takes care of the rest. Since the actual paper is eliminated, the time and tedium associated with paper work are cut down. Remember, most paper work has no immediate reward—a clerk, manager, or professional works something up on a piece of paper and puts it in the out box. When the response to this particular piece of out-box paper appears in the in-box a day or two (or several) later, it has little psychological connection with the original memo, requisition, or order. Keyed into a computer, the response to the same work is usually immediate or is at least rapid. If the response is not truly a reward, it is at least a reinforcement. The worker at a desktop computer keyboard does not have the feeling of shoveling against the tide.

Communication Develops

No matter how simply a department begins its computerization process, eventually the department will have several terminals, and next several small computers will appear. Connected together in a network configuration, the computers make up a local electronic mail system. Memos can be exchanged through the computer memory. A "mail" or "memo" program delivers each memo to its target terminal, and offers the recipient options of read (now or later), print out (local printer or main printer), file, or delete. If the office computer system is networked to the outside world—to other computers elsewhere—electronic mail (with documents of theoretically unlimited size) may be exchanged across the country or, in principle, across the world. It is a simple matter to connect any computer to a telephone line via a modem, a communications connecting and converting device.

Several small computer network services already exist. They go by names such as *Compuserve, The Source,* and Xerox's *Ethernet.* They tie the small computer into a much larger data base, which can bring fresh stock quotations (only a minute or two behind the regular ticker), commodity prices, Dow-Jones averages, headlines and complete news bulletins from United Press International (UPI) and other news services, and even electronic mail. *Ethernet* provides you with a way of having a local network, for scattered facilities of your own operation.

The small computer can also serve as an intelligent terminal for your company's corporate data center computer, giving you access to its data base and even some of its programs. Increasingly, corporate data services are installing terminals in departments for the sake of streamlining the corporate data flow. An intelligent terminal allows some reciprocity: the departments get to use the big computer on a time-sharing basis. Terminals can be "dumb," "smart," or "intelligent." A dumb terminal is simply a communications device—a keyboard and CRT screen. A smart terminal has some local data processing capabilites, but mainly or entirely for the purpose of formatting and predigesting information for input to the main computer. An intelligent terminal has considerable local or stand-alone processing capability, with a respectable random-access memory and even some local diskette storage.

Clear-sighted corporate DP services have recognized the intelligent terminal as a way of lightening the load of the central computer. An intelligent terminal closely resembles a microcomputer in every way, for the obvious reason that it really *is* a microcomputer. If you encounter real and implacable opposition to your acquiring a departmental microcomputer, try demanding an intelligent terminal and go from there. However, since the intelligent terminal can serve as a microcomputer, a microcomputer may serve as an intelligent terminal. This may be a selling point for you.

The Manager's Keyboard

Many managers shy away from having a personal terminal. A terminal, after all, incorporates a keyboard, and a keyboard is regarded as a secretarial tool. Use of a keyboard is still considered as menial by many. Use of a keyboard is seen as adversely affecting the manager's image with his peers and superiors. This may be true or may not be true in your company. In some technologically-minded companies today, the manager's terminal is seen as a status symbol ("Here's the new technology and I've got it; maybe your underlings will have something like it later.") You have to know the lay of the land in your own countryside. However, some special, nonsecretarial looking managerial terminals or keyboards have been developed.

It's a secretary's computer terminal. The secretary uses a terminal (with its ordinary secretarial keyboard) to set up the function that the boss wants from the computer. When the executive punches the requisite function key, the desired data comes up on his or her office monitor, which may be in a decorator cabinet, like a television set. (In fact, it may be an office television set.)

These little "boss-boxes" will probably enjoy quite a vogue. But for getting down the spread-sheet analysis or other managerial motivations for having a computer, the manager will, perhaps surreptitiously, use a full-function terminal with a "real" keyboard. This can be done after hours, using the secretary's terminal, or the executive may order a small hobby computer, different from the line of equipment the department is using, and have it on ostentatious display in the corner behind the desk or off to one side of the office. Since it's in full view of visitors, the executive can proclaim: "I brought in my kid's computer to get some things done around here."

At any rate, the full-function terminal, with its full-function QWERTY keyboard terminal, is going to be irresistible to most managers because it sure beats using a pencil and calculator.

CHAPTER 28

BUYING A COMPUTER SYSTEM

IF YOUR COMPANY has a computer installation in operation, or if you have purchased a small system from a computer retailer, you are probably well aware of the "pitfalls" and problems. You may or may not have lived a "horror story" based on system problems, since the majority of buyers are still satisfied no matter what you hear.

That analysis of tasks (or feasability study) that Merl Miller and Nicholas Rosa discussed previously is critical. If you are purchasing a "personal" computer to help you and your immediate staff, you can probably get what you want at a computer store. In some of these stores, you can look at several brands and you can usually see the software array that goes with each or all. If you want a TRS 80 Series unit, you will have to go to a Radio Shack. It would be best if you went to the Radio Shack Computer Center rather than your regular Radio Shack where you buy stereo equipment unless you have your order written down and know exactly what you want to buy.

You can go to an IBM retail store to buy your IBM Personal Computer, and you can go to a Digital Equipment Corporation (DEC) store to buy a small DEC system. You can also find other well-known manufacturers operating computer stores in some major cities.

Dealing with Vendors

Jim Greif, of Banner & Greif, Ltd., the agency that handles public relations for the annual Information Management Exposition and Conference produced by Clapp & Poliak, Inc., recently prepared a booklet entitled "*How to Buy that First Computer or Word Processor.*" Here is an excerpt from the booklet in the area of "Selecting the Vendor."

"The request for proposals and quotations should be sent to a number of vendors. If you are working on your own, you probably will want to send these requests to a large number of vendors. On the other hand, if a consultant is involved, he may be able to cover the ground by requesting quotations from a lesser number. Set a cut-off date for responses. If the vendor is going to be responsive to your needs in developing a system, it should respond to your initial request promptly.

"The quotations will indicate those vendors that have hardware and software close to your needs. Inspect the proposals for time tables for implementation. If your needs are highly specialized and clearly not within the range of a proposed prepackaged software system, do not permit yourself to be sold on the package. If you find a program that approximates your needs, ask the vendor for a fixed quote on the cost of modifying the software to meet your needs.

"From the quotations, whittle down the list and go back to the remaining vendors with specific questions. These might include how many support personnel are stationed in your area; the maximum response time to a service call; the cost of a service contract; the location of the parts' depot; the type of warranty; what training will be provided; the ability of the hardware and software to handle increased volume when your business grows, etc. Ask the final candidates to demonstrate how their software meets your specific needs, using sample data from your company.

"The answers to these questions will help you whittle down the list further and prepare you to talk to vendors about costs.

"If your program will need extensive customization, you may wish to send separate requests to software vendors. This process should be started early. It may even be wise to select the software first and then select the hardware to run it on.

"Here are a few specific items:

- Check references carefully. Talk to the people who are directly involved in using the system. Ask about the vendor's willingness to provide training and about service performance.

- Look at the vendor's experience in providing a system for an application similar to your company's. If your application is very unusual, you may have to be willing to be a test situation, but eperience with a situation similar to yours is preferable. Is the vendor a stable company? Does the salesperson understand your specific problems?

- Should you buy your system from one of the giants in the field or from a small company? Valid arguments can be presented on both sides of this question.

"The vast majority of vendors in the information field are small companies. This is particularly true of software houses, system houses and distributors. (Several of the computer giants sell through distributors.) Small companies often respond more quickly than larger companies to the needs of the marketplace and frequently develop creative solutions to unusual problems. Additionally, although your company is a small business, it may be an important customer to one of these smaller vendors.

"You need not fear a small company but you should be cautious. Smaller companies may be undercapitalized and suffer from cash flow problems. Look at the vendor's financial condition. It will surely look at yours.

"Buying directly from a large manufacturer has different advantages. The giants are well established and financially secure. If your system breaks down after you install it, you know that the computer giants will still be in business. Most have large research and development departments. Also, these companies have well-established service organizations (although you should carefully check any vendor's service record)."

Machines Break Down

One thing that must be faced, as with all equipment, is that computers break down. Over the years, office administrators have faced service problems with mechanical, electrical and now electronic devices that are supposed to deliver at high speeds. When they are going, the machines *do* deliver. When they are *down,* nothing usually goes on.

Because the office administrator is well aware of the problem of breakdown, he or she will also realize that a computer system, small and personal as it may be, will face moments of downtime. If the system is purchased from a local vendor (computer store), chances are good that service facilities will be available. A local dealer, who needs *local* business, might even bring out a "loaner" until the computer is fixed.

The willing, cooperative dealer is the best of possible situations. There's always the other side of the coin, so contingency planning is up to the administrator. Getting creative service is possible today, but like everything else, it costs money.

There are different types of problems. Some systems that go down frequently can be brought back up in a matter of moments by the user. On the other hand, the system might only go down once every six months, but it takes a week to get a spare part in. This can be annoying if your schedule calls for information runs within 24 hours.

Software Programs

There are literally hundreds and hundreds of business application programs for sale that fit almost every type of microcomputer made in the United States. Most administrators will have to use such programs to accomplish the jobs designated for the computer. The first thing, of course, is to be sure the program to be purchased is compatible in terms of the computer. The next consideration is whether or not the program will provide the necessary base desired for the work you want accomplished. Following that, you will have to check the "documentation" on the program—the manual that tells you how the program is supposed to work and how to make it work.

In far too many cases, however, this documentation is not well-presented, and this is usually a reflection of the program itself. Most of the large distributors of micros, on the other hand, do have good programs available. There are also companies which provide programs for other companies' computers. There is *VisiCalc, SuperCalc, Execuplan,* etc., etc. For the Apple II and III, alone, there is a book of hundreds of pages of programming available for many needs. You can get programs for law offices, accounting, doctors, small business, bankers, drug stores, secretaries and real estate offices among others.

From Radio Shack, you can get time management programs, personnel manager programs, word processing programs, general ledger, mailing lists and inventory control—as a beginning.

Once you get going, you will also begin to think about custom-designed software packages to meet your specific needs. Then there is the consideration of where to go for such programs. There are "software houses" and "systems houses" for you to choose from. Now you think about the reliability factor of the company, the accessibility and the price of the package needed. You might make use of the data processing department personnel in your own company (maybe even getting custom software via the "moonlight" route. You also may end up with a programmer of your own (someone who does all of the custom work for you). Remember, however, most customized programming costs money, and if you want to know why, try a little yourself when you get familiar with the operation of your micro.

The Challenge for Tomorrow

If, as an administrator, you have been using a microcomputer in your office for some time now, you are well aware of what it can and cannot do for you. You probably know how to run it in a simple language format or you are capable of using the more sophisticated languages. You know that you are working with a machine that has changed your office and your job forever.

If you are *thinking* about getting a computer for your office operations, you had better come to a conclusion—in a hurry. There are few offices where a computer couldn't help (as noted at the beginning of this chapter). The cost is high, but not too high in terms of office equipment. The point is to *understand* what the computer can and will do.

Peripherals

Basically speaking, peripherals are generally input/output devices which are attached to the computer. The most important of these units is probably the printer which is necessary if you want a hardcopy (paper) of your computer efforts. The printer, however, can often cost more than the computer if the original micro is a simple unit.

Although the vendor of the computer system will be more than willing to show you various printers, you might be aware that there are about 1,250 to 1,300 different printers available which use between 10 and 15 different printing techniques. There are about 120 original equipment manufacturers in this area.

Printers are classified into three main categories of two choices each. There are (1) impact and nonimpact printers—the choice of how the printer works, (2) dot matrix and fully formed character printers—how the words appear, and (3) line or serial printers—the speed and sequence of the printing on the page.

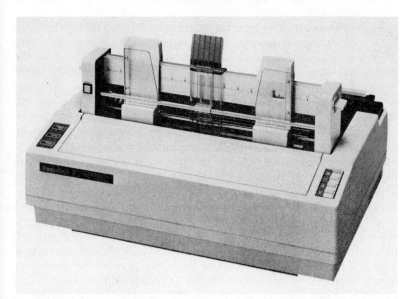

The Panasonic KX-P1160 is a bidirectional, dot matrix impact printer with a "logic seeking head" that is designed to print up to 165 characters per second in Pica and 196 characters per second in Elite. This model is shown with an optional front inserter.

Impact printers (which most resemble the typewriter technique) have either front-or rear-striking mechanisms. With the front-striking mechanism, a typeface character or the set of matrix pins strikes a ribbon against the paper to form the image—such as the typewriter does. The elements in this method include the daisywheel device, the embossed sphere, the cylinder or dot matrix printhead. In the rear-striking units, the hammer-like mechanism forces the paper and ribbon against the typeface character to form the image. The font characters are on bands, drums, trains, or chains.

Nonimpact printers are classified by the type of paper used to accept the characters. There are thermal, electrostatic and electro-sensitive techniques, all of which require special paper (much like copy machine systems before the introduction of "plain paper" units. The cost for this paper, of course, is higher than plain paper and there is no way to produce a duplicate on the spot (without taking the copy to a copying machine).

Quality Is Important

While the dot matrix fonts provide a degree of flexibility in that the type can be changed within the memory of the machine, it is still not acceptable to many administrators as "letter quality" so most companies use the format only for reports and internal development of forecasts and the like.

The high speeds of some printers are important to those who need data rapidly. Serial printers produce one column at a time in a sequence across the paper. Line printers print lines across the paper. It takes nonimpact printing to obtain high speeds. Here again, if you want a business or communication to go out, you will sacrifice ultra-high speed for quality of printing. You can get full character printing on either serial or line printers.

You can get a printer for your computer as low as $500 and you can spend $10,000 for a high-sophisticated, programmable unit. Most daisywheel printers come in at a minimum of $1,000, but in this day and age, that doesn't always hold either. Sometimes it appears like new printers are coming on the market almost weekly.

One example of the radical and rapid-fire development in this area is an *Electric Typing Fingers* unit which was developed by Personal Micro Computers, Inc. in California. This device attaches to an IBM Selectric typewriter or a similar machine. When it is attached by cable to a TRS 80 or an Apple II or to the company's own computers, it becomes a printer. There is also an adaptor that makes it usable with an IBM Personal Computer. This unit came on the market at slightly over $500, so it is a possible alternative to an administrator who has electric typewriters in the office.

Other Equipment

As you begin to use a computer, or if you are using a computer system now, you are aware that this is not a final purchase. As you buy software packages, you also think about adding disk drives for additional, faster memory as well as extra computing power. You will want, in many cases, acoustical covers for your printers, and you will be purchasing floppy diskettes and hard disks.

You can buy plotters and graphics printers for your charts, tables and colored presentations. You can add extra terminals for multi-performance, so you buy cables and interconnect units. You can buy interfaces and modems. The latter will put you in touch with other computers and/or information services throughout the U.S.

All of these units cost money—some cost much money. However, you usually don't buy one or the other or all until you discover that you have a need and something is available to solve your problems. You can choose your own speed in personal computing.

Things to Remember

In his presentation on buying computers and word processing systems, Jim Greif hits on several key areas or problems that seem to arise on a regular basis. They don't appear in any particular time sequence, but they usually show up. You have to watch for them:

- Computers have been getting smaller and more powerful and they are certainly less expensive. This doesn't mean that you buy the cheapest, smallest computer you can get. If you have laid out your needs, you can quickly learn what kind of power you will need to complete your job. If you visualize your $2,000 computer as the future hub of a 10-station operation, you had better make sure that the unit will expand to that kind of capacity. Remember, too, that price-conscious shopping is much different than price shopping.

- Choose an automated system realistically. The benefits can be extraordinary, but do not underestimate the costs. Consider, as well, the time for switching from a manual to an automated system. And, consider the time for training your employees who may have little knowledge of the new technology.

- Be certain your system has adequate accounting control. Some systems will allow changes in financial information without a proper balancing accounting transaction. The accounting integrity of your system is vital. If critical numbers can be changed by accident or without proper authorization, your accounting system can become unworkable.

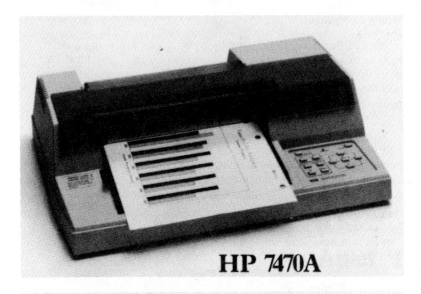

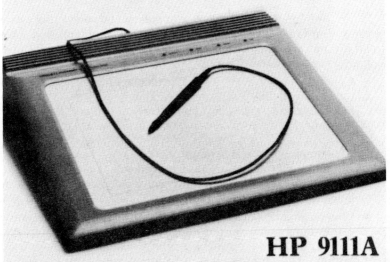

Today, low-cost graphic plotters put the visual impact of computer graphics to work for presentations of charts, graphs and the like. Two built-in pen stalls make two-color plotting simple. The HP Graphics Tablet helps you interact with the graphics display. As you move the pen-like stylus on the tablet's surface, the tablet translates your movements into X,Y coordinate points and transmits the points to the computer.

- Be sure that back-up procedures for vital records are performed. Every system should have a mechanism for copying and storing important records. Part of the memory of your system may be subject to being wiped out by electrical surges or power outages. It is essential that critical records be stored on some form of magnetic media and kept in a place separate from the computer itself.

- Be very sure you receive adequate written instructions from the vendor(s) on how to use the system. This may seem obvious, but do not overlook it. You should also require documentation for any software packages you wish to purchase. If you try an operation by yourself, using the documentation, and the operation works, then you probably can use the package.

- Don't surprise your associates and staff with the installation of a computer system unless it is *only* going to be used by you. Be sure their concerns are voiced and dealt with. For example, secretarial and clerical employees may fear for their jobs with the advent of automated systems. You should find, especially in smaller offices, that electronic systems rarely lead to lay-offs because the new systems lead to greater productivity and consequent growth.

- Be prepared for your system to go down occasionally. Any experience with electronic equipment (especially copiers for many offices) indicates that the machines will crash or go down. The idea is to be prepared and to have plans made. An arrangement with a vendor for immediate service is a good way to keep going. Some vendors will lend you a system or a component while yours is being repaired if parts must come from some distance. If it is critical, you may be able to run your program on a vendor's system at the store site or you might have an agreement with a fellow user to borrow some time. You should be flexible and accept the fact that these systems do go down.

To Sum UP

The microcomputer is fast becoming a replacement for the hand-held calculator in many business areas. It is an *expensive* replacement, but it can do much more for you and your office staff. It will free you from the worry of not having access to a large, mainframe computer or it will assure you that you can keep going when you don't have access to your company's system.

The minicomputer *is* a *management* tool, which means it is to be *used* by managers. It is not a wild statement to say: "There is *nothing* the computer can't do for a manager except manage."

It can retain important information for near-instant retrieval. It can help produce business correspondence, reports or memos. It can provide a manager with colorful and meaningful charts and graphs. It can help in forecasting, inventory, accounting and checkwriting. It can help with taxes, provide instant mail to distant points and call upon remote data libraries thousands of miles away for information that is needed instantly. Each of these functions costs money in terms of additional equipment or service rental, etc., but each function costs money under any circumstances.

Properly applied, a small computer can perform beyond the wildest claims of the salesperson who sells it, unless that person uses the computer on a daily basis.

CHAPTER 29

THE "USER-FRIENDLY" OFFICE

IN THE LAST CENTURY, scientific technology has accelerated rapidly and created a machine age in which studies of man, his limitations and his safety were often neglected. Engineering and architectural schools were oriented towards teaching students how to use materials rather than sensitizing them to the condition of equipment users.

According to Brian Grosselin, industrial designer responsible for Philips/Micom information processing systems, concern for pilot comfort and a greater awareness of his physical position in relation to aircraft equipment was first manifested during World War II. It generated a postwar concern for employees across a broad spectrum of industry. The preliminary results were the development of closer interfaces between man and machine and man and his working environment.

The emerging awareness of the human element, first in the cockpit and then in industry was the result of studies conducted by anthropologists, behaviorial psychologists, medical doctors and physiologists who provided assistance and information on man's size, strength and endurance, vis-a-vis his environment.

Human Engineering/Ergonomics

According to Grosselin, the efforts of scientists in relating man to machines are making the working environment a safer place. Their science is called "human engineering."

In North America, it is referred to as "human factors engineering," "biotechnology," or "life sciences engineering." In Europe, it is called "ergonomics," a word derived from the Greek words "ergos," meaning work and "nomos" meaning surroundings. Ergonomics is becoming popular because it is a neutral word which does not imply priority for physiology, psychology, functional anatomy or the several other considerations of the industrial designer.

The word also works well for the office situation, since it doesn't imply machines in factory terms. Most human engineering work was done on the factory floor before the office was even considered as an environment for work.

Increasingly, Grosselin continued, the user is becoming actively involved in the design process. The office worker, of course, cannot be expected to do the designer's work. What the worker does is provide information that the designer needs to arrive at a solution.

The Harris Survey

As the "office of the '80s" became a reality, Steelcase, Inc., makers of office furnishings, commissioned the Louis Harris organization to conduct a second major survey of office workers to expand its study of office environmental needs.

One of the major findings was that office workers still perceive their pay to be inferior to that of blue-collar workers, but they still believe their physical comfort on the job and their ability to communicate with management makes them better off.

Sixty-nine percent of the office workers polled thought they were physically more comfortable in the office than their counterparts in factories, and only 5 percent thought they were less comfortable. Sixty-five percent thought their general surroundings (in the office) were superior to factory surroundings, but only 23 percent thought they were paid better.

Like Temperature Control

Fully 71 percent of the office workers said that improvements in the temperature and circulation of the air in their offices would contribute to helping them produce more work in a day than they do now. Sizable majorities also cited the need for more quiet when it is essential to concentrate on the job, and more than half (54 percent) reported the need for more office equipment while 53 percent felt the need for more desk and file space. More than one-third complained about summer temperatures being too warm (under the former Carter thermostat rule). The chart following sums up workers' attitudes:

Lighting Is Important

Fully 85 percent of office workers feel that good lighting affects their comfort on the job a great deal, and a nearly identical 84 percent say they now have good lighting. While 73 percent of office workers feel that having a comfortable chair affects their comfort a great deal, an even greater 84 percent say they now have a comfortable chair.

THE "USER-FRIENDLY" OFFICE

Changes which can help increase office worker productivity.

Q.: A lot of people these days are very concerned about improving productivity—that is, allowing the same number of people to produce more than they used to during the same time period. There's a lot of discussion about what ways are best for improving productivity, and I'd like to know how each of the following alternatives would help you personally to produce more work during a day than you do now. Which do you feel would help a great deal, somewhat, only a little, or not at all in allowing you personally to produce more work in a day than you do now?

Total Office Workers (1,004)	A Great Deal	Some-what	Only A Little	Not At All	Not Sure
	%	%	%	%	%
Knowing that if you (they) produce more in a day, you'll be paid better	48	19	8	23	2
More comfortable heat, air conditioning, and ventilation	45	26	12	17	*
More quiet when you (employees) need to concentrate on your (their) job	40	27	13	20	*
More encouragement from managers and supervisors	37	29	13	21	1
More experience with your (their) job	37	22	16	25	*
More desks and files that store papers where you (employees) can easily find them	29	24	13	34	1
Better or more office equipment such as more photocopiers, computer terminals, or typewriting machines	28	26	17	29	*
More stability in the office—less moving around of people	26	25	15	33	1
A more comfortable chair with good back support	26	20	13	40	1
Better lighting	22	19	13	44	1

*Less than 0.5%.

Most executives with office planning responsibilities are aware of the importance of lighting and chairs to the comfort of office workers: Eighty-three percent feel lighting affects officer workers' comfort a great deal, and 82 percent feel a comfortable chair does the same.

Looking in more detail at office worker's satisfaction with the lighting in their offices, it can be seen that a substantial 81 percent feel their lighting is about right, not too bright nor too dim, and 88 percent feel very or somewhat comfortable with their office lighting as it is now set up.

Similarly, 73 percent are satisfied with the chair they now have, and 89 percent feel it is very or somewhat well designed for someone in their job. In most cases, however, office workers recognize that other office workers in their office who perform different jobs than they do, have chairs that are not very different from their own, while their supervisors and the management of their companies have chairs that are very different. If given a choice, most office workers would choose what looks like an executive (37 percent) or managerial chair (28 percent) for their own office or work-space; they would choose a particular chair because it looks comfortable (43 percent of replies), has arm support or back support, and is well padded, as well as having mobility and wheels.

Office Layouts Change

Since the 1978 study, there seems to have been a dramatic decrease in the use of conventional offices and an increase in the use of the open plan and bullpen types of offices. According to this new 1980 study, 29 percent of the office workers report they work in a conventional office, down ten percentage points from the 39 percent who reported it in 1978. The percentage of workers working in the open plan type of office has increased from 30 percent in 1978 to 36 percent in 1980, while increases in the bullpen or pool type of office show percentage gains of 14 percent to 20 percent during the same period.

While increases in open offices were forecast by executives surveyed in the 1978 study, such major percentage swings in just two years indicate an even more accelerated use of open offices than was anticipated.

The second *Steelcase National Study of Office Environments* adds some significant dimensions to previous findings about office workers' satisfaction with and role in shaping their office surroundings. It can be seen first that office workers draw strong connection between their comfort in the office and their job performance, just

The open office has been modified and unified to provide most of the comforts and conveniences once available only in a private office. Workstations, from executive areas to clerical areas, are tailored to meet the needs of the individuals.

Courtesy Haworth, Inc.

as they do between their overall satisfaction with their surroundings and job performance.

A majority feel that improvements in their comfort on the job will add to their productivity, and both office decisionmakers and the office workers affected by their decisions recognize that there is a potential for fewer errors and more concentration if comfort is improved.

While pay incentive is still the strongest stimulus to productivity, more comfortable heat, air conditioning, and ventilation is a continuing demand among office workers, who feel it is very important to them, who want to have a say in deciding their most comfortable temperature, who feel a more comfortable temperature would contribute to their productivity a great deal, and who feel they do not now have the right work temperatures.

Need to Concentrate

The other element of discomfort to which office workers are powerfully attuned is the unmet need for a place to work when they need to concentrate without distractions. As was found in the first study, the need for quiet and privacy is a deeply felt one, and one which many office workers feel is unfilled. Confirmed in this study is the fact that not only is it felt that this affects productivity (67 percent feel more quiet would contribute to their productivity) but it is a cause for complaints about physical discomfort and inhibits job performance. And again, this unfilled need is less prevalent among office workers in conventional offices than among those in open plan or pool type offices, although clerical workers in pool type offices suffer by far the most. The common problem of office crowding in inflationary times has had a measurable impact.

Smoking also has an effect on worker comfort and productivity. Forty-five percent of the non-smoking employees surveyed said they were bothered by those who smoke near them. Persons who are most bothered by smokers are professionals and those employed in the health and educational fields.

On the positive side, what is more reassuring is that both good lighting and a comfortable chair, given top priority by office workers for adding to their comfort, are widely available to office workers, and are not causes for dissatisfaction. A significant number of office workers are attracted by chairs that are specially designed for orthopedic support, but very few attribute backstrain or tiredness that they might experience to an uncomfortable office chair.

Overall, office workers are given far more say in the factors in the office which affect their personal comfort than they are in the larger decisions about office planning that were asked about in the first national study. Nevertheless, this study confirms that most office workers want to be involved in all decisions that affect them, and for good reasons; they perceive that their involvement will contribute to their productivity and general job performance, and to improving the offices in which they work.

Comfort Affects Performance

Over half of the office workers (58 percent) and executives (57 percent) feel that employees' job performance is affected a great deal by how comfortable they feel in their office. (See table No. 1)

According to 53 percent of the office workers and 63 percent of the executives, employees would be able to do more work in a day if conditions in their offices were changed to make them more comfortable.

Younger employees are more optimistic than older employees about being able to do more if their office conditions were changed to make them more comfortable. For example, 61 percent of the

Table 1

How comfort affects the job performance of office workers.

Q.: Generally, would you say that how comfortable you (your employees) feel in the office affects how well you (your employees) do your job a great deal, somewhat, hardly at all, or not at all?

(Number of respondents)	Total Office Workers (1,004)	Total Executives (203)
	%	%
Affects a great deal	58	57
Somewhat	34	40
Hardly at all	6	3
Not at all	2	—

employees in the 18-to-29 age group feel this way, compared to 56 percent of the employees in the 30-to-39 age group, and only 45 percent of the employees 40 years and older.

Other workers who more often associate improvements in comfort with productivity are employees who work in a bullpen (pool) type of office (63 percent), regular workers (58 percent), persons employed in the business and professional services industries (60 percent), and persons employed in the banking and investment industry (61 percent). (See table No. 2)

According to 48 percent of office workers and 59 percent of executives, the quality of employees' work would improve if their offices were made more comfortable. Once again, younger employees are more optimistic than older employees, with 53 percent of those in the 18-to-29 age group feeling the quality of their work would improve, compared to 49 percent in the 30-to-39 age group, and only 42 percent of those 40 years and over. (See table No. 3)

Office workers volunteer that, if office conditions were changed to make them more comfortable, the quality of their work would improve due to better concentration on the job (32 percent), increase of productivity (27 percent), fewer errors (20 percent), more efficiency (17 percent), and more effort put into their work because of increased motivation (17 percent).

Executives have somewhat different opinions about how the quality of the employees work would improve if they had improved office conditions. The largest number felt that there would be fewer

Table 2

Impact of comfort on doing more in a day; demographic data.

Q.: If conditions in your office were changed to make you more comfortable, do you feel you would be able to do more in a day, or not?

	(Number of Respondents)	Would Be Able To Do More	Would Not Be Able To Do More	Not Sure
		%	%	%
Total Office Workers	(1,002)	53	40	7
Age				
18–29 years	(309)	61	31	7
30–39 years	(281)	56	37	7
40 and over	(411)	45	49	6
Type of Office				
Conventional	(289)	47	48	5
Bullpen	(198)	63	31	6
Open plan	(365)	57	36	8
Job Type				
Executive, manager, supervisor	(23)	48	48	4
Professional	(162)	57	37	6
Secretarial	(89)	53	39	8
Clerical	(383)	55	38	8
Job Level				
Senior manager	(54)	50	43	7
Manager	(206)	46	50	4
Supervisor	(171)	49	43	8
Regular worker	(562)	58	35	7
Industry				
Manufacturing	(189)	51	42	7
Government	(147)	56	35	9
Health and education	(74)	45	47	8
Communications and public services	(94)	51	43	6
Business and professional services	(82)	60	35	5
Insurance and real estate	(108)	51	44	6
Banking and investments	(79)	61	28	11

Table 3

Impact of comfort on the quality of work.

Q.: If your office were made more comfortable, do you feel that the quality of work would improve, or not?

Q.: If your company's offices were made more comfortable, do you feel that the quality of work would improve, or not?

(Number of respondents)	Total Office Workers (1,003)	Total Executives (203)
	%	%
Quality would improve	48	59
Quality would not improve	46	34
Not sure	7	7

errors by employees (42 percent), followed by an increase in productivity (29 percent), better concentration on the job (25 percent), more effort into work because of increased motivation (20 percent), and increased efficiency (12 percent). (See table No. 4)

Workers feel they now have at least some say in getting whatever they need to feel comfortable in their job (58 percent), having a place to work without being distracted (42 percent), and the type of desk surface and filing equipment and storage they use (42 percent). They feel they have little or no say in determining the most comfortable working temperature (73 percent), the type of lighting that's best for the work they do (67 percent), having a place to relax (66 percent), and the type of office chairs they have (64 percent). Of the executives, 63 percent feel that office workers have at least some say in the office with regard to getting whatever they need to feel comfortable in their job, 45 percent that they have a say in the type of desk surface and filing equipment and storage they use, and 45 percent that they have a say in the type of office chairs they have.

Most executives agree that office workers have little or no say in determining the most comfortable working temperature (83 percent), having a place to relax (68 percent), the type of lighting that's best for the work they do (62 percent), and the amount of space that they need for their job (62 percent). (See table No. 5)

Having a Say

Office workers indicate that it is very important for them to have a say in the type of lighting that is best for the work they do (54

Table 4

Ways in which the quality of office workers' work would be improved if conditions were made more comfortable.

Q.: In what ways do you feel that the quality of your work (office work) would improve?

(Number of respondents)	Total Office Workers (477)	Total Executives (119)
	%	%
Better concentration on job	32	25
Increase of productivity	27	29
Fewer errors	20	42
Efficiency	17	12
More effort into work, increase motivation	17	20
Work faster	10	5
Less stress, strain	7	5
All other mentions	7	9
Do not know, no answer	2	3

Note: The percentages refer to respondents who say the quality of their work would improve if their office conditions were made more comfortable.

percent), having a place to work without being distracted (48 percent), the most comfortable working temperature for their job (47 percent), and the type of chairs they have (45 percent).

Executives, in most cases, correctly estimate the importance to office workers of having a voice in these areas, but somewhat underrate "having a place to work without being distracted" as important to them. (See table No. 6)

If office workers could make changes in the physical aspects of their office, they would more often improve the heating and air conditioning, regulate the temperature to make it more comfortable, obtain more space, get more privacy, reduce the noise level, and obtain new, better, or more comfortable office and lounge chairs.

If executives had the power to make changes, they would, in rank order, reduce the noise level, improve the lighting, obtain more space, get more privacy, and regulate the temperature better.

If office workers had a choice between a pay raise with no office improvements and a smaller raise with an office which had various

THE "USER-FRIENDLY" OFFICE

Table 5

Office workers say in determining various office conditions.

Q.: How much of a say do you and your work group (your employees) have in the following? Do you and your work group have a lot to say, some say, not too much say, or no say at all in (ITEM)?

(Number of respondents)	Total Office Workers (1,004)					Total Executives (203)			
	A Lot Of Say	Some Say	Not Too Much Say	No Say At All	Not Sure	A Lot Of Say	Some Say	Not Too Much Say	No Say At All
	%	%	%	%	%	%	%	%	%
Getting whatever they/you need to feel comfortable in their job	18	40	21	21	*	12	51	24	11
Having a place to work without being distracted	15	27	23	35	1	8	33	43	14
The type of desk surface and filing equipment and storage they/you use	15	27	22	35	1	7	38	33	21
The amount of space they/you need for their/your job	13	26	24	36	1	6	32	39	23
The type of office chairs they/you have	14	20	19	45	1	12	33	29	25
Having a place to relax	12	20	20	46	1	9	23	36	32
The type of lighting that's best for the work they/you do	12	20	18	49	1	10	29	34	28
The most comfortable working temperature for their/your job	9	16	20	53	1	5	12	30	53

*Less than 0.5%

Table 6

Importance of determining various office conditions to office workers.

Q.: How important is it for you personally (your employees) to have a say in (ITEM)—very important, somewhat important, hardly important, or not at all important?

	Office Workers (1,001)					Executives (203)				
	Very Important	Somewhat Important	Hardly Important	Not At All Important	Not Sure	Very Important	Somewhat Important	Hardly Important	Not At All Important	Not Sure
	%	%	%	%	%	%	%	%	%	%
The type of lighting that's best for the work you/they do	54	32	8	6	*	39	39	11	8	1
Having a place to work without being distracted	48	37	10	5	*	25	58	12	2	2
The most comfortable working temperature for your/their job	47	41	8	5	*	29	48	17	5	*
The type of office chairs you/they have	45	38	10	7	*	34	44	15	6	1
Getting whatever you/they need to feel comfortable in your/their job	44	47	6	3	*	27	56	10	5	1
The amount of space you/they need for your/their job	38	45	11	6	*	17	60	15	7	1
Having a place to relax	32	42	17	9	*	23	42	26	8	2
The type of desk surface and filing equipment and storage you/they use	28	46	17	9	—	18	57	16	7	1

improvements, over half of the office workers would choose a raise with no improvements.

Some of the office workers, however, would choose a smaller raise if they had control over the air conditioning and heating (30 percent), improvements in the general comfort of their office (27 percent), and a specially designed chair for their back support and comfort (26 percent), a door they could close for privacy (21 percent), and a quieter office (20 percent).

Somewhat fewer office workers would choose a smaller raise if they had a window with a view, office furniture that they had chosen themselves, an office decorated to their taste, carpeting, an office that was more accessible to the people they work with, and one that was in an executive area.

Items which executives feel that their company would consider giving office workers as a reward for performance are decoration to their taste, a door they could close for privacy, carpeting, office furniture that they had chosen themselves, more quiet, and more comfort in general.

Willing to Sacrifice

Although having air conditioning and heating that they could control ranks first among office workers who would be willing to have a smaller raise with improvements, it ranks eleventh among executives as an item that they feel their company would consider as a reward for job performance.

As stated, having a specially designed chair for back support and comfort is an item for which office workers would be willing to take a smaller raise. While this factor was mentioned by 26 percent of the office workers and ranks third, only 9 percent of the executives feel a specially designed chair would be most attractive to office workers for smaller pay raises and ranked it ninth in importance. Additionally, only 7 percent of the executives feel that the company would consider a specially designed chair as a reward for job performance.

Executives underrate the importance to office workers of having a specially designed chair for back support and comfort, and they overestimate office workers' desire to have an office decorated to their taste. (See table No. 7)

Management Concern

Almost three-fourths (73 percent) of the office workers feel that their management is very or somewhat concerned with the way comfort affects employees' *job performance*. A higher 94 percent of

Table 7

Office workers willingness to sacrifice pay for office improvements.

Q.: If you were offered a choice between a pay raise with no office improvements and a smaller raise with an office that (ITEM), which would you choose?

Q.: Some people have suggested that one alternative to large pay raises is to allow employees a greater say in the furnishing and decorating of their personal office or work-space. Which 2 or 3 of the following options concerning the office environment do you feel would be *most attractive* to the employees of your company?

Q.: And, which 2 or 3 of these office options, if any, do you think your company would be most likely to consider as an incentive or reward for job performance?

	Total Office Workers (1,004)			
	Raise With No Improvements	Smaller Raise With Improvements	Already Have (Vol.)	Not Sure
	%	%	%	%
Had air conditioning and heating that you could control	58	30	11	1
Was generally more comfortable	60	27	11	2
Had a specially designed chair for back support and comfort	56	26	17	1
Had a door you could close for privacy	59	21	18	2
Was much quieter	69	20	9	1
Had a window with a view	59	19	20	2
Had office furniture that you had chosen yourself	72	19	6	3
Was decorated to your taste	73	15	10	3
Had carpeting	56	10	32	2
Was more accessible to the people you work with	61	10	27	2
Was in an executive area	71	9	18	3
None	—	—	—	—

the executives feel that top management is very or somewhat concerned with the way employee comfort affects job performance.

Almost one-quarter of the office workers and 5 percent of the executives feel that the management of their company is hardly or not at all concerned with the way comfort affects the employees' job.

Government employees are particularly vocal in expressing their views regarding management's lack of concern: almost one-third (30 percent) of them say that their managers are hardly or not at all concerned with the way comfort affects job performance.

Forty-one percent of the office workers feel their immediate supervisor is very concerned about their comfort on the job, 38 percent feel their supervisor is somewhat concerned, and 13 percent say their supervisor is hardly concerned. Asked about how much *management* is concerned with office worker comfort on the job, 29 percent of office workers say that management is very concerned, 44 percent say somewhat concerned, and 26 percent say hardly or not at all concerned.

Of the executives, 63 percent feel that top management is very concerned with employee comfort, 33 percent feel it is somewhat concerned, and only 4 percent think that management is hardly or not at all concerned with office worker comfort on the job.

Three-fourths of the executives report that their company is in general very concerned with employee comfort, 22 percent feel it is somewhat concerned, and only 3 percent of them feel the company is hardly or not at all concerned.

It is obvious that office workers and executives have rather different opinions about the concern of management for office workers' comfort.

The Office Chair

When office workers and executives are asked about the importance of office chairs to employees, out of the context of other factors, 62 percent of the office workers and 72 percent of the executives say that the office chair is very important. Over three-fourths (78 percent) of the executives feel their own chair is very important.

Over two-thirds of the employees 40 years of age and over feel their office chair is very important to them, as do 69 percent of the women employees, 70 percent of the office workers who spend 75 percent or more of their day sitting at their desk, a high 82 percent of secretaries, 69 percent of the employees in the health and educa-

Office chairs designed to relieve pressure points and offer built-in lumbar support are a part of the ergonomic approach to improving office productivity. These chairs by All-Steel, Inc., are also available in a broad range of fabrics.

tion industries, and 70 percent of those in the communications and public services industries.

Executives, unlike office workers themselves, seem to feel that the office chair is very important in showing the status of an office worker; 78 percent of the executives (compared to only 17 percent of office workers) believe this is so.

Fifty-two percent of the business executives volunteer that if office workers were given the opportunity to personally select one piece of their office furniture, they would select a chair, and 47 percent say they would select a desk. But they feel if executives themselves were given the same choice, 35 percent would select a chair and 62 percent say they would select a desk.

Satisfaction. Nearly three-fourths (73 percent) of the office workers are satisfied with their present chair. However, 26 percent say they would prefer some other kind of chair, if they were given the choice. Office workers who are particularly anxious to have another kind of chair are employees 18 to 29 years of age (34 percent), employees in a bullpen (pool) type of office (31 percent), persons at the supervisor job level (31 percent), and persons employed in the government (31 percent). (See table No. 8)

Herman Miller Research

Over the past several years, the office furnishing firm of Herman Miller, Inc., has spent a great deal of time studying the technological, procedural, and ergonomic aspects of automated offices. Some of this research has been conducted by its marketing department and some by the Herman Miller Research Corporation (HMRC), which Robert Propst set up in the sixties in Ann Arbor, Michigan.

Table 8

Worker Satisfaction with Office Chair

Q.: If you were given a choice, would you say that you're satisfied with the chair you now have, or would you prefer some other kind of chair?

	(Number of Respondents)	Satisfied With Present Chair	Would Prefer Some Other Kind of Chair	Not Sure
		%	%	%
Total Office Workers	**(1,003)**	**73**	**26**	**1**
Age				
18–29 years	(309)	64	34	1
30–39 years	(281)	70	29	*
40 and over	(412)	81	18	*
Type of Office				
Conventional	(289)	75	25	*
Bullpen	(197)	69	31	*
Open plan	(366)	73	27	1
Job Type				
Executive, manager supervisor	(23)	83	17	—
Professional	(162)	73	26	1
Secretarial	(89)	73	26	1
Clerical	(383)	69	30	1
Job Level				
Senior manager	(54)	89	11	—
Manager	(206)	80	20	*
Supervisor	(172)	69	31	—
Regular worker	(562)	70	29	1
Industry				
Manufacturing	(190)	77	23	—
Government	(147)	69	31	1
Health and education	(74)	74	23	3
Communications and public services	(94)	77	23	—
Business and professional services	(82)	67	32	1
Insurance and real estate	(108)	70	29	1
Banking and investments	(79)	73	25	1

*Less than 0.5%

Several of HMRC's findings have been delivered at symposia and panel presentations such as NIOSH's* conference on VDT Issues Affecting the Occupational Health of Clerical/Secretarial Personnel (Cincinnati, Ohio, July 21–24, 1981). (See page 729)

The knowledge gained from this research is funneled to the design and development function at Herman Miller, and has been a major factor in the design of the company's continuing line of its office components, the latest of which is called Information Processing Support Equipment.

Because the numerous conditions emerging in automated offices interrelate and affect not only the design of components but their application by facility managers and their actual use by employees— from clerical to managerial—the company outlined some of the most relevant issues which could be useful to office administrators:

The Change Factors

- Information processing equipment itself is constantly changing as a result of technological improvement. However, that technology is failing to reach its projected cost-benefit in organizations today. One reason: it is not adequately considering user requirements or limitations, or environmental support needs.

- The ratio of terminals, both hard copy and video display, to users is decreasing at differing rates in different industries. In 1970 the national ratio was greater than 60 to 1. By 1980 this ratio had diminished to around 15 to 1. By 1990 the ratio is projected to decrease to 3 to 1. But in some service industries the goal was being attained as this report was written. By 1990 some departments within these industries will be operating at a ratio of 1 to 1.

- The turnover rate of personnel in some of these industries is as high as 70 percent. This, plus multiple shifts, is creating a great range of physiological accommodation requirements at the work station level.

- The proficiency of users varies from managers who hunt and peck for the 5 percent of their time spent at terminals to operators with great proficiency who spend 90 percent of their time at VDT's.

Bruce Reinhart, director of marketing for Herman Miller's Office/Institution Division, offered this observation—which can also be summarized as a segment of corporate philosophy for Herman Miller:

*National Institute for Occupational Safety and Health

THE "USER-FRIENDLY" OFFICE

"A workplace which can adjust easily and inexpensively to new processes, equipment, and user requirements can allow people to be more comfortable and systems more productive in less time. Sensitivity to workers' social, status, health, and safety needs can be expressed through the workplace.

"There must be a recognition of the physical and psychological needs of individuals who vary widely in age, body size, and in degrees of apprehension or enthusiasm at the prospect of working with computer systems.

"If human considerations are given a high priority in the design, implementation, and physical support of a new computer system, people are more likely to view the introduciton of new technology as an opportunity—an enhancement of the daily work experience and a contribution to the quality of working life, rather than resisting the change.

"An adaptable physical environment can play an important role in the smooth integration of people, process, and equipment. At Herman Miller, we consider the workplace a central issue, not easily divorced from other major issues of systems design, organizational structure, and management style."

Layouts and Ergonomics

Traditionally, the use of VDT's (*video display terminals*) has been introduced to offices through three types of terminal use environments: community, cluster, and dedicated.

In community use—the most "elementary" setup—20 to 30 terminals are arranged in long rows agains outer walls. Each device usually supports five percent or less of each user's requirements which ninety-five percent of their time is spent in non-electronic transactions using paper, the telephone, or face-to-face meetings at their permanent work station location. This is often up to 100 feet away.

This setup has severe ergonomic problems; some users will be tall, some short, and some heavier than others. Work patterns will differ as will space and privacy needs. (Two or three persons may need to discuss information on a single terminal next to others who require privacy and quiet to concentrate.)

Little can be done to provide users with good environments in community layout. At a minimum, easily adjustable, ergonomic seating and adjustable height tables can be provided; and it may also be possible to place carrels or narrow panels between terminals. Luckily, in the transition to the second stage of terminal usage, cluster environments are created.

727

Cluster Use

A terminal in this type of environment supports the needs of two to ten users. There are two types of cluster uses: the first uses one terminal for two or four persons (rarely three or five). Each user is seated in his/her permanent work station, each of which is distributed evenly around a centrally located terminal usually on a turntable.

Each user is within arm's reach of the terminal and rotates the turntable until it faces him or her.

The second type of cluster arrangement is usually located several feet from five to ten users who take a few steps from their work station to the terminal. In both types of cluster setups, terminals usually serve from five to fifteen percent of each user's total transaction needs.

To accommodate cluster use, Herman Miller introduced, in 1981, both square and triangular work surfaces that can support a 200-pound load. These, together with turntables with adjustable tilt keyboard trays, create two-way, three way, and four-way clusters. They can be straight-line, T-shaped, an arc, a cross, a Y-shape, or any combination of these.

Although users begin to utilize the terminal more often, they cannot bring it closer to them for more convenient use. It continues to reside outside the primary source of work involvement, inhibiting, rather than encouraging, its effective utilization. Some workers also find it stressful to work all day facing others at close range. In that case, the cluster layout can use panels plus a pass-through construction which will give users easy access as well as a sense of privacy.

Dedicated Use

The dedicated environment is a one-on-one setup: one terminal to a user. It's located in the user's work station and provides between ten percent and twenty percent of the user's total processing-transaction requirements.

The chief problem with the dedicated setup is that while it may contribute to up to twenty percent of the transaction processing workload, it consumes as much as forty percent of the available work surface area. Users must gain back twenty percent to thirty-five percent more work surface for that part of their work that still must be done manually on paper, by face-to-face meetings, and on the telephone.

One answer to this problem is a corner work surface which increases the usefulness of a 90-degree corner in a work station and can be used as a writing surface or to support a VDT.

As electronic equipment becomes more prevalent, the work station assumes an increasingly important role in office productivity. For one thing, users, to be most efficient, must find ways to adapt their physical environments to the postural and work process needs. The work station's role in providing process and postural support, as well as psychological satisfaction in terms of status and social needs, becomes more crucial.

In addition, rapidly changing information processing technology requires support equipment and a work station which can adapt easily to support a constantly evolving work process. Thus work station design—and the design of information processing support equipment itself—is best begun with an analysis of the work process and the user's personal physical characteristics in relation to the work process.

The VDT Workplace

The cathode ray tube is more popularly called the VDT or video display tube or terminal in office use. As stated previously, it is the heart of the information processing operation in the office, and the number of units in various uses is growing. Along with this growth is a new concern that this type of equipment may be dangerous or even damaging to the human users.

Excluding the almost continuous flow of rumors connected with the use of CRTs—increased amounts of radiation, etc.—there has been some justification for concern. A study by the National Institute for Occupational Health and Human Services was performed primarily because of concern on the part of the workers and unions that the CRTs were emitting hazardous radiation. However, it was ultimately discovered that the real danger lay not in radiation but in simply adjusting to what is a novel—and all too unnatural—new work situation.

When VDT workers or operators were matched up with a control group of non-operator office personnel, the NIOSH study found that: "the VDT operators experienced a number of health complaints, particularly related to emotional, optical and gastrointestinal problems, more so that the non-operators." The study concluded that a "greater level of emotional stress" was being suffered by the operators "which could have potential long-term health consequences." The table following presents the basic health complaints of both groups of workers.

This points to a real problem which must be faced in the office, and the application of ergonomic solutions seems to be the way to go. The development of one set of guidelines with universal applica-

HEALTH COMPLAINTS OF VDT USERS

Complaint	VDT Users	Non-VDT Users
Eyestrain	91%	60%
Painful/stiff neck or shoulders	81	55
Burning eyes	80	44
Irritability	80	63
Back pain	78	56
Fatigue	74	57
Irritated eyes	74	47
Blurred vision	71	35
Sore shoulder	70	38
Painful/stiff arms or legs	62	35
Neck pressure	57	34
Skin rash	57	31
Neck pain into shoulder	56	19
Stomach pains	51	35
Nervous	50	31
Swollen muscles and joints	50	25
Hand cramps	49	16
Numbness	47	18
Stiff/sore wrists	47	7
Change in color perception	40	9
Pain down arm	37	20
Fainting	36	17
Loss of strength in hands/arms	36	14
Loss of feeling in fingers/wrists	33	11

Source: National Institute for Occupational Safety and Health, "An Investigation of Health Complaints and Job Stress in Video Display Operators," 1980.

tions is not possible, at least at this point, since the nature of the task being performed must be taken into account when selecting ergonomic approaches. This means the office administrator should attempt to approach the design problem with an open mind. The administrator should look at the VDT hardware itself, consider the potential for eyestrain, provide the best legibility on the display screen, provide environmental lighting and provide a work station that helps the operator in every way possible.

Many of today's offices are not properly lighted for the use of VDTs. The bright, overhead fluorescent lights create a glare. The friendly, large windows in many offices also bring in too much light in some cases. The offices are not designed for the use of such equipment in many cases, and unless redesign has taken place there are many physical problems.

THE "USER-FRIENDLY" OFFICE

Eye to Screen Relationship

Successful interaction between an operator's eyes and the VDT display necessitates a juggling of human engineering and technical objectives. Focus, resolution, brightness and contrast all contribute to the correct and clear image on the screen. The focus produces the sharpness of the characters in terms of contrast on the screen, while the resolution provides more detail within the display and affects the legibility of the characters. Most human factor studies indicate that the minimum eye-to-screen distance should be at least 500 mm or 18 inches because of the eye's ability to "accommodate" to various focusing distances.

The colors available include white on black, amber, green and blue. Studies, again, indicated that the green was preferred by operators, but there is a new consideration of black characters on a white screen to simulate the normal document.

A major problems also appears to be the movement of the eye between the dark screen and the light document (when that is necessary). All of these problems are real to varying degrees and indicate that operators cannot be expected to work too steadily on the equipment without sufficient breaks for the eyes. Eyestrain is considered the most common operator complaint associated with visual display. The placement of the display at 18 inches seems to be helpful, so this should be a major factor in designing the work station.

According to other studies and research by Systems Furniture Company, "the increasing integration of video applications in today's office set-up can no longer be isolated—or ignored. Today, installation of VDT units must become an integral element in the total office design, which is why designers must be aware of problems peculiar to the new automated office.

"However," the report continued, "it is wrong to believe that fixed criteria can be applied to these problems: there are simply too many variables. In its study of VDT terminals, NIOSH stressed the importance of ergonomic solutions—that is, design arrangements which are adaptable to a variety of individual users. 'The development of one set of guidelines with universal applications is not possible since the nature of the task being performed must be taken into account when selecting ergonomic approaches to solving VDT problems.' "

The Equipment

Video equipment currently available can be roughly divided into the following categories:

- VDTs with an integrated keyboard
- VDTs with a separate keyboard
- Microfiche viewers and readers

VDTs with an Integrated Keyboard—The monitor and keyboard form a single apparatus and cannot be independently positioned. This makes for an unwieldy arrangement since it is impossible to achieve good (or more "user friendly") hardware positioning when operating distance and viewing distance cannot be adjusted independently of one another.

VDTs with a Separate Keyboard—In this type of unit, monitor and keyboard are joined only by a cable, which is usually flexible. Thus the system is more adaptable to user needs, as it is much easier to create an ideal video work station for any user. Fortunately, the

This Steelcase Ultronic Articulated Keyboard Shelf represents the ergonomic approach to providing keyboard access from many different positions to meet the needs of the terminal operator.

use of this type of equipment is on the upswing. Both types of VDTs are marketed in many sizes, weights and models, for a variety of applications. VDTs are familiar to most in the form of terminals of an interconnected computer system, with a centralized data base (contained in a large mainframe computer). However, VDTs are increasingly being used as elements in computer sub-systems for data entry applications and as components of word processor or telecommunications (telex) systems—activities in which user and machine are much more highly interactive.

Microfiche Viewers and Readers—These sorts of VDTs differ markedly from VDTs described above. They are not usually operated by means of a keyboard. The display originates in a completely different way. Display quality, to a great degree, is determined by the information medium—whether film, jacket or diazo. Though such equipment is used for tasks of a different nature than the VDT, it should nonetheless be included in design considerations, as most design aspects related to VDT stations also apply here.

Needless to say, the degree to which the work station must be adapted to the worker rests in large part on the nature of his activities. The longer someone works at a VDT without interruptions, the more difficult it is to maintain concentration—and the greater the need to provide an optimum work environment.

Room Lighting

Lighting is a crucial factor when planning an office which includes VDT work stations. Unfortunately, where VDT work stations are integrated amongst other types of stations, not enough attention is being paid to their specific lighting requirements. In general, the following undesirable lighting effects should be avoided:

- Excessive illumination
- Reflection

Excessive Illumination refers to an excess of light falling directly or indirectly on the display screen surface. Wherever possible, light fixtures should be positioned directly above the VDT work station, in such a way that the angle of incidence of the light on the monitor does not exceed 45 degrees. Louvers on lighting fixtures can be very useful in this respect.

Reflection—occurs when lights, natural light sources, or reflecting objects are mirrored in the shiny surface of the display screen. Any influx of natural light from windows behind a work station can be effectively regulated with the help of horizontally or vertically louvered blinds. The same solution can be applied to windows in front of the work station, which frequently form a highly unfavorable background for the video display.

The NIOSH study makes the following general recommendations regarding room lighting in or around VDT work areas:

- Drapes, shades and/or blinds over windows should be closed, especially during direct sunlight conditions.
- Terminals should be properly positioned with respect to windows and overhead lighting so that glare sources are not directly in front of the operators, nor reflected in the VDT screen.
- Screen hoods may be desirable to either completely or partially shield the screen from reflections.
- Anti-glare filters may be installed on the VDT screen.
- Direct lighting fixtures may need to be recessed, and baffles may be used to cover light fixtures to prevent the luminaries from acting as a glare source. Light should be directed DOWNWARD rather than be diffused in VDT work station areas.
- Properly installed indirect lighting systems will limit the luminaries from acting as a glare source.

NIOSH further recommends that lighting levels be set at 500–700 lux, depending on the visual demands of other tasks performed in the same work area.

Working Position

The following factors are important in providing the proper working position for operating video equipment:

- Seat height
- Position of the forearms
- Direction of vision
- VDT positioning

Seat Height—should be such that both feet can be placed flat on the floor and blood circulation in the thighs is not obstructed by the front edge of the chair in which the user is seated. The best solution is to use a typist's chair which satisfies the CEN standards (CEN pr EN90 and prEN91). Then the height of the seat will be adjustable from 17 to 20 inches.

In addition, NIOSH suggests that chairs have "an adjustable seat height, adjustable lumbar support height and an adjustable backrest to provide support to the lower back. Chairs should (also) have armrests . . . or tables should have an edge that will support forearms to minimize fatigue in forearms."

Position of the Forearms—while operating any keyboard, should be horizontal.

Direction of Vision—from the eyes to the center of the display screen should ideally slant downward approximately 15 degrees below the horizontal plane. However, where the material and the keyboard play a more important part in determining the direction of vision, the primary concern is to ensure that the different components remain within reach of the eye to minimize vertical or horizontal head movements. All the various components of the VDT task should be brought within a 30 degree angle of the line-of-sight.

To achieve this, various arrangements of keyboard, display screen and material-holder are possible, depending on the individual visual powers and wishes of the VDT user:

- The most obvious arrangement is with the keyboard directly in front of the user, with the monitor above and behind it and the material-holder to the left or right.

- Another simple arrangement is with the keyboard directly in front of the user, with the monitor above and behind the keyboard and the material-holder between the two. In this position, a certain amount of vertical head movement is inevitable.

- A less well-known arrangement—which nonetheless has enjoyed wide use in Scandinavian countries—positions the keyboard directly in front of the user, with the monitor below and behind it and the material holder above the monitor.

- In general, the greater the distance between eye and monitor, the lower the monitor should be positioned in relation to the keyboard. The lower the monitor is, the greater will be the user's ability to tilt it to come as close as possible to the ideal angle of vision. Tilting can also eliminate undesirable reflection, but this is not its primary function.

VDT Positioning should provide for maximum flexibility. Thus, both keyboard and display screen should be fully adjustable to ensure an optimum level of comfort for the VDT user.

Steps must be taken to avoid any tendency on the part of the operator to lean forward to see either the display screen or the material. Ideally, the operator must at all times be able to work in a stationary yet comfortable position.

His body should be SURROUNDED by support.

The Change Factor

The new, sophisticated, automated equipment being moved into the business office has triggered much in the way of change—change in the way people do things, where they do them and who does them. Some expect the executive of tomorrow to function (interact) with the new machines. He or she will be seated in a comfortable chair at a large console-like desk punching buttons that command screens, people and communication devices.

There will be some of this, to be sure, but the executive still must function as a decision-maker, not a machine operator, and the office will more closely reflect this factor. There will be a VDT present as well as a television monitor or receiver (perhaps combined). The executive will probably have access to a video recorder as well as telecommunication devices. But most of this equipment will be unobtrusive. Ideas are exchanged in the executive office more often than simple information, and the office will reflect this concept.

Office space will face design changes. The open area plan will be present where this is compatible with privacy and noise abatement needs. As jobs change, work stations will have to change, and as work stations change, the flow of information must be accommodated as well. The office administrator will be responsible for instigating change.

CHAPTER 30

OFFICE/COMPUTER SECURITY

OFFICE security and office-building security are products of our times. Born from the problems of the late 1960s, they evolved from a cursory management consideration to a present-day administrative responsibility. In fact, in many large offices, security administration is now a staff function. Rising with the responsibility we see new employees, whose titles range from security guard to corporate security director.

On another level, supporting the receptionist, if not replacing her, we now have electronic buzzers, two-way mirrors, unbreakable glass, a variety of electronic locks and a host of new I.D. cards. Such equipment, though once totally unrelated to machines such as electric typewriters, calculators, adders and dictating units, are now necessary tools for planning the protection of today's offices.

Highlighting this change is the new emphasis placed on the word security, for no longer is it just thought of in terms of stocks, bonds, collateral, or one's job, but instead it has become synonymous with such words as protection and loss prevention.

Crime in the Office

"Your desk is not a safe and our office is not Fort Knox." These words, headlining a security poster, best describe why the average business office has become a Happy Hunting Ground for a variety of criminals. And well motivated they are, for never before has there been so much worth stealing. In becoming rich in appointments, furniture, office machines, and the purses of well-paid employees, the office has become a plum ripe for picking—and so it is, every day.

In being unprepared for attack, the office became fair game for all sorts of crimes. From New York to San Francisco, within the million and a half offices across the nation, employees' purses and wallets were being ripped-off regularly. The purse on the desk, the wallet in the jacket left behind the door, were the daily casualties of rising crime. Then too, office machines, now smaller and more expensive, were being carried out of office windows, over rooftops, and often merely in a shopping bag right through the front door. Nor were rape, robbery, mugging, fraud, loansharking, or embezzlement only occasional visitors to the office. Every day, in just about every city in our land, you read reports of these things happening in offices like yours and mine. Progressively worse, crime in the office, a problem received with shock in the sixties, is now in the eighties an almost predictable event in many offices.

Another Major Problem: Fire

While rapidly increasing crime was the primary need for office protection, further fueling that need was the problem of fire. People, not short circuits or boiler explosions, are the principal cause of fires. Also, contrary to popular opinion, statistics show that most fires occur during the day—when people are awake and active. By accident, negligence, or design, more fires occur while people are up and about and able to cause them. Therefore, with offices now housing more than half of the total working force, the chance of fire has increased drastically. With more people, we have more paper, glue, ink, chemicals, machines—all potential ingredients for fire. To say nothing of careless smokers!

Fortunately high-rise office fires do not occur everyday—but they do occur. It is therefore necessary that we plan to make them impossible. Failing in that goal, we must know how to respond promptly and efficiently before a small fire becomes a holocaust. Despite "fireproof" construction, with buildings sealed with almost unbreakable glass and interiors furnished with more and more combustible material, the potential for disaster grows greater. Add to that dangerous combination the use of man-made materials susceptible of producing poisonous fumes when burning and our concern for the future is well justified.

Other Reasons for Concern About Security

While the primary reasons for the rapid rise of concern about office security are crime and fire, problems such as brown-outs, power failures, bombs, and civil disturbance are hardly less critical. Business language has expanded; the term "contingency planning," once solely legal or financial jargon, is now a section in a security manual.

In security, contingency planning has become more important as we move into an uncertain future—a future that is already programmed to shock. In brown-outs, power failures, and energy crises, elevators will stop between floors, lights will go out, alarms will not sound, heat and air conditioning are affected, fumes accumulate behind immobile windowpanes.

Not too long ago, a Chicago loop office building filled with carbon monoxide gas, and it was only through good fortune that the building's janitor learned about it in time to warn incoming office workers.

The Security Field

A recent study ranked the security field as the 5th-fastest-growing industry in the United States. Any growth industry invites unskilled adventurers to hop on the bandwagon, and adds to the hazards of selecting competent advice. "A little security can sometimes be worse than none."

To the later embarrassment of management, this statement has often been borne out in situations where a single guard has been placed in a building lobby merely as a symbol. In such situations, tenants have assumed a great deal more security existed than in fact did. In considering nothing more than just the problems of fire, such an assumption can be deadly.

It is curious but true that in security matters, there is frequently reluctance on the part of top management to think beyond the last incident—Maginot-line thinking, in which France planned for the 1940 war in terms of the 1918 war. Some top executives will commit extensive funds to track down a thief or repair the damage of a fire but will find a lot of reasons for not spending money for an all-around security program.

In office security, being a little safe is synonymous with being a lot unsafe!

Make Loss Prevention a Full-Time Occupation

One trouble with routine is that it deadens the mind. S. D. Astor, Security Consultant, tells of an aircraft company where two "control clerks" were responsible for checking the numerical sequence of invoices and other documents. The clerks were hardworking and diligent. But when a document was missing, they didn't bother to inform their supervisor, since, when they *had* notified him in the past, he had often been too busy to follow through. Observing this, the employees reasoned it couldn't be too important whether they told him or not.

Obviously the control procedure, though well conceived, had deteriorated into a meaningless routine. The supervisor was aware of the weakness and kept meaning to correct it. But here-and-now priorities made him put off taking action for so long that postponing the matter became habitual.

The supervisor's negligence and the clerks' routine disregard of the lack of followup did not go unobserved. Shrewdly alert to the situation were a couple of other stockroom clerks. Working together, these employees cashed in on the loophole to methodically rob the company for several years, until a new supervisor took over and tightened up the paperwork.

A similar case occurred in a candy company. The procedure here called for employee A to list the missing shipping copies of invoices and for employee B to track down the reasons. But employee B normally performed what he considered to be a higher level of work, and regarded this extra chore as a useless nuisance. Obviously, the purpose and significance of the task had never been explained to him. As a result he "got out of the job" by instructing employee A to reproduce, from another file, copies of missing invoices and to insert them in their proper sequence.

During the course of a management survey, an outside security-firm investigator questioned the presence of the photocopies. This led to a more searching probe and the eventual apprehension of a smoothly operating team of employee crooks.

Such discoveries by outside consultants are by no means unusual. The experienced dishonesty-prober is adept at zeroing in on strategies of circumvention, whereas it is the primary function of the public accountant or the conventional auditor to concentrate on orthodox systems, checks, and balances.

In another recent case described by Mr. Astor, outright theft was strongly suspected, but none was brought to light. Uncovered instead was a serious situation of inventory distortion. Behind the action was an incentive-production system which paid a substantially higher rate for item X than for item Y. What investigators found were falsified records padding item X at the expense of item Y. The result was serious indeed: wage overpayments, and inventory mixup that fouled shipping and production schedules, and misrepresentations on the company's financial statements.

Loss-prevention management it not a part-time proposition. Audit and review under a proper LPM system is thorough, detailed, and continuous. "Loopholes," says a partner in one of the major public-accounting firms, "are bound to develop in virtually every operation as methods become jaded, as situations change, as employee vigilance is permitted to relax." But under LPM, loopholes are systematically spotted and plugged before appreciable damage can be done.

COMPUTER SECURITY

Whether you use a computer, a service bureau, or timesharing, or will consider a computer application in the future—and most companies probably will—you should know about computer security.

Webster's Dictionary defines security as a "freedom from exposure to danger" and as a "means of protection." A system of internal control is such a device. Computer security is a brand new term used to encompass all aspects of protection; but the concepts are not brand new and are an adaptation of the principles of internal control, which are nothing more than good common sense.

Frequently, the obvious is overlooked and it takes a disaster to awaken us.

Disaster can come in many forms, such as the following:

Fire
Flood
Storms
Earthquakes
Power failures
Interruption of telephone or telegraph service
Air conditioning and heating failures
Mechanical mishaps of all kinds
Arson
Vandalism
Malicious mischief
Acts of revenge
Employee fraud
Inadvertent errors
Innocent acts

Disaster Planning for Computers

Planning to cope with a flood, an earthquake, a bombing, a riot, or a fire can all be listed under disaster planning, and yet in many companies nothing could be more disastrous than the destruction of their computer installation. Within the last 15 years, we have moved rapidly toward a computerized society. For instance, in today's business world, manual systems are now often thought of in historical terms—"how we did it before we automated."

With each passing day we have become more dependent upon machines, so much so that should they break down or be destroyed, we could face the possibility of the total collapse of our business—at least for a time.

On the other side of this potential nightmare we have computerized crime. Security consultants throughout the world are saying that colossal business "rip-offs" of the future will be accomplished by attacking a company's computer. Unfortunately, it's a prediction that already seems all too real.

Here too, then, is another very important area for office security. Where you house your computer and how you control access, both physically and electronically, can, in a very real sense, be considered disaster planning, a problem you should deal with immediately.

Program for Disaster

Recognition of the potential for disaster is the first step towards preventing it. Even though there are catalogs filled with these incidents, it is difficult to sell management on inaugurating a disaster prevention program. Yet the alternative to persistence is to wait its occurrence.

A disaster protection program has three aspects to it:

Prevention

Back-Up

Recovery

Prevention consists of those measures designed to prevent disaster or reduce its consequences by fighting it. Back-up involves providing alternative measures to continue operations after a mishap occurs. Recovery measures provide the means to a return to normalcy.

The actual program which is inaugurated should be the product of value analysis, whereby the security measure is weighed against the relative risk. However, without a complete check list, important risks can be overlooked.

Other significant factors worthy of lengthy consideration are those aspects related to EDP auditing. EDP auditing should be far broader in significance than only its computer security aspects and involves performance, development, management controls and financial auditing. Can the reader detect elements of computer security in these aspects as well? Therefore, in weighing costs versus benefits, benefits must be construed broadly.

A computer security program should be the product of the efforts of a variety of experts and be supported and coordinated by someone in top management. These experts should include:

1. EDP manager
2. Programmers and systems analysts

3. EDP auditors
4. Physical security experts
5. Insurance cousel

Physical Security Checklist

1. Building design:
   a. Fireproof
   b. Floodproof
   c. Construction should limit earthquake damage
   d. Fire doors
   e. Adequate exits
   f. Adequate smoke removal
   g. Automatic sprinklers
2. Radio interference shielding
3. A good system of fire prevention, detection and fighting measures which should be periodically reviewed by insurance, building and fire department inspectors.
4. Emergency power shutoff
5. Emergency pumps
6. Fire drill procedure and practice drills
7. Fire and smoke alarms
8. Access control:
   a. Restricted access
   b. Zone security
   c. Intrusion detection
9. Smoking restrictions
10. The hardware should be serviced by qualified engineers regularly
11. Manufacturer's recommendations should be followed for:
    a. Cleaning of the computer center
    b. Temperature and humidity requirements
    c. Storage of tapes
12. Adequate heating and air conditioning facilities

Back-Up Security Checklist

1. Provide for alternative hardware at an alternate location.
2. Provide for duplicate copies of programs, data and files at an alternate location.
3. Create an emergency power supply source.

4. Provide for emergency operating procedures and for the post-ponement of less urgent functions in case of emergency.
5. Cross-train personnel.
6. Provide up-to-date printed records.
7. Maintain your own spare parts inventory.
8. Obtain assurance of prompt and competent repair service.

HOW TO SHORT-CIRCUIT COMPUTER CRIME

By Daniel A. Janko, national manager of Computer Auditing, and Frederich S. Atkari, director of Computer Services Group, for Alexander Grant & Company, Chicago Certified Public Accountants.

It's 7 p.m. An assistant bookkeeper in a small wholesaling company is working late into the evening to help settle numerous outstanding accounts. On the pretext of needing additional invoice data, the bookkeeper enters the office of the company's president where he finds the firm's master record-keeping system—a $6,000 micro-computer purchased at a local electronics store.

Having bought and studied a copy of the computer's instruction manual, the bookkeeper has little trouble programming a personal entry code into the machine's electronic memory. Three minutes later he's back at his desk, diligently working away.

In the months that follow, the bookkeeper, sitting at home before his own low-cost computer terminal, dials up his company's machine via telephone and enters phony invoices in the names of bogus suppliers. Checks are then automatically generated by the system and mailed to a local post office box.

Although the bills only average between $100 and $200 each, they will cost the wholesaling company many thousands of dollars until the fraud is detected.

If it ever is.

The above scenario demonstrates that computer crime is no longer the sole province of multi-million-dollar corporations. Any business, large or small, that uses a computer to pay bills, issue payroll checks, inventory merchandise or perform any other accounting function, is vulnerable to this relatively new and often underestimated avenue for sophisticated theft.

Responsibility for preventing this kind of abuse falls squarely upon the shoulders of management. The Foreign Corrupt Practices Act of 1977 affirms the precept that company executives alone must see that controls are imposed to protect the integrity of internal auditing systems, this idea being just as relevant to data processing even for those companies not doing business with foreign nations. It is, after all, a matter of practicality. Any administrator who pleads ignorance and leaves the responsibility for computer operations to a subordinate, no matter how trusted, is a prime target for electronic chicanery.

Although still rare, the incidence of computer crime is growing rapidly. Newspapers have carried numerous stories of enterprising students who have played havoc with academic records in their attempts to master supposedly restricted institutional computer systems. Here the motive is not material gain, but the precious computer time itself with which these sophisticated youngsters can expedite their own pet projects and investigations.

As easy-to-use, low-cost computers proliferate, the number of related crimes is expected to increase. As reported in the April 20, 1981, issue of *Business Week,* only 1,500 personal computers were sold in the United States prior to 1975. International Data Corp. now estimates that total to be close to 500,000 and will probably skyrocket to three million by 1985.

Estimates of losses due to computer crime now range anywhere from $100 million to $3 billion annually. This number is expected to grow substantially, not through major thefts on the Equity Funding or Wells Fargo scale, but by a rapid increase in the incidence of small-time fraud. Still, regular losses of $100 or $1,000 can be just as devastating to a small business as a multi-million-dollar embezzlement will be to a major national corporation.

Clearly, the need for firm and effective controls exists wherever a computer is present. The type and level of sophistication of these controls will depend on the size and complexity of the system involved and the functions it has been designed to perform.

Physical Security

Physical security is one of the simplest and most effective deterrents to electronic crime for businesses employing personal-sized micro-computer systems. It is also one of the most overrated and useless barriers to fraud in larger main-frame operations.

Microcomputers

If a company utilizes a micro system, the kind that can be purchased in most any computer shop for under $10,000, then physical access should be restricted to those directly responsible for its operation. When not in use, the computer should be locked away in a secure location.

Some micro systems have telephone hook-ups (modems) so that company personnel can communicate with the computer from terminals in their homes. While this is a desirable convenience, it also leaves the computers vulnerable to anyone who has learned or, as was the case in our fictitious scenario, can manufacture a password. Remote links to micro systems should therefore be avoided unless other more sophisticated safeguards have been instituted.

Which brings us to mainframe computers, those cybernetic leviathans that daily exchange countless billions of bits of information via the common telephone line. Although there is a flourishing industry selling ways to protect such computers from intruders, magnetic passes and other high-tech devices are a poor defense against a clever programmer with a telephone and terminal of his own.

This does not dismiss totally the need to shield computer hardware. Direct physical assaults on company computers are not unheard of, and while a two-inch steel door and electronic deadbolt may do little to prevent subtle tampering with internal programs, they can be quite effective against a disgruntled employee with a tire iron.

Even if the possibility of vandalism is remote, managers should take steps to protect their most valuable commodity—their computer software—from loss or damage, be it accidental or intentional. As a matter of course, all computerized master files should be copied twice, one copy kept on the premises and another removed to another location. This latter step will insure company continuity even in case of destruction of the physical plant by fire, storm, earthquake, or other disaster.

Segregation of Duties

For larger companies with data processing budgets over $10,000 a month, dividing design and operational responsibilities among numerous employees is one of the simplest and surest ways to keep a computer system honest. Systems analysts, programmers, computer operators and data entry personnel should be limited in their knowledge to only that information that is necessary to their specific areas of activity. No designer should have access to programs or data files. No programmer should be regularly involved in daily computer operations. No computer operator should be entering transactions via terminal; this should be done only by data entry personnel.

When no single employee knows how the entire computer system operates, chances are remote one will be sophisticated enough to abuse it for his or her own ends.

Unfortunately, in small companies, such segregation is not always feasible. In businesses with 10 or less employees, the designer, programmer and operator are often one and the same person. Such concentration of responsibility, unless in the hands of the company president, places the business in a very precarious position. While it may limit the number of suspects should fraud occur, it also greatly lessens the chances that such fraud will ever be caught.

The extreme vulnerability of simple micro-systems is the reason physical security, as discussed previously, is so essential in small business.

Internal Safeguards

Beyond physical and organizational procedures, there are numerous measures that can be taken within the computer system itself to prevent unauthorized use.

The most common of these is the password. In this case, the terminal operator must enter a specific code before access to computer software can be gained.

In more sophisticated systems, special passwords may be required to perform any number of individual operations. Also, specific terminals may be delegated to a predetermined set of functions and are forbidden access to other programs. These procedures help insure that no individual can perform a function for which he or she is not authorized.

To maintain the effectiveness of such a preventive system, passwords should be changed periodically along with the access phone number. This helps negate any information gathered by unauthorized parties. Also, should an employee resign or be terminated, his or her access codes should be changed immediately.

The Role of the Auditor

In years past, it was not the responsibility of auditors to look for computer fraud. Recently, however, as business computers have proliferated and their operation has become simpler, many auditors have become not only authorities in the detection of electronic abuse, but experts in its prevention as well.

An auditor will begin by studying all computer functions, eliminating those operations not significant to the accounting process, such as word processing, statistical analysis, graphics generation or any other program not directly involved in the dollars and cents aspects of doing business.

There will then be an evaluation of how well the computer has actually performed the functions to which it has been assigned. Sample financial transactions are selected by the auditor via computer-assisted procedures. These records are then checked with original source material to see, for example, that bills paid correspond to actual invoices received. Likewise, the auditor will verify that bills, invoices, orders and other source material indeed generated appropriate responses from the computer.

Financial records are always removed from the company under investigation and placed on independent computer systems for processing by the auditor. This circumvents any faulty programs or tamperings with the original system and helps turn up any discrepancies that may have occurred.

Just as auditors can scrutinize existing systems, so can they design or recommend safeguards for new computer operations. Even small computer systems, where software is often programmed with a total disregard for controls, should be inspected by a knowledgeable accountant before being allowed into a business environment.

Opportunities for electronic fraud are growing more numerous every day. Colleges and universities are now graduating students with more knowledge of data processing than seasoned experts had a mere 10 years ago while at the same time computers themselves are becoming simple enough to be operated by a competent 10-year-old.

Unless business management assumes personal responsibility for policing internal computer operations, we will likely see a veritable explosion of electronic theft and fraud in the years to come. The victims will be none other than the managers themselves.

Here are 10 steps to guard against computer crime in your business, as recommended by Alexander Grant & Co.:

1. Situate computers in a secure location.
2. Restrict access to only those individuals directly involved with computer operations.
3. If you use a micro-computer, lock it away securely when not in use.
4. Avoid telephone links with micro-computers unless other safeguards are in place.
5. Copy all computerized master files twice. Keep one on the premises and remove the other to another location.
6. Segregate responsibilities for system design, programming, computer operations and data entry among various individuals.
7. Use passwords not only for computer access, but assign specific entry codes to individual functions and operations. Likewise, individual terminals can be assigned to specific operations. Void personal passwords immediately should an employee resign or be fired.

8. Implement programs that will flag accounting operations that do not conform to an established norm.

9. If using telephone lines for data transmission, install signal scramblers to inhibit wire taps and prevent unauthorized entry. Also, change the access phone number periodically.

10. Have an experienced auditor examine your computer system and recommend safeguards tailored to your individual needs.

CHAPTER 31

OFFICE MACHINES

AS THE U.S. ECONOMY continues to change from a manufacturing orientation to a service orientation, the number of offices and office workers has shown a concomitant increase. That rise in the number of white-collar workers has brought with it a renewed interest in the productivity of office workers. Office workers—the direct labor portion of the white-collar work force—constitute the largest, single expense item in operating today's office. Consequently, for office managers to be effective, they need to direct their attention and a greater share of their capital expenditures to the office workplace. Because in today's information-based society, it is the office that can produce the greatest impact on worker productivity.

One of the primary activities of most offices is communications of one sort or another. Sales figures, production figures, attendance figures, or whatever the information, is largely communicated on paper. It is that paper which remains one of the major costs of office operations today. Much of that paper is produced by any one of a number of stand-alone machines commonly found in the office. The office of the future, if it ever arrives, will interconnect those stand-alone machines so that all information can be moved, stored and retrieved electronically. When that day comes, it will mean a change from the familiar, individual machines to networks of interconnected systems, which will lead to higher capital outlays for equipment per employee.

The National Office Machine Dealers Association, based in Wood Dale, Ill., points to the recent experience of a large bank in Chicago, which has adopted such "office-of-the-future" technology, as an example of the changes that could take place. By building a network of interactive small computers along with a large mainframe computer, the bank has developed a central library that contains the bank's huge data base. Remote telephone dictating facilities are linked to the bank's word processing machines so that bank managers can be linked to the office while they are at home, at the airport, or in a hotel room. These bank managers can now communicate without paper memos by using an electronic mail system;

messages are stored in an electronic filing cabinet. These facilities permit managers to have an office wherever there is a telephone.

As the cost of moving people from place to place, and the costs of paper and office space continue to escalate, the machine dealers organization believes it is obvious that such remote working arrangements will evolve as the costs of required technology decrease due to competition among manufacturers. As a result of such scenarios most new pieces of office equipment feature multifunctional designs that have been engineered to:

- **Cut paper flow.**
- **Capture data and reuse it.**
- **Decrease marginal costs such as travel and space utilization.**
- **Improve clerical, support, and managerial productivity.**

New Equipment Purchasing

Purchasing new office equipment is an investment in the future—it is an investment that can pay for itself in a reasonable amount of time through reduced labor costs. Making the investment in new office equipment, however, often depends on more than just the purchase price of the equipment. Such decisions can hinge on altering or replacing existing methods of communications, personnel administration, or service. And yet, the benefits of new equipment often far outweight the drawbacks. Often the replacement of old equipment with newer, more efficient models or the purchase of a piece of equipment not previously utilized can lead to any number of benefits. Among these are:

- **Increases in employee output (productivity).**
- **Reduction in human errors.**
- **A lessening of task difficulty.**
- **Increases in service or product quality.**
- **Decreases in response time.**
- **Better utilization of office space.**
- **Fewer worker distractions.**
- **A reduction in the number of workers needed; hence, lower labor costs.**

Greater Ease, More Capability

The most recent breed of office machines offers vast improvements over older models, due, in part, to semiconductor technology. Today's office machines feature a good deal of automated and self-diagnostic functions that make the machines easier to use, easier to care for, and more productive in any office environment. Additionally the use of solid-state circuitry and microprocessors has eliminated many moving parts and made the designs more efficient. What's more, most machines have been reduced in size and weight, which makes them easier to locate and move around.

It is not at all uncommon today to find calculators that are available with enhanced memory capacity, new display techniques, and a variety of advanced programmable features. Copiers come with microprocessors to monitor and control a number of functions, and electronic typewriters are equipped with automated page formatting capability, among a host of other features. These and similar advances have been made possible through the use of microelectronics.

Payments, Trade-ins, and Depreciation

If a good deal of time has passed since the last time machines were purchased for the office, then it is quite likely that the old machines in service may be overdue for replacement. Yet, a company cannot indiscriminately purchase every new machine that reaches the market. Some plan is needed to determine which new machine is best-suited for the job and how long that machine can be used before its efficiency has been reduced and it is time to trade it in on a new machine.

Normal accounting procedures frequently depreciate office assets over a period of 10 years. Some special purpose machines, such as addressing and labeling machines, may depreciate through obsolescence much sooner. But for income tax purposes, most office machines may be depreciated over a period of 10 years. Under such circumstances, it might be wise to establish a depreciation policy that will permit absorbing the cost of the machines and making them available for trade in at that time. While a great many machines may be capable of providing satisfactory service beyond the depreciation period, the costs of repairs, trade-in values, and tax considerations should induce office managers to study the use of each machine carefully.

When it comes to the actual purchase of new office machines, office managers need to investigate price and conditions of purchase carefully to avoid paying more than is required in order to obtain the desired capability. Outright purchase of the machines, often, offers the most advantageous price and the elimination of any interest payments, but this is not, necessarily, the most economical route to follow. Leasing, for example, offers the opportunity to pay lower monthly charges and makes funds, that would have been invested in new equipment, available for other profit making ventures.

Renting office machines is another consideration, but frequently this method can be more expensive than either leasing or purchasing. Sometimes, however, rental is the only option available. In some instances renting can be preferrable, because the agreement can be canceled at any time. Renting can be a good way to avoid getting stuck with equipment that is not perfectly suited to the work situation or that isn't working as expected. Some rental plans also can be converted to leasing arrangements.

Once all of the factors have been considered, leasing is still, often, the most economical method. A long-term lease of office equipment cuts the price paid down to reasonable monthly payments; allows for the preservation of existing credit lines; conserves working capital for other uses; and protects against obsolescence—if technological breakthroughs make new models more attractive the lease can be terminated and a new piece of equipment can be acquired.

Criteria for Selection of Office Machines

Just because a new piece of equipment has been introduced that will automate a task that was previously done manually or that improves upon the equipment presently used for that task, in itself, will not justify the purchase. Quite possibly very good reasons exist for performing certain operations manually, or they would have been mechanized long ago. While machines offer advantages, a careful determination of the need for a machine should be made before it is purchased.

To help in this decision-making process of selecting office machines, here are some factors to consider before making any purchase:

- **Volume of work.** Will the labor savings, better service, or faster completion of the work justify the new machine?
- **Need for accuracy.** Is a high degree of accuracy required? Will the machine improve the accuracy of job performance through the elimination of checking and rechecking?
- **Speed.** If an operation is time sensitive a machine often can be justified because it moves up deadlines, speeds up rush jobs, and improves peak-time work performance.
- **Improved job satisfaction.** Some tasks are so monotonous that it can be difficult to find and keep competent employees. Even when no savings in speed or accuracy is gained, a machine can be justified for the benefits it makes possible in improved employee relations and morale.

- **Cost reduction.** This area is often given the most consideration when the purchase of a machine is contemplated. If the machine will reduce clerical costs sufficiently to pay for itself in three years or less, it is usually considered a good investment. The clerical labor it releases, of course, must be utilized in other work areas before the use of the new machine can actually be considered a saving.

Sometimes, it is difficult to distinguish among several machines that will do a particular job well, but the selection still must be made. When faced with such alternatives here are some additional factors to take into consideration:

- **Reliability.** In most user surveys reliability scores at or near the top of the list of desired qualities. Does the machine work consistently, providing scheduled maintenance is performed, without frequent down time and need for service? Experience can vary from one manufacturer to another and even among different models from the same manufacturer. It is recommended that purchasers consult independent equipment studies or with current users of that equipment to determine the reliability rating of any office machine.

- **Ease of operation.** Fewer errors, less worker fatigue, and faster task completion can all be considered to fall in this category. Generally speaking, the newer the equipment and the more automation it features, the easier the operation will be. Some additional factors to consider include: operator instructions printed on the machine; self-diagnostic capability; operator interrupt warnings; automatic feeding; simplified replacement of paper or other supplies. Simplicity of operation is also an important factor when it comes to training operators.

- **Training.** With the increasing sophistication of functions and features has come a certain complexity of operation. While many types of machines can be operated after a five to ten minute training period, after reading an abridged guide to operations, or a combination of the two, in order to achieve maximum productivity and utilization of the machine, some operator training may be necessary. Supplier offerings in this category should be compared.

- **Service.** Reliable and continuous performance depends upon speedy repairs and expert maintenance. In some cases service will be provided by the supplier; in others, it will be the responsibility of a third party. Various types of contracts can be offered—everything from basic repairs to the use of a replacement machine if major repairs become necessary. The costs for service contracts generally range between 10 and 20 percent of the total equipment cost.

- **Operating cost.** To be considered here are questions such as: How much space will the equipment occupy? Must any special equipment or options be purchased for the equipment to operate to specifications? What is the cost of those options, special equipment, or both? How much will service cost? What will the expected outlay for supplies be? It is important to note that the cost of machine supplies purchased from the supplier can be more expensive than the cost of those same supplies purchased from another vendor. Machine supplies can be purchased from a wide variety of sources and very often lower costs are obtainable.

- **Adaptability.** What does the installation of the new equipment entail? Is the changeover to the new machine going to require new procedures, new forms, extensive retraining, or other potential disruptions to day-to-day office operations? If so, it might be better to opt for a machine that will not cause so much upheaval, even when that choice reduces the capability of the equipment. The trade off here can be intricate and needs to be monitored carefully.

- **Supplier reputation.** Because few office managers are expert when it comes to the inner workings of office machines, it is necessary to rely on the integrity of the manufacturer or dealer furnishing the equipment. How well claims and guarantees are supported, and the degree of service competence contribute to any suppliers's reputation. Many sources can be queried to determine this kind of information including other users and any number of commercially available business surveys.

- **Styling.** Today's office requires machines that are pleasing and modern in design and compatible in color. Besides being pleasing to the eye, there are further considerations that should be taken into account: has the unit been ergonomically designed (bio-engineered) to provide the maximum degree of worker comfort and safety; are all the controls—buttons, switches, and levers—easy to reach and operate; is the machine excessively noisy during operation; does it require large amounts of electricity or its own electrical circuit; is it truly state-of-the-art equipment?

- **Costs.** Final consideration should be given to the costs of purchasing, installing, and implementing the use of the new equipment. Usually the cost of a machine takes in more than the purchase price. Often a machine that has a higher purchase price than another will prove to be the better buy when hidden costs, such as service and supplies, are taken into account. If two machines still appear to be comparable after comparing labor savings, maintenance costs, durability, and the rest, then the net purchase price should be looked at. The net price takes into account the trade-in allowance for current equipment and expected residual values after depreciation is taken into account.

Control Of Office Machines

Records covering all machines should be carefully administered and maintained in a centralized location. This machine file should identify each machine in the office as to make and model number, the name of the manufacturer, the date of purchase, whether the unit was bought new or used, its purchase price, and location.

One method of record keeping that is widely used is to record all this information on separate index cards for each machine. Space on the machine report card should be provided for service information such as the name, address, and telephone number of the service company, date and descriptions of service calls, and repair charges. Such service records can help ensure that machines are inspected regularly and maintained at peak operating efficiency.

Service and Maintenance

In the days of adding machines, manual typewriters, and mimeo machines, before office machines became automated, it was entirely possible for a company to maintain its own equipment. Maintenance personnel could be readily trained to service and repair such mechanical equipment, and it was not at all uncommon to find businesses that did not rely on outside sources for their maintenance. The nature of the largely automated equipment available today makes it necessary, however, to utilize highly skilled technicians for the repair of such equipment.

For the most part, two kinds of service agreements are generally available: time and materials or contract maintenance. Time and materials service refers to service at a fixed hourly rate plus the costs of any materials and replacement parts. This kind of service is best used in situations where there is not a high demand for machine usage, if the operation is not time sensitive, or if a great deal of service expertise is not necessary for the majority of service requirements.

Contract maintenance refers to service agreements where a fixed, monthly charge is assessed for any or all maintenance. The charge takes in how much labor, parts, and materials will probably be needed and is most usually based on machine usage, such as the number of copies or keystrokes recorded in a specified period. If an operation cannot afford any down time, then a contract maintenance agreement is probably warranted.

In larger organizations it might be advisable to train an in-house technician to perform the majority of service functions when a great many similar or related machines are being utilized. Such training is expensive, but if enough machines are involved or if the operation is so time sensitive that even short periods of down time must be kept to a minimum, then the cost can be justified. Most major manufacturers offer service training today, but before such a course of action is undertaken it should be thoroughly investigated, and all the various service options should be weighed.

Strategies for Limiting Machine Down Time

While the servicing and repair of today's highly automated office machines should be left to the skilled technicians, there are still procedures that office managers can implement to keep machines operating efficiently. It is possible, through prudent use and appropriate preventive care, to keep machine maintenance time down to a minimum and extend productive time.

- **Use the Manual.** For any office machine to last longer and work more efficiently it is important for operators to take the time to acquaint themselves with the unit's operator manual. Always operate the equipment to the manufacturer's instructions as they are stated in the manual and follow the suggested preventive maintenance schedule. Today's office machines, for the most part, are both specialized and sensitive, and they represent a substantial capital investment. Consequently, employees should be encouraged to handle machines properly and instructed not to use them as shelves for coffee cups or ash trays. Employees should be instructed never to leave small objects, such as paper clips, laying on the machine; such objects could fall inside and cause severe damage to electrical components.

- **Power Supply.** Some, more sophisticated office machines, may exhibit a sensitivity to power line transients (spikes), which can cause intermittent failures, accompanied by false warning light indications. Usually, if the machine requires this degree of protection, such disturbances can be controlled by adding controlling devices to the power supply. At the very least, before installing any new piece of equipment, make certain that the available electrical receptacle and the power supply meet the manufacturer's requirements. Be certain to check with the supplier before the machine is installed as to any special power or plug requirements.

- **Supplies.** The question of supplies can be a devilish one because of the many low-cost suppliers and "look-alike" products that have entered the market. In truth, a great many of these products and suppliers are entirely reputable and no more than ordinary vigilance need be taken when ordering from these sources. However, a number of unscrupulous suppliers do exist, and inferior copies of cartridges, ribbons, and other regularly ordered supplies are readily available. A low supplies price may be tempting, but inferior quality supplies can end up costing more through frequent replacements. When in doubt, the manufacturer or some other known supplier should be depended on as a supply source. For cost effective purchasing be sure to take advantage of quantity discounts when making any supplies purchase, particularly if the machines are being used in a high-volume application.

- **Static Control Problems.** Static is most usually caused by incorrect temperature and humidity levels in the working environment and can cause any number of problems, particularly on machines that have paper transport systems. Some equipment is available with built-in static eliminators; alternatively, a variety of products—antistatic sprays, mats, gloves, and the like—can be employed to help keep static problems to a minimum.

- **Temperature Considerations.** Overheating can be a major cause of malfunction for any motorized piece of equipment. Types of equipment that generate heat, including copiers, facsimile machines, and computer printers, need to be installed in an air-conditioned environment. Equipment of this type should never be placed in a confined areas, such as a closet. Always leave enough room around the machine to allow for proper ventilation. Some automated models come equipped with special thermal sensors that signal for operator intervention should the machine overheat.

- **Housekeeping Considerations.** Airborne particulates such as dust, paper fragments, and ribbon dust can adversely effect the performance of many office machines. Dust and paper residue, if allowed to collect on moving parts such as bands, chains, and drums can create drag on a unit's motor, which can lead to a breakdown.

- **Emergency Action.** When a piece of equipment suddenly stops working, check first for power line interruptions. Are the lights still on in the work area? If so, wait a few minutes and then try to restart the machine. If it won't restart refer to the operator's manual for diagnostic instructions and for the location of any internal fuses. If all these efforts fail to restart the machine, it is time to call for service. Under no circumstances should anything but the most basic repairs be attempted by the operator.

OFFICE COPIERS

Copiers have become a basic business tool of almost every office. Today's machines with their faster speeds, larger capacities, better copy quality, and lower costs offer a tremendous amount of utility for diverse purposes—from correspondence copies to systems documentation. The latest copier machines incorporate the most recent advances in microcircuitry and solid-state electronics to offer automated functions and operator checks that were unheard of 10 years ago. Such features as microprocessors that monitor copying machine systems, single-element cartridge toner systems that greatly simplify routine maintenance, and cold-pressure fusing techniques that provide instant-on operation are just some of the advantages available on the majority of copiers available today.

There are two basic copier types: coated paper units, which use paper impregnated with a photoconductor and eliminate the need for a permanent photoconductor in the unit; and plain-paper copiers. Although coated paper units are still being sold, the reduced costs of plain-paper units, along with the convenience they offer and their vastly improved copy quality, make them a good buy for even the smallest office. There are some coated-paper machines, however, that use dry toner, offer acceptable quality for some record keeping applications, and consume less electricity than plain-paper units, which makes them desirable in some applications.

Copying Volume

For the majority of purposes, copying machines can best be classified by the volume of copies they are meant to produce. All copiers are engineered with a specific duty cycle, that is, they have been built to tolerances and specifications with a definite copying volume in mind. For best results in terms of usage costs, performance, and reliability it is good practice to stay within the limits of the manufacturer's duty cycle specifications. If it is found that these limits are routinely surpassed, it is time to replace that copier with a higher volume unit or to restructure the work routine and redistribute the work load to other machines or departments.

This plain paper copier (the first from Canon for the small office environment) produces up to 12 copies a minute at the touch of a copying key.

The types of copying machines by the amount of copies they have been designed to produce are:

- **Low-volume copiers.** These units, also called low-speed or convenience copiers, are designed to handle roughly 10,000 or fewer copies per month and run at speeds between one and 20 copies per minute. Very-low volume units, under 5,000 copies—so-called personal copiers—offer even slower copier speeds.

- **Mid-volume copiers.** Copiers in this classification can produce between 10,000 and 50,000 copies monthly at speeds up to 50 copies per minute.

- **High-volume copier/duplicators.** These copying systems are capable of producing copies at speeds up to and above 90 copies per minute at volumes of 300,000 copies a month and greater. Some units at the top end of this category do not require originals and can be used to make multiple copies of computer printout.

The designations of copiers by copying volume is a useful categorization that can be utilized to determine which copier to pur-

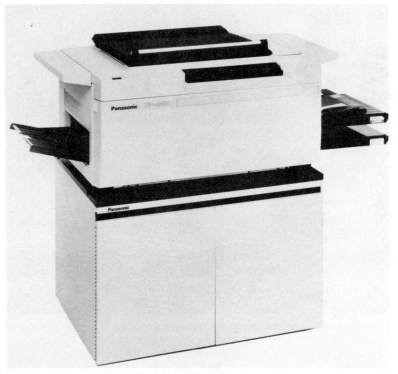

This very new copier from Panasonic produces copies at 45-copies a minute, and it features four modes of reduction and three modes of enlargement.

chase. However, copier purchase decisions should not be based strictly on speed and volume considerations. The ranges given above, and those promulgated by equipment manufacturers are meant to be used only as a guide; it is not necessary to follow them exactly. Medium-volume copiers can be safely used for smaller volume requirements as can the high-volume units.

However, because manufacturers most usually determine copier pricing based on a formula heavily weighted to copying volume, it is best to use and purchase copying machines for those applications that closely match the manufacturer's suggested volume levels. If a copier is consistently operated at reduced volume levels the cost per copy, based on the manufacturer's pricing policy, may not be cost effective. Alternatively, if a copier is consistently operated at volumes that exceed its suggested copying capacity, its reliability can be severely impaired.

Copier Abuse

Most office managers agree that copiers are an indispensable office tool that can be used to increase office efficiency and productivity. Many managers would also agree that copiers are, perhaps, the most abused and overused piece of office equipment. In a survey of more than 1,000 businesses, conducted by *Inc.* magazine in 1980, 56 percent of the respondents felt this was true. Responses were received from top executive officers—chairman, president, vice president, chief financial officer, director—general manager, office manager, purchasing agent, and other titles, from manufacturing industries, wholesale and retail trade, and service organizations.

The executives surveyed agreed that copier abuses were a problem but also believed that, for the most part, such misuse was unavoidable. Reasons given for abuse and overuse were:

- **Excessive copying—80 percent.**
- **Personal copying—69 percent.**
- **Unwarranted copying—63 percent.**
- **Sloppy copier operation—23 percent.**
- **Excessive recopying—29 percent.**

Thirty percent of the firms surveyed reported that they had instituted a variety of procedures in an effort to reduce the misuse of copiers. Manual logging of copier use was the primary control, employed by 18 percent of the respondents. Another 10 percent made use of some kind of controller device. A controller device limits the use of copiers to certain authorized personnel who need a key or control card to operate the machine. Such measures can be extremely effective if unauthorized use for personal or unnecessary copies is a problem. Interestingly, 23 percent of survey respondents, presumably those without any control system, state that they would be interested in a controller or other monitoring device on their next copier in order to reduce copier misuse.

Copier Features and Options

Today's copiers, from the lowest volume units to the high-volume copier systems, all offer advanced features made possible through the use of microelectronics. Although only the most expensive units come fully equipped, even the lowest priced models are apt to incorporate at least some of the new features. Such features include:

- **Self-diagnostic systems.** Such systems automatically monitor copier use and signal the operator to take corrective action when supplies are low; pinpoints malfunctions; and even instructs the operator on clearing jams and other problems.

- **Document handling systems.** These paper transport systems take the handling of originals out of the operator's hands and automate paper feeding. Such features expedite the copying of multipage reports.

- **Pause/interrupt mode.** Enables the operator to interrupt long runs to make a few quick copies of another job.

- **Automatic duplexing.** Two-sided copying is a feature that enables the copier to reproduce copies on both sides of a sheet. Duplexed copying can make filing more efficient, reduce postage expenses because of the reduction in the number of sheets being mailed, uses less paper, and lowers the cost per copy.

- **Reduction/enlargement capabilities.** Some copiers can reproduce over-size originals on small-size copying paper. Such features can reduce filing space needs and make it possible to make copies of computer printouts in a more manageable size. Less popular enlargement capabilities offer the ability to enlarge or blowup originals for special applications.

- **Finishing equipment.** Whether standard or purchased as options a variety of finishing equipment—sorters, collators and binders—are readily available for most copiers. Such units can be useful for long-run, multipage jobs and can help increase productivity and work flow in copying operations.

- **Large capacity paper trays.** Such add-ons hold a greater volume of paper than normal size units and, thus, reduce the frequency with which paper must be reloaded into the copying machine.

Selection of a Copier

Features aside, many of the criteria cited by copier users used in selecting which copier model to purchase are based on the cost, service, and reliability factors. In survey after survey of copier buyers the top selection criteria turn out to be the copy quality (one) and machine reliability (two). Other factors cited, in descending order of importance, include:

- **Ease of operation.**
- **Service available from the supplier.**
- **Ease of maintenance.**
- **Speed.**
- **Availability of duplexing (two-sided copying).**
- **Cost of supplies.**

For those who copy computer forms, this Kodak Ektaprint 200 copier-duplicator and Kodak Ektaprint continuous forms feeder unit can handle the job. Speeds up to 5,500 images an hour can be reache with various combinations of feeders and copier-duplicator units.

- **Reduction capability.**
- **Document feeder.**
- **Reputation of supplier.**
- **Pause/interrupt capability.**
- **Self-diagnostic features.**
- **Enlargement capability.**
- **Available financial arrangements.**
- **Quality of vendor's sales effort.**

Copier Applications

The fact that almost every office today has some kind of copying equipment is proof enough that the copying machine has become indispensable. The very nature of copy machine usage and the fact that a great many manufacturers are competing for copier sales in a crowded market makes copier selection particularly difficult. A number of independent sources of information have entered the market to provide various ratings of the different copier models.

One such source is Datapro Research Corp., Delran, N.J., which publishes yearly ratings of copiers based on user surveys. A 1982 Datapro survey found that copiers were currently being used for a variety of reproduction applications. According to the survey, low and mid-volume copiers were used most frequently to produce file copies of correspondence and documents and to create documents for internal distribution. High-volume copier/duplicators were used primarily to copy documents for internal and external distribution.

Other applications for copier machines, in descending order of use, included:

- **Production of business forms.**
- **Copies of magazines and books.**
- **Copies of checks.**
- **Labels.**
- **Production of transparencies.**
- **Production of offset masters.**
- **Reductions/enlargements.**
- **Copies of halftones and graphics.**

ELECTRONIC TYPEWRITERS

Introduced just a few years ago, electronic typewriters, sometimes called intelligent typewriters, are automated versions of the familiar electric typewriters. In size and general appearance the electronic units resemble their electromechanical cousins. But that resemblance stops there.

In the vast majority of cases an electronic typewriter can be used to replace conventional typing machines. Their use does not require a change in office procedures, work flow, or the typist's normal routine. At the same time, electronic typewriters provide typists with a means to extend office productivity beyond the capability of a conventional typewriter. In some instances, electronic typewriters can even be considered as replacements for first and second generation word processors, which have no display and use either magnetic tape or cards for input, or as low-cost alternatives to display word processors.

Electronic typewriters can be divided into three classifications based upon their capabilities and cost. Low-end electronic typewriters come closest in appearance to standard electric models. These units offer an electronic keyboard to improve keyboarding speed, limited memory capacity, and the automation of some basic typewriter functions: centering, paper feeding, column settings, and carrier return. Such low-end units are meant as a straight replacement for standard electric models and offer the advantages of greater productivity through faster typing speeds and neater typing due to error correcting functions.

One step up from the low-end electronic typewriters are a number of mid-range units. These typewriters offer expanded memory capacities, a text-entry mode that allows corrections to be made in memory before any text is printed, an increase in the number of automated features, and the capability of performing some basic word processing-type functions. Some electronic typewriters in this range offer the capability to insert or delete material, move lines around, and to search for and replace words or phrases.

The third level of electronic typewriters, the high-end units, offer greatly expanded memories—as much as several pages—and have features that come close to those available on low-end word processing systems. Some units available in this category come with such capabilities (either as standard components or available as options) as video display screens and magnetic disk drives for off-line storage of text. When such peripherals are added to these high-end electronic typewriters, they become nearly identical to low-end word

The Olivetti ET intelligent typewriter has a permanent memory of 800+ characters and a working memory of 16,000 characters (10 pages). It has a daisy wheel print unit with four pitches. Memory search can be done by paragraph, line or character.

processors—prices, features, and capabilities come very close to duplicating each other.

One of the biggest differences between electronic typewriters and the electric versions is in the typing element that they use. The electrics, for the most part, utilize some variation of the ball element, or rely on mechanizing the single-action typing made commonplace by manual typewriters. The electrics have changed all that. They make use of daisy-wheel technology.

A daisy-wheel is an impact printing device which uses a wheel having numerous radial spokes; each spoke bears type to produce characters. Daisy-wheel devices have been used in computer printers for a number of years, and have subsequently been adapted for use in typing. In some ways, electronic typewriters are identical to such computer printers that have been modified by the introduction of keyboards and different paper transport systems. In fact, some electronic typewriters even can be substituted for computer printers.

One definite advantage of the electronic typewriters appears to be the reduced cost involved in maintaining and repairing these units. While the various products have not been in use long enough to establish a definitive service record, the construction of the electronic typewriters, makes them, at least in theory, less prone to break downs. Generally, the electronics have roughly 85 percent fewer mechanical parts than their electric counterparts, and the electronic components used in these units, historically, have proven to have greater reliability. Many repairs can be made simply by replacing a circuit board. Cost-conscious managers on the lookout for low-maintenance typing machines would be well advised to consider some version of the new electronic typewriters.

Electronic Typewriter Features

The high degree of automation offered by electronic typewriters along with the memory offered and the displays available with some units make them powerful tools for increasing clerical efficiency and productivity. As office workers move up from one level of typewriter to the next, increasing capabilities become possible in terms of more automation, greater memory, and advanced editing functions. Features available on electronic typewriters include:

- **Automatic error correction.**
- **Automatic carrier return.** When the carrier comes within a certain limit of the right margin a certain action, usually the next use of the space bar, returns the carrier to the left margin.
- **Automatic indent.** Creates temporary margins for complex indentations.

- **Bold print.** Creates boldface type for emphasis without having to change printwheels or use additional keystrokes.
- **Automatic centering.** Offers automatic centering between margins or at any point selected by the operator.
- **Automatic underline.** Underlines text while typing to avoid backspacing and separate underlining.
- **Decimal tab alignment.** Eliminates spacing and backspacing steps when typing columns of figures.
- **Pitch selection.** Offers the option of 10, 12, or 15 character per inch typing.
- **Phrase storage/recall.** Allows for the retrieval of stored phrases and formats that can be called up by typing a single alphabetic character.
- **Automatic table layout.** Calculates column width automatically based upon the longest line in each column.
- **Index/reverse index.** For entering subscripts and superscripts vertical spacing is possible in amounts less than half a line.
- **Automatic form layout.** Stores complete formats for complex forms typing and enable the carrier to move to the starting of each entry with a single keystroke.
- **Scrolling.** This feature moves the display forward or back through the text to review or make corrections.
- **Right justification.** Automatically aligns words or phrases flush with the right margin.
- **Search/replace.** Will replace words or phrases automatically throughout the entire text or a portion of the text.
- **Communicating capabilities.** Allow the typewriter to be used as a communicating terminal to a computer or other piece of peripheral equipment.

DICTATION MACHINES

For the most part, dictation equipment has lagged behind most other office machines in terms of user acceptance and, to some degree, innovation. Yet, research consistently demonstrates that very real savings in time and money accrue when executives substitute dictating machines for writing out reports and communications longhand or dictating to a secretary using shorthand. Studies on document origination have shown that an executive can write in longhand at an average rate of 15 words per minute; dictate to a secretary at a speed of 30 words per minute; and compose with a dictation machine at a rate of 60 words per minute.

Some businesses, such as insurance concerns or health care establishments, find a greater need for dictating use because of the large amount of documentation required. Dictating equipment users, however, come from every size and type of business organization. As a rule, most professionals can find an effective use for dictating equipment.

Despite the impressive statistics cited above, a significant number of potential users have been reluctant to trade in pencil and paper or the interaction between secretary and manager for the more impersonal dictating machine. Still, those managers who are using dictating equipment have been satisfied with the equipment. Studies indicate that those dictating equipment users expect to make repeat purchases to get additional equipment, replace older equipment with update technology, or both.

Types of Dictating Units

Current dictating units make use of a variety of magnetic media to record and playback. Both mini- and micro-tape cassettes, continuous magnetic tape loops, magnetic belts, and magnetic disks are all used; but cassettes are far and away the most common recording medium in use today. If dictating machines are currently in use or the prospective purchase is for multiple dictating units it would be suggested that the media being used can be interchanged among the various pieces of equipment in use.

Dictating machines can be differentiated by the type of use they receive and their placement. The three main types of dictating units are:

- **Central dictating systems.** Equipment can be accessed from remote locations and can be configured in various sizes to meet the needs of different organizations. Such central systems are recommended for light to moderate use only because heavy dictating users are liable to monopolize such a centralized system which could prevent other users from gaining access. The most recent versions incorporate microprocessors to make assignments and report work status.
- **Desk-top dictating systems.** These units come as separate dictation-only units, transcription-only units or as combination dictation/transcription units. These units are recommended for use in situations with heavy dictating requirements.
- **Portable dictating units.** These are small, lightweight dictating machines that can be used either in the office or while traveling. In many cases these units are capable of recording only; for transcription a desk-top or other unit must be used.

This sleek Norelco Century dictating machine puts electronic indexing directly on the cassette.

In the majority of office situations, dictating equipment from all three of these classifications are combined to meet a variety of work needs.

FASCIMILE MACHINES

Facsimile machines are essential tools of any office that needs to transmit graphic images. These devices provide an alternative to regular postal service; an alternative which many times is preferred, because the transmission time is much faster than either postal service or specialized couriers. In addition, facsimile provides the recipient with a document that is an exact copy of the sender's original. Other types of transmission devices cannot dupli-

771

cate this capability. For instance, a telephone conversation can contain the same information, but at the end of the conversation there is no hard copy of what transpired.

Organizations such as banks, insurance companies, brokerage houses, and other financial institutions frequently have a need to transmit applications, transfers, letters of credit, and other forms requiring a legally valid signature. Because many businesses utilize widely dispersed branch offices, the transmission of such documents by other means besides facsimile can be a slow and, in some instances, a costly process. Also, by not having to rekey data, facsimile eliminates one of the principal sources of errors.

Types of Facsimile Devices

Currently, there are three basic types of facsimile devices available, although the first group, the analog units, are declining in popularity. The three categories are:

- **Low-speed units.** This group includes devices that scan, transmit, and print out at the receiving end in four to six minutes. These were the first machines introduced and they use analog technology.
- **Medium-speed units.** Devices in this group have transmission speeds that range from one to three minutes and use either analog or digital technology. Many units in this category are compatible with units in the slower category and, hence, can also transmit at slower speeds.
- **High-speed units.** Devices in this category use digital technology exclusively and feature transmission speeds of less than one minute.

Facsimile Machine Selection

Historically, most facsimile devices have been available through rental only. But as new suppliers enter the market and as technology brings the cost of these machines down, more and more units are becoming available for purchase.

Before replacing a machine currently in operation it is recommended that requirements be carefully examined. A slow-speed machine that has been in use for a number of years might be traded in on a newer unit, but because those older machines make use, primarily, of analog technology, their trade-in value is relatively low. An alternative approach would be to shift such slow-speed units to lower volume applications, and replace them with higher-speed devices.

OFFICE CALCULATORS

The printing and display calculators offering the basic four functions have changed dramatically over the last few years, due, primarily, to the use of semiconductor technology. As in the case of other office machines, calculators have been given greater capacity, more features, and greater reliability with the introduction of micro-circuitry. Today's calculators offer expanded memories, new display techniques, and a variety of advanced, programmable functions.

Three new print and print/display calculators make up the Monroe 2700 Series. These are considered to be much less expensive then the models they are replacing.

The basic types of office calculators include:

- **Desk-top, non-programmable calculators.** These basic units normally feature four functions keys (add, subtract, multiply, and divide) and ten numeric keys for data entry. This category can be further differentiated into units that display only, print only, or offer both print and display capabilities. Some units are available with memory and additional calculation functions.

- **Desk-top, programmable calculators.** These units resemble the desktop units and perform all of the same functions. Additionally, they can be programmed to handle a variety of special applications. These units can accept a predetermined number of calculations with which to compute a value, and can hold intermediate figures in memory to be used at a later point in the calculation.

- **Hand-held programmable calculators.** These units offer the same utility as the desk-top programmable units with greater portability. They are popular with scientists, engineers, accountants, and marketing managers. Prices of units in this category and other calculator groups are expected to drop as hand-held computers become more prevalent.

The programmable calculators are still used mostly by advanced engineering students and professionals, but it can be used in the business world when compact size is needed for out-of-office travel. Most of the key functions, however, are for scientific or engineering use.

Suggestions for Calculator Selection

Calculators are one category of office machines that offers more for less. As manufacturers introduce more function and greater capability, calculator prices have continued at the same level or even dropped because of the introduction of electronic technology. Although care should be taken in the selection of any office machine, the technology in this group is not as involved and purchasers can usually reach a decision in a comparatively short time.

When selecting a new office calculator here are some factors that should be referred to:

- One of the primary differences in calculators is in different keyboard arrangements. Look for units where frequently used keys or combination of keys are grouped together to further simplify use.

- Three types of displays are common: LCD, liquid crystal display; LED, light emitting diodes; and gas discharge or plasma displays. LCDs use the least power and are typically found on hand-held units. Plasma displays are, perhaps, the easiest to read, but use more power.
- More expensive calculators which feature a greater selection of functions should be preferred to low-cost units on a strictly utilitarian basis.
- Calculator printers are of two basic types: impact printers and thermal (non-impact) printers. Impact printers cost more, but tend to last much longer. The paper used in thermal printers is more expensive, and images printed on the paper are not permanent.
- The cost of new office calculators is so low, in many cases, that replacement, rather than repair, can be considered as a cost-effective strategy.

PART 6

THE OFFICE
ENVIRONMENT

CHAPTER 32

THE OFFICE-LANDSCAPING CONCEPT

By Leslie Llewellyn Lewis,
Former Vice President, the New Bauhaus,
Chicago, Ill.

IN a nation now so computerized that almost any question on animal, mineral, or vegetable matter can be answered while you wait, there are still no "hard" data on the ratio of companies owning total office buildings for their exclusive use in (1) metropolitan areas, (2) suburbs, or (3) rural districts, and those renting offices in similar categories of distribution.

If, however, one were to imagine a flight across the fifty states, it is easy to imagine that, for every superspectacular highrise occupied by a single company, there are x-thousands of offices occupied on one or more floors of a multiple-company office building, or within or attached to a manufacturing plant, or along highways or byways.

Yes, this diversified pattern offers at least one element of unity in diversity: An interest in how "others" have made the most efficient use of the space available, whether in a Sears Tower, a World Trade Center, a "Japanese Temple in Alabama," or in three rooms behind the shop.

One Helpful Source of Information

Of making books on office design there is no end, but as of this writing, one book can be highly recommended to every seeker: *"Interiors Second Book of Offices,"* edited by John Pile, of Brooklyn's Pratt Institute and published by the Whitney Library of Design.*

The book will interest every office administrator concerned with office-building design, interior arrangement, and/or interior decora-

---

*Whitney Publications, Inc., 18 E. 50th St., New York, N. Y. 10022.

tion. Even if you are interested only in a concise but fascinating history of the evolution of the office from its warehouse origins to the Glossy Parlors of today, the book is delightful.

Author Pile tells us that the first "office buildings" were built in the 1880s; that when architects Adler and Sullivan built the Schiller Building (1891) in Chicago, it was constructed so that it might be turned into a hotel if not enough offices could be rented; Frank Lloyd Wright's 1904 Larkin Building had a central court into which were built rows of 12-foot desks, each seating six clerks, facing each other, three on a side. (They were not yet, however, called work stations.)

Mies Van der Rohe, Charles Edouard Jeanneret (Le Corbusier), and Walter Gropius were among the most prominent European pioneers in office-building design, as were, in the United States, Adolph Meyer, Louis Sullivan, and Dankmar Adler. Pile describes the Philadelphia Savings Fund Society Building, built in 1932 by William Lescaze and George Howe, as the "first fully modern tower office building," although the New York Flatiron Building, one of the world's first "skyscraper" office buildings, was completed in 1902.

Today, spectacular office structures are so commonplace, from Bahrain to Bahia, Montevideo to Montreal, Melbourne to Milwaukee, that a book larger than this one would be needed to describe them. Therefore, leaving the subject of size, let us inspect more closely some of the more intimate details of modern arrangement and design.

THE OFFICE-LANDSCAPE PROGRAM

Nearly 30 years ago, a brilliant mathematician, Norbert Wiener, borrowed from medicine the word "cybernetics," (from the Greek kybernetes, helmsman) to describe a theory of communications control. Originally applying to studies of the nervous system and to a mathematical theory of the neurophysiologic basis of human behavior, the term cybernetics was extended to bioengineering and social psychology, opening a new area of relationships between man and the burgeoning field of electronics.

In a greatly oversimplified yet concise definition, cybernetics may be grossly defined as the application of the scientific method to human organizations and, as a sequel, to the adoption of planned versus haphazard organizational structures.

A decade after the introduction of Wiener's work, a small group of German social scientists in Quickborn, a city near Hamburg, saw the implications of applying cybernetics to management consultancy

All types of open office systems are seen today, some featuring wood furniture and dividers, some using laminates and plastics, even some using metal. Lighting, sound-proofing and power outlets are key factors in all layouts.

Courtesy Haworth, Inc.

in general and to office planning and organization in particular. To these men, the static "bullpen" type of central office, with its surrounding cell-like cubicles, was, in an age of computers, as great an anachronism as the quill pen.

Out of the proposals of these men, known as the Quickborner Team, was born a highly scientific program of office-organization studies, termed by German journalists "Burolandschaft," literally, "office landscape."

Understandably, the word suffered a sea change in transit to the United States, where "landscape" suggests lawns and flowers. A catchy phrase, the term was adopted by some architects as just that: atria, fountains, and gazebos in the garden; by some interior decorators as flowers in crannied interior walls; by some furniture manufacturers as exotic furniture design; and by many others, who, like the fabled blind men and the elephant, mistook a part for the whole.

Because of such confusion of interpretation of a subject that has aroused great interest in office administrators, Dartnell editors went to the source, asking a principal of the Quickborner Team, Erhard Weisner, for a definitive description of the correct meaning of Office Landscaping, which follows.

THE OFFICE ENVIRONMENT: A PSYCHO/SOCIO-TECHNICAL SYSTEM

Introduction

The term "office environment" means different things to different people. In simplified terms:

To a developer or owner, who leases the office to a tenant: it is an investment that will maximize the return on the invested capital. It should be an adjustable environment in order to suit and attract a variety of potential tenants. In addition to the return on investment and the rentability of the offices, the developer/owner should be concerned with the operational costs of the spaces during the life cycle of the investment.

To an owner/tenant: it is a costly necessity that accommodates the office workers. Although many owner/tenants are not aware of it, the office environment has, among others, the following two aspects:

a. Hardware and facilities efficiency; i.e., the ratio of costs of building and office features to generated output; for example, ratio of energy consumption to lighting level generated (lighting efficiency), or ratio of space rented to space used (space efficiency; space usage to include the amount of space as well as the quality of space: e.g., a luxuriously equipped office space that contains mostly filing equipment or other "dead" material would be considered low in space efficiency).

b. People efficiency; i.e., does the office environment stimulate the employees, increase their productivity, help to reduce turnover, etc.?

To an employee: it is a place where a person consciously spends more time than in any other room during the major part of his adult life. It influences his happiness in and out of the office, can or cannot be an enjoyable place to go in the morning, etc.

To an architect: it is an expression of his creativity and professionalism, satisfying his—normally, in these matters, uneducated—client. The visible result attracts most of the public's attention; thus esthetic considerations rank high in the building design, i.e., the "monument effect."

To an interior designer or decorator: it is a space that has to be beautified, to appeal to the visual perception of everyone in it.

To a systems analyst: it is a framework in which people are active, paper is being shuffled and moved, and decisions are made. The office environment can support or hinder the functions performed within it.

Any one of the above views *alone* is incomplete and will produce undesirable results if followed exclusively. "Office environment" is more encompassing, as will be explained below.

The Progressive Approach to the Office Environment

Inasmuch as the office environment is more than a mere facility, it requires a more complex way of thinking. Progressive planners see the office environment as what may be called "Psycho/Socio-Technical System," actually a tool for management. This system consists of the following categories of elements:

A. **Organization**
B. **Information**
C. **Personnel**
D. **Environmental conditions**
E. **Facilities and Hardware**
F. **Financial aspects**

The elements of the psycho/socio-technical system are interdependent, i.e., they often act together: a change in one element may—and usually does—affect one or more of the other elements with feedbacks. A change in one of the categories of elements requires, therefore, a complex consideration of all elements in all categories, analysis or planning that must be simultaneous. A sequential approach would not identify the cause or effect of any change, thus making it difficult to take the proper corrective action.

Conventionally, a critical look at the office environment is given only in case of a change in the category "Facilities and Hardware," e.g., typically in cases of office arrangements, remodelling of an existing facility, or planning of a new building. As outlined above, the office environment would deserve the same critical look in a change of any of the other categories.

The simultaneous analysis or planning of all factors would ideally require a complex simulation model. However, prerequisites for such a model include some kind of quantifications of all factors and functional relationships. Especially because of the psychologic and sociologic elements, the model would necessarily be incomplete; the relatively new behavioral sciences cannot yet deliver many satisfactory explanations and quantifications. Therefore, rather than pretending an exactness that is not possible by using simulation models, we have developed a "complex, interdisciplinary and participatory" planning approach (more about this later) that has proved successful with clients of all sizes and in all kinds of industries.

In the following, the different categories of elements making up the office environment will be briefly explained and examples of interdependence will be given.

A. ORGANIZATION

The office environment is occupied by an organization made up of people. These employees are grouped in work groups, sections, departments, divisions; they are organized according to reporting and command relationships that may or may not be identical with functional relationships.

The reporting relationships can be diagrammed by an organization chart. The structure, generally formalized in a pyramidal hierarchy, can distinguish different levels in the organization; these levels are rarely shown on such a chart but they are important because they represent differences in personal accomplishment, responsibility, income, status, etc., all of which are elements of the psycho/socio-technical system.

In addition to the *formalized* structure, there exists also an *informal* organizational structure. Employees do not necessarily follow the formal lines in the organization but interact also informally; for example, working communication crossing or short-cutting the formal lines, social contacts, spreading of rumors, etc. As a rule, however, only the formal organization structure is consciously used by management as a tool. A few examples of how changes in this area can affect other elements in the psycho/socio-technical system are:

1. **A change in the formal organization structure is intended to alter the flow of information and the process of decision making, thus immediately affecting the flow of paper and materials.**

2. **A change of reporting relationships as part of a reorganization affects the element "Personnel" because of personal likes and dislikes, professional jealousies, new social groupings, all of which can affect employee efficiency.**

3. **Environmental conditions can be affected because of different privacy requirements in cases of new job assignments; power and telephone lines may have to be redistributed, etc.**

4. A promotion means higher status, which is often reflected in office size, location, furnishings, and otherwise, thus affecting the element of "facilities and hardware."

5. The financial element is regularly affected by making a change, e.g., costs of retraining an employee, moving departments, etc., as well as benefits through shorter, more efficient work flow, quicker decision making, savings in personnel, etc.

B. INFORMATION

The category "Information" contains the elements—
- administrative or structural communication, following the organizational lines of report and command, for administrative or decision-making purposes
- operational or functional communication
- informal flow of communication

The media of information transmission are—
- paper and materials (forms, cards, micrographics, COM, tapes, discs, etc.) resulting in paper flow and materials movements
- face-to-face interactions, personal visits, conferences, resulting in people traffic
- technical means (telephone, telecopier, remote computer access, CRTs, etc.) requiring technical installations

Different aspects to plan or improve in this category are:

1. Generation of information, i.e., decision-making process.

2. Facilitate and improve the media, i.e., conference facilities, Word Processing, Systems and Procedures.

3. Analyze and improve the sequence of senders and receivers of information, which should result in proper physical adjacencies if the media are paper, materials, visits, and possibly even for technical transmitters. Work flow and communication studies are essential ingredients of a systematic planning.

4. Speed of information flow, which should be increased by effective procedures and services.

5. Waiting time before and after the processing of the information at a work station should be reduced (systems, manpower allocation; having the information at the right place at the right time).

6. Content of the information, requiring forms control (having the right information—not too little, not too much—at the

right station at the right time). Unnecessary copies, duplicates, or redundancy requires additional time, space, storage
facilities, material costs etc. and should be avoided.

7. Storage procedures and facilities (individual work-station file,
work-group file, central file, archives/warehouse storage), filing, retrieval and disposal procedures, retention schedules as
part of a records-management program should be optimized.

8. Suitability, efficiency, and usage of machines.

Some examples of how the element "information" interrelates
with the other elements in our total system are:

1. A significant change in the operational or functional communication will sooner or later result in a change of the organizational structure; also, the existence of informal channels, if
they make sense functionally, can bring about a change in the
formal organization.

2. The effectiveness of all kinds of communication, especially of
the face-to-face kind, certainly influences personal relationships and cooperation, and vice versa.

3. Special environmental conditions may be require for information processing or storage; implementation of new technical
media will necessitate new wiring, etc., thus changing environmental conditions.

4. Facilities and hardware are directly affected by the element
"information," e.g., storage space and units, conference and
visitor facilities, installation of required machines. Furniture
has also a significant functional (ergonomic) aspect for handling, storing information, and should not be designed in a
detrimental way—which it unfortunately quite often is.

5. The impact of the "information" element on financial aspects
is self-evident.

C. PERSONNEL

The category "personnel" is a part of the office system that is,
strangely enough, frequently overlooked. Modern findings in the
behavioral sciences, including psychologic and sociologic aspects,
are essential for optimizing the total system.

Psychologic aspects are concerned with the individual employee
and include—

• personal preferences
• "ego-needs" (status, pride, responsibility, self-actualization,
territoriality, are some key words)

- physiologic needs (food, air, comfort, relaxation, recuperation) and also psychologic effects
- social needs (affection, recognition, understanding, acceptance, involvement, sociability, aggression characteristics)
- safety needs (protection from physical or mental dangers, surprises or shocks, economic needs)

The sociologic aspects are concerned with group behavior and role-playing and include:

- group identification (group ego, formal versus informal groups)
- group dynamics ("gatekeepers," opinion leaders, who may be more instrumental in getting a job done than the formal supervisor) the rest is implied
- friendships
- cultural characteristics

Motivation and attitude studies (questionnaires, interviews, group sessions) are means to analyze and characterize individuals and groups. Programs like Job Enrichment, Management by Objectives, by Motivation, by Exceptions, by Participation, by Results, Organizational Development, and others, can be designed to increase the worker's satisfaction and thus effectiveness, reduce absenteeism, turnover, etc.

Other means are the different elements as part of the psycho/socio-technical system, the office environment.*

Examples illustrating the interdependency of personnel, organization, information, were given in the preceding paragraphs. Examples relating personnel to the remaining elements follow.

The importance of the element "personnel" in a planning project becomes clear when one realizes that the cost of an office building over an assumed life cycle of 30 years breaks down into—

- 2 percent building cost
- 6 percent maintenance cost
- 92 percent operational costs, including employee salaries

The building costs include a marginal proportion for planning and design costs. Improving the "people efficiency" of the office envi-

---

*A major problem with all office environment projects is the resistance to change inherent in the human nature. Methods of how to start to overcome this problem are part of the "complex, interdisciplinary and participatory" planning approach. I only say "start to overcome," because as a rule, 100% success is impossible, and trying to achieve a high percentage would be rather costly and time consuming. It has been our experience that our approach will "sell" the opinion leaders and make everyone willing "to give it a try"; with proper planning, time and experience while open minded and being "educated" will then do the rest.

ronment is significant, since an improvement by only 1 percent in the operational costs, i.e., 92 percent, is still larger than a 10 percent improvement in the other two categories, i.e., 8 percent thus making the effort well worth the costs.

D. ENVIRONMENTAL CONDITIONS

Environmental conditions include—

- heating
- ventilating
- air conditioning
- humidity control
- lighting
- acoustics
- fire protection
- cabling and wiring (power, telephone, data lines, etc.)
- color, texture, form of all exposed materials (interior design and decoration)

Requirements for most of these elements are specified by national, professional or governmental agencies or codes. It is up to the planner to tighten the performance specifications or custom-tailor them for the company's special needs.*

Of particular interest are considerations in areas where regulations are still missing or too general, such as—

- security of information, materials, people
- environmental protection, including noise and visual pollution
- energy conservation
- materials availability and recycling
- technologic obsolescence, requiring exchangeable, modular, or adjustable systems or elements

As a rule, the environmental elements as listed, once designed and installed—with the possible exception of color—will not be changed willfully but only in response to changes in other elements of the office system; e.g., if a reorganization or promotion results in shifting, putting up or tearing down floor-to-ceiling partitions, lights, air conditioning, etc., will normally also have to be adjusted.

However, with the stronger emphasis on the personnel element in our progressive approach, the environmental elements can also be-

---

*Zoned HVAC (Heating, Ventilation and Air Conditioning) systems, variable air flow, task-oriented lighting (which can not only save lighting energy, but also energy for air conditioning, reduce the scale of the A/C installation, etc.) are examples. However, as with all these elements, their affect as part of the total office system needs to be investigated before any decision can be made. A measurement that is beneficial in one case can be detrimental in another.

come instruments whose change can induce desirable changes in other elements of the total system, especially in the personnel category: The individual person is responsive to environmental stimuli, as has been recognized at least since the Hawthorne experiments (Elton Mayo, 1927). The findings were, for instance, one basis for the introduction of self-regulated rest and vending machine lounges as part of the office environment, as well as the development of color and interior design maxims that became part of our modern Office Landscape concept.

Carrying the same principles even further, one can expect stimulating effects in an individual's alertness and efficiency in two ways:

1. **by changing the environmental conditions in different zones on one office floor, and**
2. **by changing the environmental conditions during the course of a working day, a week, etc.**

Different stimuli are received by the human senses:

- visual (color, form, texture, of furniture, furnishings, decorative items such as growing or artificial shrubbery, pieces of art work, sculptures, fountains, etc.)
- auditory (P.A. system, background music, white noise)
- taste
- temperature sensing
- tactile (e.g., airflow)
- olfactory
- balancing sense

None of the foregoing is at present being fully exploited, and some may not even be feasible. In fact, except for the visual and auditory, the senses have not even been recognized as potential stimuli in the design of office environments.

E. FACILITIES AND HARDWARE

This category includes such elements as:
- office buildings
- office floors
- furniture
- working equipment (office machines, telephones, etc.)
- furnishings and decoration

All these elements must be designed or selected for the particular need within a specific company. Some planners have developed lists of "maxims" aiming at an optimum solution in each case; as an example, Quickborner Team's building maxims specify requirements with respect to:

- function
- interior flexibility
- exterior flexibility
- zones in the building
- building cores
- economic efficiency (investment, operational costs, energy-conservation aspects)
- work environment
- interior traffic flow
- building accessibility
- building security

Not really new but still amazingly often overlooked are the aspects of ergonomics and anthropometrics, dealing with the relationships of physical characteristics of office workers and facilities/hardware.

The psycho/sociologic aspect of office work definitely needs more attention. The employee's satisfaction, can, for instance, be increased by possible improvements in attitudes, efficiency, absenteeism, turnover, by facilitating the individual's self-expression (as described under "personnel" above); a start could, for instance be to provide space and surfaces for personal pictures or documents (diplomas, photographs), as are commonplace in the president's office but rare elsewhere.

The most visible element in the catagory "facilities and hardware" is the furniture layout. It must reflect the organizational groups, hierarchical differences, the flow of information, work and traffic, shows furniture and storage items on a floor plan, and also considers the installed technical environmental systems.

F. FINANCIAL ASPECTS

Financial aspects are involved in any one of the previously discussed elements of the office system. Sometimes such simple tools of capital budgeting as the pay-back-period method are sufficient for deciding between alternative investments. However, larger capital outlays should be based on more complex financial tools, such as one of the discounted cash-flow methods. In addition to resulting in better investment decisions, these methods also encourage the thinking in terms of the life cycle costs and benefits rather than in mere initial capital outlays.

THE OFFICE-LANDSCAPING CONCEPT

As should be clear from the foregoing, the thinking of an office environment as a psycho/socio-technical system with numerous interdependencies will also lead to consideration of some "hidden" costs that may otherwise have been overlooked, i.e., costs because of delayed decision making, inefficient work flow, personnel turnover, retraining, absenteeism, waste of energy and materials, to name just a few. Such a complex cost-benefit analysis can be an excellent way to determine an investment's financial feasibility; in reality, it will be much simpler than it may seem.

Three more factors frequently overlooked are:

1. **"Opportunity or alternative costs," which represent financial advantages if another alternative investment object had been chosen. Those profits that might have been encountered with a different choice should enter the cost-benefit analysis as a cost factor in the selected alternative.**

2. **"Social costs," which are costs that the community or economy will have because of a single company's decision. One should be aware of such costs; they may have to be carried by the company in the not-too-distant future. Environmental protection legislation and "social accounting" regulations are just a start.**

3. **Planning Approach for the "Office Environment" System. The foregoing, although by no means complete, may seem to make the planning of a total office environment appear an unsurmountable task. In the past, the isolated views of one responsible person determined the type of environment; it was either design-oriented with enclosed offices for almost everyone (inflexible, hindering the work flow, a "cover-up" solution) or it was function-and-efficiency oriented, with "bullpen" office areas or multiperson rooms (with a dismotivating effect on the employee in the first alternative and lack of privacy and individuality, plus inflexible and potentially hindering work-flow effects in the second).**

The newer "Office Landscape" environmental plan (originated by the Quickborner Team in 1960 and constantly improved since, although still not perfected) is the visual result of a planning effort, endeavoring to implement the psycho/socio-technical system, as discussed above.

To facilitate such an undertaking, a "complex, interdisciplinary, and participatory planning approach" has been developed. "Complex" because it deals with an interdependent system of elements; "interdisciplinary" because it involves and coordinates representatives of all disciplines concerned (e.g., architects, engineers, designers, systems analysts, behavioral scientists, and other specialists), as no one single person or discipline would be capable of considering all elements simultaneously, while proper planning and coordination will result in additional synergistic effects; "participatory" because it includes favorably affecting the employees, even during the planning process, thus ensuring better results and helping to gain employee acceptance.

The approach and the methods included have been applied in numerous projects, making them readily available without having to "reinvent the wheel" each time.

A partial list of American companies which have been involved in Quickborner Team "Office Landscaping" include:

Bethlehem Steel Corporation, Bethlehem, Pennsylvania; Caterpillar Tractor Corporation, Peoria, Illinois; Credit Life Insurance Company, Springfield, Ohio; Ginn-Xerox Corporation, Boston/Lexington, Massachusetts; IBM Corporation (RECD Division), Harrison/Armonk, New York; Mercedes-Benz of North America Corporation, Fort Lee/Montvale, New Jersey; Ontario Hydro Corporation, Toronto, Canada; Ray-O-Vac, Division of ESB, Inc., Madison, Wisconsin; Ryder System, Inc., Miami, Florida; Southwest Educational Development Laboratory, Austin, Texas; The Toledo Edison Company, Toledo, Ohio.

CHAPTER 33

OFFICE BUILDINGS, LAYOUTS AND FURNISHINGS

MORE THAN 35 million people in the U.S. and 10 million Canadians go to and from offices every day of the workweek. These offices are located in the heart of "downtown" metropolis cities, at the fringes, in the suburbs and even in the country. Some are in "industrial parks" and some are now located in "office campuses." Many are part of the manufacturing facility of a company, but the largest number are not.

By name, of course, there are headquarters offices, district offices, branch offices and field offices. Today, a headquarters office can have fewer people in less space than a branch or district office, and certainly fewer people than the combined work force in such outlying offices.

If your company has had the opportunity to build its own office building in recent years or has moved to a "far out" location in a park-like setting, you surely have excellent environment that was planned by professional designers. But there are many, many offices located in "downtown" buildings in cities that may be facilities erected at the turn of the century or just a few years later. These are, however, coming down at a rapid rate and giving way to new, gleaming towers of reflective glass. From the office administrator's point of view, this may be a mixed blessing but probably to the advantage of the administrator and the staff that occupies the space.

Older Buildings

One doesn't have to tour too many older office buildings to note the concessions necessary to occupying the quarters. In many cases the ceilings are too low or too high, the electric service is barely adequate, and the elevator service and floor loadings are planned to handle minimum, not maximum loads. In some cases, there are no underfloor ducts or steel reinforcements, so it is all but impossible to improve the situation. Central air conditioning is probably not available, lighting is poor, and parking facilities are limited. It is

793

usual, too, for these buildings to be built on the "core" concept which adds to existing problems.

The core-type office building is one where the elevator, stairway, shafts for mechanical services, toilets, and such are in the center of the floor plan, and a corridor around these services leads you to the office space which is usually 20 to 30 feet in depth. This permits the floor space to be divided up into smaller units for rental, giving each tenant independent access to building services.

A building of this type is often unsuitable for a large corporation. The 20- to 30-foot deep space does not permit grouping of large departmental units, or allow for the compactly planned office space which is possible when the office is planned on three or four floors of a large, open-floor-type building.

A most important factor in office building space planning is the module used in regulating proportions. It is a fallacy to use a 3-, 3½-, or 4-foot module for windows and continuous glass windows, since it is too costly to coordinate the office lighting and air conditioning on a module smaller than 8 to 10 feet. Furthermore, the space administrator has a much easier job of apportioning the space when there is less choice in the size of private offices. The continuous glass window, even when used with treated glass, breaks down the economical modular principle for the space administrator. There are also added costs for cooling and heating the area.

Office in the City Highrise Building

The main reason a firm chooses a large city for its location is so that it will be convenient to related businesses, transportation, or its branch offices. Availability of office personnel, shopping, banking, and transportation are no longer major advantages of a city location.

After having been located in a city for a long time, a company will often find its executives and general office personnel so scattered that moving out of the city would inconvenience three-fourths of its employees. Some cities, fortunately, do not present this problem to the corporation. For example, they might have industrial activity to the south, industrial housing to the east, and a river to the west. The white-collar residences, main highways, and transportation to the north then make a natural setting for the office to the north of the city on adequate acreage.

Today's older city office buildings are mainly of the core-type plan. When a corporation builds on city property, it is too costly to have expensive property remain idle for future use. So space planned for expansion is usually rented. This practice restricts the entire building planning. Therefore, high ground values, high taxes, and related problems of city real estate make the office in the city highrise one where concessions are made that are often costly to the office efficiency and overhead.

Leasing Space in the Office Building

In all relations between the tenant and landlord, it is wise to use the services of a competent lease broker, a real-estate lawyer, and an office-planning architect. Their fees are inconsequential when compared with the many savings in time and money that can be brought about in the original leasing negotiations and during the term of the lease.

The office space lease has many typical clauses, and there are many standard forms of leases, but several essential factors to check upon in leasing of space are:

1. *Amount of Space.* The total area leased should be calculated as summarized in "Standard Method of Floor Measurement of the National Association of Building Owners and Managers."

2. *Space Description.* A reduced floor plan, or plans, should be marked to show the location of the office space agreed upon, and the plans made part of the lease.

3. *Rental.* The rental figure can best be checked by comparing it with other quotations for similar space and terms in the neighborhood, allowing a variance of 10 to 20%.

4. *Length of Lease.* Office leases normally commence on May 1 and expire on April 30 of any year. Loft leases commence on February 1 or May 1. Considering the inconveniences and costs of moving, and a nominal period to live out any investments in floor covering and miscellaneous installations in the preparation of office space by the tenant, a lease of five years should be a fair term for offices of approximately 15,000 square feet or less, and 10 to 20 years on larger areas. Longer leases with renewals, or even options on ownership of the building, should be considered by larger tenants.

5. *Expansion, Contraction, and Termination.* Arrangements should be provided in the lease for expansion through options on additional space, contraction through rights to re-lease or sublease, and termination through right to cancellation by compensating the landlord for alterations and loss until re-renting of the premises.

6. *Services.* Agreement between landlord and tenant as to services that the landlord is to give the tenant, and those the tenant is responsible for, should be made a part of the lease.

7. *Alterations.* Before signing a lease, the tenant should arrange for working drawings and specifications clearly describing what partitions, doors, electricity, plumbing, heating, ventilating, air condi-

tioning, painting, and the building standard alterations he expects of the landlord, and have them included in the lease, together with unit prices, in order to make adjustments as the work progresses, or during the term of the lease.

Any alterations the tenant proposes during the term of the lease should be approved by the landlord before the work is undertaken and paid for by the tenant.

8. *Miscellaneous.* The new tenant should try to favor installations of machines, materials, and services that have already been established in the building. Typical of these are water coolers, fans, towel service, building signs, and electric current.

Repainting of the leased premises should be done every three years and be referred to in the lease.

9. *Copies of Leases.* It is customary to prepare three copies of leases, one each for the landlord, tenant, and broker, (a fourth where states require registering of leases).

The typical office lease has many standard clauses of restrictions directly and indirectly imposed upon the tenant, but the tenant can further investigate whether his organization tenancy is affected by the following restrictions or rules and regulations.

a. Buildings built for offices, stores, lofts, factories, or warehouses are often occupied by other tenants than the type for which they were originally designed, due to changes in neighborhoods and tenants of the buildings. It is wise to check any original and current restrictions.

b. Restrictions imposed by local zoning of business functions should be studied.

c. Local building department, labor department, and fire department rules and regulations should be investigated to determine their effect upon the proposed use of space.

The landlord usually requires that the tenant check with his building engineer before making any special installations such as air conditioning or electric machines, because electricity, water, and steam capacities in a building are not always adequate for the desired installations.

The Home Office Building

Elements of importance to the office—beyond the normal considerations in the construction of a new office building—are planned flexibility of space, adequate building maintenance conditions, and provision for growth.

The amount of window space, general office space, private office and storage space required for present and foreseeable expansion of an organization, and typical architectural and mechanical conditions of a building can be well planned for by an architect experienced in office layout requirements (or an architect and an office layout consultant working in collaboration).

These experts are the interpreters of the problems of the office. They create the solution, supervise the work to completion, and are on hand when preplanned growth is to be undertaken. This relationship extends over a period of many years, if not indefinitely. The architect should coordinate the physical elements of the building with the functional requirements of the company.

Care should be taken to make physical surveys of the site, such as test borings and analysis of electric power, steam, gas, plumbing (water and sewers), telephone facilities, roads, sidewalks, and municipal limitations of the property. Transportation and shopping centers should also be investigated.

If the building is new, then department heads should be consulted on the needs of their departments in physical terms. What would they like to have in terms of physical layout? What do they think they can accomplish with this type of layout?

Several of the more important factors in the construction of an office building are:

1. *Number of Floors.* Where size of the property does not limit the area of a floor, it is wise to limit the horizontal distances from 100 to 200 lineal feet. An escalator, ramp, or stairway of a 15-foot rise to the next unit of space above or below, can be used up to five floors.

2. *Type of Construction.* Considering the constant changing of office layouts and the use of heavy machines and safes, files, and equipment, fireproof steel frame or reinforced concrete construction is believed most suited to modern office buildings.

3. *Shape.* Since the office is a combination of window, general office, and storage space, the shape of the building usually evolves from these requirements, limitations of the site, imposed design, and office functions.

4. *Expansion.* Foreseeable expansion in private offices can be provided for by spare offices, conference rooms, or large offices that can be cut in two as new ones are needed.

Expansion in general offices can be provided through general offices areas which are large enough to allow for future expansion, arranged more comfortably to suit today's needs.

Provision can be made for the growth of a building by planning additions to the building, or by adding additional floors.

5. *Mechanical Facilities.* Electric light and power, heating, air conditioning, plumbing, and special devices such as underfloor ducts and intercommunication comprise the mechanical facilities of an office building. Electrical devices which will be added from time to time will require additional power, and this should be provided for when the building is planned, by providing spare electric service facilities.

6. *Services.* Cafeterias, car parking, recreation rooms, rest rooms, first-aid rooms, and similar employee service facilities should be provided for in original planning. Too often they are forgotten, and then provided for later at the expense of valuable office space.

7. *Maintenance.* Adequate storage for cleaning materials, locker room facilities, mechanical service access, and storage require coordination with maintenance people during the original planning.

Suburban Offices

Some of today's suburban office complexes look like downtown has been transplanted to the country. From the 20th floor, you can still see a midwestern corn field or waving fields of grain. Office parks and "campuses" are getting to be rather substantial complexes serving thousands of people five days a week. They attract other service firms, including major hotels, restaurants and in some cases retail stores.

The original idea was to avoid the hustle and bustle of a city location, to avoid traffic jams and crowds as well as high-cost space rentals. A decision to move "to the country" might result in all three of the problems, so the site chosen should be carefully mulled.

Today, many of the suburban office sites have good hotels nearby, which is a plus for your company if you have a constant stream of visitors, both company personnel and others. Most have good restaurants in the neighborhood as well, and usually these are easy to get to and it is easy to park, helping to simplify and speed up any entertaining executives might have to do.

The Open Office

One of the problems with renting space in older buildings is the ability to match the space with the needs of the modern, automated or semi-automated office. It is necessary to remove walls and other barriers, and sometimes it is impossible to move pillars and posts. Dreams of an "open office" may be severely restricted.

As previously indicated, there may be problems with air conditioning and electrical power. All of these mean that the taking of a lease on a building space should be approached with care. All questions should be asked in advance and all promises put into writing.

The open office, if there is sufficient room for the layout, can be as attractive for the building ownership as it is for the user. It might be suggested that the ownership be asked to initiate the first steps in planning to be sure that the concept can be achieved. Much can be done with open space if the floor is sound and the area is not too broken up. This must be considered before any agreement is signed.

OFFICE LAYOUTS

In most cases, the layout of an office should be in the hands of an office space planner with plenty of input from the office administrator and some from employees themselves. The office administrator

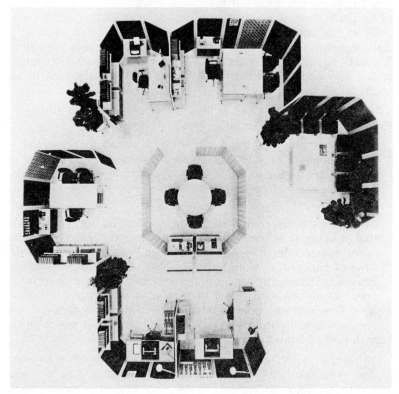

Office Landscape furniture, designed here by Facit-Addo, Inc., is called Ergonomic II because of its attention to human work needs in terms of the design of color, size, shape, sound control and flexibility. The furniture is mobile and can be changed or converted to meet any type of new situations.

799

knows if it will be necessary to provide private offices, and for whom they will be provided.

The entire plan for an office is based on (1) the equipment which will be used, and (2) the people who will use it. If some equipment is noisy (printers, bursters, etc.) they should be carefully placed to avoid total distraction. There are covers for printers that do a good job if the printer has to be right in the office area where people work on projects that require silence. Bursters should be placed as far away from work areas as is possible or feasible. Copy machines, often, are both noisy and flash bright lights for certain types of copying. These should not be placed where people can be totally distracted from their jobs.

There are versatile soundscreens and partitions or structural panels available to meet most needs for privacy and noise or sound control. These are a part of the "open office" concept which helps to keep the flow of work at a maximum while cutting costs, especially in the cubicle or private office area. People can work very close without seeing or hearing each other, and the privacy afforded is nearly equal to that of a room with a door closed. Of course, ceiling and floor treatment are a must to achieve the goal of an open, productive office.

In his publication, *"The Office, A Facility Based on Change,"* Robert Probst of Herman Miller wrote:

"Office planning has frequently treated human beings as a hydraulic quantity of sideless, senseless particles. These moveable particles are arranged to the best advantage of a geometric submissive to the architectural statement or simply a desire for non-objective order.

"We all have this desire for formal order. The only problem is that it conflicts severely with the more organic kind of spatial order human interchange uses best. The egg crate concept, with rows of enclosures connected by corridors, fits an organizational behavior format already rare and certainly obsolete: a form of linear communication based on almost totally vertical organization. Research into communication structures show that the real communication patterns in an organization almost never agree with linear hierarchy.

"Moreover, rigid spatial pre-arrangement can only agree by accident with the huge variable of how people should be grouped together. Obeying forces responsive to human communication needs would first cause variation in space enclosure to allow specific grouping, such as task group participants who need direct and continuous access to each other with no barriers whatsoever.

"This visual cueing of individual to individual is then extended to related activities or groups . . . i.e., what groups should have proximity to each other. This is the plain objective of making access efficient by reducing distance. In the super complex problem of retaining communications fluency, there is no substitute for having visual access on a demand basis to those you need to see. We are afflicted by memos as a poor substitute.

"It is true that until recently organizational mechanics and management norms have not embraced a capacity to plan space on a communications matrix basis. This ability now exists and will make this new spatial order possible.

"The word *order* is important because we are not talking about imposing visual or design chaos on space. There is a danger in disorientation, identity confusion and traffic meandering if concern for geometric order is not reconciled with needs for eloquence in space expression.

"Planning for the office requires an expanded set of skills. Planning is an exercise in futility unless it produces a knowledgeable structure built on an understanding of the key variables: the purpose of the organization; the support of individual performance; the role of facility planning and the art of pre-gaming."

If the office you work in now has limitations due to space, structure, or type of business, your responsibility lies in making it as comfortable to work in as is possible. There are changes which can be made in lighting, in noise control and in privacy which will not entail architectural changes or structural changes.

Proper lighting for the office is essential today, perhaps more than at any time in the past. The new units being used by office workers—CRTs, micrographic readers, etc.—can be all but wiped out by poor lighting, especially glare lighting.

Both the quantity of light and the quality of light are necessary ingredients in terms of keeping the work flow going. As we know, light is measured in terms of foot candles. There are 8,000 to 10,000 possible foot candles of light outside on a bright sunny day. This count drops to 100 FC at the window of a building and often descends to as little as 20 away from the window.

For years, the fluorescent light was used in offices, often in banks stretching across both open office areas and private offices as well. In many cases, this lighting provided as much or more light than was necessary for the tasks at hand. That's why the "quality" of light is measured today. Many offices have the required quantity of light, but the quality is so badly distributed that it becomes a menace to the health of the employees and contributes to energy waste. This is called "negative light" or more commonly, glare. It affects employees no matter where they are stationed, sometimes because pillars and partitions block the light and sometimes even when they, themselves, block the light by creating shadows.

On the other hand, "positive" light is scientifically placed so that the full quota required to light the area is focused on the work, and shadows and reflections are eliminated. Most office administrators have learned over the years that much of the negative light could be converted to positive light through the use of proper reflecting equipment, good distribution of the light and intelligent attention to the placing of light where it is needed.

Task Lighting

What was needed, and is now being used, is individual job or task lighting. This is especially important in any type of open office arrangement. The traditional ceiling lighting systems can be used with more reflective or bounce power, and there is a resurgence in the use of "pendant lights" which were popular several decades back. These figures are attached to ceiling grids which permit their use anywhere they are actually needed. For example, one can be

The introduction of new equipment such as video screens, microfilm readers and the like called for new lighting approaches in the office. This Zapf System work area shows the CRT and keyboard in one lighted area and the work surface of the desk in another. The task lighting utilizes internal reflectors to direct the proper amount of light on the visual task and a batwing lens to minimize veiling reflections.

Courtesy Knoll International, Inc.

placed above and just behind the workstation to provide no-glare bright light and no reflective light to interfere with a video display or CRT unit.

The lighting of special work areas is now being covered by units such as the Steelcase "Variable Intensity" task light. This lamp gives the employee personal control over the brightness level as well as the location. Adjustability is achieved with a plastic cylinder, patterned with a network of dark lines, which encases a fluorescent lamp. Light is blocked according to the density of the line patterns, and the brightness levels are adjusted by rotating the cylinder.

The light's reflector is designed to distribute illumination evenly across the entire worksurface, an improvement over ordinary fixtures which intensify light at the center of the worksurface.

Westinghouse Electric Corporation's "open Office Lighting System" incorporates some of the same concepts. It utilizes indirect ambient lighting and task lighting to improve the quality of illumination while reducing the quantity of fixtures needed.

The system is also designed to be an energy-saving alternative to direct overhead lighting. Placing the light sources closer to the work areas means less light is needed. The fixtures do not have to be installed in a rigid structure such as the ceiling and can be both saddle-mounted on the tops of workstation panels or integrated under shelves and cabinets.

Meeting Priorities

According to the American Society of Interior Designers, lighting designers can no longer uniformly illuminate work surfaces with a quantity (as opposed to a quality) of light without regard to the occupants of that space. The visual environment must allow the worker to operate with the greatest degree of visual acuity, while utilizing the least amount of physical effort for prolonged periods. To accomplish this, designers must evaluate and prioritize lighting design considerations.

The priorities first consider the factors affecting the worker, then take the influence of the facility into account. Creation of the best possible *task visibility* in the work area is the number one priority. Good task visibility is achieved when veiling reflection (reflected glare) is minimized on the task work force surfaces and VDT screens. This is the key element in productivity. It is possible to achieve this end with proper use of ambient and accent (task) lighting.

The second priority should be the creation of a comfortable *visual environment.* The key elements here are controlling window brightness and lighting system brightness in an entire environment.

Brightness ratios greater than three to one between task-lit space and its immediate surroundings or five to one between task-lit space and the general surrounding can cause visual stress and fatigue. It's also important that the ceiling have reasonable luminance to insure that the visual environment is a proper work environment.

Quality vs. Quantity

The third priority is to provide quality lighting so employees can handle all the visual tasks at the work station. The lighting system must be designed for a *"dynamic worker."* Quantity lighting is no longer acceptable for optimum results.

Flexibility is the fourth priority, and it is important in a lighting system to allow for different seeing requirements (i.e., the aging eye), and to permit the relocation of work stations as office needs change.

The ASID set as the fifth priority, *energy costs.* These must become a major consideration in lighting design because of environmental impact, energy legislation and a rapid escalation of costs. It is a reasonable assumption that energy costs will rise faster than inflation, therefore, energy conservation will be more important in a competitive industry. The sixth priority is *initial cost.* It is the least significant aspect of lighting system cost on a life-cycle basis, but it *is* the first money spent and is generally overemphasized. When comparing it with people and operating costs, the initial cost seems very small, but it must be closely evaluated with investment and energy tax credits and accelerated depreciation. The effect that lighting system cost has on other systems must also be considered. A good lighting system does not necessarily dictate an expensive system, nor is the opposite true.

The seventh priority, aesthetic integration into the overall space design, is also considered essential by the ASID. Lighting design should not be confused with fixture selection. Most often, fixture selection does not begin until the lighting concept is complete or in the final design step.

Successful Lighting

The successful lighting design, as indicated by the ASID, is the final step in the process. For maximum productivity, a luminous environment must be created that has *high visibility* (i.e., seeability). The lighting effectiveness of a direct fluorescent system is generally about 53 percent and very non-uniform. This means that 47 percent of the light at the task-lit space creates reflections that decrease visibility, while the other 53 percent is usable light. On the other hand, a well-placed indirect lighting system can create at least 50 percent greater visibility. Also, there is less reflected glare as compared to the direct system, which in turn is a potential for greater productivity.

The ASID recommends that task lighting come from the side to reduce reflections that are typically inherent with a three-foot or four-foot fluorescent strip mounted under an overhead cabinet. An undershelf-mounted fluorescent strip produces too much glare on the task-lit space and results in very poor visibility.

For good *visual comfort* comfort it is important to have an illuminated ceiling, but not a glare reflecting area. Bright-lens, direct fluorescent fixtures do not provide satisfactory visual comfort, but this is possible with properly designed and installed indirect lighting. The ASID suggests that you can check this out in a space with direct fluorescent if you are there for a short length of time. Shield the glare from the fixture with your hands and notice how the muscles around your eyes relax after you have removed the glare from your field of view. Then you try the same experiment in an indirectly illuminated space to literally see the difference and feel the difference.

Deep cell, parabolic, low brightness louvers can provide better glare control, but a dark ceiling is inappropriate for a work environment and gives the feeling that the ceiling is lower than it actually is. The answer, then, is indirect lighting for a comfortable ambient system.

Lighting "Dynamic Workers"

According to the ASID, the entire work station must be illuminated with ambient and/or accent lighting to allow for the varying tasks of the "dynamic worker." This doesn't require uniform lighting, but it is necessary that approximately 50 percent of the work station lighting come from the ambient lighting system. The remaining 50 percent must originate from the localized accent lighting. In a work station without overhead cabinets, as much as 100 percent of the lighting may be ambient. This ambient/accent approach, in general, does help to balance the luminance ratios in the work station, so it is usually suggested.

There are other important factors in lighting the office. Flexibility, for example is as important here as it is in furniture selection. Flexibility takes into account people with different seeing abilities and provides additional lighting for difficult tasks. Portable lights can be mounted on panel systems or used as floor standing lights to enhance flexibility where needed.

A final, but major, consideration is cost. The cost involved is usually the initial priority for most administrators when lighting changes are being considered. It should be remembered, however, that the lighting system cost is inconsequential when compared to the cost of the people who work in the space. Also, a good lighting system need not be expensive, while an expensive lighting system need not be good. An evaluation of costs involved, especially energy costs, must be made, probably by an expert in the field if the work to be done is extensive. There can be energy tax credits involved as well as investment tax credits that balance the basic costs of installation and use of corporate money.

The full impace of illumination on employees' productivity, attitudes and fatigue is not yet completely understood, the ASID admits, but studies are being conducted on a continuing basis to provide this information.

MANAGING TOMORROW'S WORK PROCESS

The report following is from the Herman Miller organization (Herman Miller, Inc., Zeeland, Michigan) which has been on the leading edge of office design and furniture for over 20 years.

Technology. It's growing, advancing, and maturing. And almost as quickly as it's introduced to the marketplace, it's placed in the hands of workers.

Introducing the equipment to the work place with hopes of improving everyone's productivity is one thing. *Managing* the connections among the technology, the people who use it, and the environment in which it is placed, is quite another.

It's the latter—the managing of the work process—that Herman Miller has made its business, because we realize that today, technology is a fact of life. But technology alone is just a potential; only when it's coupled with acceptance by the worker, only when it supports the needs of the worker, and only when the environment adequately supports it, can it be truly effective.

In the past, people, facilities, and other criteria for increasing productivity in the work place have been considered simply costs rather than equal participants necessary to make this technology really work. But today, that's changing—workers are making it change. They're demanding that their work-related problems and concerns are recognized and satisfied.

Specifically, they are concerned with the inability of the physical environment to support the use of video display terminals; the lack of non-adjustable desks to place keyboards and screens at proper working heights and angles; glare on screens; heat build-up where terminals are used; and uncomfortable or unsupportive chairs.

These are concerns, like it or not, managements cannot overlook. In December, 1980, nearly 1,200 clerical workers went on strike against a major insurance company in California. It was the first time in the history of white collar work (in the United States) that the lack of adequate human factors in the work place had become a reason to strike. And several other large and visible insurance companies have been confronted with dissatisfied workers who believe management should and could be more concerned with making the work place a more humane place.

These problems can't be solved by increasing benefits, allowing flexible working schedules, and the like, without really addressing the issue at hand: the critical need for improved relationships between technology and those who use it, for considering human factors in the very design of the work place.

People and Technology

Differences abound in the work place: People are different, so are the tasks they typically perform, and the way they perform them. And when electronic equipment is introduced into the process, a whole new set of differences result, and it's crucial that they be recognized.

For example, consider the following: Because workers' ages vary, eye fatigue levels vary. Some workers are used to working with electronic equipment, and know exactly what to expect; others have never been exposed to such technology. Some jobs require workers to perform only one task, and therefore sit in one basic position; other jobs require the worker to perform a variety of tasks, and therefore allow free movement within the work station. And the differences go on and on.

Being aware of these concerns is the first step in righting the wrongs that exist between workers and technology; assuring that workers will be included in making decisions that affect their jobs and that work stations and facilities will meet these needs is the second, and most important step.

The Work Process and Technology

The work process of office workers is no longer the rigid procedure it once was. It has entered, instead, into an evolutionary process that is changing every day.

Consider, as proof, the following statements:

- Approximately five percent or less of a senior manager's work volume is done on a computer terminal today. The projection for both middle and senior managers is that by

1985, they may be doing as much as 25 percent or more of their work on terminals.

- Approximately 15–20 percent of work performed by professional and technical workers can be done on a terminal today. And by the mid-1980s, that figure could rise to 50 percent for many.
- Clerical workers and clerks today do about 40 percent of their work on a video display terminal. By 1985, many of them will be processing 80–90 percent of their work through terminals.

More and more work is done electronically, and this trend will continue. Thus, organizations must make even greater attempts to bridge the growing mismatch between workers, the facilities, the environmental support, and technology.

The Facility and Technology

Electronic equipment in the work place has produced a significant impact on facilities, since they must be able to support the technology and the workers if productivity is going to increase—or at least remain constant.

Numerous issues must be addressed in each facility. Some of them include:

- Work environments using community terminals. These are work areas in which one terminal supports the information processing requirements of between 10 to 20 workers. Generally, such configurations are unable to support all of the users. To satisfy their diverse needs, the work environment must be adjustable and flexible enough to meet seating, work surface, storage, terminals and keyboards, and lighting requirements.
- Environments using cluster terminals. These are work areas in which one terminal supports the requirements of between two and 10 workers. Often, the terminal is placed in a location which is accessible to *all* users, but is not optimal for any one of them. Users, then, are often made to wait their turn to use the equipment, and then are forced to use the equipment in a less-than-ideal arrangement.
- Dedicated use environments. These are configurations in which one terminal supports the information processing requirements of a single worker. The most critical problem in this situation is that when terminals are initially introduced into dedicated work stations, they are typically used only 10 percent of the worker's time. Yet, the terminal takes up 40 percent of the available work surface. This means that users are doing their usual tasks with less work surface space.

- Special lighting for visual display terminals. Conventional ceiling illumination from a fixed place, designed for reading, just won't work for users of CRTs. More adaptive lighting is necessary in order to gain control of screen glare, contrast ratios, and natural light.

- Heating, ventilation and air conditioning (H.V.A.C.) systems. Because terminals can get hot, H.V.A.C. systems must be able to accommodate heat build-up from the terminals if users are to be comfortable. But the H.V.A.C. systems in most buildings today are having to retro-fit their systems to bring better air flows to specific areas where terminals are placed.

- Electrical, telephone, and data cables. The need to accommodate them is rising as quickly as the rate of terminals in work environments. And the traditional spaces allotted within the buildings to house cables and wires are already becoming satiated, while the cable volume continues to climb.

- Local networks, terminals, and computers. Linked together by a common set of cables, they are also on the increase in offices. Digital data and communication cables are required for terminals, and each terminal can require an additional 25–100 feet of new cable. In the short term, the cable proliferation problem will get worse before it gets better. One way of storing the abundance of cables is the raised floor. But within the next two years, undercarpet coaxial cable and fibre-optic transmission lines should be tested and ready to use in offices.

How Herman Miller Manages the Work Process

People, equipment, and facilities. They're all equally critical components in dealing with the problems of tomorrow's work place and work process.

Herman Miller began emphasizing its focus on people, the work process, and the work place back in 1968, when we introduced the Action Office® system, the first human factored open-plan office system. All system components are modular, which means that work stations can be designed according to the worker's needs and wants, and changes in the office design can be easily made.

The system was so successful in meeting the needs of the office worker and his or her individual work process, that we applied the same principle to the health care, laboratory, and light-industrial work environments, and introduced Action™ environments, Action™ lab, and Action Factory.® All provide workers with the same opportunities to make the work process more personalized, more productive, and more pleasant.

Our concern for the worker and the work process goes beyond just hardware, though: We're the only systems manufacturer to own and operate its own research facility. The Facility Management Institute, located in Ann Arbor, deals with the workers' needs in today's work place and technology-related issues facing facility managers today. And the professionals who comprise the Institute are continually researching, analyzing, and applying information related to tomorrow's worker and work process.

To further accommodate tomorrow's worker, Herman Miller has established strong relationships with several manufacturers of electronic equipment for the work place. We realize that their forte is technology, and that they can design equipment with great potential for the future. But without strong regard for those who will use tomorrow's technology, it can be of little benefit.

Technology is going to be integrated into work environments (as well as home environments), inevitably. Whether that integration takes place smoothly or traumatically; whether people accept it openly or grudgingly; whether or not it can achieve its potential to improve productivity—these are the issues. And Herman Miller takes a clear stand on the leading edge of designing the human-factored environments that can help technology fulfill its promise.

Keeping the Office Clean

It's not necessary to repeat how important it is that working offices must be kept clean for an efficient environment. While many of the jobs formerly done in offices have changed, and the amount of some types of paper have diminished, other trash-makers have taken up the role.

Tile floors, where used, should be cleaned regularly, including washing and buffing (see Standards for Cleaning Office Buildings). Carpeting can collect dust and spills quickly and must be constantly swept. Coffee stains, by the way, are hard on rugs and carpeting no matter the amount of added protection in the fabric. If coffee is taken at individual work stations, employees should know that they must alert someone or clean up a spill on their own.

When employees eat at their work stations—and this is done in many operations—the trash problem can be increased. Instead of paper and bent paper clips, the trash may contain actual garbage. After a while, in some locations, this can invite visits from unwanted pests. If a lunchroom is provided, it should be used as a matter of company policy.

On the next few pages are *Standards for Cleaning Office Buildings* which were developed by the General Services Administration as a

STANDARDS FOR CLEANING OFFICE BUILDINGS

The standards appearing below, and on the pages following, were established by the General Services Administration as a guide to determining staffing and equipment requirements in office buildings operated by GSA. They are based on the experience of the Public Buildings Service in Washington, D. C., and other cities. To apply the standards to a particular building, the entire work load is figured (square feet of floors, number of windows, etc.) and the number of man-days is then divided into day and night forces.

Job Description	Performance	Equipment	Qualifying Factors	Production Per Man-Day	Normal Frequency in Work Days
FLOOR SCRUBBING WITH POLISHING MACHINE	Place cleaning agent on floor and agitate with machine. Pick up dirty solution and rinse. (Floor swept by zone cleaner.)	1. Floor scrubbing machine 2. 2-compartment mop tank and wringer 3. Dust pan and brush 4. Three mops 5. Rags and steel wool 6. Cleaning agent 7. Hair sweep 8. Electric water pick-up in lieu of mop (optional)	15" divided wt. (rotary) polishing machine 15" concentrated wt. (rotary) polishing machine	20,000 sq. ft. 20,000 sq. ft.	Main floor corridors daily Secondary floor corridors every 5 days Other space as required
FLOOR SCRUBBING WITH POWER SCRUBBING MACHINE	Machine applies cleaning agent to floor, agitates it with revolving brushes and picks up dirty solution with vacuum device, rinsing optional. (Floor swept by zone cleaner.)	1. Power scrubbing machine 2. 2-compartment mop tank and wringer 3. Dust pan and brush 4. Two mops 5. Rags and steel wool 6. Cleaning agent 7. Hair sweep 8. Hand squeegee 9. Gum scraper 10. Garden hose (5' length) 11. Measuring cup	Machine covers strip 26" wide	25,000 sq. ft.	Main floor corridors daily Secondary floor corridors every 5 days
FLOOR MOPPING	Sweep and then place cleaning solution on floor and work with mop. Pick up dirty solution and rinse as required with mop.	1. 2-compartment mop tank and wringer 2. Two mops 3. Cleaning agent 4. Gum scraper 5. Hair sweep		20,000 sq. ft.	Main floor corridors daily Secondary floor corridors every 5 days

STANDARDS FOR CLEANING OFFICE BUILDINGS (Cont.)

Job Description	Performance	Equipment	Qualifying Factors	Production Per Man-Day	Normal Frequency in Work Days
FLOOR WAXING	Mop or scrub, apply new wax, polish. (Floor swept by zone cleaner.)	1. Dust pan and brush 2. Floor polishing machine 3. 2-compartment mop tank and wringer 4. Three mops 5. Cleaning agent 6. Gum scraper 7. Rags and steel wool 8. Mopping unit for wax 9. Wax, spirit or water emulsion	15″ divided wt. (rotary) polishing machine 15″ concentrated wt. (rotary) polishing machine 16″ cylindrical drum polishing machine	5,000 sq. ft. open area 3,000 sq. ft. office area 8,000 sq. ft. open area 3,500 sq. ft. office area 5,000 sq. ft. open area	Every 66 days˙
FLOOR BUFFING	Polish the floor to remove traffic marks without applying additional wax. (Floor swept by zone cleaner.)	1. Polishing machine 2. Steel wool (hand pad)	15″ divided wt. (rotary) polishing machine 15″ concentrated wt. (rotary) polishing machine 16″ cylindrical drum polishing machine	40,000 sq. ft. open area 30,000 sq. ft. office area 40,000 sq. ft. open area 30,000 sq. ft. office area 40,000 sq. ft. open area 30,000 sq. ft. office area	Every 22 days
FLOOR SWEEPING	Pick up loose paper and trash, sweep, clean telephone booths and dust surfaces that can be reached while standing on the floor. (Usually assigned to zone cleaner.)	1. 24″ hair sweep 2. Dust pan	Open space	50,000 sq. ft	Daily
RUG VACUUMING	Vacuum rugs with domestic, portable, or central vacuum machines.	Vacuum machine, or vacuum hose and tools for central system	Closely grouped rugs	80 (12′×15′)	Daily

812

STANDARDS FOR CLEANING OFFICE BUILDINGS (Cont.)

Job Description	Performance	Equipment	Qualifying Factors	Production Per Man-Day	Normal Frequency in Work Days
STAIR CLEANING	Sweep, dust, and scrub.	1. Broom 2. Bucket 3. Scrub and deck brushes 4. Rags 5. Cleaning agent 6. Gum scraper	Sweep and dust Scrub	60 flights (floor to floor) 20 flights (floor to floor)	Daily Every 5 days
HIGH CLEANING	Clean lights, transoms, pipes, high files, and dust venetian blinds and other objects high enough to require the ladder and too high for zone cleaner to reach while standing on the floor.	1. Ladder 2. Buckets 3. Cloths 4. Radiator brush 5. Vacuum cleaner 6. Cleaning agent 7. Wall brush 8. Push broom 9. Dust pan		10,000 gross sq. ft. floor area	Every 66 days
TOILETS, CLEANING AND SERVICING	Empty waste containers, fill soap dispensers, towel and toilet paper holders. Clean fixtures, sweep floors and mop or scrub as required.	1. Mopping unit 2. 12 qt. bucket 3. Mop 4. Radiator brush 5. Hair sweep 6. Toilet brush 7. Scrub brush 8. Gum scraper 9. Rubber gloves 10. Cleaning agent 11. Cloths 12. Polish 13. Toilet supplies		80 fixtures (Wash basins, water closets, urinals)	Clean daily Service as required
LOBBY AND CORRIDOR POLICING (Includes adjacent stairs)	Sweep up scraps of paper and cigarette butts. Mop wet spots, keep jardinieres presentable.	1. Long-handled dust pan 2. Long-handled dust brush 3. Cloths	Main corridor Secondary corridor	300,000 sq. ft. of corridor area 300,000 sq. ft. of corridor area	4 times daily Daily
LOBBY CLEANING	Sweep, mop, dust, polish metal, and clean glass.	1. Hair sweep 2. Mops 3. Gum scraper 4. Cloths 5. Metal polish 6. Chamois	Main (Large) Secondary	16 32	Daily Daily

STANDARDS FOR CLEANING OFFICE BUILDINGS (Cont.)

Job Description	Performance	Equipment	Qualifying Factors	Production Per Man-Day	Normal Frequency in Work Days
ENTRANCE CLEANING (Outside)	Sweep, police, clean glass and push plates. (Snow and sleet are removed by special work crews detailed from regular cleaning force.)	1. Broom 2. Hose 3. Cloths 4. Metal polish 5. Dust pan 6. Chewing gum scraper	Main Secondary	16 32	Twice daily Daily
PAPER AND TRASH COLLECTION	paper is bagged or boxed by zone cleaners and placed in corridors for the trash man to collect and take to trash room.	1. Twine for bags 2. 4-wheel push truck for bagged paper 3. 4-wheel box push truck for collecting loose paper		600,000 sq. ft. gross area	Daily
WINDOW WASHING	Windows washed inside and outside.	1. Safety belt (when needed) 2. Counter brush 3. Sponge or cloth 4. Chamois 5. Scraper 6. Sill pad 7. Cleaning agent 8. Bucket 9. Squeegee 10. Stepladder	Double hung 2-pane 4'×7' Double hung 4-pane 4'×6' Double hung 8-pane 3.5'×5.5' Double hung 12-pane 2.5'×5.7' Double hung 16-pane 4'×6' Industrial 20-pane 4'×7' Austral Casement 6-pane 6'×7'	60 55 45 40 35 30 35 35	Every 22 days
ELEVATOR CLEANING	Scrub, wax, and buff floors, dust interior of car, polish brass.	1. Hand truck 2. Two mops 3. Radiator brush 4. 14" hair sweep 5. Dust pan and brush 6. Dust and scrub cloths 7. Cleaning agent 8. Mopping unit 9. Short stepladder 10. Steel wool 11. Wax 12. Metal polish 13. Polishing machine (small)	Passenger elevator Freight elevator	25 25	Daily Every 5 days

guide for government buildings. Many of these guidelines can be used in your office area and in your office building.

Furniture in the Office

The open office plan, which has been discussed, is here to stay and will be growing in the future according to the National Office Products Association. Because of the flexibility offered, this type of office layout or design will influence 52% of all office furniture purchased by 1990. Nearly one-third of today's offices are open.

One reason suggested for the transition is that it might cost $1 a square foot to move a flexible department as compared to moving a traditional office at $20 a foot. Also, except for the *very* private executive offices, the flexible office offers much more privacy than the "bullpen" approach used for so many years.

Office furniture will be more modular in the future (and, it is right now). A desk or working area is now frequently called a work station, and the equipment within the station area may be shared by two or more people. For example, a recently-introduced, centrally-located turntable from Conwed Corporation gives two or three employees access to one computer. Westinghouse designed a WESTECH Series for the electronic office which builds on the inherent flexibility and cost-effectiveness of open office systems. The new system components include free-standing desks that can be joined in many configurations. These, in turn, can accommodate drawers, keyboards and bins to meet specific needs. Cluster tops can join two or more desks and can be in square, triangular, quarter round or trapezoidal shapes.

Wood is Coming Back In

Wood furniture, which disappeared from many offices with the advent of steel and laminated units, is coming back according to Conwed. "The use of wood for computer support furniture is growing," the company contends, "and many customers are specifically asking for attractive wood" in place of metal for work spaces. The line of thinking is that people such as programmers are very valuable to the company and they are being given wood furniture that "implies value and achievement."

Laminates and plastics are not exactly missing from the scene, and in many cases, office administrators are combining laminates with metal for durability and attractive work surfaces and areas. The laminates can be oak, walnut or in colors such as dusty rose. The tops can have finishes such as Morocco Sand, Khaki Green, Rose-dust, or even Mauve Mist (titles courtesy of Tibbet, Inc.).

This oak-finished "cluster" work station is designed to supply computer access for a number of employees. The use of wood in such an area is growing in popularity, especially since the new "breed" of technical employees seem to have more value to many companies. Courtesy Conwed Corporation

Most offices are being designed with "ergonomics" in mind (See Chapter 30), which means terminal stands, work surfaces (desks included), chairs and partitions are all conceived as integral parts of the work station as well as the office. It doesn't matter if the area is designated for a chief executive officer, a programer or a clerk. The biggest fuss is made over the positioning of the CRT terminal in relationship to the keyboard for the comfort and convenience of the operator. Obviously, if one doesn't have a terminal, there is little problem with this.

Executive Offices

The office of an executive still reflects the title and the job of the individual involved. Although design changes on a regular basis, there are still very basic approaches to furnishing the executive office, or, as is now the case, the executive work station.

Young and old executives alike have similar tastes for furnishings in the office . . . some like traditional decor and some favor con-

Here's the super technological executive work station of the future produced by Specification Built Corporation. It contains such capabilities as two microcomputers, a satellite video-conferencing facility, digitizing pad, an information retrieval and high speed printer and a few extra electronic amenities. Actually, seven different electronic firms supplied the equipment.

temporary. Obviously, if the offices are located in a very modern building with open office layouts throughout, a very traditional setting is going to be out of place. However, a good designer/decorator can even work this out if a request is made.

Normally, quiet elegance is what most executives want to reflect their position and their work. This can be achieved today with wood desks or combinations of metal and wood, lighting, executive chairs, credenzas and other furnishings, including pictures and plants. Color plays a major role, as it always has. Traditional woods for desks and tables are currently oak, walnut and mahogany. These woods are also contemporary, sometimes with a more exotic wood tone. Wood has and always will be, a warm, rich material. Some executives, especially newly-appointed, feel that desk size is a reflection of title. There are just as many people today, however, who want more function than size. Some want built-in electronics, some want special work surfaces. Others use the desk as a meeting place, thus it is more like a table.

Some Problems Arise

If the office administrator must work directly with a newly-named executive, one of two problems can arise. The executive can be taking over in someone else's position, or the new executive can be assuming a "new" company title or position.

If it is a simple case of "moving in" to an already functioning office space, the administrator should have some company policy regarding the offices. Is the replacement executive entitled to a newly-decorated office, a newly furnished office or a change of pictures? Chief executives can usually solve this problem when they move in, but it's not as easy for vice presidents or managers.

A clearly stated company policy covering furnishings/decorating could be based on expenditure allowed, space allocation, or even a company image. Many companies reserve the right to coordinate and control office decor and furnishings, sometimes to the point of pictures on the wall. Others feel the individual should be given leeway within "bounds" if a new office is to be designed.

This is why the office administrators should not be forced to become too involved in this type of situation. This is also why it is almost necessary to use the services of an office designer. A good

If an executive wishes to keep his or her use of microcomputer as a private function, it is possible to obtain this executive model CRT table and cabinet from R-WAY. It will discreetly keep the machine from view when it is not in use.

Harvey Probber developed a new Banker's system of desks and workstations for one of the country's most prestigious banks. It features a lavish use of mahogany solids and veneers, antique bronze inserts in leather, plush chairs, etc. There is no mistaking the area as an executive workstation.

designer can quickly see the "atmosphere" of the offices in the area and provide furnishings and lighting to blend into the previous or existing motif.

The office administrator usually provides the liaison between the executive and the designer or decorator and provides the sources for furnishings.

Executives in the Open

The high rental costs of commercial space has prompted many firms to opt for the open-plan office and the flexibility it affords. According to a report in *Administrative Management* magazine (now entitled *Office Administration and Automation*), vendors have made sure that the executive can keep his or her status in tact despite the absence of permanent walls.

In an open-plan environment, an executive can enjoy almost as much privacy as with a closed office. Panels as high as 80 inches surround wood-grain desks and furnishings. Many of the panel systems can be mounted with doors, and most provide a wide variety of possible fabrics and materials, including glass (curved or straight), which defines personal space while allowing visual supervision of subordinates if necessary.

Chances are the executive will not have to make too much of a sacrifice in the size of his or her office because of the open-plan. The major difference will be in the furnishings themselves since open-plan furnishings tend to be more streamlined and integrated rather than traditional. In many cases, the panel-hung cabinets and other components are highly efficient when compared to traditional units and more pleasing to the executives, especially younger managers.

PART 7

HOW TO IMPROVE ADMINISTRATIVE SKILLS

CHAPTER 34

GUIDELINES TO CURRENT MOTIVATIONAL THEORIES

IN order to successfully direct the work of other people, managers need a basic knowledge of current motivational theories and research and a wide variety of skills in applying their findings on the job. The following sections provide a summary of the findings of well-known behavioral scientists and some general guidelines for use by managers in developing their skills.

Current Theories and Research

Today there is a great amount of information available about human behavior. Hundreds of books, articles, pamphlets, and newsletters, and dozens of speakers at workshops, seminars, and courses provide tons of data about behavioral science findings, concepts of motivation and the management of people. All of this is helpful to managers in understanding why people behave the way they do and in developing strategies of managing which will obtain the best results for the organization and, at the same time, meet the needs of the people in that organization.

A foundation of these current motivational theories and research is essential for managers who are interested in developing their skills in managing and motivating other people. Most managers, however, are not trained psychologists or psychiatrists. Consequently, the dilemma managers face is how to sort out all of the data that's available and select those theories or research findings that would be the most useful to them in carrying out their managerial job.

In recent years, the findings of six behavioral scientists have received a great amount of attention from managers throughout business and industry.* Their works have served as cornerstones or platforms for an increased understanding of human behavior in the world of work. These six men are:

---

*Some of this popularity is no doubt due to the excellent work done by Dr. Saul W. Gellerman, a behavioral scientist, who summarized the findings of these six men in layman's language in his prize-winning book *"Motivation and Productivity,"* and in his BNA film series of the same name.

Abraham Maslow
Frederick Herzberg
David McClelland
Chris Argyris
Douglas McGregor
Rensis Likert

This chapter provides a capsule review—in three parts—of the contributions made by each of these six men.

NEEDS

As a start, if the "fuel" for the human engine is "Needs" it is essential to know something about the nature of such needs. Human needs have been the subject of studies by men and women for generations. Depending upon whose works you study, different names and varying numbers of needs are discussed. While knowledge of the many different approaches to human needs is valuable for those who are preparing to become specialists in human behavior, it becomes too complex and confusing for managers who are merely seeking a basic understanding of the nature of needs and their impact on a person's behavior. The works of Maslow, Herzberg and McClelland have helped to simplify some of this confusion.

Maslow's Hierarchy of Needs

Abraham Maslow's approach to the subject of human needs is frequently referred to in management literature today because it clearly illustrates some of the fundamental characteristics of needs. Maslow made two basic observations concerning human behavior:

1. Some needs appear to be more powerful—more potent—than other needs.
2. Needs don't seem to lie around in a disorganized, hit-or-miss fashion. Instead, there seems to be an underlying relationship—a linkage—an interlocking of needs—which forms an overall structure. This relatonship has become identified as Maslow's "Hierarchy of Needs."

At the base of this structure are *Physiologic Needs*—air, water, food, drink, elimination of body wastes, sexual satisfaction, and, in short, the needs of animal survival. These are what science calls autonomic: due to internal causes and influence, and taken for granted.

Now another set of needs, *Safety or Security Needs,* causes the person to act. These refer to the need for protection from physical harm as well as protection from mental harm—in other words, physical security and psychological security; a feeling of being safe from injury; the desire for the known vs. the unknown, the sure vs. the unsure, the familiar vs. the unfamiliar; the protection of things a person has accumulated. However, once again there is a decreasing loss of impact as these needs start to become satisfied.

Now a third set of needs, called *Belongingness,* starts to have an impact on the person's behavior. These needs are often called "Love Needs," which are frequently misconstrued in a romatic connotation; sometimes they are called "Social Needs," which are frequently misconstrued in a society connotation. Belongingness needs to refer to the desire of man to identify or affiliate with others with whom he feels he has something in common, or would like to have something in common. We often call this the "gregarious nature of man"—or the "herd instinct—i.e., the desire to be part of something bigger than oneself, to feel part of a group, to be with "my kind"; the need to give and receive love. But, as was seen with the lower-level needs, as Belongingness Needs begin to become satisfied, they no longer have a stong effect on the person's behavior.

Now a fourth set of needs, *Esteem* or *Ego Needs,* start to influence the individual's behavior. These are the needs for self-esteem and the esteem of others; self-respect and the respect of others; a feeling of personal worth, adequacy and competence; the need for respect, admiration, recognition and status in the eyes of other people. In essence, each person has a mental picture of what he or she is like, what sort of a person he or she is. This prompts action to have others see the same picture, in the same light. As was true before, the same phenomenon begins to occur. As these needs start to become satisfied, another set of needs begins to affect the person's behavior.

This fifth set of needs is called *Self-Actualization* or *Self Realization.* This refers to the desire to become as capable as you can become. It's like the saying that a person has an eight horsepower motor and is only using two horsepower. You want to use the other six. You have certain abilities you want to put to use, and you want to become that "person" you know you really are. As the person acquires additional knowledge, skills, experience and insight, he or she wants to put these increased capabilities to further use.

How Maslow's Approach Applies Today

Let's take a look at Maslow's hierarchy to see how it seems to apply in our general business or industrial scene today. Sadly enough, the first two needs are in the limelight and probably won't disappear for some time.

1. **Physiological Needs.** As the United States goes through a new stage in the concept of the workforce, many problems have arisen which have not yet been solved. After years of working at close to top capacity with only intermittent recessions, the country now faces some real changes. Manufacturing in many areas will never be the same in terms of the workforce. The fear of being replaced by a "robot" is not a science-fiction concept.

   While whole segments of the workforce—in computer operations, in high technology, etc.—are flying high, other segments have had to face drastic changes. Legislation guaranteeing subsistence at a minimum does exist, but many people don't get the full advantage of some programs. Neither companies nor government can *guarantee* anything more than the promise of trying.

2. **Safety Needs.** These are finely tuned and very diverse motivating factors for today's workforce. In more than a few instances, the health and safety fears of employees are strongly felt. While the government has provided recourse through OSHA, there is still a group of areas that bother some workers.

   The very real possibility of layoff and unemployment strikes fear in the hearts of many people at many levels. The unemployment compensation protection worked well during the 1970s when there was still an opportunity for the laid-off or fired worker to look for another job, but now many companies cannot hire or do not need additional employees. Managers, laborers, even computer programmers in some cases, find themselves without work. Entire groups of American workers find themselves with skills that are no longer needed, and some are too old to be retrained.

   Managerial and corporate strategies to alleviate these problems have had mixed success. For one thing, too many companies relied on government to solve the problem and too many employees were that sure that government would solve the problem. When this doesn't happen, the impact of these needs is strongly felt.

3. **Belongingness Needs.** These still appear to be fairly strong motivating factors in our work scene; however, the ways in which these needs are satisfied seem to be changing. In years past many employees identified with their companies—with where they worked. Today many people seem to identify more readily with their profession or their field of work.

   Americans are often referred to as "great joiners." We see

evidence of this all around us—people joining with others who share their thoughts, ideas, interests and/or objectives. It ranges all the way from fellow sportsmen to trade and professional associations, to social clubs, trade unions, and communes of individuals who are seeking a new way of life together.

4. **Esteem Needs.** These are definitely strong motivating factors in a large segment of our society today. Marketing and advertising people have been focusing on these needs for years. A quick review of many current advertisements will provide evidence of the extent to which people seek certain products and services in an attempt to reinforce their image of themselves and to have others see them in the same light. The feeling of self-respect and seeking the respect of others remains a very strong motivating factor in our society.

5. **Self-Actualization.** In recent years we are beginning to see evidence that some people are operating on this level, at least part of the time. We hear comments such as "I want to do my own thing," "I want to be a manager *now*," and "I have talents and I want to use them on something meaningful on the job." People whose lower-level needs are fairly well taken care of are now devoting more attention to becoming "that person" they believe they really are—to utilizing *all* of their talents and capabilities.

Where Needs Are Met

When you consider the lower part of Maslow's hierarchy, it becomes quite evident that these needs are primarily satisfied at work, in the home, and in various organizations to which the individual may belong. On the other hand, the upper level needs are primarily met within the individual himself. *Self*-esteem, *self*-actualization are very personal, very individual types of needs. They are ideas contained within the individual's own mind.

Four Primary Characteristics of Needs

Obviously all of the above represent a very simplified view of the nature of human needs. In reality needs do not lend themselves to such a precise or pat approach. They are much too complex for easy division into five simple categories with such clear-cut lines. However, the reason Maslow's approach has become so popular with many managers today is because it does clearly illustrate the nature of needs, or the "characteristics of needs." In order to understand needs and how they affect a person's behavior, it is essential that we know something about the characteristics of needs. So let's tally out the four key characteristics which Maslow's approach provides:

1. Some needs are more powerful or potent than other needs. Therefore in a situation where the more powerful need is not being met or satisfied, it will tend to take over the person's behavior.

   A man who is busy impressing people on a small boat with his importance (Self-esteem) will probably suddenly forget that need if he falls overboard and he can't swim. At that moment, the more fundamental need (Physiological—in the case the need for air in his lungs) will dominate or control his behavior as he thrashes around in the water.

2. A satisfied need no longer motivates. Once a person has had enough of an item, offering her some more of it will not cause her to act. For example, if you just finished a large meal and someone asked you if you'd like a large steak dinner, you would probably say, "No, I'm full." Offering you some more to eat, once your stomach was full, would not motivate you. But later on when you are hungry again, an offer of a steak dinner might very well motivate you.

   However, this is not as simple as it may first seem, because there is a big question as to what is meant by "satisfaction." We find that there are two elements that seem to have a bearing on satisfaction. One is that satisfation appears to be culturally determined. For example, the level of sustenance in the United States is quite different from what people consider to be the level of sustenance in a back village of India. In other words, as we grow up in this world of ours, our "cultural noises" tell us what we should expect in the way of satisfaction.

   Our culture is the first element in determining what satisfaction is. The second element is that satisfaction seems to be personally determined—one person may want more security than another, want more friends than another, want more to eat than another, etc.

   If we are to understand the second basic characteristic of needs, we should restate it as follows:

   "A satisfied need no longer motivates: *but* satisfaction may differ from person to person."

3. Needs are dynamic, not static. Needs are constantly changing. An individual moves up and down the hierarchy in the course of a week, a day, even over a few moments.

4. There appears to be an upward thrust to many of us. And as more and more people operate more and more frequently at

the higher level of needs, it becomes tougher and tougher for organizations to meet or satisfy those needs on a rigid, highly-organized, highly-authoritarian, redtape basis. This is because the higher level needs are much more individual in nature (Self-esteem; self-actualization). This makes it more difficult to meet them in a general, by-the numbers, "all-together-now" group basis.

Whether or not managers agree with the overall approach used by Maslow in analyzing human needs, we do have to thank him for helping us to better understand the above four key *characteristics* of needs. By understanding the nature of needs, we can better determine which types of managerial action or strategy will be effective and which will be ineffective with different individuals, in different situations and at different times.

The Meaning of Money

One question that often arises is, "Where would you place money on Maslow's hierarchy?" At first glance, it seems to relate directly to the lower-level needs, physiological and safety. A closer examination, however, discloses the fact that money could represent any one of the five needs. This is what makes the idea of money so difficult to work with; we don't know what it may mean to a specific individual.

It does represent food and something to drink (Physiological), or a roof over a person's head and perhaps a nestegg for a rainy day or retirement (Safety). Or it might be a simple statement, "Hey fellows, I'll buy the next round" as a way of seeking the warmth of friends (Belongingness); or perhaps driving a new luxurious car past a neighbor's house (Esteem). It could even mean getting away from a boring job and doing something else, such as fishing, painting, traveling or some other activity to utilize the person's untapped skills and capabilities (Self-actualization).

Often we assume money means only one thing, because that's what it means to us. Then we are surprised when someone else acts differently from what we expected because money represents something different to him.

Herzberg's Two-Factor Approach

A second approach to understanding human needs has also become very popular in recent years. This is the work of Frederick Herzberg.

Back in the early 1950's a group of businessmen in Pittsburgh became very disenchanted with the various managerial strategies they were using to try to motivate their employees. The strategies didn't seem to be working as well as they used to. The men asked Professor Herzberg if he would conduct a study of various books, research findings, reports, articles, etc. which had been written over the years to see if there were some answers to the question, "What motivates man?"

Herzberg's Findings

Herzberg and his staff set to work reading over 2,200 studies. Their findings seemed to provide two general answers. Approximately half of the studies indicated that we are motivated because we are attempting to avoid pain or discomfort. Yet the other half seemed to say we are motivated because we have a desire to grow and to develop—to become more than we were yesterday. In effect, we are growing, wanting animals. Both answers seemed to be correct. There were just too many studies in support of each answer to discount one or the other. There appeared to be *two* sides to human kind.

Herzberg decided to check out these findings in industry. To do so, he asked employees two questions. (You might wish to answer them for yourself to see how your own answers compare with Herzberg's findings.) Here are the two basic questions:

1. Think back to a time in your work experience when you were particularly satisfied—happy—felt exceptionally good. Jot down the event or the occurrence, i.e., what was happening at that time?

2. Think back to a time in your work experience when you were particularly dissatisfied—felt exceptionally bad—were disgruntled—perhaps it's when you quit your job. Jot down the event or the occurrence, i.e., what was happening at that time?

The answers Herzberg received to his first questions were primarily descriptions of what people did in terms of:

Achievement. They felt it was a time when they accomplished something. They had personal satisfaction as a result of having completed a task, solved a problem, etc.

Recognition. It was a time when they received recognition for an achievement. They had the feeling of a job well done.

Interesting Work. What they were doing, they usually found interesting.

Responsibility. They had responsibility for accomplishing tasks and had control over their jobs.

Growth and Advancement. They felt they were growing and advancing—were learning more—gaining additional insight, experience, know-how—experiencing changes in their job status—as a result of their efforts.

Such experiences caused people to be *satisfied* on the job.

The answers to what caused people to be dissatisfied on the job were *not* the opposites of the satisfiers. Instead, an entirely different set of experiences was mentioned. What caused people to be dissatisfied related mostly to the environment in which they did their job in terms of:

Company Policies and Administration. The sort of policies a company had and the way in which they were begin administered—the adequacy or inadequacy of those policies.

Supervision. The sort of supervision a person received on the job—the competency of technical ability of their supervisor.

Working Conditions. The type of conditions in which a person worked—the physical environment of the job.

Interpersonal Relations. The sort of relationships a person had on the job—with his superiors, subordinates and peers.

Money, Status, and Security. The amount of money, status and security a person received for doing the job.

Such experiences caused people to be unhappy and *dissatisfied* on the job.

(How did these answers compare to your own?)

In summary, Herzberg's findings might be diagrammed as follows:

DISSATISFIERS	SATISFIERS
Environment	**What People Do—The Task**
Company Policies & Administration	Achievement
Supervision	Recognition
Working Conditions	Interesting Work
Interpersonal Relations	Responsibility
Money, Status & Security	Growth and Advancement

Characteristics of Satisfiers & Dissatisfiers

In understanding these findings, it is helpful to look at the characteristics of each grouping. Look at the Satisfiers. These relate to what a person does. They are very individual in nature (it's the individual's *own* sense of achievement; it's the recognition *he* or *she* receives, etc.). They seem to relate to that side of a person that says one is a growing, wanting animal who seeks opportunities to become more than what one was yesterday. They are difficult to satiate because as a person acquires additional experience, knowledge and skills, that person wants an opportunity to utilize these newly-acquired capabilities. Hence they seem to be unending in nature. For that reason we call them *motivators*.

Look at the Dissatisfiers. These seem to be administered on a group basis; we have policies that affect many people, we have supervisors who may direct many employees, etc. They seem to relate to that side of people that says they will take action in an attempt to avoid pain or discomfort. They might be termed "deficit" needs because their importance is felt only when they are absent. These needs can be satisfied, but they soon become dissatisfying experiences again. They seem to be cyclical in nature. For example, a company policy of providing 10 paid holidays may not be a dissatisfying item until the employees hear of another place where a company provides 11 holidays. When their own company changes its holiday plan from 10 to 11 holidays, the employees are not motivated, they are just no longer unhappy about their company's holiday policy. The deficit has been removed. But, chances are the employees will become unhappy about their holiday policy once again when they hear of another case where employees now receive 12 holidays. No matter how generously a manager may treat employees at one time, they will eventually feel that they deserve more.

Consequently, we see that the Dissatisfiers don't seem to motivate an employee, they merely seem to sustain or maintain. Because of these characteristics, these elements have been identified as "Hygiene" or "Maintenance" factors. Maintenance seems to be a good term for managers to use because we are all conscious of the necessity to maintain our physical assets. Unfortunately, we don't think about it often in the context of maintaining our human assets.

Two Key Messages

The reasons why Herzberg's findings became popular were two-fold:

1. We used to think that the things that caused people to be dissatisfied were the same things that caused people to be satisfied. Herzberg's research has begun to show us that what causes people to be happy or satisfied on the job are not the same things that cause people to be unhappy or dissatisfied on the job. You cannot substitute a satisfier for a dissatisfier.

It is not possible to find happiness by avoiding pain. Nor can a person avoid pain or discomfort by finding happiness. These are entirely different feelings or experiences. Therefore different approaches are required in order to maintain human beings and to motivate them.

2. For years, organizations have concentrated on the maintenance side of the picture. Over the years, more and more money is being spent for these items and less and less is being received in return. Now managers are beginning to see that the real payoff may be on the other side of the picture, the Motivators. In effect, a manager not only has to be concerned about *maintaining* his employees, he also has to be concerned about *motivating* his employees. Motivation comes from what he gives his people to do—the nature of the task.

Connection Between Maslow and Herzberg

A definite connection begins to appear between the approach developed by Maslow and the approach developed by Herzberg. If Maslow's hierarchy is placed on its side, an interesting relationship appears:

Maintenance	Motivators
Company Policies & Administration	Achievement
Supervision	Recognition
Working Conditions	Interesting Work
Interpersonal Relations	Responsibility
Money, Status & Security	Growth & Advancement

It becomes apparent that even though these two men may have approached the question of human needs from two different starting points, their findings begin to tie together. Because of the nature of man, a manager can never forget about those aspects of the work which meet man's lower-level needs (Maslow) or his maintenance needs (Herzberg). If they are not treated well, employees will become very disgruntled, unhappy, irritated and cause all sorts of problems in an organization.

If they *are* treated well, however, adding further maintenance items will not cause them to be motivated. To be motivated, they must have something motivating to do. Consequently, a manager must also provide an opportunity for each person to meet more individual needs—those relating to his desire for self-esteem and self-actualization (Maslow), or those which relate to the various elements listed under Herzberg's motivators.

A Manager's Two Roles

Herzberg's findings highlight the fact that every manager has two primary responsibilities, two hats to wear:

1. **Maintenance hat** —which is a reminder to keep employees from hurting—to keep them in "good repair" so to speak.
2. **Motivation hat** —which is a reminder to provide opportunities for employees to utilize their skills and capabilities—to develop, to grow.

The Achievement Motive—David McClelland

There is one aspect of human needs (found in Herzberg's list of Motivators), that has had perhaps more study than any other. It has to do with the achievement motive. Thanks to the work of David McClelland, we now know more about what causes some people to be highly motivated, to possess a great deal of energy, drive and enthusiasm—the people we call "achievers."

For years it was thought that achievers were fortunate individuals who had inherited certain traits or behavior patterns from their parents. The feeling was that only a small percentage of the people had these traits; most did not. Consequently, the task was to seek out these "special individuals" and bring them into the organization. If a company could assemble a group of achievers, it would have a tremendous asset and a definite advantage over competitors who weren't as lucky. It was felt that these certain highly-motivated people were achievers; i.e., that motivation led to achievement.

McClelland's Findings

As a result of McClelland's research, we now understand that highly-motivated people—the achievers—may act the way they do as a result of the overall environment in which they grew up or in which they now find themselves. The research findings seem to say that a person who has an opportunity to achieve will become motivated; i.e., achievement leads to motivation. If this is so, the question arises, "How can we create an opportunity for people to achieve?" There seem to be six key elements which provide an atmosphere for achievement:

1. **Set Own Goals** The individual has a say in what he is going to do and the methods he will use in doing it.
2. **Personal Responsibility** The individual has responsibility for attaining the goals she has helped to establish. She clearly understands her role and has control over the key variables. Other people don't interfere in what she is to do.

3. **Moderately Risky Goals** There is an element of chance or risk in what a person does. It is not too easy, nor is it too difficult. As a result there is some fun or a sense of success when the person makes it.

4. **Prompt and Meaningful Feedback** The individual receives information on how he is doing as he is doing it. The information he receives is in a format that is usable. It is received frequently enough so that the individual has an opportunity to make some adjustments in what he is doing, based on the clues he receives, as he is performing his task. Therefore he has an opportunity to improve as he goes along.

5. **Rewards and Recognition Tie-in** The rewards and recognition an individual receives have a direct relationship to her achievement or accomplishment. A major accomplishment results in a major reward or recognition; a minor accomplishment merely warrants a simple comment or pat on the back.

6. **Support and Encouragement When Desired** The individual receives help when he wants it. On the other hand, when he wants to do the job alone, he is left alone.

There are many examples of situations in business, in sports, and in off-hours activities where these elements exist. They seem to explain why some people are alive on the job while others seem to be "dead on their feet," or why some people who appear listless on the job suddenly become very energetic and active after work.

If these six elements in a job or environment cause people to begin to act like achievers, then the key to motivation lies in building these elements into the work situation. To the degree that work can be changed so that an individual can find all six elements on the job, he may begin to act in a more highly-motivated fashion. He may begin to act like an achiever.

THE ENVIRONMENT

The works of Maslow, Herzberg, and McClelland focus primarily on the nature of needs. They are helpful to managers in understanding the driving forces in each person's behavior. How each person acts—the choice of behavior—is determined by how he sees himself (his self-perception) and how he sees the situation he is in (his perception of the environment).

Although a manager can't do much to directly change an individual's perception of himself, she can change some of the elements in the environment. Therefore it's helpful for a manager to have some understanding of the impact of the work environment on individuals. The findings of Chris Argyris and Douglas McGregor focused on this aspect of motivation.

The Effect of Organization Structure—Argyris

One person who has done a considerable amount of research on the effect of organization structure on human behavior is Chris Argyris. Argyris has observed how people grow up in our society, how they seem to be trained and developed from childhood to adulthood, and how they seem to behave at work. One of his interesting analyses is the process which young children go through as they grow older and become mature adults. When children are very young they are frequently described in terms such as these:

Passive
Dependent
Subordinate
Submissive
Lack self control
Have a short time perspective
Have a short span of interest

Their parents, teachers, youth leaders, etc., help them to become mature adults. As adults, they are expected to change their behavior.

From that of a child	**To that of an adult**
Passive ⟶	Active. (Able to behave in many different ways.)
Dependent ⟶	Independent. (Learn to stand on your own two feet.)
Subordinate ⟶	Equal or Superior. (You're just as good as anyone else; in fact, even better than many.)
Submissive ⟶	Dominate (Don't let others push you around. Stand your ground. Be assertive.)
Lack Self-Control ⟶	Exercise self-control. (Get hold of yourself. Be a captain of your own destiny.)
Short time perspective ⟶	Long time perspective. (Learn to think ahead; think of tomorrow.)
Short span of interest ⟶	Long span of concentration. (Once you start something, finish it. Learn to stay with things.)

This seems to be the maturing process from childhood to adulthood. It is the general direction in which people move as they grow up in our society. When we examine how people act at work, we find that some people seem to be behaving as adults—they are active, independent, dominant, etc.—as they should be; yet others seem to be behaving like children—they are passive, dependent, lack self-control, etc. At first this might be attributed to the fact that some people never grow up. They continue to be children through all of their lives. These very same people, who act like children on the job, may act quite differently off the job or when placed in another job—they act like adults.

This raises an interesting point. Perhaps the childish behavior often seen on the job is not due to the inherent nature of the employees themselves (they are really only children); instead, it may be their reaction to the situation in which they have been placed. It could be a normal reaction to the unhealthy environment in which they find themselves; they have learned to act this way as a form of attack or withdrawal from a situation they view as negative, unpleasant demeaning, etc. The organization has not given them an opportunity to act like adults and, in fact, may be actually thwarting their opportunity to meet some of their higher-level needs. As a result, the organization is badly underutilizing its employees!

How to Change Employee Behavior

In organizations where employees have some control over their environment and are involved in some of the planning as to where, when and how they are going to do their jobs, they tend to behave in a more mature, adult fashion. This type of behavior is often seen among top management people. On the other hand, where employees have been thwarted in their desire to act like an adult, where they have very little involvement or control over their environment, where they are expected to "do or die and don't ask why," and to merely perform as an extension of a piece of equipment, they tend to behave in a much more childlike fashion. They either rebel and fight back or they withdraw and become apathetic, disinterested and detached.

These findings give managers some clues as to how they might change the behavior of their employees by changing the way they have organized the work environment. If they can build in a greater degree of involvement by their employees on the job, and if they can give their employees an opportunity to have more say on how to do their jobs, i.e., more control over their environment, their employees may begin to act in a much more positive, self-reliant, independent and mature fashion.

A Theory Bin

It has been noted that as we grow up, we seem to accumulate an array of ideas, theories, hunches and exceptions concerning ourselves and the world around us. Early in life each person begins to develop some ideas about self (what sort of person one is), and about one's system of values (what's good, what's bad; what's right, what's wrong, etc.) Each person also accumulates a great variety of notions about other people (what they are like and what can be expected from them). One may deduce that fat people are jolly, redheads have a temper, bankers are conservative, etc.

All of these ideas reside in the mind in a "theory bin," so to speak, and help to effectively deal with the various events and experiences encountered each day. They serve to speed reaction time to the world. One doesn't have to think through all of the various aspects of a situation. By having programmed thinking ahead of time, one can quickly react to whatever may be encountered. These theories, ideas and assumptions, which have accumulated over a person's lifetime, underlie behavior, sometimes consciously, but often unconsciously. They frequently get in the way of reality.

Ideas About Roles

When it comes to dealing with people, we find that a person's bin of accumulated theories is also a major factor in helping decide how to behave in different situations. One decides what role he should play based on his notions of what's expected by others and what can be expected of him in any given situation. Most people play many different roles in the course of a day. At different times during the same day, they may play the role of a subordinate, a manager, a peer or associate, a father or mother, a brother or sister, a spouse, and a son or a daughter. In each role a person may act differently based on what he or she believes is appropriate when wearing that "role hat." A person may act quite differently when "out with the boys or girls" (the role of a peer), than when chatting with a son or daughter about a poor report card (the role of the concerned parent).

When a person functions in the role of manager a person acts in certain ways based on what one believes a manager should do. Actions are also based on what one thinks his subordinates are like, how one sees them behave, and what one thinks they will or will not do in the future. Different people seem to act differently when they perform the role of a manager.

838

GUIDELINES TO CURRENT MOTIVATIONAL THEORIES

The Effect of Assumptions

Students attempted to find out why some managers organize their departments and treat their employees in certain ways, while other managers follow a different approach. What was found is that the differences in action were due to differences in assumptions or expectations that managers had about people. The notions about what people are like, which one manager carried around in that personal theory bin, were different from the notions held by another manager.

Some managers had a set of notions or expectations regarding people which were rather static and quite pessimistic. They can be summarized as follows:

- People are lazy.
- People do not want responsibility.
- People are indifferent to the needs of the organization.
- People resist change.

Because of these assumptions, managers felt that it was necessary for them to direct people's efforts, control their actions and reward and penalize them in order to get them to work as the manager desired. Consequently, when a person had to assume the role of a manager, the task was to exert external control—to do things *to the people* supervised in an attempt to modify their behavior. These sets of assumptions about people, which led to specific strategies of organizing and managing, McGregor classified as "Theory X."

Other managers, however, seemed to organize their departments and manage in a different way. When McGregor asked them "Why?" he heard a different set of notions about people which were much more dynamic and optimistic. They could be summarized as:

- People are not inherently lazy, but they may act that way at times.
- People do seek responsibility.
- People are concerned about the organization's needs to the degree that they are committed to them.
- People do not resist change, but they do resist *being* changed.

This set of assumptions, which McGregor labeled "Theory Y," resulted in a management approach which was much more adaptive and flexible. Instead of prejudging what people were like, the manager spent more time trying to find out what they were really like. He or she then attempted to manage in a way that made sense in view of what was found, i.e., to fit reality. Efforts were primarily designed toward the integration of the needs of the organization and those of the individual. In effect, the manager tried to *modify the environment* in order to enable individuals to have a greater say, more involvement, more opportunity for self-direction and self-control.

Whereas the manager who operated from a Theory X set of assumptions seemed to focus efforts on *modifying the people,* the manager who operated from the Theory Y set of assumptions focused efforts on *modifying the situation.* McGregor's contribution, therefore, was to help managers see how some of their own preconceived notions about people could affect the way they organize and manage. Different assumptions about people led to different ideas about managing. Therefore, if a manager was interested in changing his or her style of managing, a helpful starting point would be to examine basic notions and expectations about people. If one changed some of those ideas, one might, in fact, decide to manage in a different way.

The Self-Fulfilling Prophecy Phenomenon

One of the intriguing aspects of McGregor's findings is the phenomenon of the self-fulfilling prophecy. What he found is that the way a manager feels about another individual's abilities, reliability, commitment, etc., is frequently communicated to that other person through not only the words the manager uses, but also through gestures, facial expressions, tone of voice and many similar subtle clues. In effect, a manager "telegraphs" to another person some personal expectations of that person. These telegraphed signals tend to tell the other person how to act and that person acts accordingly. In essence, people tend to become what is expected of them; they tend to live up to the expectations of others. If a person is treated as if he or she were stupid, lazy, irresponsible, etc., the person tends to act that way. If one is treated as intelligent, ambitious, responsible, the person tends to act *that* way.

In summary, what McGregor found is that a manager may prophesy how subordinates will act and "telegraph" that prophecy by revealing feelings about them. Based on these "signals" from their boss, the subordinates begin to act according to how they believe their boss expects them to act. The manager then says, "See, I told you that's how they would act." In effect the prophecy has come true. The manager is now convinced that subordinates are acting as prophesied.

A Key Point To Consider

The essential message to a manager from McGregor's findings is that the behavior seen may be a direct result of the way in which one is managing people—a developed management style. That style is based on underlying assumptions about people. The manager telegraphs these assumptions or expectations to subordinates in all sorts of ways. If a manager wants to change the way people are behaving, it may be necessary to start with assumptions about people and how these assumptions may be affecting style of managing. The key question is, to what extent is he or she seeing a self-fulfilling prophecy at work? If one starts with some of the same assumptions about self and applies these to others, will one manage in a different way? In order to change employee behavior, a manager may first have to start with his or her own notions about other people.

CHANGING BEHAVIOR

The works of Chris Argyris and Douglas McGregor have helped managers to look at *how* they organize, the impact organization structure has on employee behavior, and the effect their own assumptions about people have on their strategies of organizing and managing.

If they changed some of their notions about people, they would organize and manage in a different way, and as a result might bring about a change in the behavior of their employees. Behavioral change however, appears to occur quite slowly.

The Elements of Change—Rensis Likert

Changing employee behavior is a difficult thing to do. Rensis Likert has described what seems to occur. Managers attend courses or read books on the behavioral sciences. Then they decide to try some new approaches in an effort to bring about an improvement in the way their employees act on the job. After the first few attempts, there are frequently no tangible results. Consequently, many managers give up. They conclude that the information they acquired in the training course or from the book was too theoretical, not practical, or not appropriate for their particular situation. Therefore, they quickly revert back to their old style of managing. The work of Rensis Likert has given us some insight as to why tangible results are often so difficult to observe.

A Sequence of Events

Likert has noted that the end result of any activity is usually measured in the form of some type of criteria: dollars, units produced, percentages, etc. In a large number of organizations, the measurement of success is the profit and loss report. Let's indicate that by the dollar symbol—$.

This end result ($) is directly attributed to the combined efforts of a group of .people working together, either efficiently or inefficiently, in an attempt to accomplish certain goals and objectives. It's the group's behavior on the job. This step might be diagramed as follows:

Group
Behavior ――――――――――――――――――――→ $

The way a group of people behaves is based on how all of them view the situation in which they find themselves, their perception of their environment.

Group's
Perception ―――――――――→ Group ―――――――――→ $
of the   Behavior
Environment

A major determinant of the environment is the way the place is being managed; i.e., the management style in effect.

                              Group's
Management ――――→ Perception ――――→ Group ――――→ $
  Style   of the   Behavior
                           Environment

In an attempt to change the behavior of a group of employees, managers often start with the employees themselves. They try different means by urging them, exhorting them, and enticing them to act differently. The way employees are acting, however, is based on their perceptions of the environment; and their perceptions are based on how the place is being run. Therefore, if a manager is going to change employee behavior, he or she must start at the *beginning* of the whole process, which is management style.

The Time Lag

Unfortunately, Likert's process doesn't work as easily as all that. A manager may try to change style, but until employees begin to *see* the difference and perceive it as a real difference, not a new gimmick or a game, they will not change their behavior. Because of past experience, having been kidded or conned before by latest fads after their manager attended a training course or read a book, many employees may be quite suspicious of what they see and may not believe that any change has really occurred. Because of this skepticism, a manager has to continue to operate in this "new style" for quite a period of time, even when no results are seen at first, in order to add credibility and assurance that it represents a real change. Only when the employees finally see it as a change will they decide to act in a different way, based on their new perception of the situation. It will be even later before the new perception held by the employees begins to be reflected in any tangible results. In some large organizations, it may take as many as five, six or seven years before a conscientious attempt to change management style is finally picked up in something as concrete and measurable as the profit and loss column, units produced, waste reports, etc. In smaller organizations, the time lag might be much less.

The Need for Sensors

The time lag phenomenon would seem to indicate that managers have to operate with a great amount of blind faith that eventually their change in management style will pay off. However, most managers know that in the competitive business world, they had better have something more concrete than "blind faith." Actually, there are some monitoring or sensing factors that managers can use to tell how they're doing and in what direction their organization may be moving. By creating a self-examining organization where readings are continuously being taken as to how management actions are being received and interpreted by employees, i.e., how people perceive the situation, managers can have an on-going reading of the direction in which their organization is going. To use an analogy from the computer field, the organization begins to operate in "real time"—continuously sensing the actions, reactions, attitudes and feelings of its human resources and modifying its own actions as a result of this feedback. Perceptions of the environment are actually leading indicators of what will follow at a later time. Therefore, managers who spend more time receiving and interpreting what these perceptions are, will have a much clearer picture of where they are heading and how well their organization is functioning. They don't need to operate in a vacuum, to operate on blind faith. The clues and cues which employees are always sending forth will give them some measurements of whether or not they are on course.

The Manager As A "Linking Pin"

To be successful as a "sensor" of a change, a manager must serve as the main link between his or her group of employees and the rest of the organization. The manager must really serve in two different roles, as the communication link downward and as the communication link upward. The manager is the channel for information to subordinates concerning organizational goals, objectives, policies and practices. On the other hand, he or she is the channel for information to superiors concerning the needs, goals and feelings of subordinates. In effect, the manager is a leader of the work team and a member of the boss's work team. He or she is a "linking pin" between the two.

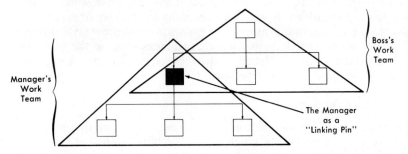

Managers who see themselves in this two-fold role are better able to keep abreast of the gradual changes in their employees' perceptions and behaviors.

Summary

If a manager is going to successfully motivate other people, he must have a sound knowledge of the basic findings from behavioral research. Studying in more detail the works of the six men mentioned in this chapter, examining the findings of many additional behavioral scientists, and staying up to date on new behavioral findings and applications will help prepare the manager for the most difficult, yet most rewarding, aspect of the job.

CHAPTER 35

A CASE STUDY: SELECTING NEW SUPERVISORS

By David G. Coverdale, Director-Industrial Relations, for the Kearney & Trecker Corporation, of Milwaukee, Wisconsin.

IN 1976 Kearney & Trecker studied supervisory needs of the Corporation based upon growth and attrition. It was anticipated that several new supervisors would be required in each 12-month period from 1976 through 1981. This was prior to the Age Discrimination Act which raised the mandatory retirement age for Kearney & Trecker employees from 65 to 70.

There are five basic steps in the successful process of selecting new supervisors. These steps are: (1) Determining the need for future supervisors, (2) Developing specifications for the positions to be filled, (3) Recruiting candidates, (4) Screening candidates, and (5) Communicating with those selected and not selected.

I. Determining the Need for Future Supervisors

Many sources provide information with which to predict the number of supervisors needed in the future. They include: (1) Mandatory retirements, (2) Voluntary retirements, (3) Terminations due to death, resignation and discharge, (4) Promotions and transfers, (5) Planned growth of the organization, and (6) Seasonal and marketing fluctuations.

The Age Discrimination Act of 1979 has, for most organizations, prohibited mandatory retirement prior to age 70, a change for those who previously used age 65 for mandatory retirement. If your organization has a mandatory age at which supervisors are required to retire, factual data can be readily obtained. All organizations, even those without computers, can check birthdates of supervisors to determine the year and month in which they will retire.

For example, at the Kearney and Trecker Corporation an annual computer printout of all management employees is provided to the training and employment departments. This printout shows each employee's birthdate, division, department, date eligible for early retirement, and date of attainment of age 70. From these data, it is simple to determine who will retire each year. Of course, all supervisory retirements may not create an opening in the supervisory ranks. Management may decide, for example, to combine functions previously supervised by two individuals. Where it is known that one or more replacements will be needed, the list of future needs has begun.

Voluntary Retirements, because they are at the option of those supervisors who have met the necessary criteria, cannot be predicted with certainty. However, projections may be made from information available.

In larger organizations, actuarial data or statistics may be used to predict voluntary retirements. Companies can analyze past voluntary retirements related to age, length of service, financial situation, attainment of maximum retirement benefits and personal health data when known. They can then project with reasonable accuracy how many supervisors will voluntarily retire in a given year.

Smaller organizations, without the data collections system of larger ones, may have an advantage. It is closer personal contact with supervisors. This day-to-day contact allows management to be informed when supervisors are contemplating early retirement. This can come about through periodic performance appraisals or casual conversation. All organizations should be alert to such signs of early retirement contemplation as:

- Exploration of actual retirement benefits.
- Significant changes in personal finances.
- Changes for the worse in health of the employee or spouse.
- Consideration of purchasing property in another area.
- Date the last child leaves home, gets married or graduates.
- Achievement of maximum pensions benefits.

These and other clues can lead managment to explore with the supervisor any plans for early retirement.

Deaths cannot be projected with accuracy. Actuarial statistics can aid organizations in estimating how many supervisors in specific age brackets will die in a given year. Also, the current health of supervisors will provide some clues. At best, this is an educated guess, but a projection to consider.

Resignations, too, are somewhat unpredictable. Unlike voluntary retirement candidates, supervisors contemplating resignation tend to be secretive about plans, fearing retaliation if the news is released that they plan to quit.

A CASE STUDY: SELECTING NEW SUPERVISORS

Resignation contemplation is less likely where supervisors are properly compensated and well motivated. In considering the likelihood of resignations from your supervisory team, study your compensation programs, looking for supervisors who perceive themselves to be compensated unfairly.

Secondly, look to the nonmotivated supervisors. Symptoms to watch for include:

- Lack of promotional growth in a significant time period.
- Budget performance problems on a sustained basis.
- Constant dissatisfaction exhibited by poor performance, negative attitudes and frequent complaints.
- Friction with peers, subordinates and superiors.

While these are not all the signs, they indicate the attitude and behavior pattern that could result in resignation.

Armed with information collected on "unhappy" supervisors, do not leap to the conclusion they are all candidates to take employment elsewhere. Actually, few will move, and as the length of service increases, likelihood of resignation decreases with the possible exception of those in the 50–60 age bracket. When most or all children have left home, employees may decide to change organizations, particularly when improved climate is a consideration. Middle and upper-level managers often pick up clues of these upcoming resignations.

Discharges are more predictable from the organization's view because the company makes the decision on whom to release and when. However, these decisions are sometimes immediate because of malfeasance, insubordination or dishonesty. Also certain discharges may be postponed for reasons such as lack of successor, health problems, employee morale, and reluctance to make unpleasant decisions.

By carefully examining terminations due to death, resignations and discharges, an organization can fairly closely predict the number of future supervisors needed.

Some supervisors may be promoted to higher level management or transferred to other supervisory or nonsupervisory jobs. Regarding promotion, an organization needs to study middle and upper-level positions to predict turnover here. Which jobs will be filled from among present supervisors and how many openings will this create? As to transfers (including demotion), the organization must study performance levels of present supervisors and predict supervisory openings created by job changes.

Growth in sales, products or services and number of clients or markets should be reviewed. Organizations must determine the manpower, capital and other resources required to create and maintain their growth. It is the amount of each that will help determine the need for new supervision. For example, if 30 new employees will be required on each of two shifts, the organization must determine the number of new supervisors required. Planning should include new supervisors to carry out growth plans.

In the canning industry, seasonal factors indicate peak employment and production. In vegetable canning in Wisconsin, late summer and fall are peak periods. Fruit packing in California also has seasonal requirements. If additional supervision is required for peak periods organizations must plan accordingly.

II. Developing Specifications for the Positions to be Filled

I. What makes an effective supervisor motivated and growth oriented?

Some factors are, proper pay and treatment, status, training and development, number of people and amount of equipment and geography he or she can be expected to effectively supervise, and responsibility and equivalent authority.

Quantum jumps in the capability and performance of a total management team are possible through the overall improvement of the supervisor and other first-level managers.

The largest cause of the very poor first level of management today is senior management. The first-level manager-supervisor is the alpha and omega of the management structure. The supervisor-first-level manager is the amplifier or the choke point of all ideas, instructions and information of higher management up to and including the CEO. He/she amplifies, interprets, passes on and implements information from higher management; or lets it die; or worse still, allows it to be misinterpreted.

Minimum requirements to be an effective first-line supervisor are:

1. Ability and willingness to accept the fact that personal performance must be through his/her employees. The supervisor must accept the fact that he/she can never be any better than the composite capability and attitude of employees.
2. The supervisor must understand, speak and write the language of employees as well as the language of peers and the boss.
3. The supervisor must demonstrate leadership abilities.
4. The supervisor must be a good listener.
5. The supervisor must be a good communicator—with employees, peers, and the boss.

6. The supervisor must be willing to take an unpopular position when necessary.

7. The supervisor should enjoy the role of being "the boss." One can never be an effective supervisor unless one truly enjoys the job of being the boss.

8. The supervisor must have good coaching abilities, since training and developing employees is one of the most important responsibilites.

9. The supervisor must understand and accept the responsibility for safety, health and performance of each employee.

10. The supervisor must accept the responsibility for all activities in his/her area—employees, equipment, schedules, production, cost, quality, and housekeeping.

11. The supervisor must keep employees, peers, and the boss informed regarding all work activities for which he or she is responsible.

He/she must be able to pass the following test:

1. *Wants* to be an effective supervisor—demonstrated *desire*.

2. *Has* the demonstrated *ability* to be an effective supervisor.

3. *Has* the demonstrated *will* and determination to be an effective supervisor.

III. Recruiting Candidates

Once needs are determined, and specifications established, the process becomes one of uncovering candidates. Two basic sources of candidates for supervision are: external candidates (those from outside the organization) and internal candidates (present employees of the organization).

Every organization should consider both sources to be sure it is not limiting qualifications of supervisory candidates. A good principle to follow: Consider as many candidates as practical in order to pick the best.

The cliché "new blood" is trite, perhaps, but the concept it conveys is valid. Organizations which never hire supervisors or managers from outside risk the ills of ancient European monarchies. The external labor force provides well-educated, technically-trained, properly-motivated candidates who, if selected, bring fresh experiences and ideas to the organization. They are not stifled with the NIH syndrome (*Not Invented Here*) and are more likely to experiment, try new ideas, create new ideas, or retry ideas once rejected that may have become workable.

The sources of external candidates are enormous. To list a few: newspaper advertisements, trade journal advertisements, college campus recruiting, professional societies, co-op programs, college or high-school level, employee referral, professional employment or executive search firms, governmental placement agencies, and unsolicited applications—walk-ins or mail-ins.

A word of caution, however. When jobs are scarce and applicants plentiful, if you advertise or use an employment agency, be sure your specifications are clear so you prescreen applicants who are unsuited or unqualified. An ad, for example, headed, "Supervisory Trainees" will, in a slack labor market, elicit many unqualified candidates. By heading the ad, "Supervisors—Experienced," and listing tight criteria for qualification, you prescreen many and improve the group from which you select.

Most organizations prefer to promote from within. This has proven practical and effective for many, if not followed slavishly. Most organizations find a proper balance of promotion from within and the selective recruiting of external candidates keeps the organization at its peak. At the first-line supervisory level, however, promotion from within is usually the best approach.

Some organizations have used their present supervisory and higher-level management people to recruit candidates from the non-supervisory work force. They are asked to recommend workers they feel would be good supervisors. Criteria have typically been high productivity, long seniority and cooperative attitude.

This approach eliminates many candidates who might become successful supervisors. Present supervisors are often a "bad screen" who select some people lacking in one of the three criteria of productivity, seniority, and cooperative attitude.

A better approach (and easier to justify) is to publicize the openings and encourage anyone interested to apply. It's also a good idea to tell your present supervisors to *encourage* application by those subordinates they feel would be good candidates. The objective is to recruit *anyone* who has a strong desire to be a supervisor.

A description of the supervisory job gives employees a good idea of what they are applying for and requirements that go with it.

There are two basic approaches for recruiting internal candidates: (1) Post the job opening on bulletin boards and have those who are interested apply at the personnel department. (2) Send a letter and application blank to the homes of all employees and have them complete application blanks and return it to the personnel department, if interested.

A CASE STUDY: SELECTING NEW SUPERVISORS

Keep in mind the fundamental principle of recruiting. Recruit those who have a strong desire for the job. And within reason, the more candidates the better.

IV. Screening Candidates

Screening is a matter of comparing the candidates to the job specifications and selecting the best fit. To screen candidates is to "screen out" candidates until the best remain, and then decide which of the best, if any, will be selected. "If any" is significant, because a common trap many fall into is to select the last remaining candidate to come through the screen, even if that candidate did not meet all specifications. There might be more qualified candidates that the recruiting process did not turn up. Therefore, screening not only helps decide which candidate should be selected, but also determines if we must go on recruiting more candidates.

There are many approaches for screening candidates. Each has good points and limitations. An effective screening process uses several methods, probably the more the better. But time, money, and qualified screeners necessitate a practical instead of an ideal approach. A list of possible screening techniques and sources of data would include the following: Personnel File (application blank showing age, experience, education, and other data), educational records, transcripts, military records, present and past supervisors in your organization (information on performance, dependability, leadership qualities, etc.), outside activities (professional organizations, churches, community groups, evidence of leadership?), union activity (evidence of leadership?), personal interview (to determine knowledge, attitudes, desires, etc.), reference checks employment: getting information on past job performance, personal: getting information on character, personality, etc., tests (to determine knowledge, intelligence, interests, personality, etc.), medical records, evaluation by outside psychologists and other professionals, and assessment centers.

NOTE: Care must be taken to comply with the requirements of the Equal Employment Opportunity Commission (EEOC).

Some selection specifications, such as age, education and previous work history may readily be determined from forms already on file such as the application blank. Other criteria, however, such as intelligence, aptitude, knowledge of management principles and their application, must be measured by other means. People trained and qualified to administer and interpret tests can provide data for some of these characteristics. The value of these tests depends on their validity, which means that responses and scores *must relate to job performance.* The competency of the test administrators is also important. Also, the tests *must not discriminate* against any legally-defined minority group.

Insights into personality may well be gained from analyzing past performance, references, performance evaluations and the interview. These methods may have more validity than personality tests, especially if accurate and honest data are available. Health status may be determined from medical records. Management abilities such as leadership can be evaluated by analyzing the individual's performance in leadership roles at work and off the job. An applicant's attitude may be determined by an analysis of job performance as well as by a personal interview.

One of the newest and most sophisticated approaches to selection is the Assessment Center. The continuing search to find a better way to predict future performance in a particular job led to development and extensive use of assessment centers by many organizations. The basic idea is to provide a simulation of the situations new supervisors face. Candidates go through a series of activities and challenges while trained observers assess their conduct to predict how the candidates would behave in real situations. According to William Byham, writing in the *Harvard Business Review,* companies use assessment centers when one of three situations affects promotional decisions:

1. Where it is difficult to make comparative judgments because candidates are evaluated by different people who have varying standards and are in varying local situations, e.g., promoting from insurance salesman to management.
2. Where it is impossible or impractical to assess all qualities needed because job requirements of the positions from which the candidates are drawn differ from those of the position to be filled, e.g., promoting from most manufacturing positions to foreman.
3. Where it is not possible for the person making the decision to personally evaluate or know the candidates' abilities in the areas of concern, e.g., hiring . . . from the outside.

Assessment centers can be effective in these situations because all candidates who are assessed:

1. Have an equal opportunity to display their talents.
2. Are seen under similar conditions in situations which are designed to bring out their particular skills and abilities that fit them for the position under consideration, and

A CASE STUDY: SELECTING NEW SUPERVISORS

3. Are evaluated by a team of trained assessors who are unbiased by past associations and who are familiar with the new position's requirements.

By far the largest application of the assessment center approach, according to Byham is in selecting applicants for first-level management positions. In these situations, the company is primarily interested in estimating managerial potential even though such centers may also produce training and development recommendations. The unique method of the assessment center is the *simulation exercise.* In it, actual conditions—whether for a present or future job—are simulated. While the participants perform the simulated exercise, their behavior is carefully observed by line or staff superiors.

The following steps are typically followed in the assessment center procedure:

1. *The company defines its purposes and expectations.*

There are many questions that need clear answers right here: What kind of behavior is required for effective performance on the first-level supervisor's job? What personal qualities and background are required? Now? Later? What specific uses are to be made of the findings of the assessment center: hiring, promotion, determination of training needs, counseling?

2. *Appropriate simulation exercises and activities are developed.*

Because you have already developed the elements of behavior required by the supervisory job, you must next select available simulations which will elicit those behaviors in your assessment center. If standardized and validated exercises are not available, you must custom-build your own. Often this requires the input of a psychologist because not only must a specific ability be identified and the activity designed to simulate this behavior on the job, but also the validity of this simulation should be experimentally or statistically made sure of.

3. *Observers are trained.*

Senior managers (usually two ranks above the participants) are then trained in observing the way the candidates act in response to the exercises. Such training most usually consists of a workshop. The observers learn about the assessment center technique, become familiar with the actual content of exercises, and by role-playing and, where possible, watching video tapes of their own performance, improve their skills in observing behavior of others. Those who have done it verify that skilled observing is neither a simple nor a casual matter. In the assessment process, the observer is trained to focus on very specific behaviors to show the presence or the absence of such predefined supervisory qualities.

4. *Candidates complete activities and exercises in the assessment center.*

The participants in one group should be selected on the homogeneity of their organizational level, e.g., all nonsupervisory employees who are candidates for the first-level supervisory job. The actual process in the assessment center may take one, two or even three days, depending on the objectives, the experience and expertise of the observers, and the time available for the task. The procedure might run like this:

- Get written applicant background information. This might include usual employment data plus reasons for wanting this supervisory position. The fact that this is repetitious of prior application information is not limiting because the willingness to do such things becomes part of the test itself.

- Have a leaderless discussion by the candidates as a group. Pose some realistic management problem, then let the group initiate discussion and carry it to some solution within prescribed time limits. Note who emerges as the leader, the talker, the follower, or the nonparticipant.

- Provide an "in-basket" exercise. Here it is possible to find out individual orientations to a variety of problems posed. Note participants' ability to determine relative importance of items as well as techniques of organizing material.

- Have a planned luncheon. Get several applicants together with one evaluator in an unstructured atmosphere to see how they interact with one another.

- Answer a questionnaire. Provide an exercise in solving of a key management problem. Candidates work as individuals on such pencil-and-paper tasks.

- Provide business games for teams. Roles are assigned by positions within the company organization (Manager, Vice-President, Engineer and the like) for a specific problem involving input by each position. Observe not only how problems are solved, but how interpersonal relationships are handled.

- Speak to the group. Each participant makes an oral presentation to all others in defense of a product, a budget or some organizational matter. Each will speak extemporaneously, from limited information provided, and for a specific, short period of time.

- Give psychological tests. (*This is an optional procedure*). Company or outside psychologist may be used. Due regard to EEO strictures must be observed—mainly that the qualities looked for are related to job performance on that supervisory job and that all applicants are treated exactly the same.

- Have in-depth interviews. Using a patterned-interview technique, have an experienced interviewer get as much information as possible to make the same predictive evaluation made on job applicants from outside.

5. *The trained observers discuss the candidates*

After participants have completed their assessment procedures, they are dismissed from the center while the panel of assessors meets. During the assessment process, each observer had been assigned specific participants to watch during each exercise. By the conclusion of that exercise, each observer had watched each participant for some of the time. Now panel members share their observations and discuss each participant's behavior in detail.

Panel discussions specify the strengths, limitations, needed areas for growth, and long-range potential of each participant. The panel's *findings* on each participant are then assembled by one designated observer who, in addition, becomes responsible for explaining results of the experience to the participants.

6. *Results are communicated to the candidates.*

Shortly after concluding the exercise period, each participant will have a "feedback session" with his designated observer. The observer will give the participant the panel's specific observations of his or her behavior during the process. How well he or she interprets this behavior depends on the observer's experience, knowledge, insight and communications skill. But, in any event, the participant is entitled to get a helpful reflection of his or her own behavior during the assessment center period. The evaluation of other candidates is not discussed.

7. *The evaluations are fed into the screening process.*

Then the organization makes its determination of the successful candidate for the supervisory opening using the assessment center results as another—probably major—tool.

An assessment center cannot produce or reveal supervisory caliber people if they do not already exist within the organization. But it can pinpoint and identify such prospects if they are there. The assessment center concept, involving as it does the method of simulation to elicit behavior critical to the supervisor's job, essentially increases any company's professionalization in its manpower development area. Under examination as to its validity, and looking at the experience of companies who have used it, the assessment center method stands strong as a significant tool for use in an organization's selection procedure.

In summary, a number of different techniques should be used to help predict future performance. Factual data should be supplemented with interviews, tests, performance appraisals and other devices or techniques such as the assessment center. If the organization does not have people qualified to assess the qualifications of applicants, ouside professional help should be used.

Almost every company—large or small—has its stated nondiscrimination policy. Top management has declared there shall be no discrimination in hiring, training, promotion, transfer, layoff or discharge by reason of race, creed, color, national origin, sex, age or handicap. Management means it and trusts the policy will be observed.

Frequently, such policies are carefully observed in the hiring process. But race discrimination and sex discrimination are too often given scant attention in the procedures usually used for the selection of new supervisors. One recent review by the government showed that *less than one percent* of the "officials and managers" in the U.S. manufacturing industries were black. As a result of such findings, certain government agencies, as well as the courts, have been looking critically at any selection procedures which may be less than equal.

The Bakke Case and, more recently, the Weber Case involve claims of discrimination and reverse discrimination. These highly-publicized cases indicate some of the EEO areas which management must know about when they develop and use any internal selection procedure.

Among principal agencies of the government involved in compliance processes are EEOC (Equal Employment Opportunity Commission), OFCC (Office of Federal Contract Compliance), and various states' EEO commissions. Their findings and decisions, in turn, have been monitored by courts up to and including the U.S. Supreme Court. By this process, the most common problems of discrimination have been identified as: (1) Failure to let employees know there are opportunities for promotion from within. (2) Relying solely on the nomination of first-line supervisors. (Bethlehem Steel case) (3) Failure to provide uniform, published standards for selection. (Rowe vs. General Motors) (4) Using vague or subjective selection standards. (Savannah Sugar Refining Company case) (5) Using tests that are not limited to "job-related tasks." (Duke Power Company and Georgia Power Company cases)

In the supervisory selection process, job-related evaluation of applicants (whether by test, interview or otherwise) not only can be in compliance with equal employment opportunity laws, but is also a sure way of selecting well-qualified supervisors for the future.

Some suggestions, offered by Professor William E. Fulmer of the Harvard Graduate School of Business Administration,* which will help managements minimize chances of discriminating against minorities are:

- Develop formal procedures that have adequate checks and balances to preclude any individual from biasing the outcome of the process.
- Identify job-related criteria that are to be used in the selection process, making the criteria as objective as possible.
- If tests are used in the selection process, make sure they have been validated.
- Communicate to all employees how the selection process works and how one can be considered for supervision.
- Make the selection system as open as possible. By enabling employees to nominate themselves, it is possible to ensure that no one is intentionally or unintentionally excluded from consideration and that only interested people are considered.
- Monitor the system so as to ensure that the procedures are being followed consistently and that affirmative action goals are being achieved.
- If minorities and women seem reluctant to apply for supervisory openings, encourage those with supervisory potential to apply.
- Document each promotion decision, including the identification of people considered and the reasons for rejection.

Each organization, when it is about to set up its new selection and training procedure, can probably avoid making changes in that program later by advance planning in this sensitive EEO area. One way for management to quickly "get a handle" on its internal practices is to review its procedures against this checklist. This list—developed from current laws and decisions (1979)—emphasizes what employers SHOULD and SHOULD NOT do in this process of selecting new supervisors.

What Employers *Should* Do

1. Determine in advance what minimum standards to apply, then apply them uniformly.
2. Check the promotion standards against the employees who are currently on the supervisory job.

Personnel Magazine, November-December 1976, page 45. American Management Association.

3. Publicize the job openings in order that *all* employees may learn about the opportunity to become a supervisor.

4. Process and evaluate *every* employee who applies for promotion consideration.

5. Base promotion selection on objective factors which measure job-related potential.

6. Use prior job performance records if supervisory job performance requires such background.

7. Use physical standards only if they are specifically required by the supervisory job. If physical exams are given, they must be given uniformly to all candidates.

8. Make complete records of your contacts, discussions, requests and responses to all candidates. Keep such records—on ALL applicants—male and female, minority and nonminority—in exactly the same way.

9. Document your reason for selection of the candidate chosen.

10. Advise all employees who were NOT selected of the reason why and be sure to keep the records on file of those reasons for nonselection. You may recommend to those who have failed what they may do to improve their chances in the future.

What Employers *Should Not* Do

1. Do not yield to stereotyping of race, color, sex, age or handicaps as a limiting factor. (Example: Women are only interested in this job until they get married.)

2. Do not use different standards for different applicants.

3. Do not close the line of promotion to any minority or to either sex.

4. Do not base selections on purely subjective standards (such as "loyalty").

5. Do not use "attitude" tests or other standards for promotion which are not related to the job which is being filled.

6. Do not give preferential consideration by allowing some to take tests a second time or to be reinterviewed, unless all candidates are given the same opportunity.

7. Do not set up practices that limit candidates from consideration (such as "experience in the field" as a prerequisite—women employees are rarely sent out into the field).

8. Do not automatically reject a handicapped person unless the job requires specific physical characteristics and those requirements are being met by the present supervisors.

9. Do not bar an applicant who "failed" from trying again in the future when you announce another opening.

V. Communicating with Candidates

It is important to communicate with candidates as they progress or are eliminated during the selection process. Experience at several major companies has shown, for example, that the number of candidates who complete all of the requirements of the selection program may be as little as 60–70% of those who initially apply.

The organization must decide at what intervals it will communicate with the applicants as well as the method to use. Each organization must constantly be aware that possibly some rejected candidates are still employees and positive attitudes are important. Particularly for organizations with consumer products, external candidates are also potential customers, as well as stockholders, community leaders and possible future employees. How and when to communicate with rejected candidates must be a well-planned program.

Exhibit A provides guidelines to use in communicating. They should be modified if necessary to fit specific organizations.

In some organizations, the selection process will actually pick the person to be promoted. In other organizations, the process will select a pool of candidates to be trained and ready to take over a supervisory position if they are finally picked. Candidates in the pool are not promised a supervisory job. They have passed the screening and have been declared "potential supervisors." But they must wait until an opening occurs and the position is offered.

The Personnel Department and line management have jointly developed and implemented the screening process. They generally agree the candidates could handle supervisory positions. When the opening actually occurs, line management has the responsibility and authority to pick a specific candidate for the specific opening. Information on all candidates will be carefully studied by the appropriate line managers.

Line manager will look at experience, technical knowledge, skills, performance appraisals, medical records and any other data which will help match the applicant to a job. They will probably conduct a personal interview with the best candidates to determine attitudes and other personal qualifications. They should look at the present compensation of the worker and compare it with the compensation

EXHIBIT A
COMMUNICATING WITH CANDIDATES

Situation	WHEN	HOW	TO WHOM
1.	After all applications for the program have been received (cut-off date).	Letter from person who received applications acknowledging receipt, and outlining selection	All applicants.
2.	Seven days prior to the date set for any step in the process.	Notices reminding candidate of event, when, where, etc.	All applicants remaining in process.
3.	Immediately following a candidate's failure to appear or qualify in a step in the process.	Letter confirming the applicant's failure to appear or to qualify and informing him of a make-up date, if any, or dropping him/her from further consideration.	All candidates who do not complete all steps of the selection process.
4.	Immediately after completion of the selection process.	Letter confirming the candidate's completion of the process and informing him/her how and when final selection will be made.	All remaining candidates.
5.	When selection is made.	Letter to successful candidates informing them of their selection.	All those selected.
6.	When selection is made.	Letter to unsuccessful candidates notifying them of who was selected, and what they can do to prepare for the next opportunity. Also, information on whom they can talk with to find out why they weren't selected.	All those rejected.

they can offer for the new position. In other words, they will make the final selection and offer on the basis of all available data.

A major goal of this chapter is to provide a practical approach to the selection of new supervisors. From the examples given, an organization should be able to select the approaches and methods on which to build a successful program. The first step is to carefully and systematically determine the number of new supervisors needed. Next, specifications must be established for screening the candidates. Using the internal and external sources available, candidates will be recruited. By applying the specifications of the open positions to the qualifications of the candidates, the best candidates can be selected. Finally, communication with successful and unsuccessful candidates is important in order to support good customer and/or community relations, sustain interest in the program for the future, document the personnel files of the candidates, and maintain high morale among all employees.

CHAPTER 36

MORE THAN 120 IDEAS
FOR CUTTING COSTS

IN THIS CHAPTER are more than 120 suggestions for cutting costs in the administration of an office.

All of the methods and the short-cuts recorded here have been tested on the firing line of practical experience. They were gleaned from surveys and reports conducted by The Dartnell Corporation over a period of years.

Some of the suggestions can be put into practice with immediate savings in any office. Others are more appropriate for the small office; still others are tailored to the largest enterprises.

Not all of the suggestions can promise immediate savings of X dollars and X cents—some even require the investment of money in new equipment or remodeled working space before savings can be realized.

The topics presented were not arranged in any particular order or sequence. This was done deliberately. It is the hope of Dartnell's editors that the most significant purpose this chapter can serve is to make office administrators, managers, and supervisors *think creatively* about their own methods and procedures. The best creative thinking, psychologists say, is apt to occur in an atmosphere away from the immediate problem. Studies have shown that ideas for solutions to problems of filing, for example, may occur while thinking about office environmental problems, and vice versa.

Thus, the best way to read this chapter might be simply to browse among the suggestions, receptive to the spark of an idea which might solve a problem in your own operations *entirely unrelated* to the particular item you were reading.

There are other suggestions, of course, which you may want to follow "right out the window." What worked for others (and all of these ideas did) could well work for you!!

Review your insurance programs for possible savings. Installation of a sprinkler system might cut your fire insurance premiums drastically. Compare the premiums you pay for collision insurance on a company fleet with the claims collected in the past. You may want to cut out this protection or go to a higher deductible basis and a lower premium. Don't insure parcel-post shipments automatically; limit to really valuable shipments.

Does your company make contributions to organizations which may not be all they pretend? Baker Properties, Inc., of Minneapolis cut its contributions by $750 annually by investing in one employee the authority to OK contributions. Fast-talking "boiler room" salesmen for dubious organizations were eliminated, including those who misled the firm previously by pretending an officer of the firm had authorized an ad. The centralized control permits checking and verification.

One plant foreman used prominent signs to peg the exact dollars-and-cents value of scrapped materials, and the cost of each rejected unit. In this way he impressed upon his employees that production alone is not the only profit measure. Production might be good, but costs could be out of line because of excessive rejects or wasted materials.

Work assignments should be brought to people at their desks, instead of permitting people to go after work. While there may be exceptions to this rule, it is most efficient to deliver supplies, work, and all other materials to each desk.

Assemble all the office printing now done piecemeal and show it all to your printer. Ask him to "gang up" the pieces so that most of them can be printed on one sheet in one press run. The savings achieved over a year on letterheads, purchase orders, memo forms,

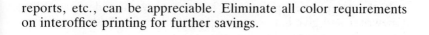

reports, etc., can be appreciable. Eliminate all color requirements on interoffice printing for further savings.

Check outgoing mail and see if more window-type envelopes can be used. Much duplicate addressing will be avoided.

Savings of time are possible in writing bills of lading by using continuous forms on an electric typewriter. An attachment holds the carbon paper instead of the typist inserting it between sheets in the usual way. In addition to serving as a uniform straight bill of lading, carbon copies of the original provide an office record, invoice, salesman's advice, and record for the accounting department. The edge of each roll of forms can be tinted a different color to designate usage.

If names are used only two or three times a year, as for example to mail catalogs, multiple stickers save time. Stickers are typed on perforated gummed sheets, about 30 to the sheet. As many carbons or other duplicates are made as will be needed. Names on each sheet are keyed for ledger account number and mailing-list code to permit testing the list. While labels are hardly acceptable for use on first-class letters, they do very well on circular letters, catalogs, announcements, etc.

Take a detached look at the physical setup of your office or plant for possible savings. When the controller of Gifford's, of Elmont, New York, did this, he saw three office departments totaling only 50 employees in separate parts of the plant. Each had its own supervisor. Consolidating the departments into one unit under a single supervisor saved many thousands a year.

If the telephone operator is not too busy, provide her with a typewriter and give her routing typing work to do. Addressing envelopes and statements, for instance.

A worker had indicated on a job analysis form that it had taken her about 300 minutes to do a filing job which could be finished in no more than 20 minutes.

The worker went to a stack of forms, took one off the top, walked 20 or 30 feet to a shelf containing a number of loose-leaf binders, selected one, returned with it to a desk, unlocked the binder at a selected page, inserted the form, locked the binder, and returned it. That completed the operation.

All this was required to file a relatively unimportant form in numerical sequence in binders. The operation was changed considerably: The form was redesigned so that it is now filed in a standard cabinet. The binders are no longer used. The operation takes less than a tenth of the time formerly required.

If labor costs are important to management as a control mechanism, consider breaking the year down into 13 four-week periods. This simplifies the spreading of overhead, since each period has an equal number of days. In the calendar month basis, the cost of overhead per unit is greater in the short month than in the long month. Under the two-week payroll period and four-week financial accounting period, a western lumber company was able to produce complete labor cost analysis, including salary overhead, every two weeks. The labor analysis covered cash and every operation showing production, man-hours, labor cost, cost per man-hour, man-hours per thousand feet produced, and labor costs per thousand feet of lumber. These reports were comparable. Semimonthly accounts were not.

This report system has been a great aid to top management and has given management more facts on which to base decisions. And while the cost is considerable, the better figures proved well worth the expense necessary to produce the numerous reports.

By standardizing the size of invoices, statements, shipping notes and forms, ledger invoices, etc., it will be possible to save on printing and paper costs.

If you already have an offset press with idle time in your office or factory, consider using it to print company stationery and envelopes. The Minot Federal Savings and Loan Association of Minot, North Dakota, saved an estimated hundreds yearly by printing its own stationery and envelopes, formerly done by a commercial printer.

Consider converting stockholder records from Addressograph files to a magnetic tape file, as did the Public Service Electric and Gas Company of Newark, New Jersey. This provides automated processing of dividend checks, reconciliation of cleared checks via optical scanning, and automated production of form followup letters which used to be typed. The system will pay for itself in work hours and in accuracy, utility officers declared.

Study the consolidation of facilities which are used only a few hours a day, for example, salespeople's rooms or desks. When the Occidental Life Insurance Company of California planned its new agency offices, the conference room was so arranged that salesmen could use the big table for their paperwork. Each salesman has a filing drawer for his prospect cards, records, and correspondence. It is unusual for more than one or two salespeople to be in the conference room at one time, although 15 are employed by the agency.

Each piece of furniture needs to be studied by someone skilled in the application of functional furniture to modern office methods. For example, the U.S. Government Printing Office effected a considerable saving of space, and at the same time speeded up the handling of clerical work, by designing a new type of desk especially suited to each operation. By making the desk lower as well as narrower, thus bringing the sorting compartments above the desk nearer to the operator, the task of sorting papers was made easier and the work could be done speedily. The new desk was 44% smaller than the kind formerly used. It permitted better arrangement and used much less space. With functional furniture receiving more and more attention from office furniture manufacturers, opportunities for cutting office costs by its use are many.

Correspondence file folders can be used twice or more by doubling back and/or using gummed slips over previous names.

Among important innovations in photocopying is reduction of oversize originals to standard 8 1/2 x 11 in. size. This unit delivers 3 copies in less time than older models required for 1 copy. Courtesy, 3 M Company

If you tear down a wall, consider replacing it with movable partitions. Many an office is "frozen" into most inconvenient and inefficient units which are not changed because of the expense. Every year, more and more offices are equipped with movable interior partitions that can be moved without too much difficulty.

It is the practice in most offices to replace old equipment only when somebody decides it is so badly worn it can no longer be repaired, or when it has been written off via the depreciation route. As a result, nearly every office is paying dearly to keep obsolete appliances on the floor, when actually the company would save money by selling the worn-out machines and buying new ones, to say nothing of the satisfaction which goes with using up-to-date equipment.

The use of half-and-half memos, one side for the message and the other for the reply, will save time and money in interoffice and salesmen's correspondence.

Many companies, selling through branch offices, have been able to cut expenses sharply by consolidating certain operations in the home office, thus permitting the use of modern equipment and providing better supervision.

A periodical check of the use made of office records, systems, and procedures should be made by the controller. Such a check should determine the approximate time spent annually to maintain the system, the cost of materials used over a year's time, the rent of the office space, and a fair charge for supervision and other overhead expenses. Against that expense a computation should be made of the probable savings or other benefits resulting from the use of the system, as compared with doing the work in some other way or not doing it at all. Audits of this sort put the finger on systems which

This desk-top computer, only slightly larger than a typewriter, can "write," store, and run programs calling for as many as 120 mathematical steps and instantly print out results on paper tape. Courtesy, Olivetti Underwood Corp.

have not been properly maintained, and on which a considerable amount of work must be done to make them fully effective.

By numbering vouchers with the number of the month and starting each month's batch at "one," using a cipher letter as a buffer, it is possible to save considerable time in filing and locating vouchers.

Another "leaking faucet" in most offices is the time lost by relatively high-salaried employees acting as office messengers. Interoffice envelopes, printed with the names of the employees or departments, should be used to facilitate the transfer of papers from one desk to another. These are usually punched with a few holes so that it is quickly evident whether there are any papers in the envelope or not. Each desk is provided with a supply of such envelopes, which are returned when empty to the sender's desk.

In order that a salesperson calling on an account could have a history of what the customer had previously bought, it seemed desirable to the sales manager of a publishing house to set up a card record on which all purchases were posted each month. On the theory that any customer who once had made a purchase was always a prospect for future sales, a customer had to die or request that his name be removed from the list before his card was removed from this file. Inside of a few years, this file contained more than 100,000 cards, required the full-time services of two clerks, plus the cost of floor space, supplies, supervision, etc.

A new sales manager took over. Having no preconceived ideas, he soon discovered that this sales record was being used very little. So he scrapped it, and there was never a single complaint from any of the salespeople.

Eliminate mailing of duplicate letters from different departments to the same branch office, district manager, or salesmen, by having all such mail collected and sent in one daily envelope.

Attach a postcard to the first statement asking customers to check "yes" or "no" whether they want monthly statements.

Avoid the use of two-color printing on invoices, statements, etc. It usually is quite unnecessary and does not add to their effectiveness one bit.

Mailing pieces can be addressed, separated, and stacked for bundling at a rate of 7500 an hour with this addressing machine. An electronic scanner "senses" code marks on EDP-printed address forms to separate the pieces automatically into stacks on the conveyor for each ZIP-code series or other grouping.

Courtesy, Chesire, Inc.

An ordinary electric light under a piece of ground glass will help clerks opening mail to see that envelopes are empty.

There is practically no operation in the office which involves the repetitive writing of names and amounts which cannot be done by machine better, and less expensively, then it can be done by hand. One of the major projects of the company's committee on the improvement of office methods, should be to make a thorough study of the high cost of writing in an office, and be prepared to make recommendations for doing it by machine. It may well be that no additional equipment is needed. Very often equipment already used for some other purpose can be made to do double duty, and thus add to the efficiency of the office.

To get the widest acceptance for an office-practices manual, it should be a joint undertaking by employees and management, rather than a list of bare "verbotens." Employees can be invited to offer suggestions for the solution of certain problems which arise in the management of the office and these suggestions can be considered by a committee of executives. Even if only a few of the suggestions are good enough to include in the manual, the fact that employees participated in preparing it will have an important bearing on its acceptance and use. It might be desirable to publish in the foreword of the manual the names of employees contributing to it.

The correction of lost time (and its counterpart, overtime) is partly a function of personnel. The time when employees could be threatened with dismissal if they persisted in coming in late or staying away without permission is past. That technique might do at a time when jobs are hard to find, but when there are more jobs than people to fill them, something more than a scolding is needed to stop this loss. One way is to install attendance "scoreboards" either for the whole office or in each department. By means of moving signals a visual record shows up those who are lax about their attendance and the "old reliables" who are on the job regularly at starting time.

To simplify the disbursement of funds in the treasurer's office, consider installing one of the several machines now on the market for writing as well as signing checks. Checks can be signed in gangs, several at a time, or a signature-etching attachment, kept under lock and key, can be used for signing all checks of $100 or less.

Printed slips are often just as effective as personally dictated collection letters. A good series of such "stickers" will eliminate many collection letters and bring the checks in just as quickly.

In smaller offices, where there are not enough employees to justify the cost of printing the office-practices manual, or book of rules, consider publishing it as a series of loose-leaf bulletins, one subject to a sheet, over a period of time. Comment should be invited, and when the series is complete, the bulletins can be edited to include worthwhile suggestions or ideas, and then reissued in a more permanent form. If the manual is to be kept in a desk, it should not be too large. While the 8 1/2-by 11-inch size is most popular, 5 1/2-by 8 1/4-inch (half-letterhead size) has much to recommend it. The smaller size is more likely to be kept and used.

Nearly every business wastes thousands of dollars annually writing unnecessary data on forms. It is usually possible to simplify forms so that a minimum of writing is required and still give all the really important information. For example, squares can be provided for checking information rather than writing it out over and over again.

By making the office manual loose-leaf and using the Dewey decimal system of numbering pages, it can be kept up to date by merely substituting new pages for old, and supplementary data covering a particular operation can be inserted in the binder. For example, manuals for use by stenographers might include a back-of-the-book section relating to style, punctuation, and other data concerning company correspondence. Similarly, a section of special value to those engaged in selling might be included. Another possibility is a section on the right and wrong ways to use the telephone for those who contact the public by telephone.

This commercial-type telephone unit automatically records calls, takes orders, and provides for multiple-line answering.   Courtesy, The Magnavox Company

Even in a relatively small office, it pays to get out some sort of newsletter for white-collar employees every two weeks or oftener. Such a letter disseminates all kinds of information which might interest employees, such as news about important sales that were closed during the period, new products that are being developed, items about new employees—who they are and where they came from—and, most important of all, news about staff promotions. Without making it too evident, the aim of the newsletter should be to take the employee into the confidence of the management, make him feel that he is a member of a champion team, and demonstrate by concrete cases that the company does reward good work and that its policy is to promote from within the organization rather than to go outside when there is a good job to be filled.

To dramatize the importance which the company attaches to the ideas of rank-and-file employees as well as those of the "top brass"—and at the same time getting many valuable suggestions for cutting operation costs—some companies favor the idea of a junior board of directors, composed mostly of younger men and women.

One such plan which has worked out well is that of the David C. Cook Publishing Company. Modeled after the famed McCormick multiple-management plan, the Cook system concentrates questions of plant management in the senior board and questions of administration and office management in the junior board.

The vacation season can set back office production, if all employees' work is allowed to pile up while they are away. If the vacationing person's tasks can be divided among the remaining workers, well and good. If not, it might be wise to call upon one of the services that supply temporary help to break vacation bottlenecks and level overloads during peak periods. In the long run, hiring outside help may prove more economical than paying employees overtime to catch up with their work. Besides this, the psychological effect on the vacationer when he returns to a clean desk will be well worth the cost.

Invoices may be enclosed with goods if inserted in a special envelope printed in red—"Warning—Do Not Destroy—This Is Your Invoice."

A factor in turnover of office employees—and especially female employees—is office noise, lack of clean rest rooms, and other conveniences now common to better-equipped offices. In many offices housed in old buildings it would be profitable to lower ceilings, install acoustic tile, improve lighting. Errors would be reduced, production would increase, and what is perhaps most important of all—turnover would decrease. Many resignations are inarticulate protests against noise, dirt, overcrowding, and poor tools in offices. People object to these things without realizing exactly what it is that makes work disagreeable. High turnover rates and high absenteeism are often nothing more than unvoiced protests against an unpleasant working atmosphere.

If you do not have an established plan for periodically rating employees on the work they are doing, you will find it profitable to establish one, even if it is quite informal at its inception. Test the idea carefully. But lean over backwards to make the employee feel he or she is getting a square deal. Ratings should be used to supplement a salary administration plan, and not made the exclusive basis for making salary adjustments.

One company sets up department standards for attendance. Every week a bulletin is issued and posted, showing the number of "lost hours" in each department and scoring each department against "bogey." The department which ends the month with the highest score is awarded an attendance banner, and each member of the department is credited with a certain number of attendance points or credits. These are accumulated and cashed in at the end of the year for merchandise prizes from a previously circulated prize book. (This plan requires granting credits for other performances as well as good attendance, such as production, conservation, suggestions, etc.) These prize books may be purchased at a nominal charge from companies which specialize in supplying prizes for industrial and sales use.

Hand-to-mouth buying of office supplies runs up prices and costs. Long-term contracts for essential supplies will yield extensive savings in the form of quantity discounts. Drop shipments can be arranged if storage is a problem.

Analysis of employment records will usually show that a comparatively few workers are responsible for the bad average "lost time" record of an office. Some office managers claim that 20% of the office staff create 80% of the absenteeism. If this is the case, it is advisable to isolate these offenders and not nag the entire organization about a situation caused by a few.

One Chicago company solved the problem, both in the office and the plant, by requiring employees who were chronically late or ab-

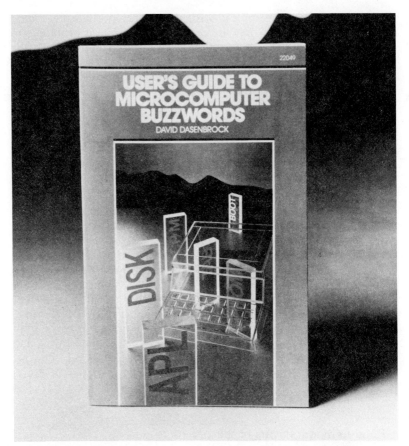

Today, there are many publications that help administrators keep abreast in touch with many of the latest developments in office automation. This "User's Guide to Microcomputer Buzzwords" is written for people who don't necessarily care what happens inside a microcomputer, but who want to be able to communicate with people who do. It is from Howard W. Sams & Co., Inc. Dartnell has "Management's Guide to Desktop Computers," which is a detailed description of the workings of the small business computers.

sent to attend a meeting where the problem was discussed constructively. For example, most employees according to innumerable surveys, attach great importance to "job security." It usually ranks ahead of wages. If employees can be made to understand that the security of their jobs and their future with the company depend upon their doing their part, as well as the company doing its part, much can be done to stop time losses. Announcement of promotions, especially at the lower levels for example, should be accompanied by an explanation that one of the reasons for the promotion was the employee's good attendance record.

As a first step in cutting down time lost by the infraction of office rules, such as those covering tardiness, visiting on the job, fighting, loafing, etc., consider setting up a committee or review board to get out a periodical report on rules violations. Such reports can be issued annually or semiannually. If the company publishes a newsletter for its office employees, the report can be included with monthly issues of that publication.

While most of the loss that comes from paying overtime for doing work which should be done on regular time is due to time wasted or lost during the day, some of it can be laid at the door of inefficient tools. Businessmen will usually invest in any new piece of equipment for the plant, if it will pay for itself within a few years, but when it comes to buying up-to-date equipment for the office they take the position, "We have always done it the hard way, why change?" Instead of considering the proposed equipment or appliance from the standpoint of what it might save in overtime, they regard it with a fishy eye, and treat it as an unnecessary expense.

Analysis shows that in departments where overtime has become a chronic habit, the introduction of timesaving machines and methods will usually put an end to overtime once and for all.

Establish some sort of overtime control system which will automatically bring to the attention of the controller, or the proper company officer, the amount of money paid out each month for overtime (the premium pay, not the base pay) by each department, or if the organization is small, to each employee. These reports tell top management which operations are bottlenecking production in the office, and show up inefficient department managers. If the department is understaffed, steps can be taken to add to the personnel. If the system or distribution of work is at fault, it can be corrected. If labor-saving equipment or appliances are needed, they

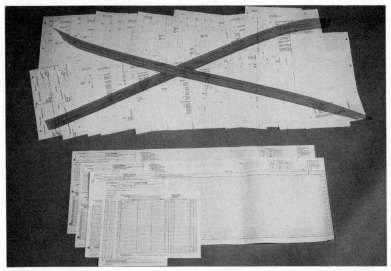

Five simple forms replace the many-paged "narrative" of the systems analysis in this NCR innovative data-processing system, planned to improve communications and documentation in systems development.

can be purchased. The important thing is to have some means of finding the leaking faucets so they do not become permanent profit seepages.

Check unnecessary use of airmail postage. Letters mailed on Fridays or Saturdays will usually reach their destinations by first-class mail as quickly as airmail. Many people now feel first class is as fast as airmail except in unusual cases.

A regular quarterly inspection of office lighting should be made by a qualified person using a light meter. Most public service companies will provide this service, or the company maintenance man can make the check. Very often the only thing that is needed to bring the light up to the required standard is washing the fixtures and putting in new bulbs. If incandescent lighting is still being used, the use of fluorescent lighting from concealed fixtures should be considered. Fluorescent lighting, unless properly installed in fixtures which shield the eyes from glare, can aggravate eyestrain. Saving in current used by fluorescent lights should, over a period of years, liquidate the cost of the better light. Offices should be floodlighted to avoid spotlighting of desks, which produces eyestrain.

The use of lightweight paper for letterheads, envelopes, catalogs, and forms can save postage expense.

Excessive overtime is a direct reflection on the management of the department in which it occurs, or top management, or both. Usually it has its roots in faulty organization. When the office is efficiently organized, with good supervision and the responsibilities of each executive clearly defined and understood, overtime is kept at a minimum.

The well-organized office recognizes the ever-present danger of changing conditions and the effect these have on the work load of different employees. Studies are being made constantly to determine which employees have too much work, and which have too little work. This is done before overtime on any operation is necessary. Overloads can usually be corrected by a redistribution of work and by the installation of appliances or systems which permit short-cutting the operation.

It is hard to measure the cost of noise in an office in dollars, but the loss is probably much greater than management realizes. Before moving into its new building some years ago, the Aetna Life Insurance Company made a careful study of the effect of noise on office production. After it had moved into its new quarters the walls and ceilings of which were noiseproofed (acoustically treated), the study was continued for several years. The results were as follows:

1. The noise level was reduced 14.5%
2. Employee efficiency was increased 8.8%.
3. Errors were reduced 29% for typists, and 52% for office machine operators.
4. Employee turnover was decreased 47%.

5. Absences were decreased 37.5%.
6. Personnel requirements were lowered about 10%.

Check employee's personal telephone calls. In some offices these are quite high. A tactful bulletin will effect a reduction.

When mailing regularly to the same address, such as a branch office, it is profitable to print or multigraph a supply of addressed envelopes in advance. Preprint similar envelopes for all regular customers.

Keeping desks well stocked with needed stationery and supplies avoids the necessity of frequent trips to the stockroom, which are time-consuming and money-wasting. Some companies have found that it cost more to handle the supplies than it did to purchase them! A Chicago utility cut expenses once by requiring every employee to requisition one week's supplies each Monday morning. If the worker underestimated her needs or wasted supplies and therefore ran short during the week, the supervisor had to sign her extra requisition.

It might pay to undertake an educational campaign to teach employees the importance of proper desk organization. See that typewriters and calculating machines are located within the normal working area. Equipment such as numbering machines, paper clips, racks holding forms, etc., should be located within the maximum area. Periodical checks should be made of all office desks to see that they are properly arranged, that each desk contains the necessary conveniences, and that the drawers are clean and tidy.

Some offices find music, piped from a central station, helpful in relieving fatigue. It makes working more pleasurable. Music can be most effectively used in departments where the work is monotonous, such as filing, addressing, tabulating, and typing. Play the records for periods of an hour, one in the morning, one in the afternoon, and one during overtime periods. Music is seldom used in all departments of the office, the usual coverage being about 15%.

In the shop any employee who found it necessary to work to the one-thousandth of an inch, and did not have the proper tools for measuring thousandths of an inch, would have such a high spoilage rate that he would be too expensive to keep. So the company usually makes available to those employees the proper gauges, micrometers, and other tools for accuracy. But that same company might conceivably require employees in its office to keep books by hand, write names over and over again, and add up long columns of figures and make complicated calculations without benefit of the tools now available for doing such work speedily and accurately.

To attain a high level of quality performance throughout an office requires, above all, supervisors who have the ability to teach others how to be accurate. It is not enough to fire employees who grow careless and make mistakes. That may be necessary as a last resort. But any person of average intelligence, who is willing to learn, can be trained to do accurate and dependable work by a capable supervisor. It may require a lot of patience, but it is worth it. Not only should supervisors be selected for those qualities, but they too must be constantly reminded that the accuracy of those for whom they are responsible is their responsibility. When a mistake is made they are to blame as much as the employee who made the mistake.

Valuable time is lost by transcribers proofreading their own letters. All stenographers are not good proofreaders. If the volume of transcription warrants it, consider employing a proofreader, who may not be a typist, to check all outgoing letters for style, grammar, and spelling before delivering them to the dictator for signature.

While every well-managed office has some method of controlling errors and getting rid of costly mistakes (so far as is humanly possible), the process can be speeded up by establishing error ratios for each department, or each operation, making monthly samplings of specific operations and then posting the result for all to see. Such a practice tends to (1) keep the organization mistake-conscious, (2) show up lax departmental management and sloppy supervision, and (3) locate weaknesses in methods which may be causing recurrence of the same type of mistakes.

In offices where dictating machines are used, and where the transcribing of letters is done in a central department, the installation of a bonus plan should help to increase output. It involves keeping an accurate record of lines typed by each operator by means of a key-stroke counter on the typewriter. Bonuses may be paid to individuals or to groups of operators, a method which tends to stop complaints that certain girls get the most difficult work.

Send a bulletin to employees showing total expense for light bills for 12 months. Ask them to cooperate in reducing this expense by switching off unnecessary lights. Hang a "Turn off the Light" tag on light cords and save energy.

Consider an office messenger service for picking up letters to be transcribed, and delivering letters for signature at regular 30 minute intervals. Most offices have messengers, but usually the pickups are so irregular that a dictator who wants to get his mail out as soon as possible, will take the recording to the transcribing department himself. Rush letters should be tagged with a red signal for immediate attention when delivered to the transcribing department.

If window envelopes are used to save addressing envelopes, print or lithograph a very faint period at the place on the letterhead where the address must begin to make it fit the window of the envelope. To avoid unbalanced letters, it is customary to type the address in the proper space to fit the window, then skip enough lines to center the letter in the remaining space. Window envelopes not only eliminate addressing, but save having the envelope tag along with the letter and the danger of getting letters in wrong envelopes.

Another way to cut the cost of both dictating and transcribing is to provide "difficulty slips" which the transcriber can check and return to the dictator. "Difficulty slips" should be in duplicate; an extra copy for the stenographic supervisor, who if the difficulty persists, can request the dictator to correct the fault.

A regular bulletin on the high cost of office waste should be posted on the bulletin board to encourage economy in the use of supplies, stationery, etc.

Where the volume of outgoing mail is not sufficient to warrant the use of an electrically operated mailing machine, or where the nature of the business is such that affixed postage stamps are desirable, considerable savings are possible through the use of hand metering machines and hand stamp-affixing machines. In offices where considerable overtime is put in by stenographers, and where it is necessary to stamp mail at times when the power machine may not be available, it is a good plan to have a sealing machine for general use.

Another opportunity for speeding the mail, particularly in the case of those companies that use any quantity of printed sales literature or advertising, is mechanical folding. One concern in Iowa reports savings in one year sufficient to pay for the folding machines used in its mailing department.

When an order is approved for processing, make one master copy, and then as many copies as may be required on an office duplicator. By designing special forms, where the wording is different on each form but the arrangement of the data is the same on all, savings up to 40% of the time usually spent writing acknowledgements, invoices, shipping notices, commission statements, inventory record copies, purchasing-department advices, credit-department advices, etc., can be saved. The master record, with a little blocking out and rearrangement of the form, does for all. These, of course, are in addition to the copies from which the order is filled. Once the master copy has been proofread and found correct, all duplicated copies are sure to be correct. Different color paper can be used for rush orders, regular orders, or back orders as the case may be.

Check present invoice and statement forms. Much wasted time and effort are caused through repetitive typing of dollar signs and even more in constant typing of one particular item of merchandise.

Consider employing a firm of management engineers to come in and study the duties assigned to each employee, in relation to what other employers in the same area are paying for similar work. Such a job audit, in the hands of top management, serves as a place to begin making payroll adjustments within established job classifications.

Taking inventory used to be a two-man operation, one counting and calling and the other writing. The modern way to take inventory is to use a tape recorder. It then becomes a one-man job, since by using a lapel "mike" the person taking the inventory merely has to "talk" the item number and quantity on hand into his "mike," and the recording can be transcribed at any time convenient to the typing department.

A weakness of most employee communications, and especially letters to employees, is that there is no real reason (in the eyes of the employee) for the letter except to "pep him up." It is possible to double and triple the readership of a letter by a good peg on which to hang it. For example, one company holds meetings at which management problems are discussed by employees with a qualified company executive. Minutes of these discussions, complete with questions and answers, are mailed to all employees. A poll showed that 81% of the employees read the minutes, and about 50% of them passed them along to members of their families to read.

If your company has a profit-sharing plan, it may help to issue quarterly progress reports. If the reports take the form of personal letters, rather than duplicated bulletins, they have a high interest value and are carefully read because they discuss a matter of mutual interest—the company's profits.

As an aid to top management in forecasting the long-range growth of the business, the office might prepare graphic charts on which such items as sales in units as well as dollars (bypassing the inflationary price gap), profits by departments, gross profits, taxes, profits after taxes, ratio of profits to sales volume, ratio of working capital to sales volume, etc., are plotted for 10 or more years back. While it is true these data represent "water over the dam," having the information in chart form when important decisions are to be made can be very useful. It helps not only in charting trends but also in stimulating thought. It keeps the thinking of a group on the track.

It is less difficult to forecast business growth over the near term—that is, for the next 12 months—than for the long term. But the more data which can be picked up from office records and used, the more reliable the forecast is likely to be. One of the most satisfactory methods of estimating sales for the next 12 months, for example, is to maintain a visible card record of sales by accounts. These cards are posted from invoices. Prior to the time of preparing the annual sales forecast, the sales manager discusses with the territorial salesmen, in person or by letter, what he considers a reasonable quota of business for each account.

Some salesmen will be too optimistic. Others, according to their nature, too pessimistic. The sales manager levels off each "loading," which becomes the territorial quota. The sum of the territorial quotas becomes the company's sales expectancy for the next 12 months. When approved by the board of directors, it becomes the production quota as well. While the quota is but an "educated" guess, it at least provides a target for production, sales, and finance.

In order to manage a business competently, top management should receive frequent and entirely reliable reports on the operations of each department. Such reports should be so set up that the chief executive can get the "meat of the coconut" without having to browse through a lot of figures, yet if any total looks out of line, the facts needed to localize the trouble should be there. Too many reports supplied top management are mere summaries, which may show the cash, sales, inventory, or receivables position of the company, but do not enable a chief executive to put his finger on profit leaks, without calling a meeting of the accounting department.

While drawing a budget is relatively simple, drawing it in such a way that it can be easily operated is something else again. The office must not only provide all the needed controls, but also make the needed information available without too much "red tape" and costly recordkeeping. While it is advisable to let each operating unit draw its own tentative budget, these should be assembled, checked, and revised by a control committee before being presented to top management for adoption. Budgets should be set up with a three-point decimal system of classification, designed to bring all related classifications in all departments under a common designating number.

The weakness of the budget system is that it tempts department managers to spend all their budgeted funds lest they have their budget cut next year. Consideration should therefore be given to some sort of departmental bonus based on savings. "Beat the Budget" competitions are especially desirable at a time of easy money and high taxes, when the urge to save is not great.

Budgets are supposed to stimulate the interest of key executives in profit control. But that means each executive must be informed from month to month as to the results of this operation and the operations of other departments. Consider issuing a confidential monthly budget summary showing prorata income and expense, but adjusted according to the seasonal flow of business. Large nonrecurring expenses, for example, should be spread over the year rather than allowed to fall in any one month. These summary sheets should be marked "Return to the President," and should be followed up to see that they are returned and not allowed to drift around the office.

Over 7 billion copies are made on office copying machines a year. The average currently is between 90 and 320 copies-per-year-per-employee. If your average is running high (say more than 185 copies per employee with 500 employees) then you should institute controls. One idea is to limit access and another is the possibility of substituting a lower cost offset duplicating machine for longer runs.

Think about using the BAD approach for involving employees in cutting costs on a day-by-day basis. BAD stands for "buck a day" and it has been a success in many operations because of its simplicity. Employees are encouraged to come up with suggestions that might save as little as $1 a day. This doesn't mean big cost-cutting ideas are ruled out, but the low goal helps employees to get into the swing of the program.

Consider flowcharting every operation in the office to have a graphic record of all the daily activities. A flowchart is, in effect, a road map which shows the route or flow of paperwork. With a graphic display, you might find a quicker or shorter route to the goal. A flowchart should not be complicated or complex or it loses its effectiveness. A template of symbols can be purchased at an office equipment supplier. That's all you need, except for the information.

The not-so-old-fashioned rubber stamp can be a cost fighter in terms of forms production. If one form has to grow to two or three or more before action is taken, perhaps a rubber stamp with pertinent data can keep one form down to one form throughout its travel. How many forms are used that require another form to back it up?

Devise either standard letters or standard paragraphs that can be used over and over again. This saves much time in creating original material when it really isn't needed. Insurance firms find this particularly beneficial in answering standard inquiries, complaints, etc. If you are mimeographing these letters, leave spaces for names, addresses, or specific information.

There are many applications for color coding in today's office with an eye toward saving time, money or both. Some firms use different colored gummed labels for their various files. It helps clerks find the sections they are interested in. Others print forms on various sheets of colored paper—an inexpensive way to guarantee forms aren't mixed up. Other firms define department areas by different colored walls, office furniture, etc. Study your office with an eye to determining where colors might clarify things.

Reduce office theft and you'll reduce costs. Consider items or areas that are vulnerable and institute changes. Lock up petty cash every night. Keep costly supplies, equipment in one area, and assign one person to handing them out. Insist on identification of all unidentified people. Many thefts of late have been by professionals, disguised as repairmen, movers and the like. From time to time, inspect your waste materials before pick-up. Many an insider has smuggled valuable goods out in this manner, only to return later to get them.

Your firm can lose untold dollars through revelations of company secrets, either by accident or through industrial spying. Like it or not, paper shredders might be in order for your executives. They are available commercially. You may even wish to contract for the services of an electronics firm to "sweep" your place for electronic "bugs" from time to time. If you do, don't have a regular schedule, for obvious reasons—insiders could anticipate the event, remove the "bug" and replace it later.

Company secrets can be revealed accidentally through loose-lipped suppliers, costing thousands. Caution them of the importance of maintaining secrecy, when required. Art studios might be drawing pictures of new products. Metal fabricating firms or tool and die shops might be providing new parts which, if competitors studied, could reveal your next moves. Select suppliers with this in mind, and caution them to which projects must be kept under tight wraps.

Order materials intelligently. And try to make use of everything, even if it means special ordering a container for your items to arrive in, etc. When Henry Ford ordered certain metal parts, he asked that they be packed in wooden containers of a certain size. Those containers, when disassembled, became running boards for his Model "T." Can you apply this lesson to your ordering habits?

In these days of high interest rates and high initial costs, the more you can do to control inventories—both of finished products and supplies, the more money you'll save. Bone up on some of the sophisticated inventory control methods available today and select the one best suited to your operations. Keep track of when you are reordering items so you won't run out. Are there peaks and valleys? Can charts be established? Can you take advantage of volume discounts or would they cost you more in tied-up capital than they are worth? You've got to be on your toes, because your competitors are.

Paid time off is the most expensive employee benefit, concluded a management study by Hayes/Hill, Inc., recently, and managers should try to keep it in bounds. Paid time off includes vacations and holidays (typically 25 days which translates to 10 percent of the work year) and all sorts of personal time off. Tighter controls offer a major cost reduction.

Check items you buy to spot too stringent specifications. Relaxing them may expand your sources of supply and cut procurement costs. One company discovered its specifications were so tight only one supplier could fill the need. After specs were reviewed and realistically revised, competitive bids were obtained at a much lower cost.

Improve your customer relations and perhaps boost sales as well. Let good customers know when a price hike is emminent. They'll buy in quantity to beat the increase—you'll enhance goodwill and the present balance sheet as well. Many firms have this policy.

Are you paying employees too much or too little? Each could be costly, but for different reasons. Too much means just that—and you're out more money than necessary. Too little means you might have excessive turnover—itself a costly item. The solution: Participate in local salary surveys, especially within your industry. These give you a handle on which to judge your present salary structure—and make any needed adjustments. Sometimes only certain job titles are "out of whack"—sometimes the entire schedule of pay needs rearranging upward.

Analyze what your customers or clients want. Provide that and only that and you'll most likely reduce costs and increase sales too. Value analysis is a technique which analyzes a user's wants from a product and limits its unnecessary characteristics without curtailing reliability, quality or performance. Have your most qualified people study alternate materials, newer processes and more simplified approaches.

If your company has a purchasing department, use it, even if it is in another city. Even if allowing them to order for you would be inconvenient and time-consuming, they could still share expertise with you on what products are good buys, what ones aren't, and maybe even where to shop. If you've got one locally, so much the better. Purchasing agents and their staffs are trained and knowledgeable—but they can't help you if you don't let them.

It should go without saying, and yet much money is squandered each year on air fares for trips decided on at the last minute. With some prior planning, usually bargain air fares can be utilized.

Consider putting labels on all the many items in your office supply cabinet. This could help your employees become more aware of their costs. Once aware, they may be more sparing.

Word processing equipment manufacturers often charge premium prices for their word processor supplies. You can improve on those costs by shopping around, dealing with independents and even utilizing mail order firms, which might save you upwards of 30 percent.

It's always good office practice to check up on the ability to pay on the part of a new customer. To do so, secure financial statements.

With the increased cost in gasoline, has your firm considered selling its product or service either by telephone or by direct mail? Now may be the ideal time. Even if the entire product line cannot be handled this way, perhaps certain items could—on an experimental basis, at first, if you like.

More and more businesses are encountering slow payers these days. You can combat that situation by: (1) Increasing your discount for prompt payers, (2) Creating an in-place system for slow payers, with a series of letters and a determination of when to send them, (3) Tightening up on your due dates, and (4) Installing penalties (or increasing them) for slow payers.

Don't always consider buying new equipment. You might be better off leasing it. Perhaps you don't have a year-round need for an item, but it would help in Spring to have it. Or you're not certain a certain piece of equipment is the answer, but you'd like to find out. Lease it.

Contests aren't just for salespeople. You can structure one to meet or exceed some goal. It could be so many letters a day produced by word processing, or so many orders filled in a day or whatever you decide. Consider contests as a way to enhance the bottom line. Give each contest a specific theme the staff can relate to and provide strong promotion to make that theme come alive. If possible, select prizes that people dream of—exotic vacations, microwaves and the like.

If your people deal with customers, be sure they know what buying signals are. This knowledge can really increase profit. Common "I'm ready to buy" questions include: (1) What is the price? (2) When can you make delivery? (3) Does it come in (mention sizes, colors, etc.?) (4) What size order gives the best price? (5) When will there be a new model? and (6) What terms do you offer? These are buying signals that tell your people to close the sale.

Incentive pay may be the answer to motivate your people, especially executives. It's becoming more prevalent in the banking industry, for instance, says Towers, Perrin, Forster & Crosby of New York. About 94 percent of respondents in a recent survey presently use incentive compensation compared with 78 percent in a 1977 study. It may be applicable to your industry. Peg increases so they'll be more than offset by profits.

Consider changing company rules against rehiring ex-employees, and save money in the process, assuming you weren't previously unhappy with the individual involved. Most likely you'll get back an experienced employee, a more mature one, and perhaps even one with greater skills than when he or she left. Employers are finding rehires are among their most loyal workers.

If you want insurance cost increases to be less erratic, and perhaps to enjoy increased cash flow, self-insurance is an option to investigate. Big manufacturers have self-insured themselves against product liability claims. Hospitals have done the same for medical malpractice. An increasing number of companies are at least partially self-insuring their employee group health coverage. In a study of 500 large businesses, Hay Associates found 26 percent utilized some kind of self-insured medical plans, up from only 18 percent three years ago. Advocates don't claim it will save money but do cite less erratic cost increases because the expense for self insurance should more closely match increases in medical costs and not insurance company adjustments, and cash flow improves since the company itself holds the reserves against potential losses. Such a move, it should be noted, requires much study.

It's not enough to know that temporary workers are available to you . . . you've got to know when to use them. Temporary workers should be used for work overloads caused by: (1) peak loads, (2) cyclical conditions, (3) inventories, (4) vacations, (5) sickness, and (6) unfilled job openings.

Ever consider creating a corps of your own temporary workers by tapping your retirees? Here's a group that knows your company and often the job at hand. One large Chicago insurance company has done this with excellent results. The golden-agers are given a day or two of advance notice, and an outline of the assignment. If one or two turns it down, others are called until all openings are filled. Work is kept to under six hours a day, usually, and the assignments last a week or two at most. For the oldsters, it's pocket money and a chance to visit with old friends while feeling productive—for the company, a needed source of temporary workers, at a reasonable price.

Many firms have found it profitable to reward employees who refer their friends or relatives for employment. This payment may take many forms, such as cash, government bonds, time off and the like. Be certain your prize costs less than advertising the job, an employment agency fee, or other built-in costs. Employees who sell the company to someone else resell themselves on the firm in the process—a hidden benefit.

If you're in a position of hiring people, give serious consideration to hiring older workers and you probably will save money. In their favor are these points: (1) Salary requirements are realistic, (2) Experience makes them tolerant, less likely to buck the system, (3) More likely to be prompt, (4) Content with their job and less likely to job hop (check previous record here), (5) Fulfill the role of mentors to younger employees, and (6) More reliable, with fewer absences.

In a situation where attracting many applicants for jobs is a problem, consider an open house for prospects. Keep your office open on a Saturday, or in the evening. Invite interested applicants to drop in, via either newspaper or radio/TV ads, or both. Serve refreshments, show a film or slides about the company, and have staff members on hand to greet visitors, answer questions. Sure you'll encounter over-time expenses but experts say these are more than offset by savings in employment agency fees or advertising for help costs.

Promoting or hiring the wrong person to a management job can be a very costly error. Yet determining what factors one should promote on are sometimes "fuzzy" in the promoter's mind. Use these guidelines, which National Personnel Associates, a network of employment agencies, uncovered when it asked its members to rank ten reasons why one managerial candidate is chosen over others. They are: (1) Know-how, track record, (2) Being personable, making the best impression, and having the best chemistry with the employer, (3) Outstanding in dealing with subordinates, (4) Being highly motivated and career oriented, (5) Exhibiting best growth potential, (6) Impressive reputation, references, (7) Showing the most enthusiasm for the job, (8) Being the most imaginative, innovative, (9) Willing to accept a lower salary than others, and lastly, (10) Available at an earlier date than others.

APPENDIX

GLOSSARY OF ELECTRONIC CALCULATOR TERMS

ADD MODE:

Allows entry of numbers to two decimal places without the need to enter the decimal point.

ADDING MACHINE LOGIC:

The function key is pressed after the number is keyed in. For example, to perform the problem $(-5+4-3)$, the following sequence is followed. Depress (5), depress $(-)$, depress (4), depress $(+)$, depress (3), depress $(-)$. The great majority of office desk electronic calculators use Adding Machine Logic.

ALGEBRAIC LOGIC:

The problem is entered as it would be written. To perform the problem $(-5+4-3)$, the following sequence is followed. Depress $(-)$, depress (5), depress $(+)$, depress (4), depress $(-)$, depress (3). To perform the problem $(7-6)$, depress (7), depress $(-)$, depress (6). Algebraic logic is found on some mini-calculators and the large programmable machines.

Figuring machines used in offices before the introduction of electronic calculators (Electromechanical machines), all use the Adding Machine Logic. Office personnel accustomed to these machines might have difficulty in using a machine with algebraic logic and *serious mistakes can be made*. Machines with algebraic logic are more suited for the consumer market, or the programmer who has to enter very lengthy equations on the machine.

BACKSPACE KEY (SHIFT KEY):

Shifts all digits one place to the right, dropping the last digit on the right.

BUFFERED KEYBOARD (OPEN KEYBOARD):

Allows entry of numbers while calculator is executing previous calculations.

CAPACITY:

The capacity of a calculator is the maximum number of digits that can be entered in one factor or obtained in a result. In most machines, the capacity is equivalent to the number of digits in the display. In a few machines, it is larger than the number of digits in the display and a flip-flop key is used to show the full result. Where this is the case, it is noted in the table.

CHANGE SIGN KEY:

Changes the sign of the number from positive to negative and visa-versa.

COMMA INDICATOR:

A means of separating numbers into threes for easy reading, with decimal point as the base.

CONSTANT FOR MULTIPLICATION AND DIVISION:

Allows multiplying or dividing a series of numbers by one number without reentry of the number.

DECIMAL:

FLOATING:

Puts no restrictions on the position of the decimal point.

FIXED:

Restricts the number of decimals to that preselected.

FLEXI MODE:

Allows for entry of numbers to any decimal setting without the need to enter the decimal point.

ITEM COUNTER:

Counts the number of calculations preceding the final result.

MEMORY LIGHT:

A light which indicates there is a number in the memory.

MEMORY + AND − KEYS:

These keys provide direct access to the memory for storing numbers.

MEMORY REGISTER:

A register in which the contents can be added to or subtracted from. The contents are available until the register is cleared.

NON-ADD KEY:

(Found on printers.) Enters numbers that do not affect calculations, used for entering dates and notations.

PERCENT KEY:

A key which divides the number entered by 100. In some machines, it reduces the steps required in percentage calculations.

PROGRAM:

A sequence of detailed instructions for the operations necessary to solve a problem. Programmable electronic calculators can "learn" the steps of a problem, so that after the first sequence of entries only the variable numbers need to be entered on the keyboard without manual activation of the control keys. Some programmable machines store programs on cards or tapes.

REPEAT ADDITION AND SUBTRACTION:

Ability of the machine to repeat adding or subtracting a number by mere depression of the plus or minus key without reentry.

REVERSE KEY (EXCHANGE OR RECALL KEY):

Reverses positions of two numbers such as dividend and divisor.

ROLL-OVER INDEXING:

Allows depression of a key before releasing the previous key.

ROUND-OFF:

The last digit displayed in an answer is increased by one if the following digit would have been a 5 or greater.

ROUND-UP:

The last digit displayed in an answer is increased by one if the following digit would have been a 1 or greater.

SCIENTIFIC NOTATION:

The number is entered or a result is displayed in terms of a power of 10. For example, the number 1234 is entered as 1.234

$\times~10+^3$ and the number 0.001234 would appear as 1.234 $\times$ $10-^3$.

SUM OPERAND:

Automatically sums first factors of sequence multiplication or division problems. Used when obtaining average unit price and standard deviation.

UNDERFLOW:

Machine will accept the full listing capacity of the display for multiplicand and multiplier when using whole number digits, and will display the left hand digits of the answer correctly. For example, in a 12-digit machine, 12 whole number digits can be multiplied by 12 whole number digits (24 digits) and the machine will display the 12 left hand digits of the answer correctly.

ZERO SUPPRESSION:

Only entered zeros will appear on display.

Courtesy, Buyers Laboratory, Inc., Hackensack, N. J. 07601

GLOSSARY OF COMMUNICATIONS TERMS

ACCESS LINE (WATS)

A telephone line connected to the user's premises either to establish or to receive calls to or from a particular WATS service area.

ADDRESS

In communications, the coded representation of the destination of a message.

ALPHA-NUMERIC

Contraction of alphabetical-numerical. A system including letters, numbers, and symbols.

ALTERNATE ROUTE

A secondary communications path used to reach a destination if the primary path is unavailable.

ALTERNATE USE

The provision of facilities which may be used for separate purposes, e.g., voice and data.

AMA (AUTOMATIC MESSAGE ACCOUNTING)

Equipment that automatically records all data concerning user-dialed long distance calls necessary for billing purposes.

AMPLITUDE DISTORTION

Distortion in the amplitude of a wave form, particularly due to attenuation.

AMPLITUDE MODULATION

A method of transmission whereby the signal wave voltage is impressed on a carrier wave of higher frequency so that the amplitude of the carrier wave is varied proportionately with the amplitude of the signal wave.

ANALOG

Signals which make use of electrical analogies (e.g., varying voltages or frequencies) to produce a signal of a continuous nature rather than of a pulse nature.

ANC (ALL-NUMBER CALLING)

A system of telephone numbering that uses seven digits within a Numbering-Plan Area (NPA).

ANI (AUTOMATIC NUMBER IDENTIFICATION)

Equipment that automatically records the calling number. This is a part of AMA.

ANSWERBACK (DATA)

A signal or tone sent by the receiving business machine or data set to the sending station for identification or to indicate it is ready to receive transmission.

AREA CODE

The three-digit code used when dialing long distance calls from one Number-Plan Area (NPA) to another.

ASR

Automatic send and receive.

ASSEMBLE

In communications, to accumulate in main or auxiliary memory portions of an incoming long message.

ATTENUATION

The difference between transmitted and received power due to transmission loss through equipment, lines, or other communications devices.

AUDIO

Frequencies which can be heard by the human ear (usually between 15 Hz and 20,000 Hz).

AUTOMATIC ALARM EQUIPMENT

A device to automatically initiate a signal to indicate a changed or troubled condition.

AUTOMATIC CALLING UNIT (ACU)

A dialing device supplied by the communication common carriers which permits a business machine to automatically dial calls over the communications network.

BANDPASS FILTER

A filter which permits free passage to frequencies within a specific range and which bars passage to frequencies of that range.

BANDWIDTH

The difference, expressed in Hz, between the highest and lowest frequencies of a band.

BASEBAND

In the process of modulation, the baseband is the frequency band occupied by the aggregate of the transmitted signals when first used to modulate a carrier.

BATCH PROCESSING

A method of processing in which a number of similar input items are accumulated and processed together.

BAUD

A unit of signaling speed. In an equal length code, one baud corresponds to a rate of one signal element per second. Thus, with a duration of the signal element of 20 milliseconds, the modulation rate is 50 bauds (per second).

BAUDOT CODE

A code for the transmission of data in which five bits represent one character. Standard 5-channel teletype code.

BINARY

Consisting of two conditions (Yes: No, Off: On). Each element is called a bit.

BINARY CODED DECIMAL (BCD)

A system of binary numbering where each decimal digit is represented by 4 bits.

BIT

A unit of information content. Contraction of "binary digit," a bit is the smallest unit of information in a binary system of notation. It is the choice between two possible states, usually designated one and zero.

BIT RATE

The speed at which bits are transmitted, usually expressed in bits per second.

BLOCK

A group of words or characters considered or transported as a unit, particularly in reference to input and output.

BLOCKING

A condition where connections cannot be made due to "all lines" busy.

BREAK

Telegraph term to denote interruption of a sender.

BROADBAND

See Wideband.

BROADCAST

The dissemination of information to a number of stations simultaneously.

BUFFER

An isolating circuit or system used to avoid or delay reaction between and the corresponding driving circuit.

BUFFER STORAGE

A storage device used to compensate for a difference in rate of flow of data or time of occurrence of events, when transmitting data from one device to another.

BUSY HOUR

The peak 60-minute period during a business day when the largest volume of communications traffic is handled.

BYTE

A sequence of adjacent binary digits operated upon as a unit and usually shorter than a word.

CAMA (CENTRALIZED AUTOMATIC MESSAGE ACCOUNTING)

Similar to AMA, this equipment serves several central offices in recording data of user-dialed long distance calls. When ANI is not included, an operator records the calling number at the beginning of the call.

CARD COLUMN

One of the single digit columns on a tabulating card. When punched, a column contains only one digit, one letter, or one special code.

CARD DIALER

Automatic dialer and regular telephone combined in one desktop unit. Phone numbers coded on plastic cards are inserted in the dialer slot for fast, accurate dialing, or touch-tone entry of fixed data into a data processing system.

CARD FIELD

A set of card columns, established as to number and position, into which the same information item is regularly punched.

CARRIAGE RETURN

In a character-to-character printing mechanism, the operation that causes the next character to be printed at the left margin.

CARRIER SYSTEM

A means of obtaining a number of channels over a single path by modulating each channel upon a different "carrier" frequency and demodulating at the receiving point to restore the signals to their original form.

CCSA

Common control switching arrangements. Designed for users having extensive private line communications requirements.

CENTRAL OFFICE

The place where communications common carriers terminate user lines and locate the equipment which interconnects those lines.

CENTREX

A type of private branch exchange in which incoming calls can be dialed direct to any extension without an operator's assistance. Outgoing and intercom calls are dialed direct by the extension users.

CHAD

The small pieces of paper which are punched out of a paper tape are called chad. A tape punched in this manner is called "fully punched tape."

CHANNEL

A path for electrical transmission between two or more points. Also called a circuit, facility, line, link, or path.

CHARACTER

The actual or coded representation of a digit, letter, or special symbol.

CHECK CHARACTER (OR DIGIT)

One or more characters (or digits) carried in a symbol, word, or block; coded, depending on the remaining elements, in such a way that if an error occurs it will be detected (excluding compensating errors).

CIRCUIT

See Channel.

CIRCUIT, 4 WIRE

Communication path using one channel for each transmission direction.

CLOCKING

A reference source of timing for a machine or system.

COAXIAL CABLE

Consists of a conductor suspended in the center of, and insulated from, another tubular conductor. One or more may be used within a single cable.

CODE

A system of symbols and rules for use in representing information.

CODE CONVERSION

The conversion of data from one code to another.

COMMUNICATIONS COMMON CARRIER

A company which provides communications services to the public and whose charges and service are subject to public utility regulation.

COMPANDOR

A device used on telephone channels to improve voice quality and reduce noise.

COMPILE

To produce a sequentially ordered machine language program from a series of symbolic operation codes or statements. A special compiling program is used to perform this transformation from a nonmachine to machine language.

COMPUTER UTILITY

A term sometimes applied to service bureaus, particularly those which use communications channels to permit remote access.

CONTENTION

A condition on a multipoint communication channel when two or more locations try to transmit at the same time.

CONTROL PROGRAM

The program responsible for handling input/output for both terminals and file storage, establishing processing priorities, maintaining waiting lists of work in process, activating operational programs, and performing other supervisory functions in a real-time system. Words sometimes used synonymously to designate such a program include driver, executive, monitor, and supervisor.

CONVERSATIONAL MODE

A procedure for communication between a terminal and computer in which each entry from the terminal elicits a response from the computer, with the terminal "locked out," or inhibited while the response is being prepared.

CONVERTER

Device for changing one form of information language to another so as to render the language acceptable to a different machine; (e.g., card to tape conversion, or Baudot to another code form).

COUPLING

The connecting of two or more devices in such a manner that information or energy is transferred from one to the other.

CROSSBAR

Dial switching system using mechanism called "cross-bar switches." These consist of contact spring units operated in coordination by horizontal and vertical members.

CROSSTALK

Voice communication in one circuit being overheard in another circuit.

CRT

Cathode ray tube. A television-like picture tube used in visual display terminals.

CYCLE

Interval of one completion in a recurrent period. In alternating current, the time for a change of state from a zero to a zero through a positive and negative maximum.

DATA

Any representations, such as characters or analog quantities, to which meaning may be assigned.

DATA COLLECTION

The act of bringing data from one or more points to a central point.

DATA COMMUNICATIONS

The movement of encoded information by means of electrical transmission systems.

DATA ORIGINATION

The earliest stage at which the source material is first put into machine-readable form or directly into electrical signals.

DATA PROCESSING

Any operation or combination of operations on data.

DATA SET

A device which converts the signals of a business machine to signals that are suitable for transmission over communication lines. The device also may perform other related functions.

DECIBEL

Unit of measurement of transmission loss, gain, or relative level, based upon a logarithmic scale.

DEGRADATION

A condition in which the system continues to operate, but at a reduced level of service. Unavailability of major equipment subsystems, or components is the usual cause.

DELAY DISTORTION

Distortion resulting from nonuniform speed of transmission of the various frequency components of a signal through a transmission medium.

DEMODULATION

The process of retrieving an original signal from a modulated carrier wave. This technique is used in data sets to make communication signals compatible with business machine signals.

DIAGNOSTIC ROUTINE

A routine designed to locate and identify errors in a computer routine or hardware component.

DIAL SWITCHING EQUIPMENT

An automatic telephone system whereby one user can establish, through electromechanical or electronic equipments, a connection to another telephone user without the assistance of an attendant.

DIGIT

One of the symbols, 0, 1 to 9. Also used in telephony to describe the impulse sequence produced by the telephone dial.

DIRECT DISTANCE DIALING

A telephone service which enables a user to dial directly to telephones outside the user's local area without the aid of an operator.

DISPLAY UNIT
A device which provides a visual representation of data.

DISTORTION
Change in the received signal waveform (or pulse shape) as compared with the original transmitted signal.

DOUBLE PARITY
A system using both vertical and horizontal parity schemes.

DROP
The wire that leads to the user's premises—as from a pole to a building.

DUPLEX
In communications, pertaining to a simultaneous two-way and independent transmission in both directions (sometimes referred to as full duplex—as contrasted with half-duplex).

ECHO
A portion of the transmission signal returned from a distant point to the transmitting source with sufficient time delay to be received as interference.

ECHO SUPPRESSOR
A device used on a voice circuit to suppress the reflected energy of an echo.

EDGE PUNCHED CARD
A card of fixed size into which information may be recorded by punching holes along one edge of the card.

ENTRANCE FACILITY
The facility between the user's premises and the telephone company central office; or the user-provided interexchange facilities.

ENVELOPE DELAY
Characteristics of a circuit which result in some frequencies arriving ahead of others, even though they were transmitted together.

EQUALIZER, DELAY

A corrective network which is designed to make the phase delay or envelope delay of a circuit or system substantially constant over a desired frequency range.

ERROR

Any discrepancy between a computed, observed, or measured quantity and the true, specified, or theoretically correct value or condition.

ERROR CODE

A specific character which may be punched into a card or tape to indicate that a known error was made in the associated block of data, and which is read for action by the receiving device.

ERROR CONTROL

An arrangement to detect the presence of errors. In some systems, refinements are added that will correct the detected errors, either by operations on the received data or by retransmission from the source.

ERROR CORRECTION

System which detects and inherently provides correction for errors occasioned by transmission equipment or facilities.

ERROR DETECTION

System which detects errors occasioned by transmission equipment or facilities.

ESS (ELECTRONIC SWITCHING SYSTEM)

A communications switching system which uses solid state devices and other computer-type equipment and principles. It operates in millionths of a second.

EXCHANGE

A defined area, served by a telephone company, within which the carrier furnishes service at the exchange rate and under the regulations applicable in that area as prescribed in the carrier's filed tariffs.

FACSIMILE (FAX)

Transmission of pictures, maps, and diagrams. The image is scanned at the transmitter, reconstructed at the receiving station and duplicated on some form of paper.

FILTER

Devices used to either suppress unwanted frequencies or noise, or to separate channels in communication circuits.

FINAL ROUTE

The last choice route in the automatic routing of DDD calls.

FOREGROUND PROCESSING

High-priority processing, usually resulting from real-time entries, given precedence by means of interrrupts over lower-priority "background" processing.

FOREIGN EXCHANGE SERVICE (FX)

A service which connects a user's telephone to a remote exchange. This service provides the equivalent of local service from the distant exchange.

FORM FEED

Device to permit correct positioning of documents or business forms on a teletypewriter or business machine to ensure that the form is in the correct position on the machine to receive data.

FREQUENCY

Rate of alternations expressed in cycles (kilocycles or megacycles) per second, or Hertz. One Hz equals one cycle per second.

FREQUENCY MODULATION

A method of transmission whereby the frequency of the carrier wave is changed to correspond to similar changes in the signal wave.

FUNCTION CODES

Codes inserted in tape or cards to effect specific machine functions (e.g., tabulate).

GANG PUNCHING

High-speed parallel method of reproducing fixed information from a master card into a whole series of detail cards.

HALF-DUPLEX

Pertaining to an alternate, one-way-at-a-time, independent transmission (sometimes referred to as "single"—as contrasted with duplex).

HARD COPY

A printed copy of machine output in readable form for people, as contrasted with machine-readable only.

HARDWARE

Items of equipment used in a communications or data processing system.

HEADER

1. A file record containing common, constant, or identifying information for a group of records that follows.
2. The first part of a message, containing all necessary information for directing the message to its destination.

HERTZ (Hz)

Cycles per second.

HOLDING TIME

The length of time a communication channel is in use for each transmission. Includes both message time and operating time.

HOLLERITH CODE

Standard twelve-level code used by business machine tab cards.

HOLOVISION

Transmission of a three-dimensional image.

IMPULSES

The making and breaking of a circuit by pulsing contacts to sympathetically operate remote devices.

INFORMATION
The meaning assigned to data by known conventions.

IN-PLANT SYSTEM
A data handling system confined to one building or a number of buildings in one locality.

INPUT
1. The data to be processed.
2. The state or sequence of states occuring on a specified input channel.
3. The device or collective set of devices used for bringing data into another device.
4. A channel for impressing a state on a device or logic element.
5. The process of transferring data from an external storage to an internal storage.

INPUT OUTPUT
A general term for the equipment used to communicate with a computer and the data involved in the communications.

INTERCOM
Communications between locations on a user's premises.

INTERFACE
A shared boundary. For example, the boundary between two sub-systems or two devices.

INTERFERENCE
Presence of undesirable energy in a circuit.

INTERRUPT
A break in the normal flow of a system or routine such that the slow can be resumed from a point at a later time. An interrupt usually is caused by a signal from an external source.

KEYBOARD DEVICES
Teleprinters and other devices that use a keyboard for manual entry of information.

KEY SET

Another name for pushbutton telephones, wherein the buttons are used for intercom, holding, signaling and/or pickup of additional telephone lines.

KSR

Keyboard, send and receive.

LDX

Long distance Xerography. A name used by Xerox to identify its highspeed facsimile system. The system uses Xerox terminal equipment and a wideband data communication channel.

LINE FEED

A teletypewriter function code which rotates the platen of a page machine to a position to accept the next printed line.

LINE SWITCHING

The switching technique of temporarily connecting two lines together so that the stations directly exchange information.

LINK

See Channel.

LOADING

The addition of an inductive element to a circuit to counteract capacitive characteristics which distort the signal.

LOCAL CHANNEL

A channel connecting a communications subscriber to a central telephone office.

LOOP

In communications, loop signifies a type of facility; normally the circuit between the subscriber and the central telephone office.

MACHINE LANGUAGE

The instructions and information used by a computer to perform an operation. The language consists of characters and symbols recorded on tape and cards.

MANUAL SYSTEM

A system whereby telephone or other connections are established with the assistance of an attendant.

MARK

A term which originated with telegraph to indicate a closed-key condition. Present usage implies the presence of current or carrier on a circuit or the idle condition of the teletypewriter. It also indicates the binary digit 1 in computer language.

MARK SENSE

Process of using pencil to mark preprinted cards with information. In electronic data processing, a machine responds to the graphite penciled marks as though they were punched holes in the cards.

MASER

A device capable of amplifying or generating radiation. Maser amplifiers are used in satellite communication ground stations to amplify the extremely weak signals received from communications satellites.

MASTER STATION

The main station in a group of stations that controls the transmission of all the stations.

MCS

Microseconds.

MEGA

A prefix meaning million. A mega bit equals one million bits.

MESSAGE

A communication, prepared for information interchange, in a form suitable for passage through the interchange medium. It includes:

1. All portions of the communication, such as machine sensible controls.
2. An indication of the start of the message and the end of the message.
3. A heading containing routing and other information, one or more texts containing the originator-to-addressee communication(s), and the end-of-text indicator.

MESSAGE FORMAT
Rules for the placement of such portions of a message as message heading, address, text, and end of message.

MESSAGE NUMBERING
The identification of each message within a communications system by the assignment of a sequential number.

MESSAGE SWITCHING
The switching technique of receiving a message, storing it until the proper outgoing circuit and station are available, and then retransmitting it toward its destination.

MICR (MAGNETIC INK CHARACTER RECOGNITION)
Machine recognition of characters printed with magnetic ink.

MICROSECOND
One millionth of a second.

MICROWAVE
All electromagnetic waves in the radio frequency spectrum ranging from approximately 1,000 to 300,000 megahertz.

MNEMONIC
A simple code that has some easily remembered relationship to the actual meaning or function, e.g., LA for Los Angeles, or Sub for subtraction instruction.

MODE
The manner or way a particular device is acting or functioning.

MODEM
Contraction of modulator-demodulator. A device which modulates or demodulates signals transmitted over communication facilities.

MODULATION
The process by which some characteristic of one wave is varied in accordance with another wave. This technique is used in data sets to make business machine signals compatible with communication facilities.

MODULATION, AMPLITUDE
A method of transmission whereby the signal wave voltage is impressed upon a high frequency carrier wave, which is varied in accord with amplitude variations of the signal wave.

MULTIPLE ADDRESS MESSAGE
A message to be delivered to more than one destination.

MULTIPLEX
Use of a common channel in order to make two or more channels, either by splitting of the frequency band transmitted by the common channel into narrower bands, each of which is used to constitute a distinct channel; or by using time or phase division.

MULTIPLEXING
The division of a transmission facility into two or more channels.

MULTIPOINT CIRCUIT
A circuit interconnecting several stations.

MULTISTATION
Any network of stations capable of communication with each other, whether on one circuit or through a switching center.

NARROWBAND
A communications channel with a bandwidth less than that of voice-grade channel.

NCSU
See Network control signaling unit.

NETWORK
1. A series of points interconnected by communications channels.
2. The switched telephone network is the network of telephone lines normally used for dialed telephone calls.
3. A private line network is a network of communications channels confined to the use of one customer of the telephone company.

NETWORK CONTROL SIGNALING UNIT

Normally a telephone set that controls the transmission of signals into the telephone system which perform supervision, number identification and control of the switching machines.

NOISE

Disturbing electrical impulses introduced in a circuit by equipment components, manually—introduced interference, or natural disturbances.

OCR (OPTICAL CHARACTER RECOGNITION)

The machine recognition of printed or written characters based on inputs from photoelectric or other transducers.

OFF-LINE

Pertaining to equipment or devices not under direct control of the central processing unit of a computer. Also may be used to describe terminal equipment which is not connected to a transmission line.

ON-LINE

Pertaining to peripheral equipment or devices in direct communication with the central processing unit of a computer. Also may be used to describe terminal equipment which is connected to a transmission line.

ONE-WAY CHANNEL (SIMPLEX)

A channel which permits transmission in one direction only.

OPERATING TIME

The time required for seizing the line, dialing the call, waiting for the connection to be established, and coordinating the forthcoming transaction with the personnel or equipment at the receiving end.

OUTPUT

1. The data that has been processed.
2. The state or sequence of states occurring on a specified output channel.
3. The device or collective set of devices used for taking data out of a device.
4. A channel for expressing a state of a device or logic element.

5. The process of transferring data from an internal storage to an external storage device.

PARALLEL TRANSMISSION

Method of information transfer in which all bits of a character are sent simultaneously. See and contrast with Serial transmission, page 926.

PARITY BIT

A means of detecting transmission errors. Basically, this consists of using only those codes with an even number of bits, or only those codes with an odd number of bits. The even or odd counting of bits is done electrically. As each code is received, a malfunction or transmission error is then detected immediately. In an odd parity check, the appearance of an even code would indicate a transmission error.

PARITY CHECK

A check in which a one or zero is carried along in a character or group of characters depending on whether the total number of ones or zeros, in the character or group, is odd or even.

PASS BAND

Range of frequency spectrum which can be passed with low attenuation.

PAX

Private automatic exchange.

PERFORATOR

A tape punch unit activated mechanically from a keyboard.

POINT-TO-POINT COMMUNICATIONS

Communications between two fixed locations.

POLAR OPERATION

Circuit operation in which mark and space transitions are represented by a current reversal.

POLL

A flexible, systematic method, centrally controlled, for permitting stations on a multipoint circuit to transmit without contending for the line.

POLLING

A centrally controlled method of calling a number of points to permit them to transmit information.

PRIORITY OR PRECEDENCE

Controlled transmission of messages in order of their designated importance, e.g., urgent or routine.

PRIVATE LINE OR PRIVATE WIRE

A channel or circuit furnished by the telephone company to a subscriber for his exclusive use.

READER (TAPE)

A device associated with a teletypewriter or other business machines that has the function of a transmitter.

REAL-TIME COMMUNICATIONS

Information transmitted, processed and received, concerning an event taking place in time, to take action to influence that event if desired.

REDUNDENCY

The portion of the total information contained in a message which can be eliminated without loss of essential information. (This term has a different meaning in connection with the design of electronic equipment.)

REMOTE ACCESS

An arrangement whereby distant terminals have access to a central computer via communications channels.

REPEATER STATION

An intermediate point in a transmission system where line signals are received, amplified or reshaped, and retransmitted.

RESPONSE TIME

The amount of time elapsed between generation of an inquiry at a data communications terminal and receipt of a response at that same terminal. Response time, thus defined, includes: (1) transmission time to the computer and (2) processing time at the computer, including access time to obtain any file records needed to answer the inquiry, and transmission time back to the terminal.

REVERSE CHANNEL

A portion of the communications channel that is reserved for supervisory signals returned from the receiving station.

RO

Receive only.

ROTARY DIAL

A telephone that sends dial pulses to the telephone switching equipment to establish a connection.

ROTR

Receive-only typing reperforator.

RT

Reperforator-transmitter.

SAMPLING

1. A technique of systems analysis whereby traffic volumes, file activity, and other factors are estimated, based upon a representative sample.
2. A method of communication line control whereby messages on a circuit are sampled by a computer that selects only those for which computer processing is required.

SCAN

To examine the status of communication lines or other input/output channels, in order to determine whether data is being received or transmitted.

SELECTIVE CALLING

The ability of a transmitting station to specify which of several stations on the same line is to receive a message.

SERIAL TRANSMISSION

A method of information transfer in which the bits composing a character are sent sequentially. See and contrast with Parallel transmission.

SERVICE BUREAU

An installation where the user can lease processing time on a central processor and peripheral equipment. Programs as well as data may be made available to the user or the user may supply the programs and the center will load both program and data to be processed, process the data, and deliver the results to the user. The program and data for processing may be delivered or sent between user and center in any of several forms: cards, punched tape, or magnetic tape. Data communications may be used between the user and the center to move the information electrically. The service bureau also may provide such services as key-punching the data and preparing it for processing.

SIDEBAND

A band of frequencies containing components of either the sum (upper sideband) or difference (lower sideband) of the carrier and modulating frequencies.

SIGNAL ELEMENT

That part of a signal which occupies the shortest interval of the signaling code.

SIGNAL-TO-NOISE RATIO

The ratio of the power of the signal to that of the noise.

SIMPLEX CHANNEL

See One-way channel.

SINGLE ADDRESS MESSAGE

A message to be delivered to only one destination.

SINGLE SIDEBAND

Carrier system in which one sideband is transmitted and the other is suppressed. The carrier may or may not be transmitted.

SKIP CODE

A function code which directs a machine to omit certain fields of information.

SOFTWARE

The totality of programs and routines used to extend the capabilities of computers. Contrasted with hardware.

SPACE

A term which originated with telegraph to indicate an open-key condition. Present usage implies the absence of current or carrier on a circuit. It also indicates the binary digit "0" in computer language.

SPIRAL PARITY

A system whereby the check character is developed by making diagonal rows, either odd or even.

STAND-ALONE CAPABILITY

A multiplexer designed to function independent of a host computer, either all of the time or some of the time.

STATION

One of the input or output points on a communications system.

STATUS REPORTS

A term used to describe the automatic reports generated by a message switching system generally covering service conditions, such as circuits and stations out of service and back in service.

STEP-BY-STEP

Automatic dial system in which calls go through the central office by a succession of switches which move a step at a time, each step being made in response to the dialing of a number or letter.

STORAGE

A general term for any device capable of retaining information.

STORE-AND-FORWARD

Process of message handling used in a message switching system.

STUNT BOX

A device to control the nonprinting functions of a teleprinter terminal. Control characters can be sent to it over the communications channel.

SUPERVISORY CONTROL

A system to control the operation of remote equipment. (This term has a different meaning in terms of computer process control.)

SWITCHED MESSAGE NETWORK
A network of telephone lines and switching equipment normally used for dialed telephone or data transmission calls.

SWITCHING CENTER
A location where an incoming message is automatically or manually directed to one or more outgoing circuits.

SYNCHRONOUS
A property of transmission where speed of operation is fixed and related to the system involved.

TARIFF
A schedule published by a communications common carrier and filed with a public service commission describing the services provided by the carrier, the rates thereof, and the conditions under which they are offered.

TELECOMMUNICATIONS
The reception and/or transmission of information of any nature by telephone, telegraph, radio, or other electro-magnetic systems.

TELEGRAPHY, PRINTING
A method of telegraph operation in which the received signals are automatically recorded in printed characters.

TELEPRINTER
Term used to refer to the equipment used in a printing telegraph system. A teletypewriter.

TELE-PROCESSING
A form of information handling in which a data processing system utilizes communications facilities.

TELETYPE
A registered trademark of the Teletype Corporation. Usually refers to a series of different types of equipment, such as transmitters, tape punches, page printers, utilized for communication systems.

TELETYPEWRITER (TTY)
A name used by the Bell System to refer specifically to telegraph page printers. The equipment transmits and/or receives

typed records or perforated tapes at speeds from 60 to 150 words per minute.

TELPAK

A service offered by communication carriers for the leasing of wideband channels between two or more points.

TERMINAL

1. A point at which information can enter or leave a communication network.
2. An input/output device designed to receive or send source data in an environment associated with the job to be performed and capable of transmitting entries to and obtaining outputs from the system of which it is a part.

TIE LINE

A private communication channel of the type provided by communications common carriers for linking two or more points together.

TIME DIVISION

Interleaving several message channels which are separated from each other in time on a single transmission media.

TIME SHARING

A method of operation in which a computer facility is shared by several users for different purposes at (apparently) the same time. Although the computer actually serves each user in sequence, the high speed of the computer makes it appear that the users are all handled simultaneously.

TORN-TAPE SWITCHING

Manual teletype switching system in which tapes received at a center are carried to a transmitter for retransmission to their final destination.

TORN-TAPE SWITCHING CENTER

A location where operators tear off incoming printed and punched paper tape and transfer it manually to the proper outgoing circuit.

TOUCH-TONE

A registered service mark of the A.T. & T. Company which identifies its pushbutton dialing service.

TRAFFIC

The total information flow in a communications system. This includes conversations, written messages, facsimile, and data.

TRANSCEIVER

A device which is capable of transmitting and receiving.

VOICE COUPLER

A voice connecting arrangement that permits direct electrical connection of user-provided voice transmitting and receiving equipment to the telephone network.

VOICE-GRADE CHANNEL

A channel suitable for transmission of speech, digital or analog data, or facsimile, generally with a frequency range of about 300 to 3000 Hz.

VOLATILE DISPLAY

The nonpermanent image appearing on the screen of a visual display terminal.

WATS (WIDE AREA TELECOMMUNICATIONS SERVICE)

A service provided by telephone companies which permits a customer by use of an access line to make calls to or to receive calls from telephones in a specific zone on a dial basis for a flat monthly charge.

WIDEBAND

A term applied to facilities or circuits whose bandwidths are greater than than required for one voice channel.

WIDEBAND CHANNEL

A channel wider in bandwidth than a voice-grade channel.

WORD

In telegraphy, six characters (five characters plus one space). In computing, an ordered set of characters which is the normal unit in which information may be stored, transmitted, or operated upon within a computer.

WPM

Words per minute.

METRIC PAPER SIZES

This is a system of sizes having aspect ratios of 1:1.414. The unique property of rectangles with this aspect ratio is that when cut in half, the two halves have the same proportion as the whole. To integrate the sizes with the metric system the basic (A-0) size has an area of very close to one square meter. This produces a rectangle with the dimensions of 841 × 1189 mm and an area of 0.999949 square meter. Succeeding sizes are developed by repeated halving so that we get:

	Millimeters	Inches
A0	841 × 1189	22.11 × 46.81
A1	594 × 841	23.39 × 33.11
A2	420 × 594	16.54 × 23.39
A3	297 × 420	11.69 × 16.54
A4	210 × 297	8.27 × 11.69
A5	148 × 210	5.83 × 8.27
A6	105 × 148	4.13 × 5.83
A7	74 × 105	2.91 × 4.13
A8	52 × 74	2.05 × 2.91
A9	37 × 52	1.46 × 2.05
A10	26 × 37	1.02 × 1.46

The 1798 French "Grande Registre" paper of 0.4204 × 0.5946 meters expressed in even millimeters becomes the A2 size.

The ISO standard includes a subsidiary series of sizes to be used when sizes are needed intermediate between any two adjacent sizes of the "A" series. The "B" sizes are:

	Millimeters	Inches
B0	1000 × 1414	39.37 × 55.57
B1	707 × 1000	27.83 × 39.37
B2	500 × 707	19.69 × 27.83
B3	353 × 500	13.90 × 19.69
B4	250 × 353	9.84 × 13.90
B5	176 × 250	6.93 × 9.84
B6	125 × 176	4.92 × 6.93
B7	88 × 125	3.46 × 4.92
B8	62 × 88	2.44 × 3.46
B9	44 × 62	1.73 × 2.44
B10	31 × 44	1.22 × 1.73

The B3 size of 353 × 500 mm compares with the 1798 Grand Papier size of 0.3536 × 0.500 meters.

The "B" sizes provide sheets with one dimension an even fraction of one meter and an aspect ratio of 1:1.414. The "B" sizes are therefore not midway between adjacent sizes of the "A" sizes, but each "B" size has an area 41% greater than the corresponding "A" number.

The Japanese believed that it was more important to establish a subsidiary size system midway between the "A" sizes than to achieve the convenience of even fractions of a meter as one dimension. Japanese Standard P 0138 lists this "B" series:

	Millimeters	Inches
B0	1030 × 1456	40.55 × 57.32
B1	728 × 1030	28.66 × 40.55
B2	515 × 728	20.28 × 28.66
B3	364 × 515	14.33 × 20.28
B4	257 × 364	10.12 × 14.33
B5	182 × 257	7.20 × 10.12
B6	128 × 182	5.04 × 7.20
B7	91 × 128	3.58 × 5.04
B8	64 × 91	2.52 × 3.58
B9	45 × 64	1.77 × 2.52
B10	32 × 45	1.26 × 1.77

These sizes have an aspect ratio of 1:1.414 and are 50% greater in area than the corresponding "A" sizes. This may be a more useful principle than the 1:1.414 area difference in the ISO size system as "B" sizes are regularly used in Japan and very rarely used in Europe.

Although the 1798 French standard size was limited by the handcraft method of making paper, the dimensions were more precise than those adopted in Germany in 1922. The area of the French A0 sheet, by projection, is 0.999988 sq. m. compared with 0.999949 sq. m. in the 1922 German version.

The ISO size system is also imprecise in halving. One half of 1189 becomes 594 and one half of 297 becomes 148. As a result of this dropping of fractions, if we regenerate the A0 size by multiplying the A10 sizes by 32, we get 832 × 1184 mm as compared with the standard A0 size of 841 × 1189 mm. These errors are not important except they make it impossible to fit the system into continuous form depths without change.

GLOSSARY OF MANAGEMENT TERMS, PHRASES AND CONCEPTS

by: Charles Leon Lapp, Ph.D.

Adaptive subsystems

Perform those activities within an organization which are designed to monitor or sense the nature of the world in which the organization operates.

Administrative theory school

These theorists did the most extensive early analysis of what functions executives perform in whole or in part.

Age-salary ratio

The relationship between an individual's age and the salary he or she receives.

Ambiguity

A condition in which individuals may not be clear as to what the role requirements are. Distinguish between task ambiguity and social-emotional ambiguity.

Analysis of performance

The last phase of decision making; a manager's assessment, once a decision is made, of how well organizational members, organizational subsystems, and the entire organization are functioning as a result.

Aptitude

A potential talent for a particular type of work.

Assessment centers

Workshops in some large companies for new managerial trainees, designed to assess a candidate's managerial potential and counsel him or her on ways to become successful in the organization. Typically, candidates are put through a series of simulated exercises, group discussion sessions, and extended psychological interviews for a few days. Their performance is normally evaluated by both psychologists and successful line managers in the organization.

Attitude

A predisposition to respond to a certain type of stimulus.

Barnard's unit concept

Chester Barnard's idea that an organization should be composed of small units, each consisting of 10 or fewer members.

Barometric indicators

Historical and current economic data used to predict future trends of business activity; a forecasting method of planning.

Behavioral processes

Motivation, leadership, group behavior, and communication—the interactions between and among organizational members that enable the organization to move toward its goals. One of the four dimensions of management.

Behavior modification

Increasing desired patterns of behavior, or decreasing undesirable behavior, by using scientifically determined rewards or punishments.

Boundary

Spanning subsystems carry on the environmental transactions in procurring the input, disposing of the output, or assisting in these functions.

Bounded rationality

Administrative theorists said, the manager would have to select the best of all possible alternatives. But an "administrative man" is limited by his own perceptions.

Bounded discretion

The area within which managers are free to make decisions, limited by social norms, rules, and policies within the organization; legal restrictions; and moral and ethical norms.

Break-even analysis

A decision-making technique based on determining the point at which the income a product brings in equals the cost of producing it, at varying prices and levels of demand.

Bridge

In Henri Fayol's theory, the path by which someone in one part of a hierarchy can communicate with his or her equals in other sections without going through supervisors.

Budget

An allocation of specific amounts of money to various departments or groups for the purpose of controlling expenditures and monitoring activities.

Bureaucracy

A hierarchical organization characterized by specialized functions, staff, record keeping and rigid lines of authority.

Capital budgeting

A decision-making technique in which a manager evaluates the relative attractiveness of various projects in which an initial lump payment generates a stream of earnings over a future period.

Capitalism

An economic system of private ownership of capital with competition in a free marketplace determining price, supply, and demand.

Centralization

The extent to which responsibility and authority in an organization are vested in a core executive group or office. (Contrast decentralization.)

Classical management

The first identifiable modern school of management. It includes scientific management, functionalism, and bureaucracy.

Closed system

A set of processes that operate in a recurring cycle and in which feedback provides a self-correcting mechanism. (Contrast open system.)

Collateral subsystems

Carry out support and coordinating activities (similar to the concept of staff—managerial—administrative—and maintenance).

Conditional values

What you can expect if a particular strategy is chosen and a particular state of nature occurs.

Cognitive dissonance

An uncomfortable feeling that arises when an individual perceives a conflict between two of his or her ideas or cognitions, leading the person to abandon one of the ideas.

Conference approach

A group-discussion session similar to T-groups, focused on the solution of a specific organizational problem. (See organizational development.)

Consideration

One of the two key dimensions of leader behavior, involving being supportive of subordinates and constructing a friendly organizational climate.

Consultative

Sharing opinions with no obligation to act on them. (Contrast directive.)

Contingency theory of leadership

Fred Fiedler's theory that a task-oriented style of leadership is successful when the environment or situation is either very uncertain or very certain, and a considerate style is successful under moderate certainty.

Contingency theory of management

An approach that assumes the type of management that is successful depends on such factors as the kind of technology used to create the final product or service and the degree of external environmental uncertainty the organization faces.

Control

The monitoring of plans and the pinpointing of significant deviations from them. In some situations, the control system contains an action device that automatically corrects these deviations; in others, managers must determine what corrective action is appropriate. Both organizational subsystems and organization members must be controlled for plans to be accomplished.

Control, feedback

Diagnosis of an error after it has occurred.

Control, feedforward

Diagnosis of an error before it has occurred.

Co-optation

A method an organization uses to reduce the uncertainty it faces: Management attempts to influence its external environment by seeking out representatives from the community to become members of the organization.

Critical incidents

A method of rating that a manager keeps a record of the positive and/or negative behaviors of each subordinate over a period of time.

Critical path

The path in a PERT network that requires the longest time to complete, and which thus determines the project's completion time.

Decentralization

The extent to which responsibility and authority are delegated to lower levels in the organization. (Contrast centralization.)

Decision making

A problem-solving activity that comes into play when the individual realizes that the gap between *what is* and *what should be is too great.* It involves recognizing a problem exists, searching for alternative solutions, evaluating these solutions, and selecting and implementing a solution.

Decision theory

Is a set of concepts generally mathematically based which describes what decision should be made in order to achieve some objective.

Decision tree

A decision-making technique appropriate when a series of decisions must be made but their outcomes are unknown. (See expected value.)

Delphi technique

A forecasting technique in which the organization polls at periodic intervals a small number of experts who make predictions about long-run technological and market changes that eventually will affect the organization. (See nominal group technique, page 946.)

Departmentalization

Division or grouping of organizational jobs and subunits on the basis of a common characteristic, such as product or purpose, function or specialization, place or clientele.

Descriptive

Based on actual practice rather than theory or ideals; as a descriptive model of decision making. (Contrast normative.)

Deterministic

Based on exact, known quantities; as a deterministic model of decision making. (See probabilistic.)

Dimensions of management

Four areas within which managerial activities take place: organizational design, planning and control, behavioral processes, and decision making.

Directive

Involving orders that are to be followed. (Contrast consultative, page 937.)

Distributive bargaining

Involves a situation where one party's loss is another's gain.

Dynamic organizations

The environments are characterized by more uncertainty than others.

Econometric model

A complex computer simulation of the entire economy used to forecast future levels of economic activity.

Economic man

A normative model of decision making, developed by Adam Smith, in which the manager is assumed to understand all the alternatives he can pursue to accomplish particular goals, from which he chooses the most desirable alternative. (See satisficing, page 950.)

Entrepreneur

An individual who starts a new enterprise consisting of eight or more employees. According to Joseph Schumpeter, one who combines given resources so as to radically alter the consumption and production patterns of a society.

EOQ (Economic order quantity) model

An inventory decision-making method used to establish a formula for answering two questions: *When* should supplies be ordered, and in *what quantity?*

Ergonomics

The study of ways to make work less taxing physiologically.

Equity theory

A motiviational theory that assumes an individual must see a relationship between the rewards he or she obtains (outcomes) and the amount of work he or she performs (inputs).

Expectancy theory

A theory that assumes an individual's motivation is a function of *two expectancies:* that *effort* will result in successful performance, and that successful performance will lead to desired outcomes.

Expected value

A decision-making technique that indicates probable profit by multiplying possible future outcomes and the probabilities of their occurrence, and summing the totals.

Fast track

A term for the path taken by certain individuals who are picked for rapid advancement while the remainder of the managerial workforce is essentially by-passed.

Federal decentralization

A combination of departmentation by product and by function, in which operating units that are largely self-contained draw personnel from functional departments as needed. (General Motors.)

Flexitime

A way of scheduling the work under which employees must be present during a "core" period, but can begin work any time before the core period; their starting time determines their quitting time.

Forecasting

Planning focused on the prediction of future occurrences that may affect the organization. Forecasts can be long-range, short-range, or rolling (integrating long and short-range).

Functional foremanship

In scientific management, a system whereby each aspect of an employee's job is examined by a specialized foreman. The worker thus reports to several functional foremen. (Frederick W. Taylor.)

Functionalism

An approach to management that focuses on the functions of management.

Functions of management

According to Fayol and other writers in the classical management school, the specific activities that a manager must perform (such as planning) to be successful.

Group behavior

Interactions within and among work groups; one of the behavioral processes in an organization.

Hard criteria

Viewed as ends or levels of attainment.

Hawthorne effect

The change in workers' behavior that automatically occurs when they are studied.

Heuristic

Helping to discover or learn.

Hierarchy

The set of levels of power in an organization that makes some individuals subordinate to others in authority, earnings, and/or status.

Horizontal integration

A company's attempt to dominate a market at one particular stage of the production process by monopolizing resources at that stage. (Contrast vertical integration.)

House management development model

A systematic approach to the problem which seeks to specify the minimum conditions required for successful change efforts.

Human relations

A school of management whose basic proposition is that the attitudes individuals develop in informal groups within an organization critically influence their commitment and level of productivity.

Human resource accounting system

A means of assessing an organization's employees in terms of replacement costs, selection costs, and the like.

Hygiene factors

In two-factor theory, extrinsic sources of motivation, which do not relate directly to the nature of the work (for example, working conditions), and which affect the rates of absenteeism and turnover. (Herzberg.)

Integrative bargaining

A situation where the possibility of a solution that will benefit both parties is reached.

Intervention

The process in organization development by which planned changes are implemented. (See process intervention; structural intervention.)

Job design

Consists of specifying the content of the job, the methods used on the job and how the job relates to other jobs in the system.

Job enlargement

Increasing the number of operations an individual performs in a job cycle.

Job enrichment
>   Increasing the amount of responsibility an individual can exercise in his or her job.

Leadership
>   The ability of a superior to influence the behavior of subordinates; one of the behavioral processes in an organization. (Clout.)

Linear programming
>   A decision-making technique that is an extension of break-even analysis. It is particularly appropriate when an organization manufactures two or more products and uses two or more resources.

Linking pin
>   Rensis Likert's term for a member of two work groups whose work overlaps, responsible for coordinating the work of the two groups.

Machine-controlled systems
>   Technology in which machines rather than human beings control or monitor the work processes, as in an oil refinery.

Management audit
>   A control technique that assesses the overall quality of management by means of methods such as questionnaires, interviews, and analysis of "hard" data elements (turnover, productivity, and so forth).

Maintenance subsystems
>   Seek to smooth out the problems of operating the other subsystems, and to monitor their internal operations.

Management by objectives (MBO)
>   An organization-wide planning system in which top management typically defines four or five general objectives it wishes to achieve within a given period. Managers throughout the hierarchy refine these objectives into subobjectives for their own units. Each employee's performance is then evaluated in terms of individual objectives that relate directly to the unit's objectives. (Cascading of Objectives.)

Management information system (MIS)

Any system of data collection and analysis that will help the manager perform his or her job more effectively.

Managerial grid

An O.D. approach to changing organization; it assumes that managers should be both *task-oriented* and considerate. Blake & Mouton puts people and task orientation dimensions together into five basic styles.

Managerial subsystems

Comprise the organized activities for controlling, coordinating and directing many subsystems of the structure.

Maturity curves

Developed from an analysis of salary levels attained by professionals of a certain type after certain time periods upon receiving their final college degrees.

Managerial team

A group of managers who successfully coordinate their efforts so that they and their respective organizational units benefit.

Manager pair

Two managers, a specialist and a generalist, who work together, the specialist digging more deeply into the problems the generalist diagnoses.

MAPS (Multivariate analysis, participation, and structure)

An approach to organization development design that allows the members of the organization to define the major task groups or units and to select the individuals most suitable for working in them.

Maximum principle

Strategy selected that has the greatest payoff.

Minimax principle

The decision maker selects the strategy which returns to him the greatest amount under the worst conditions.

Matrix organization

An organization design that combines departmentation by product and function: Functional managers exercise technical authority over projects, while the product managers have responsibility for budgets and the final completion of projects. The functional managers lend employees to product managers as needed.

Mechanistic structure

An organization having a high degree of *functional specialization of jobs,* a *centralized hierarchy,* formal and standardized jobs and procedures, economic sources of motivation, and authoritarian leadership style, formal and impersonal relations between individuals and groups, and vertical and directive communication. (Contrast organic structure, page 946.)

Michels' Iron Law

Michels' statement that whoever says organization, says oligarchy, or rule by the few.

Model

A simplified or concrete representation of a complex or abstract process or idea.

Motion study

Scientific management's analysis of the specific motions of workers at a given job, through the use of films and other devices, so as to determine what motions are necessary for the job's completion. (See time study.)

Motivation

The physical and mental state that propels an individual to act in a particular manner, or the deliberate creation of such a state; one of the behavioral processes in an organization.

Motivators

In two-factor theory, intrinsic sources of motivation, relating directly to the nature of the work (for example, interesting and challenging assignments), which affect rates of productivity.

Must objectives

Specify the outcomes that have to be achieved.

Need hierarchy

Abraham Maslow's theory of motivation, which holds that the human needs are arranged in a hierarchy; the individual seeks to satisfy basic and elementary needs first, and then higher-order needs.

Nominal group technique (NGT)

A forecasting technique in which 7 to 10 experts meet to share and discuss their ideas and predictions.

Nonprogrammed decision

A solution to a problem that cannot be found by using a standard routine or program, but demands a creative response.

Nonzero-sum situation

A competitive situation in which when one group wins, the other group also wins or its position remains unchanged. (Contrast zero-sum situation.)

Norm

A standard or ideal pattern, e.g., of behavior.

Normative

Reflecting a norm; as a normative model of decision making. (Contrast descriptive.)

Office of the president

A system by which two or three co-equal chief executives in an organization divide the work and coordinate their respective efforts.

Open system

A set of processes whose recurring operation is influenced by outside factors. (Contrast closed system.)

Operant conditioning

Involves stating the goal of learning—measuring the individual's behavior prior to learning—and then behavior directed toward goal is rewarded.

Organic structure

An organization design having enriched jobs, a decentralized hierarchy, flexible jobs and procedures, economic and noneconomic sources of motivation, democratic leadership, informal and personal relations between individuals, and both vertical and lateral consultative communications. (See mechanistic structure.)

Organization design

The structure of an organization which provides a framework for its activities and delineates the basic lines of authority and responsibility.

Organization development (O.D.)

The introduction of planned and systematic change into an organization within the dimensions of organization design and behavioral processes.

Parity principle

The idea that the amount of authority an individual possesses should be equal to his or her responsibility.

Participative management

A system by which employees are allowed to have a voice in decisions that bear directly on their work.

Payback period

The length of time required for the net revenues of an investment to cover its initial cost.

Perception

Is the chief mechanism by which human beings come to know the world outside themselves. Perception translates the stimuli received by the senses into impressions of the world.

Personal space

The physical area around an individual within which other people generally do not trespass.

Planning

Specifying organizational goals and the means to be used to achieve them. There are two kinds of means: *strategies* and *tactics*.

Planning-programming-budgeting system (PPBS)

An organization-wide planning system that includes definition of objectives, analysis of anticipated costs and benefits of each program, allocation of resources to authorized programs, completion of authorized programs, and analysis of the results of each program.

Policy

A general guide management employs to direct organizational activities.

Polyspecialist

A manager who is neither a generalist nor a specialist, but rather is very knowledgeable in several areas.

Power

The source of a superior's ability to persuade subordinates to follow a particular course of action. There are *five* types of power: *legitimate, reward, expert, coercive,* and *referent.* (Force one can use to obtain compliance.)

Primary subsystems

Are the production, boundary-spanning and adaptive subsystems (similar to the concept of line organization).

Psychological contract

Refers to the mutual expectation between an organization and its members about what is expected of each.

Principles of management

Certain guidelines that Fayol and other members of the classical management school held that a manager should follow to achieve success. (See, for example, span of control.)

Procedures

Plans that establish a customary method of handling future activities. They normally accompany policies.

Process intervention

In organization development, an attempt to change the attitudes of organizational members so that organizational objectives can be accomplished more successfully. (See structural intervention.)

Process or automated technology

Technology in which the organization invests heavily in capital equipment but does not spend much money on labor.

Program evaluation and review technique (PERT)

An organization-wide planning technique particularly appropriate for a project that consists of a number of interrelated steps or activities, some of which must be finished before others can begin.

Programmed decision

A solution to a problem found by using a program, routine, or procedure that has been successful for similar problems in the past.

Project management

An organization design in which each subordinate is employed only for the life of the project; when the project is completed the subordinate is either assigned to another project or let go.

Protégé

An individual whose career is advanced by the help of an older and successful executive.

Protestant ethic

The idea that worldly success is a necessary but not sufficient condition for salvation.

Questionnaire data banks

Computer stores of information collected from a large number of questionnaires, used to pinpoint problems in an organization. Normally each organizational unit is compared to the norm or average on each questionnaire item.

Rational criterion

This approach is based on the idea that for decisions under conditions of uncertainty, it is impossible to make a reasonably adequate estimate of the probability of a particular state of nature occurring, but that if there is no cause to believe that one state of nature is more likely to occur than another, it can be reasonably assumed that they are equally likely to occur.

Rectitude power

Respect for moral uprightness.

Regret criterion

Suggests the amount of regret that might be measured by the difference between the payoff actually received and the payoff that could have been received if one had known that the state of nature that was going to occur.

Risky shift phenomenon

    The finding that the behavior of individuals as individuals often is radically different from their group behavior. In some situations, individuals take a riskier position; in others, a more conservative position.

Rules

    Specific procedures that individuals and operating divisions of an organization should follow to be in conformity with organizational policies. However, some rules are not specifically related to policies.

Satisficing

    Choosing a solution to a problem by examining only four or five alternatives that are minimally acceptable, and picking one that will be adequate, rather than taking additional time and effort to find the best possible solution. (See economic man.)

Scientific management

    The approach within the school of *classical management* whose proponents argue that there is an ideal way of performing any job, which can be pinpointed scientifically through time and motion study.

Sensitivity training

    A group-discussion method used to give individuals insight into their strengths and weaknesses. Although a psychologist is present, the group starts off its discussions in an unstructured and "leaderless" fashion; gradually the psychologist intervenes to help members understand their attitudes and behavior.

Simulation

    Building and testing models that use mathematical relationships between critical, "real-world" factors to create a facsimile of real conditions; normally done on a computer.

Socialization

    Is the process by which a culture or society, or other institutions condition the behavior of individuals.

Soft criteria

    Involves not a particular level of achievement, but determination that an event or condition has or has not occurred.

Span of control

> The number of subordinates a manager supervises or should supervise. (Unit of supervision number of operator employees one person can supervise.)

Staff

> Managers and employees who advise and assist line managers and employees, and are not directly involved in the production of the final good or service of the organization.

Standard cost system

> A control technique that estimates anticipated costs for a particular product or level of volume.

Stereotypes

> Preconceived notions about people, often based on superficial characteristics, which can distort communication between individuals.

Strategy

> The means that an organization uses to achieve its overall objectives.

Streams of management

> The major schools of management have developed within two major streams, economics and behavioral science.

Structural intervention

> In organization development, altering the structure of an organization so that individuals relate to one another in a *new and different way.* (See process intervention.)

Subordinate goals

> Goals which are desired by two or more groups but can only be reached through cooperation of the groups.

Synectics

> Concept association—study of environmental interrelationships.

System Four

> A total organizational intervention stressing participative management: Managers express complete confidence and trust in

their subordinates, obtain subordinates' ideas, and try to implement them if possible, delegate a great amount of responsibility, and use group decision making as much as possible.

Systems theory

An approach to management that assumes: (1) an organization is a system consisting of subunits that interact with one another and depend on one another; and (2) an organization is an open system interacting with its external environment and dependent on it.

Tactic

The means used to attain specific objectives that relate directly to the overall objectives of an organization.

Task Force

A group set up within an organization to accomplish a specific objective, after which it disbands. It differs from a temporary committee in that its members are drawn from various departments in the organization interested in the outcome of the task force's work.

Task orientation

One of the two key dimensions of leader behavior, involving focusing on *initiation of structure, assignment of tasks,* specification of the manner in which tasks are to be completed, and clarification of schedules.

Team building

In organization development, an intervention focused on improving the effectiveness and efficiency of one group or unit.

Technology

The means that an organization uses to produce its goods or service.

Theory X

The managerial assumption that human beings are lazy, avoid responsibility, need direction, and must be coerced.

Theory Y

The managerial assumption that human beings seek responsibility and want to use their abilities.

Time study

Scientific management's method of determining the time a worker needs to complete a given job cycle, by the use of the stop watch. (See motion study.)

Total organizational intervention

In organization development, an intervention focused on improving the efficiency and effectiveness of an organization.

Training groups (T-groups)

Sensitivity training groups, which can be used to train managers in interpersonal insight and relations.

Trait theory

A view of leadership that assumes leaders differ from average people in traits like intelligence, perseverance, and ambition.

Two-factor theory

Frederick Herzberg's idea that job motivation has two independent sources: hygiene factors and motivators.

Unit technology

Technology in which an organization spends a great amount of money on labor relative to capital investment in equipment.

Values

Are more deeply ingrained than attitudes. They are what are an individual considers good or bad—important or unimportant.

Vroom—Yetton Model (V-Y)

Takes into consideration a number of factors which influence the degree of success in using a participative approach.

"Want Objectives"

These are objectives that are not necessarily critical, but are desirable.

Vertical integration

A company's attempt to dominate a market by controlling all steps in the production process, from the extraction of raw materials through the manufacture and sale of the final product. (Contrast horizontal integration.)

Work group

The formal group of individuals assigned to perform a particular task or function in an organization.

Zero-sum situation

A competitive situation in which resources are finite, so that what one group wins, the other necessarily loses. (Contrast nonzero-sum situation.)

Zone of indifference

Means substantially that a person is willing to comply.

INDEX

INDEX

INDEX

INDEX

INDEX

INDEX

INDEX

INDEX